Worldwide Destinations

Worldwide Destinations

The geography of travel and tourism

Third edition

BRIAN G. BONIFACE

CHRIS COOPER

BUTTERWORTH
HEINEMANN

OXFORD   AUCKLAND   BOSTON   JOHANNESBURG   MELBOURNE   NEW DELHI

Butterworth-Heinemann
Linacre House, Jordan Hill, Oxford OX2 8DP
225 Wildwood Avenue, Woburn, MA 01801-2041
A division of Reed Educational and Professional Publishing Ltd

A member of the Reed Elsevier plc group

First published as *The Geography of Travel and Tourism* 1987
Reprinted 1988, 1990, 1991, 1993
Second edition 1994
Reprinted 1994, 1995, 1996 (twice)
Third edition 2001 (twice)

British Library Cataloguing in Publication Data
Boniface, Brian G.
    Worldwide destinations: the geography of travel and
    tourism. – 3rd ed.
    1. Tourist trade   2. Travel
    I. Title   II. Cooper, Christopher P.
    338.4'791

ISBN 0 7506 4231 9

For information on all Butterworth-Heinemann publications
visit our website at www.bh.com

Composition by Genesis Typesetting, Rochester, Kent
Printed and bound in Great Britain

FOR EVERY TITLE THAT WE PUBLISH, BUTTERWORTH-HEINEMANN
WILL PAY FOR BTCV TO PLANT AND CARE FOR A TREE.

Contents

List of figures   ix

List of tables   xi

Preface   xiii

Part One   The Elements of the Geography of Travel and Tourism   1

1   Introduction to the geography of tourism   **3**
Case study: Other forms of travel   10

2   The geography of demand for tourism   **12**
Case study: The new tourist   20
Case study: World patterns of international tourism flows   21

3   The geography of resources for tourism   **25**
Case study: The Galapagos Islands, Ecuador: a case study in resource conservation
and tourism development   34

4   Climate and tourism   **39**
Case study: Climate change and tourism   50

5   The geography of transport for travel and tourism   **53**
Case study: Managing transport at the tourism destination   65
Case study: Airline strategic alliances   67

Part Two   The Regional Geography of Travel and Tourism in the World   71

6   An introduction to the tourism geography of Europe   **73**
Case study: European policy and tourism   78

7   An introduction to the tourism geography of Britain   **81**
Case study: Strategic planning for destinations: Bournemouth's tourism strategy   89

8   The tourism geography of England and the Channel Islands   **97**
Case study: London Docklands: waterfront regeneration and tourism development   104
Case study: The New Forest: managing tourism in an environmentally sensitive area   107

9   **The tourism geography of Scotland, Wales and the Isle of Man**   109
Case study: The Isle of Man   114

10 **The tourism geography of Ireland**   117
Case study: Dublin   122

11 **Scandinavia**   124
Case study: Adventure tourism in two areas of Arctic Scandinavia – Swedish Lapland
and Svalbard   131

12 **The Benelux countries**   134
Case study: The impact of tourism on a historic city: Bruges   140

13 **Central Europe: Austria, Switzerland and Germany**   144
Case study: Berlin: the revitalization of a European capital   153

14 **France**   155
Case study: The French Riviera: fashion as an influence on resort development   164

15 **Spain and Portugal**   167
Case study: Madrid as a centre for cultural tourism   180

16 **Italy**   182
Case study: Venice: heritage in danger   189
Case study: The Italian Lakes   192

17 **Malta, Greece and Cyprus**   195
Case Study: A SWOT analysis of Greek tourism   202
Case Study: Rhodes   203

18 **Eastern Europe and the CIS**   206
Case study: Tourism as an agent of economic restructuring   223
Case study: Prague   224

19 **The Middle East**   226
Case study: Tourism in the Republic of Yemen   236
Case study: Nile cruise tourism   237

20 **Africa and the islands of the Indian Ocean**   240
Case study: Local community involvement in safari tourism: the CAMPFIRE project
in Zimbabwe   257

21 **South Asia**   259
Case study: Adventure tourism in Nepal: environmental and social impacts   268
Case study: The Maldives   271

22 **East Asia**   273
Case study: Bali and Lombok   285
Case study: The Asian currency crisis: the impact on tourism   288

23 **North America**   292
Case study: New York City   309
Case study: Nunavut: Tourism in the Canadian Arctic   311

24 Latin America and the Caribbean   **315**
     Case study: Tourism plans in the Caribbean   334
     Case study: The regeneration of Rio de Janeiro   335

25 Australasia   **338**
     Case study: Kangaroo Island   350
     Case study: Hawaii   351

26 The future geography of travel and tourism   **355**
     Case study: Space: the final tourism frontier?   361

Sources   363

Bibliography   371

Selective place name index   373

Subject index   383

List of figures

1.1	Leisure, recreation and tourism	4
1.2	The tourism system	5
1.3	Classification of travellers	11
2.1	Stages in economic growth	13
2.2	The demographic transition	16
3.1	Tourism planning flow chart	28
3.2	The recreational business district	33
3.3	The tourist area life cycle	33
3.4	The Galapagos Islands	35
3.5	The growth of tourism to the Galapagos	36
3.6	Stakeholders in the Galapagos Islands	37
4.1	World climate zones	40
4.2	Bioclimatic chart	42
4.3	Tropical lowland and highland climates	49
4.4	The relationship between climate change and tourism	51
5.1	The historical development of transport and tourism	55
5.2	The five freedoms of the air	59
5.3	IATA traffic conference areas	60
5.4	Publicity poster	66
7.1	Bournemouth tourism consultation document	91–6
8.1	London Docklands	104
12.1	Growth of tourism to Bruges	141
16.1	Venice	190
21.1	Map of Nepal	269
23.1	Nunavut	312
26.1	International tourism in metamorphosis	360

List of tables

1.1	Smith's typology of tourists	8
1.2	Leisure and business tourism	9
2.1	Economic development and tourism	14
2.2	The international tourism shares of the developing countries and those at high mass consumption	15
2.3	Domestic age and tourism demand	18
2.4	Cohen's classification of tourists	19
2.5	International tourism arrivals: the historical trend	21
2.6	International tourism arrivals: the changing regional picture	23
3.1	Carrying capacity	26
3.2	The benefits of tourism planning	27
3.3	A classification of recreational resources	31
4.1	Temperatures and clothing: holiday travel in January	41
4.2	World climates and tourism	44–5
5.1	Characteristics of transport modes	57
9.1	The relative contribution of the tourism and finance sectors to the Manx economy, 1971 and 1995	115
12.1	Characteristics of tourism to Bruges	142
18.1	Development obstacles to tourism in Eastern Europe	223
19.1	Floating hotels on the Nile, 1995	238
19.2	Average daily number of visitors at the key sites in the Nile Valley in December	239
22.1	The effect of the Asian currency crisis on tourism	289

Preface

In the mid-1980s when we set out to write the first edition of *The Geography of Travel and Tourism* there was a pioneering feeling, as we followed in the footsteps of a very small number of geographers who had previously entered the territory of tourism. Fifteen years later, embarking on this third edition, *Worldwide Destinations: The Geography of Travel and Tourism*, the territory has been well and truly explored, not only by ourselves, but also by many other authors writing books, reports, and journal papers.

Indeed, writing the first edition presented real problems of sourcing accurate information and statistics about each country – yet for this edition, the information is much more readily available, not only in print form but also on the Internet. This creates both problems and opportunities – it certainly means that this edition can draw upon up-to-date material and the gaps that were evident in our first edition can be plugged. However, it does also raise issues both of the reliability of the information and also the sheer quantity of material creates information overload for students. Here the challenge is to transform that information into knowledge. To this end, we have changed the layout of the book to be more reader-friendly and introduced detailed case studies in each chapter to allow the reader to investigate key issues in more depth. We also hope that the book has a less Eurocentric focus than previous editions, and in so doing, we have included new and emerging destinations that were not on the tourism map – including space travel! – when we wrote the first edition.

Nonetheless we have retained many of the ingredients of the successful first two editions. In particular we have retained our comprehensive coverage of each region and country in the world, written to a flexible template including demand, supply, organization and regional tourism resources. We make no apology for this comprehensive approach, as we feel that not only is it still needed, but also it complements the more detailed treatment of other texts, reports and papers that deal with particular themes or regions of the world. For schools and colleges in particular this raises a real issue of library resourcing and we hope that this text provides an all-embracing framework from which students can build their knowledge of world travel and tourism. We also feel that many tourism courses are demanding geographical knowledge, not only in terms of traditional travel geography, but also through the analysis of destinations and other supply elements of tourism. It is here that geography can make a real contribution to the study of tourism. Many tourism modules and courses have titles such as tourism impacts, sustainable tourism, tourism development, tourism destinations ... In effect, they deal with a geographical analysis of tourism, though are not necessarily so labelled. We therefore hope that this book will be used by a wide variety of readers, whether geographers or not.

This new edition will be accompanied by an online tutor resource (due July 2001). Email the Butterworth-Heinemann Marketing Department at bhmarketing@repp.co.uk for further details.

As ever, a large number of family, friends and colleagues have assisted us, wittingly or unwittingly, in writing this edition – Mrs Cooper senior has typed much of the manuscript with her characteristic enthusiasm and accuracy, helped by Diane Hibbert in the International Centre for Tourism and Hospitality Research at Bournemouth University; Diana Ferry of the Institute of Commercial Management; Maria Boniface helped with the research for this book; Lionel Becherel compiled the list of destination web sites; the library at Bournemouth University has been a comprehensive source of material; and our students and colleagues from many countries around the world have been an invaluable source of information and trends. Kathryn Grant at Butterworth-Heinemann has been a supportive and professional editor and as always a delight to work with.

Brian Boniface and Chris Cooper
December 1999

Part One

The Elements of the Geography of Travel and Tourism

1

Introduction to the geography of travel and tourism

LEARNING OBJECTIVES

After reading this chapter, you should be able to:

1 Define and use the terms leisure, recreation, and tourism and understand their interrelationships.
2 Distinguish between the different forms of tourism, and the relationship of different types of tourist with the environment.
3 Appreciate the importance of scale in explaining patterns of tourism.
4 Identify the three major geographical components of tourism – tourist-generating areas, tourist-receiving areas and transit routes.
5 Explain the push and pull factors that give rise to tourist flows.
6 Appreciate the main methods used to measure tourist flows and be aware of their problems.

Leisure, recreation and tourism

What exactly is meant by the terms 'leisure', 'recreation' and 'tourism', and how are they related? *Leisure* is often seen as a measure of time and is usually used to mean the time left over after work, sleep, and personal and household chores have been completed (Figure 1.1). In other words, leisure is free time for individuals to spend as they please. This does, however, introduce the problem of whether all free time is leisure. A good example of this dilemma is whether the unemployed feel that their free time is in fact 'enforced' leisure. This has led to the view that leisure is as much an attitude of mind as a measure of time, and that an element of 'choice' has to be involved.

Recreation is normally taken to mean the variety of activities undertaken during leisure time (Figure 1.1). Basically, recreation refreshes a person's strength and spirit and can include activities as diverse as watching television or holidaying abroad.

If we accept that leisure is a measure of time and that recreation embraces the activities undertaken during that time, then tourism is simply one type of recreation activity.

It is, however, more difficult to disentangle the meanings of the terms 'recreation' and 'tourism' in practice. Perhaps the most helpful way to think about the difference is to envisage a spectrum with, at one end, recreation based either at home or close to home and, at the opposite end, recreational travel where some distance is involved and overnight accommodation may be needed. This is based on the time required for the activity and the distance travelled, and it places tourism firmly at one extreme of the *recreation activity continuum* (Figure 1.1). The idea of a continuum is helpful as, for example, it allows us to consider the role of same-day visitors or excursionists. These travellers are increasingly a consideration in the geography of tourism – they visit for less than twenty-four hours and do not stay overnight. In other words, they utilize all tourism facilities except accommodation, and place pressures on the host environment and society.

Clearly, tourism is a distinctive form of recreation and demands separate consideration. Many different definitions of tourism exist, and the international debate as to the definition of tourism still continues. The United Nations Statistical Commission now accepts the following definition of tourism: 'The activities of persons travelling to and staying in places outside their usual environment for not more than one consecutive year for leisure, business and other purposes.'

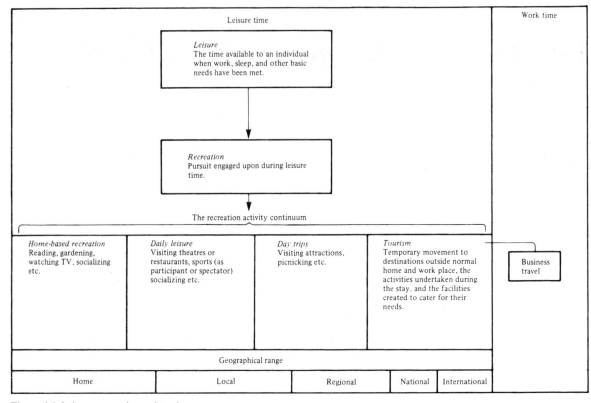

Figure 1.1 Leisure, recreation and tourism

This definition raises a number of issues:

- It is a *demand-side definition*, more concerned with identifying the 'tourist' than the tourism sector or industry. The debate to define tourism is now firmly focused on the *supply-side* – locating tourism businesses and activities on to internationally accepted classifications of industries and employment categories.
- What is a person's *usual environment*?
- The inclusion of business and other *purposes of visit* demands that we conceive of tourism more widely than simply as a recreation pursuit.
- Certain types of traveller are excluded from the definition (see case study in this chapter). Of course, tourism itself is only one part of the spectrum of travel, which ranges from daily travel to work or for shopping to migration, where the traveller intends to take up permanent or long-term residence in another area.

Geography and tourism

When we study the geography of travel and tourism, three key concepts need to be considered:

- spatial scale
- the geographical components of the tourism system
- spatial interaction between the components of the tourist system.

Spatial scale

Geographers study the spatial expression of tourism as a human activity, focusing on both tourist-generating and tourist-receiving areas as well as the links between them. This study can be undertaken at a variety of scales, ranging from the world distribution of climatic zones, through the regional assessment of tourist resources, to the local landscapes of resorts.

The idea of scale has been used to organize the material presented in this book because at each different scale a distinctive perspective on and insight into tourism is gained. Simply, as a more detailed explanation is required, attention is drawn to ever smaller parts of the problem. This idea of scale, or geographical magnitude, keeps in focus the area being dealt with, and can be likened to increasing or decreasing the magnification on a microscope or the scale of a map. Burton (1991), for example, provides a good example of the importance of scale when considering tourism flows. At the international scale in the Northern Hemisphere the dominant flow of tourists is north to south, but at the regional scale a variety of other patterns emerge such as travel between cities, or out of cities to the coast and countryside.

The geographical components of the tourism system

From a geographical point of view tourism consists of three major components which are; first, the places of origin of tourists, or *generating areas*; second, the tourist destinations themselves, or *receiving areas*; and, finally, the routes travelled between these two sets of locations, or *transit routes* (Leiper, 1979). This simple model is illustrated in Figure 1.2 and the components form the basis for Chapters 2 to 5 in this book.

- *Tourist-generating areas* represent the homes of tourists, where journeys begin and end. The key issues to examine in tourist-generating areas are the features that stimulate demand for tourism and will include the geographical location of an area as well as its socioeconomic and demographic characteristics. These areas represent the main tourist markets in the world and, naturally enough, the major marketing functions of the tourist industry are found here (such as tour operation, travel retailing). Tourist-generating areas are considered in Chapter 2.
- *Tourist-destination areas* attract tourists to stay temporarily and will have features and attractions that may not be found in the generating areas. The tourist industry located in this area will comprise the accommodation,

retailing and service functions, entertainment, and recreation. In our view, tourist destination areas are the most important part of the tourism system, not only attracting the tourist and thus energizing the system but also where the impacts of tourism occur and therefore where the planning and management of tourism is so important. Features of tourist destination areas are examined in Chapters 3 and 4.

- *Transit routes* link these two types of areas and are a key element in the system as their effectiveness and characteristics shape the size and direction of tourist flows. Such routes represent the location of the main transportation component of the tourist industry and are considered in Chapter 5.

Spatial interaction between the components of the tourist system

Tourist flows

While the study of the geography of tourism should include the three components identified above, there is a danger that, in conveniently dissecting tourism into its component parts, the all-important interrelationships are lost. The consideration of tourist flows between regions is therefore fundamental to the geography of tourism and allows the components of tourism to be viewed as a total system rather than a series of disconnected parts.

Tourist flows are a form of spatial interaction between two areas with the destination area containing a surplus of a commodity (tourist attractions, for example) and the generating area having a deficit, or *demand* for that

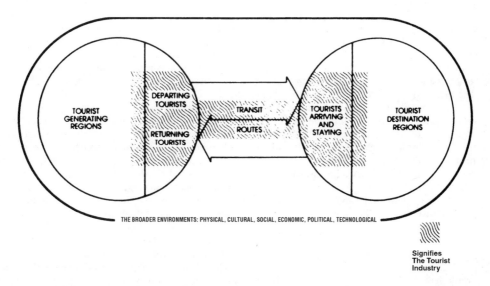

Figure 1.2 The tourism system
Source: Leiper (1979).

commodity. In fact, it is possible to detect regular patterns of tourist flows. They do not occur randomly but follow certain rules and are influenced by a variety of push and pull factors:

- *Push factors* are mainly concerned with the stage of economic development in the generating area and will include such factors as levels of affluence, mobility and holiday entitlement. Often, too, an advanced stage of economic development will not only give the population the means to engage in tourism but the pressures of life will provide the 'push' to do so. An unfavourable climate will also provide a strong impetus to travel.
- *Pull factors* include accessibility, and the attractions and amenities of the destination area. The relative cost of the visit is also important, as is the marketing and promotion of the receiving area.

Explaining tourist flows

The flows, or interaction, between places are highly complex and are influenced by a wide variety of interrelated variables. A number of attempts have been made to explain the factors that affect tourist flows and to provide rules governing the magnitude of flows between regions. An early attempt was made by Williams and Zelinsky (1970) who selected fourteen countries that had relatively stable tourist flows over a few years and which accounted for the bulk of the world's tourist traffic. They identified a number of factors that helped to explain these flows. These included:

- distances between countries (the greater the distance, the smaller the volume of flow)
- international connectivity (shared business or cultural ties between countries)
- the general attractiveness of one country for another.

A second means of explaining tourist flows is offered by the *gravity model*, based on two main factors that influence flows. The first of these are the push and pull factors which generate flows, and the gravity model states that the larger the 'mass' of the pushing or pulling regions, the greater the flow between them. The second factor is a restraining one, based on the distance between the origin and the destination of the flow. Here, the time and cost involved in travel act to reduce flows with distance. This is known as the friction of distance.

Other, more complex, multivariate models can also be used to explain tourist flows. The work of Witt (see Sources) is notable here.

Measuring tourist flows

As tourist flows have grown in prominence, national governments and international organizations have introduced the measurement of both international and domestic flows. Burkart and Medlik (1981) have identified three main reasons why this statistical measurement of flows is important:

1 Statistics are required to evaluate the magnitude of tourist flows and to monitor any change. This allows projections of future flows and the identification of market trends to be made.
2 Statistics act as a base of hard fact to allow tourism planners and developers to operate effectively and plan for the future of tourism.
3 The statistics are used by both the public and private sectors as a basis for their marketing.

Measurement of tourist flows can be divided into three main types:

1 *Statistics of volume* give the number of tourists leaving an area or visiting a destination in a given period of time and provide a basic count of the volume of tourist traffic. Volume statistics also include the length of stay of visitors at their destinations.
2 The second category of statistics is that of *tourist characteristics*. While statistics of volume are a measure of the quantity of tourist flows, this second category measures the quality of the flow and will include information on types of tourist (sex, age, socioeconomic group, etc.) and their behaviour (structure of the trip, attitudes to the destination, etc.). It is not uncommon for statistics of tourist characteristics and volume to be collected together.
3 The third type is *expenditure statistics*. Tourist flows are not simply movements of people but they also have an important economic significance for the destination, the generating region, and the transport carriers. Quite simply, tourism represents a flow of money that is earned in one place and spent in another. To make comparisons easier, expenditure is usually expressed in US dollars rather than the national currency.

A variety of methods are available to measure tourist flows. For volume statistics, tourists can be counted as they enter or leave an area and immigration figures will often provide this information. Obviously this is relatively straightforward for international flows, but much more problematical for domestic tourism. For destination areas, an alternative method is to enumerate tourists at their accommodation by the use of registration cards. This method is only effective with legal enforcement and normally omits visitors staying in private houses, or with friends or relatives.

Statistics of domestic tourism volume may be obtained by national travel surveys or destination surveys. National travel surveys involve interviewing a representative sample of the population in their own homes. Questions are asked on the nature and extent of travel over a past period and the results not only provide statistics on the volume of domestic tourism but also may include expenditure and the character of the flows. Examples of national travel surveys include the UK Tourism Survey (UKTS) and the German *Reiseanalyse*. In destination surveys visitors to a tourist area, specific site, or attraction are questioned to establish the volume, value, and characteristics of traffic to the area or site.

Surveys of tourist characteristics have evolved from straightforward questioning which gives basic factual information (for example, the age profile of visitors) to surveys which now concentrate on questions designed to assist the marketing and management of a destination, or to solve a particular problem. Statistics of tourist characteristics are obtained in a variety of ways. Additional questions can be added to accommodation registration cards or border checks, but more commonly a sample of travellers is asked a series of questions about themselves, their trip, opinions of the destination, etc. (An example of this approach is the UK International Passenger Survey (IPS) which measures the volume and value as well as the characteristics of UK inbound and outbound tourism.)

Measurement of tourist expenditure can be obtained by asking tourists directly how much they have spent on their holiday, or indirectly by asking hoteliers and other suppliers of tourist services for estimates of tourist spending. For international expenditure statistics, bank records of foreign currency exchange may be used as another indirect method.

Despite the variety of methods available to measure tourist flows, it is not easy to produce accurate tourist statistics. In the first place, the tourist has to be distinguished from other travellers (e.g. returning residents) and, while internationally agreed definitions of tourists do exist, they are not yet consistently applied throughout the world. At the same time, until recently there has been no real attempt to co-ordinate international surveys. To add to these problems, survey methods change over the years, even within single countries, and comparisons of results from year to year are difficult. A further problem is that surveys count 'events', not 'people', so that a tourist who visits a country twice in a year will be counted as two arrivals. Those on touring holidays may be counted as separate arrivals in various destinations and will inflate the overall visitor arrival figures. The relaxation of border controls, especially within groups of trading countries – such as the European Union (EU), compounds the tourist statistician's problem and makes it difficult to enumerate tourists.

Forms of tourism

The geographical components of tourism, allied to the idea of scale and tourist flows, combine to create a wide variety of different forms of tourism. These forms of tourism can be organized according to:

- type of destination
- the characteristics of the tourism system
- the market
- the distance travelled.

Type of destination

Tourism can be classified according to the type of destination visited. Here, from a geographical point of view, an important distinction is that between international and domestic tourism:

- *Domestic tourism* embraces those travelling within their own country.
- *International tourism* comprises those who travel to a country other than that in which they normally live. International tourism can be thought of as:
  - *inbound tourism* – non-residents travelling in a given country
  - *outbound tourism* – involving residents of a particular country travelling abroad to other countries.

International tourists invariably have to cross national frontiers and may well have to use another currency and encounter a different language. Clearly, the size of a country is important here. Larger countries are more likely to have a variety of tourist attractions and resorts and, quite simply, the greater physical distances, which have to be overcome, may deter international tourism. This is exemplified by the volumes of domestic tourism in the USA (almost 90 per cent of all tourism) compared to the Netherlands (around 50 per cent). Increasingly, too, the distinction between these two forms of tourism is diminishing as the facilitation of movement between countries is increased and barriers to travel lowered. In the EU, for example, from 1 January 1993 all travel between member states has been classed as domestic.

Concern for the environmental impact of tourism has focused attention on ways of classifying tourists according to their relationship with the destination. Smith (1978), for example, groups tourists along a continuum ranging from explorers, with virtually no impact, to mass tourists where the impact may be considerable (see Table 1.1).

The characteristics of the tourism system

In the above section we considered forms of tourism based on the destination. Taking this idea further we can consider forms of tourism based dominantly on the destination visited, but also where the destination visited will influence the other components of the tourism system – the market and its motivation to travel, and the means and form of transport used. In other words, the tourism product determines the nature of the tourism system. For example:

- rural tourism
- urban tourism

- heritage tourism
- cultural tourism
- eco-tourism.

The final form of tourism on the list – eco-tourism – exemplifies this approach.

- In the *generating area* for example, the eco-tourist characteristically will be motivated by the responsible consumption of nature-based tourism products and will be educated to an above average level.
- In the *destination area*, nature will be the main attraction and the ancillary services (accommodation, transport, etc.) will be well managed and 'green' or 'environmentally friendly'.
- In the *transit zone*, the eco-tourist will seek locally owned companies who attempt to minimize the impact upon the environment caused by their transport operations.

The market

A further basis for classifying forms of tourism relates to the market itself. This can be in terms of the purpose of visit of the tourist:

- *Holiday tourism* is perhaps the most commonly understood form, where the purpose of visit is leisure and recreation. Holiday tourism can be divided into the 'sun, sea and sand' type where good weather and beach-related activities are important or the 'touring, sightseeing and culture' type where new destinations, and different life styles are sought (Holloway, 1989).
- *Common-interest tourism* comprises those travelling with a purpose common to those visited at the destination (such as visiting friends and relatives [VFR], religion, health or education reasons). Common interest tourists – especially those visiting friends and relatives – may

Table 1.1   Smith's typology of tourists

Type of tourist	Numbers	Adapt to local destination	Tourist impact decreases	Tourist volume increases
Explorer	Very limited	Accepts fully	↑	⎤
Elite	Rarely seen	Accepts fully		
Off-beat	Unknown, but visible	Adapts well		
Incipient mass	Steady flows	Seeks Western amenities		
Mass	Continuous influx	Expects Western amenities		
Charter	Massive arrivals	Demands Western amenities		↓

Explorer
These include academics, climbers, and true explorers in small numbers. They totally accept local conditions, and are self-sufficient, with portable chemical toilets, dehydrated food, and walkie-talkies.

Elite
Travelling off the beaten track for pleasure, they have done it all, and are now looking for something different. While they use tourist facilities, they adapt easily to local conditions – if they can eat it, we can.

Off-beat
Not as rich as the elite tourist, they are looking for an added extra to a standard tour. They adapt well and cope with local conditions for a few days.

Incipient mass
A steady flow of tourists but in small groups or individuals. They are looking for central heating/air conditioning and other amenities, but will cope for a while if they are absent, and put it down to part of the 'experience'.

Mass tourism
Large numbers of tourists, often European or North American, with middle-class values and relatively high incomes. The flow is highly seasonal, with tourists expecting Western amenities and multi-lingual guides.

Charter tourism
This is full-blown, down-market, high volume tourism. It is totally dependent upon the travel trade. The tourists have standardized tastes and demands, and the country of destination is irrelevant. This type of tourism is less common in developing and undeveloped countries.

Source: Smith (1978).

make little or no demand upon accommodation or other tourist facilities at the destination.

- *Business and professional tourism* makes up the final purpose-of-visit category. Included among business tourists are those attending trade fairs and conferences or participating in incentive travel schemes. The inclusion of business travel complicates the simple idea of tourism being just another recreational activity. Clearly, business travel is not regarded as part of a person's

leisure time and cannot be thought of as recreation. Yet, because business travellers use the same facilities as those travelling for pleasure and they are not permanent employees or residents of the host destination, they must be included in any definition of tourists (Figure 1.1). The business traveller, unlike the holiday-maker, is highly constrained in terms of where and when to travel. The differences are summarized in Table 1.2.

Table 1.2 Leisure and business tourism

	Leisure tourism	*Business tourism*	*But . . .*
Who pays?	● The tourist	● The traveller's employer or association	● Self-employed business travellers are paying for their own trips
Who decides on the destination?	● The tourist	● The organizer of the meeting/incentive trip/conference/exhibition	● Organizers will often take into account delegates' wishes
When do trips take place?	● During classic holiday periods and at weekends resulting in seasonal demand	● All year round, no seasonal fluctuations, but less demand at weekends	● Peak holiday months are avoided for major events
Lead time? (period of time between booking and going on the trip)	● Holidays usually booked a few months in advance; short breaks, a few days	● Some business trips must be made at very short notice	● Major conferences are booked many years in advance
Who travels?	● Anyone with the necessary spare time and money	● Those whose work requires them to travel, or members of associations ● Generally over 75 per cent of business travellers are men	● Not all business trips involve managers on white-collar duties ● In the USA women account for 40 per cent of business travellers
What kinds of destination are used?	● All kinds: coastal, city, mountain and countryside	● Little choice of destination, except for conferences etc. ● Largely centred on cities in industrial countries	● Incentive destinations are much the same as for up-market holidays
How important is price in influencing demand?	● Sensitive to price, resulting in elasticity of demand	● Less sensitive to price – time is more crucial	● Economic recession can cause a downturn in demand or a switch to cheaper transport (e.g. from business to economy class)

Source: Adapted from Davidson (1994: p. 4).

A further market-based approach is to consider:

- the *nature of the tourists* themselves such as
  - youth tourism
  - grey tourism
  - gay tourism
- the type of travel arrangement purchased such as
  - an *inclusive tour* where two or more components of the tour are purchased together and one price is paid
  - *independent travel* arrangements where the traveller purchases the various elements of the trip separately
  - *tailor-made*, which is a combination of the two.

Distance travelled

A final basis for a classification of tourism is by the distance travelled:

- *Long-haul tourism* is generally taken to be journeys of over 3000 kilometres.
- *Short-haul tourism* comprises journeys below that distance.

The distinction is important in terms of aircraft operations and for marketing.

In all of these approaches to the identification of forms of tourism it is important to recognize that each particular form of tourism will still involve all of the geographical components but that each component will be configured in a distinctive way and take on particular characteristics.

Summary

Leisure has come to be accepted as a measure of free time, while recreation is seen as the activity undertaken during that time. Tourism is a distinctive form of recreation including a stay away from home, often involving long-distance travel and encompassing travel for business or other purposes.

The geography of travel and tourism focuses on three key concepts. First, tourism consists of three main geographical components: the tourist-generating areas, the tourist-receiving areas and transit routes. Second, from a geographical point of view, tourism can be considered from a number of scales, from the world scale, to the regional and local scales, depending upon the level of detail required. Finally, the spatial interaction that is generated between the components of the tourism system, and at different spatial scales, is conceived of as tourist flows. Understanding of these flows is fundamental to the geography of tourism and can be achieved by considering the push and pull factors that give rise to these flows, and how they can be measured.

Different forms of tourism can be distinguished, based upon the destination chosen, components of the tourism system, the market, purpose of visit, the distance travelled, and not least, the nature of the tourists themselves.

Case study

Other forms of travel

Drawing up definitions of tourism is problematic, simply because certain forms of travel have to be excluded from tourism statistics. Figure 1.3 shows in diagrammatic form the various classifications of travellers who are both included and excluded in official tourism statistics, but we need to look more closely at the following:

- *Travellers.* Travel, if we include the nomadic wanderings of hunters and herdsmen, is older than civilization itself. In all periods of history some travellers have been motivated by 'wanderlust' or curiosity, in contrast to the majority whose journeys were regarded as essential – merchants, missionaries, diplomats, soldiers and sailors. Visitors to remote parts of the world often see themselves as 'travellers' or even 'explorers' rather than tourists, and their journeys as 'expeditions' or 'treks' rather than tours or excursions. They would argue that conventional tourism has become altogether too commercialized, comfortable and predictable, and that 'real travel' should involve an element of hardship and improvization, as in the past. However, from an official statistical point of view these self-styled *travellers* still count as tourists, however much they dislike the term.
- *Migrants.* Migration is clearly different from tourism. You could define migration as travel with a commitment to live and work in another country or region. People leaving their home country or region are emigrants, whereas on arrival in their place of adoption they become immigrants. On an international level, they require special documentation to legally enter, reside and work in that country. Emigrants provide a great deal of business for many airlines and shipping companies, and they may require specialized freight forwarding and resettlement services. Migration between specified countries is subject to more restrictions nowadays than during the nineteenth and early twentieth centuries – for example, both the USA and the EU place strict controls on immigration. Migration to these regions is often for the purpose of finding employment for a few years rather than with the intention of making a permanent home in another country. The *guest workers* of Germany are one example of such short-term migrants. Much smaller numbers of *expatriates* from countries like Britain are working in areas such as the oil-rich Gulf States as highly paid professionals. These people generate a considerable demand for tourism in their country of temporary residence.
- *Refugees.* Although economic pressures are the motivation for most immigrants, refugees are forced by

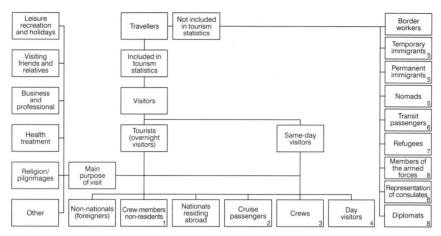

1 Foreign air or ship crews docked or in lay over and who use the accommodation establishments of the country visited.

2 Persons who arrive in a country aboard cruise ships (as defined by the International Maritime Organization, 1965) and who spend the night aboard ship even when disembarking for one or more day visits.

3 Crews who are not residents of the country visited and who stay in the country for the day.

4 Visitors who arrive and leave the same day for: leisure, recreation and holidays; visiting friends and relatives; business and professional; health treatment; religion/pilgrimages and other tourism purposes, including transit day visitors en route to or from their destination countries.

5 As defined by the United Nations in the Recommendations on Statistics of International Migration, 1980.

6 Who do not leave the transit area of the airport or the port, including transfer between airports and ports.

7 As defined by the United Nations High Commissioner for Refugees, 1967.

8 When they travel from their country of origin to the duty station and vice versa (including household servants and dependants accompanying or joining them).

Figure 1.3 Classification of travellers
Source: World Tourism Organization.

war or political oppression to find sanctuary in another country or region. In the second half of the twentieth century, the volume of refugees worldwide has remained persistently high at about 15 million annually, although their origins and destinations change as new 'trouble-spots' appear on the world scene. The protection of refugees is one of the responsibilities of the United Nations, which attempts to persuade member states to be more generous in extending the right of asylum to those fleeing from persecution. Solutions to the problem include:

– voluntary repatriation to the place of origin (although Article 37 of the United Nations Charter forbids the return of a refugee if their life or liberty are at risk)
– integration in the country of present residence
– resettlement in other countries which have greater resources.

2
The geography of demand for tourism

LEARNING OBJECTIVES

After reading this chapter, you should be able to:

1 Explain the term 'tourist demand' and distinguish between its components.
2 Understand the concepts of travel propensity and frequency.
3 Identify the determinants of demand for tourism.
4 Explain the influence of stage in economic development, population factors and political regimes on demand for tourism.
5 Understand the influence of personal variables on the demand for tourism.
6 Appreciate the main barriers to travel which lead to suppressed demand.

Leisure, recreation and tourism: a basic human right?

Leisure, recreation, and tourism are of benefit to both individuals and societies. The United Nations (UN) recognized this as early as 1948 by adopting its Universal Declaration of Human Rights, which states that everyone 'has the right to rest and leisure including . . . periodic holidays with pay'. More specifically, in 1980 the World Tourism Organization declared the ultimate aim of tourism to be 'the improvement of the quality of life and the creation of better living conditions for all peoples'. In other words, statements by such organizations suggest that everyone has the right to demand tourism; however, more recent statements are tempered by the need to recognize

that such demands should have a positive impact upon host societies and environments: 'Tourism: a leading activity of the 21st Century for job creation and environmental protection' (World Tourism Day declaration by the World Tourism Organization, September, 1997).

This chapter examines how participation in tourism differs between nations and between individuals and explains why, despite declarations to the contrary, tourism is an activity highly concentrated among the affluent, industrialized nations. For much of the rest of the world, and indeed many disadvantaged groups in industrialized nations, participation in tourism, and particularly international tourism, remains an unobtainable luxury.

The demand for tourism: concepts and definitions

Geographers define tourist demand as 'the total number of persons who travel, or wish to travel, to use tourist facilities and services at places away from their places of work and residence' (Mathieson and Wall, 1982). This definition implies a wide range of influences, in addition to price and income, as determinants of demand and includes not only those who actually participate in tourism but also those who wish to but, for some reason, do not.

Demand for tourism consists of a number of components:

● Effective or actual demand comprises the numbers of participants in tourism, i.e. those who are actually travelling. This is the component of demand most commonly and easily measured and the bulk of tourist statistics refer to effective demand.

- Suppressed demand is made up of that section of the population that does not travel for some reason. Two elements of suppressed demand can be distinguished:
  - potential demand refers to those who will travel at some future date if they experience a change in circumstances, e.g. their purchasing power may increase.
  - deferred demand is a demand postponed because of a problem in the supply environment, i.e. scarcity of a good or service (e.g. travel opportunities).
  In other words, both deferred and potential demand may be converted into effective demand at some future date.
- Finally, there will always be those who simply do not wish to travel, constituting a category of no demand.

Effective demand

Travel propensity

In tourism, a useful measure of effective demand is travel propensity, meaning the percentage of a population that actually engages in tourism. Net travel propensity refers to the percentage of the population that take at least one tourism trip in a given period of time, while gross travel propensity gives the total number of tourism trips taken as a percentage of the population. Clearly, as second and third holidays increase in importance, so gross travel propensity becomes more relevant. Simply dividing gross travel propensity by net will give the travel frequency, in other words, the average number of trips taken by those participating in tourism during the period in question (see Appendix 2.1). The suppressed and no-demand components will ensure that net travel propensity never ap-

proaches 100 per cent and a figure of 70 per cent or 80 per cent is likely to be the maximum. Gross travel propensity, however, can exceed 100 per cent and often approaches 200 per cent in some Western European countries where those participating in tourism take more than one trip away from home.

Determinants of travel propensity

Travel propensity is determined by a variety of factors which, for the purposes of this chapter, can be divided into two broad groups. First, there are the influences that lie at the national level of generalization and comprise the world view of travel propensity, including economic development, population characteristics, and political regimes. Second, a personal view of variations in travel propensity can be envisaged in such terms as lifestyle, life cycle and personality factors. In fact, a third group of factors relating to the supply of tourist services is also important. This group encompasses technology, the price, frequency and speed of transport, as well as the characteristics of accommodation, facilities, and travel organizers. These factors are dealt with in Chapters 3 and 5.

The world view

Stage in economic development

A society's level of economic development is a major determinant of the magnitude of tourist demand because the economy influences so many critical, and interrelated, factors. The economic development of nations can be divided into a number of stages, as outlined in Table 2.1 and Figure 2.1.

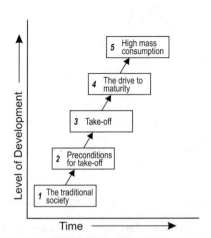

Approximate date of reaching a new stage of development

Stage Country	2	3	4	5
UK	1750	1820	1850	1940
USA	1800	1850	1920	1930
Japan	1880	1900	1930	1950
Venezuela	1920	1950	1970	-
India	1950	1980?	-	-
Ethiopia	-	-	-	-

Figure 2.1 Stages in economic growth
Source: Waugh (1995: 574).

Table 2.1   Economic development and tourism

Economic stage	Some characteristics	Examples
Traditional society Long-established land-owning aristocracy, traditional customs, majority employed in agriculture. Very low output per capita, impossible to improve without changing system. Poor health levels, high poverty levels	*The least developed countries of the Third World.* Economic and social conditions deny most forms of tourism except perhaps domestic VFR	Parts of Africa and southern Asia
Pre-conditions for take-off Innovation of ideas from outside the system. Leaders recognize the desirability of change	*The more advanced developing countries of the Third World.* From the take-off stage, economic and social conditions allow increasing amounts of domestic tourism (mainly visiting friends and relatives). Outbound international tourism is also possible in the drive to maturity. Inbound tourism is often encouraged as a foreign exchange earner	South and Central America[a]; parts of the Middle East[a], Asia and Africa
Take-off Leaders in favour of change gain power and alter production methods and economic structure. Manufacturing and services expand		Mexico; parts of South America
Drive to maturity[b] Industrialization continues in all economic sectors with a switch from heavy manufacturing to sophisticated and diversified products		
High mass consumption Economy now at full potential, producing large numbers of consumer goods and services. New emphasis on satisfying cultural needs	*The developed world.* Major generators of international and domestic tourism	North America; Western Europe; Japan; Australia; New Zealand; parts of South East Asia

Notes: (a) Countries which are members of the Organization of Petroleum Exporting Countries (OPEC) are a notable exception in these regions; examples include Algeria, Libya, Nigeria, Kuwait, Saudi Arabia, Ecuador and Venezuela.
(b) Other countries that merit a special classification are:
    (i)   Former Eastern European and Soviet Bloc countries which are in the transition stage to market economies
    (ii) Centrally planned economies, although most are at the drive to maturity stage; examples include China and North Korea.

Source: Adapted from Chubb and Chubb (1981), Cleverdon (1979) and Rostow (1959).

As a society moves towards a developed economy a number of important processes occur. The nature of employment changes from work in the primary sector (agriculture, fishing, forestry) to work in the secondary sector (manufacturing goods) and the tertiary sector (services such as tourism). As this process unfolds, an affluent society usually emerges and numbers of the economically active increase from around 30 per cent or less in the developing world to 50 per cent or more in the high mass-consumption stage of Western Europe or the USA. With progression to the drive to maturity, discretionary incomes increase and create demand for consumer goods and leisure pursuits such as tourism.

Other developments parallel the changing nature of employment. The population is healthier and has time for recreation and tourism (including paid holiday entitlement). Improving educational standards and access to media channels boost awareness of tourism opportunities, and transportation and mobility rise in line with these changes. Institutions respond to this increased demand by developing a range of leisure products and services. These developments occur in conjunction with each other until, at the high

Table 2.2   The international tourism shares of the developing countries and those at high mass consumption

Economic stage	1990 Share of international tourist arrivals (%)	1997 Share of international tourist arrivals (%)
Developing countries stage	28	31
High mass-consumption stage	62	57

Note: Shares do not total 100 per cent due to other categories not included in the table.

Source: WTO (1998).

mass-consumption stage, all the economic indicators encourage high levels of travel propensity. Clearly, tourism is a result of industrialization and, quite simply, the more highly developed an economy, the greater the levels of tourist demand. Indeed as the World Tourism Organization (WTO) clearly states: 'The combined share of developing countries in the global tourism market . . . is still less than half that of developed countries in respect of arrivals, and only just in excess of one third of tourist receipts' (WTO, 1995: 11).

However, the share of the developing countries is increasing in terms of both volume and expenditure (Table 2.2). As more countries reach the drive to maturity or high mass-consumption stage, so the volume of trade and foreign investment increases and business travel develops. Business travel is sensitive to economic activity, and although it could be argued that increasingly sophisticated communication systems may render business travel unnecessary, there is no evidence of this to date. Indeed, the very development of global markets and the constant need for face-to-face contact should ensure a continuing demand for business travel.

Population factors

Levels of population growth, its development, distribution and density affect travel propensity. Population growth and development can be closely linked to the stages of economic growth outlined in Table 2.1 by considering the demographic transition, where population growth and development is seen in terms of four connected phases (Figure 2.2).

- The *high stationary phase* corresponds to many of the least developed countries in the Third World with high birth and death rates keeping the population at a fluctuating but low level.
- The *early expanding phase* sees high birth rates but a fall in death rates due to improved health, sanitation, and social stability leading to population expansion characterized by young, large families. These countries are

often unable to provide for their growing populations and as a result are gradually becoming poorer. Clearly, tourism is a luxury that most cannot afford, although some nations are developing an inbound tourism industry to earn foreign exchange: indeed low-income countries have shown the highest growth in inbound tourism in the 1990s.
- The *late expanding phase* sees a fall in the birth rate rooted in the growth of an industrial society and advances in birth control technology. Most developing countries fit into these two categories with a transition to the late expanding phase paralleling the drive to maturity.
- The *low stationary phase* corresponds to the high mass-consumption stage of economic development. Here, birth and death rates have stabilized to a low level. At this stage, it is the changing characteristics of the population which have important implications for tourism demand in terms of:
  - populations are ageing
  - these ageing populations have a high discretionary income
  - the post-Second World War baby boomers are an important population cohort who, as discerning travellers will be able to exercise 'grey' power and influence demand
  - household composition is changing with increased numbers of single and childless households and fewer families in the traditional sense.

Population density has a less important influence on travel propensity than has the distribution of population between urban and rural areas. The densely populated rural nations of South-East Asia have low travel propensities due to the level of economic development and the simple fact that the population is mainly dependent upon subsistence agriculture and has neither the time nor the income to devote to tourism. In contrast, densely populated urban areas normally indicate a developed economy with consumer purchasing power giving rise to high travel propensity. The urge to escape from the stress of the urban environment –

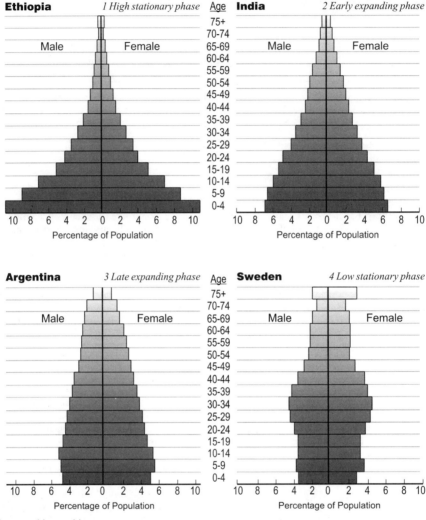

Figure 2.2 The demographic transition
Source: Waugh (1995).

'to get away from it all' – is particularly strong in large cities or conurbations.

The distribution of population within a nation also affects patterns, rather than strictly levels, of tourist demand. Where population is concentrated into one part of the country tourism demand is distorted. This asymmetrical distribution of population is well illustrated by the USA, where two-thirds of the population live in the eastern one-third of the country. The consequent east-to-west pattern of tourist flow (and permanent migration) has placed pressure on the recreation and tourist resources of the western states. At the regional level concentration of population into cities

also has implications for demand patterns, with a recreation and tourism hinterland often developing around the city.

Political influences

Politics affect travel propensities in a number of ways:

● *Political complexion* In democratic nations the degree of government involvement in promoting and providing facilities for tourism varies. Typically, 'conservative' administrations subscribe to the principles of the free market and act to nurture an environment in which the tourism industries can flourish, rather than the administration being directly involved in tourism itself. Socialist administrations, on the other hand, encourage the involvement of the government in tourism and often provide opportunities for the 'disadvantaged' to participate in tourism. Democracies may also control levels of propensity for travel abroad by limiting the amount of foreign currency that can be taken out of a country. Commonly this occurs when a nation's own currency is weak or the economy faltering. A weak currency will also deter people from travelling abroad. Currency controls are more common in planned economies, where levels of control of international tourism can be considerable. In planned economies tourist organizations are centralized and act as an arm of the administration. The people's freedom of movement is often curtailed, and inbound tourism is inhibited by the need to obtain visas.

- *Political groupings* Politics is also influencing tourism demand in terms of political and economic groupings of countries and the increased facilitation of travel between members of such groupings. The member countries of the EU for example, are committed to the effective abolition of border controls, a move which has boosted demand for intra-European travel.
- *Deregulation* The political environment for deregulation and privatization also encourages tourism demand through such initiatives as the deregulation of transportation which can act to reduce fares and thus increase demand for travel; and the increased efficiency of the sector, which again acts to boost demand through lowered prices and higher quality.
- *Political instability* In a more general sense, unstable political regimes where civil disorder or war is prevalent may forbid non-essential travel, and inbound tourism will be adversely affected.

The personal view

Two sets of personal factors influence travel propensity and therefore act to condition access to tourism. The first group of factors can be termed *lifestyle* and include income, employment, holiday entitlement, educational attainment and mobility. A second group comes under the term *life cycle*, where the age and domestic circumstances of an individual combine to affect both the amount and type of tourism demanded. Naturally, these factors are interrelated and complementary. A high-status job is normally associated with an individual in middle age with a high income, above-average holiday entitlement, education and mobility. The interweaving of these variables, coupled with their rapid growth throughout the latter half of the twentieth century, have combined to make leisure, recreation, and tourism a major force in the developed world.

Lifestyle determinants

Income

Tourism is a luxury, an expensive activity that demands a certain threshold of income before an individual can choose to take part.

- *Gross income* is the total amount earned, but gives little indication of the money available to spend on tourism.
- *Disposable income* represents the money that actually reaches the public's hands to dispose of as they please, but demands on disposable income include essentials such as housing, food, and clothing.
- *Discretionary income* is the most useful measure of the ability to participate in tourism. Discretionary income is the income left over when tax, housing and the basics of life have been accounted for. Clearly, two households with the same gross incomes may have very different discretionary incomes.
- The relationship between income levels and consumption of tourism is known as *elasticity*. As we would expect, the higher the income, the higher is the demand for tourism. Of course, different generating regions have different degrees of elasticity – it tends to be higher for the North Americans and Japanese than for Europeans. This means that, a low discretionary income markedly depresses travel propensity. As discretionary income rises, the ability to partake of tourism is associated with the purchase of leisure-orientated goods, until, with a high discretionary income, travel may reach a peak and then level off as the demands of a high-status job, and possibly frequent business trips, reduce the ability and desire to travel for pleasure.

Employment

The nature of employment not only influences travel propensity by determining income and holiday entitlement but also has an effect upon the type of holiday demanded. A more fundamental distinction is between those in employment and those unemployed. The impact of unemployment on tourism demand is obvious, but the nature of demand is also changed, with the threat of job insecurity among the workforce encouraging later booking of trips, more domestic holidays, shorter lengths of stay and lower spending levels.

Paid-holiday entitlement

A variety of holiday arrangements now exist worldwide, with most nations having a number of one-day national holidays, as well as annual paid holiday entitlement by law or collective agreements. Individual levels of paid-holiday entitlement would seem to be an obvious determinant of travel propensity, but in fact the relationship is not straightforward. However, it is possible to make a number of generalizations.

- Low levels of entitlement do act as a real constraint upon the ability to travel, while a high entitlement encourages travel. This is in part due to the interrelationship between entitlement and factors such as job status, income and mobility.
- As levels of entitlement increase, the cost of tourism may mean that more of this entitlement will be spent at home.
- Patterns of entitlement are changing. Entitlement is increasingly used as a wage-bargaining tool and the introduction of flexitime, work sharing and long week-ends will release blocks of time which may be used for short holiday breaks.

Other personal factors

Level of educational attainment is an important determinant of travel propensity as education broadens horizons and stimulates the desire to travel. Also, the better educated the individual, the higher his or her awareness and susceptibility to information, media, advertising and sales promotion. In addition, education enhances the ability to utilize technology and will facilitate demand for travel through access to the Internet and computer reservation systems. Personal mobility, usually expressed as car ownership, is an important influence on travel propensity, especially with regard to domestic holidays. This variable will be discussed in Chapter 5. Finally, other variables such as gender and race act to condition access to tourism.

Life-cycle determinants

The propensity to travel, and indeed the type of tourism experience demanded, is closely related to an individual's age. While the conventional measurement is chronological age, domestic age better discriminates between types of tourist demand and levels of travel propensity. Domestic age refers to the stage in the life cycle reached by an individual and different stages are characterized by distinctive holiday demand and levels of travel propensity (Table 2.3). The concept of domestic age works well for Westernized, industrialized tourist generating countries and is therefore a useful generalization. However, it has its critics as it:

- is less well suited to other cultures
- in the industrialized world, changing household composition and social norms mean that the concept has to be treated with care.

Personality factors

No two individuals are alike and differences in attitudes, perceptions and motivation have an important influence on

Table 2.3   Domestic age and tourism demand

Adolescence/young adult
At this stage there is a need for independence and a search for identity. Typically, holidays independent of parents begin at around fifteen years, constrained by lack of finance but compensated by having few other commitments, no shortage of free time and a curiosity for new places and experiences. This group has a high propensity to travel, mainly on budget holidays using surface transport and self-catering accommodation. They are seen as opinion leaders and the tourism sector actively seeks their custom hoping to gain their loyalty in later years.

Marriage
Before the arrival of children young couples often have a high income and few other ties giving them a high travel propensity, frequently overseas. The arrival of children coupled with the responsibility of a home mean that constraints of time and finance depress travel propensity. Holidays become more organizational than geographical with domestic tourism, self-catering accommodation and visiting friends and relatives increasingly common. As children grow up and reach the adolescence stage, constraints of time and finance are lifted and parents' travel propensity increases. In the industrialized countries this, post-Second World War 'baby boom' group are the vanguard of the *new tourist* – discerning, experienced and seeking quality and value for money.

Retirement
The emergence of early retirement at fifty or fifty-five years is creating an active and mobile group in the population who will demand both domestic and international travel. In later retirement lack of finance, infirmity, reduced personal mobility and often the loss of a partner act to offset the increase in free time experienced by this group. Holidays become more hotel-based and travel propensity decreases.

---

travel decisions. Attitudes depend on an individual's perception of the world. Perceptions are mental impressions of, say, a place or travel company and are determined by many factors, which include childhood, family and work experiences. As perceptions will be influential in making the decision to travel, it is important for planners and managers in tourist destinations to foster favourable 'images' of their locations in the public's mind.

Attitudes and perceptions in themselves do not explain why people want to travel. The inner urges, which initiate travel demand, are called travel motivators. Gray (1970) has outlined a classification of travel motivators:

- *Wanderlust* is simply curiosity to experience the strange and unfamiliar. It refers to the basic trait in human nature to see, at first hand, different places, cultures and peoples.
- *Sunlust* can be literally translated as the desire for sun and a better climate, but in fact it is broader than this and refers to the search for a better set of amenities than are available at home.
- Other motivators include status/prestige and people – the desire to meet new people or to travel with others.

It is unusual to travel for one motivator alone and, instead, some combination which includes sunlust and wanderlust is more likely.

The interaction of personality attributes such as attitude, perceptions, and motivation allow different types of tourist to be identified. One classification by Cohen (1972) is particularly useful. He uses a classification based on the theory that tourism combines the curiosity to seek out new experiences with the need for the security of familiar reminders of home. Cohen proposes a continuum of possible combinations of novelty and familiarity and, by breaking up the continuum into typical combinations of these two ingredients, a fourfold classification of tourists is produced (Table 2.4).

Suppressed demand

Throughout this chapter the concern has been to identify factors which influence effective tourist demand. Yet tourism is still an unobtainable luxury for the majority of the world's population, not just in undeveloped and developing countries but also for many in the developed world. Indeed there are considerable inequalities of access to tourism, which are rooted in the personal circumstances of individuals. Lansing and Blood (1960) have identified five major reasons why people do not travel:

- expense of travel
- lack of time
- physical limitations (such as ill health)

Table 2.4 Cohen's classification of tourists

The organized mass tourist Low on adventurousness he or she is anxious to maintain his or her 'environmental bubble' on the trip. Typically purchasing a ready made package tour off-the-shelf, he or she is guided through the destination having little contact with local culture or people.	Familiarity ↑
The individual mass tourist Similar to the above but more flexibility and scope for personal choice is built-in. However, the tour is still organized by the tourism industry and the environmental bubble shields him or her from the real experience of the destination.	*Institutionalized tourism* Dealt with routinely by the tourism industry – tour operators, travel agents, hoteliers and transport operators.
The explorer The trip is organized independently and is looking to get off the beaten track. However, comfortable accommodation and reliable transport are sought and while the environmental bubble is abandoned on occasion, it is there to step into if things get tough.	
The drifter All connections with the tourism industry are spurned and the trip attempts to get as far from home and familiarity as possible. With no fixed itinerary, the drifter lives with the local people, paying his or her way and is immersed in their culture.	*Non-institutionalized tourism* Individual travel, shunning contact with the tourism industry except where absolutely necessary. ↓ Novelty

Adapted from: Cohen (1972).

- family circumstances
- lack of interest.

It is not uncommon for individuals to experience a combination of two or more of these barriers. For example, a one-parent family may find that lack of income and time will combine with family circumstances to prevent tourism travel. As it is just these groups who would most benefit from a holiday, tourism planners are increasingly concerned to identify these barriers and devise programmes to encourage non-participants to travel. Perhaps the best known example of this is the *social tourism movement*, which is concerned with the participation in travel by people with some form of handicap or disadvantage, and the measures used to encourage this participation.

Summary

Tourism is a major contribution to the quality of life in the twentieth century, and demand for tourism is made up not only of those who participate but also those who do not travel for some reason. Travel propensity is a useful indicator of tourism participation, as it gives the proportion of a population who actually engage in tourism. Travel frequency refers to the average number of trips taken by those participating in tourism during a specified period. Travel propensity is determined by a variety of factors that can be viewed at two scales. At the world scale, those countries with a high level of economic development and a stable urbanized population are major generators of tourism demand. The political regime of a country is also relevant here. At the individual scale, a certain level of discretionary income is required to allow participation in tourism, and this income, and indeed the type of participation, will be influenced by such factors as job type, life-cycle stage, mobility, level of educational attainment and personality. Even within the developed world, many are unable to participate in tourism for some reason. Demand for tourism is therefore concentrated into developed Western economies and predominates among those with high discretionary incomes.

Case study

The new tourist

Introduction

As the tourism market has matured in the last quarter of the twentieth century, a new type of tourist has emerged. Poon (1993) for example argues that the standardized mass tourism of the 1960s and 1970s is being superseded by a new tourism revolution. This represents a sea change in the nature of tourism demand that has implications not only for the planning and management of tourism destinations, but also for the way that the tourism sector operates.

The key influences

A range of key influences can be identified which have encouraged the growth of *the new tourist*:

- Trip frequency (both leisure and business), and therefore experience, has increased.
- New destinations, particularly long haul, are within reach of the mass market.
- The selling of travel has become technologically driven, allowing individual access to computer reservation systems and the Internet.
- The media and pressure groups (such as Tourism Concern) have taken a real interest in the responsible consumption and development of tourism, raising the profile of sustainability and placing issues such as the environment and concern for host populations centre stage.
- Deregulation in the tourism sector has allowed the individual consumer access to efficient direct reservation systems.
- Concentration in the industry has meant that one group of companies can offer a complete range of travel options.
- Emergence of the knowledge-based society creates a demand for authentic and well-interpreted experiences.
- Changing demographics in many key tourist-generating regions with ageing populations, smaller household sizes and higher discretionary incomes all combine to change lifestyles and the nature of tourism needs.

The nature of the new tourist

These developments have created a tourist who:

- is critical and discerning
- is able to make comparisons
- has considerable consumer skills
- is motivated by *wanderlust* – curiosity and cultural reasons to travel
- is motivated to seek out activity and adventure vacations and involvement in the destination
- is motivated to search for the authentic and the natural
- seeks quality, good service and value for money
- has values which encourage the *ethical consumption* of tourism
- has values orientated to the environment and which reflect a changing lifestyle

THE GEOGRAPHY OF DEMAND FOR TOURISM 21

- is prepared to be flexible in travel arrangements
- is prepared to adopt *high-satisfaction/low-loyalty* travel purchasing behaviour
- is independently minded
- is prepared to travel at short notice or even spontaneously.

The implications of the new tourist

Poon sees the new tourist as the driving force of change behind the new tourism revolution as the sector metamorphoses from the rigid, packaged tourism of the 1960s and 1970s to a new flexible form of tourism. This revolution in tourism demand has implications for both destinations and the tourism sector itself.

1 *Destinations* will need to recognize that these *critical consumers* seek quality, sound environmental and sustainable practices, ease of access to reservation systems, and authentic, well managed experiences. As Poon (1994: 91) states 'travellers are increasingly prepared to shun over-commercialised and polluted resorts'.
2 *The tourism sector* will need to rethink its marketing strategies and provide tailored, customized vacations which demonstrate an understanding of the motivations and needs of the new tourist – in other words understand the way that the new tourist thinks, feels and behaves. This will involve sophisticated approaches to the *segmentation* of the tourism market as well as development of customer databases and relationship marketing where customer loyalty is encouraged. In addition, the new tourist renders traditional market research techniques of classifying individuals by age or occupation redundant. Instead, more sophisticated (and expensive) techniques are needed to expose underlying values and motivations.

Case study

World patterns of international tourism flows

This case study is confined to *international* tourism flows and receipts, as the collection and estimation of statistics of international tourism is more accurate than that for *domestic* tourism. The collection and aggregation of statistics into six world regions by the WTO necessarily means that their regions, while failing to conform to geographical logic, are used throughout this case study.

The historical trend at the world scale

The end of the Second World War represented the beginning of a remarkable period of growth for international tourism, with an annual average growth rate approaching 7 per cent per annum for the second half of the twentieth century (Table 2.5). International tourism has been remarkably resilient to factors that may have been expected to depress growth – recession, oil crises, wars and terrorism.

- *The 1950s* – in 1950, international tourist arrivals stood at 25.3 million. Growth of international tourism was sluggish as the world recovered from the Second World War. However, the adoption of the jet engine in the closing years of the decade provided an important technological enabling factor for international travel.
- *The 1960s* – by 1960, arrivals had reached 69.3 million. The decade of the 1960s saw demand for international tourism realized by:

Table 2.5   International tourism arrivals: the historical trend

Year	International tourism arrivals (millions)	International tourism receipts (US$ millions)
1950	25.3	2 100
1960	69.3	6 867
1970	159.7	17 900
1980	284.8	102 372
1985	321.2	116 158
1990	454.8	255 000
1995	567.0	372 000
Forecast for 2010	1046.0	N/A

– *Demand-side factors* – large numbers of those living in the developed world had the desire, time and income to travel.
– *Supply-side factors* – the response by the tourism industry to develop the 'standardized' approach of inclusive tours offered at a competitive price.

Business travel too, was becoming significant and emerged as an important sector of the market.

1 *The 1970s* – in 1970, international arrivals had risen to 159.7 million. Growth slowed due to the oil crisis in 1974 and economic recession at the end of the decade. However, recession demonstrates the 'ratchet' effect of tourism demand with an increasing rate of growth in times of prosperity, and at times of recession, demand remains fairly constant, as consumers are reluctant to forego travel.
2 *The 1980s* – by 1980, international arrivals had reached 284.8 million and growth rates began to slow as the market moved towards maturity. The mid-1980s were a period of substantial travel with European destinations experiencing record years. However, in 1986 the Chernobyl incident, the Libyan bombing and the fall in the US dollar saw a shift in demand away from Europe and North Africa. The late 1980s saw a return to the normal pattern of tourism flows, and accelerating growth, only to be disrupted by the Gulf War.
3 *The 1990s* – in 1990 international arrivals stood at 454.8 million. The decade opened with the Gulf War that severely depressed international travel and had a long-term impact upon tourism enterprises such as airlines. Over the decade, growth of arrivals was strong and a shift in patterns of demand was evident with the opening up of the former Eastern Bloc, and the expansion of tourism in the Pacific Rim countries. In the closing years of the decade, the Asian currency crisis depressed intra-regional travel in Asia, though inbound travel was boosted as prices fell.

It is difficult to generalize about the pattern of international tourism flows as individual countries display marked differences and contrasts. Similarly, each destination receives a distinctive mix of tourist origins and modes of transport. On a world basis it is estimated that:

(a) 80 per cent of international arrivals are by surface transport
(b) 20 per cent are by air
(c) 30 per cent of international arrivals are for business purposes
(d) 70 per cent are for pleasure.

The changing regional picture

The determinants of tourism demand, we discussed earlier, allied to the characteristics of the mosaic of tourism destinations around the world, combine to produce global rhythms and patterns of tourism. International tourism arrivals and departures are concentrated into relatively few countries, mainly in Europe and North America. This produces an unbalanced picture that favours developed western economies and disadvantages the developing world which is left to compete for the long-haul market – which accounts for a minor share of the total market.

Generators

The major tourism-generating countries are those in the *high mass-consumption stage* of economic development, although as countries reach the *drive to maturity stage* they become significant generating markets. For any particular country, a typical list of the top generating markets would contain neighbouring states together with at least one from a list containing Germany, the UK, Japan and the USA. In part, this is explained by two conflicting trends:

● the importance, though declining, of short-haul travel to neighbouring countries which represents up to 40 per cent of total international trips
● a substantial growth in long-haul travel occurred in the last two decades of the twentieth century. This is due to both consumer demand for new, more exotic destinations and the response from the travel industry to package long-haul destinations. Aircraft technology and management can now deliver these at a price and length of journey acceptable to the consumer.

Destinations

The postwar period has been marked by the rapid emergence of the East Asia and the Pacific region (EAP) as an international tourism destination, largely at the expense of the Americas and Europe (Table 2.6).

East Asia and the Pacific

In 1950 the EAP region had a share of less than 1 per cent of international tourism; yet by the year 2010 this share is forecast to exceed 20 per cent. This has a number of explanations but the key to the region's success is due to:

● rapidly developing countries with large populations
● well-managed airlines based in the region
● perceived exotic culture
● world-class natural attractions

Table 2.6   International tourism arrivals: the changing regional picture (percentage share of international arrivals by WTO region)

Region	1950 (%)	1960 (%)	1970 (%)	1980 (%)	1990 (%)	Forecast for 2010 (%)
Europe	66.5	72.5	70.5	68.4	63.5	50.2
Americas	29.6	24.1	23.0	18.9	18.8	18.6
East Asia and Pacific	0.8	1.0	3.0	7.0	11.4	22.1
Africa	2.1	1.1	1.5	2.5	3.4	4.4
Middle East	0.9	1.0	1.4	2.4	2.1	3.5
South Asia	0.2	0.3	0.6	0.8	0.7	1.0

- good quality tourism infrastructure such as airports
- a dynamic, enthusiastic tourism region with newly emergent destinations such as China
- favourable exchange rates
- competitively-priced inclusive tours
- high-quality accommodation products and cuisine.

Europe

Europe's share of international tourism has been eroded in the postwar period. While Europe is still pre-eminent in terms of total volume of international arrivals, growth has been at a slower rate than regions such as EAP. The trend of new destination regions taking market share from the traditional destinations such as Europe is clear and will continue into the next millennium. Nonetheless, Europe still dominates world tourism flows simply because it contains:

- many of the world's leading generating countries
- a number of relatively small but adjacent countries generating considerable volumes of cross-border travel
- a mature travel and transport industry
- natural and cultural attractions of world calibre
- new themed attractions such as Disneyland Paris
- attractive capital cities
- newly emerging destinations such as the former Eastern Bloc countries

- a variety of tourism products from beach to winter-sports holidays
- a mature tourism infrastructure, including the Channel tunnel and other transport developments
- highly trained personnel
- a developing pan-European currency in the form of the Euro
- an integrated industrial base which is important for business tourism.

Elsewhere in the world

The *Americas* account for a significant share of international tourism activity, with an increasing volume of overseas travel to supplement the huge domestic market. In *Africa*, due to the prevailing political instability and poor infrastructure, tourism growth is relatively stagnant. The majority of arrivals are in North Africa, but the newly emergent and 'politically acceptable' South Africa is shifting the emphasis of tourism. In the *Middle East*, the stop-go nature of the peace process inevitably has an impact on tourism demand and supply, while in *South Asia* – a region with poor infrastructure and political instability – most activity focuses on India.

Note: This case study has drawn heavily upon the statistics of the World Tourism Organization and papers by John Latham in Cooper and Lockwood (1989–) and 'databank' in *Tourism Economics*.

Appendix 2.1 Calculation of travel propensity and travel frequency

Out of a population of 10 million inhabitants:

3.0 million inhabitants
take one trip of
one night or more   i.e. $3 \times 1 = 3.0$ million trips

1.5 million inhabitants
take two trips of one
night or more   i.e. $1.5 \times 2 = 3.0$ million trips

0.4 million inhabitants
take three trips of
one night or more   i.e. $0.4 \times 3 = 1.2$ million trips

0.2 million inhabitants
take four trips of one
night or more   i.e. $0.2 \times 4 = 0.8$ million trips

5.1 million inhabitants
take at least one trip   8.0 million trips

therefore:

Net travel propensity =

$$\frac{\text{Numbers of population taking at least one trip}}{\text{Total population}} \times 100 = \frac{5.1}{10} \times 100 = 51 \text{ per cent}$$

Gross travel propensity =

$$\frac{\text{Number of total trips}}{\text{Total population}} \times 100 = \frac{8}{10} \times 100 = 80 \text{ per cent}$$

Travel frequency =

$$\frac{\text{Gross travel propensity}}{\text{Net travel propensity}} = \frac{80\%}{51\%} = 1.57$$

A further refinement to the above calculations is to assess the capability of a country to generate trips. This involves three stages. First, the number of trips originating in the country is divided by the total number of trips taken in the world. This gives an index of the ability of each country to generate travellers. Second, the population of the country is divided by the total population of the world, thus ranking each country by relative importance in relation to world population. By dividing the result of the first stage by the result of the second the 'country potential generation index' (CPGI) is produced (Hurdman, 1979).

$$\text{CPGI} = \frac{(N_e/N_w)}{(P_e/P_w)}$$

where N_e = number of trips generated by
country
N_w = number of trips generated in world
P_e = population of country
P_w = population of world

An index of 1.0 indicates an average generation capability. Countries with an index greater than unity are generating more tourists than expected by their population. Countries with an index below 1.0 generate fewer trips than average.

Adapted from: Schmidhauser, H., 'Travel Propensity and Travel Frequency', pp. 53–60 in Burkart, A. J. and Medlik, S., *The Management of Tourism*, Heinemann, London, 1975; and Hurdman, L. E., 'Origin Regions of International Tourism', *Wiener Geographische Schriften*, **53/54**, 43–9 1979.

3

The geography of resources for tourism

LEARNING OBJECTIVES

After reading this chapter, you should be able to:

1 Appreciate the nature of resources for tourism.
2 Distinguish the methods used to classify and evaluate resources for tourism.
3 Outline the main factors favouring the development of tourist resources.
4 Understand the way that destinations evolve.
5 Appreciate the need for tourism planning and sustainable development.

Introduction

Technology now allows tourists to reach most parts of the world, yet only a small fraction of the world's potential tourist resource base is developed. Nonetheless, with a growing demand for tourism focused on a small resource base, tourist destinations are under pressure. In part this is because tourism does not occur evenly or randomly in space – pressure is focused seasonally and at special and unique places. This demands the effective planning and management of tourist resources and in particular the recognition that appropriate tourists should be attracted to each type of resource. Of course, different types of tourism will have distinctive requirements for growth, and certain sites, regions or countries will be more favourable for development than others. This chapter examines tourist resources at three scales: the world, the national and the local.

Resources for tourism

Tourist resources have three main characteristics:

1 The concept of tourist resources is normally taken to refer to tangible objects which are considered of economic value to the tourism sector. The sector, and indeed the tourist, therefore has to recognize that a place, landscape or natural feature is of value before they can become tourist resources. For example, sunshine was not seen as a tourist resource until the 1920s and, with the increased threat of skin cancer, may not be viewed as a resource in the future.
2 Tourist resources themselves are often not used solely by tourists. Apart from resort areas or theme parks where tourism is the dominant use of land, tourism shares use with agriculture, forestry, water management or residents using local services. Tourism is a significant land use but rarely the dominant one, and this can lead to conflict. Tourism, as a latecomer, is 'fitted in' with other uses of land. This is known as *multiple use*, and needs skilful management and co-ordination of users to be successful.
3 Tourist resources are perishable. Not only are they vulnerable to alteration and destruction by tourist pressure but, in common with many service industries, tourist resources are also perishable in another sense. Tourist services such as beds in accommodation or ride seats in theme parks are impossible to stock and have to be consumed when and where they exist. Unused tourist resources cannot be stored and will perish, hence the development of yield management systems to maximize the consumption of resources.

Planning for tourism resources

Inevitably, tourism is attracted to unique and fragile resources around the world. In the early decades of the postwar period this was actively encouraged and international tourism was sought by many countries as an ideal solution to economic problems. Tourism was seen as an 'industry without chimneys' which brought economic benefits of employment, income and development. However, the economic imperative overlooked the environmental social and cultural consequences of tourism in a number of developed and developing countries. In part, this was due to the ease of measuring economic impacts of tourism and the difficulty of quantifying other types of impact. However, as we approach and enter the new millennium, we are seeing environmental and host community considerations complementing the economic need of destinations. Consumer pressure is shunning ethically unsound destinations and environmental impact assessments are being completed

for major tourist developments. Sustainable tourism will therefore become acceptable; in other words, *tourist development will not compromise the ability of future generations to enjoy tourist resources*. A key concept here is that of carrying capacity – in other words, planners determine the levels of use that can be sustained by a tourist resource and manage to that level (see Table 3.1).

Tourism planning must be central to these issues. Such planning has evolved from an inflexible, physical planning approach to a flexible process which seeks to maximize the benefits and minimize the costs of tourism. The benefits of tourism planning are clear (Table 3.2). Ideally, tourism planning:

● is based on sound research
● involves the local community in setting goals and priorities
● is implemented by the public sector in partnership with the private sector.

Table 3.1 Carrying capacity

The concept of carrying capacity has a long pedigree. It was originally developed by resource managers in agriculture and forestry to determine the cropping levels that pieces of land could sustain without nutrients and other food sources being depleted.

Of course, in tourism the concept has a similar meaning. Quite simply, carrying capacity refers to the ability of a destination to take tourism use without deteriorating in some way. In other words it defines the relationship between the resource base and the market and is influenced by the characteristics of each. One of the best definitions is by Mathieson and Wall (1982: 21): 'The maximum number of people who can use a site without unacceptable alteration in the physical environment and without an unacceptable decline in the quality of experience gained by visitors.'

This definition raises two key points:

1 Carrying capacity can be managed and there is no absolute number for any destination. For example, *open heathland* can appear crowded with very few visitors present, while a *wooded area* can absorb many more visitors before appearing crowded.

2 There are different types of carrying capacity:
   (a) From the point of view of the resource:
      (i) *Physical carrying capacity* refers to the number of facilities available – aircraft seats or car parking spaces for example. It is easy to measure and can be calculated on a simple percentage basis.
      (ii) *Environmental or biological carrying capacity* is more difficult to measure and refers to limits of use in the ecosystem. There is increasing interest in the capacity not only of the flora to take tourism use but also in terms of fauna – such as tourism based on whale or dolphin watching, or in the African game reserves.
   (b) From the point of view of the visitor:
      (i) *Psychological or behavioural carrying capacity* refers to the point at which the visitor feels that additional tourists would spoil their experience. This is less straightforward than may appear at first sight. For example, completely empty spaces are just as problematic as crowded ones, and the type of tourist also has an effect on perceptions of crowding.
   (c) And from the point of view of the host community:
      (i) *Social carrying capacity* is a measure of the ability of the host community to tolerate tourism. It is a more recent addition to typologies of capacity and will become an important issue in the future.

Table 3.2   The benefits of tourism planning

For those involved in delivering and developing tourism at the destination, tourism planning:

- provides a set of common objectives for all at the destination to follow
- co-ordinates the many suppliers of tourism at the destination
- encourages partnerships between stakeholders at the destination
- encourages effective organization at the destination
- provides an integrating framework for future actions and decisions.

For the destination itself, tourism planning encourages a high-quality tourism environment because it:

- optimizes the benefits of tourism to a destination
- minimizes the negative impacts of tourism on the economy, environment and host community
- encourages the adoption of the principles of sustainable tourism at the destination
- provides a land-use based plan for zoning areas for development, conservation and protection
- encourages design and other standards for the tourism sector to work to
- encourages careful matching of the development of the destination and its markets
- allows for the consideration of issues such as manpower and investment
- upgrades the destination environment
- encourages a monitoring system to be implemented at the destination.

Despite the many approaches to tourism planning, the planning process can be reduced to six basic questions:

- What type of tourist will visit?
- What is the scale of tourism?
- Where will development take place?
- What controls will be placed upon development?
- How will development be financed?
- What will be government's role?

The answer to these questions will depend, from place to place, on the government's approach to tourism and the importance of tourism to the economy. The planning process is summarized in Figure 3.1.

Unfortunately, despite the emergence of tourism planning as a profession, plans for tourism still either fail or are opposed. They may fail because policy changes, demand changes, unforeseen competition emerges, investment is not available or the plan was too ambitious or inflexible. Opposition often comes from the private sector, which objects to planning interfering with its business, or from those who object to the cost of the process.

If tourism planning does not succeed then:

- the quality and integrity of the tourist resource are at risk
- the role of tourism in multiple land use may be threatened as other uses dominate
- the tourist suffers from a poor quality experience.

Tourism resources at the world scale

Physical features

Nearly three-quarters of the earth's surface consists of sea, including the five oceans – namely the Pacific (by far the largest), the Atlantic, Indian, Southern and Arctic Oceans. The remaining 29 per cent comprise the seven continents and associated islands, namely Asia (the largest both in land area and population), followed by Africa, North America, South America, Antarctica, Europe and Australasia. (Strictly speaking Europe is part of the greater landmass known as Eurasia). Almost 40 per cent of the Northern Hemisphere, but less than 20 per cent of the Southern Hemisphere, is made up of land. This uneven distribution of land and sea has important implications for climate, population distribution, economic development, communications and, thus, tourism.

The land surface of the earth is composed of a variety of landforms which you can broadly group into four categories: mountains (areas of elevated, rugged terrain), more gently sloping hill lands, elevated plateaus, and lowland plains. Within each landform category there are features resulting from natural forces and variations in the underlying rock. Volcanoes, crater lakes and calderas, lava formations, geysers and hot springs, are geothermal features caused by disturbances from deep within the earth's' crust. Even in areas where volcanic activity ceased long ago, springs rich in minerals have in turn given rise to the type of health resort known as a spa. Another important group of features is found in *karst* limestone areas, where surface

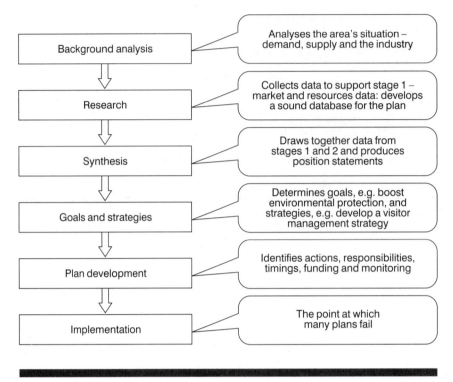

Figure 3.1 Tourism planning flow chart
Source: Based on Mill and Morrison (1985).

streams have 'disappeared' underground to carve out impressive caves, sinkholes and gorges which are used for recreation and adventure tourism.

Although mountains and hill lands account for 75 per cent of the land surface, they are occupied by only a minority of the world's population. Mountain ranges are found in every continent but are particularly associated with geologically unstable areas characterized by earthquakes and volcanic activity. This explains why some of the world's most spectacular mountains are situated in the 'Pacific Ring of Fire' close to the western and eastern margins of the world's largest ocean. Those mountain areas in middle latitudes affected by glaciation during the last Ice Age are particularly attractive for tourism development. This is due to the variety of scenic features, including spectacular peaks, glaciers, cirques, lakes and waterfalls, as well as the crisp clear air which encourages a range of activity and adventure holidays. Most of these involve limited numbers of visitors and are the concern of 'niche' tour operators dealing directly with their customers. In contrast, skiing has attracted a mass following and a major winter sports industry has burgeoned in most developed countries. Much of the demand is generated from densely populated countries where suitable resources are in short supply. This

has resulted in the development of a multitude of ski resorts in the more accessible mountain regions: some of these are based on existing rural communities but a growing number are purpose-built at higher altitudes for the skiers' convenience. In summer these same regions attract tourists interested in sightseeing for a 'lakes and mountains' holiday. In southern Asia, the Middle East, Africa and Latin America mountain resorts cater more for health tourism, providing relief from the oppressive summer heat of the cities in the lowlands.

The sparse population of most mountain regions has made it easier for governments to designate areas as *national parks* for their outstanding natural beauty, unique geological features or wildlife. Nevertheless, few suitable areas are pristine wilderness, so that tourism has to compete with other demands on resources including forestry, pasture for grazing, hydroelectric power generation and mineral extraction. Since mountain areas have a limited carrying capacity, overdevelopment involving the construction of roads and cableways is a matter of growing concern. This has led many authorities to discourage the more popular forms of tourism in favour of *eco-tourism* (tourist activities in harmony with the natural environment), which will sustain the resource for future generations.

The coast continues to be the most popular location for holidaymakers worldwide. The beach, more than any other environment, appeals to all the physical senses and is associated in people's minds with carefree hedonism. Sandy beaches and sheltered coves providing safe bathing with a protective backland of sand dunes or low cliffs, will encourage tourism development and a wide range of recreational activities. More rugged and exposed coastlines might attract surfers, but would deter other water sports enthusiasts and families with young children. Although beaches have a high carrying capacity compared to most 'natural' environments, they are prone to pollution and erosion by winter storms. Small islands, and the coral reefs found along many tropical coastlines, are particularly vulnerable to the ecological damage caused by excessive numbers of tourists. Coastal plains are ideal for large-scale resort development, but such locations are also sought after as sites for major industries, and you would agree that oil refineries do not make good neighbours! Most destinations are now aware of the tourism potential of attractive beaches, so that the developers' attention has turned to the wetlands – estuaries, marshes, swamps and tidal mud flats, which are not valued as a tourist resource. Although ecologically important as a wildlife habitat, the world's wetlands are increasingly under threat. In many tropical countries for example, mangrove swamps have been dredged to provide harbours and yacht marinas. Elsewhere, wetlands have been reclaimed for use by airports, industry and intensive agriculture.

Inland water resources for tourism can be viewed as nodes (lakes, reservoirs), linear corridors (rivers, canals), or simply as landscape features (such as the Victoria Falls). Lakes are particularly numerous in recently glaciated areas such as the Alps, Northern Europe and North America. Where lakes are accessible to major cities they attract second-home owners and a wide range of recreational activities which may not be compatible (for example, anglers and water-skiers). Spatial zoning and temporal phasing of these activities may be necessary to avoid conflict. Water pollution is also a problem, as unlike the tidal nature of the sea, lakes have no natural cleansing mechanism. Rivers are more widely available than lakes but, in most cases, tourism and recreation take second place to the needs of industry, commerce and agriculture. Even so, cruises on the world's great rivers are growing in popularity, as are boating holidays on the inland waterways of Europe, for example. At the other extreme, rivers previously regarded as unnavigable are sought out by adventurous tourists for the challenge of whitewater rafting and canoeing.

The world's forest resources also deserve special mention. In most developed countries forests and woodlands are valued for recreation and wildlife protection, in contrast to the exploitation which occurred in the past. Multiple use is characteristic of such areas, and careful management is essential to protect the resource.

Cultural features

Culture is an increasingly important tourist resource, reflected in the cultural differences across the world in terms of language, art, festivals, folklore, handicrafts, food, music and the way of life of different peoples. On a world scale, we can recognize a number of cultural regions, where there is a broad similarity in lifestyles, architecture, agricultural systems, and often a shared historical background and religion. These regions rarely correspond to continental divisions. For example, European or 'Western' culture since the Renaissance has spread well beyond the confines of Europe, as a result of overseas trade, colonial expansion, emigration and advances in technology. However, in most countries of Africa, Asia and, to a lesser extent, Latin America, 'Western' influence is superficial and strong cultural differences persist. This is evident in the Islamic countries of Africa and the Middle East, as well as the countries of South-East Asia where Buddhism has long been the dominant influence. Every tourist needs to respect these differences in lifestyle, and business travellers especially should be aware of the host country's social conventions and taboos to avoid causing offence. In many countries, so-called primitive tribal groups live outside the mainstream culture. Identified as the 'Fourth World' (Graburn, 1976), these tribes are increasingly seen as a unique resource by tour operators and included on the backpackers' itinerary. Unfortunately tourism could present another threat to a way of life which is already endangered.

Tourism thrives in the absence of barriers to communication, so the existence of a common language is an advantage – although the ubiquitous use of English poses a threat to other, minority languages. A shared religion can also encourage travel between countries. Most of the great religions have shrines or holy places, and some of these – Lourdes, Rome, Jerusalem and Mecca – annually attract millions of visitors worldwide. Pilgrimages – journeys with a religious motivation – were arguably the first form of organized mass tourism. Although, or perhaps because, we live in a world dominated by secular, materialistic concerns, this type of tourism would appear to be on the increase. Cultural tourists in a wider sense are attracted to destinations noted for their art treasures, historic sites and buildings, or even their literary associations. These visitors, including the young backpackers taking a year out from work or college, are following in the tradition of those élite travellers who took the Grand Tour in the eighteenth century, but on an altogether vaster scale in terms of their numbers and the extent of their travels.

Although *heritage* is a vaguely defined word, it has become the focus of a major form of tourism – *heritage tourism* – which has grown with tourists' curiosity about places, the past and nature. In its wider sense heritage includes those natural as well as human-made features which are considered worthy of preservation. Some features are so unique, spectacular or well known that they are of worldwide significance and their loss would affect human-kind as a whole. For this reason the United Nations Educational, Scientific, and Cultural Organization (UNESCO) has designated most of these for special protection as World Heritage Sites. However, while this designation does bring with it management responsibilities, lack of the ability to enforce conservation means that some monuments are in a poor state of preservation.

Many tourists, especially those in the younger age groups, are less attracted by a country's past achievements than its contemporary culture, as reflected in sport, fashion and entertainment. Here, the influence of the media is evident. The national tourist organization of a country may spend a vast budget on a promotional campaign, but this may have considerably less impact than the free publicity and exposure provided by a movie or television series seen by a worldwide audience of millions.

Tourist resources at the national scale

At the level of individual countries, tourism development involves either finding suitable regions to develop or, in areas already established, alleviating problems of conges-tion or overuse. These activities demand accurate methods of classifying tourism resources and evaluating their potential.

Classification of resources for tourism

Tourist attractions

Attractions are the *raison d'être* for tourism; they generate the visit, give rise to excursion circuits and create an industry of their own. The simplest approach to identifying attractions in an area is to draw up an inventory or checklist, by defining the range of attractions, counting them, and either listing or mapping the result. Swarbrooke (1995) has classified attractions into four main categories which can be defined as:

- natural – including beaches, caves, scenic features and wildlife
- human-made, but not originally designed to attract tourists, such as historic houses, castles and cathedrals
- human-made and purpose-built to attract tourists; this includes museums, art galleries, exhibition centres, casinos and a growing range of leisure attractions for a 'day out' such as theme parks and water parks
- special events. These 'event attractions' differ from the others, which are 'site attractions', in that they occur only periodically and in some cases, change locales. The latter category include sporting events, such as the football World Cup and the Olympic Games. These present unique opportunities to promote the host country and

have a spin-off effect encouraging other attractions nearby. They also require considerable investment, planning and organization to safeguard the health, safety and security of both visitors and participants. Other event attractions include for example, markets, festivals, folk-lore events, ceremonies, pageantry and religious processions.

Quite clearly different forms of tourism are based upon different types of attraction. The younger tourist for example, is more likely to be attracted to theme parks with their emphasis on exciting rides and entertainment, than to most heritage attractions, such as 'stately homes', museums and cathedrals. Business travellers will have differing needs from the rest of the travelling public. They gravitate toward major commercial centres which are highly accessible, and offer facilities for conferences and trade exhibitions, as well as a range of complementary attractions and services.

Some attractions have a greater 'pulling power' than the rest, so that in many countries we can recognize a hierarchy of attractions. At the apex of the pyramid are those 'must see' attractions of international calibre; rela-tively few in number, they attract tourists worldwide. In the second tier are those which might be visited as part of an excursion circuit focusing on one or two major 'sights'. At the base of the pyramid are many minor attractions which currently draw their visitors from within the immediate region. Increasingly, tourist attractions, and the tourism resource base in general, are suffering from increased use and need effective visitor management. This can only be achieved if these attractions are considered as an integral part of the tourism resource base rather than dealt with in isolation.

A broader view of the tourism resource base

One of the most useful classifications of the total resource base for tourism and recreation is that of Clawson (Clawson and Knetsch, 1966). This sees resources as forming a continuum from intensive resort development at one extreme to wilderness at the other, and, therefore, incorpor-ates both resource and user characteristics. Clawson's three basic categories are:

- user-oriented areas of highly intensive development close to population centres
- resource-based areas where the type of resource deter-mines the use of the area
- an intermediate category, where access is the determin-ing factor.

As you are probably aware, there are hundreds of outdoor recreation activities which have relevance for the tourism industry, ranging from abseiling to zoological expeditions. In Table 3.3 an attempt has been made to relate some of these activities to Clawson's classification.

Table 3.3 A classification of recreational resources

User orientated	Intermediate	Resource based
Based on resources close to the user. Often artificial developments (city parks, stadiums etc). Highly intensive developments. Activities often highly seasonal, closing in off-peak.	Best resources available within accessible distance to users. Access very important. Natural resources more significant than user-orientated facilities, but these experience a high degree of visitor pressure.	Outstanding resources. Based on their location, not that of the market. Primary focus is resource quality. Often distant from users, the resource determines the activity.
Reproducible $\longleftrightarrow$		**Non-reproducible**
Activity paramount $\longleftrightarrow$		**Resource paramount**
Artificiality $\longleftrightarrow$		**Naturalness**
$\longleftarrow$	**Intensity of development**	$\longrightarrow$
Proximity $\longleftarrow$	**Distance from user** $\longrightarrow$	**Remoteness**
Examples of activities:	**Examples of activities:**	**Examples of activities:**
Golf	*Yachting*	*Sightseeing*
Tennis	*Windsurfing*	*Mountain climbing*
Spectator sports	*Boating*	*Trekking*
Visits to theme parks,	*Camping*	*Safaris*
zoos, resorts, etc.	*Hiking*	*Expeditions*
	Angling	*Surfing*
	Field sports	*Whitewater rafting*
	Downhill skiing	*Canoeing*
	Snowboarding	*Potholing*
		Scuba diving
Typical resource:	**Typical resource:**	**Typical resource:**
Theme park	Heathland	Unique historical monument National park

Another way of thinking about resources, related to Clawson's ideas, is to classify them into:

- reproducible (can be replaced, for example, theme parks)
- non-reproducible (they cannot be replaced, such as elements of the natural and cultural heritage mentioned earlier).

Evaluation of resources for tourism

Measurement of the suitability of the resource base to support different forms of tourism is known as resource evaluation. The main problem here is to include the varied requirements of different users. For example, pony-trekkers need rights of way, footpaths or bridleways, and attractive scenery. Combination of these various needs is

the aim of a resource evaluation system which is often tabulated into a matrix or put on to data cards, each one of which relates to a location. They can also be combined into the so-called recreation opportunity spectrum.

The tourism product

An area may have tourism potential – a favourable climate, attractive scenery, hospitable people and a range of resources awaiting discovery. However, it will not become a viable tourist destination until its attractions are complemented by a range of facilities and conditions to support the visit. For example, it will need to have accessibility to the major tourist-generating countries and favourable conditions for development, which means the provision of basic infrastructure, and a measure of political stability. A destination therefore needs to have attractions, accessibility, amenities and ancillary services in place to lure the tourist. These elements combine to provide the *tourism product*. Individual enterprises within the tourism industry supply products to the consumer – hotels and airlines are notable examples. These various sectors of the tourism industry contribute to the tourism product of a destination, which can then be marketed to potential customers. This involves the marketing of places, where a very different approach is needed to the marketing of tangible products such as motor cars. Equally, the marketing of the destination will be different depending upon the target market: for example, domestic and foreign tourists may find different aspects of the destination attractive, as may younger and older visitors. To make its product more appealing, each destination should be able to offer a *unique selling proposition* (USP) – an attribute which gives it an advantage over the competition. Some destinations already have a clearly defined tourist image, which consists of a set of well-known attractions, or a special ambience as regards say, food, customs and entertainment. However, the mental picture that tourists have of a destination may well be unrepresentative of the destination as a whole, and bear little relation to economic and social realities. This is particularly true of mass tourism, where the 'environmental bubble' simply reinforces prejudices about national stereotypes.

Tourist resources at the local scale

For the tourism resource to be developed, someone or some organization has to act. These agents of development can be either in the private sector, or in the public sector – central government, state-funded organizations acting on its behalf and local authorities.

The public sector is involved not only in tourism development at the local scale, but at all levels, including the international. Developing countries receive assistance for projects through agencies such as the World Bank, the United Nations Development Programme and the European Bank for Reconstruction and Development. Many governments actively encourage tourism projects in their own countries by providing finance at generous rates and tax breaks to developers. Typically at the national and international levels, government involvement is with the planning and co-ordination of tourism development. At the local level the role of the public sector is usually limited to providing the initial infrastructure; this includes all development on or below ground, such as roads, parking areas, railway lines, harbours and airports, as well as the provision of utilities. The importance of adequate water supplies for example needs to be emphasized, and where basic services have failed to keep pace with a spate of hotel-building, a destination will suffer bad publicity regarding its standards of health and safety. The public

sector is also responsible for ensuring adequate security against crime and terrorism. Even an isolated incident affecting tourists can receive widespread coverage by the media in the generating countries.

As tourism projects are costly, private sector developers typically provide the superstructure. This includes the accommodation sector, of which hotels are usually the most important component, entertainment, sport and shopping facilities, restaurants and passenger transport terminals. Clearly this division of responsibilities reflects the motives of the two sectors: the private sector looks for profit and a return on investment, while the public sector is anxious to provide the basic services in an environment favourable for tourism development. In some developed countries the *voluntary sector*, consisting of non-profit-making organizations, plays a subsidiary role in the development process. As their main interest is conservation, they are much more likely to oppose large-scale tourism projects than to initiate development. The National Trust is an outstanding British example but differs from most such organizations by being a major landowner.

At the local scale accessibility is all-important and may be the deciding factor in the success of a tourism project. Resorts in destination areas such as the Mediterranean owe much of their popularity to their location near an airport with direct flights to the major tourist-generating areas. However, accessibility is a relative term which is determined by cost as well as distance. Exclusive 'up-market' resorts are often located in areas away from the main tourist routes.

Other factors encouraging the development of tourism resources at the local level include land availability, suitable physical site attributes (soil, topography) and a favourable planning environment with zoning for tourism. Normally undeveloped '*greenfield*' sites are chosen, but there are an increasing number of tourism projects in inner city areas, often utilizing a waterfront location previously occupied by dockyards and industry. Such '*brownfield*' sites normally require costly treatment before building work can take place.

Finally, tourism development should take place with the consent of the local community. However, in most developing countries (and some developed ones) democratic structures of government are weak and even the ownership of land may be the subject of dispute. Local authorities may lack the expertise and financial 'muscle' to curb the activities of business interests from outside the region, such as multinationals, when these may have a negative social and environmental impact.

Tourist resorts and tourist centres

At the local scale the development of tourist resources leaves a distinct imprint on the landscape. This is particularly evident in the *resorts* of the developed countries

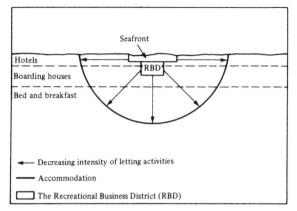

Figure 3.2 The recreational business district
Source: Wall, 'Car owners and holiday activities', in Lavery (1971).

which have evolved in response to the needs of tourists. They are distinct in layout and townscape from other urban and rural settlements. In Western Europe alone, over 400 resorts can be identified including spas, winter sports resorts and cultural/historic centres, as well as holiday resorts of varying size, whose clientele ranges from the popular to the exclusive. Historic towns and cities are usually multifunctional, and tourism is a latecomer. Such places are *tourist centres*. In true resorts, tourism is the *raison d'être*, although other functions may be added later when the resort has reached maturity. Spas and holiday resorts are often characterized by eclectic styles of architecture in contrast to more workaday communities.

Typically you would find a concentration of tourist-orientated land and building uses close to the main focus of visitor attraction. This area of tourist-related functions is termed the *recreational business district* (RBD), distinct from the main office and shopping area, which in larger towns is termed the central business district (CBD). The RBD develops under the twin influences of the major access route into the resort and the central tourist feature. For example, in seaside resorts the RBD often develops parallel to the beach, behind a promenade (boardwalk in the USA) and contains premier hotels and shops. Beyond this, the intensity of tourist functions and land values decreases in a series of zones around the RBD (Figure 3.2). In the case of historic centres, the RBD usually corresponds to the ancient core of the town, which in most European examples is centred on a castle, university or cathedral. It is here that conservationist's efforts are concentrated and *interpretation* may be used to bring alive the 'heritage experience' for the tourist. However, as Ashworth and Tunbridge (1990) point out, 'the attraction may be medieval, but few tourists are prepared to sleep, eat and travel in medieval conditions', so modern support facilities, while necessary, may be an intrusive feature in the skyline of the historic city. Authenticity has its limits and living in a museum-city may also be highly inconvenient to the local inhabitants. In large cities, especially capitals such as London, the historic/cultural area is polycentric. Tourist facilities are more widely dispersed between a number of areas catering for different types of visitor (for example, Soho, Covent Garden), while the business traveller is attracted to the CBD with its range of financial and commercial services (in this example, the City of London).

The development of resorts over time is an important consideration for tourist geographers. Butler (1980) has suggested a tourist area life cycle where resorts evolve from discovery through development to eventual decline. Although the life-cycle approach has its critics – who feel it is difficult to operationalize – the main utility of the approach is as a way of thinking about resorts, an explanatory framework for their development, and as a means of integrating supply-side developments with the

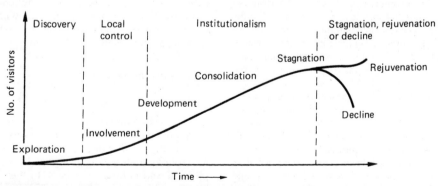

Figure 3.3 The tourist area life cycle
Source: Butler (1980).

evolving market of a resort. After all, the type of tourist who visits at introduction will be very different from that visiting in consolidation or decline (Figure 3.3). The tourist area life cycle is as follows:

- Exploration: small number of adventurous tourists, main attraction is unspoilt nature or cultural features.
- Involvement: local initiatives provide facilities and some advertising ensues. Larger numbers of visitors, a tourist season and public sector involvement follows.
- Development: large numbers of tourists and control passes from locals to national or international companies. The destination begins to change in appearance. Overuse may begin.
- Consolidation: the destination is now a fully-fledged part of the tourist industry – the rate of increase of visitors is reducing. A recognizable recreational business district has emerged.
- Stagnation: peak visitor numbers have been reached and the destination is unfashionable with environmental, social and economic problems. Major promotional efforts are needed to maintain visitor numbers.
- Decline: visitors now visit newer, rural resorts as the destination goes into decline. It is dependent on a smaller geographical catchment and repeat visits.
- Rejuvenation: here the authorities attempt to 'relaunch' the destination by providing new facilities, attracting new markets and re-investing.

Summary

Certain factors favour the development of tourist resources and this explains why the world pattern of tourism supply is uneven. Developed tourist resources are cultural appraisals, considered by society to be of economic value. They are usually shared with other users and are both fragile and perishable. As the negative impacts of tourism are realized, tourism planning for resources will become vital. Planning aims to minimize the costs of tourism and to maintain the integrity of the resource base. At the world scale both physical and cultural features are key factors influencing tourist development. Of the range of physical features in the world, coasts, mountains, and inland water are the most popular locations for tourist development.

At the national scale, classifications of tourist attractions which include the whole tourist resource base are useful. Evaluations of the potential of the resource base to satisfy tourists' demands allow possible future areas for recreation and tourism to be identified. These evaluations can then be applied to the local scale where resultant resort developments have a distinctive morphology and mix of service functions. It is also possible to identify a cycle of resort development.

Case study

The Galapagos Islands, Ecuador: a case study in resource conservation and tourism development

Introduction

The Galapagos Islands lie in the Pacific Ocean about 1000 kilometres west of Guayaquil on the South American mainland (see Figure 3.4). The unique wildlife of the Galapagos is a world-class attraction and a non-reproduceable resource, which has been given international recognition as a World Heritage Site and Biosphere Reserve. Most of the animals have no fear of man, as there are no natural predators. Although the islands are situated on the Equator, penguins and sea lions flourish alongside species more closely associated with the tropics, due to the cold ocean currents offshore. The best known animals are the marine iguanas and giant tortoise, of which there are 14 distinct species on the different islands. This provided the inspiration for Darwin's theory of evolution and the islands' scientific value has long been recognized. Until recently the Galapagos were protected by their remoteness, and the human impact was relatively slight. Since the 1970s the growing popularity of eco-tourism has focused public interest on the islands, providing support for conservation but posing a greater threat to the fragile ecosystems than the occasional havoc wreaked by pirates and whalers in the past. The widespread perception that the islands are a 'tropical Eden' is far from the reality. The climate is dry and since the islands are volcanic, the scenery is for the most part barren and rugged. The plants and animals are well adapted to the conditions, including the periodic heavy rains and warmer temperatures resulting from El Niño (see Chapter 4), but their survival is affected by a number of serious problems due to human interference with the environment. Introduced plant and animal species may soon outnumber those native to the islands.

Managing the resource

National park designation

In Europe and North America conservationists and even representatives of the travel industry are seriously considering the introduction of 'no-go areas' for tourists as a solution to the damage caused by tourism to fragile physical and cultural resources. In the Galapagos this has been the policy for many years and you might investigate whether this is feasible or even desirable for

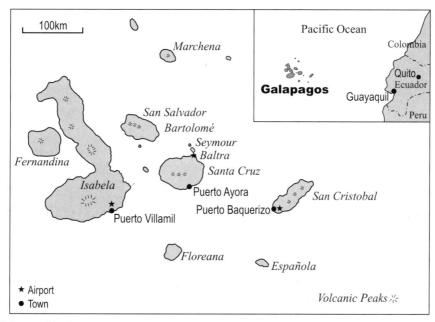

Figure 3.4 The Galapagos Islands

other areas. As early as 1959, when the number of visitors was less than 1000 a year, the Ecuadorian government designated 97 per cent of the archipelago, excluding only those areas already settled, as a National Park. In 1968 the Charles Darwin Foundation, an international non-profit organization, was established to protect the islands' ecosystems in co-operation with the Galapagos National Park Service (GNPS), a government agency. Organized tourism began at about this time and in 1974 a master plan for the national park set a limit of 12 000 visitors a year, later expanded to 40 000 for economic reasons, with a maximum visitor stay of six days.

Zoning

The National Park was divided into five zones to give varying degrees of protection and balance the needs of tourists against the primary objective of conservation, as follows:

1 For the use of local residents for agriculture and forestry.
2 Tourist zone, but access restricted.
3 Access restricted to a maximum of twelve visitors at a time.
4 Access for scientific research only.
5 Access prohibited without special permit.

Visitor management

Strict regulations are in force to ensure visitors do not destroy the wildlife they come to see. Access is also controlled by price; it costs almost as much for foreign tourists to reach the Galapagos by air or cruise ship from the mainland of Ecuador as it does to fly from Europe to Quito or Guayaquil. Visitors to the National Park have to pay a hefty entrance fee (currently $100). Tourists are restricted to some sixty visitor sites designated by the GNPS; most of the islands' land area is off limits for visitors and, indeed, residents as well. At each visitor site a rough waymarked trail gives you the opportunity to see the wildlife, unusual plants and volcanic mountain landscapes of the Galapagos. Tourists are always accompanied by a naturalist guide licensed by the GNPS with a maximum of twenty visitors per guide. Itineraries for tourists on cruise ships visiting a large number of sites, or on day excursions based on island hotels, are arranged well in advance by the tour operator. Those arriving in chartered yachts and other small vessels are allowed some flexibility in organizing their own itineraries subject to a maximum number of sites per boat.

Visitor impacts

Thanks to this system of visitor management, tourism has made little direct impact on the island's ecosystems.

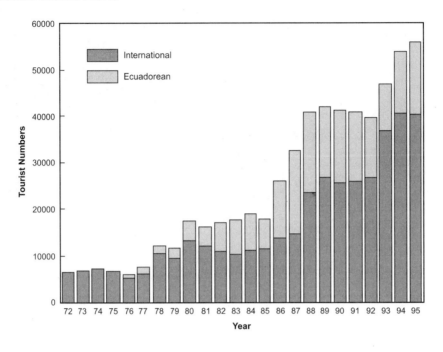

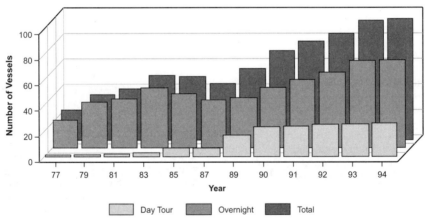

Figure 3.5 The growth of tourism to the Galapagos
Source: Galapagos National Park Service, in Jackson (1997: 251).

Eco-tourism in the Galapagos was worth an estimated $105 million to Ecuador in 1995. Most foreign visitors are high-income, middle-aged Europeans and North Americans. The value to the national economy is even greater if we consider that most of these tourists spend three days in mainland Ecuador, principally in the cities of Quito and Guayaquil, as part of their holiday. However, only a small proportion of the visitor spend actually benefits the local economy, as most tourist requirements have to be imported from the mainland, and eco-tourism creates relatively few jobs. Conservationists are concerned that this 'educational tourism' could grow to become conventional tourism, where visitors are less sensitive about their impact on the environment. There are, for example, no clearly defined limits on the annual number of visitors (the planned limit of 40 000 has long been exceeded), or the number of tourist boats operating in the islands, which have increased steadily over the years (see Figure 3.5). Few recreational activities are available except for scuba diving, snorkelling and sport fishing, which has the potential to attract the luxury market. Further growth will generate a demand for more shore-based facilities. At present Puerto Ayora and two other small towns offer little more than basic amenities and support services; so

far proposals to build high-rise or luxury resort hotels have been resisted.

Ecuadorians and foreign visitors evaluate the island's resources in different ways. Domestic tourists, for example, are much more likely to buy black coral souvenirs from local traders, which is illegal. Tourism has resulted in an influx of workers from the mainland, helped by subsidized domestic air fares. They are attracted by the prospect of short-term financial gain and

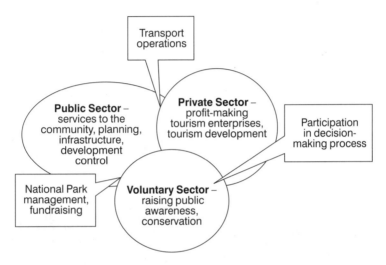

The Public Sector includes:

- The Ecuador Government and its agencies:

  - The Forestry Service
  - Ministry of Agriculture
  - The Armed Forces (who operate the TAME airline)
  - The Galapagos National Park Service
  - The Instituto Nacional Galapagos (INGALA)

- The municipios (local authorities).

The Private Sector includes:

- Tour operators
- Hotel owners
- Some small businesses catering for tourists
- The SAETA airline
- Shipping services
- Yacht charter
- The fishing industry.

The Voluntary Sector includes:

- The Charles Darwin Foundation (CDF) – an international body
- The World Wide Fund for Nature (WWF)
- The Galapagos Conservation Trust in the UK and similar organizations in different countries, affiliated to the CDF.

Figure 3.6 Stakeholders in the Galapagos Islands

a climate which is free of tropical diseases. The population is growing at the rate of 8 per cent a year. This puts pressure on scarce resources such as water, foodstuffs and building materials, and increases the risk of oil spillage from the supply ships, all of which further tips the balance against the survival of the islands' wildlife.

The stakeholders

Conservation is also vital for the surrounding seas, and tourism has to share use of this resource with the important fishing industry – this includes both small-scale local operators and large, well-equipped ships based on the mainland and supplying international markets. In 1986 the government established the Galapagos Marine Resources Reserve, reputedly the world's largest, covering an area of over 130 000 sq. km. In 1995 a concerted effort was made to ban commercial fishing, especially of sea cucumbers which are valued in the Far East as an aphrodisiac. In protest, islanders threatened the staff of the GNPS and the Charles Darwin Research Station at Puerto Ayora, and deliberate damage was caused to wildlife habitats. Similar incidents have occurred in other national parks where local communities feel excluded, the Coto Doñana in Spain is another example. In the case of the Galapagos the government has taken on board the principle of local involvement. The 'Special Law for the Galapagos' passed by the Ecuadorian Congress in 1998, recognizes the importance of sustainable development. Its main points are:

- Greater co-operation between the organizations concerned with conservation and tourism development. The various stakeholders are shown in Figure 3.6.
- Promotion of locally based nature tourism.
- Greater control over tourism development by INGALA, the regional planning agency, which will require environmental impact statements from developers.
- Stabilization of population growth by making it more difficult to obtain rights of residence in the islands.
- Allocation of 40 per cent of the visitor entrance fee to the GNPS for conservation.
- Protection of native island species to be achieved through prevention – by stricter quarantine regulations against plant and animal imports – and damage limitation – by eradication of introduced species.

It remains to be seen how effective the Special Law will be in practice. Like other developing countries, Ecuador takes pride in its heritage, but has limited financial resources to set aside for conservation when there are more pressing economic and social problems. It may also be difficult to find experienced professional workers to enforce the regulations in the face of opposition from local politicians, an inefficient bureaucracy, and the multinational corporations. It is clear that there are many interests in the conservation of the islands of which tourism is an important, but not the only, stakeholder.

4

Climate and tourism

LEARNING OBJECTIVES

After reading this chapter, you should be able to:

1 Understand the importance of latitude and the distribution of land and sea areas in determining climatic differences.
2 Be aware of the major climatic elements and explain how these affect the various types of recreational tourism.
3 Understand the problems of classifying world climatic zones.
4 Describe the distribution of world climates and their significance for tourism.

Introduction

We can view climate either as a resource encouraging the development of tourism or as a constraint limiting the appeal of a destination. Despite the widespread availability of air-conditioning and other forms of climate control, tourists are bound to spend much of their time in an outdoor environment, which may be considerably warmer or colder than their country of origin. As air travellers, with a limited range of clothing, we need accurate information on the climate of the destination. Many types of recreation, from sunbathing to skiing, are weather dependent. On a world scale the importance of climate is shown in the broad pattern of movement from the colder, cloudier tourist-generating countries to warmer, sunnier destinations; on a local scale it is seen in the decision of

urban families to visit a nearby beach on a hot summer's day. For a resort, climate largely determines the length of the holiday season (although this is also influenced by external factors such as the timing of school holidays in the generating areas). Climate also determines factors such as a resort's development and operating costs; sales of beverages and leisure equipment are affected by weather changes, while the providers of tourist services have to cope with seasonal variations in demand. In most destinations, the problem of *seasonality* seriously affects profitability and employment in the tourism industry. Finally, the traditional relationship between climate and tourism may be changing as evidence linking skin cancer with exposure to sunlight is publicized and associated with issues such as global warming.

The world climate scene

Climate is the long-term average of weather conditions at a particular location. It is defined by three main factors: latitude; the distribution of land and sea areas; and relief.

Latitude or distance from the Equator is the primary factor, as this determines the angle of the sun's rays at any given time of the year; if this is too oblique the sun's heating power will be limited. Due to the earth's rotation the Northern Hemisphere is tilted toward the sun in June, when it is overhead at noon on the Tropic of Cancer (latitude 23.5° North). North of the Arctic Circle (latitude 66.5° North) there is daylight for at least twenty-four hours at midsummer, while Antarctica (south of latitude 66.5° South) is experiencing continual darkness. By December, on the other hand, the sun's overhead path has moved south of the Equator to the Tropic of Capricorn (latitude 23.5° South).

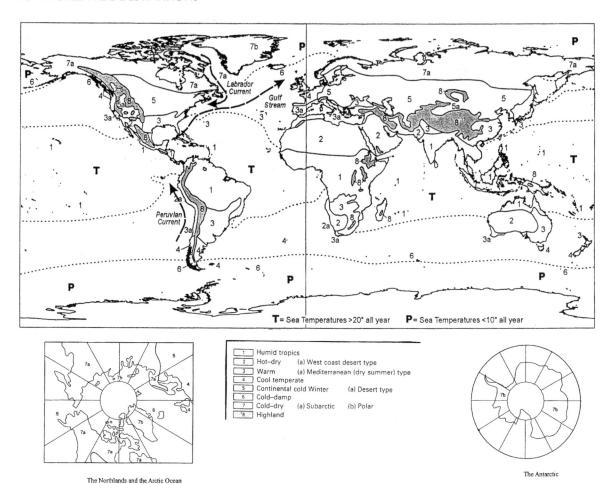

T = Sea Temperatures >20° all year   P = Sea Temperatures <10° all year

Humid tropics
Hot–dry   (a) West coast desert type
Warm   (a) Mediterranean (dry summer) type
Cool temperate
Continental cold Winter   (a) Desert type
Cold–damp
Cold–dry   (a) Subarctic   (b) Polar
Highland

The Northlands and the Arctic Ocean

The Antarctic

Figure 4.1 World climate zones

This marks the onset of summer in the Southern Hemisphere and, in contrast, a period of continuous cold and darkness north of the Arctic Circle. The zone between the tropics enjoys a warm climate all year round as the sun is high in the sky for most of the day. The result of increasing distance from the Equator is a shorter summer and a greater difference in day length between the seasons.

The simple model of a steady decrease in temperature from the Equator to the poles is complicated by the fact that most of the world's landmass is concentrated in the Northern Hemisphere. Land surfaces heat and cool more rapidly than large areas of water. The oceans therefore act as a reservoir of warmth, so that windward coasts and islands have a *maritime* climate which is equable. Furthermore, warm ocean currents, notably the Gulf Stream and North Atlantic Drift distribute some of the warmth of tropical seas

to higher latitudes (see Figure 4.1). As a result, Britain and Ireland have a much milder climate than their position relatively near the Arctic Circle would suggest. Elsewhere, cold currents have a chilling effect, the most well known example being the Labrador Current off the east coast of Canada. (Icebergs carried by this current caused the 1912 *Titanic* disaster). The heartlands of Eurasia and North America at similar latitudes to Britain are far removed from the influence of the sea and experience a *continental* climate, characterized by extreme variations in temperature.

In many parts of the world, where there are high mountains, *relief* has a major effect on weather patterns. Climbers are well aware that air temperatures are considerably lower on the summit of a mountain. There is also a reduction of barometric pressure with increasing altitude;

at 5000 metres the density of the air is less than 60 per cent of its sea-level value. The thinner atmosphere at such altitudes means that, although more solar radiation reaches the ground by day, heat is lost more rapidly to the sky at night. Because there is less oxygen in the air, physical exertion becomes more difficult. Great contrasts in temperature, moisture and sunshine are found within short distances in mountain regions, providing a variety of habitats for plants and animals. Mountain barriers profoundly modify the climates of adjacent lowlands since moist air from the sea is forced to rise over them, becoming drier and warmer as it descends. At a local scale, the position of a slope or valley in relation to the direct rays of the sun has important consequences for land use and resort development, as in the Alps.

Climatic elements and tourism

Temperature

Temperature is the element of climate which has the greatest influence on tourist activity, and the type of clothing worn (Table 4.1). Water sports such as swimming, surfing, and diving are essentially warm weather activities. At the beach, both the air temperature and the sea temperature (which is normally cooler during the daytime) should be above 20°C. You should be aware that water cools the body by conduction thirty times faster than dry still air at the same temperature. Other activities are less suitable in high temperatures, especially when humidity is taken into account. This is normally expressed as the *relative humidity*, which measures the moisture content of the air as a percentage of the total amount it could contain at a given temperature. Thus tropical air at 35°C can hold nine times more water vapour than cold air at 0°C. A dry heat, where the relative humidity is less than 30 per cent, is widely recognized as being more tolerable than the humid heat typical of many tropical destinations. When moisture levels

Table 4.1 Temperatures and clothing – holiday travel in January

	Average daytime temperature (°C)	Clos (units of thermal resistance)
Oslo	0	2.0
Paris	5	1.6
Alicante	15	1.2
Tenerife	20	0.8
Barbados	30	0.1

in the air are nearing saturation it is difficult to keep cool despite profuse sweating, and failure to maintain the body's heat balance will result in heat exhaustion and, in extreme cases, heatstroke. A more common problem, due to the wearing of unsuitable clothing, is the skin condition known as 'prickly heat'. The effect of humidity on how hot the weather feels can be expressed as a value called *effective temperature* which also takes into account air movement, or more simply as the *apparent temperature*, as used in the bioclimatic chart (Figure 4.2). The importance of this for human well-being can be demonstrated if you compare conditions in Delhi and Aswan, as shown by the climographs on the chart, using average daytime values of temperature and relative humidity for each month of the year. The weather in Delhi would be more uncomfortable in August than in Aswan, although the actual air temperature is 5°C lower.

Tourists do, however, vary considerably in their ability to acclimatize, according to their age, gender, body build, rate of metabolism and ethnic origin. Although the human body can adapt fairly readily to tropical conditions – by an increase in the sweat rate, for example – much depends on alterations in patterns of behaviour and lifestyle. This is also true of severely cold conditions where the physiological response (such as shivering) is much less effective. Human comfort is also greatly influenced by factors such as radiant heat from the sun and air movement.

Sunshine

The effect of sunshine is particularly important at the seaside, where ultraviolet light is reflected from the water surface and the sand, adding to the heat load which the exposed skin is receiving from the sky. The British Isles, despite the advantage of having long summer days, experience a cloudy climate compared to that of southern Spain, where the sun shines for as much as 80 per cent of the daylight hours. Ultraviolet radiation is even more intense in low latitudes, although the duration of bright sunshine may be less than in the Mediterranean. The safe length of exposure to the sun will depend on the holidaymaker's skin type and the strength of suntan preparations. These protect the outer skin from the short-wave UVB rays, which cause burning but allow through the long-wave UVA rays to stimulate melanin production. Skiers and mountain climbers at high altitudes also risk sunburn since the air is clear and sunlight is strongly reflected from snow and bare rock. Such incident radiation can provide considerable warmth to the skin even though the air temperature may be as low as 0°C. On a global scale there is increasing evidence of a depletion in the ozone layer in the upper atmosphere; this could cause a dangerous increase in ultraviolet radiation. Already in the 1980s the growing incidence of skin cancer was worrying health authorities in the USA, Australia, and South Africa. However, in Britain and other

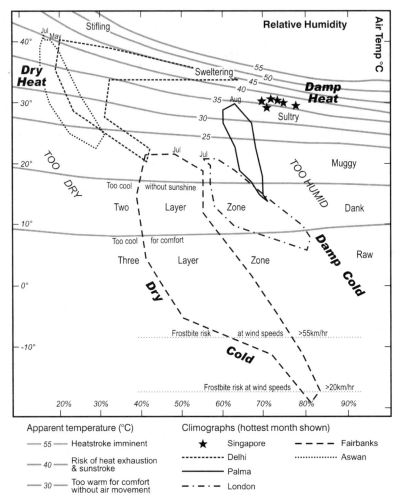

Figure 4.2 Bioclimatic chart

northern countries there are as yet few signs that the cult of sunbathing, which first became fashionable in the 1920s, will lose its popularity.

Wind

Winds are influenced in their direction and strength by the gradient between high and low pressure areas (shown by the spacing of the isobars on a weather map), by the Earth's rotation, and by topography. A world view of air circulation shows that in low latitudes the trade winds are blowing from an easterly direction. This simple model is greatly modified, especially in the Northern Hemisphere, by the great seasonal contrasts in temperature and pressure between the continents and the oceans, which result in notable shifts in

wind direction. At a local scale, onshore sea breezes during the daytime and weaker offshore land breezes at night are a feature of many coastal areas. A knowledge of these winds is essential for the sailing and surfing enthusiast, while the glider pilot is interested in the peculiarities of mountain winds such as the Föhn of the Alps. In the tropics, sea breezes have a cooling effect, so that effective temperatures in islands such as Singapore are at times more comfortable than indicated by the bioclimatic chart (Figure 4.2). In high latitudes, and in middle latitudes during the winter months, strong winds combined with low temperatures have a pronounced chilling effect on exposed skin, leading in extreme cases to frostbite. Even in the relatively mild conditions typical of maritime locations such as the British Isles, this *wind-chill* factor is a major constraint on outdoor recreation.

Precipitation

We can also regard precipitation in its various forms of rain, hail, sleet and snow as a constraint. Much, however, depends on its intensity, duration, and seasonal distribution. In the tropics there is usually a well-defined division of the year into 'wet' and 'dry' seasons. *Rain* typically falls in short heavy downpours, following strong convectional heating of the air and the build-up of cumulus clouds during the afternoon. In contrast, most of the rain that falls in Britain is cyclonic in origin; it may be smaller in total amount but is spread over many more rainy days.

We can view *snow* as an expensive hazard for transport or as a valuable recreational resource. Suitable locations for ski resorts are found mainly in accessible mid-latitude mountain regions, where there is adequate snow cover for at least three months of the year. As the provision of facilities for 'downhill' skiers is costly, the resort operator needs accurate information on the local climate, including temperature, sunshine, wind speeds and relative humidity. For example, where monthly average minimum temperatures are below $-2°C$ snow falls are likely to be frequent. The type of cover is also important and 'powder' – loose, low-density snow – is favoured by skiers. Although the introduction of winter sports has brought economic benefits to remote mountain communities, it has also led to environmental degradation, especially in the Alps. Deforestation to create ski runs has increased the risk of avalanches.

Air quality

Last but not least, the monitoring of air quality is increasingly crucial as part of the concern about environmental issues and the quality of life generally. Most of you are aware of the motor vehicle as a major polluter, emitting nitrous oxide, hydrocarbons and ground level ozone (not to be confused with the ozone in the stratosphere). An older problem in most of the world's large cities, especially in the less developed countries, is the emission of sulphur dioxide from 'smoke-stack' industries. Smogs, or severe episodes of air pollution are particularly common in regions where anticyclonic conditions, inhibiting air movement, prevail for much of the year. Examples would include the Mediterranean countries and California in summer, and the continental heartlands of North America and Eurasia in winter. An unpleasant cocktail of gases poisons the air of our cities, reducing visibility, blighting vegetation, eroding historic monuments and threatening the health of people suffering from respiratory problems. Moreover, the effects of 'acid rain' have degraded forests and lakes in many areas downwind of sources of industrial pollution in North America and Europe.

World climate

Classifying climates

Even in a small country like Britain, temperatures, rainfall and exposure to wind or sunshine vary a good deal, resulting in many local climates. However, these differences are less significant on a global scale than those between, say, the South of England and the French Riviera. It is also true that areas of the world separated by vast distances have such similar features that they can be regarded as belonging to the same climate zone. Thus the climate of California resembles that of Spain, and the South Island of New Zealand shows broad similarities to England, once the reversal of the seasons in the Southern Hemisphere is taken into account.

It is relatively simple to draw a series of world maps showing the various elements of climate, but much more difficult to synthesize this information in order to determine the best overall conditions for tourism. A number of attempts have been made to classify climates from a human rather than an agricultural standpoint. Of particular relevance is the work of Lee and Lemons (1949), who devised a scheme relating temperatures to clothing requirements. Terjung (1966) utilized data on temperature and relative humidity to produce a Comfort Index for each month of the year for both day and night-time conditions. This was further refined, where the data were available, to take account of the effects of wind-chill and solar radiation. Terjung's classification is the most comprehensive but has the disadvantage of producing an excessive number of climate zones, even when the features of the Comfort Index are summarized for the year as a whole. Another interesting approach is the 'climate code' devised by Hatch (1985). This is an index of overall climatic favourability ranging from 0 (abysmal) to 100 (idyllic), calculated from prorated monthly values of temperature, rainfall, sunshine and relative humidity. This index is particularly useful for assessing the suitability of a destination for beach tourism, as it is biased towards dry, sunny, and warm climates.

The bioclimatic chart (Figure 4.2) was the starting point for the classification scheme adopted in this book. You can use it to investigate the suitability of an area's climate for tourism, once you have obtained the average monthly daytime values of temperature and relative humidity and plotted the co-ordinates on an overlay superimposed on the chart. We can think of the world's climates as a continuum, from hot humid conditions at one extreme to cold and dry at the other. However, most parts of the world have climates which lie somewhere between these extremes, and which are characterized by distinct seasonal variations. This is shown by the climographs for Delhi, Palma, London and – in an extreme form – for Fairbanks, Alaska. Such climates are conventionally described in terms of their temperature and rainfall characteristics. They have been grouped into eight major climate zones,

Table 4.2   World climates and tourism

Zone	Physical characteristics	Significance for tourism	Type location N = Northern Hemisphere S = Southern Hemisphere
(1) *Humid tropics* (a) Equatorial	Day and night equal in length year round. Extensive cloud cover and abundant rainfall. Temperatures in range 23–33°C with high humidity. Weather enervating.	Generally unfavourable. Scope for river-based expeditions.	Amazonia
(b) Trade wind type	In Northern Hemisphere north-east trades bring heavy rainfall December–May: in Southern Hemisphere south-east trades bring heavy rainfall June–October. More sunshine than (a) especially in the 'dry season'.	Generally favourable for beach tourism. Risk of cyclones/hurricanes during rainy season.	Barbados (N) Mauritius, Tahiti (S)
(c) Tropical wet dry	Much greater seasonal variations, especially in rainfall. A long dry season often divided into the 'cool dry' (warm days and cool nights) and the 'hot dry' where the high temperatures are usually associated with low humidity. The rainy season typically lasts from June to November in the Northern Hemisphere and from December to May in the Southern Hemisphere. The parched landscapes of the dry season contrast with the lush vegetation resulting from the rains.	Rainy season can be unpleasant due to sweltering conditions, while storms may disrupt communications. Dry season suitable for sightseeing, safaris and beach tourism except during the periods of 'highest sun'.	Goa, Bangkok (N) Darwin (S)
(2) *Hot dry*	Little or no rainfall. Great daily variations in temperature due to intense solar radiation and strong nocturnal cooling. Low humidity except in some coastal areas. In northern Hemisphere the cool season lasts from November to March, in the Southern Hemisphere from April to September.	The moderate temperatures and abundant sunshine of the cool season favour winter-sun tourism, especially in coastal areas. Summer conditions can be unpleasant. The desert environment attracts trekking expeditions.	Aswan, Bahrain (N) Alice Springs (S)
(a) West coast desert subtype	Moderate temperatures year-round but offshore dust-laden winds, especially at night.	Less favourable. Scope for water sports, especially fishing.	Tarfaia (N) Mollendo, Swakopmund (S)
(3) *Warm*	In Northern Hemisphere long warm season May to October, in Southern Hemisphere November to April.	Highly favourable; weather permits outdoor recreation year-round. Summers ideal for beach tourism.	
(a) Mediterranean type	Cool winters with moderate rainfall, warm to hot dry summers. Abundant sunshine		Palma, Los Angeles (N) Cape Town, Perth (S)
(b) Warm temperate humid summer type	Cool winters with moderate rainfall; in the Northern Hemisphere occasional outbreaks of cold weather. Summer tends to be the rainy season with much hot, humid weather.		New Orleans, Shanghai (N) Buenos Aires, Sydney (S)
(4) *Cool temperate*	Mild to raw winters. Weather highly variable. Rather cool cloudy summers; in the Northern Hemisphere June to August, in the Southern Hemisphere December to February.	Winters unfavourable. Short season for beach tourism; suitable for the strenuous types of outdoor recreation. All-weather facilities desirable at holiday resorts.	Dublin, Vancouver (N) Wellington (S)
(5) *Continental cold winter*	Cold winters with extensive snow cover. Warm summers with moderate rainfall June to August. Pronounced seasonal changes.	Winters suitable for skiing and other snow-based activities. Short season for beach tourism; lakes are likely to be more important for water sports than coastal areas.	Chicago, Montreal, Stockholm, Sapporo (N)
(a) Mid-latitude desert type	Little or no rainfall due to the 'rain shadow' effect. Differs from the 'hot dry' in having very cold winters.	Generally unfavourable. Scope for trekking expeditions in summer.	Ulan Bator (N)
(6) *Cold damp* Subarctic Maritime (N) Subantarctic (S)	Raw winters, no real summer, Overcast skies and strong winds prevalent year-round	Unfavourable, but rich bird and marine animal life attracts nature-lovers.	Faeroes, Aleutians (N) South Georgia (S)

Table 4.2   Continued

Zone	Physical characteristics	Significance for tourism	Type location N = Northern Hemisphere S = Southern Hemisphere
(7) Cold dry (a) Subarctic continental	Very cold winters, spectacular spring thaws, short summers.	Generally unfavourable. Winter temperatures below −20°C curtail outdoor recreation. Permafrost inhibits the construction of tourist facilities. Skiing and other snow-based activities possible in late winter; canoeing and fishing in summer.	Fairbanks, Rovaniemi (N)
(b) Polar climates	Bitterly cold dark winter months with high wind-chill. Air temperatures in summer rarely rise above 10°C despite almost continuous daylight, poleward of latitude 70° from May to August in the Arctic and from November to February in Antarctica. Incident radiation from snow and ice-covered surfaces.	Unfavourable – but scope for expeditions entailing a high degree of preparation. Cruising in Arctic and Antarctic waters during summer months.	Spitzbergen (N) Deception Island (S)
(8) Highland climates (a) Tropical highlands	Great differences in temperature between day/night and sunlit/shaded locations. Intense ultraviolet radiation, low humidity, absence of dust and pollen at high altitudes above the cloud level. A mosaic of climates and life-zones at different altitudes. Permanent snowline above 4500–5000 metres.	Very favourable at altitudes between 1500 and 3000 metres as the cool air gives relief from the heat of the tropical lowlands, encouraging the development of health resorts such as the 'hill-stations' of southern Asia. At higher altitudes increasing risk of 'altitude sickness' will restrict skiing and other activities to acclimatized individuals. Scope for trekking, climbing, and nature study, but mountain ecosystems are vulnerable to the impact of tourism.	Addis Ababa, Quito Darjeeling (N) La Paz (S)
(b) Mid-latitude highlands	Much greater seasonal differences of temperatures than in (a). Cold snowy winters contrast with warm rainy summers, but weather is highly variable. Importance of mountain and valley winds. Life-zones include coniferous forest with alpine meadow above the tree-line. Permanent snowline above 2500–3000 metres.	Generally favourable but conditions vary with altitude and aspect. A reliable snow cover in winter at altitudes of 1500–2500 metres encourages the development of ski resorts. Lack of air pollution favours health tourism and a wide range of outdoor activities in summer.	St Moritz, Denver (N)

related more closely to human physiology. Figure 4.1 shows the distribution of world climates, but you should be aware that the boundaries drawn on the map indicate wide areas of transition rather than abrupt changes. A summary of these climates and their suitability for tourism is set out in Table 4.2.

World climate zones

The humid tropics (zone 1)

This is perhaps the most important zone, in view of its extent and potential for tourism development. Here the main problem is keeping buildings and their occupants cool, as temperatures rarely fall below 20°C even at night,

while humidity is generally high. Buildings should be designed to take advantage of any breezes; usually an open plan is adopted with rooms having access to a veranda. Sometimes buildings are elevated on stilts to capture any air movements above the vegetation. For the tourist, clothing should be lightweight, of open texture and made of absorbent materials. Most of the diseases for which the tropics are notorious are mainly due, not to the climate, but to the poor standards of sanitation prevailing in many Third World countries. Nevertheless, the hot moist environment favours the growth of harmful bacteria and parasites, while diseases such as malaria are carried by insects which cannot thrive in cold temperatures. Visitors can protect themselves from malaria by taking prophylactic drugs and by preventative measures, such as not exposing legs and arms in the evenings when the mosquitoes are active. For other tropical diseases such as yellow fever, vaccination is essential. (It is worth noting that highland areas in the tropics not only enjoy a cooler climate but also are malaria-free.)

With the exception of the equatorial zone, most parts of the tropics have a 'dry season' of varying length when conditions are not unfavourable for tourism. It is then that the savannah grasslands, typical of much of Africa, provide the best conditions for game viewing or 'safari tourism'. In the beach destinations of the Caribbean, West Africa and southern Asia the dry season coincides with the winter months in North America and Europe, so that they are well placed to attract winter-sun seekers from the main tourist-generating countries. Tropical countries south of the Equator are less favoured as their best months coincide with summer in the countries of the Northern Hemisphere.

Extensive coral reefs fringing the coastline are a feature of many holiday destinations in the tropics (they cannot flourish where sea temperatures fall below 20°C). These provide an ideal setting for water sports, particularly scuba diving. The exuberant vegetation and diversity of species found in the tropics is increasingly perceived as a resource for eco-tourism. Here is it worth noting that tropical Africa is generally much richer in the 'big game' animals, sought by safari enthusiasts, than similar environments in South and Central America, southern Asia and Australasia. Each of these regions has distinct species occupying equivalent niches in the ecosystem. Most tropical habitats are threatened by the growing pace of economic development in the Third World countries of the 'South', which is often geared to supplying raw materials for the developed countries of the 'North', such as Japan, the USA and the EU. The disappearing rainforests of the Amazon Basin and Indonesia are two well-known examples, with environmental consequences that may well be serious, not just for the tropical zone, but for the Earth as a whole.

The hot dry climates (zone 2)

Areas of constant drought account for about one-third of the Earth's land surface. They occur mainly in tropical and subtropical latitudes wherever the air is dry as a result of subsidence from the permanent high-pressure belts.

The hot dry regions include the sunniest places on earth – Upper Egypt and Arizona both receive more than 4000 hours of bright sunshine annually. They are also subject to extremes of temperature. Due to the intensity of the solar radiation, air temperatures often reach 45°C by mid-afternoon in the summer but fall rapidly after dark as a result of radiation from the ground to the clear night sky. During the winter months frost may occasionally be recorded before dawn. The humidity is generally very low during the daytime. The main exceptions are coastal areas adjoining an enclosed sea where relative humidities are high due to evaporation from the water surface. Very little of this moisture is able to rise to produce rainfall, making the summer climate of places like Bahrain and Aden particularly oppressive. Other coastal areas, with a cold ocean current offshore, experience much cooler temperatures and a good deal of mist – the rainless Namib Desert is a good example.

The dryness of the air, aggravated by strong dust-laden winds, results in rapid evaporation from the skin and the risk of dehydration. The intense glare from the sky can cause eye disorders. The clothing most suited to the climate should be loose fitting, to allow evaporative cooling from the skin; the material should be of close texture and moderate thickness. It should also be light in colour to reflect radiation, and cover as much of the body as possible. A variety of shading and insulation devices are used by architects in hot dry regions to even out the daily variations of temperature and reduce the impact of solar radiation.

Areas of sand dune devoid of vegetation account for only a small proportion of the desert regions, which support a surprising variety of plant and animal life adapted to drought conditions. Strong winds and 'flash floods' after the sporadic rains have, over the millennia, produced many spectacular landforms by erosion. In the few places where ground water is available the vegetation can be luxuriant. Some of these oases can support large urban communities on the basis of complex irrigation systems.

The more accessible areas of the deserts are increasingly sought after by tourists, who value the space, the sunny winter climate, and the scenery, which they can offer. Some dry regions such as Arizona are perceived to have a healthy climate free of respiratory diseases, whereas in the irrigated areas of the Sahara and the Middle East there is a substantial risk of malaria. Development has taken place in those regions where adequate supplies of water and power can be provided at reasonable cost and where good external communications are available to the main tourist-generating countries. Coastal areas have the best prospects as water can be obtained from the sea by desalinization, although this is expensive.

The warm climates (zone 3)

Situated mainly between latitudes 25° and 40°, these regions come under the influence of air masses of tropical origin in summer and the westerly winds of middle latitudes in winter. Unlike the tropics, there is a definite cool season, but winters are rarely cold enough to prevent outdoor activities such as golf and tennis from being enjoyed in comfort. One standard layer of clothing (or 1 clo of thermal resistance, equivalent in insulation value to a business suit) is sufficient for winter temperatures that range between 10°C and 20°C. Most of the zone is, however, too cool for beach tourism in winter, despite the impression given by some 'winter sun' holiday brochures. The main exceptions are the Canary Islands, Madeira, Bermuda and southern Florida, which can be described as 'subtropical'.

Within this zone the Mediterranean climate, with its dry summers and abundant sunshine, provides the best all-round conditions for tourism and outdoor recreation. As the name implies, this climate is best developed around the Mediterranean Sea, which allows the influence of the Atlantic Ocean to penetrate as far as south-west Asia. It is also found in California and in equivalent latitudes of the Southern Hemisphere. During the autumn and winter months these regions lie in the path of depressions which bring a good deal of rain. The summers are very warm, although the afternoon heat is modified by sea breezes and fairly low humidities, while the nights are pleasantly cool. Lack of rain, however, causes problems in ensuring adequate water and power supplies to meet the needs of farmers, manufacturers and the tourism industry. The dry evergreen vegetation characteristic of these climatic conditions is frequently subject to devastating fires.

On the eastern margins of the continents in these latitudes the warm temperate humid summer climate has adequate rainfall throughout the year. In some areas, notably southern China and Japan, summer is the rainy season and winters are relatively dry, thanks to the monsoon. Summers can be oppressively hot due to the high humidity and there is generally less sunshine than in the Mediterranean. However, the prevailing warm moist conditions are very favourable for agriculture.

The cool temperate and continental cold winter climates (zones 4 and 5)

These climates of middle latitudes are significant mainly as generating areas for sun-seeking tourism. The main difference between the maritime climates of the western margins of the continents and the continental climates of their heartlands and eastern margins is the relative mildness of winter in the former compared to its severity in the latter. In Europe the westerlies and their associated depressions can penetrate far to the east, in the absence of any significant north-to-south mountain barrier. It is therefore difficult to draw any meaningful boundary between the maritime climate of Western Europe, best exemplified by the British Isles, and the continental climate of Eastern Europe. Indeed, anticyclones centred over Scandinavia can occasionally 'block' the westerlies and bring spells of very cold winter weather to parts of Britain. In North America high mountains run parallel to the west coast, shutting out the moderating influence of the Pacific Ocean and confining mild, moist climatic conditions to a narrow coastal strip. You may be surprised to find that the coastal areas of eastern North America and East Asia have a severe winter climate, but this is because the prevailing winds are offshore, bringing very cold air from the continental interiors. The Atlantic and Pacific Oceans do, however, have a slight warming effect, and this is sufficient to trigger off heavy snowfalls in the mountains of New England and northern Japan. The situation is quite different at equivalent latitudes in the Southern Hemisphere, where there are vast expanses of ocean, interrupted only by the southern extremity of South America, Tasmania and New Zealand. These areas experience a maritime climate which is milder, more equable and much less prone to air pollution than that of the British Isles.

In the maritime or cool temperate zone, winter temperatures are generally in the range of 0°C to 10°C and there is little snowfall except on high ground. Two standard layers of clothing (1.6 clos) are normally sufficient for these conditions. However, the mild temperatures are often associated with overcast skies, drizzle, fog and strong winds. Due to the continual progression of warm and cold fronts, the weather is very changeable. There is generally adequate rainfall at all seasons, and it is often excessive on west-facing coasts and mountains. Summers tend to be rather cool and cloudy, with afternoon temperatures rarely exceeding 25°C. Such a climate is invigorating, but it is not well suited to the more popular forms of outdoor recreation.

In the continental zone, winter temperatures are below 0°C for one to five months, so that snow, icy roads and frozen waterways are to be expected – and dealt with – as a matter of course. Buildings are well insulated and in some regions have traditionally been designed to withstand heavy snowfalls. Winter clothing consists of three standard layers (equivalent of 2 clos) separated by 6 mm of trapped insulating air. An overcoat, adequate head covering and protection for the extremities are essential in these cold temperatures. However, the winter weather is generally more settled, due to the prevailing anticyclonic conditions, than in the cool temperate zone. This provides opportunities for a variety of snow-based activities such as cross-country skiing and snowmobiling. Summers are appreciably warmer than in the British Isles with daytime temperatures frequently exceeding 25°C. Nevertheless, a good deal of rain falls during this season and hailstorms are frequent. Autumn in forested areas is a colourful season and is characterized by keen, stimulating weather.

The cold damp climates (zone 6)

Small in terms of land area, these essentially maritime climates are dominated by the permanent low-pressure belts over the North Atlantic, North Pacific and Southern oceans, which generate a great deal of stormy weather throughout the year. These regions receive less sunshine than any other part of the world, while temperatures rarely fall much below −5°C in winter or rise much above 10°C in summer. The climate is too cold and windy for tree growth and there is much boggy terrain due to the constant precipitation. Rain or wet snow can easily penetrate clothing, robbing it of its insulating qualities. Heat loss also occurs from the feet if these are not adequately protected from the wet ground, causing serious skin damage or 'trenchfoot'. Suitable clothing for these bleak conditions consists of material with small air spaces which prevents heat loss due to the wind and, at the same time, allows the skin to 'breathe' freely, plus a water-repellent outer layer which can be easily removed. The weather of the more exposed upland areas of Britain, so popular with hikers, approximates to these conditions for much of the year.

The cold dry climates (zone 7)

The cold climate regions account for a third of the earth's land surface, including 10 per cent (mainly in Antarctica and Greenland) which is permanently ice covered. Although temperatures in the subarctic zone can reach 25°C during the brief summers, the length and extreme severity of the winters is the dominant fact of life in high latitudes. In the Arctic zone the sun's rays are oblique even in summer, counteracting the advantage of continuous daylight at this season, while for several months the sun scarcely appears above the horizon. In the Southern Hemisphere, Antarctica has an even colder climate than that experienced by the northern lands adjoining the Arctic Ocean. Although the icy seas of both polar zones are surprisingly rich in marine life, the species representing the Arctic are distinct from those of the Antarctic. The Arctic supports a variety of mammals, with the polar bear at the top of the food chain. In contrast, the continent of Antarctica is virtually sterile and only its coastal fringes provide a habitat for penguins and other bird life.

Provided the weather is calm, temperatures as low as –40°C are bearable as the air is very dry. However, this causes dehydration, as moisture is lost from the body to the atmosphere in exhaled breath, and this, together with heat from vehicles and buildings, produces 'human habitation fog' in built-up areas. Extreme cold has a punishing effect on people and materials – for example, steel becomes brittle and shatters like glass. Under blizzard conditions exposed flesh can freeze in less than a minute, due to wind-chill. The extremities have to be protected from frostbite; the ears by a fur-lined hood; and the hands and feet by two insulating layers. Arctic clothing tends to be bulky as several layers are needed under a windproof parka; with physical exertion large quantities of sweat are produced. The clothing should fit fairly loosely when active but can be drawn in when at rest to trap insulating air. However, no amount of clothing will keep an inactive individual comfortable for long at temperatures below –15°C.

Throughout the Arctic and most of the subarctic the summers are not warm enough to thaw more than the topsoil, so that the moisture beneath the ground remains frozen. This condition, known as *permafrost*, presents costly engineering problems. Buildings and even utilities must be insulated from contact with the ground, otherwise the permafrost would melt and the structure subside.

Because moisture cannot drain down, there is much surface water in summer, which attracts swarms of biting insects. The southern part of the subarctic zone is dominated by vast, rather sombre forests of spruce, birch, or larch, which can withstand a short growing season and poor soils. As summer temperatures decrease, these are replaced by the stunted vegetation of the tundra and the polar deserts of the Arctic zone. Fur trapping has long been the only source of income for the native peoples of Alaska, northern Canada, Greenland and Siberia. Tourism could now offer an alternative as they could provide guiding and outfitting services to groups of hunters, anglers, and expeditioners from warmer climate zones. So far, tourism has made an impact in those areas, such as Lapland, the Mackenzie Valley and Alaska, which are accessible by road as well as by air from the major population centres to the south.

This situation may change for a number of reasons. First, there is a growing awareness of the wildlife and spectacular mountain scenery of some Arctic regions such as Baffin Island, and this could form the basis of adventure holidays. Second, the growth in popularity of winter sports will lead to development in parts of the subarctic zone. Third, the opening up of Russia to Western tourism will lead to a reappraisal of the tourism potential of Siberia and the Arctic sea route to the north. The cold climate regions will continue to appeal to only a small section of the travel market. However, there is evidence that even minimal numbers of tourists can have a damaging impact on the fragile ecosystems of the polar regions, even where tourist movements are strictly controlled, as in Antarctica. This is a problem simply because the ecosystem takes such a long time to recover from damage.

The highland climates (zone 8)

These are scattered throughout other zones wherever high mountains or plateaus rise more than 1500 metres above sea level, as this is the altitude at which the effects of reduced air pressure first become noticeable. Many important cities in Latin America, East Africa and the Himalayas are situated at altitudes of between 1500 and 4000 metres, where it is necessary for the tourist and business traveller to spend a few days adjusting to the rarefied air. Above 4000 metres acclimatization is more difficult and the symptoms of 'altitude sickness' may occur. Temperatures at these high altitudes are, on average, 20°C lower than those recorded near sea level in the same latitude, although the seasonal rhythm is similar (see Figure 4.3). Ascending a high mountain in the tropics involves passing through a range of climates from warm to cold, depending on altitude, and with humid or dry characteristics according to exposure on windward or leeward slopes. At the highest levels the vegetation superficially resembles that of the Arctic tundra, but the climate of high altitudes differs from that of high latitudes in receiving a large amount of solar radiation

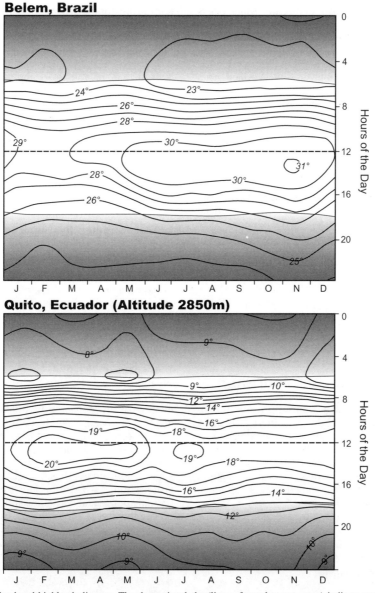

Belem, Brazil

Quito, Ecuador (Altitude 2850m)

Figure 4.3 Tropical lowland and highland climates. The thermoisopleths (lines of equal temperature) indicate variations in temperature (°C) during the day throughout the year. As both Belem and Quito are situated at the Equator, seasonal variations in temperature are very small compared to the differences between day and night, with a rapid rise in temperature after sunrise.
Source: Trewartha (1954: 243, 271).

throughout the year. Notable examples of a 'cold region where the sun is hot' would be Tibet and the Altiplano of Bolivia, where the Indian poncho is the garment best suited for the conditions. In the middle latitudes both the snowline and the treeline are at much lower altitudes than in the tropics and, as mentioned earlier, mountain regions in these zones are favourable for skiing in winter.

Summary

At the world scale, climate is one of the key factors influencing tourism development and holiday travel. Climatic conditions are determined by latitude, altitude and the interrelationship of coasts and mountains. Climate is made up of several factors, of which temperatures and humidity are the most significant for human well-being, while others strongly influence particular types of recreational activity. Seasonal variation is an important characteristic of most climates and this is used as a basis for classification, so that useful comparisons can be made between different destinations. The optimal climate for tourism is the Mediterranean type.

However, tour operators are increasingly seeking out 'exotic' locations where conditions are much less favourable. The hot climates, formerly regarded as unhealthy, are now highly regarded as destinations for beach holidays. The cold climates of high mountain regions and high latitudes are attracting the more adventurous tourists who value the unpolluted, natural environment despite its hazards.

Like other tourism resources, climate is subject to change. It remains to be seen whether these changes will be beneficial to the tourism industry, or to tourists themselves. Some destinations will gain as a result, whereas others, dependent on beach tourism, will lose out. It is certain that tour operators and tourism generally will have to adapt, as the climate is beyond human control.

Case study

Climate change and tourism

The impact of climate change upon tourism is potentially very significant and is already being felt in some parts of the world. Whereas in the past, climate changes took place over long periods of time, there is now considerable evidence that the rate of change is accelerating, due to man's interference with the natural environment. The two key dimensions of climate change can be thought of as:

● global warming
● thinning of the ozone layer.

Global warming: the causes

Since the beginning of the twentieth century, average temperatures worldwide have increased by about 0.5°C and may rise by another 2.0°C in the next century. The causes and effects of this *global warming* are as yet not fully understood. Some scientists link the rise in temperature directly to major increases in emissions of carbon dioxide, methane and nitrous oxide into the atmosphere. These in turn have resulted from the burning of fossil fuels such as oil and coal by transport, industry and domestic consumers, or from the widespread forest clearance that is taking place throughout the tropics. It is known that carbon dioxide is largely

responsible for the *greenhouse effect* of the atmosphere, which prevents excessive radiation of heat from the earth's surface back into space.

The evidence for climatic change is not one-way and is capable of several interpretations. Some scientists believe that the release of methane from the thawing permafrost beneath the tundra and greatly increased snowfall resulting from higher temperatures in the Arctic might lead to another Ice Age. According to this scenario the flow of the iceberg-laden Labrador Current would strengthen, deflecting the warm Gulf Stream well to the south of its present path across the North Atlantic. It is not difficult to predict areas in northern latitudes such as the British Isles experiencing a general deterioration of the climate.

Global warming: the impact on tourism

Ski resorts

The effects of global warming appear to be most obvious in mountain regions, where glaciers have retreated and many ski resorts, especially in areas such as Scotland, are becoming unprofitable.

Rising sea level

The Antarctic Peninsula is a good example of the situation in high latitudes; here the ice cap is melting back rapidly and possibly becoming unstable. Full-scale melting of the polar ice would result in a rise in sea levels worldwide, spelling disaster for many low-lying island destinations, such as the Maldives and Micronesia. The Mediterranean zone would become hotter and drier, aggravating already serious water shortages in some resort areas. These would be less popular with visitors from northern Europe, who conceivably could bask in subtropical warmth in their own seaside resorts, benefiting from an extended summer season. The relationship between tourism and global warming is summarized in Figure 4.4.

Undesirable side-effects include:

● invasions of insects, and pathogens spreading disease
● possible ecological disaster for native plants and animals
● prolonged heat waves, especially in cities, with episodes of poor air quality
● increased storm activity and consequent coastal erosion
● increased algal growth at the coast depleting water quality
● air travel likely to become more expensive due to the penalties imposed on the use of environmentally damaging aircraft fuel.

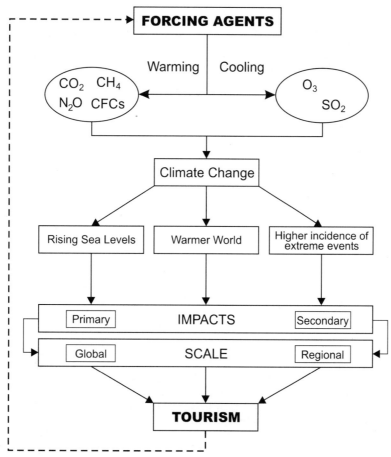

Figure 4.4 The relationship between climate change and tourism
Source: Giles and Perry (1998: 76).

El Niño

A graphic reminder of the power of ocean currents and minor shifts in the atmospheric circulation to influence the weather is shown by the El Niño phenomenon in the eastern Pacific. In some years, December brings a weakening of the trade winds, a reversal of the surface ocean currents, and a surge of abnormally warm water toward the west coast of South America. El Niño displaces the cold offshore Peru Current, bringing heavy rain to the arid coastal belt and destruction of marine life. This spells economic disaster for the beach resorts and the vital fishing industry of Ecuador and Peru. The effects of El Niño are not confined to the Pacific coast of South America, as the weather system characterized by the trade winds is generally stable and spans the entire tropical zone and beyond. The collapse of this system has almost a global impact, affecting areas as far apart as California, southern Africa, Indonesia, Australia and Polynesia with unseasonal floods, droughts and hurricane-force winds. The El Niño of 1997–8 was blamed for the intensity of the forest fires and smog conditions that afflicted South-East Asia. Elsewhere, heavy rains combined with warmer temperatures are putting greater numbers of people at risk from diseases such as *dengue fever*. In the Pacific Ocean corals which can only tolerate a small range of temperature have been devastated. The severity of El Niño episodes in the 1990s increases the probability that the world can expect more extreme fluctuations in weather conditions and this poses serious problems for resort planners, developers and the tourism industry generally.

Thinning of the ozone layer: the causes

The thinning of the ozone layer in the stratosphere was first discovered over Antarctica in winter but is now noticeable year-round, and to a lesser extent over the Arctic. The causes of the thinning are thought to be the emission of chloro\fluorocarbons (CFCs) from devices such as air conditioners, refrigerators, freezers and aerosols. Of course, tourism must be a contributory factor here. In the meantime action is being taken by governments, industry and consumers, mainly in the developed countries, to curb the use of CFCs, but it remains to be seen whether a worldwide ban of CFCs can be made effective. A start was made in this respect with the adoption of the First International Protocol for Control of Greenhouse Gases at Kyoto, Japan, in 1996.

Thinning of the ozone layer: the impact on tourism

The ozone layer filters out the lethal UVC rays and reduces the impact of the harmful UVB rays of the sun. As so-called *ozone holes* have been identified certain destinations already pose a health hazard to visitors – for example parts of the Southern Hemisphere such as Australia, New Zealand, South America and even the Falkland Islands are problematic. Scientists believe that increased ultraviolet radiation is causing a higher incidence of skin cancer and eye cataracts worldwide. If you are fair-skinned you risk sunburn within fifteen minutes of initial exposure, while the use of oils and creams with a high sun-protection factor (SPF) will not prevent long-term damage to the skin. Media interest in the problem may eventually affect attitudes to sunbathing, and to beach tourism in the following ways:

- excessive exposure of the skin may become unfashionable as holidaymakers see the advantages of clothing with a high SPF
- destinations that have traditionally relied on beach tourism will need to diversify by offering *beach plus* products and tours.

The El Niño website is at http://www.enn.com/elnino/ news.htm

5

The geography of transport for travel and tourism

LEARNING OBJECTIVES

After reading this chapter, you should be able to:

1 Appreciate the close relationship between tourism and transport.
2 Understand the principles of spatial interaction between places and understand their importance to tourism geography.
3 Describe the four main physical elements of a transport system – the way, terminal, carrying unit and motive power.
4 Identify the costs involved in running a transport system.
5 Describe the distinguishing features of the main transport modes and recognize their particular contributions to tourism.
6 Identify the Greenwich Meridian, the various time zones and the International Date Line, and illustrate their importance to the traveller.
7 Outline the characteristics of each mode of transport for the different types of traveller.

Introduction

In Chapter 1 three components of tourism were identified: the tourist-generating areas, tourist-destination areas and the linkages between them. This chapter introduces some of the basic principles of transport geography and illustrates their application to tourism.

Tourism and transport are inseparable. Tourism is about being elsewhere and transport bridges the gap between origin and destination. We need to consider transport for these reasons:

- In a historic sense, transportation has developed hand-in-hand with tourism. Improvements in transport have stimulated tourism and, in turn, tourism demand has prompted such transport developments as the growth of charter air services to serve the leisure market.
- Transportation renders tourist destinations accessible to their markets in the tourist-generating areas. All tourism depends on access. Indeed, accessibility, or lack of it, can make or break a destination.
- Transport for tourism involves considerable public and private investment and represents a major sector of the tourist industry in terms of employment and revenue generated. Tourism then is transformed by, and has helped to transform, the world communications map.

However, although estimates suggest that up to 40 per cent of leisure time is spent travelling, we should bear in mind that increased mobility is the means to achieving an objective, rather than as an end in itself.

Principles of interaction

In Chapter 1 the basic principle of spatial interaction between two places was outlined in terms of a supplying area containing a surplus of a commodity and the origin area having a demand for that commodity. In geography this is known as spatial differentiation, with transport linking the two areas.

Ullman (1980) has suggested that three main factors are responsible for spatial interaction and, therefore, transport development:

1 *Complementarity* This is a way of saying that places differ from each other and that in one place there is the desire to travel and in the other place the ability to satisfy

that desire. This complementarity of demand and supply will produce interaction between areas and a transportation system will be required. Examples of complementarity are the flows of tourists from north-eastern states of the USA to resorts in the western states and Florida; or from north-west Europe to the Mediterranean coastal resorts.

2 *Intervening opportunities* While Ullman's idea of complementarity makes interaction possible, there may be competing attractions. For example, for a resident of Munich wishing to take a summer holiday in a Spanish resort, mainland Spain is closer than one of the Canary Islands. Mainland Spain is, therefore, an intervening opportunity, even though perfect complementarity exists between Munich and the Canary Islands.

3 *Transferability or friction of distance* This refers to the cost (in time and money) of overcoming the distance between two places. If the time and money costs of reaching a destination are high, then even perfect complementarity and lack of intervening opportunities will not persuade movement to take place.

Ullman's three factors explain why interaction takes place between places and, if two places have no interaction, it can usually be explained by referring to complementarity, intervening opportunity, or transferability.

The elements of transport

If interaction does take place a transport system will be needed. Faulks (1982) has identified four basic physical elements in any transport system:

● the way
● the terminal
● the carrying unit
● motive power.

For each mode of transport, the characteristics of these elements vary and it is, therefore, useful to examine each in turn.

The way

The way is the medium of travel used by the various transport modes. It may be purely artificial such as roads, railways, tram-tracks or cableways; it may be a natural way such as air or water; or it can be a combination of the two (such as inland waterways). A variety of distinctions are important:

● If the way has to be provided artificially a cost is incurred.
● The cost of the way is influenced by a second distinction: whether the user shares the way with others (for example, roads) or has sole use of a specialized way (for example, railways).
● A further distinction is that on roads and inland waterways, vehicles are controlled almost exclusively by their drivers or operators with a minimum of traffic control (such as traffic signals). In contrast, air traffic, railways and, to some extent, shipping are subject to traffic control, signals or some other navigational aid. This adds to the cost of the way.

The nature of the way is an important consideration for the carrying units, terminals and motive power. For example, while aircraft have the freedom of the skies, they have to be robust to ensure safety and comfort, and the carrying unit is thus expensive. Also, specialized terminals are required which are both costly and often located at some distance from the destination which they serve.

The terminal

A terminal gives access to the way for the users while a *terminus* is the furthest point to which the transport system extends – literally the end of the line. Terminals can also act as interchanges where travellers may transfer between modes (train to bus, aircraft to train, or, in the case of the Channel tunnel, bus/car to train). Terminals vary considerably in their design and the amenities they provide, as these are determined by the length and complexity of the journey, and the expectations of the passengers. You have only to compare the facilities available in an international air terminal with those in a coach terminal.

The carrying unit

Each 'way' demands a distinctive form of carrying unit. Some carrying units such as aircraft, ships, and road vehicles are very flexible as their use of the 'way' rarely restricts other vehicles. However, trains, monorails and trams are confined to a track where overtaking is virtually impossible and breakdowns can cause extensive delays. A second consideration is whether the carrying unit can be adapted to other purposes (for example, some cruise ships are converted passenger liners).

Motive power

The historical development of motive power technology reads almost like a history of tourism (Figure 5.1). As we enter the new millennium, tourism is reliant almost exclusively on artificial power for reaching a destination, although activity holidays such as cycling, pony-trekking and sailing are increasingly popular and environmentally acceptable. Motive power combines with the 'way' and the carrying unit to determine the speed, range and capacity of the transport mode in question.

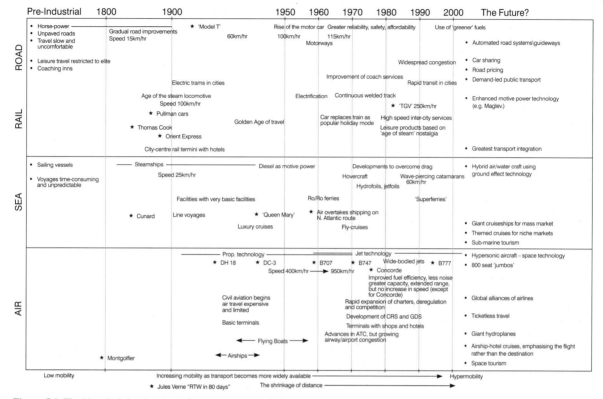

Figure 5.1 The historical development of transport and tourism
Source: Adapted from Cooper et al. (1998).

Finally there is the question of size. Here the most important consideration is to find the combination of carrying unit and motive power that can hold the maximum number of passengers while still allowing efficient utilisation of the transport system. Increasing size does bring its own problems. Jumbo jets, for example, require longer runways and larger charter aircraft reduce the flexibility of tour operations.

Transport costs and pricing

Transport costs and pricing are fundamental to the geography of tourism. The distinctive cost structure of each mode influences consumer choice and thus determines the volume of traffic on a route. There are two basic types of transport cost:

1 *Social and environmental costs* These costs are not paid for by the user of the transport but are borne by the community. An example of this is the unquantifiable cost

of aircraft noise to residents living near international airports.

2 *Private costs* Those who use or operate the transport system, directly or indirectly pay private costs. When considering the private costs of operating transport a basic distinction needs to be made between fixed and variable costs:

(a) *Fixed costs* (or overheads) are incurred before any passengers are carried or, indeed, before a carrying unit moves along the 'way'. These costs are 'inescapable' and include items such as interest on capital invested in, and depreciation of, the transport system. The most important feature of fixed costs is that they are not only inescapable, but that they do not vary in proportion to the level of traffic on a route, the distance travelled, or the numbers carried. For example, the control tower of an airport has to be manned irrespective of the number of aircraft movements at the airport.

(b) *Variable costs* (or running costs) do depend upon the level of service provided, distance travelled and the volume of traffic carried. Here costs include fuel, crew wages, cleaning and the maintenance of carrying units. These costs are 'escapable' because they are only incurred when the transport system is operating and can be avoided by cancelling services.

The distinction between fixed and variable costs is a very important one because each mode of transport has a different ratio of fixed to variable costs. Railways, for example, have to provide and maintain a track. This means that the total costs of a railway system contain a high proportion of fixed costs whereas for road transport the fixed costs are low. This means that the cost per passenger-kilometre decreases rapidly for rail but more slowly for road transport. In other words, railways are uneconomic if they are only carrying a few passengers because each has to make an unacceptably large contribution to fixed costs. On the other hand, road transport is much more competitive as the greater part of the costs are variable, and vehicles can be deployed more readily to meet changes in demand.

The distinction between fixed and variable costs is not a sharp one and in fact the two types of cost do blur. For example, costs of staffing and equipping a terminal may increase with the volume of traffic. These costs are known as semi-fixed. Clearly, the time period has to be defined in distinguishing between fixed and variable costs. While it can be said that crew wages are a variable cost, in fact crew are retained and have to be paid irrespective of the utilisation of the transport system in the short term. Their wages are therefore a short-term fixed cost but in the longer term staffing can normally be adjusted to the volume of business.

The ratio of fixed to variable costs is an important consideration for transport operators in the tourism business. Compared to many activities transport has a high proportion of fixed costs. Its product is also perishable because, if a seat is not sold on a flight, it cannot be stored and sold at a later date. These two factors mean that operators must achieve a high utilization of their systems. This involves not allowing carrying units to be idle for long periods of time without making a contribution to fixed costs and achieving a high *load factor* (i.e. the number of seats sold compared to the number available).

The *marginal cost principle* is of particular interest to the transport operator. Simply, marginal cost is the additional cost incurred in order to carry one extra unit of output (for example, a passenger). The operator determines a load factor that covers the fixed costs of the journey and the variable cost of each passenger carried. If the journey is budgeted to break even at, say, a load factor of 80 per cent then every extra passenger carried over this level will incur a small marginal cost (because variable costs are low) and therefore represents a substantial profit for the operator. Unfortunately, the opposite also applies.

For every passenger below the 80 per cent level a loss will be incurred.

A related problem is the fact that tourist demand tends to be highly peaked on a daily, weekly and an annual basis. This means that air transport fleets may only be fully utilized at certain times of the year. Both in Europe and North America one solution to this was the creation of the winter holiday market in the late 1960s to utilize idle aircraft and make a contribution to fixed costs. Another solution is to use *differential pricing*. Here operators offer low fares for travel in the off-peak period to increase the traffic at these times. Increasingly, all transport modes are carefully matching fares to distinctive market segments each of which have their own travel requirements.

Transport modes, routes and networks

Modes

In transport the term 'mode' is used to denote the manner in which transport takes place. Each mode has distinct operational characteristics, based on the different ways in which technology is applied to the four elements of any transport system. Technology determines the appropriateness of each mode for a particular type of journey. It also ensures that some modes overlap in their suitability for journeys and this may lead to competition on certain routes. In other cases, transport modes are complementary as in the case of rail or road links from airports into cities, or fly-drive holidays, where the advantages of air transport are used to reach the destination and the flexibility of motor transport for touring the destination (see Table 5.1).

Routes

Transport routes do not occur in isolation from the physical and economic conditions prevailing in different parts of the world. Mountain ranges, extensive hilly terrain, river valleys, waterlogged ground or, even, climatic factors influence transport routes, as do the location of major cities, political boundaries, and the tourist-generating and destination areas. However, not all modes of transport are equally affected by these factors. For example, mountains do not deflect air transport routes although they will influence the location of air terminals. In contrast, railways are very much influenced by topographical features. These factors, combined with considerations of technology and investment, ensure that transport routes remain relatively stable channels of movement.

The fact that some modes of transport have a restricted 'way' – road, railway tracks, or canal – will automatically

Table 5.1   Characteristics of transport modes

Mode	Way	Carrying unit	Motive power	Advantages	Disadvantages	Significance for tourism
Road	Normally a surfaced road, although '*off road recreational vehicles*' are not restricted.	Car, bus, or coach. Low capacity for passengers.	Petrol or diesel engine. Some use of electric vehicles.	Door-to-door flexibility. Driver in total control of vehicle. Suited to short journeys.	Way shared by other users leading to possible congestion.	Door-to-door flexibility allows tourist to plan routes. Allows carriage of holiday equipment. Acts as a link between terminal and destination. Acts as mass transport for excursions in holiday areas.
Rail	Permanent way, with rails.	Passenger carriages. High passenger capacity.	Diesel engines (diesel/electric or diesel/hydraulic). Also electric or steam locomotives.	Sole user of the way allows flexible use of carrying units. Suited to medium or long journeys, and to densely populated urban areas. Non-polluting.	High fixed costs.	In mid-nineteenth century opened up areas previously inaccessible for tourism. Special carriages can be added for scenic viewing, etc. Trans-continental routes and scenic lines carry significant volume of tourist traffic.
Air	Natural.	Aircraft. High passenger capacity.	Turbo-fan engines; turbo-prop or piston engine.	Speed and range. Low fixed costs. Suited to long journeys.	High fuel consumption and stringent safety regulations make air an expensive mode. High terminal costs.	Speed and range opened up most parts of the world for tourism. Provided impetus for growth of mass international tourism.
Sea	Natural.	Ships. Can have a high degree of comfort. High passenger capacity.	Diesel engine or steam turbine.	Low initial investment. Suited to either long-distance or short ferry operations.	Slow. High labour costs.	Confined to cruising (where luxury and comfort can be provided) and ferry traffic.

confine movement into a series of channels. For navigational purposes those modes of transport which use natural ways – the sea or the air – are also channelled and movement does not take place across the whole available surface of the earth. We can look at transport route systems at a variety of scales:

- At the world scale there is a network of inter-continental air routes, and to a much lesser extent destinations are linked by the long sea routes (line routes) nowadays used mainly to transport cargo.

- At the regional scale, most countries have nationwide coach and rail networks.
- At the local scale excursion circuits based on a particular city or resort.

Networks

Each transport network is made up of a series of links (along which flows take place) and nodes (terminals or interchanges). The accessibility of places on a network is of particular interest to tourist geographers as, once a node is linked to another, it becomes accessible. It must be noted, though, that scale is important here. For example, at the local scale many places may be highly accessible but when viewed at the world scale they become relatively inaccessible.

Geographers analyse and describe these route networks in a variety of ways:

● The most straightforward technique is a flow map, which shows the volume of traffic on each route. Examination of the map gives a rough indication of major nodes and links.
● A more accurate approach is to analyse and summarize the network using graph theory with a series of descriptive measures. However, before this can be done the transport network must be reduced to its essential elements of nodes and links. A good example of this is the map of the London Underground system, which reduces the network to its essential structure, disregarding actual distances. In theory, the more links there are in a network, the greater the connectivity of that network. But in fact even very dense transport networks can be badly connected, making some cross-city or cross-country journeys difficult.

The remainder of this chapter will provide a detailed consideration of each of the modes, routes and networks for travel and tourism.

Air transport

The most influential developments for international tourism since the Second World War have occurred in the air transport mode, where technological advances have opened up many parts of the world to tourism. Indeed, no part of the world is now more than twenty-four hours' flying time from any other part and it is estimated by the World Tourism Organization that around 20 per cent of international tourism uses air transport. Of the many technologies used by tourists, it is the jet aircraft that has captured the imagination, since it has opened up many formerly remote areas as holiday destinations. It must be emphasized that only a small percentage of the world's population have ever used airlines, and even in developed countries surface modes of transport carry many more times their volume of passengers. However, air transport has done most to bring about far-reaching changes in the nature of international tourism and the structure of the travel industry since the 1950s.

The following are the main advantages of the air transport mode:

● The way allows the aircraft a direct line of flight unimpeded by barriers such as mountain ranges, oceans, deserts or jungles.

● Superior speeds can be reached in everyday service.
● Air transport has a high capacity to carry passengers and is ideally suited to movements of over 500 kilometres, for journeys over difficult terrain, and also short journeys where a change of transport mode would otherwise be necessary (for example, a journey from the North Island to the South Island, New Zealand, where Cook Strait has to be crossed).

Air transport does, however, have disadvantages:

● The need for a large terminal area that may be some distance from the destination that it serves.
● It is expensive due to the large amounts of power expended and the high safety standards demanded.
● Aircraft are dependent on petroleum which, like most natural resources, is far from evenly distributed among the nations of the world, with a heavy concentration in one of the world's trouble-spots – the Middle East. There is the ever-present possibility of another energy crisis and oil reserves are being depleted – not only by demand from civil aviation but also from the private motorist, other transport modes and the rest of the economy.

The world pattern of air routes

The shortest distance between two places lies on a great circle which, drawn on the surface of the globe, divides it into equal halves, or hemispheres. Aircraft can utilize *great circle routes* fully because they can ignore physical barriers. For example, the great circle route between Western Europe and the Far East is over Greenland and the Arctic Ocean. Aircraft can use great circle routes due to improved technical performance, pressurized cabins and greatly increased range. Aircraft can now fly 'above the weather' in the extremely thin air, uniformly cold temperatures and cloudless conditions of the stratosphere at altitudes of between 10 000 and 17 000 metres. In middle latitudes pilots take advantage of upper-air westerly winds which attain speeds as high as 350–450 kilometres per hour. These *jet streams* reduce the travel time from California to Europe by over an hour compared to the time taken on the outward journey.

However, the 'freedom of the air' is, to some extent, an illusion. The routes are influenced not only by the operational considerations of jet streams but also by safety factors. The movement of aircraft, particularly over densely populated countries, is channelled along designated airways or corridors. The development of air routes is determined by:

● the extent of the demand for air travel
● the existence of adequate ground facilities for the handling of passengers and cargo
● international agreement.

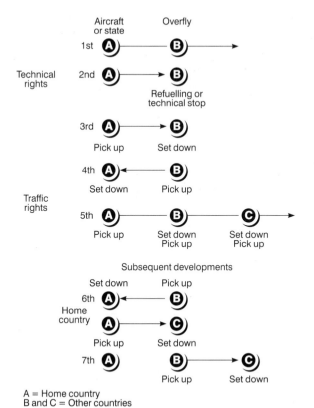

A = Home country
B and C = Other countries

Figure 5.2 The five freedoms of the air

The Chicago Convention in 1944 defined five freedoms of the air that are put into practice by bilateral agreements between pairs of countries (Figure 5.2). These freedoms are:

● The privilege of using another country's airspace.
● To land in another country for 'technical' reasons.
● The third and fourth freedoms relate to commercial point-to-point traffic between two countries by their respective airline.
● The fifth freedom allows an airline to pick up and set down passengers in the territory of a country other than its destination.

In many parts of the world these freedoms are greatly affected by international politics. Commercial considerations are also important. For example, as countries such as Russia and the Third World have tried to compete against established airlines in order to gain foreign exchange, new 'freedoms' have emerged. The sixth and seventh freedoms allow an airline to pick up in another country, take passengers back to its home base or 'hub' and then take

them on to another destination. For example, Swissair may pick up passengers in London, take them back to Zurich where they change Swissair planes and are taken on to, say, South America or Africa. This is known as 'hub and spoke' operations and has encouraged the development of both world and regional hub airports.

The importance of international and national agreements is decreasing as *deregulation* of the air transport system takes place. This means that governments are no longer allowed to control routes, fares or volumes on flights within and across their borders. The first major country to deregulate was the USA in the late 1970s, followed by the EU in the 1990s. Deregulation:

● encourages competition amongst airlines
● encourages the building of 'strategic alliances' amongst airlines
● encourages growth of regional airlines and regional airports
● has led to the development of low-cost 'budget' airlines on busy routes.

The routes and tariffs of the world's scheduled international airlines are, to an extent, controlled by the International Air Transport Association (IATA) to which most of them belong. The International Air Transport Association has divided the world into three Traffic Conference Areas for this purpose (see Figure 5.3).

Most of the world's air traffic is concentrated in three major regions – the eastern part of the USA, Western Europe and East Asia. This is due partly to market forces originating from their vast populations and partly because of the strategic location of these areas. The situation of London is especially advantageous as it is almost at the centre of the earth's 'land hemisphere' in which over 90 per cent of the world's population – and an even higher proportion of the world's industrial wealth – are concentrated.

The 'air bridge' between Europe and North America across the North Atlantic is the busiest intercontinental route, linking the two greatest concentrations of wealth and industry in the world. The capacity provided by wide-bodied jets and vigorous competition between the airlines has brought fares within reach of the majority of the population, while the Atlantic has shrunk, metaphorically speaking, to a 'ditch' that can be crossed in a few hours.

Time zones and air travel

Much international travel necessitates a time change if the journey is in any direction other than due north or south. These differences in time result from the Earth's rotation relative to the sun; at any given moment at one locality it is noon, while half the world away to the east or west it is midnight. The sun appears to us to be travelling from east to west and making one complete circuit of the earth every twenty-four hours. If we could see it from a vantage point in

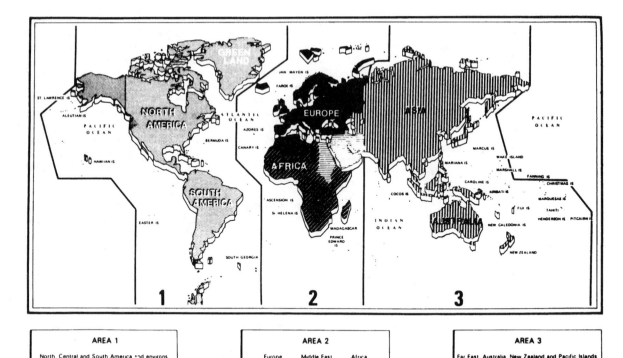

AREA 1	AREA 2			AREA 3
North, Central and South America and environs	Europe	Middle East	Africa	Far East, Australia, New Zealand and Pacific Islands

IATA traffic conference areas

For organizational purposes, the world is divided into three main IATA traffic conference areas, each with geographical subdivisions (see map).

No. 1 (TC1) For the Western Hemisphere (North, Central and South America, including Hawaii and the Caribbean)

No. 2 (TC2) For Europe, Africa and the Middle East

No. 3 (TC3) For Asia and the South-west Pacific

There are also four traffic conferences covering routes between the various conference areas:

Nos 1 and 2 (TC12) North, Mid and South Atlantic Routes

Nos 2 and 3 (TC23) Routes between Europe/Africa/Middle East and South-west Pacific

Nos 3 and 1 (TC31) North, Central and South Pacific Regions

Nos 1, 2, and 3 (TC123) Round the World Routes

Figure 5.3 IATA traffic conference areas

space, the earth is in fact making a complete turn on its axis through 360º of longitude. This means that for every 15º of longitude the time is advanced or put back by one hour; places that lie east of the Greenwich Meridian have a later hour, those to the west an earlier hour due to this apparent motion of the sun.

Theoretically, every community could choose its own local time. It was primarily the development of the railways that made it necessary to standardize timetables, using an international system of time zones based on the Greenwich Meridian. Since 1884 the world has been divided into twenty-four time zones in which standard time is arbitrarily applied to wide belts on either side of a particular meridian which is usually a multiple of 15º. Travellers passing from one time zone to another will therefore adjust their watches by exactly one hour (with the exception of a few parts of the world where the standard time differs by thirty minutes or so from neighbouring areas). Countries in the Western Hemisphere have time zones that are designated with a minus number as so many hours 'slow' behind Greenwich Mean Time (GMT). Greenwich Mean Time is the standard time on the Greenwich Meridian passing through London. Countries in the Eastern Hemisphere have time zones designated with a plus number as so many hours 'fast' on GMT. Only when it is noon on the Greenwich Meridian is it the same day worldwide; at all other times there is a twenty-four hour difference between each side of the 180° meridian. In 1884 the International Date Line was established as the boundary where each day actually begins at midnight and immediately spreads westwards. It corresponds to the 180° meridian (except where deviations are necessary to allow certain territories and groups of Pacific islands to have the same calendar day). The calendar on the western (Asian) side of the International Date Line is always one day ahead of the eastern (American) side.

Fast jet travel across a large number of time zones causes disruption to the natural rhythms of the human body that responds to a twenty-four hour cycle of daylight and darkness. This effect of *jet lag* differs considerably between individual travellers, and seems to be more disruptive on long west-to-east flights than on westbound journeys.

The location of international airports

The growth of civil aviation has placed demands on the world's major airports that were not anticipated at the time they were built. A major international airport now needs several passenger terminals, adequate car parking, hotels with conference facilities, a cargo terminal, warehousing and servicing facilities, and has all the problems associated with large urban areas such as traffic congestion on the access road, crime and pollution, plus the ever present need for security.

The largest jet aircraft in operation need runways of at least 3000 metres in length. In tropical countries, and especially at high altitudes, runways have to be even longer, as the lower density of the air means that jets have to make longer runs to obtain the lift to get airborne. A major international airport, therefore, requires a good deal of land. The physical nature of the airport site is important. It should be as flat as possible with clear, unobstructed approaches. Such land is not abundant in the small islands that are popular with holidaymakers or, for that matter, near many of the world's cities. In both Rio de Janeiro and Hong Kong airports have been built on land reclaimed from the sea. Runways are aligned so that aircraft can take off against the prevailing wind and airports should be located up-wind of large concentrations of industry, which cause 'smog' and poor visibility. The local weather record is therefore important.

At the same time, the airport must be in a location that is readily accessible to the large centres of population it is primarily meant to serve. However, most are between 20 to 30 kilometres distant, and sometimes as much as 50 kilometres away (e.g. Narita serving Tokyo). Investment is needed to construct or improve a rapid surface transport link between the city centre and the airport to minimize total travel time. This is particularly important for business travellers on short-haul flights. Generally, there is a motorway link or, in densely populated areas, a high-speed railway – separated from the main network – and sometimes a helicopter link for business travel.

The growth of air traffic has meant that many airports are now reaching, or have exceeded their passenger and aircraft capacity for safe and efficient operation. This is beginning to pose a real constraint on the development of air transport. Yet, despite their value for tourism and the national economy, proposals for both new airports, or for airport expansion, are fiercely opposed in developed countries. This is mainly due to the problem of noise pollution and because land is scarce, especially in Western Europe. Consequently, on short- and medium-haul routes there is a definite role for short take-off and landing (STOL) aircraft and possibly for seaplanes and airships, none of which require extensive ground facilities. Helicopters are manoeuvrable but noisy and expensive to operate, and have only a limited range and capacity. The helicopter is not widely used for sightseeing excursions, except in North America, where it is also used for heli-hiking and heli-skiing.

Surface transport

Unlike air transport, which is truly worldwide in its scope, road and rail communications are constrained by national boundaries to some extent, and subject to a greater degree of control by national governments. Road and rail networks are therefore described in more detail in the regional chapters.

Road transport

The main advantage of road transport is the door-to-door flexibility it allows. This means that travel by other transport modes almost invariably begins or ends with a road journey. This, combined with the fact that road vehicles can only carry a small number of passengers and have a relatively slow average speed, makes them particularly suitable for short- to medium-distance journeys. Also, the development of 'recreational vehicles' (RVs) allows a form of motorized accommodation. The main disadvantage of road transport is that many users share 'the way' and this can lead to congestion at times of peak demand. With an industry subject to annual and weekly peaks like tourism this can be a major handicap. Despite this, however, since the Second World War the private car has become the dominant transport mode for most types of tourism. Similarly, coaching has grown to provide not only a change of transport mode to transfer passengers from airports or other terminals to their final destination but is also used as the basis for excursions from resorts, and touring holidays as a product in its own right.

The main impetus towards an international system of highways has come about through the demands of an increasingly motorized population and the development of long-distance coach services and road haulage. The popularity of the car is due to the fact that it provides comfort, privacy, flexibility in timing and the choice of routes and destinations – and, theoretically, door-to-door service – except in cities where parking is a growing problem. The private car, especially in North America, has resulted in a completely new tourism landscape of motels and drive-in facilities dedicated to the needs of the mobile traveller. Current trends suggest that there will be 1 billion cars worldwide by 2030, with the largest increases taking place in the Third World.

Currently, car ownership in many developing countries remains a luxury, and buses and even trucks are the recognized means of conveying passengers as well as mail and freight. Vehicles are specifically adapted for the local terrain and climatic conditions, so that scheduled bus services can operate in desert and dry grassland areas, where there are no conventional roads. In the humid tropics there is a fairly extensive network of dirt roads that are viable during the dry season but impassable after the rains. Many countries, notably Brazil, have largely bypassed 'the age of the locomotive' and are very conscious of the value of airports and highways as a means of achieving national unity and economic progress. International road projects in developing countries include the Pan-American Highway system in Latin America and transcontinental systems in Africa and Asia that can be used, when the political situation allows, by overland expeditions and the more adventurous type of traveller.

In Western Europe and North America a growing network of motorways connects most major cities and industrial areas, though holiday resorts are generally less well served. Motorways have shortened journey times and have appreciably reduced accident rates. Roads designed especially for sightseeing have been built in scenically attractive coastal and mountain areas. However, too much road building and the development that invariably goes with it can destroy the very beauty that the tourist has come to see.

Rail transport

In contrast to the road, the railway track is not shared and extra carrying units (carriages) can be added or removed to cope with demand. This is particularly important in holiday areas where special trains may be run. Also, special facilities can be provided on rolling stock such as dining cars or viewing cars for scenic routes. The railway's main

disadvantage, however, is that the track, signalling and other equipment has to be paid for and maintained by the single user of the 'way'. Providing railway track is particularly expensive as the motive power can only negotiate gentle gradients. This means that moving earth, blasting rock cuttings and constructing tunnels is a major cost consideration, especially on long routes and in mountain regions. Railways are, therefore, characterized by high fixed costs and a need to utilize the track and rolling stock very efficiently to meet these high costs. The railway's speed and ability to carry large numbers of passengers make it suitable for journeys of, say, 200–500 kilometres between major cities.

In the nineteenth century the introduction of railways revolutionized transport and enabled large numbers of people to travel long distances relatively cheaply. The great transcontinental railways were built in the period before 1914 when there was no serious competition from other modes of transport. The first was the Union Pacific between Chicago and San Francisco, completed in 1869, which helped to open up California and the American West. The Canadian Pacific railroad between Montreal and Vancouver was built for political as well as economic reasons, because otherwise British Columbia would not have joined the Canadian Confederation. Similar motivations were behind the Australian Trans-continental from Sydney to Perth that links Western Australia to the rest of the country. The longest railway of them all – the Trans-Siberian linking Moscow to Vladivostok – took fifteen years to complete (1891–1905) and still remains the vital lifeline of Siberia. Since the 1930s new railway construction has virtually ceased in most countries, with the significant exceptions of Russia, China and some African states – notably Zambia and Tanzania.

Since the 1950s the railways have come under increasing competition from the airlines for long-distance traffic and the private car for short journeys. The decline has been greatest in the USA, where most communities are now without any passenger train service. In France and Japan, on the other hand, there has been considerable government investment in applying new technology to developing high-speed trains and upgrading the trunk lines between major cities. In Western Europe, the Channel tunnel link between England and France has encouraged the development of rail-based tourism products and may prompt a modal switch from congested airspace and roads. The growth of environmentalism, coupled with concern at another future energy crisis, may accelerate this trend and lead to a rail revival in other developed counties. (However, it is ironic that high-speed trains themselves have been opposed by environmentalists, mainly the TGV in France and the Transrapide in Germany.) It is significant that major cities throughout the world from Miami to Hong Kong and Kuala Lumpur to Bangkok are investing in 'rapid transit' – automated light railway networks – rather than urban motorways to handle the immense numbers of commuters and tourists. In mountain regions specially designed railways have been used, as in Switzerland, to overcome the problem of steep gradients and are tourist attractions in themselves, although aerial cableways are nowadays more versatile and cost-effective, as well as being faster in transporting large numbers of tourists.

Sea transport

Sea transport lacks the speed of air travel – an aircraft can cross the Atlantic twenty or more times while a ship makes a single return journey. Most of the long-haul passenger traffic has, therefore, been lost to air simply because the ship is so slow. Also, many travellers dislike the vagaries of the sea and the six types of motion to which a vessel is subjected. However, the advantage of this mode is that:

● Ships expend relatively little power.
● Ships can be built to much larger specifications than any vehicle or aircraft, to carry thousands of passengers at a time.
● They can provide a high degree of comfort. This has led to the development of the cruise market, which is travel for travel's sake in 'floating resorts'.
● Sea transport is ideally suited to short sea crossings, providing a roll-on, roll-off facility for motor vehicles.

Technological advances are beginning to overcome some of the conventional disadvantages of sea transport. For example, a conventional vessel has to 'push' out of the way a volume of water equal to its own weight. This can be partly overcome by vessels using the hydrofoil principle (where the hull is lifted clear of the sea by submerged foils acting like aircraft wings) or hovercraft (where the entire vessel uses a cushion of air to keep it clear of the water). So far, neither hydrofoils nor hovercraft are used on long ocean voyages due to their vulnerability in rough seas and strong winds, as well as their limited capacity and range of operation. Nevertheless, they are successful on short sea crossings where their speed (up to three times that of a conventional ship), manoeuvrability, and fast turn-round in port give them the advantage. Wave-piercing catamarans have been shown to be more versatile than hovercraft or hydrofoils on some routes, and there is obvious potential for high-speed craft combining the advantages of both air and sea modes currently under development.

The world pattern of shipping routes

We must make a distinction between the long-haul or line routes plied by shipping and the short sea routes, especially those of Europe and the Mediterranean, where ferries provide vital links in the international movement of travellers by road and rail. Cruising needs a separate category here since it is essentially waterborne tourism rather than a point-to-point voyage.

Long-haul routes

Despite having the advantage of 'the freedom of the high seas' outside a country's territorial waters, ships rarely keep to great circle routes. Instead they ply 'sea lanes' determined by the availability of good harbours en route and physical conditions – sea areas characterized by persistently bad weather, floating ice, reefs and sandbars are avoided. Economic considerations are foremost: the most important routes are those linking Europe with its main trading partners overseas. Tourists and emigrants now account for only a minute fraction of the business due to competition from the airlines and the high labour and fuel costs involved in operating a passenger liner. (Some cargo liners do however take a limited number of passengers.) The Panama and Suez Canals are vital links between the oceans on these routes, avoiding a much longer voyage around Cape Horn or the Cape of Good Hope.

Short sea routes

Passenger traffic on the short sea routes is increasing rapidly throughout Western Europe largely as the result of the popularity of motoring holidays and the growth of trade between the countries of the EU. The introduction of roll-on roll-off facilities has enabled ports to handle a much greater volume of cars, coaches and trucks, and most ferries now operate throughout the year with greatly improved standards of comfort and service. With the opening of the Channel tunnel in 1994 many cross-Channel ferry companies are moving their investment into the western English Channel. Ferries are often the only transport option available in groups of small or remote islands where airports may be few and far between. In the case of the Aegean islands of Greece, a popular holiday destination, large capacity ferries provide a link to the mainland ports, while smaller vessels offer an inter-island service, especially during the peak summer season. Similarly, shipping services, making greater use of hydrofoils, connect the many islands along the Adriatic coast of Croatia. In the case of Hawaii, however, inter-island ferries have long been replaced by air services. In island nations of the Third World such as the Philippines, ferries are popular due to their low fares, although safety standards are below those considered acceptable in Western countries. In most parts of the world, ferries are not widely used by business travellers; one notable exception is the jetfoil service linking Hong Kong to Macau.

Cruising

Cruising represents a purely leisure-based use of sea transport. The chartering and operation of ships for inclusive tours began in the 1860s and reached its heyday in the 1920s. Typically, such cruises lasted for several months and catered exclusively for upper-income groups with abundant leisure and wealth. The sea voyage, often undertaken for health reasons, was more important than the places visited. In the postwar period, cruising again increased in popularity and has helped to offset the great decline in scheduled services offered by the passenger liner. Since the 1950s shipping lines have diversified into cruising, although this has not always been an easy transition, as the ships were often unsuitable.

Cruising has developed into a luxury, floating package with a high standard of service and accommodation. The introduction of fly-cruising in the 1960s was important as it allowed the cruise ship to be based in a port in the cruising region. Cruise ships then became smaller as few ports of call can accommodate 30 000-ton passenger liners. The cruise market has proved resistant to recession with a loyal, repeat clientele. The industry is also developing new products and experiencing considerable new investment. For example, large purpose-built cruise ships are designed with a great deal of open deck space for warm-water voyages and provide themed, special-interest cruises with sports, activities and entertainment. At the same time the cost of cruising has decreased and the average age of customers has fallen, to become less of a 'grey market'. The growth of other activities – such as whale and dolphin watching – is seeing the development of new areas of the oceans for tourism, although the impact upon the animals is little understood.

The Caribbean is the most popular cruising destination. Its popularity is based on its position close to the North American cruise market (the largest in the world), its ideal climate and island scenery, and the wide choice of shore excursions. Cruise ships operate out of Jamaica, Puerto Rico and Barbados, as well as Florida where Miami acts as the main port. Winter is the main cruise season but early summer is also popular. Increasingly, cruise ships are based on the west coast of the USA at the ports of San Francisco, Los Angeles and San Diego – convenient for visiting Mexico and the Panama Canal.

The two other main cruising regions are the Mediterranean and the Far East/Pacific. The North European market dominates cruising in the Mediterranean. There are many ports of great cultural, historic, and natural interest that can be visited. In the Pacific, cruises off the east coast of Australia, taking in New Zealand, Hawaii and Tahiti, are popular, while in the Far East cruising off the east coast of Asia is popular with Australians and Japanese.

Areas for summer cruises include the Baltic and the Norwegian coast in northern Europe and the equally spectacular coasts of British Columbia and Alaska in North America. New cruising routes are beginning to be pioneered in South America, the Arctic Ocean and Antarctica.

The location of seaports

The ideal seaport should have:

- a harbour with a good depth of water close inshore and free from obstructions such as reefs, sandbanks or dangerous currents
- a climate free from severe winter freezes, fogs and strong winds

- land available for development
- a productive hinterland with easy surface access to the main population centres.

In fact few ports satisfy all these requirements. In many parts of the world – the Mediterranean and West Africa are important examples – good harbours are few and far between, and it has been necessary to construct artificial ones at great expense. Historically, many seaports have developed on estuaries or the tidal sections of large rivers, to serve cities located upstream. Unfortunately, ports located on estuaries require constant dredging because of silt brought down by the rivers. The finest harbours are often located in mountainous regions, but suffer from the handicaps of poor hinterlands, difficult communications and little room for expansion (the Norwegian fjords are a good example).

Summary

Transport is created or improved because it satisfies a need for spatial interaction between two places. This interaction may be explained by three basic principles: complementarity, transferability and intervening opportunity. Once spatial interaction exists, a transport system will be required and, in general terms, the main physical elements of the system will comprise: a way, a terminal, a carrying unit and motive power. The costs of the transport system can be divided into social costs, which are those to the community, and private costs, which are borne by the user or operator of the system, and which comprise fixed and variable costs. The combination of the physical elements and cost structure of a system result in the suitability of different transport modes for different types of journey. Each transport mode operates along a route, determined by the nature of the 'way', or navigational convenience. Transport networks are therefore made up of stable links, along which movement takes place, and nodes, or terminals.

The development of rapid means of communication, especially in the field of civil aviation, has done much to revolutionize the scale and structure of the travel industry. It has also meant that almost all countries of the world have adopted a system of time measurement based on the Greenwich Meridian. Air transport and shipping services form a worldwide network that is based largely on market forces and needs to be examined on an international scale. This is less true of road and rail communications, which are subject to more detailed control by national governments and are therefore best dealt with on a country-by-country basis. Airports are closely integrated with surface forms of transport. The expansion of major international airports leads to demands on scarce land, energy and human resources that are increasingly difficult to resolve. The jet aircraft is but one of many modes of transport, some of which have highly specialized roles (such as the hydrofoil and hovercraft) while others such as the private car, bus and train are competing for a wider market.

Case study

Managing transport at the tourism destination

Introduction

The vast majority of travel at the destination takes place by surface transport, dominantly in the car but also by coach. This immediately creates a number of issues and problems for tourism destinations:

- *Safety* – motor transport is dangerous, with an average of 250 000 deaths and 7 million serious injuries worldwide every year. Clearly, unrestricted use of the car is not conducive to safe and secure holiday destinations or attractions.
- *Speed* – holiday driving is on average 10 per cent slower than normal driving and visitors are often uncertain of their route.
- *Facilities* – cars need facilities such as car parks that can also be visually intrusive. Also, the building of roads along seafronts acts to separate the tourist accommodation, retailing and other activities from the beach.
- *Visual intrusion* – cars parked en masse are brightly coloured and reflect light, often creating an eyesore adjacent to a natural or historic attraction, or within a resort or historic town.
- *Congestion* – cars cause traffic congestion en route and at destinations.
- *Environmental impact* – cars are a source of pollution in destination areas – with their visual intrusion, noise and fumes.

Yet, the reasons why cars are used at the destination are compelling:

- They allow door-to-door flexibility, providing tremendous freedom.
- They are perceived as an inexpensive form of travel, especially for family groups, because running costs and depreciation are not seen as part of the cost of individual trips.
- They allow unparalleled viewing.
- They can comfortably contain luggage, pets, recreational equipment and people (including the elderly or the handicapped who otherwise may not have access to tourism destinations).
- They can be used to tow caravans, trailer tents or boats.
- They act as a secure base for the tour – while picnicking, or enjoying an attraction.

Management solutions at the destination

Nonetheless, the impact of the car has become severe at many tourism destinations and management solutions are now being adopted to solve these problems and balance the needs of local community traffic and that of visitors. However, these solutions are relatively recent, as motorists are often resistant to restrictions. We seem able to accept restrictions on motoring for business or everyday domestic travel, but are rather less willing to accept it when we are 'at leisure'. However, the increasing desire for a quality experience at destinations will demand that leisure traffic is also 'managed'.

There are two key management approaches:

Separate visitors from their cars

1 *Park and ride schemes* Park and ride schemes involve the provision of an alternative form of transport for the visitor. Normally, the visitors are invited to park their car and to travel to the attraction by bus, or some other form of transport. Park and ride schemes need a number of conditions to be successful:

   (a) A road configuration that prevents 'short circuiting the system'.
   (b) Local resident and business community support – often such schemes are seen as an infringement of residents' freedom and businesses worry that trade will be lost.
   (c) Effective and visible marketing, publicity, signage and information (see Figure 5.4).
   (d) Visitors who are prepared to sacrifice their own freedom to benefit from an enhanced experience at the destination.
   (e) A safe and screened parking area with weatherproofed waiting areas/bus stops.
   (f) A regular shuttle service to the attraction – a key benefit of park and ride schemes is that the volume and speed of visitors arriving at the attraction can be controlled.

   Park and ride schemes are well suited to destinations such as historic towns and villages where the streets are narrow and access is difficult; natural attractions where the presence of traffic is intrusive; family-based attractions; or destinations where the presence of children is common. Park and ride is a flexible management option, as it can be used only at peak times if necessary – weekends and busy holiday periods for example.

2 *Provision of alternative forms of transport* The imaginative provision of alternative forms of transport also acts as an effective management tool at the destination to separate the visitor from the car. In particular

the creation of more attractive public transport systems is common at destinations. For example:

(a) Circular sight-seeing city bus and boat tours with regular 'hop-on-hop-off' stops at key tourist sights as in London and New York, many historic cities and also rural areas such as the UK's Peak District National Park.

(b) Public transport that meets the needs of the user, as for example at Hadrian's Wall in the north of England where a bus service calls at key points along the wall to save visitors doubling back to their cars.

(c) Journey planner computer discs to make the public transport system 'legible' at tourist destinations.

(d) Novelty forms of transport such as cable cars, horse-drawn trams, recreational road trains or steamboats. Monorails are used in some theme parks and exhibition sites but tend to be too intrusive and costly for most attractions.

Welcome to the
Moors Green Passport Scheme

If you're planning to visit the North York Moors, why not:

Park your car at the selected car park or Park and Ride site

Join the bus - departure every 10 minutes from the Park and Ride site

Save money by staying longer and using the discount offers at local attractions

and:

Help the environment by minimising the number of car journeys and reducing pollution, delays and congestion

● The bus ticket includes special discounts
  (sample price £2.50 for an all day Family Passport ticket)

● The scheme will operate on

Sunday 6 August 1995
Sunday 13 August 1995
Sunday 20 August 1995
Sunday 27 August 1995
Monday 28 August 1995
Sunday 3 September 1995

● Parking charges will vary according to the site that you choose:-

1. *Hutton le Hole car park*, adjacent to the Ryedale Folk Museum - the longer you stay, the less you pay (£1 for 3 hours or more, £1.50 for up to 3 hours, £2 for up to 2 hours and £2.50 for up to 1 hour - all including one free Moorsbus ticket).

2. *Off A169 Malton Road Park and Ride Site*, just south of Pickering - free parking (the Moorsbus leaves every ten minutes from this site for locations around the National Park).

Parking attendants will be available to offer assistance at the selected car park and Park and Ride Site - so your car should be SAFER too!

Please remember:

"The longer you stay the less you pay"

Need any more information? Pick up a leaflet from the car park or Park and Ride site (see above), the bus drivers, or the following tourist information centres:-

Helmsley Tourist Information Centre　　Tel: 01439 770173 (0930 - 1800hrs)
Pickering Tourist Information Centre　　Tel: 01751 473791 (0930 - 1800hrs)
The Moors Centre, Danby　　　　　　　Tel: 01287 660654 (1000 - 1700hrs)

The Moors Green Passport Scheme is being run by Oxford Centre for Tourism and Leisure Studies, a supported by the North York Moors National Park, North Yorkshire County Council, Royal Automobile Club, Rural Development Commission, Ryedale District Council and Countryside Commission.

Produced by: Oxford Centre for Tourism and Leisure Studies at Oxford Brookes University
Designed by: The Spare Room, Oxford
Printed by: Noel Richardson & Co. Ltd. York on Renato Recycled Paper

Figure 5.4 Publicity poster
Source: OCTALS (1998).

Separate visitor traffic from local traffic

1 *Scenic drives* The creation and development of scenic drives allows the separation of touring traffic from local traffic. Given that tourism traffic drives more slowly and is seeking to enjoy the drive, rather than simply to get from A to B as quickly as possible, it is logical to create special linear attractions for the car-borne tourer. These are known as scenic drives and are designed primarily to provide a distinctive driving experience for pleasure travel. They allow the destination manager to control the numbers of vehicles entering the drive and environmental impact can be reduced, as visitors tend to stay within their vehicles. Scenic drives are often provided with a range of facilities and features:
(a) Interpretation and information for the visitor.
(b) Frequent stopping places for views, picnics and barbecues.
(c) Landscaped and purpose-designed driving experiences to maximize views and scenery.
(e) Motels, shops and cafés.

Scenic drives are found mainly in North America – the Blue Ridge Parkway is a good example, snaking through Virginia and North Carolina, it is often used in car advertisements. They are much less common in other parts of the world, including Europe.

Case study

Airline strategic alliances

Background

In the USA in the late 1970s, there were pressures for greater liberalization and for the introduction of freer competition within air transport operation. The US Airline Deregulation Act of 1978 led to the reorganization of domestic air transport within the USA and also it led to attempts to create a freer international market for transport by air. The result was the development of many new domestic carriers in the USA and the emergence of new international operators based in that country. By the 1990s a similar number of carriers existed as before but their size and market dominance were very different.

In the intervening period a series of mergers occurred between larger successful operators and the smaller, nearly bankrupt, carriers. A tendency for further mergers could lead to say ten 'mega-carriers' in operation worldwide by the year 2005. Various relationships have developed:

- Financial – acquisitions, mergers, cross-share holdings, partial-share holdings and equity swaps, these tended to be of a financial nature.
- Other actions include franchising and code sharing. However, governments do not welcome the idea of their national carrier being owned by a foreign enterprise, nor do they wish to see bankruptcies of their own airline; considerable government subsidy of state airlines has resulted.
- Small airlines have had to merge with other operators, especially in terms of their computer reservation system (CRS) activities. Large carriers such as American Airlines (AA) have a major interest in the Sabre CRS, and British Airways (BA) in the Galileo CRS.
- A merger between AA and BA has been subject to much discussion and concern by the US government and the European Commission because it will lead to a very large and dominant carrier.
- Alliances have developed without investments in equity across national borders; these alliances focus on marketing agreements and technical co-operation.

Alliances can be horizontal, vertical or external in nature. In air transport there have been horizontal alliances for a long time such as pooling agreements or revenue sharing arrangements between airlines. New airline alliances now involve selection of partners to complement networks and increase market coverage. Vertical alliances involve links with other suppliers in the tourist industry such as travel businesses; external alliances involve joint ventures or marketing promotions such as frequent flier programmes (FFPs), relationship marketing and telephone calling cards.

New types of alliance: the Star Alliance and Link

Link

Potentially the most powerful alliance will be BA embracing AA and drawing in other airlines to provide both market coverage and pooling of facilities such as booking, staff and aircraft:

- BA, with its direct investment policy, already has TAT and Air Liberté in France, Deutsche BA and Quantas. It has many franchised partners in the UK from Manx Europe and City Flyer Express to Maersk UK, Loganair and Brymon, all operating now as BA Express. BA has an alliance or part alliance with a further eleven airlines.
- AA has a direct investment in Canadian Airlines International, plus co-operative or code sharing agreements with some twenty-three other carriers. AA

is also developing an alliance with Iberia and two Argentinian carriers.

- Other airlines in the alliance include Cathay Pacific, Japan Airlines, American West, GB Airways and Finnair.

Star Alliance

Among the most threatening alliances to BA and AA is the new Star Alliance; this pledges a more unified, high-quality product while retaining individual brand identities.

Thai Airways International and five other major international airlines have formed nineteen working groups to implement the Star Alliance programme, which will unify operations worldwide and could lead to joint purchases of aircraft and components in the near future. The Star Alliance is the world's largest single airline group. Over 230 000 staff members will make flights to 642 destinations in the world.

The six carriers are:

- Thai
- United Airlines
- Scandinavian Airlines
- Lufthansa
- Air Canada
- VARIG.

In addition, the alliance plans to persuade South Africa Airlines and British Midland to join the programme to cover South Africa and the British Isles.

These carriers will implement the programme by integrating products, airport lounge services, on-board/in-flight services, customer relations, corporate communications, marketing communications, reward and recognition. These areas will be implemented by separate working groups. In addition, the six companies will form a joint management committee to settle disputes while the integration is being completed.

- In terms of joint facilities, the airlines will introduce a combined counter for customers of all six carriers. At the moment, Thai has a ticketing counter inside Lufthansa's premises, while Lufthansa operates a ticketing office on Thai's premises. This will be integrated to allow all six carriers to operate joint facilities.
- On network connectivity, a working group will be set up to ensure that passengers of all six carriers have convenient access to transfer flights across carriers.
- Another working group will formulate a 'people' policy to ensure that employees of all six carriers understand how to achieve the objectives. To this end, the airlines will introduce a joint training programme.

- On safety, the companies will ensure that they maintain uniform standards.
- On sales and distribution, they will ensure that pricing is uniform on the same routes to avoid competition among members of the alliance.
- On aviation regulations, they will work together to ensure that the members achieve the best possible results in negotiations for international aviation rights.
- In the near future, alliance members will prepare to adopt a common policy on aircraft, spare parts and related acquisitions, but this is subject to further negotiations.

Star Alliance partners

Thai Airways International is Asia's leading airline, operating out of Bangkok, the aviation hub of Asia and one of the world's most popular tourist cities. The airline enjoyed its thirty-second successive year of profitable operations in 1996. Within Asia, Thai now fly to more countries than any other airline, with convenient connections to the world's fastest growing economies. Thai tradition and culture are evident, wherever Thai fly. Each day, over 10 000 female passengers are presented with an orchid corsage before embarking. Thai's wines and Asian speciality meals are second to none and their traditional *wai* greeting has become a legend, while their corporate vision statement, 'The First Choice Carrier, Smooth as Silk First Time Every Time' is fast becoming a reality.

United Airlines began its first scheduled service outside North America in 1983 with a non-stop flight to Tokyo. Since then United has grown to become one of the largest international carriers in the world. In the mid-1990s, after nearly seventy years of passenger and cargo service, United is the largest majority employee-owned company in the world. Their network covers 140 destinations in thirty different countries.

The German carrier *Lufthansa* founded in 1919, is one of the ten largest airlines in the world. In terms of passenger numbers on international scheduled flights, it occupies second position in the world airline ranking. The airline's success owes a great deal to Lufthansa's technical expertise. Lufthansa's fleet is one of the youngest and most environment-friendly in the industry and the airline offers passengers the comfort of the most modern aircraft. For an airline to be successful, it is essential that it has a global route network. The airline supplements its own network through co-operation with other major airlines. Passengers benefit additionally from an extensive frequent flyer programme and improved ground services.

Scandinavian Airlines System (SAS) was founded in August 1946, as a consortium of the national airlines of Denmark, Norway and Sweden. The airline's products and service are based on simplicity, choice and care. SAS was founded in the spirit of international co-operation. Today, this same spirit has been applied when forging alliances with other quality airlines. With its partners, SAS now offers travellers to and from Scandinavia convenient connections throughout an integrated global traffic system.

Air Canada's predecessor, TCA, inaugurated its first flight in the 1930s carrying mail aboard an L10A from Vancouver to Seattle. Today, Air Canada is Canada's largest carrier and has established itself as a leader in global air transportation by pursuing an aggressive strategy based on value-added customer service, technical excellence and unsurpassed passenger safety. Together with its regional airlines, Air Canada provides air transportation to 125 destinations across Canada, the USA, the Caribbean, Europe, the Middle East and Asia. With its Star Alliance partners, Air Canada's reach has been extended still further. With the addition of forty-one new aircraft in 1998, Air Canada has one of the youngest fleets in the world.

Latin America's largest airline, VARIG Brazilian Airlines, has a proud seventy-year history. With its fleet of over eighty medium- and wide-body jets, the airline has accumulated more than 6 million flight hours over the years. VARIG maintains a route network covering eighty-seven cities within Brazil, as well as thirty-five cities in twenty-three countries throughout the Americas, Africa, Asia and Europe. VARIG's employees are dedicated to providing quality customer service, which has been recognized by many international awards. Today, VARIG has established itself with world travellers through its customer-oriented frequent flyer programme, which offers loyal customers a wide range of generous benefits.

(*Source*: John Westlake, Bournemouth University, kindly provided this case study.)

Part Two

The Regional Geography of Travel and Tourism in the World

An introduction to the tourism geography of Europe

LEARNING OBJECTIVES

After reading this chapter you should be able to:

1 Appreciate why Europe continues to dominate world tourism.
2 Understand the major patterns of tourism demand in Europe.
3 Be aware of the major physical and social features in Europe and their implications for tourism.
4 Appreciate the role of the EU in tourism organization and development.
5 Recognize the major geographical influences on the distribution of tourism resources in Europe.
6 Recognize the role of improvements in transport infrastructure in encouraging a freer movement of tourists throughout Europe.

Introduction

As a region, physical features – mountains, rivers and seas – prescribe Europe's boundaries, yet within these boundaries Europe is a region of immense economic, social and cultural diversity. In part this diversity explains why Europe continues to be a crucible of conflict, with two world wars in the twentieth century which ended with a civil war in the Balkan region. Europe is also under economic pressures from both North America and the newly industrializing countries of South-East Asia. Here, Europe's failure to perform as a region is brought into clear focus when shares of international tourism are examined:

● In 1960 Europe accounted for 72 per cent of international tourism arrivals.
● By 1998 this share had fallen to 50 per cent.

Nonetheless, Europe continues to dominate world tourism. This is despite the fact that Europe accounts for less than 10 per cent of the world's population and an even smaller share of its total land area. During the late 1990s it received over 320 million of the world's 620 million international tourist arrivals, and accounted for almost 60 per cent of the world's receipts from international tourism. The strong economies in the region account for most of the world's top tourist-generating countries, dominating the outbound flow of international travel, and are also estimated to generate massive demand for domestic trips. On the supply side, tourists are provided for by over 11 million bedspaces in hotels and similar establishments, representing 40 per cent of the world's bed stock.

Europe is pre-eminent in the world's tourism system for the following reasons:

● Most of the region's economies are in the high mass-consumption stage, or in the drive to maturity. The population, though ageing, is in general affluent, mobile and has a high propensity to travel.
● Europe consists of a rich mosaic of languages, cultural resources and tourist attractions of world calibre.
● Europe comprises many relatively small countries in close proximity, encouraging a high volume of short international trips.
● The region's climatic differences are significant, leading since the 1950s to a considerable flow of sun-seeking tourists from northern Europe to the south.
● Europe's tourism infrastructure is mature and of a high standard.
● The tourism sector throughout most of the region is highly developed, and standards of service – though not the best in the world – are good.
● Most European governments have well-funded, competent tourist authorities with marketing and development powers.

With a few striking exceptions, Europe's political and economic structures are stable, providing a safe environment for investment in tourism. Since the 1980s, the dismantling of the Iron Curtain and the opening up of Eastern Europe, along with the advent of the Single European Market, have removed barriers to tourism movement within Europe.

Physical features

Physically, but not culturally, Europe is in effect a western extension of Asia, a peninsula surrounded on three sides by sea. The eastern boundary is much more indeterminate, being marked by the not very impressive Ural Mountains, and the narrow waterways linking the Mediterranean and Black Seas. A glance at a map of the area will show you that this boundary is in fact straddled by two important nations – Russia and Turkey. Within Europe we can distinguish two major physical/climatic divisions – north and south – separated by a series of mountain ranges such as the Alps.

The dominant feature of Northern Europe is a plain, crossed by many rivers, and extending from southern England to Russia, with the remnants of worn-down mountain systems along its periphery. It is on this plain that the major industries and cities are located, and therefore it acts as the source of many tourists to the rest of Europe. Southern Europe on the other hand is hilly or mountainous, containing only small pockets of fertile lowland, and with few inland waterways of any length.

Europe's mountain ranges act as a major influence on weather systems, in the past were barriers to communications, and nowadays are seen as a recreational and tourism resource for winter sports and 'lakes and mountains' summer holidays. The most important are:

- The Alps – a series of high mountain ranges extending in an arc from south-eastern France to Austria and Slovenia. Their great height is due to geologically recent earth movements, while the valleys were widened and deepened by glaciers during the last Ice Age. A number of large lakes were formed as a result of moraines – accumulations of glacial debris – blocking the valleys.
- The Pyrenees – three mountain ranges extending from the Bay of Biscay east to the Mediterranean, and forming the boundary between France and Spain.
- The Balkan mountain ranges form a very rugged peninsula in south-eastern Europe bordered by the Adriatic, Aegean and Black Seas. Earthquakes are frequent in this region. There is a striking contrast between the coastlands that enjoy a Mediterranean climate, and the interior that experiences harsh winters.
- The Carpathians – a series of mountain ranges forming a crescent around the Danubian Plains in the heart of Europe.
- The Caucasus lie far to the south-east, between the Black Sea and the Caspian Sea (which is not really a sea, but a vast salt-water lake). These mountains rise to even greater altitudes than the Alps.
- The Kjolen mountains form the spine of the Scandinavian Peninsula. They differ from the other ranges in being geologically stable, the remnants of a much older mountain system than the Alps, and over the ages have been worn down to a series of high plateaus rather than rugged mountain peaks.

Europe's seas also deserve consideration in view of the importance of coastal tourism – in most countries with a coastline more than two-thirds of the accommodation stock is found at the seaside. Tourism is, however, only one of many uses of the coast, with the result that pollution and degradation of the marine ecosystems are serious problems.

- This is especially true of the Mediterranean, which, although virtually an inland sea, is the focus of much of Europe's tourism. Not only are there a number of large industrial cities on the coast but the Mediterranean also attracts over 120 million holidaymakers each summer, far in excess of any other body of water of similar size. In other words, the Mediterranean accounts for only 0.7 per cent of the world's sea area but its shoreline attracts over 20 per cent of all international tourism arrivals. Over 500 rivers flow into this enclosed sea, carrying all manner of pollutants. The natural cleansing action of the sea is reduced by the weakness of the tides, and the fact that the water is changed only once in every ninety years, through the Mediterranean's only outlet – the Straits of Gibraltar – to the Atlantic Ocean. The scope for international co-operation to mount clean-up operations and prevent further pollution is limited, and less than a half of the shoreline belongs to EU countries.
- The Baltic Sea is a major focus for tourism but also the repository of many rivers and much industrial waste, particularly from the countries of the former Soviet bloc, where environmental controls are less stringent than those of Scandinavia.

Climatically, Europe is very varied – on the western fringes of the European plain Atlantic influences keep the climate mild, but unpredictable, while the further east we travel, the more extreme are the temperatures in both summer and winter. In the mountains long periods of high pressure bring clear skies and excellent visibility, while the Mediterranean climate is judged to be just about perfect for most tourism activities, with hot sunny summers and mild winters.

Cultural features

Europe does not represent a homogenous population or society – there is a mosaic of languages, traditions and cultures. To Asian or African eyes, there are many cultural similarities between the countries of Europe, but these are much less obvious to a North American, or for that matter a British tourist, visiting the Continent. These cultural differences are rooted in history and partly determined by language and religion. The most striking differences in lifestyles, cultural traits and perhaps national temperaments are:

● Those between northern Europe and the 'Latin' south-west, so called because its languages – notably French, Italian and Spanish – are derived from Latin, the language of the Roman Empire, which once dominated southern Europe, and later the language of the Roman Catholic Church. Whereas the Protestant Reformation of the sixteenth century came to dominate most of northern Europe, it failed to take root south of the Alps.
● Between Western and Eastern Europe. The differences here go much further back in time than the 'cold war' division of Europe between Russia and the Western powers between 1945 and 1989. Whereas Western Europe in the Middle Ages was influenced by Roman Catholicism, the eastern part of the continent was much more influenced by the Orthodox version of Christianity based at Constantinople, and disrupted by mainly Moslem invaders from Asia. The differences between east and west are shown in their starkest form in the former Yugoslavia in the conflict between Catholic Croatia and Orthodox Serbia. In contrast, in Western Europe, the tensions between Catholics and Protestants have, to a large extent, disappeared, with the notable exception of Northern Ireland.
● Many of the mountain regions of Europe contain communities that are culturally different from those of the surrounding lowlands. Their former isolation helped preserve traditional lifestyles, but these are now increasingly under threat, partly as a result of tourism and second home development by affluent city-dwellers.

A complex history of interaction between the different cultures spanning more than two millennia has left a rich architectural heritage throughout Europe that is now an important tourist resource. At least as far as Western Europe is concerned, we can distinguish the following stages of cultural development as expressed by those monuments that survive.

● *Prehistoric* The long preliterate period, embracing the Stone, Bronze and Iron Ages that includes Stonehenge and similar megalithic structures in Minorca, Brittany and Malta.
● *Greco-Roman* The heritage of the Romans – which in turn was influenced by ancient Greece – as expressed in their engineering achievements, such as bridges and aqueducts, as well as their temples, baths and arenas. These can be found throughout the Roman Empire which stretched from Hadrian's Wall to Palestine, and from the

Rhine and Danube to the edge of the Sahara Desert in North Africa.
● *Romanesque* The so-called 'Dark Ages' which followed the break-up of the Roman Empire and the invasions of barbarian peoples from northern and eastern Europe, eventually produced the Romanesque style of architecture, expressed mainly in churches and monasteries of a simple but robust design. In the eastern Mediterranean, centred on Constantinople, the more elaborate Byzantine style developed, which eventually spread to Russia and other parts of eastern Europe.
● *Gothic* In the twelfth century this was replaced by the Gothic style of architecture. This originated in northern France at the times of the Crusades, when the Catholic Church was at the height of its power. It is characterized by an emphasis on the vertical – notably soaring spires, and by an abundance of stained glass.
● *Renaissance–Baroque* The Renaissance (rediscovery of classical learning) which started in Italy in the fifteenth century, was inspired by the design of classical Greek and Roman temples. This was followed by the Baroque style of architecture that emphasized colour and exuberant ornamentation.
● *Industrial Revolution* The technological changes that took place in the nineteenth century resulted in the use of mass-produced building materials, and this was an age of great engineering achievements, particularly applied to transport.
● *Post-Industrial* During the twentieth century, social as well as technological changes have led to a great emphasis on individuality of design in architecture and experimentation with new materials. (Examples of these different stages in architectural development can be seen on the ECU banknotes for the EU, introduced in 1999.)

Tourism demand

Europe's population exceeds 500 million people and represents a major tourism market for both the region and elsewhere in the world. There are a number of demographic trends that will impact upon tourism:

● Decreasing propensity to marry.
● Increasing diversity of lifestyles and living arrangements.
● A trend to marrying later in life.
● A decline in fertility.
● An increase in the number of divorces.

This means the traditional family holiday will no longer be the norm in many countries, the elderly will become an important consideration in tourism, and the European market is not growing as fast as other regions of the world.

To some extent, the rise of the Eastern European market will offset the slower growth characteristic of Western Europe.

These social and demographic factors have resulted in a complex pattern of tourism demand in Europe, although the methods of collecting tourism statistics do differ between countries, making comparisons difficult. Western Europe takes the lion's share of international tourism with almost 40 per cent, followed by southern Europe, with a share of around one-third. However, there are signs that the traditional flow of tourists from the northern industrial areas to the south is diminishing for the following reasons:

● consumers are tiring of the inclusive-tour format
● the Mediterranean is becoming increasingly polluted
● long-haul destinations are growing in popularity
● competing destinations have become increasingly available.

The bulk of tourism in Europe is generated from within the region and only the USA is a significant market from outside it. Most countries are significant destinations in their own right but Spain, Italy and France are clearly in the lead, not just for the region but for the world as a whole. Estimates suggest that two-thirds of European international tourism is for leisure purposes, around 15 per cent is VFR and 20 per cent business travel. The car is the dominant mode of transport because of the many short, cross-border trips, followed by air travel.

Of course, international tourism is an important feature of the European economy with a redistribution of wealth from north to south, which varies in significance from country to country. For example, in Spain and Portugal tourism is a significant source of export earnings in the form of foreign exchange, yet for the major generators of tourism (such as the Netherlands and Germany) tourism only represents a small percentage of imports, despite the volume of out-bound travel. Tourism is therefore a vital ingredient in Mediterranean economies and the fall in arrivals is a major problem for these countries, demanding imaginative solutions. It is also these countries in southern Europe – particularly Portugal, Spain and Greece – which still have low levels of holiday-taking by populations who are less urbanized, and with larger families than other parts of Europe. Seasonality is a major issue in European tourism, fuelled not only by climate but also by traditions. Although beach tourism (increasingly augmented by sports and activities) still dominates the European product, other sectors of tourism are on the increase. These and other trends include:

● Europeans will continue to take more, but shorter tourism trips.
● Short-break city and cultural tourism is growing rapidly.
● Traditional north-south holidays are still a significant feature of European tourism, but we are also seeing east-west and west-east travel growing rapidly.

● Significant market segments for the growth of tourism will be those aged over fifty-five years, and those aged under twenty-five years of age.
● Intra-regional flows of tourism represent over three-quarters of Europe's international tourism, but their share is decreasing.
● The market is moving increasingly towards taking holidays which involve active pursuits, and/or exposure to local society and culture.
● Decreasing popularity of the car for leisure-based trips and an increase in the use of air travel.
● Demand for business tourism in Europe will continue to be strong despite the growth of communication technologies.
● Ceilings of growth are being reached in some Western European countries, whereas countries in eastern and southern Europe have considerable growth potential.

Supply of tourism

Tourist attractions

The range of tourist attractions in Europe is impressive and many are of a high quality. Despite the drive to a unified Europe, very significant differences exist between the constituent countries, and this very diversity in a small area is a major part of Europe's attraction to tourists. A division can be seen in physical and cultural terms between the countries north and south of the Alpine ranges, and between those of Eastern and Western Europe.

● Southern Europe is the most climatically favoured area with *a pleasure periphery* of resorts developed in almost every country fringing the Mediterranean. Add to this the cultural and historic attractions of many of these Mediterranean countries – for example, Greece and Italy – and the classic mix of a tourist destination is created. The climate is ideal for tourism, with hot and sunny summers followed by mild winters. It is therefore doubly tragic that the pollution and low-cost development in much of the Mediterranean has detracted from these natural and cultural attractions.
● The mountains of Europe, extending from the Pyrenees to the Carpathians, are also a major summer and winter destination. They are complemented by the uplands of northern Europe which tend to cater for a regional or local, rather than an international, market for outdoor recreation.
● The lowlands of Europe are climatically less ideal for tourism, but many of Europe's major cities are located here so business tourism and short sightseeing breaks are popular. It is also here that we see the development of theme parks and other market-based attractions. Examples include Disneyland Paris, Parc Asterix, Futuroscope and the Guggenheim museum in Bilbao.

Accommodation and transport

The accommodation and food and beverage industries are dominated by small businesses across Europe: in the UK over one-half of accommodation establishments are independently owned; in the Netherlands two-thirds of accommodation establishments have less than sixteen rooms. This lack of concentration is changing as a number of large hotel chains – such as the French group, Accor – continue to develop units across the region, and hotel companies expand into the former Soviet bloc. However, there is a clear trend in the European tourist industry for dominance by larger companies who will be able to take advantage of the international opportunities offered by both globalization and the EU.

Transport

The transport sector in Europe has been heavily influenced by deregulation.

- For air transport, deregulation has encouraged the development of regional airports and airlines and is taking pressure from the very busy routes between major cities, and from the north to southern holiday destinations. The rapid growth of budget airlines in the 1990s for example is one result of increased competition on routes. However, congestion in the skies over Europe is likely to become acute, partly due to the ineffectiveness of Eurocontrol in Brussels in co-ordinating national air traffic information.
- Although deregulation also applies to other modes of transport, its impact on surface transport is less obvious, but other events will be important. The cross-Channel ferry industry, for example, has moved its activities to the western Channel to counter the effect of the Channel tunnel; the European rail network is investing in high-speed routes which will eventually link the major European countries and could conceivably extend into Eastern Europe. Indeed, the continued investment in rail transport will see a gradual switch from road and air to rail travel. Although this is being done partly for environmental reasons it is not clear whether these lines will be cost-effective and they may even create their own pollution problems. For road transport, the disappearance of border controls, which will extend across the region as more countries are drawn into the EU, will encourage international travel. There is already a network of continental highways bearing the 'E' designation (for example, E1 running from Le Havre to Sicily and E2 from Paris to Warsaw via Nuremberg). Mountain ranges act as a constraint on overland transport, although the Alps separating northern and southern Europe are no longer a formidable barrier, with a number of tunnels and passes allowing year-round travel. However, any further road developments in the Alps will exacerbate the environmental problems which are already acute.

On the supply side in Europe there are trends towards:

- A more deregulated and liberal environment for transport and other tourism sectors.
- Improved quality of existing provision of tourism supply in the former countries of the eastern bloc.
- Diversification of products in established destinations, such as coastal resorts.
- Special interest, city-based, activity-centred developments will grow at the expense of traditional beach resorts.
- Cruising combined with special interest activities is a growth area.
- Business tourism facilities in the former Eastern Bloc are expanding.

The organization of tourism in Europe

The organization of tourism in Europe is complex. Each country has its own distinctive administration and traditions that influence both the public and private sector in tourism. Every country in Europe has a national tourism organization, supported by both regional and local organizations. Generally, the functions of these organizations are to develop and promote tourism, although in some cases their powers are more wide-ranging and include the registration and grading of accommodation as well as education and training. There is an identifiable trend towards devolution of tourism powers from the national level to regions, and a move to involve the private sector in the activities of the tourist boards. The individual organizations and their powers are described in the relevant chapters, but since the early 1980s, the EU has also become involved in the organization and administration of tourism. The background to EU involvement is described in the case study in this chapter.

Summary

Europe is pre-eminent in world tourism representing around half of international world arrivals, and has a large outbound and domestic tourism industry. This is because most of the region's economies are either in the high mass-consumption stage or the drive to maturity, so the population, though ageing, is in general affluent, mobile and has a high propensity to travel. Europe also comprises many relatively small countries in close proximity, encouraging a high volume of short international trips. The region's climatic differences are significant and have led to a flow of tourists from industrialized northern Europe to the south. In terms of the organization of tourism in Europe, most

governments have well-funded, competent tourist authorities with marketing and development powers and, as the
region attempts to compete with other world destination
regions, the role of the EU will become increasingly
important to tourism. Europe's tourism infrastructure is
mature and of high standard, with a fully developed
transport network. The tourism industry is also highly
developed, with the largest regional concentration of
accommodation in the world. In terms of tourist attractions,
Europe's rich mosaic of languages, culture and physical
features produce attractions of world calibre.

Case study

European policy and tourism

Introduction

The impetus for a united Europe emerged from the
devastation of the Second World War. The idea of a
customs union for coal and steel dates back to 1951 and
led to the European Coal and Steel Community (ECSC).
The ECSC was successful and as more countries joined
it broadened to other sectors of the economy. This led to
the signing of the Treaty of Rome in 1957 as the basis of
all European legislation, however, tourism was not
included as a policy area in the original Treaty. The
Treaty of Rome founded the European Economic Community which became the present EU and in the ensuing
decades the number of members grew from the original
six signatories to fifteen in 1994. By the mid-1980s
impetus for a Single European Market led to the Single
European Act that aimed to abolish the following
barriers to movement in Europe by the end of 1992:

● physical barriers
● technical barriers
● fiscal barriers.

The Single European Market operates within a framework of European organizations and decision-taking
bodies, each of which has a role in tourism:

● *The European Commission* Based in Brussels, the
  Commission was created to implement the Treaty of
  Rome and is effectively the 'civil service' of Europe.
  Its remit is to provide the *European* dimension by
  initiating, implementing and policing EU legislation.
  It is made up of a series of departments – or
  Directorates. Tourism is in Directorate General
  XXIII.
● *The European Parliament* The Parliament is based in
  Brussels and Strasbourg. It is an elected body and

debates and amends European legislation. The Parliament has traditionally been supportive of tourism
initiatives at Community level.
● *The Council of Ministers* The Council makes decisions about European legislation, once it has been
  initiated by the Commission and debated by Parliament. The Council exists to balance the Commission
  by providing the *national* interest of members.
  Statements by the Council relating to tourism have
  triggered significant policy initiatives.
● *The European Court of Justice* The European Court is
  based in The Hague with the remit to interpret the
  Treaty of Rome and make judgements. The Court
  would make judgements over any dispute concerning
  tourism policy or related policy as it impacts upon
  tourism.
● *European Investment Bank* (EIB) The EIB provides
  long-term loans and supports regional development
  in the EU. Tourism projects benefit from regional
  development schemes.
● *Committee of the Regions* The Committee comprises
  representatives of regions and cities across the EU,
  and is an increasingly important forum for tourism
  initiatives.

The implications of European policies for tourism

The legislation and initiatives that have created the
Single European Market have had a number of implications for tourism. These can be considered in terms
of:

● tourism policy – which is a minor element of the
  Community's business and budget
● other policy areas – such as transport and regional
  development – which have considerable influence
  and budgets.

Tourism policy in the EU

The fact that Europe has a tourism policy that relates to
all member states is unusual on a world basis. It also
reflects the importance of tourism in the EU, estimated
to generate 9 million jobs and account for at least 5.5
per cent of gross domestic product. There are few
geographical regions that have a supra-national tourism policy. However, the tourism policy for Europe is
relatively recent and has undergone a number of
changes in the last quarter of the twentieth century;
indeed it has been criticized as being piecemeal and
ad hoc. Equally, the policy has had much less impact
upon the tourism sector than some of the other
European polices outlined in below. This is partly
because, at European level, there is no legal authority
to act in the tourism field, and the view has been that

the 'subsidiarity' principle operates – i.e. that tourism is a matter for member states and not for Europe as a whole.

Significant events in the development of a tourism policy for Europe:

- *1980* Establishment of a Tourism Commissioner.
- *1982* The *Initial Guidelines on a Community Policy for Tourism* was drafted stressing: the need for freedom of movement; importance of social tourism; improving working conditions in tourism; addressing seasonality; regional development; and the importance of cultural tourism.
- *1984* European Court judgement that the EU could intervene in tourism matters under the principle of free movement of persons, services and capital. The Council of Ministers emphasized the need for tourism to be a greater consideration in the Community.
- *1986* The *Community Action in the Field of Tourism* was published setting out the Commission's objectives in tourism as freedom of movement, addressing temporal and spatial imbalances, providing information and protection for tourists, improving working conditions and improving tourism statistics. This document firmly established tourism as an element of Community policy and saw an increase in the tourism budget.
- *1988* Proposal for the European Year of Tourism to be held in order to stress preparations for the 1992 initiative, promote knowledge of cultures and lifestyles, promote seasonal and geographical spreading of tourism, and promote tourism generally.
- *1989* Directorate General XXIII of the Commission was established to implement the European Year of Tourism. Also the Council of Ministers made a statement on the direction that tourism should take in the Community. This statement:
  - stressed the subsidiarity rule for tourism
  - called on member states to co-operate on tourism strategy
  - stressed that a Community tourism policy would benefit the individual traveller and tourism enterprises
  - stressed the need for a better distribution of tourism
  - stressed the need to invest in human resources in tourism
  - set up a statistical action plan for tourism
  - stressed the need to co-ordinate Community policies in terms of infrastructure for tourism.

  1990 European Year of Tourism – but not an unqualified success.
- *1991* The *Community Action Plan to Assist Tourism* was published based on the Council of Ministers' statement in 1989. The plan ran from 1993 to 1995, aiming to improve tourism statistics, stagger holidays,

encourage co-operation between members, provide consumer protection, cultural tourism, tourism and the environment, rural tourism, social tourism, youth training and promotion of Europe as a destination.

- *1995* A Green Paper was published on *The Role of the Union in the Field of Tourism*. This paper laid out four options for future European Commission involvement in tourism ranging from effectively doing nothing and leaving tourism to member states (option 1), to a full treatment of tourism at Community level (option 4).
- *1996* The First Multiannual Programme to Assist European Tourism – Philoxenia (literally from the Greek 'hospitality towards visitors') was proposed by the Commission as a new programme of action in tourism. Philoxenia ensured continuity of action in tourism and also addressed issues of the impact of tourism, competitiveness and quality.
- *1997* The European Parliament voted for option 4 in the 1995 Green Paper, effectively creating a new tourism role for the European Commission working together with member states. This implies that the Treaty of Rome would need to be revised to include a 'tourism competence'.
- *1999* The introduction of the 'Euro' as the EU's currency has major implications for tourism. Resignation of the Commissioner for DG XXIII along with all the other Commissioners.

Related policy issues which affect tourism

Removal of physical barriers:

- *Legislation to remove barriers to travel and the free movement of goods and services* This allows for the free movement of travellers between member states and implies the abolition of border controls and customs within the EU.
- *Transport policy* has had a major effect upon tourism in two ways:
  - through the creation of free movement by enhancing surface travel 'through routes' across Europe
  - through the deregulation of transport. The major development here has been the three-stage deregulation of European air transport, with the effect of enhancing the role of regional airports, supporting smaller airlines and changing the patterns of air travel across Europe.

Removal of technical barriers:

- *Regional development* The structural funds are designed to remove regional disparities across Europe. There are a large number of different funds and criteria of eligibility for each fund differs. Tourism plays a major role in these funds through encouragement of small enterprises, reviving rural, urban and declining industrial areas and through job creation. The structural funds have provided substantial funding to tourism in Europe.

- *Environmental legislation* A range of environmental initiatives have impacted upon tourism, in particular bathing water directives and environmental impact and auditing legislation, and benchmarking exercises such as the 'Blue Flag' beach scheme.
- *Social legislation* Here tourism is affected through the provisions to enhance the working conditions of part-time and temporary workers and the mutual recognition of qualifications across member states. This will encourage labour mobility in tourism across the EU.
- *Consumer protection policy* The EU consumer protection policy has important implications for tourism. The Package Travel Directive is designed to provide protection for those booking inclusive tours; the Timeshare Directive protects those purchasing timeshare accommodation and there is a range of information initiatives which involve tourism.

Removal of fiscal barriers:

- *Economic and monetary union* The introduction of a Single European Currency (the ECU) will facilitate pan-European travel by doing away with currency exchange and will also act as a basis for fare construction and encourage pan-European travel companies.
- *Harmonization of taxes and duties* Here there are a range of policies that aim to provide a 'level competitive playing field' across Europe. There are two areas where tourism is directly affected:
  - the removal of duty free allowances for travellers between member states. This is a contentious issue as transport operators and terminals make a large profit on duty free goods. The loss of jobs and the raising of fares are a possible consequence.
  - the harmonization of value added tax (VAT) rates across Europe will impact upon tourism enterprises and government revenue.

7

An introduction to the tourism geography of Britain

After reading this chapter, you should be able to:

1 Appreciate that socioeconomic, technological and institutional factors present a powerful force in British society enabling the demand for tourism to be realized.
2 Be aware of changes in the volume of domestic tourism in Britain, and the factors that have brought about these changes.
3 Appreciate the volume and scope both of British residents' domestic tourism and tourism overseas, and the factors that have brought this about.
4 Understand the recent influences upon the volume of inbound tourism to Britain and the nature of the overseas market.
5 Recognize the importance of physical geography in influencing the tourist resource base.
6 Demonstrate a knowledge of the key components of tourism supply in Britain.
7 Understand the way in which tourism is administered in Britain.

Introduction

Geographically Great Britain and Ireland are the two largest islands in the group known as the British Isles, lying off the north-west coast of Europe. They include two sovereign states – The United Kingdom of Great Britain and Northern Ireland (UK) and the Republic of Ireland. We use the term *Britain* to include the three nations of England, Scotland and Wales, and to exclude Northern Ireland which is dealt

with in Chapter 10. Only a narrow stretch of water separates Britain from the continent of Europe and this has given the islands:

● a strong maritime outlook with interests extending to all corners of the globe, while the naval heritage is an important part of Britain's tourist appeal
● a cultural identity quite distinct from other Western European countries. The 'narrow seas' are often stormy and in the past have acted as a constraint on visits from the European mainland.

It can almost be said that holidays in the modern sense were invented in the British Isles, with their tradition of travel and exploration. The importance of tourism is clearly illustrated by these statistics for the 1990s:

● Overseas arrivals to the British Isles approached 30 million.
● Trips overseas by the British and Irish population peaked at over 40 million.
● Domestic tourism approached 130 million trips.

Despite these impressive figures, the UK's balance on the travel account remains negative, while for the Republic of Ireland, the balance is positive.

The physical setting for tourism

The British Isles are relatively small in land area but they offer three physical regions as the setting for tourism in Britain:

1 *The highland zone* includes Central and North Wales, the Southern Uplands, and the Highlands and Islands of Scotland. Here rocks are older, often impermeable, and

high rainfall gives leached, infertile soils. Population is thinly scattered and land use dominated by livestock rearing.

2 *The upland zone* includes Exmoor, Dartmoor, the Brecon Beacons, the Black Mountains, the Pennines and, in Scotland, Caithness, Sutherland and the Orkneys. Here the rocks are younger, landforms more rounded, and distinctive regional differences are apparent (contrast the Yorkshire Dales with Dartmoor). British national parks and National Park Direction areas are mainly in the highland and upland zones where they have been designated for their natural beauty and characteristic landscapes.

3 *The lowlands* nowhere exceed 300 metres in altitude and encompass much of southern and eastern England. The lowlands are warmer and drier, and land use is dominated by intensive agriculture and sprawling conurbations.

The coasts are equally important for tourism. The western coasts are irregular with estuaries, cliffs, sandy coves and islands, in contrast to the east where smooth, low coasts are typical, with long beaches and spits, and low cliffs or dunes. Most of the more attractive stretches of coastline have been given protection as 'Heritage Coasts'.

Climate and weather

The latitudinal extent of the British Isles (from 50º North to 60º North) gives a diversity of climatic influences and conditions. The location of the British Isles off the coast of mainland Europe means that the climate is tempered by maritime influences, especially in Ireland and the South-West of England, where moist, mild conditions predominate. The British Isles are a battleground of different air masses and conditions are dependent upon either the nature of the dominant air mass at the time or the wet and stormy weather which results from the 'fronts' where the air masses meet. Low-pressure systems are constantly coming in from the Atlantic, and the western highlands and uplands bear the brunt of these systems, sheltering the lowland zone.

In winter, temperatures are lowest in the north-east of the British Isles and mildest in the south-west, but in summer the gradient changes to west–east, with cooler temperatures in the west, although sea temperatures are often lower off the North Sea coast, as the prevailing westerly winds are offshore. In the summer, too, sunshine figures are a source of keen competition between resorts. The south coast has the highest average number of bright sunshine hours per day, with the hours decreasing inland, to the north, and with altitude.

If sunshine is the goal of many holidays, precipitation is to be avoided (apart from snow in winter-sports resorts). The highest precipitation is found in the higher ground of the west (Ireland, the Lake District, Wales and the Scottish Highlands) which, at 2500 millimetres (100 inches) per year, is about four times as much as parts of eastern England. Precipitation

falling as snow is more common in the highland and upland zones, and the colder east. In the Cairngorms in Scotland snow can lie for more than 100 days of the year and has led to a major development of winter sports in the Aviemore area. Any average figures are deceptive and the variety of influences upon weather in the British Isles means that there are considerable differences from the average experience.

Changes in postwar British society

Demand for tourism and recreation in Britain has grown at a phenomenal rate since the Second World War, not only in terms of volume but also in variety. The cause of this growth is rooted in the social and economic development of Britain since the Second World War; specifically, two major influences can be identified: social/economic and technological.

Social and economic influences

Social and economic changes in Britain have combined to boost demand for both domestic and international tourism. In the last half of the twentieth century, rising per capita incomes have brought higher purchasing power. The 1960s were a particularly prosperous period of high employment in which the first real stirrings of mass demand for tourism were experienced. The following decades suffered the setbacks of energy crises, recession and unemployment but, even so, real household disposable incomes per head increased by 80 per cent between 1971 and 1990, fuelling demand for tourism.

The dramatic increase in *car ownership* has played its part in revolutionizing holiday habits. Car ownership more than doubled in the decade 1950–60, and then doubled again by 1970. In Britain in the mid-1990s car ownership stood at over 20 million vehicles, and facilities for motorists have grown accordingly. For example, in the 1990s the length of British motorway exceeded 3100 kilometres bringing many holiday destinations within reach of urban conurbations. As a consequence of these developments, passenger-kilometres driven increased considerably. However, increasing concerns about the environmental impact of traffic have slowed government road-building schemes and in the new millennium attempts will be made to curb the use of the car, especially in the cities.

Increased affluence and personal mobility have been paralleled by an increase in both educational levels and access to education. In consequence, there has been a heightened awareness of opportunities for tourism. For example, in the 1990s, 4.5 million students were in full-time higher or further education.

The *time available* for holidays has also grown with increased holiday entitlement, three-day weekends, and various flexible-working arrangements providing blocks of time for trips away from home. Through the 1960s, for example, industry and services (such as retailing and banking) moved towards a five-day working week. This in itself is significant for the shorter-holiday market, but for the traditional long holiday it is the annual entitlement that matters and this has greatly increased since the Second World War. In the 1990s, legislation at the European level has increased workers' entitlement to holiday and leisure time.

Perhaps surprisingly, the increase in demand for tourism and recreation has come more from changes in society brought about by the above factors, than by any large increase in the population itself. Indeed, between 1951 and 2001 the population in Britain grew by less than 20 per cent. More important to tourism is the changing composition of the population. For example, the postwar baby boom produced a generation that demanded tourism and recreation from the late 1970s onwards. Similarly, the population is healthier and living longer, and the retired population is rising. By 2001 25 per cent of the British population will be aged fifty-five years and over – most of whom will be active, leisured, affluent and experienced travellers.

Technology

These changes in society have gone hand in hand with technological innovations (aside from transportation, which was dealt with in Chapter 5). For example:

- Breakthroughs in product design have brought a range of leisure goods within reach of the population (such as fibreglass boats, mountaineering equipment and specialist outdoor clothing).
- Technology, too, through the media, has brought awareness of holiday and recreational opportunities to all, specifically through newspaper and magazine travel sections, television and radio programmes featuring holiday opportunities, or the guidebooks produced by tourist boards and motoring organizations.
- Computer reservation systems (CRS) have developed rapidly in the last quarter of the century, allowing the tourism industry to be more efficient and responsive to consumer demands, whilst rapid adoption of the internet in homes in the 1990s is revolutionizing access to information and purchasing habits for travel.
- Finally, not only has technology released the work-force from mundane tasks as microprocessors and robot engineering are introduced, but labour-saving devices have also helped to reduce the time spent on household chores and released that time for leisure and tourism.

Demand for tourism in Britain from overseas

Britain is a major recipient of international tourists in the global scene, ranking only behind France, USA, Spain and Italy, and nationally tourism is an important earner of foreign currency. Overseas visitors come to Britain for heritage, culture, countryside and ethnic reasons. The ebb and flow of tourist movements in and out of Britain is due to the relative strength of sterling against other currencies, the health of the economy, special events, and the marketing activities of both public and private tourist organizations.

The historical trend

The 1960s

The early 1960s saw between 3 and 4 million overseas visitors coming to Britain, but with the devaluation of sterling in 1967 Britain became a very attractive destination.

The 1970s

The number of overseas visitors had increased to almost 7 million visits by 1970. By the mid-1970s the weakness of the pound against other currencies made Britain the 'bargain basement' of the Western world and arrivals leapt to 11 million. This boom in inbound travel easily outpaced the depressed demand for overseas travel by British residents, and Britain enjoyed a surplus on its balance of payments travel account. In other words, spending by overseas visitors to Britain was greater than spending by British residents overseas. This was compounded by the Queen's Silver Jubilee in 1977, which increased arrivals to 12 million. By 1978 sterling was a stronger currency and Britain was experiencing high inflation.

The 1980s

The above two factors had the effect of increasing the real price of tourism services and goods in Britain and increased taxation on goods in the early 1980s led to a 'price shock' for overseas visitors. Britain was no longer a cheap destination and both visitor numbers and spending (in real terms) declined accordingly. This led to a deficit on the balance of payments travel account, the first for many years. World economic recession also depressed visits in the early 1980s but an upturn began in 1982, caused by a weaker pound and allied to economic recovery in the main generating areas of Western Europe and North America. Only in 1986 was this growth rate checked by the Libyan bombing, the Chernobyl incident and the weakening of the US dollar.

The 1990s

The decade saw significant events that have profoundly influenced the trend of tourism to the UK. The opening of the Channel tunnel changed the mode of transport of visitors to the UK and took market share from both air and sea arrivals, while deregulation of air travel within Europe and the emergence of budget airlines has encouraged the growth of arrivals to regional gateways. By the late 1990s, overseas visits to the UK had grown steadily to reach 26 million. General trends are:

1 The origin of overseas visits to Britain is changing. Not only are the sources of travel becoming more diverse, but also visits from all major source areas have increased steadily. Visits from Western Europe form the majority of the market at around two-thirds of the total. Visits from North America have remained relatively stable at about 15 per cent of the total, while new markets such as Eastern Europe have made a major contribution to arrivals over the decade. In the rest of the world, the major markets are Australia, New Zealand, the Middle East and Japan.
2 Length of stay is decreasing.
3 Visitor spending is increasing.
4 London dominates as a destination for overseas visitors.

These aggregate figures conceal variations in the different segments of the flow of overseas visitors to Britain:

1 Holiday visits grew rapidly up until 1977 (to almost half of total arrivals), but have declined slowly since that date with considerable annual fluctuations. In the 1990s holiday visits represented around two-fifths of total overseas arrivals.
2 Visiting friends and relatives is a reliable and growing sector accounting for 20 per cent of total arrivals in the 1990s. This is a particularly important sector of the Scottish market.
3 Business travel has also grown steadily, accounting for 25 per cent of total arrivals in the 1990s.
4 Britain attracts 2.5 million day-excursionists, with the Channel tunnel and cross-Channel ports and ferries accounting for a large percentage of this traffic.

Visitor characteristics

Within the UK, both the geographical and seasonal distribution of overseas visitors is very concentrated. Geographically, almost 90 per cent of visitors are to England, with Scotland (8 per cent) and Wales (3 per cent) taking much smaller shares. Even within England, the pattern is concentrated upon London, which takes almost half of overseas visits. Obviously, London is the capital city, a major gateway and business centre, and would be expected to receive the lion's share of overseas visits – especially first-time visits. However, tourist authorities are anxious to spread the benefits of this spending to other areas by encouraging motoring and touring holidays (especially from Western Europe). Equally, encouraging traffic through the Channel tunnel and the regional airports may reduce the concentration upon London. Indeed, there is evidence that

these measures are meeting with some success with Glasgow and Edinburgh increasing their share of overseas visits. Seasonality is reducing but the third quarter of the year still accounts for the highest percentage of overseas visitors to Britain.

Around two-thirds of visitors to Britain arrive by air and less than one-third by sea. The share of seaborne visits is declining due to:

● competition from the Channel tunnel
● growth of budget airlines and regional air services
● deregulation of Ireland/UK air services.

British residents' demand for tourism

Britain's tradition of tourism has led to a high level of travel propensity in the population. Around 60 per cent of the British take a holiday in any one year but, taken over a period of three years, this figure rises to 75 per cent as some enter and others leave the market in a particular year. Even so, there is a hard core of those who do not travel, especially the poor and the elderly. Not only is travel propensity high, but also travel frequency averaged 1.5 trips for those holidaying away from home.

The main growth in tourism has been overseas travel at the expense of the domestic long-holiday market. For the British tourism market as a whole the underlying factors fuelling growth – leisure spending, holiday entitlement and mobility – continued to rise to the end of the century. However, while outbound tourism continues to grow, domestic tourism can only share in this growth through the trend towards leisure day trips and shorter holidays.

Domestic tourism in Britain

Taking the British Isles as a whole, domestic tourism for all purposes approached 120 million trips in the late 1990s, while Britain's offshore holiday islands (the Channel Islands, the Isle of Man and the Scillies) accounted for over 2 million trips.

Although domestic tourism accounts for about 6 per cent of consumer spending, it contrasts sharply with international tourism out of Britain because it:

● has a shorter length stay
● demonstrates a lower level of spending
● is more difficult to measure – in 1989 the four UK national tourist boards launched the United Kingdom Tourist Survey (UKTS), replacing previous surveys.

The domestic tourism historical trend

Holidays in Britain are inextricably linked with disposable income and general economic health.

The 1970s

The decade began with strong demand for domestic holidays in Britain. However, over the decade demand fluctuated and, in the face of changing economic factors, the share of domestic tourism experienced an absolute decline as that of overseas tourism by British residents increased.

The 1980s

Recessions adversely affected demand for domestic tourism and a number of factors came into play. First, domestic tourism is dominated by those in the lower social grades that are more sensitive to price and changes in income or economic circumstances. Second, the industrial heartlands of the North, the Midlands, Scotland and South Wales, which traditionally generated high levels of demand for holidays at home, were particularly badly hit by the recessions. As a consequence, demand for holidays in Welsh and northern resorts fell. Finally, not only did inflation push up the cost of a holiday at home but also, at the same time, recession bred uncertainty about employment and holiday decisions were delayed. The mid-1980s saw a significant upturn in domestic tourism due to the increased cost of travel overseas, a weak pound and vigorous promotion of holidays in Britain. Hopes for the continuation of this increase were dashed in the late 1980s/early 1990s as recession and the Gulf War severely reduced domestic volumes and spending across the whole of the UK.

The 1990s

New products in the domestic market stimulated visits in the 1990s, but the pattern of holiday-taking remained stable over the decade, with the West Country strengthening its dominant position in terms of visits and the car in terms of mode of transport. In the 1990s there have been important changes in the structure of the domestic tourism market:

- a continued decline in length of stay
- growth in the shorter holiday markets
- growth of business and conference tourism
- a shift away from traditional coastal destinations towards towns and countryside
- a response by the coastal resorts to upgrade and reposition their facilities
- an increased volume of trips to friends and relatives.

Domestic tourism visitor characteristics

Aggregate totals do disguise differences between the various sectors in Britain. The UKTS shows that the holiday sector accounts for around 55 per cent of domestic tourism trips, business 12 per cent and visiting friends and relatives 28 per cent. Each of these sectors has a distinctive geographical pattern and shows contrasting trends over time.

An important distinction in the domestic market is between a long holiday (four nights or more) and a short holiday (one to three nights). For some time, the general trend has been a gradual decline in domestic long holidays and an increase in short, often additional, holidays. Clearly, many short holidays are taken as 'additional' holidays to complement the 'main' holiday (which may be taken in Britain or overseas); indeed in 1997, for the first time more 'additional holidays' were taken in Britain than 'main' holidays.

The generation of domestic holiday trips is broadly proportional to the distribution of population across the British Isles. However, some areas have a relatively high holiday-taking propensity (the South-East of England) while others are low (Scotland, the North-West of England). England is the dominant domestic holiday destination for the UK with three-quarters of mainland trips in the late 1990s. Scotland and Wales each account for around 10 per cent of trips, with Northern Ireland having just over 1 per cent of the market. Within the UK, the West Country is by far the most popular destination, with around one-fifth of total trips.

Of course, holiday choices are difficult to explain and are subject to the vagaries of changing tastes and fashion. However, the basic principle of spatial interaction is in operation in the domestic market, with a supplying area containing a surplus of a commodity and the tourist-generating area possessing a demand for that commodity. For example, the South of England and the West Country are perceived to be sunny and warm, with their added advantages of an attractive coast, fine established resorts and opportunities for touring. But set against these attractions is the problem of overcoming distance to reach the holiday destination from home.

Domestic tourism demonstrates a clear pattern in time as well as space. The trend towards short, additional holidays has gone some way towards reducing the acute seasonal peaking of domestic holidays, rooted in the timing of school and industrial holidays. Around two-fifths of long holidays begin in July or August, but for short holidays, this figure falls to one-fifth.

The business and conference sector of the domestic market has grown steadily in the 1990s representing 12 per cent of total trips, but 15 per cent of total expenditure due to the high spending nature of these tourists. Resorts, towns and cities hotly compete for this lucrative sector across the British Isles because it:

- is not concentrated in the summer peak
- tends to use serviced accommodation
- brings a high-spending clientele to the destination.

Demand for overseas travel

The British Isles are a major generator of tourism trips abroad, with the UK consistently in the top five countries in the world. Indeed, the greatest market growth in tourism has been in trips overseas which more than doubled in the decade 1978–88 and reached over 40 million trips by the late 1990s. Over the last half of the twentieth century, the holiday sector in particular has exhibited strong growth, especially inclusive tourism to short-haul (mainly Mediterranean) destinations. This growth has been fuelled by:

- competitive pricing of inclusive tours
- a strong consumer preference for overseas destinations
- an increasingly experienced outbound market.

In the future, growth will be by an increase in travel frequency rather than by new entrants to the market.

The overseas travel historical trend

Growth in the holiday sector stems from economic factors, but the activities of the travel trade since the 1950s have brought a holiday overseas within reach of a large percentage of the population. What has happened is that the increased organization of the travel industry coupled with the growth of travel intermediaries, such as travel agents and tour operators, has taken much of the responsibility of organizing a holiday away from the tourist. Add to this sophisticated marketing, pricing and reservations systems, and it is clear that the travel industry has done much to convert suppressed demand into effective demand for holidays overseas. Taking the critical twenty years when growth was at its height, in 1970 only one-third of the population had ever taken a holiday overseas; by 1990 this figure was well over two-thirds. Clearly, this has implications for both products and destinations as the market matures.

The 1970s

Between 1965 and 1972 the real price of inclusive tours fell by 25 per cent, due to increased use of jet aircraft, fierce price competition and the increased availability of winter holidays. This encouraged demand, only to see it dashed by the oil crisis of 1973–4 and the bankruptcy of a major tour operator. The mid-1970s saw fluctuations in the numbers of holidays taken overseas as higher oil prices, weak sterling, economic recession and higher holiday prices took their toll. In the late 1970s, a strong pound, cheaper holidays/airfares, and vigorous marketing increased demand to a growth rate of 20 per cent per annum. At the same time, high inflation pushed up the price of a domestic holiday, and with the British beginning to view the annual holiday as a priority, overseas holidays grew in popularity.

The 1980s

The decade of the 1980s saw virtually uninterrupted growth in overseas holiday trips. Four key underlying causes can be identified:

1 Britain was an oil-rich country with a relatively strong currency *vis-à-vis* popular holiday destinations.
2 Real discretionary income rose for groups with a preference for overseas travel (the young; higher socioeconomic groups).
3 A sophisticated tour operation and distribution system, allied to high spending on promotion, made overseas travel accessible also to lower socioeconomic groups.
4 Competitive pricing of inclusive tours.

The 1990s

The market continued to grow in the 1990s, despite the setbacks of the Gulf War. In the 1990s the market was characterized by a number of key influences:

1 Acquisition and merger in the tour operator/travel agency sector led to an increased concentration of capacity in the hands of a few companies.
2 The deregulation of European airlines blurred the distinction between charter and scheduled services and allowed the growth of budget airlines.
3 The opening of the Channel tunnel led to a response by the ferry companies in terms of new ships and routes in the western Channel.
4 The loss of destinations such as Yugoslavia.
5 The effective devaluation of the pound in 1992 when the UK left the European Monetary system.
6 The introduction of a tax on air passenger departures.
7 The introduction of the Euro as European currency.
8 Competitive pricing of long-haul destinations such as Florida and the Far East.

Overseas travel visitor characteristics

In the late 1990s British residents took over 40 million trips overseas and spent almost £16 billion, leaving a deficit on the UK's travel account. Length of stay has also increased contributing to higher spending overseas. The level of spending on overseas trips confirms the high priority given to overseas travel by the British. Examining the reason for the visit, holiday tourism represents two-thirds of trips; business tourism 15 per cent of trips; and VFR 12 per cent of trips.

In total, over 30 per cent of trips are by ferry or the Channel tunnel and more than two-thirds by air. The modal split has changed in the 1990s due to the influence of the Channel tunnel (which provided the first fixed link to the continent) and European airline deregulation. Holiday arrangement – inclusive tour or independent – has also changed with a growth in independent travel, as the relative share of inclusive tours shrinks (just over one-third of all trips in the late 1990s). The fact that a large majority of the British population has experienced a holiday overseas has led to an increased number who feel confident to travel independently. For these travellers, France is the most important destination. However, this new breed of experienced traveller is now travelling further and to a greater range of countries.

In the late 1990s the most popular destinations continued to be Spain, France, Ireland, North America, Italy and Greece. Clearly, Western Europe dominates, with the USA the only non-European country with considerable drawing power. In line with this and recent trends worldwide, long-haul destinations are a source of considerable growth. Business trips have remained buoyant over the decade and trade with EU member states generates a significant volume of surface travel for business purposes.

Three key influences will determine the volume and nature of the UK market for travel overseas in the future:

- prospects for the UK economy and relationships with Europe and the Euro
- changes in consumer habits and thinking, particularly with regard to green issues
- the growing maturity of leisure markets in terms of products offered and the response of the market.

The supply of tourism in Britain

The components of tourism

This section examines the various components of tourism in Britain from a geographical viewpoint. Tourism supports over 1.5 million jobs in Britain indirectly or directly – jobs which are distributed throughout the tourism industry.

Resources

Britain's tourism resource base is remarkably diverse for a small country. Regional resources embrace the fourteen national parks that have been designated in England and Wales and five national park direction areas in Scotland. In England and Wales, national parks are required both to preserve their natural beauty and to enhance their enjoyment by the public. Other important regional features include the forests in Britain. The British Forestry Commission is charged with opening up the forests for recreation and tourism and has developed self-catering cabins in holiday areas, and community forests on the edge of conurbations.

The British Isles also contain major inland water bodies, but demand for their recreational use on the mainland outstrips supply. This has led to intensive management of lakes such as Windermere and Lake Bala as well as the Norfolk Broads. Other linear features include rivers and canals, both of which are extensively used for recreation, as are the Heritage Coasts and long distance footpaths, such as the Pennine Way. Government provision for tourism and recreation is complemented by conservation trusts and charities, such as the National Trust (NT) which has purchased attractive areas of coast and countryside, as well as a large number of historic buildings.

Attractions

It is in areas such as national parks and the hinterlands of major resorts that the most successful point tourist attractions lie. In the 1990s, tourist attractions in the UK have received a major funding boost from the Heritage Lottery and Millennium funds, which have directed money to develop new attractions and improve many existing ones. Indeed, these initiatives, along with EU funds in Ireland, have begun to transform the leisure landscapes of the British Isles in the final decade of the twentieth century. The very diversity of size, type, and ownership of attractions make classification difficult but Patmore (1983) has identified three basic types of attractions.

1 Many attractions simply result from the opening of an existing resource – an ancient monument, stately home or nature reserve.
2 Some attractions have begun to add developments (such as the motor museum and monorail at Beaulieu Palace) to augment the attraction and broaden their appeal. The varying shades of provision in the English and Welsh country parks mean that they should also be included in this second category.
3 This type of attraction is one artificially created for the visitor, such as Alton Towers or London Zoo, or heritage attractions such as 'Wigan Pier'. The government and the tourist boards are anxious to improve the professionalism of tourist attractions and to diversify the range on offer – which now include coal-mining museums and theme parks.

Accommodation

Accommodation is concentrated into centres of demand such as the seaside resorts and the major cities. In the British Isles around two-fifths of beds in serviced accommodation are located at the seaside, especially on the southern and south-western coasts of England, and in North Wales. However, much of this accommodation is in outmoded Victorian and Edwardian buildings – establishments that do not meet the aspirations of contemporary holidaymakers. Both the public and private sectors are trying to remedy this problem and ensure that accommodation supply matches demand. The real change in holiday tastes has been for self-catering accommodation. In 1951, 12 per cent of main holidays in England used self-catering accommodation, but by the late 1990s the figure was over one-third. Self-catering developments were initially in holiday camps, later in caravans and, more recently, in purpose-built complexes of self-catering units with sports and activity provisions. This was pioneered by CenterParcs in Sherwood Forest and has expanded to other locations, as well as attracting other companies into the market such as the Oasis holiday village on the edge of the Lake District National Park. At the same time the holiday camps have had to upgrade their facilities and reposition themselves in the market place as tastes have changed. In major towns and cities demand from business and overseas travellers keeps bed occupancy rates high. Here provision tends to be in the larger, expensive hotels (often of more than 100 bedrooms).

Accommodation is also dispersed along routeways and in rural areas. Initially, accommodation was found on coaching routes and later at railway termini and major ports. More recently, airports and air terminals have attracted the development of large, quality hotels (as at Heathrow and in west London) and motorway service areas now also offer budget accommodation – the equivalent of the old coaching inns. In rural areas accommodation is concentrated in south-west England, Scotland and Wales. There is a growing demand for farm holidays, self-catering cottages and 'timeshare' developments. It is also the rural areas that bear the brunt of second-home ownership.

Transport

Travellers entering the British Isles can do so through a variety of gateways, but in fact both air and surface transport networks focus on the south-east of England.

1 *Air* Over 80 per cent of international passengers travelling by air are channelled through the London airports and airlines are reluctant to move out from these gateways. Manchester has been identified as the UK's second major airport and Glasgow's international status has stimulated major growth. Belfast and airports on the offshore holiday islands complete the network, and although holiday traffic to these islands is not inconsiderable it has a highly seasonal pattern. Overall, Britain's major airports handled around 120 million passengers in the late 1990s.

2 *Sea* For sea traffic, there is again a concentration of passengers in southern England due to the dominance of cross-Channel ferry routes, though companies are moving into the western Channel to counter the threat of the Channel tunnel. Elsewhere there is a diversification of routes such as those from Hull and Harwich on the east coast. A second concentration of routes is from the west coasts of mainland Britain to Ireland and Northern Ireland. On the sea routes the upgrading of ships and the introduction of high speed 'catamarans' is a response to both the Channel tunnel and greater expectations by travellers.

3 *The Channel tunnel* The 'Chunnel' opened in 1994 and has not only stimulated new traffic, but has also taken traffic from both air and especially sea services to Europe. Interestingly, the response of ferry operators to develop routes in the western Channel has been less successful than hoped. Other responses have been mergers on the short sea routes, closure of some routes (Newhaven to Dieppe for example) and price competition.

4 *Surface transport* In the domestic market, and for overseas travellers touring the British Isles, surface transport dominates. Significant developments have been the deregulation of coach services on 1980 leading to a competitive intercity service and privatization of the rail service. Privatization of the railways has led to regional differentiation on the routes and new services that are receiving investment – such as those serving coastal and inland holiday areas. In the British Isles there are also over forty private railways trading on nostalgia for the steam era.

Since the Second World War the use of the car has become more important than either rail or coach services, as road improvements have been completed and the real cost of motoring has fallen. Since 1955 the use of the car for domestic holidays has increased at the expense of rail and coach travel. The 1980 Transport Act revolutionized the coach business in the UK by deregulating services. Coaches pose a very real alternative to rail travel on journeys of up to 400 kilometres and the new generation of luxury coaches has increased passenger figures on coach services.

Administration

Public agencies with responsibility for tourism in the British Isles play a vital role in shaping the tourist 'product', both through their promotional activities and advice. Increasingly, government is 'devolving' these functions to regional and local organizations.

1 *National level* In Britain the 1969 Development of Tourism Act formed three statutory national tourist boards, (English, Scottish and Wales Tourist Boards) and the British Tourist Authority (BTA) which was given sole responsibility for overseas promotion and any matters of common interest between the national tourist boards. However, in recent years both Scotland and Wales received powers to undertake their own overseas promotion. The English Tourist Board (ETB) and the BTA both reported to the Department of Trade and Industry (changed to the Department of Employment in 1985, to the Department of Heritage in 1992, and then to the Department of Culture, Media and Sport). The Scottish and Wales Tourist Boards (STB and WTB) report to the Scottish Office and the Welsh Office respectively. Britain's offshore holiday islands each have small, relatively independent boards reporting directly to their island governments.

The twin roles of promotion and development are effective tools with which to shape the supply of tourism in the British Isles. On the promotion side, the national boards in Britain are charged to promote their own countries within the UK (and increasingly overseas) and have backup research and advisory powers.

For development, the boards were given the responsibility of providing and encouraging the provision and improvement of tourist facilities and amenities, although the financial incentives attached to this function have been withdrawn from the UK.

With the changes in the perception of the role of the public sector and in preparation for the devolution of power to Scotland and Wales, the tourist boards across the British Isles have been scrutinized. Scotland has undergone considerable restructuring of public agency responsibility for tourism in the 1990s with the Scottish Tourist Board changing its role and enterprise agencies taking responsibility for tourism development. In England the ETB was replaced in 1999 by the English Tourism Council (ETC), with planning rather than marketing responsibilities, as part of a rational strategy to stimulate tourism investment in the new millennium.

2 *Regional and local level* A regional tourist board (RTB) structure that reflects the increasing emphasis of funding devolved to the regions across the British Isles supports the national tourist boards. There are eleven RTBs in England, and three regional tourism companies in Wales. In Scotland, a major restructuring at the regional level has given rise to over eighteen Area Tourist Boards and development powers to the local enterprise councils. At the local level, local authorities (county and district councils) have considerable tourism powers available for promotion and development.

Summary

Britain is a major generator of both domestic and international tourism. Demand for tourism has grown rapidly since the Second World War for reasons which are rooted in the social and economic development of the countries concerned. Around 60 per cent of the British population now take a holiday in any one year but, even so, there is a hard core of those who do not travel. The majority of domestic tourism trips are to the UK mainland. Demand by residents of Britain for holidays abroad has increased steadily since the Second World War and the UK is consistently one of the top world tourism generators. A combination of economic circumstances and the response of the travel industry has converted suppressed demand into effective demand for holidays abroad. Britain is a major recipient of overseas tourists on the global scene and this demand is influenced by the relative strength of currencies, the health of the economy, special events and the marketing activities of tourist organizations.

The British Isles comprise a rich variety of landscapes and weather conditions. Physically, the three main zones are the highland zone, the uplands and the lowlands, and the climate is tempered by maritime conditions. The main components of tourist supply in Britain are a diverse group of attractions from national parks to theme parks, a wide accommodation base focused on the coasts and in the major cities and a comprehensive transport network internally, as well as international gateways of global significance, including the major innovation of the Channel tunnel. Tourism in Britain is administered by a number of tourist boards each with marketing and development powers, though their roles are being reviewed.

Case study

Strategic planning for destinations: Bournemouth's tourism strategy

Tourism destinations are increasingly thinking about developing long-term strategies, as the market becomes more competitive. Strategies for destinations need careful design and development as we are dealing with living, breathing communities where the interests of local businesses, local people and local authorities all have their part to play. Of course, the development of a successful strategy provides a number of advantages:

● a guiding set of objectives for all *stakeholders* to work towards
● an agreed set of aims for the future direction of the destination
● identifiable roles and responsibilities for all involved
● a set of standards against which the success of the plan can be gauged.

Above all, a strategic plan gives the destination a sense of purpose and provides a competitive edge against other destinations that may not have developed a well thought out marketing and planning strategy.

A critical key to a successful strategy is to ensure that all those involved in tourism are consulted, and feel that they have an input into the process – an approach known as 'inclusion'. Often such planning exercises are led by the local authority, simply because their remit is to have an overview of tourism development and marketing for a destination.

In 1999, Bournemouth, a successful resort on the south coast of England, embarked upon just such an exercise by circulating everyone in the tourism sector with a copy of the document that appears in Figure 7.1. Over 1200 such documents were circulated, followed by an open forum where the shape of the plan was discussed. The nine themes that formed the core of the consultation were:

1 Research and performance measurement.
2 Product/resort development.
3 Raising standards.
4 Protecting the environment.
5 Attracting visitors.
6 Visitor information.

7 Improving the profile of tourism locally.
8 Tourism organizations.
9 Funding.

(This case study appears with the permission of Bournemouth Tourism.)

Developing a New Tourism Strategy for Bournemouth: Industry Consultation

Time for a New Tourism Strategy?

The Bournemouth Marketing Plan has been implemented successfully over five years bringing new visitors, new investment and a great deal of positive publicity for the town. It is time to review our approach and plan new initiatives.

the trends are with us ...

over the past five years, Bournemouth has outperformed other resorts in visitor trends, occupancy and private sector investment. High value markets such as overseas visitors and conferences have grown. We are well placed to face the challenges ahead but there are threats too ~ transport policy, new attractions in the major conurbations, increased competition ...

re-positioning accomplished ?

Five years ago Bournemouth was described by comedians as "the place old people go ~ to visit their parents". Harpers and Queen magazine described us as "the next coolest city on the planet". But the wider public takes longer to convince and we still need to work on re-positioning. It's important to include the "grey" market in our target groups ~ but they are getting "younger" all the time and we must avoid reminding them too much of their parents.

a consistent brand and identity ?

We have made good progress in developing brand values which combine quality and vitality. The Bournemouth tourism logo has been developed to convey this message and we have stuck with it for three years, so it is **beginning** to work. The next step is for more local organisations and businesses to adopt it ~ the Council needs to make maximum use of this visual identity if we are serious about single-minded marketing for the town.

the snowball effect

Success breeds success and the conspicuous high performance of our leading tourism businesses is an inspiration to others. Interest for investment is buoyant and the Council needs clear objectives and priorities to make the best of this.

the interactive economy

A strong tourism sector supports successful retailing, which serves local residents well and makes Bournemouth a popular choice for other business investment. Our recent success in the conference sector is clearly due to quality facilities, good accommodation stock and a wide range of restaurants / nightlife.

The language schools and University flourish in an environment of lively activity. And everyone appreciates our award-winning gardens, beaches and leisure facilities. Bournemouth is more than the sum of its parts and the success of all sectors will remain interdependent.

small firms, key people

The Bournemouth product is only as good as its weakest link. We have a generally excellent product but all businesses need to improve constantly to stay ahead of the competition. That is why this Strategy puts a greater emphasis on business support and particularly on developing the skills of key people.

campaigns for the future

A new format Bournemouth Guide is planned for the Year 2000, supported by promotional campaigns which will make more use of direct mail and new technology. Market segmentation is being developed to help target our resources in the most effective way.

Following our initial consultations, the main themes which emerged are:

Quality assurance ~

Bournemouth sees itself as a high quality destination but visitors booking "blind" need independent assurance, particularly of accommodation standards.

Distinctiveness ~

Too many towns are offering the same shops, attractions and restaurants. Bournemouth's priority should now be to develop distinctive products, image and cultural activity.

Partnership ~

The Council, tourism, entertainment and retail sectors need to work even more closely together, in a structured partnership. A "business levy" could be considered to achieve this.

Market intelligence ~

There is need to further improve our information on target markets to achieve more effective marketing.

Figure 7.1 Bournemouth tourism consultation document

Overview of the Industry

It is clear to most observers that the changes experienced in the tourism industry over the past couple of decades are merely a prelude to the challenges the future will bring. Ever increasing customer expectations; a more complex and fast changing marketing environment and increasing pressure on limited resources will all impact upon the ability of Bournemouth's Tourism industry to prosper in the next millennium. Future success will ultimately depend upon our ability to understand these issues and manage our resources to respond to the opportunities and threats they will inevitable bring.

In recognising many of these issues and the strategic role that tourism plays in delivering the corporate aim of 'providing a framework for the sustainable economic, environmental and social development of the Borough' the Council is seeking to publish a new Tourism Strategy to ensure that the industry's contribution to that aim is maintained and enhanced. In effect the role of the strategy is to set the working agenda for our tourism industry over the next 5+years.

Value of Tourism

The 1995 Cambridge study **The economic impact of tourism in Bournemouth**' provided volume and value statistics that clearly demonstrated the strategic importance of tourism to the borough and its value to the wider economies of Dorset and Southern region. (N.B. day trips are defined as those involving a round trip of 20 miles or more and a visit of at least 3 hours). Some key facts regarding tourism in Bournemouth are summarised in the following tables:

Volume & value of tourism	Trips	Nights	Spend
Staying Visitors	1,278,000	8,186,000	£313 million
Day Visitors	4,237,000		£58 million
Total	5,515,000	direct spend	£365 million
		indirect spend	£114 million
	total spend		£480 million

Employment in Tourism by sector	Direct	Indirect	Total
Accommodation	6962	2131	6835
Retail/Shops	1346	277	1623
Restaurants/Pubs	2816	738	3544
Attractions/Ent	1165	360	1525
Transport	213	36	336
Total:	12,588	3,841	16,429

Expenditure by Sector (£000's)	UK staying Visitor	Overseas Visitor	Day Visitor	Total (%)
Accommodation	£111,909(56%)	£36,687(16%)		£147,304(40%)
Retail/Shops	£32,687(16%)	£24,392(21%)	£13,393(26%)	£70,473(19%)
Catering	£29,977(15%)	£20,561(18%)	£23,521(45%)	£74,059(20%)
Attractions/Ent	£11,207(16%)	£23,631(21%)	£6,131(12%)	£40,969(11%)
Transport	£14,695(7%)	£8,959(8%)	£8,749(17%)	£32,403(9%)
Total:	£199,475(55%)	113,939 (31%)	£51,794(14)	£365,208 (100%)

How Can You Help?

To succeed, the Strategy must be 'inclusive,' meeting the needs of the wider tourism industry (not only leisure, business and language tourism), while addressing the concerns and requirements of the local population - which necessarily requires wider consultation. This document has been published as part of that consultation process, to provide you with an opportunity to make your opinions known and shape the future direction of tourism in Bournemouth.

To provide focus for this process, three 'strategy development' meetings were organised by tourism officers in August and September and were attended by representatives of the accommodation, attractions, retail, entertainment, conference, transport and education sectors. At these sessions a variety of tourism issues were discussed under the following topic headings.

- **Where we are today?**
- **Where we are going & Where do we want to be?**
- **How do we get there?**

The key themes arising from these meetings have been summarised in the nine sections that follow and you are invited to add your comments, outlining any suggestions you may have concerning these subjects, in the space provided. We would be particularly pleased to receive additional views concerning issues that may have been overlooked together with your suggested priorities for future action.

Please return this form or your written submissions by 28th April to:

Rm 1, Bournemouth Tourism, Westover Road, Bournemouth BH1 2BU.

Some of the Current & Future Issues Affecting Tourism that the New Strategy should address

Legal & Political Issues
- *New Government 'tourism strategy' outlining ETB's future role/structure*
- *Revision of Tourist Board Boundaries and role of Regional Development Agencies*
- *Minimum Wage/New Deal legislation*
- *Environmental issues (Local Agenda 21 considerations on sustainability/green issues)*
- *Accommodation Grading Issues*
- *Local Government Review*
- *Disabled Access legislation*
- *Health & Safety*
- *Visa / Immigration issues impacting upon language students*

Economic Issues
- *Current 'short term' threat of domestic recession*
- *Recession spreading from Far East affecting 'new markets'*
- *The EURO and its effect on tourism within the European community*

Cultural Issues
- *Important issues arise regarding overseas and ethnic minority marketing*
- *Product development aspects (arts, festivals etc)*

Technical Issues
- *Improved road network from Midlands (Newbury bypass)*
- *Developing Airport links*
- *Media fragmentation*
- *Information technology developments*
- *Media Fragmentation*
- *Transport Policies*
- *Planning Policies*

Social Issues
- *Ageing domestic population*
- *Continued changing family profile - especially one parent families*
- *Polarisation of population into money rich -time poor and time rich - money poor.*
- *Increase in environmental concern and soft/passive leisure pursuits.*

Competitors
- *New 'non traditional' destinations (e.g. towns, cities and rural areas)*
- *New resort products (Oasis, Centreparks) and huge investment in traditional holidayparks.*
- *Overseas competitors threatening Short Break as well as traditional markets*
- *Travel Lodge / Budget Hotel chains*

Distribution Channels
- *IT developments (internet) accelerating challenge to traditional information delivery channels.*
- *Increased use of travel / centralised agents for purchase of domestic products by domestic consumers*

Trends
- *UK Short Breaks increasing at expense of long term holidays*
- *Growth in domestic market small*
- *Growth from overseas increasing*
- *Seaside Tourism still in decline but representing 40% of UK holiday market*
- *Late Booking*
- *Growth in Group Travel*
- *Growth in Self - Catering holidays*
- *Increase in additional holidays*
- *Reduction in repeat visits as markets widen*

1. RESEARCH & PERFORMANCE MEASUREMENT

Reliable research is a precursor for effective marketing and subsequent performance measurement. This issue is seen as a major weakness across the resort, with current studies providing interesting statistical information but failing to meet wider industry information requirements concerning the attitudes, aspirations and requirements of visitors and non visitors. There is broad support for the development of a stronger, more integrated research regime.

Which specific areas of activity do you feel require additional or new research and how might these be conducted and funded?

2. PRODUCT/RESORT DEVELOPMENT

While it was acknowledged that our resort will enter the new millennium in good order, compared to our traditional domestic competitors, concern was raised, particularly from the accommodation sector, about the deterioration of buildings in some areas and the detrimental affect this had on their businesses. The need to spread the benefits of tourism and new development more evenly throughout the resort, the closure of facilities outside of 'the main season' and transport and parking problems throughout the resort were also raised. The criteria applied by the council for approving, prioritising and encouraging new investment was also raised with the retail sector especially concerned about the affect of out of town shopping developments on the existing fabric of Bournemouth's town centre. The Council's role in encouraging and developing Events and Festivals was also noted.

Please detail areas of concern relating to product development and any suggestions you may have for future attractions including events that would improve Bournemouth's offer to attract visitors?

3. RAISING STANDARDS

Improving competitiveness centred mainly on the resort environment and the need for the accommodation sector to upgrade their facilities as customer expectations continue to rise. Training, both in customer hospitality and marketing practice was considered an important issue and the subject of compulsory grading for accommodation providers received strong support.

How might we encourage investment in training and should grading be an issue that is extended beyond the accommodation sector? How might this be applied?
Should we set a date in the future for all accommodation to be part of the National grading schemes?

4. PROTECTING THE ENVIRONMENT

Bournemouth has been credited with being the 'world's cleanest and greenest resort' and consistently wins accolades for environmental practice. However, it is clear that political pressure will increasing be applied to the tourism industry with regard to environmental protection issues, with traffic reduction through the encouragement of greater use of alternative 'greener' transport high on the government's agenda. The development of visitor management plans to reduce visitor pressure in certain areas by spreading the benefits of tourism is another recurring theme with customers developing an increasing understanding and expectation of good environmental practice.

How might Bournemouth build on its reputation of sound environmental practice and encourage individual businesses to become 'greener'? What should visitor management procedures include? How might car dependency be reduced? How might Bournemouth increase its competitive advantage by furthering green issues?

5. MARKETING COMMUNICATIONS (ATTRACTING VISITORS)

Improving and strengthening marketing communications will be an essential element of the emerging strategy and many issues were raised about the current promotional programme. There was a concern that too much activity concentrated on the 18-30 market at the expense of 'traditional' sectors. The need to identify key market segments and develop compelling propositions based on research was highlighted with the development of a comprehensive electronic (Internet) marketing and information delivery strategy considered overdue. Bookability issues and observed telephone response problems were also raised. Finance for marketing and the apparent lack of support for resort marketing initiatives from non accommodation sectors and the absence of a strategy for attracting day visitors also gave cause for concern.

How might Bournemouth increase awareness among potential visitors and which segments of our various markets should we be addressing collectively? What image should we be projecting, through which means and how might this be funded? How can IT help in any of these processes?

6. MARKETING COMMUNICATIONS (INFORMING VISITORS WHEN HERE)

The location of the Visitor Information Bureau, resort signage and the indifferent distribution of a plethora of publications lacking visual integration have all been raised as causes for review. It was observed there was a lot of information encouraging visitors to leave the resort and that little control was evident.

How might we improve the provision of in-resort information and what information is lacking?

7. IMPROVING TOURISM'S PROFILE (LOCALLY)

The accommodation sector feel quite strongly that the value of leisure tourism, in particular, was underplayed by the retail sector and it was considered that more could be done to raise the profile of the industry locally and to explain its benefits in terms of the economy, leisure, social and cultural provision. There was also concern that the non statutory status of tourism might inevitably lead to further reductions in council support.

What steps might be taken to raise tourism's profile and reputation within Bournemouth among the wider constituency of residents, councillors, industry and commerce ?

8. TOURISM REPRESENTATIONAL STRUCTURES

Clearly tourism covers more than holidaymakers and there was some discussion about the council's role in related markets including: day trippers for leisure and shopping, conference/business travel and language education. Historically Bournemouth Tourism's focus has been the 'staying' leisure market, working in partnership with the accommodation sector, with an expectation that tourism promotional activity will provide umbrella support in terms of image and awareness for other markets. Bournemouth has achieved a high level of input into national strategies and for raising the awareness of issues affecting the local industry.

Should Bournemouth Tourism's remit be extended to cover other markets, where can additional resources be found and how might current representational structures be affected ?
Is Bournemouth Tourism the 'natural agency' for executing wider tourism marketing programmes and should there be a more fundamental review of representational structures within the resort ?
Can our high national profile help in greater recognition for achieving 'Beacon Status' for Bournemouth Council ?

9. FUNDING

Funding for marketing activity is a central issue, with the accommodation sector keen to encourage greater financial participation from other sectors of the industry to support and increase resort promotion and research activity. Political pressure is reducing the ability of local government to co-fund existing tourism marketing activity. Sponsorship, accommodation commission earnings, increased income from advertising in publications, improved sales performance within the Visitor Information Bureau and telephone charges are all revenue generating activities currently being explored to maintain existing activity but cannot address the need to fund broader marketing activity beyond leisure tourism. Government proposals that might allow councils to place a levy on business rates to provide additional local funding provides an interesting solution and while this option received interest there was discussion concerning how this resource would be deployed for the benefit of all if administered by what was perceived as an accommodation focused business unit.

Do you have any suggestions that might address the present and future marketing communications funding requirements?
How might funds be better allocated to benefit all Bournemouth's tourism markets?

Please return this form or your written submissions by 28th April to:

Rm 1, Bournemouth Tourism, Westover Road, Bournemouth BH1 2BU.

8

The tourism geography of England and the Channel Islands

The South

Tourism in the British Isles is heavily concentrated in southern England where London dominates the pattern as a business and tourism centre of world significance. This is particularly the case for overseas visitors. The region is the UK's main gateway for all modes of transport, and is also a major concentration of population, wealth and commercial activity. This is one reason why it is seen as the UK's premier tourist-generating area, but also one of the most congested for both air and surface transport in the UK.

London is the focus of national communications, with the main railway termini (also the Channel tunnel terminal), coach interchange and the destination of the busiest English motorways. It is circled by airports (Heathrow, Gatwick, Stansted, London City Airport, and Luton) which are fundamental to the international network of air services.

Until the proposed single authority comes into force, London includes thirty-four local authorities which have their own strategies for tourism. This makes the task of the London Tourist Board in co-ordinating public and private sector activities a difficult one. The most important of these authorities are:

● The City – the ancient nucleus, now a major international finance centre
● The City of Westminster – the nation's administrative centre
● The Royal Borough of Kensington and Chelsea.

Both overseas and domestic tourists as well as day visitors flock to London's museums, historic buildings and many other attractions. London's appeal lies in the ceremonial and architectural heritage of its imperial past, its purpose-built tourist attractions, shopping and nightlife. For example, most of the national museums and art galleries are located in London – notably the Victoria and Albert Museum, the Science Museum and the Natural History Museum in South Kensington, the National Maritime Museum in Greenwich, and both the Tate Gallery and the National Gallery. In the last ten years a range of purpose-built attractions have been developed including:

● The Museum of the Moving Image
● The Football Association Premier League Hall of Fame, showcasing soccer
● The London Aquarium
● Rock Circus.

The millennium has provided London with a major boost in investment for tourist attractions. Millennium developments include:

- The Millennium Dome at Greenwich
- The London Eye on the South Bank of the River Thames opposite the Houses of Parliament
- The Millennium Bridge
- London Zoo's Millennium Conservation Centre.

Tourism does add to the capital's congestion, especially in the central area, where most of the attractions and accommodation are found. Efforts are being made to 'spread the load' to less well-known attractions outside central London, such as the former Docklands to the east (see the case study at the end of this chapter). Many of London's boroughs are important secondary centres of tourism in their own right (Islington is a good example here), while others see tourism as problematic and restrict tourism initiatives through development control (Westminster is often quoted as an example). Tourist pressure is a particular problem for London's historic buildings, but set against this is the fact that tourism contributes to London's economy through spending and jobs. It also helps to support the West End theatres, shops and department stores, and other amenities that Londoners enjoy. The capital is also the setting for many special events in the sporting and arts calendar which draw hundreds of thousands of visitors (notably the Notting Hill Carnival, Wimbledon, soccer finals and cricket and rugby matches).

Business and conference tourism is also focused on London and while there are a number of purpose-built facilities – the Barbican Conference Centre, the Queen Elizabeth II Conference Centre, Olympia and Earl's Court – much of the business and conference tourism activity takes place in the capital's hotels. Most of the larger hotels have conference and business facilities. Despite this, there is a shortage of accommodation in London and new developments have been built to address this problem, notably in the budget hotel sector and in converted buildings such as the former County Hall.

Outside London, the South is covered by two regional tourist boards (the South-East and Southern). Throughout the South the countryside is an important tourist resource and has received protection from the sprawl of London and other cities. Areas of outstanding natural beauty (ASONB) include the Chilterns and the North Downs, where country parks, picnic sites and trails focus visitor pressure. Tourist attractions include:

- St Albans Cathedral
- Highclere Castle
- Woburn Abbey – one of the first stately homes to attract the mass market by providing attractions
- The stately homes of Luton Hoo, Blenheim Palace and Knebworth

- Whipsnade Wild Animal Park
- Transport features such as the Grand Union Canal.

To the west, the Thames flows through several towns which feature prominently on the excursion circuit from London, notably Oxford, where the university's colleges and other important historic buildings, libraries and museums are the main attraction. In Oxford the conflict between tourist pressure and the historic townscape is recognized but as yet unresolved. Henley is a small town, famous for its regatta, and Windsor further downstream is a classic case study of the tension between tourism and local interests. Windsor's key attractions – associated with royalty over the centuries – are the Castle and St George's Chapel. Windsor, due to its proximity to London, is inundated with coaches in the summer months. Other attractions in the Thames Valley are Ascot racecourse and boating activities on the region's rivers and canals.

South-east England comprises Kent, Surrey, and East and West Sussex. The Kent countryside is studded with hop gardens, oast houses and windmills. Many of the hop farms and vineyards are open to the public. However, the 'Garden of England' has been the focus of considerable development pressure in association with the Channel tunnel and its rail link to London and the demand for 'out of town' shopping. Here new developments include the Blue Water leisure and shopping centre – the largest in Europe. The Channel ports face severe competition from the Channel tunnel and, to mitigate the loss of jobs, Dover has developed a major themed attraction (The White Cliffs Experience) and the Historic Dockyard at Chatham has been adapted to become an important tourist attraction. Although many of the coastal towns of Kent are attractive centres of tourism (Broadstairs, Ramsgate, Whitstable, Herne Bay) or historic and important resorts (Margate), the industrialization of areas such as the Thames estuary, conflicts with tourism and the area faces competition from northern France.

Inland, there are historic buildings such as Hever Castle and Leeds Castle – major tourist attractions and conference venues – as well as market towns that are shopping and historic centres such as:

- Ashford – now given added importance as a Channel rail terminal
- Tonbridge with its Norman castle
- Royal Tunbridge Wells with its chalybeate spa
- The village of Chiddingstone, wholly owned by the National Trust.

At Canterbury the cathedral and the themed 'Canterbury Tales' exhibition recalling its importance as a centre of pilgrimage are a major attraction for domestic and overseas visitors. A steam railway runs on Romney Marsh.

Westwards along the coast in Sussex, historic towns such as Rye compete for attention with the large well-established resorts of Eastbourne, Brighton, Hove, Littlehampton,

Worthing and Bognor Regis. Brighton in particular has been successful in attracting a younger clientele while other resorts have declined. In addition to the usual holiday attractions, Brighton has the Royal Pavilion, a marina and a conference centre, and is the stage for cultural events such as the Brighton Film Festival. Similarly, Hastings has developed themed attractions – the 1066 Story, Smugglers' Adventure, Shipwreck Heritage Centre and a Sealife Centre – in an attempt to gain new visitors. The coast is also an important natural and scenic resource, protected by Heritage Coast designation (as at Seven Sisters) and with natural features such as Chichester harbour.

Chichester is one of a number of historic towns in the area with its cathedral and Festival Theatre. Arundel has a castle and a cathedral in a spectacular setting, while inland, in Surrey, Guildford is an important regional centre and focus for business tourism. Nearby are historic houses – Polesdon Lacey and Clandon Park – and a number of large theme parks located to take advantage of the motorway ring around London. Legoland, Chessington World of Adventures and Thorpe Park are examples.

Hampshire and Dorset are experiencing a resurgence of cross-Channel ferry traffic as companies develop routes in the western Channel to counter the competition from the Channel tunnel. Services to France operate from Portsmouth, Southampton and Poole. Features include:

1 Portsmouth has a major regeneration of its harbour area for the millennium to create an international maritime leisure complex which focuses on England's naval heritage where visitors can see historic ships from different eras – the *Victory*, the *Mary Rose* and the *Warrior*.
2 Adjacent to Portsmouth is the resort of Southsea with its fairground, the Pyramids leisure pool, Sea Life Centre and the D-Day Museum.
3 The Bournemouth conurbation (embracing Poole and Christchurch) is the major resort in the region with one of the largest concentrations of tourist accommodation in the country. Bournemouth has survived successfully as a premier resort into the twenty-first century by updating its image and providing a major International Conference Centre, Oceanarium, and the launching of events and festivals. Poole is set on one of the largest natural harbours in the country. Its historic quay and Waterfront Museum complement the boating and watersports facilities of a tourist centre which is also a growing commercial port.
4 Swanage is an attractive, small family resort backed by the scenic Purbeck Hills.
5 Other tourist attractions include Marwell Zoo, Broadlands House and Paultons Park.
6 To the west of Southampton are a number of sailing centres (as at Lymington and Christchurch) and Beaulieu where the National Motor Museum is housed.

7 The most important feature is the New Forest, an area of heath, woods and grazing land. It was designated as a national park in 1999 but whether this will cope with the increasing numbers of visitors, mostly casual day trippers, is still questioned and the forest is subject to a series of management plans (see the second case study at the end of this chapter).
8 The region has many historic towns and cities – notably Winchester (with INTECH 2000, a hands-on learning centre), Dorchester, Wimborne, Sherborne and Bridport.
9 To the south, the Isle of Wight is an important holiday destination with several family resorts, notably Ryde and Shanklin, and new developments focusing on the island's many dinosaur finds. It is linked to the mainland by a number of car and passenger ferry services.
10 To the west of Bournemouth is the countryside of Thomas Hardy's novels and the resorts of Lyme Regis and Weymouth. Weymouth is a historic resort with twentieth-century attractions including a Timewalk exhibition and speciality shopping at Brewer's Quay.
11 The Dorset coast is a classic fieldwork area for geography and geology, and receives many educational visits attracted by such features as Chesil Beach and Lulworth Cove.

The South-West

The South-West Peninsula, consisting of Cornwall, Devon and Somerset, has the valuable tourist resources of two attractive coastlines, fine scenery and a mild, sunny climate (which has given rise to such slogans as 'The Cornish Riviera' and more recently 'The English Riviera'). Formerly the region suffered from remoteness, but the M5 motorway and increased car ownership means that it continues to be the most popular tourist region for the British tourist. Tourism is important for employment and income generation, although seasonality is a problem. The pressures of tourism are particularly acute in Cornwall, which has a separate cultural identity, high unemployment with the demise of its traditional industries, and a peripheral location.

The countryside of the South-West contains two national parks with their associated facilities for visitors:

● Dartmoor (with its treeless moorland and the granite masses or 'tors')
● Exmoor (a gentler, more wooded landscape).

There are also several ASONB including the Mendips and Quantocks. The countryside is a major attraction of the region with spectacular features such as the Cheddar Gorge and Glastonbury Tor, which dominates the Somerset Levels. Many of the villages with their craft workshops are linked by a series of themed trails. Perhaps the best known of these is the Tarka Country trail in north-west Devon which is held up as a classic example of sustainable tourism in rural areas.

The rural South-West has pioneered activity and farm holidays. The region has many market towns which also act as regional tourism centres – Truro, Taunton, Barnstaple, Tavistock, Marlborough, Salisbury and Wells. Glastonbury has special significance as an ancient centre of pilgrimage and, in more recent times, as a destination for 'new age' enthusiasts and music festival devotees.

The region's other attractions include:

- the artificial lakes of Chew Valley and Blagdon
- castles such as Powderham and Tintagel
- Bodmin Moor – which like Tintagel and Glastonbury, has associations with the legends of King Arthur
- theme parks (such as Longleat, and Flambards)
- industrial heritage sites such as the Wheal Martyn Museum, Charlestown Shipwreck Centre and Morwellham Quay
- gardens such as the Lost Gardens of Heligan in Cornwall, where the climate favours subtropical vegetation
- abbeys (Buckfast and Sherborne)
- caves (at Wookey Hole and Cheddar)
- themed accommodation developments (as at Somerwest World, Minehead)
- the Eden Project at St Austell is being developed as a landmark attraction focused on ecology and conservation
- prehistoric sites at Avebury and Stonehenge are of international importance.

Major tourist centres include Exeter, which is an important regional capital with a cathedral and Roman remains. Bristol has developed a tourism industry based on business travel, contemporary museums (for example, the Exploratory Hands-On Science Centre, Science World and Wildsceen World) and its maritime history. Bath has rejuvenated its Roman spa and is visited for its fine Georgian architecture, cultural events and shopping. Plymouth has a new aquarium and many maritime connections – its large natural harbour is a sailing centre.

The coast of the South-West is perhaps its best known feature through generations of British seaside holidays. Much of the region's varied coastline is protected by heritage coast policies, or National Trust ownership. This is to protect the coast not only from industrial development but also from insensitive tourist development. The coastline provides many recreational opportunities such as long-distance coastal paths, water sports (especially surfing), and sailing on the estuaries. In Devon the three resorts of Torquay, Brixham and Paignton are each very different and cater for differing markets, but are promoted together as the English Riviera. The resorts have been the focus for a tourism development plans and have the English Riviera

Conference Centre, which was built to help diversify into new markets. Smaller resorts in Devon are Seaton, Beer, Teignmouth, Dawlish and Exmouth. Cornwall's Celtic heritage provides a contrast to neighbouring Devon, and the Cornish coastline is spectacular and includes the attractive features of Land's End and St Michael's Mount. There are many tourist developments and resorts. These include:

- the large family resorts of Falmouth and Penzance
- the surfing beach of Bude
- the more modern developments at Newquay
- harbours at Padstow and St Ives (with its literary and artistic associations, now focused on the Tate Gallery and the Barbara Hepworth Museum)
- the small traditional Cornish fishing villages of Mevagissey, Polperro, Fowey and Looe.

The north Devon coast has beautiful scenery and good surfing beaches. The major resort is Ilfracombe, and smaller resorts include Clovelly, Lynmouth and Lynton. Off the coast is Lundy Island, a wildlife reserve. The Somerset coast has the two large resorts of Minehead and Burnham-on-Sea as well as the small and attractive harbour town of Watchet. Weston-super-Mare is a large and successful resort on the shores of the Bristol Channel, which has invested in new initiatives such as the Tropicana Pleasure Beach.

East Anglia

Facing the North Sea and within easy reach of London, East Anglia is well placed to attract continental visitors through Stansted Airport and the ports of Harwich and Felixstowe. This region largely escaped the developments of the Industrial Revolution and has preserved many of its rural traditions. Predominantly low-lying, the landscape is nonetheless varied, with market towns such as Ipswich, King's Lynn (with its 'North Sea Haven' interpreting the environment), Bury St Edmunds and Lavenham, which are well endowed with historic buildings. The major centres for tourism are:

- Cambridge, with its historic townscape and university in a beautiful riverside setting
- Ely, famous for its cathedral
- Colchester, with Roman remains, castle and museums
- the historic town and ancient regional capital of Norwich.

East Anglia's countryside was made famous by Constable's paintings which portray the area around Dedham and Flatford along the river Stour. The countryside is dotted with windmills and bulb fields, some of which are open as tourist attractions.

Although at first sight the East Anglian coastline may seem uniform, it is in fact very varied. For example, the East

Suffolk coastline is a designated heritage coast and has an internationally renowned bird reserve. The region has the major historic resorts of Great Yarmouth, Clacton and Southend as well as several smaller resorts such as Cromer and Hunstanton, and Sheringham and Holt which are linked by a coastal steam railway. On the Essex marshes and river estuaries are yachting centres such as Burnham-on-Crouch and Maldon. The Essex coastline has suffered from unplanned second-home development in the past due to its good transport links to London. This has also meant that many of the Essex resorts have become retirement and day-trip destinations for east London.

The Norfolk Broads to the west of Great Yarmouth are perhaps Britain's best known area for water-based recreation and holidays. There are over 200 kilometres of navigable waterways and over 2000 powered craft for hire. However, the commercial success of tourism in the area has been achieved at a cost to the environment, and in conflict with agriculture which makes heavy demands on water supplies in an area with one of the lowest rainfalls in Britain.

Problems include:

- detergents, human sewage, discarded fuel and a lowered water table has upset the ecological balance
- banks are eroded and wildlife disturbed by the passage of boats
- the sprawl of boatyards and development despoil the landscape.

In an effort to balance the conflicting demands of tourism, agriculture and wildlife, the area is now carefully managed by the Broads Authority as a quasi-national park.

The Midlands

For most people, the Midlands are associated more with industry than tourism. However imaginative theming of short breaks, investment in attractions and accommodation, and good marketing is attracting tourists and day visitors to the countryside, historic towns and industrial heritage of the region. For example, the Cotswolds to the west are famous for mellow limestone buildings in tourist centres such as Broadway or Chipping Campden. Cannock Chase is an important regional recreational resource located near the Midlands conurbation which is developing facilities for visitors. Other countryside areas include the Malverns, Charnwood and Sherwood Forest, and the Wye Valley near the Welsh border, which attracts canoeing and other activity holidays. Also important for water sports is Rutland Water, an artificial lake in the east of the region.

Of the region's historic towns, the best known is Stratford-on-Avon, which is popular with overseas visitors for its literary associations, underlined by the Royal Shakespeare Theatre. Other important tourist centres in the South and West Midlands are:

- Gloucester and Worcester, with their cathedrals
- the elegant spa town of Cheltenham
- the industrial city of Coventry symbolizing urban recovery after the Second World War
- former fortress-towns of the Welsh Marches (the border country with Wales) such as Hereford, Ludlow and Shrewsbury are noted for their half-timbered 'black and white' architecture.

In the East Midlands, Lincoln is the major tourist centre with a notable cathedral. Nottingham has exploited its association with the legendary Robin Hood, and Leicester is the site of the new National Space Centre. The National Exhibition Centre and National Arenas at the heart of the motorway system enhance Birmingham's importance as a centre for business and event tourism. The region's industrial heritage is now undergoing radical change with the restoration of canals and a new breed of museum such as:

- the Ironbridge Complex which interprets the beginnings of the Industrial Revolution
- the Potteries Museum at Stoke-on-Trent and 'Ceramica' at Burslem showcase the ceramics industry of north Staffordshire
- the Black Country Museum at Dudley.

Important themed attractions, taking advantage of motorway access, include Warwick Castle and the American Adventure near Ilkeston. The resorts of Skegness, Mablethorpe and Cleethorpes on the Lincolnshire coast provide traditional seaside recreation for the industrial cities of the East Midlands.

The North

The northern part of England, which includes four regional tourist boards, is one of contrasts, from industrial heartlands, through the spectacular scenery of national parks, to its bustling resorts. The region also forms an important gateway to Britain for Scandinavian, German and Dutch tourists who enter through the ports of Newcastle and Hull. The scenery of the area is evidenced by the fact that it contains five national parks – which are the focus of tourism and day trips – and a number of areas of outstanding natural beauty.

In many rural upland areas European and British regional funds are supporting the development of farm-based tourism. Tourism and recreation brings income and jobs, supports rural services and stems depopulation, but herein also lie seeds of conflict, as some argue that tourism interferes with farming operations and destroys the very communities that tourists visit. This may occur through the purchase of second homes and the reorientation of rural services towards weekend and summer visitors.

The Lake District National Park is a major tourist area which is intensively managed for tourism and recreation with 'honeypot' areas designed to take pressure (Ambleside and Bowness) along with traffic management and car-parking schemes. Access to the park from the north is through the market town of Penrith, and from the south through the historic town of Kendal. The major centre in the park is Keswick, and there is a national park centre at Brockholes. There are attractions based on the literary associations with Wordsworth and Beatrix Potter. The Lake District is popular for active tourism and recreation – walking, water sports, outdoor pursuits and mountaineering. In the past these activities have interfered with the upland farming regime of the area, but management schemes run by the park's authorities have solved many of these problems. The landscape is on a human scale with attractive towns and villages, fells (low moorland hills) and lakes, each with its own character. Windermere, for example, is intensively used, while remoter lakes and tarns are little visited.

Other tourist areas fringe the Lake District:

1 To the west the coast has golf courses; the AONB of the Solway Firth; the distinctive scenery and wildlife sanctuaries on Morecambe Bay; and historic buildings at Cartmel Priory and Furness Abbey.
2 To the east the Eden Valley is an important angling area within the newly designated AONB of the Northern Pennines, a bleak moorland region with market towns such as Alston, reputedly the highest in England.

The Northern Pennines border the Yorkshire Dales National Park, which is characterized by a relatively gentle land-scape, criss-crossed by limestone walls and dotted with field barns (some converted to shelters for walkers). Touring centres in the park include Richmond, Skipton and Settle, and popular villages such as Malham with its cove and tarn – a spectacular relic of the Ice Age. In and around the park are literary sites linked to the Brontës and also locations associated with popular series on British television. Like its southern neighbour, the Peak District National Park, the dales are popular for outdoor pursuits and field studies. The Settle/Carlisle Railway is a major scenic attraction linking two national parks.

The Peak District Park is an area of moorland, notched by deep valleys as at Dovedale. The White Peak is the southern and central area of limestone dales and crags with important centres such as Matlock and Castleton. The Dark Peak in the north is a more rugged and spectacular area with a number of lakes and reservoirs. The Peak has caverns and mines open to visitors and the industrial heritage is now a major attraction at museums such as the Crich National Tramway Museum. At Matlock Bath the Heights of Abraham is a country park with theme park attractions. Nearby is Alton Towers, one of Britain's most visited theme parks, and Chatsworth House, an important stately home. The main touring centres are at Bakewell, Ashbourne, Matlock and Holmfirth – the latter again home of a popular television series. The spa town of Buxton has revived its opera house and conference facilities.

The North York Moors National Park contains heather-covered, rolling countryside with picturesque villages. There is a spectacular coastline, summits such as Roseberry Topping, and natural features such as the Hole of Horcum, popular with hang-gliders. The North Yorkshire Moors steam railway runs through the park from Pickering to Grosmont.

The region's fifth national park – the Northumberland National Park – lies on the Scottish border and contains Kielder Forest and Kielder Water, both recent additions to the landscape. Hadrian's Wall to the south is of unique historic interest as a Roman military achievement, with associated archaeological attractions. Hadrian's Wall runs from Hexham westwards to Carlisle – an important regional centre, gateway to the Border Country and with many historic buildings.

The coasts of the North embrace major resorts and areas of scenic and conservation interest. Many of the North's resorts have faced the problem of declining traditional markets in nearby industrial cities by investing in new facilities, upgrading accommodation and marketing aggressively to new market segments. Resorts include:

1 Blackpool with its famous Tower jostled by a townscape of tourist facilities and small guest-houses and the famous Pleasure Beach, yet the resort has new attractions such as the Sandcastle Centre.
2 Scarborough is one of Britain's oldest resorts, an elegant town between two bays and its redeveloped Spa Conference Centre now adds a business dimension to its market.
3 The region has a range of smaller resorts (such as Bridlington, Hornsea, Whitby and Filey on the North Sea coast and Morecambe on the less bracing Irish Sea coast).
4 Day-trip centres close to conurbations (such as New Brighton and Southport serving Merseyside, and Whitley Bay for Newcastle).

The undeveloped coast is also an important attraction. Much of the North Yorkshire coast is within the North York Moors National Park. The Northumberland coast is spectacular and much of it is designated as heritage coast. Likewise, Flamborough Head is a designated heritage coast; Holy Island is a historic pilgrimage centre, and both the Farne Islands and Spurn Point are wildlife sanctuaries.

In the region are attractions of national importance, such as Castle Howard, spas such as Harrogate and Ilkley, and historic towns such as Chester, Durham, Beverley and York which attract overseas, domestic and day visitors alike. York, in particular, deserves special mention for the following reasons:

1 It has retained its medieval walls, city gates and street pattern.
2 York Minster is one of Europe's largest Gothic churches.
3 The Jorvik Viking Centre has turned an archaeological site into a visitor attraction.

The industrial heritage is also exploited for tourism. Bradford's tourism industry, based on the woollen textile heritage (with a little help from the Brontës), has been a notable recent example of an imaginative approach to developing tourism. Indeed, the resurgence of tourism-related developments characterises most northern cities. Regional centres such as Newcastle, Liverpool, Hull and Manchester have major tourist developments leading their drive for reinvestment. The Liverpool Garden Festival and Albert Dock schemes, for example, were designed to attract investment in other economic sectors, and Manchester has developed an exhibition centre (the GMex Centre) and an urban heritage park at Castlefield with similar motives. Important developments include:

- Wakefield's coal-mining museum
- Wigan Pier – a successful themed attraction based on life in Victorian England
- Sheffield is developing special-event tourism and hosts the National Centre for Popular Music and the major leisure and shopping complex at Meadow Hall
- Beamish Open Air Museum has many northern buildings and features that have been reassembled together on one site
- Hull hosts 'The Deep' intepreting the life of the oceans and its fishing and whaling heritage
- Doncaster has 'The Earth Centre' for environmental education and research
- Rotherham has 'Magna' a visitor attraction based on British Industry achievements
- The Lowry Centre in Salford showcasing one of the region's most famous painters
- The National Discovery Park in Liverpool.

The offshore islands

The Channel Islands

Lying off the Cherbourg peninsula, the Channel Islands capitalize on their favourable sunny climate, Norman-French traditions and culinary attractions. Jersey and Guernsey are semi-independent states with their own parliaments, tourist boards and low rates of tax, which attract business, an influx of retired people and duty-free shoppers. The islands have attractive coastal scenery, fine beaches (although strong tides and currents are hazardous to bathers) and well-developed tourist facilities. They can be reached by air and also by ferry and hydrofoil services from France and southern England. However, once on the islands, the pressure of traffic is one of tourism's negative impacts.

Jersey

The tourist centre of Jersey is the town of St Helier, with Elizabeth Castle in the bay and Fort Regent Leisure Centre above the town. St Helier has a comprehensive range of tourist accommodation, restaurants and shops, and a new waterfront and marina development. The island's military history is interpreted for visitors at a number of sites and both museums in St Helier and a new themed attraction – the Living Legend – tell the island's story. The island's key attractions are the beaches – the coves in the north, the sweep of St Ouen's Bay in the west and the large beach at St Brelade's Bay, with the cove at Portelet in the south. Jersey has lost market share to Mediterranean destinations and has a new tourism strategy to claw back tourists. A number of new, budget-priced air services will assist in this goal.

Guernsey

The focus of tourism on Guernsey is St Peter Port. Here accommodation, restaurants and retailing are found. Guernsey's tourist industry is smaller than that of Jersey but again the attraction is the coastal scenery and beaches, augmented by attractions such as butterfly farms, historic forts, museums and wildlife.

Other Channel Islands can be visited for a day from Guernsey or Jersey and some have a limited amount of accommodation. These include Alderney, Herm, Sark and Jethou.

The Isles of Scilly

Off the coast of Cornwall, the Isles of Scilly have a small tourist industry. Accessible by air or ferry from Penzance, they consist of some 200 small islands where the attraction is the mild weather, flora and fauna, and unspoilt maritime scenery. The main island is St Mary's, from which boats serve the other islands.

Summary

England and the offshore islands of the Channel Islands and the Scillies are well endowed with most types of tourist attractions and an increasingly professional approach to their management is evident. Each tourist region comprises a variety of attractions and resources which together give a unique blend. However, across them all common threads can be identified. These include the growth of heritage attractions; the increasing use of rural resources for tourism; the growth of tourism in towns and cities (such as Bradford) which previously have been more commonly associated with industry; and the often-successful attempts of the more traditional resorts to reinvest and attract new markets.

Case study

London Docklands: waterfront regeneration and tourism development

Background

In London Docklands, we have an example of tourism on a local scale, focusing on a small area. On the other hand, this is also one of the world's largest projects for inner-city regeneration, involving the redevelopment of almost 90 kilometres of waterfront, mainly for commer-

cial or residential use. Although tourism has been something of an afterthought rather than part of the original scheme, the new developments attract over 1.5 million visitors a year to a formerly neglected part of London.

As officially designated, London Docklands extends along both banks of the River Thames. As well as Wapping, the Isle of Dogs and the Royal Docks – which are generally regarded as part of the East End – it also includes a substantial area, known as Surrey Quays, extending south of the river from London Bridge to Deptford (see Figure 8.1). Although physically separate, these areas have a shared history of domination by the shipping industry, social deprivation and marginalization from the rest of London.

The first enclosed docks were built in the early 1800s to alleviate the acute congestion of the shipping in the Pool of London (the section of the Thames east of London Bridge) and thus eradicate the pilfering of ship's cargoes that had reached crisis proportions. The last of the Royal Docks – the King George V – was not completed until shortly after the First World War. In the meantime the docks played a major role in Britain's

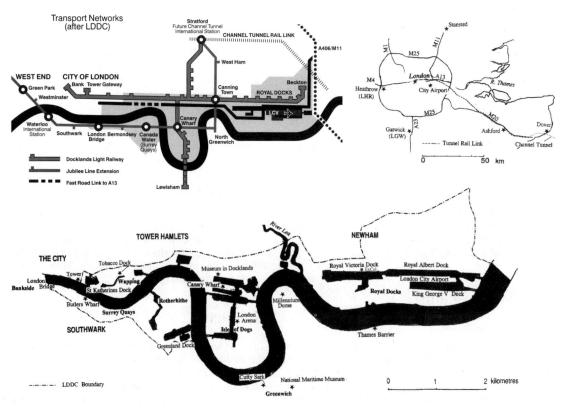

Figure 8.1 London Docklands

overseas expansion and industry grew up nearby, along with low-grade housing to accommodate a vast pool of unskilled labour. The area had few amenities other than 'gin-palaces'. St Saviours Dock in Bermondsey was the setting for one of London's most notorious slums – Jacob's Island – described by Charles Dickens in *Oliver Twist*, while Whitechapel was the location for the 'Jack the Ripper' murders in the 1880s.

Docklands suffered severely from bombing during the Second World War, and although a considerable amount of slum clearance took place in the postwar period, the area remained visually unappealing and was shunned by tourists, partly because it was perceived to be crime-ridden. Also, the docks themselves had high fortress-like walls and security arrangements that prevented public access. The same was true of the waterfront of the Thames itself, an almost unbroken barrier of wharves and warehouses. The River Thames was no longer the transport artery for Londoners that it had been in the eighteenth century. Docklands was not easily accessible by public transport, with few underground and suburban railway services compared with Central London. By the 1960s the enclosed docks had become obsolete due to the introduction of container ships requiring deepwater harbours. As a consequence, the East India, London, St. Katherine and Surrey Docks were closed between 1967 and 1970, followed by the West India, Millwall and Royal Docks in 1981. With the loss of an estimated 50 000 jobs, Docklands faced severe social and economic problems. More than 2200 hectares of wet docks, wharves and warehouses now lay derelict, but the private sector was reluctant to invest and the task of urban renewal was clearly beyond the resources of the local authorities.

The Conservative government then in power was ideologically committed to the use of market forces rather than state intervention to reverse the process of inner city decline. Nevertheless it set up thirteen Urban Development Corporations (UDCs) with wide-ranging powers to purchase land, prepare development plans and provide the necessary infrastructure. The sites were then sold or leased to private developers at market value. The London Docklands Development Corporation (LDDC) was the best known of these public agencies. Also of particular relevance to tourism were those UDCs responsible for large-scale redevelopment of inner-city and waterfront areas in Bristol, Central Manchester and Liverpool. The LDDC was able to overrule any opposition to the scheme from the Labour-controlled local authorities for the area. Part of the Isle of Dogs was designated by the government as an Enterprise Zone, where developers were granted generous tax relief and freedom from the planning controls that normally apply under the Town and Country Planning Acts. With substantial financial backing from a Canadian corporation, this became the focus of a massive new office development project, centred on Canary Wharf.

Transport

Improved accessibility has been crucial to the success of London Docklands as a business venue and as a tourist destination. It has involved the following transport initiatives.

London City Airport (LCY)

This new airport, financed by the private sector, was designed to meet the needs of business executives, at a location much closer to London's financial district than congested Heathrow. However the site, between two of the former Royal Docks, is restricted and was originally intended to be a STOL airport. The introduction of longer-range jet aircraft has enabled LCY to serve a growing number of destinations in Europe, while a costly road scheme has improved access to the City of London and the motorway network.

The Docklands Light Railway (DLR)

This rapid transit system serving the new developments in Docklands was financed by the LDDC, London Transport and the private sector. Elevated above street level, and fully automated, the DLR was a novelty when it was inaugurated in 1987 and soon became a tourist attraction in its own right. However, it has been criticized by commuters for unreliability and the system is not particularly well-connected to the London Underground network.

The Jubilee Line Extension

This is part of the London Underground system, connecting Canary Wharf to the Channel Tunnel Rail Link terminal at Stratford and Waterloo Station. The Jubilee Line therefore improves the accessibility of Docklands and Greenwich, not only in relation to Central London, but also to the national and continental rail networks. Canary Wharf station – itself a masterpiece of civil engineering – is designed to handle 40 000 passengers per hour, almost four times the present capacity of the Docklands Light Railway.

River transport

The Thames nowadays is used much more for leisure than for freight, with a variety of craft used for floating restaurants, corporate entertaining, tour boats and pleasure cruises. Regular river bus services, linking Docklands and Greenwich to the City and Westminster, are environmentally desirable but have so far proved unprofitable, for the following reasons:

1 It is difficult to find suitable craft, which are fast, manoeuvrable and yet produce the minimum of wash.
2 Operating costs per passenger are much higher than for buses.
3 Restrictions on the use of piers by the Port of London Authority, which controls most activities on the river.

One solution might be for riverbus services to be integrated with London's bus, underground and suburban train services, by including them in the 'Travelcard' facility that encourages visitors to use public transport in the off-peak at reduced fares.

Attractions and amenities

London Docklands during the 1980s and 1990s was transformed from an industrial wasteland to a new 'city on the water' dominated by ultramodern business and residential developments. Canary Wharf – boasting London's tallest building – is the flagship of the scheme, and now vies with Frankfurt as one of Europe's most important financial centres. Not only has the City spread eastwards, but also the newspaper publishing industry, formerly based in Fleet Street, has moved to Wapping and the Isle of Dogs. Many former warehouses of architectural merit have found new roles as restaurants, pubs, shops, artist's studios, apartments and museums. Some of the wet docks have become yacht marinas and provide facilities for a variety of water sports. These areas of open water, amounting to some 160 hectares – together with over 27 kilometres of waterfront now open to public access, are perhaps the most attractive feature of the new Docklands. Some 5000 beds have been added to the capital's accommodation stock, including a new youth hostel at Rotherhithe. However, jobs in the hotel and catering sectors probably account for less than 10 per cent of the employment generated by the various development projects. Not all of these have proved to be successful; for example, Tobacco Dock in Wapping was promoted as a Docklands version of Covent Garden, but its future as a leisure shopping centre appears to be uncertain.

Most attractions and amenities in Docklands were designed primarily for use by local residents and the business community. Those of most significance to visitors include:

1 *Leisure and shopping developments* – such as Hay's Galleria, Butler's Wharf and St. Katherine's Dock, which have benefited from their proximity to well-known tourist attractions such as Tower Bridge and the Tower of London.

2 *Conference and exhibition venues* – the most important of these are the London Arena, which is a major venue for concerts and sporting events, drawing audiences from all over the capital, and the ExCel Centre at the Royal Docks, which is expected to rival Earls' Court as an exhibition venue and generate a possible 14 000 jobs.
3 *Heritage attractions* – compared to other areas of Inner London, Docklands has relatively few historic buildings. There are a few eighteenth century churches, but these are far surpassed in tourist appeal by the riverside pubs in Wapping and Rotherhithe, which have traded on their past associations – real or imagined – with smugglers and pirates. More tangible reminders of the area's maritime heritage are the historic ships moored at the quays in St. Katherine's and West India Docks. The Museum in Docklands project brings together materials relating to the development of London's port and its riverside communities from Roman times to the present day. London's role as a passenger terminal for ocean voyages prior to the Second World War is recalled in the project to convert a cruise liner into a floating hotel and maritime museum at South Quay. Both these developments are close to Canary Wharf, providing a much-needed focus for tourism in the area.

Critics of the Docklands project allege that it has failed to benefit the local working-class communities in terms of job opportunities, as most of the latter are in the banking and financial sector. The new riverside apartments have been purchased by highly paid City executives and middle-class professionals, while the *gentrification* of the area is also shown by the type of restaurants and shops which are now proliferating. The opportunity to replan a large part of London on the grand scale has been missed; although there are some interesting examples of modern architecture and engineering, most of the development has been piecemeal and of mediocre design.

In our view, Docklands has the following defects as a tourist destination:

1 It is too spread out and lacks an overall focus. A survey carried out by the LDDC in 1997 revealed that the majority of visitors came simply 'to look around'. The Docklands Light Railway and Canary Wharf – which then did not offer facilities specifically for tourists – were the most popular attractions.
2 Signage for visitors is inadequate, and perhaps because of the vast amount of construction work still taking place, parts of the area are not 'pedestrian-friendly'.
3 Since the demise of the LDDC in 1998, Docklands has been the responsibility of the borough councils of

Southwark, Tower Hamlets and Newham, in association with English Partnerships, with the result that promotion of the area has been ineffective.

4 There is insufficient nightlife for visitors compared to other parts of London – for example, Canary Wharf, a hive of activity by day, is empty after office hours.

Docklands is likely to appeal to the type of visitor who is more interested in the 'new Britain' represented by Terence Conran's Design Museum at Butler's Wharf, than the 'theme park Britain' evident in London's more traditional tourist attractions. It is perhaps more realistic to view Docklands as part of a wider area of London, focused on the riverside developments which are taking place along the south bank of the Thames from Waterloo to the Woolwich Barrier, and which are now within fifteen minutes travelling time from Canary Wharf:

1 To the west of London Bridge lies Bankside, another run-down area which before the Industrial Revolution was the entertainment district for London – attractions here include the Globe Theatre, the Tate Modern Gallery and the Vinopolis wine museum.
2 To the east of the Surrey Docks lies Greenwich, with such well-established tourist attractions as the *Cutty Sark* and the National Maritime Museum, not to mention the publicity generated by the Millennium Dome.

Case study

The New Forest: managing tourism in an environmentally sensitive area

Introduction

The New Forest is an environmentally sensitive area with a unique landscape in Hampshire in the south of England. It is under severe pressure, not only from tourism and recreation, but also from other developments such as housing and transport.

Strictly speaking, the New Forest is neither 'new', nor a 'forest'. The New Forest is an area of open heathland, interspersed with woodland. The geology of the area rendered it relatively infertile and unattractive to early settlers, hence, when William the Conqueror set the area aside in 1079 as a private deer-hunting reserve, it was unsettled open land. William's 'new' hunting forest was much more extensive than the 230 square kilometres that remains as the New Forest Heritage Area, although the area's royal status as Crown land has undoubtedly protected the New Forest from development over the

centuries. Today, the New Forest landscape, flora and fauna are conserved under a variety of pieces of legislation and is set to become a national park in the early years of the millennium.

The scale of tourism

The New Forest is a very popular destination for both staying and day visitors. Visitor pressure in the New Forest arises from the adjacent conurbations of Southampton and Bournemouth and Poole, and the fact that the New Forest is easily accessible on the motorway network. Tourism in the New Forest is estimated to:

- support 3000 jobs in the New Forest area
- contribute £70 million to the local economy
- attract the equivalent of over 7 million visitor days.

The components of tourism

Attractions

The New Forest landscape, flora and fauna is the main attraction for visitors, even though less than half of the Forest is wooded. The Forest has three main landscape areas:

- the Avon Valley to the west, stretching from Salisbury to Christchurch
- the new Forest itself, with its mosaic of open heathland, woodland and villages
- the coast, stretching from Christchurch in the west to Southampton Water.

Aside from the most important attraction of the New Forest landscape and wildlife, there are a range of attractions either in or close to the New Forest. These include:

- Beaulieu – with the National Motor Museum, Palace House and Abbey
- Bucklers Hard – a preserved shipbuilding village
- Breamore House and gardens
- Paulton's Park – a small theme park close to the Forest
- Exbury Gardens
- Eling Tide Mill
- Lyndhurst New Forest Museum and Visitor Centre
- Rockbourne Roman Villa
- a range of wildlife attractions – such as the Owl and Otter Centre
- a range of farm attractions open to families such as Longdown Dairy Farm
- attractive villages with traditional thatched cottages as at Emery Down, Burley and Sway
- the annual New Forest show which is estimated to attract 100 000 visitors a year.

Transport

A key issue is the management of traffic in the New Forest. Most visitors arrive by car, although the New Forest is well served by the main railway line between Weymouth and Waterloo. Traffic management takes the form of a 40-mph speed limit throughout the unfenced roads of the New Forest, and landscaped verges, ditches and ramparts that prevent off-road parking except in over 150 designated parking zones. Until 1999 parking in most of the New Forest was free, but since that date visitors pay a car-parking fee throughout the New Forest. Other forms of transport are also available and include the ever-popular horse riding, cycle hire (mountain bikes have caused damage to parts of the Forest), horse-drawn wagon rides, and regular bus and coach services. These alternative forms of transport to the car are co-ordinated in a series of networks in an attempt to reduce the number of car-borne visitors to the Forest.

Accommodation

Much of the accommodation for visitors to the New Forest is found in the neighbouring resort of Bournemouth. However, the New Forest has a large number of camping and caravan sites providing over 20 000 bed-spaces. Serviced accommodation is in shorter supply, focused in the towns and villages and consisting of traditional bed and breakfast and small hotels/inns providing 4100 bed-spaces. Self-catering cottages and apartments provide a further 600 bed-spaces.

Managing tourism

Burgeoning visitor pressure has meant that a key issue for the New Forest has been the management of visitors and their traffic. The New Forest District Council has regularly surveyed visitor use and has in place a tourism and visitor management strategy for the Forest entitled *Making New Friends* (NFDC, 1996). This followed a 1994 consultation document, controversially entitled *Living with the Enemy* (NFDC, 1994) which mapped out the challenges for the New Forest tourism industry.

Management of tourism in the New Forest is a vitally important issue as tourism could disturb local communities and destroy the sensitive habitats that provide the New Forest's appeal and significance. One of the problems is the plethora of agencies, committees and other bodies involved in the management of the New Forest. These include:

- Hampshire County Council – with a co-ordinating role at county level
- New Forest District Council – the local authority with day-to-day responsibility for the management of all elements of the New Forest and its population
- New Forest Tourism – the local trade association representing over 250 private sector operators
- The Southern Tourist Board – the regional tourism board for the New Forest
- The Forestry Commission – with responsibility for managing the woodlands, but with important recreation and tourism interests
- The Countryside Agency – charged with managing the landscape and recreation in the New Forest
- English Nature – with responsibility for the New Forest flora and fauna
- The National Farmers Union – representing practising farmers in the New Forest
- The Country Landowners Association representing the interests of local landowners
- The Court of Verderers – which administers the Forest's commoners – people who own or rent land and thus have the right to graze animals in the New Forest. This ancient land management system means that around 5000 horses and ponies roam the New Forest and are part of its charm, though they are often to be found on unfenced roads and some are killed each year by traffic.

Clearly with so many interested and legitimate stakeholders, managing the New Forest is problematic, but has been facilitated by the formation of the New Forest Committee to co-ordinate the management tasks. The local authority recognizes the challenge of balancing everyone's interests in their mission statement: 'Our aim is for New Forest District to become a tourism destination where the visitor, tourism industry, local community and environment are in complete harmony, and thus make a significant contribution to improving the quality of life.'

This will be achieved by the tourism strategy for the New Forest that aims to:

- target and regulate visitor flow through appropriate marketing
- integrate all tourism and transportation
- research and ensure strategic information is correct and communicated to visitors
- achieve the best quality of service facility and value for money
- involve the local community
- protect and enhance the quality of the environment
- provide the right experience in the right place.

9

The tourism geography of Scotland, Wales and the Isle of Man

Scotland

Occupying the rugged northern third of Britain, Scotland was never conquered by the Romans, and throughout the Middle Ages it successfully struggled to retain its independence from England. However, a form of the English language became dominant except in the more remote western and northern parts of the country, where Gaelic speech and culture still survive. The Scots developed their own legal system and church. Scottish architecture was influenced by France, so the castles and historic towns look 'foreign' to English visitors. Outside the conurbations of Glasgow and Edinburgh, it is a much less crowded country than England, with plenty of space for outdoor recreation. Two-thirds of the country is mountainous, and the Highlands are the largest area of unspoiled mountain and lake scenery in Western Europe. Many potential visitors are deterred by the reputation of the climate such that, outside the Central Lowlands, leisure tourism is very seasonal. However, the west coast of Scotland in fact enjoys the highest amount of spring sunshine in Britain. Apart from the fine scenery, Scotland can also offer a wealth of folklore and a romantic history – portrayed by Hollywood films in the 1990s. For example, there is a strong interest, even outside English-speaking countries, in the clan system of the Highlands and in places associated with such well-known historical figures as Mary, Queen of Scots, Bonnie Prince Charlie, Robert Burns and Sir Walter Scott.

Scottish tourism is administered by a range of public agencies at national, regional and local level, co-ordinated by the Scottish Tourist Board. The Scottish tourism product is delivered primarily by small businesses and this places a question over the quality of the product at times, and has also held back investment in the sector – Scotland for example has few all-weather developments. Scottish tourism is based on scenery, cultural heritage, folklore and the large ethnic market – especially from Canada. Special interest and activity holidays are also important – particularly those based on fishing, whisky and golf. Scotland's tourists come mainly for leisure purposes, as Scotland was a late entrant into the conference and exhibition market. The overseas market has remained healthy for Scotland, with the USA and Europe providing most of the demand. Most visitors arrive by air as Scotland has no direct ferry access to mainland Europe. Scotland also attracts domestic tourists, of which around one half originate from within Scotland itself. Increasingly, Scotland faces a dilemma: the traditional image of lochs, tartan and heather is inappropriate for the newer forms of tourism developing in Glasgow and Edinburgh and based on short city-break products.

Three main tourism regions can be identified in Scotland, based on differences of geology and culture:

- the Southern Uplands, mainly high moorlands with only a few pockets of lowland
- the Central Lowlands, which is actually a rift valley formed between two faults or lines of weakness in the Earth's crust; although this region occupies only 10 per cent of the total area, it contains 80 per cent of Scotland's population of 5 million
- the Highlands and Islands of the north and north-west, where ancient rocks form rugged mountains and a magnificent coastline, and the nearest there is to true wilderness in the British Isles.

The Southern Uplands

The Southern Uplands lie between the Cheviots on the English border and the southern boundary fault of the Central Lowlands, which approximates to a line drawn between Girvan in Ayrshire to Dunbar. Granite is the rock most commonly found in Galloway in the west, forming a rugged landscape. To the east of Dumfries the hills are more rounded and broken up by areas of lowland, the most extensive being the Merse of the Tweed valley. The Southern Uplands as a whole are thinly populated, and the towns are quite small. There are few roads or railways and the main lines of communication with England keep to the valleys.

This area forms the gateway to Scotland and tourist developments at Gretna have exploited this. The main tourist attractions in the Border Country to the east include:

- the abbeys at Jedburgh, Kelso and Melrose – immortalized by Sir Walter Scott
- the spa town of Peebles
- the textile weaving towns of Hawick and Selkirk.

On the route west to Galloway, Dumfries has associations with Robert Burns and a 'Burns Trail'. Galloway has a milder climate and gardens are an attraction. The area has facilities for sailing and other activity holidays, and there are important archaeological sites and the Galloway forest park. Stranraer is a major ferry port for Northern Ireland.

North of Galloway the Ayrshire coast has notable seaside resorts, such as Girvan, and Ayr has one of Scotland's few all-weather facilities at Butlins WonderWest World. There are also golf courses, as at Troon. Northwards towards the central lowlands are the attractions of:

- Traquair House
- the Scottish Museum of Woollen Textiles near Peebles
- Chatelherault hunting lodge
- New Lanark industrial village.

The Central Lowlands

Despite the name, the Central Lowlands include a good deal of high ground, since the formation of this rift valley was accompanied by extensive volcanic activity. The isolated 'necks' of long-extinct volcanoes can still be seen, the crag on which Edinburgh Castle is built being a good example. The Ochils and Sidlaws to the north of the estuary known as the Firth of Forth, and the Pentland Hills to the south, rise to 500 metres – high by English standards. Parts of the eastern Lowlands are quite fertile, notably the Carse of Gowrie in Fife and the Lothians around Edinburgh. The western part of the Lowlands has a damper climate. The coastline is deeply indented by three great estuaries – the Firths of Forth, Clyde and Tay on which are situated Scotland's major ports, Leith (for Edinburgh), Glasgow with its outport at Greenock, and Dundee.

The Central Lowlands contain by far the greater proportion of Scotland's industry and population. The main centres – Glasgow, Edinburgh, Dundee and Stirling – are linked by a good communications system, which has involved bridging the Forth and Tay. Here, too, are the main international and domestic air gateways to Scotland. Both Edinburgh and Glasgow have shuttle services to London, while Glasgow Airport is now developing new international services since the deregulation of air services in Scotland and the demise of Prestwick. Budget airlines also operate to Luton and other regional airports in the British Isles.

The region is dominated by the two rival cities of Glasgow and Edinburgh. Both are significant cities for tourism but have very different products and approaches. Each has its own tourist board and tourism strategy.

Edinburgh

Edinburgh as the capital of Scotland, accommodates the new Scottish Assembly, and is a major cultural centre, attracting a large number of overseas visitors especially to the International Festival and Military Tattoo. The old city is built on a narrow ridge on either side of the 'Royal Mile' connecting the castle on its crag to the palace at Holyrood House, and is crammed full of picturesque buildings. It is separated from the 'New Town' to the north by the Norloch Valley, now occupied by public gardens and the Waverley railway station. The New Town, built according to eighteenth-century ideas of planning and architecture, contains Princes Street, a major shopping area, but other speciality shopping streets now compete with Princes Street's multiple stores. In particular, the area to the north of Princes Street and the Grassmarket area in the old town and Stockbridge abound with restaurants and speciality retailing. Edinburgh has a wealth of historic buildings and national attractions such as the Royal Scottish Museum and the newly developed 'Dynamic Earth' story of the planet. The Edinburgh International Conference Centre has been a major boost to business tourism. There are also many attractions on the outskirts:

- Edinburgh Zoo
- the Forth road and rail bridges
- Dirleton, Tantallon and Crichton Castles
- Linlithgow Palace
- the Scottish Mining Museum.

Across the Forth Estuary lies Dunfermline, the ancient capital of Scotland, and Fife. The Fife coast has a string of picturesque fishing villages, including Elie and Crail, and the historic university town of St Andrews with its golf course. Dundee is the regional centre and has the twin attractions of the royal research ship *Discovery* at Discovery Point and a new Science Centre. Perth is another former Scottish capital and acts as the gateway to the Highlands.

Glasgow

Glasgow is a much larger city than Edinburgh, having developed mainly during the nineteenth century as Scotland's major port and industrial centre. Glasgow's renaissance as a cultural centre was well publicized in 1990 with its selection as European City of Culture. With the vision of the local authority and the Greater Glasgow Tourist Board and Convention Bureau, a fine Victorian city now has a wealth of attractions, accommodation, and tourist facilities. In particular:

- the Burrell Collection in the art gallery and museum
- the People's Palace
- St Enoch Shopping Centre
- the Scottish Exhibition Centre
- the refurbished Pollok House
- the Clyde Auditorium
- the newly developed Glasgow Science Centre.

Stirling

Stirling with its strategically located castle played a major role in the Scottish Wars of Independence, and is now the focus of international interest due to films such as *Braveheart*.

The Highlands and Islands

Geologically speaking, the Highlands include the whole of Scotland to the north of a line drawn from Helensburgh on the Firth of Clyde to Stonehaven on the North Sea coast, which represents the northern boundary fault of the Central Lowlands. The region is made up of very old, highly folded rocks, and was severely affected by glaciation during the Ice Age, which formed its landscape of rugged mountains (the highest in the British Isles), lochs and broad, steep-sided glens. Most of the forests of Scots pine which formerly covered much of the Highlands have disappeared, with the significant exception of the Cairngorms area, leaving a treeless, heather-covered landscape.

The Highlands are divided into two by Glen More, the great rift valley extending right across Scotland from Fort William to Inverness, which is followed by the Caledonian Canal. The north-west Highlands to the west of Glen More are more rugged than the Grampians to the east. The Atlantic coast from Kintyre to Sutherland is deeply indented by sea lochs and is fringed by innumerable islands, with very little in the way of a coastal plain. Along the North Sea coast the coastline is more regular and less spectacular; there are fairly extensive lowlands in the north-east 'shoulder' of Scotland between Aberdeen and the Moray Firth, where the climate is drier and better suited to farming.

By comparison with the Lowlands, most parts of the Scottish Highlands are today sparsely populated, although population is returning. Despite a difficult climate and poor soils the glens, the coastal lowlands and islands once supported a Celtic people whose way of life was quite different from that of the Lowlands. The Highlanders spoke Gaelic and had a strong feeling of loyalty to the clan or tribal group. In the nineteenth century many such communities disappeared to make way for large private sheep farms and game reserves, the people emigrating to Canada or to Glasgow. Traditionally, many Highlanders have gained a living from 'crofting' – a self-sufficient type of agriculture on smallholdings supplemented by fishing. In some localities weaving and whisky distilling have been important activities.

Tourism has become an important source of income and provider of jobs. In 1965 the Highlands and Islands Development Board was set up by the British government to encourage public and private investment in the seven 'crofting counties' (Argyll, Inverness, Ross and Cromarty, Sutherland, Caithness, Orkney and Shetland). In the past this area was very short of quality accommodation, so the Board financed new hotels and self-catering accommodation. In 1991 it became Highlands and Islands Enterprise which is also concerned with investigating ways of extending the short tourist season, and ensuring that tourism does not damage the beauty of the scenery.

The main tourism centre for the Highlands is Inverness, where the majority of accommodation and services are found. South of the town, Loch Ness has a tourist industry based on the world famous 'monster' with visitor centres at Drumnadrochit.

Transport is a problem in the Western Highlands on account of the deeply indented coastline, so wide detours have frequently to be made to get from one place to another. The Hebrides are particularly isolated, although some of the small scattered communities are linked by 'air taxi' services and ferries operated by Caledonian MacBrayne to the mainland. The ports of Ullapool, Kyle of Lochalsh, Mallaig and Oban are the main bases for visiting the Hebrides. Islands have a great attraction for holidaymakers, despite in this instance the unpredictable weather and lack of facilities:

1 Skye is popular because of its historical associations with the clans and the magnificent mountain scenery of the Cuillins. A toll bridge links Skye with the mainland.

2 Iona is a place of pilgrimage.

3 Staffa is noted for its basalt sea caves.

4 Crossing the Minch, the Outer Hebrides or Western Isles have a bleaker environment. Harris is noted for its tweed, cloth handwoven into distinctive patterns.

5 The Orkneys and the Shetlands, separated from mainland Scotland by some of the stormiest seas in Europe, were once ruled by Norway – and in the latter (often called Zetland) the Scandinavian influence remains strong even today (one manifestation being the 'Up Helly A' festival in Lerwick). The Orkneys are fairly low lying and fertile, and contain prehistoric remains as well as the magnificent harbour of Scapa Flow, once an important naval base. The Shetlands lie 140 kilometres further north and are bleaker and much more rugged. Oil has brought wealth to a community where fishing has traditionally been the mainstay of the economy and the distinctively small, hardy island sheep and ponies are reared. These northern islands are linked by regular air services from Edinburgh and Glasgow as well as ferries from Scrabster (near Thurso) and Aberdeen.

The scenic attractions of the Grampians are more readily accessible than those of north-west Scotland to the cities of the Lowlands, although upgrading of the A9 road has reduced the isolation of the Highlands. This part of Scotland was made fashionable as a holiday destination by Queen Victoria, and the Dee Valley west of Aberdeen is particularly associated with the British royal family; however more recently, Hollywood films based on Scottish heroes have stimulated renewed interest in the area. During the nineteenth century a number of hotels were built, notably on the shores of Loch Lomond, in the Trossachs (an area of particularly fine woodland and lake scenery) and at Gleneagles near Perth, which is a noted centre for golf. The Spey Valley (famous for its whisky and salmon fishing) was another area that particularly benefited from Victorian tourism. It has good road and rail communications to Glasgow and London. After the 1960s, this area became important for winter sports, since the Cairngorms can provide a suitable climate and terrain.

Skiing takes place from December to April in the Coire Cas, a corrie or cirque that acts as a 'snowbowl', located high above the treeline on the northern slopes of Cairngorm Mountain. The Aviemore Centre in the valley below is a purpose-built resort offering a full range of services. Conferences are held in spring and autumn, while in summer the Centre is used as a base for activity holidays, including pony-trekking and nature study – for which the Cairngorms nature reserve is probably unrivalled in Britain. Unlike other Scottish resorts, Aviemore has a year-round season and adequate wet-weather facilities, so that it can take full advantage of tourism. Elsewhere, new winter sports facilities are being developed near Fort William and at Glenshee. However, proposals to expand ski facilities have received considerable opposition from environmentalists, concerned about the fragile nature of the mountain ecosystem.

Wales

Wales has maintained a separate national identity despite the union with England imposed by King Edward I and later reinforced by Henry VIII. This is evidenced by:

● the survival of the Welsh language, especially in the mountainous north and west of the country

● the Celtic heritage, expressed in a strong literary and musical tradition, and the national gatherings known as eisteddfods

● the strength of Nonconformist Christianity, with simple chapels featuring in the landscape rather than imposing cathedrals

● in the twentieth century, the Welsh language and culture have been encouraged by the British government. The country has its own Minister and government departments responsible for tourism and heritage, and a separate Welsh Assembly, all based in Cardiff.

Tourism policy and product development is the responsibility of the Wales Tourist Board, with separate regional organizations for North, Mid-Wales and South Wales.

North Wales

North Wales, consisting of the counties of Gwynedd and Clwyd, is scenically the most interesting part of the country. Gwynedd is the most important tourist region in Wales. It is often regarded as the cultural 'heartland' of Wales, where the people continue to speak Welsh as their first language. The traditional culture has persisted partly because the region is isolated to some extent by the rugged mountains of Snowdonia, which rise abruptly from the coast. North Wales contains Britain's largest national park and castles dating from Edward I's conquest of Gwynedd in the thirteenth century. A number of these castles – Conwy, Harlech, Beaumaris and Caernarfon – are World Heritage listed sites.

The mountains of Snowdonia have a craggy appearance quite different from the rounded outline of the Cambrian Mountains to the south and the Hiraethog or Denbighshire moors to the east. Radiating from Snowdon itself are a number of deep trough-like valleys carved out by the glaciers of the Ice Age – examples include the Llanberis Pass and Nant Ffrancon, which contains a number of small lakes. In such a valley is Lake Bala, a large natural lake with water sports and fishing. The beautiful scenery has encouraged touring and activity tourism in such centres as Beddgelert,

Llangollen, and Betws-y-Coed. For the less active, the Snowdon mountain railway takes visitors to the summit of Snowdon from Llanberis, and incidentally has caused serious visitor pressure problems at the summit. Dolgellau is an historic stone-built town at the foot of Cader Idris and close to the beautiful Mawddach estuary. The seaside town of Barmouth is at the entrance to the estuary.

Tourism dominates the economy of North Wales and takes advantage of both the rural and industrial heritage. Most of the high land in North Wales is of little agricultural value. In the upper valleys there are isolated sheep farms, with their characteristic stone buildings and small irregular fields separated by roughstone walls. As in northern England, hill farms cater for tourists as a way of supplementing their incomes. The other major industry is based on mineral resources. Large areas near Bethesda, Llanberis and Ffestiniog are the sites of slate quarries, some of which have become important tourist attractions – as at Llechwedd. In Llanberis the Welsh Slate Centre interprets this once important industry for the tourist. Other industrial features that are now tourist attractions are the narrow-gauge railways of Wales, exemplified by the Ffestiniog Railway which has its terminus at Porthmadog, and the redevelopment of the Welsh Highland Railway between Porthmadog and Caernarfon. Finally, Wales is a source of both power and water for England and these resources are also used for tourism as the power stations welcome visitors. In contrast, the Centre for Alternative Technology at Machynlleth is an important attraction with true 'green' credentials.

The coastline of North Wales is particularly attractive and easily reached from the conurbations of Merseyside and Manchester. There are a number of popular seaside resorts along the coast east of the estuary of the Conwy:

● Llandudno is the best known with its fine beach situated between two headlands – the Great and Little Orme
● Colwyn Bay is the site of the Welsh Mountain Zoo
● Rhyl with its all-weather 'Sun Centre' and Sea Life Centre, has undergone substantial redevelopment. Much of the narrow coastal strip around Rhyl houses large caravan sites.

These resorts, and particularly Llandudno, have benefited from the upgrading of the A55 road, traditionally the route to the North Wales coast from the conurbations of north-west England, although this does mean that the resorts are easily within day trip distance of the conurbations and do not require an overnight stay.

Anglesey and the Lleyn Peninsula are less commercialized, with smaller resorts, such as Pwllheli, devoted to sailing or other 'activity' holidays. Bardsey Island off the coast is a nature reserve. In parts of North Wales the purchase of country cottages as 'second homes' by visitors from outside the region is controversial (partly because it is felt to weaken the Welsh language culture). Although some villages (for example, Abersoch on the Lleyn peninsula) are dominated by second homes, others argue that the rural area benefits economically by bringing business to local suppliers. Holyhead, with its important ferry service to Ireland, is the only significant commercial centre.

Mid-Wales

Mid-Wales is also mountainous and thinly populated, except for the narrow coastal plain around Cardigan Bay, and the upper valleys of the Wye and the Severn. In the former area Welsh culture is strong, while much of Powys is anglicized. North-to-south communications are difficult, especially by rail, and there are no large towns. There are a number of small seaside resorts on Cardigan Bay, such as Aberdovey and Aberystwyth, which are popular with visitors from the English Midlands. Inland, there are some small market towns, such as Newtown, Llanidloes, and Welshpool, and a number of former spas, such as Builth Wells. These towns have become centres for touring the Cambrian Mountains, but are important historic towns in their own right. Montgomery, for example, has many Georgian buildings. Other attractions in Mid-Wales include Powis Castle, Lake Vyrnwy and the Glywedog Gorge.

South Wales

South Wales contains the majority of the Welsh population of almost 3 million, the only large towns and most of the industries. The region is separated from the rest of Wales by the Black Mountains and the Brecon Beacons, but is easily accessible from southern England via the two Severn road bridges. In the centre of the region lies the South Wales coalfield, which is crossed from north to south by a number of deep narrow valleys, including those of the Taff, Rhondda and Rhymney. Mining communities straggle almost continuously along the valley bottoms, and the landscape was disfigured by spoil heaps, tips and abandoned workings. Both British and European initiatives have transformed this landscape of dereliction with:

● landscaped country parks
● the development of a museum of coal mining at Big Pit, Blaenavon
● the Rhondda Heritage Park.

A similar transformation has occurred in both Cardiff, the capital of Wales and seat of the new Welsh Assembly, and Swansea, where dockland areas have been redeveloped as a maritime quarter with water sports, retailing, restaurants and hotels. West of Swansea, the Gower Peninsula is an area of outstanding natural beauty with good beaches. Cardiff is the location of major developments such as:

● the Millennium Stadium
● the Millennium Centre

- a major redevelopment of Cardiff Harbour with museums – such as Techniquest – and hotels
- national institutions such as the Welsh Folk Museum at St Fagan's, the National Museum of Wales and Cardiff Castle.

On the outskirts, Penarth is a small resort, Barry Island has a major pleasure park, Llanelli is developing a coastal park and Castell Coch overlooks the city. The city is served by Cardiff Wales Airport.

Historically, the region has a great deal to offer. There are important Roman remains at Caerwent and Caerleon; and in this area, too, the Normans built many castles to control the coastal plain and the valleys leading into the mountains of Mid-Wales. There are castles at Tenby, Pembroke, Haverfordwest and Raglan which are tourist attractions. In Dyfed, the National Botanic Garden for Wales is an ambitious project creating an attraction of international significance. In the Border Country fortifications and historic monuments are also tourist attractions – Tintern Abbey, Monmouth and Chepstow Castle are notable examples.

The Brecon Beacons National Park rises to over 900 metres at Pen-y-Fan, to the west is the old hunting ground of Fforest Fawr, in the north-east the broad valley of the River Usk and to the south spectacular waterfalls and caves. Hay-on-Wye is the touring base for the park and a centre for the second-hand book trade. On the Usk, Abergavenny is also a touring and trekking centre. East of Brecon, Llangorse Lake is developed for water sports and is an important centre for naturalists.

The Pembrokeshire Coast National Park is Britain's only linear national park. It stretches from Pen Camais in the north to Amroth in the south and overlooks the offshore islands of South Wales. Notable here is Caldey Island, where tourists can visit the monastery, and the bird reserves on Skokholm and Skomer. Fishguard is a small town with ferry services to Ireland. One outstanding cultural attraction is St David's, which was a major place of pilgrimage in medieval times. Around the park runs the 269-kilometre coastal path, taking in resorts such as Tenby and Saundersfoot, and features in the national park such as Manorbier Castle, the lily ponds at Bosherston, Pendine sands, Llaugharne with its association with the great Welsh poet Dylan Thomas, and the many beaches.

Summary

Scotland, Wales, and the Isle of Man (for the latter see the following case study) are well endowed with a wide variety of tourist attractions. Both Scotland and Wales can be divided geographically into three tourist regions, each with its own unique blend of natural and cultural resources. However, common threads can be identified across them all. These include the growth of heritage attractions – particularly those stressing the Celtic and industrial heritage – and the increasing use of rural tourism to boost the economy in remoter areas – often based on farm tourism or specialist products such as fishing – and the growth of tourism in towns and cities in terms of both cultural and short-break tourism and business tourism. In both the traditional resorts of Wales and in the Isle of Man the authorities are reinvesting to attract new markets.

Case study

The Isle of Man

Introduction

The Isle of Man is 50 kilometres long and 20 kilometres wide, situated centrally in the Irish Sea, to the east of Ireland, west of England and south-west of Scotland. The island's location in the Irish Sea is at once both an advantage and a disadvantage. On the one hand the island's location allows it to draw upon the large population catchments of the English Midlands and North, the Scottish Lowlands and the east coast of Ireland. However, on the other hand, to reach the island involves a short air journey or sea crossing, often in unpredictable weather as the island suffers from successive waves of Atlantic fronts passing over the Irish Sea.

The Isle of Man has a rich history that now provides the basis for both heritage tourism and the island's ambitions to become a major location for both film and television productions. Vikings invaded the island in the ninth century, followed by Scottish rule until the fourteenth century when the island came under English rule. Since the mid-nineteenth century the island has regained its autonomy and has its own parliament – Tynwald – its own language – Manx – and its own civil service. Although it has a high degree of autonomy it is not an independent country, as it is a dependency of the British Crown.

The island has a long history of tourism with peak numbers of visitors arriving by steamship in the early years of the twentieth century to enjoy a traditional seaside holiday. However, the Isle of Man's tourism success in the twentieth century has been one of mixed fortunes. There was a surge of visitors immediately following the Second World War, but by the 1950s the island began to experience the beginnings of a constant and sustained decline in visitor numbers. This was caused by the fact that holiday tastes and aspirations ceased to find the island's traditional holiday formula attractive. In the last two decades of the twentieth century the island has undergone something of a renaissance with a thriving offshore finance industry. This has stimulated business tourism and up-market facilities such as hotels and restaurants have been developed to serve the market.

Demand for tourism

Demand for tourism on the Isle of Man was at its height in the late nineteenth and early twentieth centuries when visitors from the north of England, the Midlands and southern Scotland were attracted to the island's traditional seaside product and value-for-money accommodation stock. In the postwar period the island's tourism authorities were slow to respond to changing tastes in holiday taking and the structural shifts taking place in the UK domestic holiday market, resulting in falling visitor numbers. However, since the mid-1980s, strong political commitment and support for tourism have seen a rejuvenation of the island's products and facilities (partly driven by the demands of the business travellers) and demand has stabilized at around 200 000 staying visitors per year. The majority of visitors are from the UK, but the Irish family market is also an important source. A small number of visitors come to the island from Europe, often as part of a northern England itinerary. Nonetheless the volume of overnight tourists is significantly less than in earlier decades and this has impacted upon the contribution of tourism to the island's economy (see Table 9.1).

Supply of tourism

Attractions

- *Douglas and the coastal towns* The main town on the Isle of Man is Douglas, with a sweeping Victorian promenade of guesthouses and terraced hotels. Douglas is the main seaport and has the Manx Museum and 'Story of Mann' exhibition. Douglas also represents the main concentration of bed spaces, restaurants and other facilities for the visitor. Indeed, despite declining numbers, tourism still supports many of the shopping and entertainment businesses in Douglas. These include the restored Victorian Gaiety Theatre, a casino and leisure centre. Other coastal towns, each with a range of small attractions and accommodation base, include:
  - Port Erin
  - Peel

  - Ramsey
  - Castletown.
- *Built heritage* The island has a rich built heritage with many remains of both Celtic and Norse origin. The key features are:
  - the Laxey Wheel to the north of Douglas, the world's largest working waterwheel
  - historic buildings such as the castle and cathedral at Peel and Castle Rushen at Castletown – the island's former capital
  - the site of the island's first parliament at Tynwald Hill near Peel
  - museums and craft centres including the Grove Rural Life Museum at Ramsey, the House of Manannan – a newly-built heritage centre on the harbourside in Peel – and the Nautical Museum at Castletown
  - Cregneash Folk Village is a recreated rural life museum with original Manx cottages interpreting the crofting way of life of the islanders in the past.
- *Natural heritage* The island has been likened to a miniature landscape of northern England featuring all the elements of beaches, fells, valleys and coast, yet within a small area. The natural heritage of the island is being interpreted and developed for special interest holidays and both walking and cycling trails are available – three long-distance footpaths have been designated. Key features are:
  - the Point of Ayre – a protected area of dune coast in the north of the island
  - the wetland habitats of the Ballaugh Curraghs with its wildlife park
  - the Calf of Man – a small rocky island and a wildlife sanctuary in the south
  - a series of seventeen mountain and coastal glens managed by the Manx Forestry Department with facilities for recreation.
- *Transport heritage* The Isle of Man is famous for a range of transport-based tourist attractions. These include:
  - the annual Tourist Trophy (TT) motorcycle races, dating back to 1904. This event takes place on a road circuit around the island and fills the island's

Table 9.1 The relative contribution of the tourism and finance sectors to the Manx economy, 1971 and 1995

	Island employment, 1971 (%)	Island employment, 1995 (%)	Island income, 1971 (%)	Island income, 1995 (%)
Tourism	7	3	11	6
Finance	3	14	21	35

Source: Web site at http://www.gov.im/tourism

bed-spaces during 'TT Week'. The circuit is used for other race events throughout the year
- the electric mountain railway from Laxey up the island's highest peak, Snaefell
- the horse-drawn *toast-rack* trams that run along Douglas seafront
- the Manx electric railway between Douglas and Ramsey
- Groudle Glen steam railway
- the Manx narrow gauge steam railway from Douglas to Port Erin in the south, with its railway museum at the Port Erin terminus.

Accommodation and transport

The Isle of Man has a varied accommodation base ranging from recently developed luxury country house hotels to value-for-money guesthouses. The Manx government has had a long-standing scheme to assist the accommodation sector both to adjust to the demands of the contemporary holidaymaker, and also to attract new accommodation stock. The tourism authorities also operate a compulsory registration and grading scheme for accommodation. However, as the staying visitor market has shrunk, so has the island's accommodation stock with many buildings being converted into health, office or residential use. By the mid-1990s there were less than 5000 bed-spaces available on the island, mostly in serviced accommodation.

Traditionally, holidaymakers reached the Isle of Man by steamship, using the Isle of Man Steam Packet Company sailing out of Liverpool, Heysham, Belfast and Dublin. In recent years fast catamarans have also been introduced, but the success of the island's airline – Manx (now a subsidiary of British Airways) has made it an important carrier for business and leisure passengers. The island's airport, Ronaldsway, is served by three airlines – Manx, Jersey European and Comed Aviation – with flights to many UK regional airports, as well as to both Ireland and the Channel Islands. Of course, as an island, it is very dependent upon its carriers for survival and the Tynwald closely monitors transport policy and scrutinizes applications from new operators serving the route network.

The organization of tourism

The Department of Tourism and Leisure has responsibility for both the promotion and development of tourism on the island and runs its own tour operation business bringing in visitors – Everymann holidays. The department's policy is 'to develop, promote and encourage tourism to optimise economic and social benefits to the Isle of Man'. The department works closely with other agencies that are responsible for transport, heritage and planning. Manx National Heritage and the Manx Nature Conservation Trust are responsible for a number of the island's natural and historic attractions.

The Isle of Man has had to adapt its tourism product to the tastes of late twentieth century holidaymakers. The island's traditional markets sought an English seaside product and while this forms an element of the island's attraction, other elements of the destination mix are now seen as more important in attracting visitors. These include the development of quality accommodation, the development of activity holidays based upon the island's natural and cultural heritage, and the development of sports tourism utilising the island's eight golf courses, excellent fishing and other facilities. It is interesting that this approach also depends upon the provision of good quality, professionally managed tourist accommodation. Traditional establishments in Douglas have struggled to meet these standards and there has been a switch in both development and demand for establishments in rural parts of the island. The Isle of Man is therefore an excellent example of a destination that is having to reposition itself to attract tourists in the twenty-first century.

10

The tourism geography of Ireland

After reading this chapter, you should be able to:

1 Demonstrate a knowledge of the main tourist regions in the Republic of Ireland and Northern Ireland.
2 Understand the distribution and importance of tourist resources in the Republic of Ireland and Northern Ireland.
3 Recognize the increasing role being played by heritage resources and attractions in the regions considered in this chapter.
4 Recognize the importance of rural resources in Irish tourism.
5 Understand the importance of the major cities of the Republic of Ireland and Northern Ireland as business and leisure tourism centres.
6 Recognize the increased importance of the border region for tourism initiatives in Ireland.

Ireland: an introduction

As an island situated at the western periphery of Europe, Ireland is geographically isolated from the world's main tourist-generating countries, with the exception of Britain, and is the only country of the EU not accessible by road or rail to mainland Europe. Since 1922 it has also been a divided island. The Republic of Ireland chose independence and neutrality, whereas the province of Northern Ireland (made up of six of the counties of Ulster) remained part of the UK. This partition never achieved widespread support among the Catholic population who form a substantial minority in Northern Ireland. In 1969, the outbreak of violence in Northern Ireland proved detrimental to both its tourism industry and that of the Republic. The division of Ireland, based largely on religious differences between Catholics and Protestants, and historical memories of British rule, remains an unsolved problem. However, the peace initiatives of the 1990s have made considerable progress toward ending 'the troubles' and are leading to the co-ordinated development of tourism on both sides of the border.

Despite the impressive economic development that has taken place since the 1970s, Ireland remains more rural than other West European countries, with few major cities. The low population density, uncrowded roads, unspoiled countryside and slower pace of life make Ireland an appealing destination. The people have a reputation for hospitality and conviviality, and the legendary *craic* is itself an attraction. It is therefore no accident that Irish 'themed' pubs are now found all over the world, while Irish music and dance have gained an international following.

The central feature of Ireland is a low-lying plain, dotted with drumlins – rounded hills of glacial origin – lakes and expanses of peat bog. This is almost encircled by mountains, which are not particularly rugged, and breached by both the valley of the Shannon and the west coast around Dublin – traditionally the gateways for visitors. Ireland's reputation as the 'Emerald Isle' is due to the mild damp climate, which favours the growth of lush dairy pasture throughout the year, and in the south-west, subtropical vegetation. However, the unpredictable weather, particularly cool cloudy summers, is one of Ireland's weaknesses as a holiday destination.

Ireland is poor in natural resources compared with Britain, and until recently, many of its young people emigrated to seek greater economic opportunities. In the eighteenth century, the Protestant 'Scots-Irish' from Ulster played a major role advancing the frontier of settlement in

North America. Following the Great Famine of the 1840s much larger numbers, mainly from the Catholic south and west, were forced to emigrate overseas. The descendants of these emigrants in the USA, Canada, Australia and Britain are now many times more numerous than the population of Ireland itself. Ethnic tourism and genealogy (tracing family roots) is therefore a lucrative business in both the Republic and Northern Ireland. The epic theme of emigration also plays a major role in the countries' heritage attractions.

Ireland's heritage is an important part of its tourism industry, though its interpretation in Northern Ireland is viewed differently by Catholics and Protestants. We can identify the following themes:

1 *Religion in Ireland as the 'Land of Saints and Scholars'* Many of Ireland's religious monuments – Celtic crosses, monasteries and 'round towers' date from the European Dark Ages when Ireland became a centre of missionary endeavour.
2 *Nation-building* The Celtic language and folklore are seen as central to Ireland's national identity. However, the great majority of the population are English-speaking, due to the long period of domination from Britain. The Anglo-Irish ruling class left a legacy of great country houses that are now important tourist attractions. In their time, these were viewed as symbols of oppression, so that the struggle for independence, particularly the 1798 rebellion, is a major theme in heritage interpretation.
3 *The literary and artistic heritage* Ireland has produced many of the great writers and dramatists of the English-speaking world.

Transport

Mode of travel to Ireland has changed in the last two decades of the twentieth century as budget airlines and aggressive marketing have seen air transport increase at the expense of the ferry services. The main sea routes to Ireland from the Continent are:

● Cork/Roscoff
● Rosslare/Cherbourg.

There is a wide choice of main sea routes to Britain:

● Rosslare/Fishguard or Pembroke
● Dun Laoghaire/ Holyhead
● Dublin/Liverpool
● Belfast/Liverpool
● Belfast/Douglas and Heysham
● Belfast/Stranraer or Cairnryan.

On many of these sea routes operators are investing in state-of-the-art vessels, including high-speed catamarans, and are also cutting fares in a bid to regain market share from the airlines.

Nonetheless, air traffic to Ireland has increased at the expense of the sea routes. Deregulated airlines have reduced fares and opened up access to Ireland's regional airports. Ryanair for example has pioneered the development of regional airports, supported by monies from the EU, namely – Waterford, Kerry (Farranfore), Galway, Sligo, Donegal (Carrickfinn) and Horan International (formerly Knock). These are in addition to the four main airports at Belfast, Dublin, Shannon and Cork. Dublin has both long- and short-haul air routes and remains the main international gateway to Ireland. Belfast City Airport is well served by air routes to the UK (including a shuttle service to Heathrow) and Europe. The expansion of air services has helped the expanding business and conference traffic to Ireland. The Republic of Ireland's national carrier is Aer Lingus. Ireland's location on the western periphery of mainland Europe does give it the advantage of uncongested skies and, with the expansion of networks of air routes between European regional airports, the authorities intend that Ireland will become less isolated from its tourist markets. In the Republic, the railways and coach/bus services are operated by Coras Iompair Irelandann (CIE), allowing integrated travel across the country.

The Republic of Ireland

Domestic and outbound tourism demand

The propensity for holiday-taking in Ireland is lower than in Britain, In the late 1990s the Irish took around 7 million domestic trips annually. The strength of the Irish economy has encouraged the growth of overseas tourism, particularly in the VFR and business sectors, and about 4 million trips overseas are made each year. The most popular destinations are the UK and the Mediterranean, but as charter flights to long-haul destinations are introduced, a greater range of destinations are in evidence. There is also a substantial volume of cross-border traffic between the Republic and Northern Ireland. Factors differentiating the nature of tourism demand in Ireland from that in Britain include:

● a much higher proportion of young people in the population resulting in an expanding market for family holidays
● although the role of the Roman Catholic Church has diminished since the 1980s, popular devotion remains strong as expressed in pilgrimages to religious shrines. The most important of these in Ireland itself is Knock in County Mayo, which even has its own airport.

Inbound tourism demand

In contrast to the UK, Ireland achieved only very slow growth in overseas tourist arrivals over the decade of the 1970s, and high inflation and unfavourable exchange rates led to slight reductions in arrivals in the early 1980s. However, deregulation of Ireland/UK air services and the development of regional airports increased arrivals to approach 4 million in the late 1990s and, as a consequence, arrivals by sea have fallen. Substantial investment in the Irish tourism product, increases in quality and improved marketing, and prospects of peace in Northern Ireland have boosted arrivals in the 1990s – particularly from North America. Features of the Irish inbound market in the 1990s include:

● heavy dependence on the British market which accounts for two thirds of arrivals
● dependence upon the peace process in Northern Ireland
● increasing domination of arrivals by air leading to a response by the ferry companies to increase quality and introduce faster services
● acute seasonality
● high percentage of 'ethnic' visits, especially from Britain and the USA.

Ireland's tourism industry employs 137 000 people and is predominantly one of small businesses. The country's tourism resource base includes three national parks, a number of forest parks and an extensive system of inland waterways. Among the most important linear attractions are the Grand Canal and the Wicklow Way, a long-distance footpath. Tourism products include:

● rural tourism that not only supports the local rural economy and helps to stem depopulation, but also keeps alive traditional activities and handicrafts such as embroidery and knitwear
● activity holidays based on sport (fishing, golf, sailing, horse riding, etc.)
● culture (theatre, folk museums and international festivals)
● ethnic activities based around the many centres of genealogy
● English language schools in competition with the UK
● culinary activities.

In the 1990s this resource base received considerable investment from EU regional funds and the Irish government.

In the Republic of Ireland the policy body for tourism is the Ministry of Tourism and Trade supported by the national tourist organization – Bord Failté Eireann. Bord Failté was established in 1955 with promotion (both domestic and overseas) and development functions. Hotels and guesthouses are classified under a statutory registration scheme and the government's business expansion scheme supports tourism enterprises. In the 1980s the Irish government recognized the importance of tourism to their economy and instituted a review of Bord Failté and tourism in Ireland. This led to Bord Failté contracting out much of its operational work and focusing on international marketing. At the same

time, a five-year planning framework for tourism was put in place with the aim of increasing both tourist volume and spending. The review was closely integrated into a successful bid for a high level of EU structural funds (from the European Regional Development Fund and the European Social Fund). These were applied to programmes of investment in extending and upgrading the range and quality of tourist facilities in Ireland. Three priority areas were identified:

● tourism infrastructure
● tourism facilities
● marketing/training.

The investment was focused on both population and spatial areas:

1 The population areas include Dublin and Killarney, Wexford and Sligo, Castlebar and Dingle, Kilkenny and Cobh, and Ballybunion and Bundoran.
2 The spatial areas include touring areas (Ring of Kerry, Boyne Valley), special-interest areas (Burren, Western Lakes), developmental areas (Shannon and the canals) and product areas where a local area can support a saleable product such as crafts.

The injection of money into the sector has increased professionalism, product range and quality in the tourism sector. It has also had the effect of changing the distribution of tourism across Ireland. While tourism is evenly spread compared to most other European countries, the west and the south-west have lost market share to Dublin. The next stage will be to sustain these initiatives. In the late 1990s, the marketing objectives for Irish tourism are to:

● extend the season
● boost air and sea access
● explore new markets
● develop new products and niche markets
● develop the marketing of the whole of Ireland through the 'All Ireland Marketing Initiative'
● encourage high-spending tourists.

Although the Republic of Ireland is organized in seven regional tourist boards, we prefer to divide the Republic of Ireland for tourism purposes into three main regions, based on the historic provinces of Leinster, Connacht and Munster:

● Dublin and the east
● Western Ireland
● The South-West.

Dublin and the east (Leinster)

Dublin remains pre-eminent as the centre for Irish tourism and is dealt with in the case study. Dublin is a good base for tourism circuits that include some of the most attractive scenery of eastern Ireland – the granitic Wicklow Mountains with their steep-sided glens. The narrow coastal plain is fertile, with a relatively dry and sunny climate. The Vale of Avoca is famous for the beauty of its landscape, and the village of Avoca attracts many visitors as the setting for a well-known television series. Along the coast are found resorts as at Bray and Tramore, and the small ports of Waterford (with its glass factory), Arklow and Wexford (with its international festivals). To the west of Dublin, Kilkenny has a particularly fine medieval heritage, also supported by international festivals.

Western Ireland (Connacht)

Western Ireland contains the greatest concentration of tourist resources. In the past, the Irish government has encouraged tourist facilities to locate in the west, which is a much poorer region economically with a high dependence on traditional peasant farming. Special incentives are available in the Gaeltacht – those areas where the people still speak the Gaelic language as their mother tongue. This is because the west is regarded as the true repository of Irish national culture, rather than the Anglicized south and east. Bord Failté encourages farmhouse holidays, and has promoted cottage rentals: a number of villages have built attractive cottages in traditional style as self-catering accommodation.

Galway is the recognized capital of the west and its airport is developing rapidly in line with Ireland's other regional airports. It is the southern gateway to the Connemara touring area and, with its adjoining resort Salthill, is an important centre for touring holidays and conferences. The main touring circuits are:

- the Great Western Lakes – Corrib, Mask and Caarra – to the north
- to the west is a superb indented coastline and the Connemara Mountains
- in the south-west, the Aran Islands can be reached by sea or air
- in the south are the cliffs of Moher and the botanically and geologically important Burren area of limestone scenery in County Clare. The interpretive centre has helped to reduce the impacts of tourism on these sensitive natural areas.

The South-West (Munster)

The South-West includes the most attractive scenery in Ireland, and three of its main tourism centres – Killarney, Cork and Limerick. The major tourist resources are Killarney, Tralee, Cork and the Limerick/Shannon area.

Killarney

Killarney was recognized as a holiday resort of international significance in the nineteenth century. Nowadays it is an ideal touring centre, including the famous scenic road known as the 'Ring of Kerry'. Killarney has the largest concentration of bed-spaces outside the capital, and its airport at Farranfore is positioned to attract the short-break market from the UK. Nearby are the lakes and mountains of the Killarney National Park, Muckross House and some of the best golf courses in Europe.

Tralee

Tralee has an important festival, deliberately promoted by Bord Failté to attract participants claiming Irish descent from all over the world.

Cork

Cork is the second city of the Republic and the centre of a development zone that includes Kinsale, Blarney and Cobh:

- Kinsale has long been an important sailing and fishing centre and is finding a niche market in culinary short-breaks.
- Blarney is world famous for its castle, housing the stone which confers the gift of eloquence.
- Cobh was the principal staging point for passenger liners and millions of emigrants en route to the USA before the jet era. The quayside has been restored with attractions recalling its role in Ireland's social and transport history.

The Limerick/Shannon area

The Limerick/Shannon area has a range of high-quality accommodation and provides good access to other areas. Shannon Airport until the 1960s was a compulsory stop on transatlantic flights and pioneered the 'duty free' concept of airport shopping shortly after the Second World War. The River Shannon is now more important as a tourism resource for sailing and fishing than as a commercial waterway, with Athlone and other smaller centres providing facilities. North-west of Limerick is Bunratty Castle which pioneered the medieval banquet idea, so popular with North Americans. Bunratty has now expanded its heritage attractions into a folk park and shopping complex.

Northern Ireland

The province of Northern Ireland is much smaller than the Irish Republic, with a population of over 1.5 million. It is, however, more urbanized with almost one-third of the inhabitants living in the capital, Belfast. This is an important port and shipbuilding centre (the *Titanic* was launched here) due to its location on a deep, sheltered estuary. The province has frequent air and shipping services to Scotland and England, and a good road and railway network. Northern Ireland's main tourism resource is the scenery of limestone uplands, lakes and the basalt plateau of Antrim. The distribution of tourism is very much a coastal one, with the exception of the Fermanagh Lakeland. Tourism promotion and development are the responsibility of the Northern Ireland Tourist Board (NITB), which was one of the first statutory tourist boards to be set up (in 1948). The NITB works closely with Bord Failté and the BTA. There are also a number of regional tourist associations.

The main tourist resources

Belfast

Since 1969, the threat of terrorism has severely curtailed tourism in Belfast but with the peace process the city is receiving an increasing number of both visitors and investment, assisted by the formation of the Belfast Visitor and Convention Bureau in 1999. The city has a pedestrianized centre, historic buildings, museums, a zoo and a rich industrial heritage, and is redeveloping its cathedral area to rival Dublin's Temple Bar district for shopping and nightlife. New developments include the Odyssey Project – a multimillion pound education, science and sporting development, and ECOs – an environmental education centre. In a bid to encourage tourism, Belfast hosts a variety of international events such as the Cutty Sark Tall Ships Race. On the outskirts of Belfast attractions include Hillsborough, with its fort, castle, and gardens, Carrickfergus Castle and the Ulster Folk and Transport Museum at Cultra.

The North

North of Belfast lies the Antrim plateau where the basalt forms impressive cliffs and includes:

● the Giant's Causeway, perhaps Ireland's most famous natural attraction, and because of its unique character, a World Heritage Site
● the nine glens of Antrim are deep wooded valleys sloping down to the sea which were carved out of the basalt by fast-flowing streams. Glenariff is the best known glen and at the foot of the glen one of the many *feiscanna* (festivals) of the region is held
● the scenic road from Larne to the seaside resort of Portrush takes in spectacular coastal scenery. Portrush, Ballycastle and Coleraine are the main resorts on the Antrim coast, which have reinvested to improve facilities for family and golf holidays.

The West

To the west is Londonderry (Derry) set on a hill on the banks of the Foyle Estuary. The town still has evidence of its medieval origins, including the walls that withstood a historic siege in 1689. South-east of Londonderry are the touring circuits of the Sperrin Mountains, where attractions include the Sperrin Heritage Centre, Springhill House and the historic town of Moneymore. To the south is the Ulster-American Folk Park of Omagh, one of the increasing number of folk museums in the province, which explores Scots-Irish links with the USA.

The Centre

In the centre of Northern Ireland the river Erne runs through Fermanagh Lakeland to provide an important resource for water-based holidays, natural history, activity and fishing holidays. Castle Archdale on Lough Erne is the main centre for sailing and hire cruising on the extensive system of inland waterways. Castle Coole and Florence Court are significant attractions run by the National Trust. The town of Enniskillen is a historic centre on the river Erne. Armagh is the spiritual capital of Ireland boasting two cathedrals and numerous Georgian buildings.

The South

South-east of Armagh rises the granite mass of the Mournes, rounded mountains sweeping down to the sea. On the coast, Newcastle is a seaside resort and a sailing and golf centre. Other resorts in the foothills of the Mourne Mountains are lively Warrenpoint and the quieter Rostrevor, both on Carlingford Lough. The Ards Peninsula is a scenic area within easy reach of the resort of Bangor and the city of Belfast. Attractions on the peninsula include Castle Ward, Mount Stewart and Kearney Village. The Ards Peninsula is separated from the rest of County Down by Strangford Lough, also a bird sanctuary and site of the Strangford Stone, erected for the millennium. Around the lough are the abbeys of Inch, Grey and Comber, and to the south, the cathedral town of Downpatrick with its new visitor centre interpreting the legacy of St Patrick.

The Border Region

The border region between Ireland and Northern Ireland is the focus of considerable tourism investment in the wake of the peace process. Local authorities on both sides of the border are co-operating under the aegis of the European Structural Funds' assistance for border regions – Interreg, and monies are also flowing from the EU's Peace Fund and the International Fund for Ireland.

Summary

Ireland is well endowed with many types of tourist attractions and can be divided geographically into a number of tourist regions, each with its own unique blend of natural and cultural resources. However, common threads can be identified across them all. These include the use of European funds to develop tourism, the growth of themed heritage attractions – particularly those stressing the Celtic contribution – the increasing use of rural tourism to encourage the economy in remoter areas, often based on farm tourism, and the growth of tourism in towns and cities – in terms of both cultural and short-break tourism and business tourism as in Dublin. In some traditional resorts the authorities are reinvesting to attract new markets.

Case study

Dublin

Introduction

Dublin's setting on the wide Dublin Bay is backed by the Wicklow Mountains and the Dublin area contains over one-third of Ireland's 3.6 million population. The city of Dublin itself has not only become a major European tourist city on the world stage, but it is also the most important gateway to Ireland with both air and sea access (through Dublin's port at Dun Laoghaire). This is reflected in the statistics – the Dublin region saw the highest growth of visitor numbers in Ireland in the 1990s, such that by the late 1990s Dublin received 3 million overseas visitors and over 1 million domestic visits, contributing a spend of well over I£500 million.

Tourist resources of Dublin

The main tourist resources of Dublin are its history, literary heritage, national institutions and the character of the old city with its fine eighteenth-century buildings. This was celebrated in 1991 when Dublin became the 'European City of Culture'. As a city, Dublin has ancient origins dating from a Viking settlement in the ninth century AD, which developed into a medieval walled city, before being followed by a major period of prosperity and expansion in the eighteenth century, when many of Dublin's finest buildings were erected. Some of the finest examples of Georgian architecture can be seen today along the canals and in the wide streets and spacious squares. The tourist resources of

Dublin are focused in a small geographical area, ideal for exploration on foot using the themed trails available.

Recent refurbishment and redevelopment has been careful to maintain both the streetscape and detail of Dublin, while enhancing the townscape for both residents and visitors. This has been aided by the Historic Heart of Dublin Project. The project has EU funding to document Dublin's building stock and reverse areas of urban decline, social disadvantage and unemployment. The project aims to encourage the economic viability of the heart of Dublin as a truly sustainable city where the heritage is respected and restored and the economic and social needs of the community are met in the spirit of Agenda 21.

Geographically, the tourist resources of Dublin have two foci – the River Liffey and Trinity College.

The River Liffey divides the city into the northside and the southside and was the focus for Dublin's city-wide initiatives to celebrate the millennium including:

- the Millennium footbridge across the River Liffey
- a boardwalk along the banks of the River Liffey.

On the southside of the river, Trinity College houses the Book of Kells and is central to Dublin's emergent tourist zones:

- To the south and south-east of Trinity College lie attractive Georgian squares such as Fitzwilliam Square and important national institutions – the National Museum, the National Gallery of Ireland, the National History Museum and the Genealogical Office – an important resource for the ethnic tourism market retracing their Irish roots, and two exhibitions of Dublin's history and background – The Dublin Civic Museum and Dublina.
- To the west lies Temple Bar, a newly emerging left bank area of the Liffey with art galleries, shops, pubs, restaurants and street entertainers.
- Beyond Temple Bar is Dublin Castle – the former seat of government under British rule – and the two cathedrals – St Patrick's and Christ Church.

Across the river on the northside is one of Ireland's most famous streets – O'Connell Street with the General Post Office – leading to a cluster of attractions including:

- the Hugh Lane Municipal Gallery of Modern Art in a Georgian mansion in Parnell Square
- the Dublin National Museum
- Dublin Writers Museum featuring the lives and works of Dublin's literary celebrities, such as Joyce, Wilde and Sheridan
- Phoenix Park – Europe's largest enclosed park, in the centre of the city.

Transport, accommodation and organization of tourism

Dublin Tourism is responsible for the organization of tourism and is a regional tourism authority affiliated to Bord Failté. Its duties include designing and implementing tourism strategy and action plans, new product development and tourism marketing, as well as operating the tourist information offices.

To ease traffic congestion, Dublin has the Dublin Area Rapid Transit (DART) system running on 38 kilometres of track.

There is a wide range of accommodation in and around Dublin, including 6500 serviced accommodation beds in country houses, castles, hotels and guesthouses, also farmhouses, university accommodation, hostels and campsites. Dublin's 1000 or more pubs are also a significant Irish export to the rest of the world.

Dublin is an important shopping and entertainment centre for both domestic and international visitors. Significant entertainment venues and festivals include:

- the refurbished National Concert Hall, home of the National Symphony Orchestra
- the Abbey Theatre
- the restored Gate Theatre
- the Olympia Theatre
- the Irish Film Centre
- cabaret at Jury's Cabaret and Doyle's Irish Cabaret
- festivals and events such as the Irish Film Festival, Dublin Theatre Festival and, in 1998, Dublin hosted the first start of the Tour De France to be held outside France.

(Web sites at http://www.dublincorp.ie/dublin/ and http://www.visit.ie/dublin/)

11

Scandinavia

LEARNING OBJECTIVES

After reading this chapter, you should be able to:

1 Describe the major physical regions and climate of the Scandinavian countries and understand their importance for tourism.
2 Understand the nature of Scandinavian economies and society, and their significance for tourist demand.
3 Outline the major features of demand for both domestic and international travel in Scandinavia.
4 Describe the major features of the Scandinavian tourism industry including transport, accommodation, and promotion.
5 Be aware of the importance of eco-tourism in the Scandinavian environment.
6 Demonstrate a knowledge of the tourist regions, resorts, business centres and tourist attractions of Scandinavia.

Introduction

Strictly speaking, Scandinavia consists of only three countries – Denmark, Norway and Sweden. However Finland is usually included. Although they are geographically isolated in the North Atlantic, Iceland and the Faroe Islands (which belong to Denmark) have been added, as they share with the other countries a similar culture and outlook. All these countries are members of the Nordic Council (Norden) which is responsible for a high level of co-operation in policies affecting transport, tourism, education and the environment. The Scandinavian airline – SAS – which is jointly owned by the governments of Denmark, Norway and Sweden is one such example of international co-operation, and was the first to develop transpolar routes to North America and the Far East. Despite limited natural resources, a rigorous climate and a peripheral location in Northern Europe, the Scandinavian countries have achieved economic prosperity and stability. Their health and social welfare services are among the best in the world. High environmental standards are maintained, both in the cities, which are free of litter and graffiti, and in the countryside. Compared to the crowding which afflicts most of Europe, Scandinavia can offer vast areas of sparsely populated coast and countryside, with almost unrestricted access to a range of recreational resources. Public transport systems are usually integrated and provide a viable alternative to touring by car.

The Scandinavian landscape still bears the imprint of the glaciers of the last Ice Age. The glaciers eroded the valleys of western Norway into deep troughs and scraped bare the ancient plateau surfaces of Finland and Sweden. Here the ice sheets left masses of boulder clay, which are now covered by coniferous forest dotted with lakes and outcrops of rock. Nevertheless, the region contains a great diversity of scenery. The lush farmlands of Denmark are as different as you can imagine from the lunar volcanic landscapes of Iceland, or from the forests of northern Scandinavia. The climate also varies from cool temperate in Jutland to subarctic in Northern Scandinavia. Most of the region has a continental climate with severely cold winters and warm summers. The main negative feature affecting the development of tourism is the shortness of the summer season and the darkness of winter, due to the northerly latitude.

The Scandinavian countries have shared similar cultural features since the Viking era (approximately 800–1100 AD). Historically Denmark, and later Sweden, were the dominant countries in the region – with the result that they now have a more impressive heritage of historic buildings than the other three countries. Also, the Lutheran Church has provided a measure of cultural unity since the Reformation in the sixteenth century. Nevertheless, each country has developed a strong national identity and the differences extend to international politics. Sweden for example has pursued a policy of neutrality for the last two centuries. However in 1995 it joined the EU along with Finland, following the example of Denmark, whereas Norway and Iceland have decided not to join.

The Scandinavian countries have a total population of only 24 million, which is mainly concentrated in the towns and cities of the southern part of the region. The climate as well as social and economic conditions combine to make Scandinavia one of the major generating areas in the world for holiday tourism, especially to winter-sun destinations. The people enjoy a high standard of living, but at the same time place great emphasis on leisure, outdoor recreation and the quality of life; levels of education are high and typical annual leave entitlement is five weeks or more. Add to this a well-developed and efficient travel trade throughout the region, and it is no surprise that levels of both domestic and foreign holiday-taking are much higher than the average for Europe. Holidays abroad represent around one-third of all holidays taken by residents of Norway, Sweden and Denmark and, in consequence, these countries have a deficit on their international travel account. A large percentage of these holidays are to other countries in the region, facilitated by the abolition of passport controls for inter-Scandinavian travel. This does mean, however, that statistics for international travel between Scandinavian countries are not collected, making it difficult to measure regional tourism flows. In domestic tourism there is a growing trend for short second holidays, especially those based on winter sports and other types of outdoor recreation.

On the other hand, the relatively high cost of living, high levels of taxation and strong currencies combine to make Scandinavia an expensive destination for foreign visitors. The majority of tourists are from other parts of Europe, especially Germany. There is a widespread perception that Scandinavia is not only more expensive but also less accessible than other destinations, involving long journeys by road and car ferry, or expensive air travel. The completion of a number of bridges and tunnels connecting the Danish islands to the mainland will greatly improve transport by road and rail between Scandinavia and the rest of Europe. With deregulation under the EU, air fares are set to fall substantially, while Copenhagen is rapidly becoming a major hub for long-haul as well as inter-regional air services. Inbound tourism to Scandinavia should also increase as interest in 'green tourism' gathers momentum. The tourism products offered by the Scandinavian countries are generally more 'environment friendly' than those available in the Mediterranean and other 'sunlust' destinations. They include:

- camping and self-catering holidays in the countryside
- city breaks
- summer sea cruises along the Norwegian and Baltic coasts
- a range of activity and 'wilderness adventure' holidays.

Denmark

The smallest and most densely populated of the Scandinavian countries, Denmark lacks wilderness areas and spectacular scenery (the highest point is only 170 metres above sea level). Denmark's appeal lies in its neat, gently rolling countryside and picturesque towns and villages, immortalized by Hans Andersen. Consisting essentially of 100 inhabited islands and the Jutland Peninsula, with only a short land border with Germany, no part of the country is far from the sea. It is therefore not surprising to find that sailing is a popular pastime and that the Danes have the highest rate of yacht ownership in Europe. They also have one of the highest rates of ownership of second homes (known locally as 'summer houses'). Much of the demand is generated from the capital, Copenhagen, where most families live in flats. Cycling is also very popular – the topography is ideal even if the weather is unpredictable, and this greenest of transport modes is encouraged by a nationwide system of bikeways. Danes have the reputation for being more informal and 'continental' than other Scandinavians, with a quality of life expressed by the Danish word *hygge* (roughly translated as 'cosy'). This is experienced in the traditional inns, as drinking laws are more relaxed than elsewhere in Scandinavia. Copenhagen is particularly renowned for its exuberant nightlife and tolerance of different lifestyles.

Danes enjoy up to six weeks' annual holiday entitlement and two-thirds of the population take a holiday away from home every year:

- *Domestic travel* Over half of these holidays are domestic. People prefer to stay with friends and relatives, or in owned and rented 'summer houses' or use camping sites in preference to serviced accommodation. Along with other Scandinavian countries, Denmark encourages the principle of 'tourism for all' or social tourism for those people who for various reasons find it difficult to take a holiday.
- *Outbound travel* Nearly half of all holidays are taken abroad. Other Scandinavian countries are less popular than Spain and Germany.
- *Inbound travel* Denmark is heavily dependent upon Germany and the rest of Scandinavia for international arrivals. International arrivals are highly seasonal with most concentrated between May and September.

Apart from Kastrup, serving Copenhagen, there are some international flights from Aarhus and Billund, operated mainly by Maersk Air. However the absence of charter flights, allied to good road and ferry links, means that surface travel is predominant. The Danish Tourist Board reports to the Ministry of Business and Industry and carries out promotion of Denmark overseas, while domestic tourism is the responsibility of the regional and local authorities.

Transport within Denmark is mainly by private car using a well-developed internal and international road system with ferry connections between the islands. Stena and Scandinavian Seaways operate international ferry services to the rest of Scandinavia, Germany and the UK. However the ferries will decline in importance as a result of the completion of a number of bridge and tunnel projects. These must rank as some of the world's most spectacular engineering feats; they include the Great Belt Bridge linking the islands of Funen and Zealand, and the Oresund Bridge and Tunnel connecting Zealand to Sweden. The Oresund link, positioned close to Copenhagen, will enhance the city's role as the gateway to Scandinavia. Another project – the Fehmarn Belt Tunnel – will provide a more direct route between Copenhagen and North Germany.

The majority of Denmark's accommodation capacity is self-catering, including summer homes and campsites, and this is where most of the growth has occurred. Hotels, inns and youth hostels are widely available, with the highest occupancy levels in Copenhagen, and, during the summer peak, on the island of Bornholm. Stays on Danish farms are popular with British families, often as part of a package deal with the ferry operators.

The advantage of a small country like Denmark is that you can follow the scenic 'Marguerite Route' and see virtually all the key attractions in the course of one touring holiday, starting with the Jutland Peninsula. Much of the peninsula is covered with pine forest and large tracts of heathland, interspersed with peat bogs, which have yielded fascinating evidence from prehistoric times. Interest in Denmark's rich and varied heritage is widespread, forming the basis of a number of folk museums where buildings and traditional crafts are preserved in an authentic setting, or in reconstructed Iron Age villages, where students re-enact the lifestyles of the remote past. The preserved 'old town' of Aarhus is another heritage attraction, which can be enjoyed alongside a vibrant modern city. Denmark is also well equipped with activity parks for children known as 'Sommerlands', but the most popular attraction is undoubtedly Legoland at Billund. Jutland's west coast has fine sandy beaches backed by dunes, but bathing is often unsafe due to the changing winds and tides. The fishing port of Esbjerg is a major centre with ferry connections to Harwich in England and the islands of Fano and Romo. It is also close to the medieval town of Ribe with its Viking Centre.

The islands of the Danish Archipelago to the east offer different landscapes and attractions:

- *Bornholm* situated in the Baltic Sea, 200 kilometres east of Copenhagen is particularly appealing with its rocky granite scenery, but is remote from the rest of the country.
- *Funen* known as the 'Garden of Denmark' is especially well equipped for tourism; Odense attracts many American tourists as the birthplace of Hans Andersen.
- *Zealand* is probably the most interesting for the foreign visitor. At Roskilde there is much evidence of Denmark's Viking past and 'longship cruises' are even available. There are a number of important historic buildings, the best known being Frederiksborg Castle, and Kronborg Castle at Helsingor famous for Shakespeare's *Hamlet*. Above all, Zealand contains Copenhagen, which is a long-established city breaks destination and a major cultural centre. With its copper-sheathed roofs and spires, harbour and pedestrianized shopping streets, the Danish capital is most attractive. Specific sights include the Tivoli Gardens, Europe's oldest amusement park, with its theatres and summer festivals, the Danish Royal Ballet, the Louisiana Museum of Modern Art, and the Carlsberg Brewery. Unlike most European capitals, Copenhagen has fine beaches and resort attractions within easy reach by public transport from the city centre.

Norway

Of all the Scandinavian countries, Norway is probably the best known. For over a century, tourists have visited the fjords in the western part of the country, attracted by the breathtaking combination of mountain and coastal scenery. The land is rugged and only 3 per cent can be cultivated; so Norwegians throughout their history have turned to the sea for their livelihoods. Norway has the longest coastline in Europe, deeply cut by the fjords, with chains of offshore islands providing a sheltered coastal waterway for shipping. Norway has a substantial merchant navy and is important in the cruise market, while sailing is a popular pastime for Norwegians. The heritage of seafaring and exploration, from the Viking longships to Amundsen and Thor Heyerdahl (of *Kon Tiki* fame) is greatly valued. The former isolation of many areas, separated by mountain and fjord, explains why Norway, in contrast to Denmark, has retained much of its traditional culture, including the wearing of colourful regional costumes on special occasions. Norway's huge resources of hydroelectric power are vital to the economy, but concern about the impact of the power industry on the environment has led to demands for more areas to be set aside as national parks.

There are substantial variations in climate in such an elongated country – the North Cape is almost 2000 kilometres by air from Kristiansand in the south. Temperatures on the coast are much milder than you would expect for such high latitudes, due to the influence of the Gulf Stream. The fjords and shipping lanes remain ice-free in winter and it is possible to grow fruit and cereals as far north as Tromso, 300 kilometres inside the Arctic Circle! To experience true Arctic conditions, you need to go even further north, to Svalbard (see the case study at the end of this chapter). It is worth emphasizing that you can only see the midnight sun in summer, weather permitting, north of the Arctic Circle; at the North Cape there is continuous daylight from mid-May to the end of July. Exposed coastal areas like Bergen receive an excessive amount of rain, while the sheltered heads of the fjords are much drier, sunnier and warmer in summer – but cold in winter. In the mountainous interior, heavy snowfalls are frequent, making it possible to ski year-round in areas like the Hardangervidda east of Bergen. The Norwegians claim to have invented skiing – although as a means of travel rather than as a sport – and they probably have the world's highest participation rate in skiing, with ski trails even in cities such as Oslo.

The prosperity of the Norwegian economy, thanks largely to North Sea oil revenues, explains why holiday propensities are high. However, holiday patterns are changing as the traditional long summer holiday gives way to shorter, more frequent trips:

- *Domestic travel* Most Norwegians take holidays within their own country, largely because the ownership of holiday chalets is widespread. Many of these are situated in the *saeter*, the high summer pastures above the treeline, and are a reminder of the pastoral life style of the past. Hiking is a popular activity in summer and skiing in winter.
- *Outbound travel* The high number of Norwegians who take a holiday abroad leaves a deficit on the country's travel account. Only a small number of trips are to other Scandinavian countries, as Norwegians prefer instead to travel to the UK (attracted by shopping bargains in Newcastle, for example), southern Europe, North Africa and the Canary Islands.
- *Inbound travel* Norway has experienced a growth of inbound travel, largely due to the Lillehammer winter Olympics and the country's image as a green destination. Norway's foreign visitors come largely from Denmark and Sweden, but those from outside Scandinavia, such as the Germans, British and Americans, tend to stay longer and spend more. There is a pronounced peaking of demand during the short summer season. The importance of the US market is partly explained by large-scale emigration from Norway in the nineteenth century.
- In such a mountainous country, getting around can be a problem – it takes over a week to travel the length of Norway by car – so air transport is important. International air passengers are served by Oslo's two airports, and domestic air services, such as those operated by Braathens SAFE, link almost fifty destinations. However, the majority of foreign visits and domestic trips are by private car, taking advantage of the improved 80 000 kilometre road network and ferry links across major fjords (although the ferries are crowded during the summer peak). The rail network run by Norwegian State Railways is more limited, since it terminates in Bodo, leaving Northern Norway without a rail service. The Bergen to Oslo railway does offer the tourist one of Europe's most scenic journeys, and it played a major role in opening up Norway for tourism. However, it is the shipping services that have traditionally provided the country with a lifeline. Tourists can travel on the Norwegian Coastal Express fleet from Bergen to Kirkenes on the Russian border. Ships call at some thirty-five ports to take on or unload passengers and cargo throughout the year. The round trip takes twelve days and is an interesting alternative to the summer holiday cruises available to the Western Fjords and 'the Land of the Midnight Sun'. Large numbers of visitors also use the ferry services operated by Color Line, Scandinavian Seaways and Stena which link Norway to the UK and Denmark through the ports of Bergen, Stavanger, Oslo and Kristiansand.

In the peak season the majority of accommodation is in camping, although other types of self-catering have grown in popularity, leading to a shortage in the supply of holiday cabins. Other accommodation is available on farms and in *rorbus* – fishermen's winter cabins built on stilts over the water's edge. Relatively few tourists, other than business travellers, use hotels although these are generally open year-round. Even so, there is an acute shortage of accommodation capacity in the popular tourist areas in the peak summer and Easter periods.

The Norwegian government recognizes the importance of the industry in aiding rural communities, transport operators and the accommodation sector, and has therefore attempted to reduce the acute seasonal and geographical concentration of visits. Nortravel Marketing (NORTRA) is the government agency responsible for promoting Norway and reports to the Ministry of Trade and Industry. It is encouraging eco-tourism and tapping new markets such as Eastern Europe and and Russia.

Western Norway

Western Norway is the most popular area for foreign visitors since it includes the five most spectacular fjords (Hardanger, Sogne, Nord, Geiranger and Romsdal), the highest mountains, and the largest glacier in mainland Europe (the Jostdalsbreen). Less well known is a cultural resource unique to Norway – the *stave* churches, built entirely of wood and with Viking features in their design. The historic port of Bergen, situated between the two longest fjords – the Hardanger and the Sogne – is the gateway for exploring this region by ship, road or rail. The Geiranger Fjord is generally recognized to be the most attractive, with its towering rockfaces and myriad waterfalls. Of the many villages lining the shores of the fjords, Laerdal, Olden and Ulvik are the most popular resorts, while Balestrand has retained much of the ambience which attracted British tourists in Victorian times. A short distance inland lies the Jotunheim National Park, Norway's most visited wilderness area, and a favourite with hikers and climbers.

Southern Norway

Southern Norway offers a gentler coastline of sheltered coves and beaches that are popular with domestic holiday-makers. Although a modern city compared to Bergen, Oslo is an established destination for cultural tourists. The main attractions are the museums celebrating Viking and maritime heritage, and the Vigeland sculpture park. Oslo is the gateway to Norway's main skiing areas, and a number of resorts have developed along the railways linking the capital to Bergen and Trondheim. Lillehammer, venue for the 1996 Winter Olympics, is the most important.

Northern Norway

Northern Norway beyond the Arctic Circle is different from the rest of the country, not least because the interior is occupied by people of an age-old, distinct culture – the *Sami* (formerly known as Lapps). Lapland also includes part of Northern Sweden and Finland but the Sami of Finnmark have retained their semi-nomadic way of life, based on reindeer herding, to a greater extent. Tourism provides a welcome source of income but as with all such indigenous peoples, represents a potential disruption to a culture which is in delicate balance with the harsh environment. The coastal communities, such as those on the Lofoten Islands, largely depend on the fishing industry and tourism is of secondary importance. The regional capital Tromso boasts the world's most northerly university and brewery. It is called 'the gateway to the Arctic' as so many polar expeditions set out from here. Most tourists then proceed to the North Cape, which ranks as a mass tourism destination by Arctic standards, attracting several thousand visitors daily during the summer.

Sweden

Although it is the largest of the Scandinavian countries, Sweden lacks the clearly defined image presented by Norway and Finland. Although it shares the Kjolen Mountains with Norway, the scenery tends to be less spectacular on the eastern slopes. With 50 per cent of its area under forest, and boasting innumerable lakes, rivers and rapids, Sweden has the largest area of unspoiled wilderness in Europe. However the country is known mainly for the quality of its industrial products, from motor vehicles to furniture, rather than for any specific tourist attractions.

Sweden's tourist resources include a varied coastline on two seas, lakes and mountains, forests, inland waterways, and a rich cultural heritage. It was the first country in Europe to develop a system of national parks to protect its wilderness areas from exploitation by the important mining, timber and wood pulp industries. Public access to the countryside is guaranteed by the traditional law known as *Allemansrätt* (every man's right), which allows the visitor to camp overnight, hike, ride, cycle and picnic on private land. Although winters are severely cold with abundant snow, summers are warm and sunny, especially along the Baltic coast. Midsummer day is the occasion for festivities throughout the country.

Sweden has a very prosperous economy, although since the early 1990s growth has declined and unemployment has risen steeply. The majority of Swedes have at least five weeks' annual holiday entitlement and the Swedes not only have one of the highest holiday propensities in the world, but also they are more likely to take a second holiday than the European average.

Domestic travel

The private car accounts for the majority of holiday trips taken by Swedes, but escalating costs have reduced the amount of touring. Self-catering accommodation is favoured, especially summer cottages. Some 600 000 of these are owned, often by people who have migrated to the cities but wish to retain a link with their rural homeland. Domestic business travel is focused on Stockholm, Gothenburg and Malmö.

Outbound travel

The Swedes are important generators of international travel. Foreign destinations popular with Swedish holidaymakers include other Scandinavian countries, Germany, Spain, Greece, Cyprus and the UK.

Inbound travel

In contrast to outbound tourism, the volume of inbound tourism is small and, although it has increased gradually through the 1990s, this still leaves a large deficit on the travel account. The main generating countries are the rest of Scandinavia, Germany, the UK, the Netherlands and the USA.

Relatively little development has taken place for a number of years in Sweden's serviced accommodation stock. Demand for hotel accommodation by domestic tourists is small, with the exception of business travellers. Acute shortages of suitable hotels in cities like Stockholm has led to the development of company flats. Self-catering accommodation in the form of summer cottages and log cabins is in demand for holiday tourism; timeshare and multi-ownership schemes are being developed, as are high quality campsites.

International air transport is served by Stockholm Arlanda, Gothenburg and Malmö airports, and domestic flights are operated by SAS and Braathen SAFE to some twenty destinations. However most holiday tourists arrive by car and ferry, or hovercraft, via the main routes from Denmark and Germany. Car travel is expensive in Sweden and government policy is to favour public transport by imposing controls on car use. Swedish railways have therefore received considerable public investment to provide high-speed routes between the major cities. There is also a nation-wide system of cycle routes.

In 1992, the state-owned Swedish Tourist Board was replaced by a private sector initiative – the Swedish Travel and Tourism Council. The Council is jointly owned by 300 private companies and is responsible for promoting Sweden at home and abroad. It is supported by an independent network of twenty-two regional organizations. A small agency, the Swedish Tourism Authority is publicly funded and has the remit of co-ordinating tourism activity in Sweden.

The main tourist areas are found in the south, along the Baltic and North Sea coasts, and in the central lake district west of Stockholm.

The Göta Canal

A linear attraction linking these three areas is the Göta Canal, 190 kilometres in length, which connects Gothenburg to Stockholm and the three largest lakes – Vänern, Vättern and Mälaren. The canal was built in the nineteenth century to provide a short cut for shipping. Although it has lost most of its significance as a commercial waterway, some of the original vessels have been adapted for summer cruises.

North Sea coast

Gothenburg is Sweden's major North Sea port but offers many cultural attractions and the Liseberg theme park, one of the largest in Scandinavia. The 'golden coast' of Bohuslän nearby is popular with Swedish families, especially the resort of Tanum Strand, which is an excellent base for exploring the many offshore islands. Scania in the extreme south of Sweden has lowland landscapes similar to those of Denmark and its capital Malmö, very close to Copenhagen, is a major business centre.

Baltic coast

On the Baltic coast, the island of Gotland with its white sandy beaches and strange rock formations has a special appeal. The well-preserved medieval city of Visby is a World Heritage Site as well as being a lively summer holiday resort.

Lake district

Lying close to the Norwegian border, the provinces of Värmland and Dalarna offer scenic lake and forest land-scapes, and are ideal for activity holidays, including fishing, canoeing, and whitewater rafting in summer. Mora on Lake Siljan has hosted international downhill ski events, but is mainly noted for the Vasaloppet, a cross-country ski race which attracts thousands of participants each March. Dalarna is regarded as the cultural heartland of Sweden, offering picturesque folk customs, heritage museums and innumerable handicraft outlets. However, the most interesting place for the foreign visitor is undoubtedly Stockholm. The capital is attractively situated on a number of islands at the entrance to Lake Mälaren, while thousands more islands scattered along the Baltic coast provide ideal sites for summer homes. The well-planned modern city contrasts with heritage attractions such as Gamla Stan (the preserved old city), the Vasa Ship Museum, and Skansen, Scandinavia's oldest folk museum. Stockholm's main event attraction is the Water Festival in August.

The North

Norrland, the sparsely populated northern half of Sweden, includes a number of wilderness national parks and part of Lapland (see the case study at the end of this chapter).

Finland

Culturally, Finland (or Suomi as it is called in Finnish) is different from the other Nordic countries due to its language and the cultural links with Russia to the east. Finland offers the visitor vast expanses of lakeland blending almost imperceptibly with forest, a unique landscape associated with the music of Sibelius. Of the total area no less than 10 per cent is inland water – lakes, marshes, rivers and rapids – while forests of conifers and birch make up another two-thirds. Eskers, long sinuous ridges of material laid down by glaciers in the last Ice Age, separate the lakes and are a distinctive feature in a landscape which is for the most part lowland. Winters are long and severe, but the Finns are adept at dealing with them; fleets of icebreakers keep open the shipping lanes and a whole range of winter sports, including ice hockey and snowmobile rallies are popular during the cold season. Much of Finland's prosperity is derived from its seemingly inexhaustible forest resources which provide timber, wood pulp and furs. The exploitation of these in the past has caused concern among environmen-talists, but as in Sweden, the timber is now harvested on a sustained yield basis. The forests and lakes are much valued as a recreational resource, and great efforts have been made to maintain water quality. Most families in Helsinki and other cities own a lakeside cabin as a second home, usually with a sauna attached. In Finland the sauna is as much a social institution as a means of relaxation.

Around 50 per cent of the population take a holiday of four nights or more away from home. The proximity of Finland close to the weak economies of the former Soviet

Union, allied to devaluations of the Finnish mark, has meant that the tourism sector has suffered from overcapacity in the 1990s. In turn this led to reductions in prices and a formerly expensive destination became much more affordable. Finland has therefore experienced considerable increases in inbound travel in the 1990s. In contrast, the growth in outbound tourism has slowed since the early 1990s in response to a downturn in the national economy and the successive devaluations of the currency.

Finland has pursued an aggressive tourism policy, spearheaded by the Finnish Tourist Board, which reports to the Ministry of Trade and Industry. Tourism is seen as a means for regional development in the rural areas, and also for diversification of Helsinki's economy. Swedish and Norwegian visitors arrive mainly by sea, in preference to the long road journey around the Gulf of Bothnia, through the ports of Helsinki, Turku, and Maarianhamina in the Aland Islands. Visitors from other West European countries can take the more direct ferry route operated by Finnjet from Travemunde in North Germany. Air transport has grown steadily in importance, with Helsinki acting as the gateway and Finnair as the national airline. Domestic transport arrangements are excellent, with broad all-weather highways, an improved rail system and a network of domestic air services to over twenty destinations.

Motels and hotels are concentrated in the major cities (Helsinki, Turku and Tampere) where business travel means they can maintain a high annual bed occupancy rate (up to 75 per cent in Helsinki). Finland can also provide low-density holiday villages, concentrated in the central lakeland area, holiday cottages, farm accommodation and campsites. Seasonality is high, the majority of foreign tourists arriving between May and October with a peak in July. In consequence, roughly one-quarter of the accommodation stock is only open for part of the year. A conscious effort has been made to extend the season by developing conference and winter sports tourism. Partly because of Finland's post-Second World War neutrality in world politics, Helsinki has become a major international conference centre, offering facilities such as Finlandia Hall and first-class hotels.

Finland's appeal to foreign visitors lies in its uncrowded natural resources and it has capitalized fully on the growth of eco-tourism.

Lapland

Finnish Lapland especially offers scope for wilderness adventure holidays, both for independent travellers and for package tourists. Summer activities include rafting, canoeing, gold panning, mountain-biking – while in winter 'reindeer safaris' involving a stay in a Sami encampment, and dog-sled expeditions are on offer. Charter flights are available in December from Britain to Rovaniemi, the main tourist centre, which has been promoted with considerable success as 'the home of Santa Claus' and now has a theme park – Santa Park. As a result Finland has a larger share of winter visitors from the UK than any other Nordic country. Skiing 'under the midnight sun' is available in the far north near Lake Inari, where the forest at last gives way to barren fells and tundra.

Saimaa Lake District

The best opportunities for outdoor recreation are to be found in the Saimaa Lake District in the south east of the country. The lakes offer no less than 50 000 kilometres of shoreline and are forested down to the waters' edge; not surprisingly, this is a popular area in summer. The main tourist centres are Lapeenranta for summer cruises, and the spa town of Savonlinna which has an international opera festival. The Karelia forest region bordering Russia is culturally distinct, as shown by the many Orthodox churches.

The coasts

Both the southern and western coasts of Finland are characterized by clusters of offshore islands which provide opportunities for sailing. Seafaring traditions are particularly important in the Aland Islands which are Swedish speaking and autonomous. For this reason they are popular with Swedish as well as Finnish holidaymakers, not least for the duty-free shopping available on the ferries. Other places of interest include the resort of Hanko, favoured by the Russian aristocracy prior to the 1917 Revolution, and Helsinki. Finland's capital is noted more for its fine modern architecture than for historic buildings. It has however been designated a European City of Culture and is a convenient starting-point for excursions to St Petersburg and Estonia.

Iceland

Promoted as 'a land of ice and fire', exposed to the raw forces of nature, Iceland is geologically unique. This large island is located on one of the major fault lines in the Earth's' crust and contains over 200 volcanoes – major eruptions and earthquakes occur on average every five years. Although one-fifth of the country is covered by glaciers, Iceland is by no means as cold as its western neighbour Greenland, thanks to the warming influence of the Gulf Stream. However, its location close to the Arctic Ocean does mean that the weather is highly unpredictable, and in winter abysmal. The tourist season is short, even by Scandinavian standards, and summer temperatures rarely exceed 20°C (although it may feel warmer as the air is unpolluted and remarkably clear). Iceland's abundant geothermal resources are harnessed to heat swimming pools, buildings and greenhouses. One well-known example is the so-called 'Blue Lagoon' outside Reykjavik, which is actually an effluent reservoir from a power plant. Agriculture is largely restricted to sheep farming and the landscape is for the most part treeless. Nearly all the population lives in or near the coast, while the interior is made up of desert-like lava plateaux or rugged volcanic mountains.

With few resources other than the dominant fishing industry, Iceland is anxious to encourage tourism. Promotion is the responsibility of the Icelandic Tourist Board assisted by the national carrier Icelandair. Because Iceland is an expensive destination and relatively difficult to reach, the volume of inbound tourism is small, though growing and significant given the country's sparse population. Visitors come mainly from the USA, Germany and the UK. The volume of outbound tourism is constrained by the scant leisure time available to many Icelanders (who have to 'moonlight' at a second job to maintain their high living standards).

The bulk of the air transport services from Western Europe and Scandinavia are provided by Icelandair and SAS, while the international airport at Keflavik is often used as a stopover on transatlantic flights. Access by sea is much less convenient and comprises ferry services from Bergen, the Shetlands and Esbjerg. There is an extensive domestic air network which is necessary in view of the fact the Iceland has no railways and the least developed highway network of any country in Europe (Albania excepted). In fact, most of the roads, especially in the rugged interior, are suitable only for four wheel drive vehicles. Iceland's accommodation stock comprises hotels, guesthouses, youth hostels, farms and campsites.

Iceland's tourism appeal lies in its unspoiled natural scenery and the scope for adventure holidays. Pony trekking for example, is a successful product utilizing the native breed of horse which is small and uniquely adapted to the rugged terrain. Other activities include bird-watching, whale-watching, skidoo driving across glaciers, rafting and camping expeditions. Skiing facilities on a modest scale are available near Reykjavik and Akureyri. The most popular tourist attractions are located in the 'Golden Circle' east of Reykjavik, including the Gullfoss waterfall, the Great Geyser and the Thingvellir National Park – a spectacular natural amphitheatre where Iceland's parliament was held in Viking times. Another cluster of natural attractions in the north of the country includes Lake Myvatn and Dettifoss, Europe's largest waterfall. Human-made attractions are few, and found mainly in Reykjavik, which is an unpretentious medium size city, dominated by low-rise wooden buildings. It does contain 60 per cent of the country's population and most of its high-class accommodation. It is also remarkable for the creative energy of its young people. Some of the local foods on the menu are not for the squeamish – a reminder of the rugged lifestyle endured by previous generations of Ice-landers, who had to make do with whatever resources were available.

The Faroes

The Faroes consist of eighteen inhabited islands in the stormy North Atlantic, halfway between the Shetlands and Iceland.

They are a self-governing nation within the Kingdom of Denmark, but they have stayed outside the EU. Tourism is much less important than the fishing industry, which may explain why the Faroese have rejected calls from the world's environmentalists that they should give up their whaling traditions. The excessively wet and windy climate is a major constraint on tourism, but the islands can offer some of Europe's most spectacular cliff scenery and vast colonies of seabirds. The Faroes are accessible by scheduled flights from Copenhagen and by summer ferry services from Esbjerg, Bergen and Iceland.

Summary

Scandinavia's climate is typified by severely cold, long winters and warm, sunny summers. The varied landscapes include forested countryside dotted with lakes, indented coastlines with fjords and islands, and the volcanic features of Iceland. Social and economic conditions have combined to make Scandinavia one of the major generating regions in the world for holiday tourism, delivering a deficit on the travel account for the region. Inter-Scandinavian travel has been particularly popular, facilitated by the abolition of passport controls.

Accommodation capacity in the short summer season is dominated by the self-catering sector as serviced accom-modation is in short supply. The majority of international tourists arrive by car using the many ferry services available, though international air links are comprehensive. Internal travel will be facilitated by new tunnels and bridges, and is typified by rapid intercity rail links, broad, surfaced highways, and extensive domestic air and sea links. The most important of Scandinavia's tourist resources are the uncrowded, unpolluted countryside, the spectacular scenery of the mountains and many coastal regions, the islands and holiday beaches, and the Scandinavian culture and outdoor way of life on show in the capitals and major cities of the region.

Case study

Adventure tourism in two areas of Arctic Scandinavia – Swedish Lapland and Svalbard

Introduction

Approximately one-third of Scandinavia lies within the Arctic Circle, while the Norwegian islands known as Svalbard lie only 1000 kilometres from the North Pole. However climatic conditions are not as severe as they are in similar latitudes in Greenland, Northern Canada, Alaska and Siberia. The high northerly latitude is compensated to some extent by the warming influence of the North Atlantic Drift, which keeps the seas around the North Cape ice-free all year round, allowing the majority of visitors to Svalbard to arrive by ship rather than by air. In Swedish Lapland summer temperatures compare favourably with those of Scotland much further south.

Swedish Lapland

Of the two areas in this case study, Swedish Lapland offers much more potential for tourism and other types of economic development. Apart from a warmer climate than Svalbard, it has the following advantages over other Arctic regions:

- It is within easy reach by road, rail and air transport of the major population centres of Sweden and Finland.
- It has been settled by incomers from the south since the sixteenth century, and has a well-developed infrastructure.

Nevertheless the towns still have a frontier look about them compared to those in southern Sweden. The formerly nomadic Sami people have been assimilated into the mainstream Swedish economy and social structure, without suffering the exploitation, welfare dependency, and loss of cultural identity that have befallen other indigenous communities in the Arctic.

Mining is the main economic activity in the region. This is the basis for the prosperity of Kiruna, one of the largest cities north of the Arctic Circle, which is noted for its nightlife throughout Sweden (it also boasts the world's largest iron ore mine). Tourism in the region began in the late nineteenth century, and is growing in importance for the following reasons:

1 *Interest in eco-tourism and green issues* Swedish Lapland is one of the largest areas of unspoiled wilderness in Europe. It boasts six national parks, of which Abisko is the best known, extensive forests of pine, spruce and birch, expanses of tundra, lakes and mountain scenery, and fast-flowing, unpolluted rivers. With only 5 per cent of Sweden's population, yet covering 25 per cent of its area, the region is renowned for silence and solitude, especially in winter when the night sky is frequently lit up by displays of the aurora borealis (northern lights).
2 *Winter sports* Swedish Lapland is Europe's most northerly developed ski area, offering skiers and snowboarders the novelty of practising their sport until late June under the midnight sun. The area is guaranteed heavy snowfalls, with less risk of avalanches than in the Alpine resorts. However, the season does not start until mid-February, due to the

short period of winter daylight. Riksgränsen, situated close to the Norwegian border, on the railway linking Kiruna to Narvik, is the main centre, where Sweden's first ski school was established in 1932. There are extensive cross-country trails for ski-touring and telemarking, but with a vertical descent of only 400 metres, Riksgränsen's slopes have less appeal for downhill skiers. Other winter activities include ice-fishing, snow-scooter safaris and sledging with a team of huskies.

3 *Sami (Lapp) culture* Jukkasjärvi, whose name means meeting place in the Sami language, and Jokkmokk are the traditional centres of Sami culture, where the old ways have continued to flourish, and silver and leather handicrafts are sold to tourists. Here the Sami still wear their brightly-coloured leather clothing, and use dog teams for reindeer round-ups, whereas elsewhere they tend to use snowmobiles and mobile phones.
4 *The Ice Hotel* Jukkasjärvi also offers a truly unique winter attraction – the Ice Hotel – promoted as the world's largest igloo. This is an interesting example of sustainable tourism, using renewable natural resources. The rooms and furniture of the hotel are made from 30 000 tons of ice and compacted snow, which is taken each November from the frozen River Torne, and the structure is used until it melts, usually in early May. The temperature inside the hotel is kept at a constant −7°C, although outside it may fall as low as −35°C. Bed furnishings are made from reindeer hides and skins, whose insulating properties provide protection from the low temperatures, but needless to say, most tourists prefer to use the adjoining wooden chalet-style huts. The Ice Hotel attracts a variety of clients, from conference groups to Japanese honeymoon couples.
5 *Other outdoor activities* Summer activities include white water rafting, hiking, mountain climbing and fishing. Swedish Lapland boasts the world's most northerly golf course at Björkliden. Field sports are popular in autumn, while survival training in one of Europe's most rugged environments is available all year round.

Svalbard

Svalbard is situated 1000 kilometres north of the Norwegian mainland but is actually closer to Greenland. Spitzbergen is the name given to the largest island of the group, which is noted for its dramatic landscape of fjords, ice-sculpted mountains and glaciers, as well as for the variety of wildlife that has adapted to an inhospitable environment. Svalbard is in the High Arctic, north of latitude 75° – where winter is characterized by several months of continuous darkness as well as extreme cold. In summer, temperatures rarely rise above 10°C, despite continuous daylight from April to August, and the weather is also highly unpredictable. West Spitzbergen is much more accessible than the rest of the archipelago, which is hemmed in by pack ice for most of the year. Uninhabited at the time of its discovery, West Spitzbergen now contains three settlements, two of which are Russian and the third – Longyearbyen – Norwegian. These are based on a coal mining industry that is no longer competitive in world markets. Although the islands are under Norwegian sovereignty, they are regarded as an international zone for commercial activities.

West Spitzbergen was the base for a number of expeditions to the North Pole in the early part of the twentieth century. These played a major role in attracting international interest in the area, with visitors arriving by cruise ship from mainland Norway. During the 1990s over 20 000 cruise passengers a year visited the islands, attracted by the wild Arctic scenery. Longyearbyen offers some tourist facilities, but the main attraction is Magdalen Fjord, with its heritage of the former whaling industry and polar exploration. Some air passengers spend a few days in Longyearbyen and take part in day excursions, whereas others, mainly Norwegian, are attracted by wilderness adventures, which include:

- trekking and mountain climbing
- exploring the coast by kayak or zodiac (inflatable craft with an outboard motor)
- snowmobile 'safaris' and skiing during the spring months
- bird-watching
- survival training and leadership courses.

Most of these activities require months of planning and preparation, and tourists are usually aware of the risk in challenging the wilderness, which include the possibility of attacks by polar bears (a protected species in Svalbard). Nevertheless, the Norwegian government has imposed a comprehensive system of regulations on tour operators as well as independent travellers, to ensure the protection of the fragile Arctic ecosystems, as well as visitor safety. For example, tour operators must notify the Governor of Svalbard of their activities, and are responsible for their clients' behaviour.

Tourism in Svalbard is far from being a minor activity, as it provides employment for some 10 per cent of the population. Nevertheless, it will have to be considerably expanded if it is to replace coal mining as the mainstay of the economy, but this in turn will increase environmental impacts.

12

The Benelux countries

LEARNING OBJECTIVES

After reading this chapter, you should be able to:

1 Describe the physical regions and climate of the Benelux countries and understand their importance for tourism.
2 Understand the relationship between the individual Benelux countries and be aware of their linguistic contrasts.
3 Appreciate the scale of demand for both domestic holidays and holidays abroad, and the nature of that demand.
4 Outline the main features of the tourism industry in the Benelux countries.
5 Demonstrate a knowledge of the tourist regions, resorts, business centres, and tourist attractions of the Benelux countries.

Introduction

Three small countries in Western Europe – Belgium, the Netherlands and Luxembourg – have a much greater economic, cultural and political significance than you would expect from their size. Historically known as the Low Countries, the Netherlands and most of Belgium are made up of lowland plains adjoining the North Sea, while flat-topped uplands are characteristic of southern Belgium and Luxembourg. Areas of heathland separate the coastal lowlands from the uplands of the Ardennes, which rise to just over 600 metres above sea level. The region has a cool maritime climate similar to that of England. Near the coast the cloudy weather is unpromising for tourism with moderate rainfall throughout the year, whereas inland the maritime influence begins to fade; winters are colder, with enough snow in the Ardennes for skiing, and summers are warmer.

Culturally the Benelux countries are interesting for their heritage of historic buildings and art treasures, a reminder that the region has played a major role in European history. However, their economic prosperity has frequently led to conflict with powerful neighbours, with the result that after the Second World War Belgium, the Netherlands and Luxembourg led the way to European unity with the formation of a customs union. This means that restrictions on movement between the three countries are minimal. With a combined population of 26 million, the Benelux states are the most densely populated countries in Europe. Not only does this lead to intense competition for land use, but it also places pressure on the environment to the extent that any proposed tourist developments are very closely scrutinized. The economies of the three countries have grown steadily in the postwar period, giving rise to increasing demands for both domestic and foreign tourism. Expenditure on overseas travel exceeds the receipts from inbound tourism in all the countries of the region. Annual holiday entitlement averages five or more weeks and a typical working week is less than forty hours.

The Netherlands

The Netherlands Tourist Board promotes the country as 'Holland', although the name really applies to just two of the eleven provinces that united to resist Spanish rule in the sixteenth century. Holland has a strong identity; its landscapes and cultural features are known worldwide. The Dutch contribution to art, with painters like Rembrandt, Frans Hals, Vermeer and Van Gogh, has been immense.

Dutch achievements in seamanship, agriculture and engineering have also been remarkable. Much of the country, especially in the west, is made up of flat *polderlands* reclaimed from the sea. The story of this reclamation and the constant battle against the sea is proudly told in exhibitions and museums, as well as in the many engineering works (such as the Delta Plan) which are tourist attractions in themselves. The countryside is criss-crossed by dykes and canals, although relatively few windmills now survive along with the 'meers' (lakes) resulting from early drainage schemes. However, much of the east and south of the Netherlands is scenically different, with extensive areas of heath and woodland.

The Netherlands can also offer cultural diversity. For centuries the Dutch ruled a major overseas empire, with colonies in the Caribbean, South America, South Africa and Asia. The influence of their most important former colony – Indonesia – is evident for example in the buffet-style *rijstaffel*. Perhaps because of their maritime outlook and the pressures of living in a small, crowded country, the Dutch have a reputation for both tidiness and tolerance, and it is probably this which has attracted young tourists from all over the world. In contrast, some of the formerly isolated fishing communities around what was once the Zuider Zee (now the Ijsselmeer) have retained a strong religious outlook, along with the wearing of the traditional costumes that attract tourists. The Netherlands is also a major industrial nation. High living standards, urban pressures, excellent transport systems, and an unpredictable climate have combined to encourage the development of theme parks and innovative ideas in leisure. The best known examples are the De Efteling Family Leisure Park near Breda, and the CenterParcs accommodation concept, which uses advanced technology to create an all-weather leisure environment in an attractive woodland setting.

The level of economic development has fuelled the demand for leisure and tourism. Throughout the 1990s foreign holidays by the Dutch have eroded the share of domestic holidays, while expenditure on overseas travel exceeds the receipts from inbound tourists.

Domestic travel

Domestic holidays (particularly short trips) and day excursions are an important sector of the Dutch industry. The majority of domestic holidays are concentrated in July and August, leading to congestion in popular holiday areas. A nationwide programme to stagger holidays was introduced in 1983 to help ease seasonal congestion, while a trend to more winter holidays may also help combat the problem. Most people taking domestic holidays use the private car and tend to stay in self-catering accommodation (such as summerhouses, caravans, campsites, or holiday villages) rather than in hotels. Despite the prevalent use of the private car, the Dutch rarely take touring holidays, preferring instead single-centre stays in their small and crowded country. Business and conference tourism is an important sector of the domestic market. Good-quality conference facilities are dispersed throughout the country in both purpose-built centres and in hotels, motels and holiday villages. International conferences are seen as a growth area, especially given the Netherlands' central position in Europe.

Outbound travel

The Dutch have one of the highest holiday propensities in Europe as they take more holidays abroad than in their own country; the Netherlands are a major generator of international tourists on a world scale. New destinations such as South Africa are popular, as is the increasing trend to take winter holidays (particularly skiing). The small size of the country encourages day excursions and cross-border trips (around two-thirds of all foreign trips are to neighbouring countries).

Inbound travel

The Netherlands also receive large numbers of visitors. The majority of tourists are from Western Europe, dominated by arrivals from Germany. Inbound tourism to the Netherlands has shown modest growth in the 1990s, partly due to a range of special events (such as major art exhibitions) and the Dutch tourism authorities' promotional campaigns. The international short-break market is important in the Netherlands with most foreigners only staying for two to three nights on average. However, in contrast to the domestic market, they tend to use serviced accommodation. In consequence, serviced accommodation and foreign visitors are concentrated into a few centres; Amsterdam alone accounts for around 50 per cent of the commercial bednights spent in the country.

Tourists can enter the Netherlands through Schiphol, Amsterdam's international airport. The national airline is KLM, which, together with its subsidiary BTLM, carries domestic passengers and those travelling to neighbouring countries. Martinair and Transavia are the main tourist charter airlines. Other international gateways are Maastricht Airport and the ferry terminals at Vlissingen, Europort and the Hook of Holland, mainly handling passengers from the British Isles. Surface transport arrangements are excellent both throughout the Netherlands and also into neighbouring countries with 90 000 kilometres of road and a comprehensive intercity rail network. There is a fully integrated public transport network of buses, trams, and trains. Cycling is encouraged with a nationwide system of dedicated routes.

Accommodation in the Netherlands is dominated by self-catering with campsites, holiday villages, and a network of trekkers' huts for cyclists and walkers. This sector of the accommodation market is well developed in the Netherlands to meet the demand for inexpensive family holidays.

Also, given the extensive water resources of the Netherlands, marinas are an important source of accommodation. Overall, serviced accommodation capacity is declining, particularly in the boarding-house sector.

Tourism promotion, both domestic and international, is the responsibility of the Netherlands National Tourist Office, sponsored by the Ministry of Economic Affairs. The Office is backed by regional, provincial and local promotion, as well as by the Netherlands Congress Bureau. The government is improving tourist infrastructure by investing in bungalow parks, hotels, marinas and tourist attractions. Promotional themes focus on waterland, cultural/historic heritage, cities and the seaside. This reflects the fact that each of the provinces of the Netherlands has special appeal for foreign visitors, (except maybe for Flevoland, which is almost entirely polders reclaimed from the Zuider Zee in the 1930s). Most foreign tourists are attracted to the western half of the country, particularly to the cities of the Randstad. This is a ring of urban development that contains almost half the population of the Netherlands, but on just 15 per cent of its land area. Development in the Randstad is therefore carefully planned to preserve its 'green heart' – an area of attractive countryside inside the ring that includes the world-famous bulbfields around the historic town of Haarlem. The Randstad includes the following major tourist centres:

- The Hague (Den Haag), the diplomatic capital of the Netherlands; attractions nearby include Madurodam – Holland in miniature – the pottery town of Delft and the resort of Scheveningen
- Utrecht, famous for its university
- Rotterdam, Europe's largest port at the mouth of the Rhine. Whereas other Dutch cities tend to promote their heritage attractions, Rotterdam was rebuilt after the Second World War and is thoroughly modern in its outlook and architecture.

Amsterdam

Amsterdam is also located in the Randstat. It is the commercial capital of the Netherlands, and one of the world's top five tourist centres. Most of the historic area dates from Amsterdam's Golden Age in the seventeenth century, when the city was the hub of a vast trading empire, and there was little expansion or rebuilding in the long period of subsequent decline. The merchant's houses, with their intricate brickwork, stepped gables, and narrow frontage along tree-lined canals – now form one of the world's most picturesque urban landscapes.

Amsterdam boasts an excellent transport infrastructure that includes the famous trams, a network of cycleways and a metro system that should provide improved access to Schiphol Airport and reduce car use. The *Grachtengirdle* – the concentric ring of canals – is now mainly used for sightseeing excursions.

Compared with London or Paris, Amsterdam has few individual buildings that are internationally renowned as tourist attractions. The floating flower market on the Singelgracht, and the Ann Frank House – a reminder of the city's important Jewish community – are among the most popular with foreign visitors. Art lovers are attracted to the Rijksmuseum and the Van Gogh Museum. However, the main appeal of Amsterdam lies in its street life, shops, cafés and entertainment facilities. These include the theatres around the Leidseplein, the smoke-filled 'brown bars' of the Jordaen district, and the De Wallen area near the Eastern Docks which has a long-established sex industry.

Amsterdam faces a number of problems in competing with other European cities as a tourist destination, namely:

1 Tourism development is often given a low priority by the city government, whose policies are aimed at maintaining a large resident population in subsidized housing in the historic centre.
2 Long-established perceptions of the city relate to a particular time period – the seventeenth century – which make change and diversification difficult.
3 Since the 1960s a very different image – of Amsterdam as a city of drugs and sex – has become deeply ingrained in the popular culture, especially among young tourists. This has led in some areas to an ambience of sleaze, litter and drug-related crime that provides an unwelcome contrast to the traditional Dutch obsession with cleanliness and public order.

The North Sea coast

The North Sea coast with its sandy beaches backed by dunes is served by a string of resorts, which attract large numbers of German holidaymakers (mainly from the Ruhr conurbation) as well as the Dutch themselves. The busiest resorts are:

- Zandvoort – noted for its motor racing circuit
- Noordwijk – renowned for its flower gardens
- Scheveningen – Holland's best known seaside resort.

After a long period of decline, Scheveningen was transformed by an ambitious scheme of reinvestment in exciting new leisure facilities, and it has become a major conference venue, as a well as a classic example of the rejuvenation stage of the tourism area life cycle (see Chapter 3). Between the resorts there are conservation areas where further development is strictly prohibited. This is because the dunes, which play a vital part in Holland's coastal defences, are very vulnerable to visitor pressure. To the south lies the province of Zeeland, originally a group of islands at the mouth of the Rhine, now joined up by the Delta Plan to create an environment suitable for a wide range of water sports. In contrast, the medieval towns of Middelburg and Veere have much to attract the heritage tourist.

Friesland

In the north-east, the province of Friesland offers a more tranquil environment of small rural communities where the Frisian language is still spoken. The main attraction here is the Frisian Lake District around the resort of Sneek that offers facilities for boating and sailing. Separated from the mainland by the extensive mudflats of the Wadden See, the Frisian Islands such as Texel provide fine beaches, self-catering accommodation and a number of important nature reserves.

Gelderland

Gelderland in the east of the country is under-populated by Dutch standards, and large expanses of heath and woodland have been designated as the Hoge Veluwe National Park. The city of Arnhem was the scene of a major battle in the Second World War, as the bridging point over the river Rhine close to the German border, and now offers a number of museums and attractions focusing on the region.

Limburg

The province of Limburg in the extreme south is the only part of the Netherlands that can be described as hilly. Partly for this reason the resort of Valkenburg, with its casinos and golf courses, is very popular among domestic tourists. The attractive city of Maastricht has taken advantage of its location on the borders of three countries to become an important venue for international conferences.

Belgium

It can be difficult to define the tourism product of Belgium compared to neighbouring France, Germany and Holland. This is largely because the country is divided in language and culture between the Dutch-speaking Flemings in the north and the French-speaking Walloons in the south. Scenically too, the flat farmlands of Flanders and the heaths of the Kempen are quite different in character from the hills and forests of the Ardennes. Moreover Belgium as an independent nation did not exist until 1830. In the Middle Ages, cities such as Bruges, Ghent, Antwerp and Liège were to a large extent independent, and grew wealthy on the profits of the cloth trade. However, lack of political unity led to the region being dominated by the great powers of the time, namely Burgundy, France, Spain and the Austrian Empire. Unlike the Dutch, the Belgians were generally ready to accept foreign rule and remained strongly Roman Catholic after the Reformation in the sixteenth century. This is shown by the abundance of religious art and impressive Baroque architecture in cities such as Brussels. Because of its location, Belgium was the 'cockpit of Europe' in the frequent wars between France and other countries. Some of the many battlefields have become historic sites on the tourist itinerary, notably:

- Waterloo just south of Brussels (the Napoleonic Wars)
- the cemeteries and war memorials around Mons and Ypres (First World War)
- the 'Battle of the Bulge' museum at Bastogne in the Ardennes (Second World War).

Although it can offer beaches, attractive waterways and fine scenery, Belgium's appeal is mainly cultural, in the widest sense. Like the French, the Flemish and Walloons take food and drink seriously, and it is worth noting that the country produces little wine but over 400 different kinds of beer! As this is a Catholic country, the tourist can also enjoy many interesting festivals, although by no means all are religious in character. As in the Netherlands, theme parks are popular, which attract large numbers of tourists from neighbouring countries such as France.

About half of the Belgian population takes an annual holiday away from home and growth of holidays abroad has outstripped growth in the domestic market, equally, expenditure on travel overseas outstrips receipts from inbound tourists.

Domestic travel

For domestic holidays the most popular form of transport is the car, and self-catering accommodation (holiday villages, caravans and camping) is becoming increasingly used, as serviced accommodation declines in popularity. Social tourism is important in the Belgian domestic market. The Ardennes and the coast are the most popular holiday regions.

Outbound travel

Belgium is an important generator of international tourists. The majority of main holidays are taken abroad. Most trips are to neighbouring countries, but Italy and Spain are also important destinations. As in the Netherlands, the high number of trips abroad leaves a deficit on the travel account.

Inbound travel

The performance of Belgium as an international tourism destination has been disappointing throughout the 1990s. The majority of foreign arrivals are from other European countries – particularly the Netherlands. However, visits from neighbouring countries tend to be short compared to visits from, say, the UK or the USA. Business trips are concentrated into Brussels (particularly as it hosts the European Commission), and Antwerp; while international conferences are attracted to the seaside resorts of Ostend and Knokke, as well as to new facilities in Liège and

Bruges. Apart from these business travel centres, visits elsewhere in the country tend to be for holiday purposes.

In the serviced accommodation sector low occupancy rates mean that few new hotels are being built and, despite government assistance schemes, little investment is occurring in the existing hotel stock. Most hotel guests are business travellers while demand for self-catering accommodation comes from holidaymakers. Campsites, holiday villages, chalets and apartments are available.

Both external and internal transport links are highly developed. Brussels is the gateway to Belgium for the great majority of air travellers, although the airports at Antwerp, Liège and Ostend do have some international services. More significant from the viewpoint of price-conscious British tourists are the ferry services to Ostend and Zeebrugge, including a fast catamaran connection. The Channel tunnel is providing competition for the ferry operators and the airlines, so that the Eurostar fast train service from London to Brussels has gained a large share of the lucrative business travel market. Belgium has an extensive motorway network for such a small country (over 1250 kilometres). The environmental impact has been considerable, but it does mean that no part of the country is more than three hours' drive from the coast, and Belgium's traditional role as 'the crossroads of Europe' has been enhanced. The Belgian railway network is less convenient for touring the country, as it is focused on Brussels.

The small size of the tourism industry in Belgium has meant that government policy for tourism is low on the priority list and lacks clear objectives. There are separate promotional commissions for the French-speaking and Flemish regions, both with head offices in Brussels, while the Belgian National Tourist Office oversees the promotion of Belgium abroad.

The tourist resource base is very diverse for a country of this size, and we may summarize these resources as:

- the coastal resorts
- the art cities of northern Belgium
- the Ardennes.

The coastal resorts

The North Sea coast, like that of Holland, is sandy, flat and backed by dunes. However flooding has been less of a problem in the past than the silting up of ports such as Bruges, which now lies a considerable distance inland. The coast is only 60 kilometres in length and it has suffered from overdevelopment and lack of planning, as shown by the ribbon development of high-rise apartments and holiday villas. However the beaches are well maintained, colourful windbreaks provide protection from the constant breezes, while the resorts provide many amenities. A tramway linking all the resorts offers a safe alternative to the car in an area where traffic can reach saturation point in peak season. In addition to domestic tourists, the coast is popular with

Germans, while Ostend has long been an established favourite with the British. The resorts differ a good deal in size and character:

- De Panne with its wide expanse of beach can offer sand-yachting as an activity for the young affluent visitor
- Zeebrugge caters more for families
- Ostend and Blankenberge are the busiest resorts, providing a sophisticated holiday product including casinos
- Knokke-Heist near the Dutch border is definitely up-market.

The art cities

The main attractions for foreign tourists are the art cities, mostly situated in Flanders within easy reach of the coast. These are ideal for short breaks, or as part of an extended tour taking in Northern France and the Rhineland. The heritage of Gothic and Renaissance art and architecture is a reminder, not only of the power of the Church, but also the wealth and prestige of the merchant guilds.

1 Bruges is the best preserved of these cities and merits closer study.
2 Ghent is perhaps more typical, as it has moved with the times and remained a major centre of commerce.
3 Antwerp on the River Scheldt is Europe's second port and rivals Brussels in its nightlife and range of museums and exhibition centres. It was the birthplace of Rubens and has been designated a European City of Culture. The important diamond industry owes a great deal to the city's close links with Belgium's former colony in the Congo.
4 Brussels however has the advantage of being the capital, not only of the Flanders region and of the country, but also, in a sense, of the EU. Flemish, French – and increasingly English – are in use throughout the city. It contains the European Commission that has spawned a high-spending bureaucracy and encouraged many multinational corporations to set up their head offices near the centre of power. Brussels has one of the finest groups of Baroque buildings in Europe – the Grand Place – and the modernistic Atomium. But, not having a river as a focus, it lacks the visual appeal of most European capitals.
5 Liège is the most important city in French-speaking Wallonia and is famous for its glass and gun-making industries. It is close to the Ardennes holiday region. Much of the area to the west was blighted by heavy industry in the last century, and is now undergoing economic regeneration.
6 Namur, in an attractive setting at the confluence of the Meuse and the Sambre, is the official capital of Wallonia.

The Ardennes

The Ardennes, with its forests, limestone gorges, winding river valleys and picturesque chateaux, is Belgium's scenic resource; much of the region was, until recently, remote and sparsely populated. Field sports have been important in the past, but nowadays a wide range of activities are catered for such as riding, cycling, rock-climbing, caving and canoeing. The Ardennes attracts large numbers of Dutch tourists as well as domestic visitors, but this popularity has put increasing pressure on its resources. In the areas most accessible to the conurbations of Belgium, the Netherlands and Germany, the unplanned proliferation of second homes has caused social and environmental problems. Greater control over development and more effective visitor management are needed, and for this reason part of the Upper Ardennes has been designated a national park.

Many of the villages and market towns of the region have become resorts, the most important being Dinant, in an attractive setting on the River Meuse. Specific tourist attractions include the caves at Han-sur-Lesse, the castle at Bouillon, associated with the Crusades, and Orval Abbey, noted above all for its beer. One other resort deserves special mention, as it has given its name to similar attractions elsewhere; this is Spa, where the mineral springs set the fashion for 'taking the waters' to the rest of Europe. Like other health resorts it offers a range of cultural and sporting activities, and is the venue for the Belgian Grand Prix motor racing event.

Luxembourg

The Grand Duchy is the smallest member of the EU, but the largest of the six 'ministates' of Europe, which have somehow survived since medieval times. Since 1839 it has been closely linked with Belgium and the Belgian franc is legal tender. As you might expect from its size (slightly less than Dorset or Rhode Island), inbound tourism is of far greater importance to Luxembourg than it is to Belgium. The annual number of visitor arrivals is more than double the resident population, but the impact of tourism is less than you might expect for two reasons: the length of stay is short, and many visitors are business travellers to Luxembourg City. Others are transit passengers taking advantage of Luxembourg's low-cost international flights, while most holidaymakers tend to be campers from the neighbouring conurbations in France, Belgium, the Netherlands and Germany.

Tourism has a major impact on the economy and is Luxembourg's third foreign currency earner after financial services (banking and insurance) and steel exports. The majority of visitors are from Europe with almost half originating from Belgium and the Netherlands. Seasonality is high, most tourists arriving between June and September.

Most of Luxembourg's accommodation capacity is on campsites. Although more nights are spent in campsites than in hotels, it is the latter which are most important in terms of tourist spending. However this is affected by the nature of the business travel market, which can afford the high tariffs. Transport facilities are excellent for such a small country, which apart from the capital is made up largely of rural communities. In addition to the international airport at Findel, close to the capital, there are 270 kilometres of railway network and 5000 kilometres of road.

Tourism is the responsibility of the Ministry of Tourism backed by the National Tourism Office. The promotion of conference tourism is given a high priority; helped by the fact that the country has three official languages and its people are proficient linguists and supporters of European co-operation.

Luxembourg's tourist appeal lies in its capital city and attractive countryside:

1 Luxembourg City is an important financial centre as well as being the seat of the European Parliament (shared with Brussels and Strasbourg), and other EU organizations. The city has an attractive setting on a series of hills and valleys linked by viaducts. Although most of the massive fortifications were torn down and replaced by boulevards long ago, enough remains to explain why Luxembourg was once called 'the Gibraltar of the North'.

2 The country's other attractions lie mainly in the north, which forms part of the Ardennes. They include Vianden, a noted beauty spot with an impressive castle, Clervaux, famous for its abbey, and Echternach, a pilgrimage centre which is of unique interest for its Whitsun dancing processions. The Germano-Luxembourg Nature Park nearby is an outstanding example of international co-operation in conservation. The 'Bon Pays' in the south of the country is less impressive scenically; it does, however, contain the spa town of Mondorf-les-Bains, which has been rejuvenated to meet contemporary leisure demands.

Summary

Physically, the Benelux countries comprise three regions – the lowlands of the coast, the intermediate plateau zone and the uplands. The climate is unpromising for tourism. The Benelux countries were joined by a customs union in 1947 and they are closely integrated. Demand for tourism and recreation is high, but this does place pressures on the environments of these small, densely populated countries.

Throughout the 1990s demand for overseas travel in the Netherlands and Belgium exceeded the demand for domestic main holidays. Inbound tourism has demonstrated modest growth throughout the 1990s, but all countries in the region have a deficit on their travel account. The majority of foreign tourists are from Western Europe. Transport facilities are comprehensive and the region's position in Europe attracts many transit passengers. Accommodation provision is dominated by self-catering capacity, particularly campsites and holiday villages.

There are three main areas of tourist attraction. First, the historic towns and cities attract business and holiday tourists alike, second, the resorts of the North Sea coast are major holiday and day- trip centres and, third, the uplands and countryside are important holiday centres for campers.

Case study

The impact of tourism on a historic city: Bruges

Introduction

Tourism is of major importance to Bruges, supporting an estimated 6500 jobs directly and indirectly in the city and its surrounding area, of which two-thirds are in the hotel and catering sectors. Yet the very popularity of this small city in West Flanders has brought severe traffic problems, threatening its unique heritage. These problems are now well on their way to being resolved through a number of planning and marketing initiatives.

Bruges (or Brugge as it is known in Flemish) is one of the best preserved medieval cities of northern Europe. For this reason it has become a popular short-break destination as well as a long-established attraction on European touring circuits. Unlike modern conurbations, the townscape of Bruges is on a human scale, a picturesque composition of red-brick gabled buildings, church spires, cobblestone streets and squares and tranquil waterways set in the green Flanders countryside. A map of the city reveals the medieval street pattern threaded by a ribbon of canals which has led to Bruges being described, somewhat misleadingly, as the 'Venice of the North'. Beyond the ring road enclosing the old city lie the new residential and industrial districts, which attract relatively few tourists compared with the historic core.

There are two squares at the heart of the old city that symbolize its dual role as a trading centre and administrative capital:

- the Markt (market place)
- the Burg (the site of the fortress of the medieval Courts of Flanders).

Bruges grew rich in the Middle Ages on the wool trade with England, reaching the peak of its prosperity in the fifteenth century when it was chosen by the Dukes of Burgundy as the capital of their extensive domains in France and the Low Countries. It was then the leading commercial centre of northern Europe, boasting the world's first stock exchange. Most of the important buildings and the art treasures date from this period. Later, Bruges lost wealth and population as the result of the silting up of the Zwin estuary and the shift of international trade to Antwerp. By the early nineteenth century Bruges appeared to be in terminal decline and was described by one Romantic writer as the 'dead city', but this proved to be its salvation, as the citizens were too poor to replace the old buildings. The first tourists were attracted by the timeless atmosphere and encouraged the civic authorities to impose strict conservation measures which remain in force today. At the close of the century Bruges made an economic recovery, establishing a new port on the North Sea coast at Zeebrugge (Bruges on Sea). However, tourism continued to grow to become the basis for the city's prosperity.

The tourist resources of Bruges

Attractions

The tourist attractions of the old city include:

- The Hallen Belfry is a graceful bell tower and the main landmark of Bruges. It dominates the Markt, and has played a major role in the events that shaped the city's history.
- The Stadhuis (town hall) dominates the Burg, and is another outstanding example of Gothic architecture.
- The medieval churches, of which the most famous is the Onze-Lieve Vrouwekirk that boasts a sculpture by Michelangelo.
- The art galleries, which feature paintings by Van Eyck, Memling and other Flemish artists.
- The Begijnhof (beguinage) is the most visited of the medieval almshouses that give Bruges much of its peaceful charm.
- The Minnewater (lake of love) – once the harbour of Bruges in the Middle Ages but now a romantic backwater.
- Boat trips on the canals are very popular with visitors, some going as far as Damme, a picturesque small town 7 kilometres to the north, which has been designated as 'Bruges in miniature'. Carriage rides in the old city are also popular.
- Event attractions are focused on the medieval period. The most famous example is the 'Procession of the Holy Blood' – one of Belgium's most colourful religious festivals – that has taken place annually since the time of the Crusades. Some purists accuse Bruges of being a 'medieval theme park' and question the authenticity of some of its traditions.
- Apart from these heritage attractions, the city's shops, quality restaurants and markets are popular with visitors. The traditional lace industry would almost certainly have died out were it not for tourism, but is nowadays rarely carried on outside people's homes.

Other industries less dependent on tourism are chocolate-making (an art form in Belgium) and brewing.

Bruges is promoted jointly with Zeebrugge, which has a lively programme of events and entertainment during the summer. Attractions outside the old city in West Bruges include a theme park and dolphinarium, and a major sports complex, but these have limited international appeal, and current policy is to restrict any further development of tourism.

Bruges is by no means a 'museum-city' or provincial backwater. Many of its residents commute to Brussels, while the College of Europe is a reminder of the city's important role in the development of the EU. About 15 per cent of staying visitors are business travellers or conference delegates. Bruges is an important venue for international conferences, with many hotels providing facilities as well as the Congress Centre and historic Stadshallen.

Transport

The city has excellent transport links by road and rail to:

- Brussels airport
- the ferry terminals at Ostend and Zeebrugge
- Lille on the Eurostar route
- the Channel tunnel via the E40 motorway.

Accommodation

Bruges can offer the visitor an extensive range of accommodation. Hotels are the most important category with over 100 establishments, accounting for 70 per cent of bed capacity and over 80 per cent of tourist overnight stays in the mid-1990s. Two-thirds of the hotels have less than twenty rooms, but there has been a big increase in recent years in the larger properties with over eighty rooms. Over half the hotels are in the three- or four-star categories, the great majority offer en suite facilities and are open for at least ten months of the year. However, they face keen price competition from similar properties in Ghent, Antwerp and Brussels. As you might expect, the more expensive hotels are located near the Burg, while cheaper accommodation is generally found nearer the outskirts. These include youth hostels, – especially popular with young American visitors – campsites, private guesthouses which attract a wide range of independent travellers, and holiday villages catering primarily for the Belgian and Dutch family markets.

The demand for tourism in Bruges

Staying visitors

Bruges attracts visitors from all over the world. Judging by hotel statistics for 1984–94, Japan is an expanding market, while the USA is declining in importance. However, two-thirds of hotel guests came from neigh-

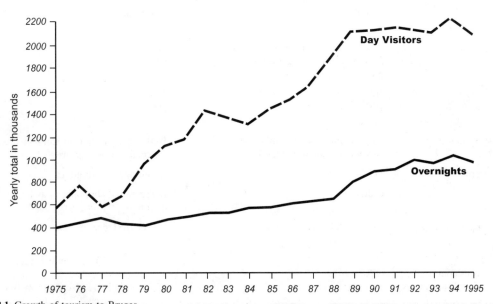

Figure 12.1 Growth of tourism to Bruges
Source: West Flanders Economic Study Bureau (WES) (1996).

bouring countries, with Britain contributing the largest numbers (almost 25 per cent) but the lowest spend per capita. Domestic tourists account for only 6 per cent of hotel stays, which is perhaps not surprising given the size of Belgium and the availability of cheaper types of accommodation.

Day visitors

The biggest growth is in numbers of day visitors, based mainly in the coastal resorts or cities of Belgium, and this has clear implications for the future direction of Bruges's tourism industry. Between 1975 and 1991, whereas overnight stays by tourists doubled, day visits to Bruges almost quadrupled, but since then the growth rate has stabilized (see Figure 12.1).

The issue

The majority of visitors arrive by car, and car ownership by Bruges residents is also increasing. The main problem, as in other historic cities all over Europe, is to find a balance between low-volume, high-spend staying tourists, and day visitors whose contribution to the local economy may be offset by their negative impact on the host community and the fabric of the historic town. Table 12.1 summarizes the differences between these two types of tourism in Bruges.

As a result of the rapid growth of tourism, Bruges in the early 1990s faced severe traffic problems that threatened to devalue both the tourist experience and the quality of life for local residents. The main problems were:

1 The concentration of visitors in a very limited area (430 hectares) of the old city. At peak periods there can be as many as 20 000 day visitors in addition to 8000 or so staying tourists.
2 The large number of tourist coaches impeding traffic flow.
3 The inability of the medieval street pattern to cope with the demands of the motor car.

A strategy for tourism

As part of an integrated plan for tourism development, it was necessary to bring together the many small enterprises that make up the private sector in Bruges and the local and regional authorities who formulate planning and marketing policies. To improve the quality of the

Table 12.1   Characteristics of tourism to Bruges

Characteristic		Staying visitors	Day visitors
Volume:	Trips	590 000	2 million
	Nights	980 000	
Spend	(US$)	120 million; high spending – over 50% on accommodation but only 16% on shopping	83 million; low spending – 33% on shopping
Transport:	Car	60%	69%
	Coach	19%	20%
	Train	21%	11%
Seasonal distribution		Fairly even; lowest numbers in November, January–March	High concentration in summer months, especially at weekends
Growth pattern		Stable	Booming, but irregular
Orientation		Culture	Recreational shopping is as important as culture
Effect on employment		High (1055 person-years)	Lower (611 person-years)
Visitor origin:			
Domestic		7%	45% (mainly from Flemish-speaking areas)
Neighbouring countries		65%	42%
Other foreign countries		28%	13% (on holiday elsewhere in Belgium)

Source: West Flanders Economic Study Bureau (WES), 1996

tourism product, a traffic control plan was implemented in 1992, with the following aims:

- to improve traffic flow within the historic centre
- the diversion of through traffic away from the city centre
- to discourage the use of the private car as the best means of transport to reach the historic centre
- to encourage the use of the bicycle as a 'green' transport mode
- to enable residents to access local services within the city centre.

The main features of the plan are:

1 A circulation system consisting of five loops, which keeps superfluous traffic away from the city centre and diverts it to a number of large underground car parks on the periphery.
2 Vehicles have been banned from certain streets and squares such as the Markt, which formerly acted as a traffic hub, and a one-way traffic system imposed elsewhere in the historic centre.
3 At the same time, the traffic flow on the ring road has been improved.
4 Tourist coaches are banned from the city centre, except to deliver tourists to and from their hotels.
5 Restrictions on car use have gone hand in hand with an efficient and frequent bus service. Visitors who use the car park near the railway station (capacity 1600 spaces) also get free tickets for the bus into the centre.
6 Cyclists are exempt from the one-way street system, and cycles are available for hire at the railway station and from many hotels.

7 Signposting has been improved, and the promotional literature makes it clear to visitors that Bruges is easily accessible by public transport and can easily be explored by bicycle or on foot.

Traffic control is a means of creating a Bruges where tourism is in balance with the needs of residents and where the emphasis is on quality. This is to be achieved by:

1 Restricting new hotels to areas outside the historic centre.
2 Encouraging repeat visitors by offering package deals, including public transport, to hotel guests from Belgium and neighbouring countries, who account for 70 per cent of the demand for hotel accommodation. Of these visitors, half choose Bruges as the sole destination for their trip.
3 Promoting seminars and small- to medium-sized conferences.

You might consider whether the example of Bruges, in dealing with visitors, might benefit other historic cities of similar size such as Oxford or York.

Acknowledgement

We are indebted to Christina Claerbout, Tourist Officer; Jean-Pierre Drubbel, Director for Tourism, Toerisme Brugge for their help.

(http://www.brugge. be/toerisme/en/index.htm)

13

Central Europe: Austria, Switzerland and Germany

Introduction

The countries of Austria, Germany and Switzerland occupy a key position in Central Europe. Both Austria and Germany were historically great empires, whereas Switzerland has always been a small country owing much of its importance to its strategic location astride the major passes over the Alps. Apart from Germany's short North Sea and Baltic coasts, the area under consideration in this chapter is landlocked. Three major physical regions can be identified:

1 The North German Plain and the coast are of relatively limited importance for tourism.

2 More important are the Central Uplands, which include areas such as the Rhineland and the Harz Mountains in Germany, the Mittelland plateau in Switzerland, and the Danube Valley in Austria.
3 The three countries contain over 50 per cent of the Alpine area.

The Alpine area is of major importance for both winter and summer tourism and offers great variety of scenery, from the high fretted ridges and peaks eroded by glaciation, snow-filled cirques and glaciers, to the lakes and forested lower slopes. Forests provide a major recreational resource throughout the region, especially in Germany.

With the exception of the North Sea coast the region has a continental climate, with winters getting colder, not only as we travel further east, but also as a result of altitude. In the mountains the climate is bracing with clean air and brilliant sunshine, but the weather varies with aspect and altitude and fogs are frequent in some valleys during the winter. The cold winters bring the snow which made possible the development of winter sports, yet the resorts on the shores of the more southerly lakes bask in almost Mediterranean temperatures. The Föhn wind frequently blows down some of the south-facing valleys of the Alps bringing unseasonal warmth and excessive dryness during the winter months.

Despite their very different historical backgrounds, all three countries are federal republics, with considerable devolution of powers (including tourism responsibilities) to the states in Germany, the provinces in Austria and the cantons in Switzerland. In fact, Switzerland is more properly known as 'the Swiss Federation'. The combined population of the countries is well over 90 million, with Germany accounting for over 80 million, followed by Austria with 8 million, and Switzerland with 7 million inhabitants. Major population concentrations include the Rühr area of Germany, the area around Vienna in Austria, and in Switzerland, Zurich, though not the capital, is the largest city. German is the dominant language throughout the region. However, in Switzerland, French, Italian and Romansh are also official languages.

The reunification of Germany has brought economic problems to that country but the economies of the three countries are nonetheless highly developed and industrialized, with a high standard of living and quality of life. This is reflected in the widespread demand for environmentally sound tourism. Both Germany and Austria are members of the EU, while Switzerland – in line with its historic tradition of neutrality – has no political affiliation. A central geographic location and good communications mean that levels of outbound tourism are high in all three countries. However, the strength of their currencies does limit the number of inbound tourists. In Austria and Switzerland the annual holiday entitlement is four weeks or more, and in Germany entitlement is five or more weeks. In Austria there is a thirty-five to forty-hour working week and in Germany forty hours is the norm, but in Switzerland working hours are relatively high and attempts are being made to reduce them.

Austria

Austria is a small country with a capital that is larger than might be expected – due to the historical fact that Vienna ruled the vast Hapsburg Empire until 1918. The lavishly decorated Baroque churches, monasteries and palaces are part of that heritage. Austrian composers – notably Mozart and Schubert – made an immense contribution to the world of music and are now celebrated through annual music festivals. But for most people, the abiding image of Austria is its scenic countryside of lakes and mountains, while its reputation as one of the world's major winter sports destinations has tended to overshadow the many cultural attractions.

Tourism is an important industry to Austria representing 6 per cent of the gross national product. Austria has the benefit of both a summer and a winter season – the winter sports market has grown steadily since the late 1950s and is now more significant in terms of tourist spending, than summer tourism, although it remains smaller in volume. For many years Austria was in the top position for skiing, having overtaken Switzerland in the 1960s, but more recently France has relegated it to second place. Much of the resort development took place in the years following the Second World War as part of the reconstruction of Austria's economy.

Demand for tourism

Inbound tourism

Over 20 million international visitors arrived in Austria's registered tourist accommodation each year in the 1990s,

giving Austria a large surplus on its tourism account. This, however, reflects a stagnating tourism sector in Austria, struggling to compete with emergent destinations in Eastern Europe, and handicapped by the strong Austrian currency. The majority are on a holiday visit and there is no doubt that proximity to Germany is important to Austria as that market accounts for almost two-thirds of arrivals. The next two countries, the Netherlands and the UK, are also important sources of tourists but together only account for a small proportion of nights. New markets in Eastern Europe, coupled with marketing initiatives also mean that Austria is receiving an increasing number of visits from this region. In addition to their proximity, Germans are attracted to Austria because there is no language barrier, their currencies have similar buying power, and yet Austria, with its more relaxed lifestyle, is sufficiently different from Germany to give a feeling of being in a foreign country. However, this reliance on one market does leave Austria vulnerable in times of recession and concentration of visits determined by holiday periods in Germany causes congestion at the borders. In popular holiday areas many resorts become totally geared to the German market.

Domestic and outbound tourism

Austrians have a low travel propensity (around 45 per cent) of which domestic holidays account for about half. There is a move towards taking more than one holiday, particularly in the form of short breaks, and this is spreading the holiday pattern away from July and August. Farmhouse stays have been successfully promoted to encourage tourism throughout the rural areas, but there is still a concentration of holidays in the Tyrol, creating considerable congestion with visitors outnumbering locals in many villages. Austria is a major generator of international tourists on a world scale, though the majority of trips are to neighbouring countries, emphasizing Austria's favourable location in Europe. The majority of holidays abroad are to Mediterranean countries – particularly Italy, Greece and Croatia.

Supply of tourism

Transport

The majority of tourists arrive by car on the 18 000-kilometre road network and congestion on the roads is experienced at the beginning and end of the main holiday periods. The tortuous nature of some of the roads emphasizes the difficulty of transportation in this elongated and mountainous country, yet the network reaches into the most remote parts, and includes Europe's highest road to the summit of the Gross Glockner. There are over 6000 kilometres of railway including twenty private railway companies, and these are well integrated with rural bus services reaching the most remote communities. There are six airports in Austria, but some argue that a restrictive policy on inbound flights to Vienna has held back the development of the tourist industry and compounded Austria's dependence on the German market.

Accommodation

The majority of the more than 1 million beds available are in serviced accommodation and the authorities are improving the quality of accommodation as a means of boosting both domestic and foreign tourism. Although business travel is relatively unimportant in Austria, the small conference market is being developed, particularly in hotels in Vienna, Linz, Salzburg, Innsbruck, Graz and Villach, as well as in the larger *schlosshotels* – castles which have been converted into hotels.

Organization

Each of the nine Austrian provinces has responsibility for tourism administered by the provincial government and a tourist board. At national level tourism is the responsibility of the Ministry of Economic Affairs. Promotion of Austria abroad is the responsibility of the Austrian National Tourist Organization which has undergone a restructuring and a refocusing of priorities in the face of stagnant demand from the international market. The Austrian government provides grants and loans for tourist development, mostly in the accommodation sector. The tourism authorities in Austria are upgrading tourist infrastructure generally, particularly in the area of sports and facilities for activity holidays, and extending the network of ski lifts and funiculars, which are rivalled only by Switzerland in scope. However, some resorts (such as Mayrhofen) have halted further development in line with Austria's green image and this may have persuaded potential skiers to choose France instead.

Tourist resources of Austria

Austria contains 35 per cent of the Alpine area (compared to Switzerland's 15 per cent) and the country is famed for its lake and mountain scenery, winter-sports facilities, and picturesque towns and villages. Trending east–west across the country and separated by the deep valley of the river Inn, the mountains are Austria's main attraction. Here, tourism is often the only economic land use, and even though it often benefits only a few communities, tourism is seen as a remedy for the problems of declining agriculture. However, this is not without environmental costs, such as forest hillsides and meadows scarred from ski-lift development or villages marred by insensitive building.

Each of the Austrian provinces can offer distinctive attractions.

The Tyrol

The Tyrol is by far the most popular destination for foreign visitors, containing the most spectacular Alpine scenery and the greatest number of ski resorts. Tyrolean folklore and costumes are the best known of Austria's traditional cultures. Most of the resorts have been developed from farming villages situated in the tributary valleys of the River Inn – the Otztal and Zillertal for example – at altitudes of between 1000 and 1800 metres. Traditional building styles, based on the chalet that is well adapted to heavy winter snowfalls, provide a pleasant ambience for holidays. Summer activities in the Tyrol include hiking and gliding, while most villages are equipped with a swimming pool and facilities for tennis and other sports. Tourist centres include Innsbruck, which is not only the capital of the Tyrol but an important cultural centre; a reminder of its former role as a summer residence for the Hapsburg emperors. This explains the many Renaissance buildings. Along with the ski resorts on the slopes nearby, the city has twice hosted the Winter Olympics. St Anton, Kitzbühl, Söll, Seefeld and Mayrhofen are all ski resorts of international significance.

The Vorarlberg

The Vorarlberg to the west of the Arlberg Pass is similar to the Tyrol, but also has some affinity with neighbouring Switzerland. Lech and Zurs offer up-market skiing, while Bregenz on the Boden See is a popular lake resort. We can include with this province the tiny principality of Liechtenstein, which is better known as a tax haven than as a winter sports destination.

Salzburg and the Salzkammergut area

The province of Salzburg and the Salzkammergut area (so called because of the historically important salt mining industry) offer gentler lake and mountain scenery. St Wolfgang is the most popular of the resorts in summer, but its entertainment scene is subdued compared to Söll or Kitzbuhl in winter. Other attractions include the Krimml waterfalls in the Hohe Tauern National Park, the Dachstein ice caves, and the spas of Bad Ischl and Bad Gastein.

Styria and Carinthia

The forested 'green province' of Styria, and the less commercialized resorts of Carinthia, are the provinces that the Austrians themselves prefer. Carinthia is also increasingly popular with foreign visitors as a summer holiday destination, where the warm sunny climate and lakes such as the Wörther See, offering many facilities for water sports, are the main attractions.

The Danube Valley

The remaining provinces of Austria, occupying the Danube Valley, are scenically less attractive, with large areas of lowland supplying most of the country's agricultural needs. The Burgenland is similar in its steppe landscapes to neighbouring Hungary, while the shallow Neusiedlersee is an important nature reserve. Both the provinces of Upper and Lower Austria contain vineyards, monasteries (such as Melk) and castles (such as Dürnstein) and it is possible for the tourist to see these on a Danube river cruise from Vienna.

Whereas Graz, Linz and Innsbruck are important regional centres, only two of Austria's cities – Vienna and Salzburg – attract huge numbers of visitors from all over the world, thanks to their heritage of music and architecture.

Vienna

Vienna is full of reminders of its imperial past. These include the monumental buildings lining the Ringstrasse encircling the old city, and the art treasures housed in the former palaces of the Hofburg, Belvedere and Schönbrunn. Music and dance are as much a part of the city's social and entertainment scene as they were in the time of the 'Waltz King' (Johann Strauss) more than a century ago. The State Opera House and St Stephen's Cathedral are also part of this musical heritage. Although Vienna trades on nostalgia for its tourist appeal, the city is an efficiently run modern conference venue, with an international role as a United Nations centre, while geographical location makes it the recognised gateway to Eastern Europe.

Salzburg

Salzburg has a flourishing tourism industry based on:

1 The summer music festival, which was further boosted in 1991 by the Mozart bicentenary celebrations. During festival time, accommodation in this relatively small city is at a premium.
2 The *Sound of Music* connection. Classical music lovers are outnumbered by those tourists who are attracted to the city and the scenic countryside of lakes and mountains nearby, through their associations with this popular film.
3 Its unique heritage of Baroque architecture – probably unrivalled outside Spain or Italy – which was brought into being by the powerful Prince-Bishops who once ruled Salzburg.

Switzerland

Switzerland is poor in natural resources and contains a diversity of languages and cultures. Yet its people have achieved a degree of political stability and economic prosperity that is envied by the rest of the world. Swiss industrial products, based on a high input of skill in relation to the value of the component raw materials, have an international reputation for quality. Similarly, the country's scenic attractions – arguably the most spectacular in Europe

– have been intelligently exploited by a hospitality industry that is renowned for its professionalism. Historically, the country developed as a loose federation of cantons – small mountain states – fighting to preserve their independence from foreign domination, and in many respects the cantons still play a more important role in Swiss politics than the federal government in Berne.

Tourism in Switzerland has a long history, and the industry was already well established in the late nineteenth century. Its development came about as a result of a number of factors:

1 From early times, Switzerland was a transit zone for invading armies, merchants and pilgrims, and later had to be crossed by wealthy travellers undertaking the Grand Tour. The Swiss were in demand as guides, as there were no serviceable roads and the Alpine passes were often hazardous. Accommodation was also needed for travellers, the most famous example being the hospice on the St Bernard Pass.
2 As a result of the Romantic Movement in art and literature at the close of the eighteenth century, the mountains were no longer seen as a barrier to be feared, but as a resource to be valued. For example, Byron and Shelley stayed for a considerable time by Lake Geneva, and summer resorts gradually developed for well-off tourists around other lakes in Switzerland.
3 From the middle of the nineteenth century the demand for tourism in Switzerland grew as the result of the Industrial Revolution in Western Europe, the improvement in road and rail communications and the growth of the middle class, particularly in countries like Britain, where Thomas Cook did much to popularize the country. The more adventurous tourists sought the challenges of mountain-climbing, following Whymper's ascent of the Matterhorn in 1865. More remote areas of the Alps were progressively opened up to tourism with the construction of funicular and cog railways, and hotels were built at the edge of the Alpine glaciers, such as the Aletsch.
4 Although Switzerland had been known for its spas since Roman times, substantial development of health tourism occurred in the late nineteenth and early twentieth centuries as a result of the spread of tuberculosis in the industrial cities of Europe. The pure mountain air in spas such as St Moritz Bad and Arosa was believed to provide a remedy for the disease.
5 Skiing and other winter sports were introduced to St Moritz and the resorts of the Bernese Oberland by wealthy British tourists at the close of the nineteenth century. At first, the existing mountain railways – now operating year-round – were used to transport the skiers to the slopes, but as demand grew from the 1930s onwards, they were largely superseded by faster, more efficient aerial cableways.
6 International trade had long been important to Swiss cities such as Geneva. The strict neutrality of Switzerland

and its multilingual character encouraged the growth of all kinds of business and conference tourism. Starting with the Red Cross, Geneva became the venue for many international organizations, while Zurich is a financial centre of worldwide significance. Berne and Lausanne also provide important conference functions.

Demand for tourism

Domestic and outbound travel

The Swiss have one of the highest holiday propensities in the world with around 75 per cent taking a holiday of at least four nights. Holiday-taking is at its highest among upper-income groups, the middle aged and those living in the larger towns or cities. Demand for domestic tourism has remained static and the high frequency of holiday-taking means that most domestic holidays are second or third holidays.

Domestic holidays contrast with those taken abroad as they tend to be winter-sports or mountain holidays, many taken in the months of January to March. Swiss holidays abroad are concentrated into the summer months of July to September and the most popular destinations are Italy and France.

Inbound travel

In the 1990s demand from foreign visitors to Switzerland stagnated, although the tourism account remained in surplus. The reasons are:

- the strength of the Swiss franc that has given Switzerland a reputation as an expensive country to visit, and this is reflected in the increasingly short length of stays by foreign visitors
- declining levels of service
- an old-fashioned image of Switzerland.

As in Austria, Germans account for the majority of visitors. Around 40 per cent of bed-nights occur in the winter season (November to April), a figure boosted by the Swiss participating in winter sports.

Supply of tourism

Transport

The private car dominates travel in both the domestic and foreign travel markets. There are 66 000 kilometres of roads, including 1550 kilometres of motorway. As in Austria, the transport networks are tortuous and the topography often demands major engineering feats – the 18-kilometre tunnel under the St Gotthard being an outstanding example – while the roads over the Alpine passes are spectacular. Even so, roads in the high Alps are often blocked by snow from November to June. While the road network brings many remoter parts of the country within reach of day visitors this has created congestion in holiday areas. Imposition of tolls may alleviate this congestion. The Swiss Federal Railways and the private railway companies operate 5000 kilometres of track (1400 kilometres are narrow gauge) and there are many mountain railways, funiculars and rack-and-pinion systems which are often tourist attractions in themselves. Although the cost is high, tunnels and snowploughs allow the railways to operate throughout the year. There are three international airports – at Zurich, Geneva and Basle and the national carrier is Swissair. Other features of the Swiss transport system, which is highly integrated, include the postal coaches – penetrating to the remotest villages – bicycle hire at many rail stations and the lake ferries.

Accommodation

The development of accommodation over the last twenty years has led to an excess of supply over demand. About one-third of the serviced accommodation capacity is only available in the winter season, particularly in the high ski resorts (such as St Moritz and Arosa). Most hotels are small with the few larger hotels found mainly in Zurich and Geneva. 'Supplementary accommodation' includes chalets, apartments, holiday camps, and camping and caravan sites. This lower-cost supplementary accommodation has flourished as foreign visitors offset the high cost of a Swiss holiday but it is also popular with domestic holidaymakers.

Organization

In the face of declining international demand for Switzerland in the 1990s, the Swiss National Tourism Organization was renamed 'Switzerland Tourism' in 1995 and underwent restructuring and a refocusing of priorities. It is responsible to the Federal Department of Public Economy and formulates and implements national tourism policy. Switzerland's maturity as a destination is reflected in the long tradition of tourist associations and information services at local and regional levels. There are also many specialist organizations such as the Swiss Travel Bank that was founded to give less privileged workers the chance to go on holiday.

The Swiss Plan for Tourism of 1979 established a national policy framework for action by the cantons. The plan envisages Switzerland as a destination for individual and small-group tourism. It also sees the development of the supplementary accommodation sector and new infrastructure development in less developed tourist regions, such as the foothills and the Jura, in a bid to spread the benefits of tourism and take pressure away from the established areas. It is aided by central government regional funds and an enhanced budget for the Swiss National Tourist Office. A subsequent report to the 1979 plan – the Krippendorf Report

– urged quality development in tourism and warned of the dangers of not pursuing a sustainable tourism policy. Since then the refocused Switzerland Tourism organization has embarked upon a new campaign to change the image of Switzerland and develop new tourism products – such as snowboarding and cycling holidays – to take the country into the twenty-first century.

The tourist resources of Switzerland

The most popular area is the Alpine zone, attracting over half of all visitor arrivals. Here lie the majestic snow-capped peaks, glaciated valleys and winter-sports developments that are Switzerland's trade mark. However, tourist development has placed pressures upon the society and environment of the area and the integration of tourism into the agricultural and forest economies has needed sensitive handling.

Each of the Swiss cantons has its own range of attractions, but several major tourist areas stand out, namely:

1 *The Bernese Oberland* The most spectacular Alpine scenery is found here, south of the lake resort of Interlaken. An excellent network of funicular railways and cableways provides access to the snowfields and glaciers, the most famous ascending the slopes of the Jungfrau and Eiger. At Lauterbrunnen there is a classic example of a glaciated valley with spectacular waterfalls. Long popular with British tourists, the area preserves Swiss rural traditions and at the same time has some of the most sophisticated ski resorts in Europe, notably Gstaad, Wengen and Grindelwald.
2 *The Valais* This includes the upper Rhone valley as far as the Simplon Pass and a number of small historic towns. The most well-known resort is Zermatt, with its views of the Matterhorn, but the most popular ski area is Crans-Montana where considerable development has taken place.
3 *Lake Lucerne and the Forest Cantons* The fjord-like Lake Lucerne is probably the most beautiful body of inland water in Europe. The cantons around it, notably Schweiz, are historically important as the cradle of Swiss independence. Lucerne is a picturesque city, famous for its medieval Chapel Bridge, but like most resorts in Switzerland it is not renowned for its nightlife.
4 *The Grisons* In some respects this is the most traditional part of Switzerland with villages where the Romansch language is still spoken. It also contains the Swiss National Park where endangered alpine species such as the *chamois* are protected. On the other hand, this canton contains a number of spas and ski resorts catering mainly for wealthy tourists, the most famous being St Moritz, Davos, and Klosters.
5 *Lake Geneva* With its southerly aspect this French speaking area is noted for its vineyards. The most well-known resort is Montreux, which has an important music festival.
6 *The Ticino* Due to its location, the Italian-speaking Ticino enjoys the warmest climate in Switzerland. The colourful towns and villages and the scenery are more Mediterranean than Central European. We are therefore treating this area as part of the Italian Lakes region in Chapter 16.
7 *The Mittelland* Most of the Swiss population lives outside the Alps in the plateau region to the north and west, and it is here that the important industries and major cities are located. Of these, Basle on the Rhine is a university city and cultural centre and Zurich contains the Swiss National Museum, but Berne is probably the most interesting from a tourist viewpoint. The picturesque old town, with its medieval shopping arcades and Clock Tower is a World Heritage Site.
8 *The Jura* The western boundary of Switzerland lies along the forested Jura Mountains. Less spectacular than the Alps, this region receives fewer foreign visitors. The small towns of the region, such as Les Chaux de Fonds, are noted for traditional Swiss crafts such as watchmaking.

Germany

Unlike Austria or Switzerland, Germany lacks a well-defined tourism image, with many people regarding it as a destination for business rather than holiday travel. This is not surprising as Germany has the world's third largest economy. Yet the country is well endowed with a variety of beautiful scenery and cultural attractions. The former division between East and West Germany tended to obscure the long-standing physical and cultural differences between the Protestant northern part of the country and the predominantly Catholic south and west. Regional differences are also a legacy of the time, prior to the nineteenth century, when Germany was a patchwork of small, virtually independent states. Berlin has strong rivals in several other major cities, which act as world-class cultural and business centres.

The picture of tourism in Germany has also been complicated by the fact that from 1945 to 1990 the country was divided, along with the capital, Berlin. The two Germanies that resulted from this division had widely differing political and economic structures:

- *West Germany*, officially known as the Federal Republic of Germany or BRD, prospered under a democratic style of government and a free market economy.
- *East Germany*, officially called the German Democratic Republic or DDR, was compelled by its Soviet masters to adopt communism and a centralized command economy. Tourist enterprises such as hotels were nationalized and the whole industry was subject to state control. East

Germans were discouraged from visiting other countries, with the exception of those in the Soviet bloc, such as Romania and Hungary. Visits from West Germans were virtually prohibited while tourism from other Western countries was subject to many restrictions.

The structure changed rapidly after 1989 with the removal of the Berlin Wall and the reunification of Germany a year later. This has meant that Germany has a range of new tourism products and domestic markets for tourism. For example, there has been a flood of West German tourists into East Germany, attracted by the low cost of accommodation. East Germans now have the freedom to travel abroad, but it will be some time before they have the financial resources to do so in large numbers. The economy of the former DDR was badly depressed because it was based on industries that could not compete with West German products. West Germany comprises 80 per cent of the population as a whole, and dominates both the supply and demand of tourism in the new Germany.

Demand for tourism

Domestic travel

The West Germans have been the world's greatest spenders on travel and tourism for many years and they attach great importance to their annual holiday, even in times of recession. For holidays of five days or more, travel frequencies are high and holiday propensities reach almost 75 per cent, though this does vary according to age, socioeconomic status, and place of residence. Residents of the former East Germany also have high holiday propensities but these are still mainly expressed in domestic trips. The domestic market accounts for the great majority of bed-nights and so dominates the industry. Domestic holidays are particularly concentrated into the summer months and in the south of Germany and on the coast. Business travel is important in the domestic market. Germans are very health conscious and over 200 spa resorts based on abundant mineral springs have long been developed to meet this demand. Most of these are located in the uplands of the Mittelgebirge in the central part of the country. Hiking is also popular and Germany was the first country to provide a nationwide network of youth hostels.

Outbound travel

Germany was for many years the most important generator of international tourists in the world but in the 1990s has been overtaken by the USA. Around two-thirds of all holidays are taken abroad, and the majority of trips are to Mediterranean countries (particularly Italy and Spain) and to neighbouring Austria. Many trips are package tours sold by the highly organized travel industry that has grown up to meet the demand for holidays abroad. Spain is by far the most important package holiday destination and long-haul travel is also important.

Inbound travel

The high volume of travel abroad keeps Germany's travel account in considerable deficit even though, in the 1990s, around 15 million foreigners arrived in registered tourist accommodation annually. The main origin countries are Germany's neighbours, now more numerous as a result of reunification – and excursionists form a significant tourism flow into Germany. Generally, average lengths of stay are short – around two days – and this means that foreign visitors contribute a small volume of the bed-nights in the country. Business travel is important in the inbound market, exceeding the volume of holiday traffic from abroad.

Supply of tourism

Accommodation

Domestic business travellers and most foreign visitors are accommodated in hotels in towns and cities. Demand for self-catering accommodation exceeds supply, as does that for most types of accommodation in the peak season. There is a concentration of hotels and guesthouses serving the holiday market in Bavaria and Baden-Württemburg, and a shortage of accommodation throughout most of the former DDR. Holiday parks – groups of chalets around a pool and other leisure facilities – are popular with German families.

Transport

The car is the most important form of tourist transport. The road network is excellent with over 7000 kilometres of autobahns (high-speed motorways) and also specially designed scenic routes for visitors. A major problem is seasonal congestion both en route to, and in, the popular holiday areas. Rail travel is the second most popular form of travel with promotional fares and inclusive package holidays available; plans for a high-speed train service (ICE) are well advanced. The larger cities have a fully integrated public transport system of trams, buses, 'U-bahn' (underground), and 'S-bahn' (fast suburban trains). Air travel is served by ten international airports, all well connected by rail with the urban areas they serve. The national carrier, Lufthansa, is based at the main gateway and hub at Frankfurt. Arrivals by sea can enter via Hamburg from Harwich, from Trelleborg in Sweden to Sassnitz and from Roby Havn in Denmark to Puttgarten. Cruises on the Rhine and the other major rivers, the canals that link these natural waterways, and on Lake Constance are also popular.

Organization

Tourism in Germany suffers from having no representation at senior level in the federal government. Tourism responsibilities are in the hands of the sixteen *länder* (states) who have considerable independence to promote and develop tourism but this does result in considerable fragmentation. There is, for example, no national tourism policy as tourism is low on the list of government economic priorities and little federal aid is available for the industry. The aid that is available is mainly used to boost accommodation in less-developed areas and to stimulate farm tourism. The states provide funds for both upgrading accommodation and for season-extension developments (such as indoor swimming pools) in resorts. The German National Tourist Board (Deutsche Zentrale für Tourismus – DZT) promotes Germany abroad and is mainly financed by the federal government. The German Tourist Federation is made up of state, city and other organizations and is responsible for domestic promotion and tourist development. A German Convention Bureau promotes conference facilities.

Tourist resources of Germany

Each of the sixteen *länder* which make up present-day Germany has a historical identity, but they vary greatly in size and tourism potential. For example, Schleswig-Holstein with its lowland scenery, and the Saar with its industrial landscapes, suffer by comparison with the mountains of Bavaria.

Northern Germany

This region includes the states of Schleswig-Holstein, Lower Saxony, Hamburg, Bremen and Mecklenburg-West Pomerania in the former DDR. In this part of Germany the main tourist attractions are found on or near the coast. Inland, there are large areas of forest, heathland and lakes – such as those of Holstein and Mecklenburg, providing some variety in the otherwise featureless expanse of the North European Plain. The North Sea is colder and rougher than the Baltic, and the coast is low-lying, with large areas of mudflats exposed at low tide. However, the North Frisian Islands have fine beaches, the most popular being those of Sylt, which is linked to the mainland by a causeway. The resort of Westerland attracts fashionable holidaymakers as well as German families, and it was here that naturism – known in Germany as *freikorpskultur* (FKK) first appeared on the holiday scene in the 1920s. The tideless Baltic coast is scenically more attractive, with sandspits enclosing extensive lagoons. With the exception of Kiel – a major yachting centre, and Travemünde, most of the Baltic resorts were situated in the former DDR. These flourished serving a captive domestic market, but their outdated facilities and substandard service practices left them ill-equipped to face the competition following German unification and the introduction of a free market economy. They are now being 'rediscovered' by West German holidaymakers, who are attracted by the lack of commercialization – caused by decades of neglect under communism. This is particularly true of the island of Rugen, with its cliffs, deeply indented coastline, beaches and beautiful countryside. Its chief resort, Warnemünde, attracted the German élite in the late nineteenth century.

Many of the cultural attractions of northern Germany date back to the Middle Ages, when the powerful Hanseatic League of merchants from Hamburg and other cities dominated trade throughout northern Europe. This heritage is exploited for tourism in the picturesque port of Lübeck, with its well-preserved city walls and gates, church spires and red-brick merchants' houses. Similar examples, but less commercialized can be found in Rostock, Wismar and Stralsund.

The major cities of the region – Hamburg, Bremen and Hanover – are primarily business centres with tourism playing a secondary role. Hanover, the capital of Lower Saxony, has historical associations with Britain, but is mainly known for its trade fairs. Hamburg deserves special mention for the following reasons:

- It is one of Europe's major ports, with worldwide trading connections, and a special economic role in relation to Eastern Europe and the countries of the former Soviet Union.
- It is a major cultural centre, with publishing as one of its major industries.
- The picturesque setting of the old city, between the harbour and the Alster Lakes, appeals to visitors.
- The vitality of its nightlife, centred on the Saint Pauli district and the notorious Reeperbahn, also appeals to visitors.

Central Germany

To the south of the North German Plain rise the forested uplands of the Mittelgebirge. For the most part they are not high or rugged enough to be regarded as mountains, but they are ideal hiking country. The towns of Hesse and the Weser Valley are rich in legendary associations, notable examples being Hamelin and the castle at Sababurg immortalized by the Grimm brothers. The German Tourist Board has promoted a tourist route from Bremen south to Marburg based on these resources as the 'Fairy-Tale Road'.

To the east, the Harz Mountains are renowned for their beautiful scenery and waterfalls. During the post Second World War division of Germany this region was bisected by the Iron Curtain which severely disrupted all communications, to the detriment of its tourism industry. Although the barriers are now gone, the picturesque medieval towns such as Goslar on the western side of the former boundary are thriving more than those in what was once the DDR (such as Wernigerode and Quedlinburg).

The Rhineland

Western and southern Germany contain the areas most popular with foreign visitors. Its people tend to be more pleasure-loving – Carnival or *Fasching* is an important festive event in many of the towns and cities, especially in the Rhineland. The Rhine is Europe's most heavily used inland waterway, and river cruises have been popular with tourists since the beginning of the nineteenth century. The most scenic stretch of the river is between Bingen and Koblenz, where it is confined in a narrow gorge. Here the Rhine, followed closely by the autobahn and railway, meanders between terraced vineyards and steep crags crowned by romantic castles which feature prominently in German legend. The northern Rhineland is less attractive as it includes the heavily industrialized Rühr Valley conurbation. Of the many tourist centres in the Rhine Valley, the following deserve special mention:

- Rüdesheim is the most popular of the wine festivals in the region.
- Düsseldorf is the leading commercial centre and is a 'must' for the serious shopper as well as business travellers.
- Cologne (Köln) boasts Germany's most famous cathedral and is an important venue for trade exhibitions. Phantasialand – one of Germany's major theme parks – is situated nearby.
- Bonn was a small university town, famous as the birthplace of Beethoven, when it was chosen as the capital of the new Federal Republic in 1949. This status gradually became defunct following the 1991 decision of the Bundestag (Parliament) to reinstate Berlin as capital of a united Germany.
- Aachen lies close to the border with Belgium and the Netherlands, and is an example of international city promotion, in partnership with Liège and Maastricht. It is historically important as the capital of Charlemagne, who founded the Holy Roman Empire – the forerunner of the German state, and in a sense, of the EU.
- Trier in the wine-producing Moselle Valley, is rich in historical monuments dating back to Roman times.
- Other important historic cities in the Rhine Valley are Mainz, Wörms and Speyer, similarly located near vineyards.
- In contrast, Frankfurt on the River Main is a thoroughly modern city and the financial capital of Germany. Its airport is one of the world's busiest, and it lies at the 'crossroads' of the autobahn network.

Southern Germany

South Germany comprises the states of Baden-Württemberg and Bavaria. Baden-Baden is Germany's most noted spa town, while the famous old university town of Heidelberg is a 'must' on the international tourist circuit. In contrast, Stuttgart is the centre of the German motor vehicle industry and attracts a good deal of business travel for this reason. Bavaria is the most popular state with domestic and foreign tourists, since it can offer a great variety of scenery and is noted for its folklore, which has much in common with the Austrian Tyrol. Major attractions of Southern Germany include:

- The Black Forest, a scenic area of pine-covered uplands, waterfalls and picturesque villages rising to the east of the Rhine, which offers ideal opportunities for skiing in winter and hiking in summer, with the world's oldest long-distance footpath – the *Westweg*. The region is also famous for its folklore and clock-making industry, carried on in small towns such as Triberg.
- The 'Romantic Road' – Germany's best-known tourist route – linking a large number of well-preserved medieval towns, including Würzburg, Bamberg and Rothenburg.
- Nüremberg, despite heavy damage in the Second World War, is a major cultural centre, along with Regensburg on the Danube – onetime capital of the Holy Roman Empire – and Bayreuth with its Wagner festival.
- The Bavarian Alps provide spectacular lake and mountain scenery. Tourist centres include Garmisch-Partenkirchen, which is a leading ski resort, and the village of Oberammergau noted for its traditions of woodcarving and fresco-decorated buildings as well as the Passion Play staged every ten years by the community.
- The romantic castles built by King Ludwig II of Bavaria in the nineteenth century are very popular with visitors, the most famous example being Neuschwanstein.
- Munich, the capital of Bavaria has a wealth of Renaissance architecture and is a favourite with art and music lovers. It is also very much a modern city with facilities provided for the 1972 Olympic Games. Its beer gardens and annual Oktoberfest are world-famous.

Eastern Germany

Prior to 1990 this region, consisting of the states of Brandenburg, Saxony, Saxony-Anhalt and Thuringia formed part of the DDR. It is crossed by the River Elbe, and cruises are now available from Hamburg to the scenic area known as the 'Saxon Switzerland' near the border with the Czech Republic. Unfortunately, much of Saxony south of the Elbe has suffered severe pollution from obsolescent heavy industrial plant using low-grade coal. Enormous investment will be required to bring environmental standards up the to level of those in West Germany. To the south of Berlin lies the Spreewald, a maze of waterways, where traditional lifestyles and the Wendish language persist. In contrast, the state of Thuringia is a forested upland region. It contains a number of historic towns, notably Weimar – important for its associations with Göethe, Germany's greatest poet – and Eisenach, where Martin Luther initiated the Protestant Reformation. As in other parts of the former DDR, there is a shortage of tourist accommodation.

Three cities in the region are major tourist centres – namely Leipzig, Dresden, and Berlin (see the case study at the end of this chapter for the latter):

- Leipzig hosts an international trade fair twice a year and has played a leading role in the cultural life of the nation, especially music.
- The same is true of Dresden, a beautiful Baroque city that was reconstructed after its devastation in 1945 (Dresden porcelain is actually made in the town of Meissen 30 kilometres away).

Summary

Apart from the short German coast, Austria, Switzerland and Germany are landlocked countries. Physically, three regions can be identified: the coastal lowlands, the central uplands and the Alps. The combined population of the three countries is well over 90 million, and with highly developed economies and standards of living, demand for tourism and recreation is high. Of particular note is the importance of Germany as one of the world's leading generators of international tourists and the issues raised by the reunification of Germany. Austria and Switzerland are both significant destinations for tourists from the rest of Europe. However, international demand has stagnated in the 1990s and led to the restructuring of the region's national tourism organizations.

Transportation in the three countries is well developed but has to overcome the harsh physical conditions and topography of the Alps. The federal organization of the three countries has led to considerable devolution of tourism powers to the states in Germany, provinces in Austria and cantons in Switzerland.

The main tourist regions are the coasts of northern Germany with its islands and resorts, the central uplands of Germany, including the Rhineland and the Black Forest, and the Alpine area of all three countries with its opportunities for both winter and summer tourism. The towns and cities of all the countries are also important for sightseeing and as business travel centres.

Case study

Berlin: the revitalization of a European capital

The reunification of Germany in 1990 brought together two major cities – East and West Berlin – that had evolved for forty-five years under two very different political and economic systems. A year earlier the Berlin Wall, which since 1962 had prevented free movement between East and West, ceased to exist except as a resource for souvenir-hunters from all over the world. At the time of the fall of the Berlin Wall the population of East Berlin was estimated to be 1.3 million, whereas West Berlin had a population of over 2 million. During the 1990s both the administrative functions of the German federal government and embassies were gradually moved from Bonn to Berlin, which had been the capital of a united Germany from 1871 to 1945. The process of reinstatement was symbolized by the opening of the new Reichstag (Parliament building) in 1998, as part of a huge government complex on the eastern edge of the Tiergarten – Berlin's central park, which also includes the new Chancellery. Another landmark in 1994 was the ending of the four-power military occupation of the city by the wartime allies (the USA, Britain, France and Russia), which also allowed Lufthansa to operate flights to Berlin's Tegel Airport for the first time since Germany's defeat in 1945.

During the period of the Cold War, East and West Berlin were deliberately promoted as showcases for the achievements of socialism and Western democracy by the respective governments of East and West Germany.

1 In East Berlin the Alexanderplatz was chosen as the centre of the DDR, the 350-metre high television tower symbolizing the power of the communist state. Before 1945 this impressive square had been the power centre of the Kingdom of Prussia and later of the Third Reich, and the East German regime was determined to obliterate this legacy of the past. East Berlin also contained what had been the most fashionable street of the prewar capital – the Unter den Linden – which had suffered massive destruction as a result of Allied bombing. The majority of prewar Berlin's cultural attractions – its great museums, cathedrals, universities, palaces and art galleries – were likewise in the communist zone.

2 In contrast, West Berlin focused on the Kurfurstendamm, which had been a secondary centre in the prewar capital. This became noted for its shops, restaurants, cabarets and hotels, while West Berlin as a whole generated cultural dynamism and prosperity under a free market economy, aided by generous subventions from the federal government in Bonn. The Europa Centre epitomized this commercial success in contrast to the greyness and the restricted shopping and nightlife of East Berlin. West Berlin was also multicultural, not only in comparison to East Berlin, but also to the rest of the Federal Republic, attracting immigrants from all over Europe. It was also a major tourist centre, whereas East Berlin placed restrictions on Western tourists.

An important point to remember is that West Berlin was an enclave, an island of democracy, completely surrounded by the Soviet controlled DDR throughout the Cold War period. This made the city a vulnerable target for economic blockade since its surface transport links could be cut at any time. The need for North Atlantic Treaty Organization (NATO) military protection also made West Berlin a potential flashpoint in any dispute between the two superpowers – the USA and the Soviet Union.

The actual heart of pre-war Berlin – the Potsdamerplatz – remained a wasteland throughout the Cold War period due to its location on the border between East and West. During the late 1990s it became the scene of one of the world's greatest building projects, part of the plan to make Berlin the European metropolis of the twenty-first century. The Potsdamerplatz is to be a new commercial centre, with a mix of theatres, hotels, shopping malls and restaurants. The rebuilding programme is itself attracting swarms of 'construction-site tourists', curious to see a city in the remaking. Most of the projects are taking place in the former East Berlin – specifically in the historic area of the city known as the Mitte lying to the east of the Friedrichstrasse. This contains the medieval nucleus of Berlin which was virtually obliterated by post World War II reconstruction, and what remains of the elegant Baroque city, centred on the Unter den Linden, laid out by the eighteenth-century kings of Prussia, especially Frederick the Great.

The rebuilding programme will transform East Berlin, and revitalize its economy, but it also raises questions as to which elements of the city's heritage should be preserved or restored. Here ideological considerations play a major part, given Berlin's role in shaping European history during the twentieth century. For example:

● Of Hitler's Chancellery and wartime bunker, no trace remains, and even the sites are left unmarked, to avoid the possibility of them becoming neo-Nazi shrines. In contrast, a museum to the Jewish Holocaust has been designated in the locality.
● Similarly many Germans would like to see the monuments of the East German regime removed, such as the Palace of the People (the DDR Parliament), which replaced the former palace of the kings of Prussia.

● The communist regime neglected the Baroque heritage of East Berlin for many years, but in the 1970s initiated a massive restoration programme following a reappraisal of the role of Frederick the Great as a national leader. More recently the restoration of Berlin's most well-known landmark – the Brandenburg Gate – stirred controversy, as the Prussian Eagle and Iron Cross were regarded by many as symbols of the old militaristic Germany.
● The medieval nucleus of Berlin is unlikely to be restored, given the high cost of land in the city centre, as building on such an intimate scale would not yield economic returns.

The new Berlin has become a centre for fashion, music and the performing arts, which makes it an interesting short-break destination. It still exerts a special fascination as a result of its recent history. It is also a green city, with much of its area allocated to recreational space in the form of parkland, woods, lakes and canals.

Transport facilities are excellent, and it is worth noting that the U-bahn and S-bahn networks which functioned efficiently during the division of the city, have now been extended. However the price of accommodation is set to rise substantially with the growth of business and conference travel to the new capital. We think the following attractions are worthy of special mention:

1 *The Berlin Wall* Only a segment remains of the original 160 kilometre-long Wall, but this is now the world's largest open-air art gallery. Near Checkpoint Charlie on Friedrichstrasse (the former entry point to East Berlin for Western visitors) a museum now commemorates the attempts made by East Berliners to escape to freedom in the West.
2 *Museum Island* This historic area of East Berlin has some of Europe's finest museums and art galleries, the most famous being the Pergamon Museum, which is a collection of art objects from the ancient civilisations of the Middle East, the most spectacular being the Ishtar Gate from Babylon.
3 *The Egyptian Museum* This museum is the equivalent in West Berlin of the Pergamon Museum, containing the 3000-year old bust of Nefertiti.
4 *The Charlottenburg Palace* This was a favourite residence of Frederick the Great, along with his ornate summer palace at Sans Souci, in the western suburb of Potsdam.

14

France

LEARNING OBJECTIVES

After reading this chapter, you should be able to:

1 Appreciate the social and economic changes that have taken place in France and understand their importance for tourism.
2 Recognize the contribution of France to world culture and the importance of the cultural heritage.
3 Recognize the variety of physical features and climates in France and understand their significance for tourism.
4 Be aware of the major role played by the public sector in the organization and planning of tourism in France.
5 Understand the importance of transport infrastructure in the development of tourism.
6 Recognize the major components of the French holiday market and the scale of inbound tourism to France.
7 Be aware of the importance of the regions in supplying distinctive tourism products.
8 Be aware of the importance of rural tourism and measures to protect the French countryside.
9 Demonstrate a knowledge of the tourist regions, resorts, business centres and tourist attractions of France.

Introduction

For many years, France has been the world's top tourist destination in terms of visitor numbers, and it is second only to the USA in terms of tourism receipts. France was one of the first countries to recognize the importance of the industry, setting up a national tourism office as early as 1910. It is no coincidence that much of the vocabulary used in tourism is of French origin, particularly as regards the hotel and catering sectors.

Among the factors contributing to France's success in tourism are:

1 It is the largest country in Western Europe, boasting a natural resource base which includes an extensive coastline facing three seas, some of Europe's finest rivers – the Loire, Rhône, Seine and Garonne – and three major mountain areas – the Alps, Pyrenees and Massif Central.
2 France is also unique among European countries in its latitudinal and altitudinal range, which gives rise to a variety of climates and landscape features. Mediterranean conditions are found in Provence, Languedoc-Roussillon and Corsica. A long dry summer with abundant sunshine, combined with mild winters, allows for a prolonged tourism season in world-famous resorts such as Nice and St Tropez. The Atlantic and Channel coasts have less sunshine and a climate favouring the more active types of recreation. Eastern France has a continental climate with cold winters, while in the mountains, snow cover is uneven and variable – especially in those ski resorts situated at low or middle altitudes.
3 French culture has been widely emulated, starting in the Middle Ages with the Gothic style of architecture and the ideal of chivalry. In the seventeenth century, Louis XIV's court and palace at Versailles was the role model for the upper classes throughout Europe, and despite subsequent wars and revolutions, France remained pre-eminent in the world of haute-couture and fashion. In the late nineteenth century, French artists and architects were responsible for many innovations, such as impressionism, cubism and art nouveau.

4 French is the most widely spoken world language after English and Spanish. Cultural and business ties between France and its former colonies remain strong, determining the patterns of tourist flows to a considerable extent.

5 France is the world's fourth economic power (after the USA, Japan and Germany) and has been at the forefront of technological advance. However, most of this industrial development has taken place since the Second World War, and many city-dwellers retain close links with the countryside. France has the largest agricultural sector in Western Europe, offering the tourist a landscape that owes much of its charm to the prevalence of small-scale mixed farming, using fairly traditional methods of production.

6 France can offer a wide variety of tourism products based on these resources. We might mention for example:

(a) Special interest holidays, including wine-tasting tours of Burgundy and culinary short breaks for gourmets – foodies – in Normandy.

(b) The Club Mediterranée holiday village concept in beach and sport tourism.

(c) The importance of health tourism. Most of the numerous spas in France developed in the nineteenth century on the basis of mineral springs, while others on the coast offer thalassotherapy – seawater treatments. Spa facilities have generally been upgraded to meet changing demands, and offer a range of sporting, entertainment and cultural attractions.

(d) The importance of pilgrimages in a country where 90 per cent of the population are, at least nominally, Catholic. Some shrines such as Mont St Michel in Normandy, Rocamadour in Aquitaine and Vezelay in Burgundy were well-established in medieval times, acting as 'gathering points' on the major pilgrim routes to Santiago de Compostela in Spain. In contrast, Lourdes and Lisieux became pilgrimage centres in the nineteenth century.

(e) Winter sports are offered in the mountain resorts of the Alps, Pyrenees and the Massif Central. France has been an innovator in ski instruction (the short ski method), and in the development of purpose-built ski resorts above the tree line to guarantee a longer snow season. It has overtaken Austria and Switzerland as Europe's leading winter sports destination.

(f) Sailing is another major activity, which has spawned a massive investment by the public and private sectors in coastal marina developments. France boasts 450 such *ports de plaisance* offering a total of over 150 000 moorings.

(g) Other activity and adventure-based types of tourism include:

(i) boating on the superb network of rivers and canals

(ii) canoeing on fast-flowing rivers, such as the Ardèche

(iii) horse-riding

(iv) cycling – here two influences are perhaps at work – the trend toward 'green tourism' and the role of the Tour de France in raising the international profile of the sport

(v) surfing along the Atlantic coast

(vi) diving, along parts of the Mediterranean coast such as Corsica

(vii) mountain-climbing in the Alps and Pyrenees

(viii) caving in the Dordogne region

(ix) hiking on the network of *grandes randonees* (long-distance waymarked trails) which penetrate the scenic areas of France

(x) golf, which is a fast-growing market, with developments in the coastal resorts of northern France.

In some of these products France has few rivals. However, the country's flair for style and innovation has not always been matched by effective marketing.

The demand for tourism in France

The French tend to take their holidays in France, due to the country's range of tourist resources, and also the tradition of spending the summer in the south. As a consequence, the propensity of the French to travel overseas is lower than other European countries. As recently as 1958, only 25 per cent of the French took a holiday. Both domestic and foreign tourism increased through the postwar years and by the late 1990s almost 60 per cent of the population took a holiday away from home.

Domestic tourism

The changing economic and social geography of postwar France has had implications for participation in tourism. Demographic changes since the Second World War have boosted the population by 19 million (to over 59 million), restored the imbalance between males and females, and replenished both the low numbers of young people and the toll of two world wars. However, as early as the 1970s, France was experiencing an increased number of old people and a decrease in average family size. At the same time, France was transformed from an essentially rural society into an industrial economy with people leaving the countryside for urban manufacturing and service centres. Accompanying these changes has been a growth in the numbers employed in the service sector, increased car ownership, social tourism initiatives, and substantial rises in both disposable and discretionary incomes. This has led to an expansion of leisure spending as recreation and tourism have become significant in French life.

In this respect, an important enabling factor has been the increased leisure time available to the French. Successive reductions of working hours have left a statutory working week of less than forty hours. Also, the minimum school-leaving age has been raised to sixteen years and there is continuing pressure for early retirement. Since, its introduction in 1936, annual holiday entitlement has grown to five weeks and many workers have six or more weeks. The fact that at least two of the weeks have to be taken between May and October has led to congestion in this peak holiday period. With the new millennium the working week was reduced to thirty-five hours – the lowest in Europe, further increasing the leisure time available. The downside of the social legislation affecting labour is that employers may be reluctant to recruit staff, resulting in a high rate of unemployment compared to the USA or the UK.

France has a very high proportion of domestic holiday-taking, with trips demonstrating a number of characteristics:

1 They are lengthy, often three or four weeks, although there are signs that the traditional month away in August *en famille* is decreasing.
2 They are concentrated into the peak summer months (the majority of holidays are taken in July and August) although efforts are being made to spread the load with promotional campaigns, staggering of school holidays and the growth of winter holidays.
3 In a country with such varied holiday opportunities, a wide distribution of holiday destinations is evident, though a general movement from north to south, as well as to the periphery, can be discerned, with a concentration in the mountains and at the coasts.
4 The car is the most common means of domestic holiday transport.
5 Self-catering, second homes and visiting friends and relatives account for the majority of holidays – simply because their cost commends them to families in peak season.
6 The majority of holidays are arranged independently, but works councils and other non-profit-making organizations play an important role. These range from professional organizations that own fully equipped holiday accommodation and rent to members at competitive rates to those involved in social tourism.

Social tourism represents a very strong movement in France and is significant for French domestic patterns of demand. There was a spectacular growth in social tourism initiatives in the 1960s, and in the late 1990s the government established a new fund to allow the unemployed and poorer citizens to take a holiday, using spare capacity in the coastal resorts. Examples of social tourism initiatives include:

● children's hostels – *colonies des vacances*
● family holiday villages *villages vacances familiales* (VVF)
● government schemes such as the *cheque vacances* to boost holiday opportunities for the disadvantaged groups in society.

Second homes – *residences secondaires* – continue to play an important role in domestic travel, accounting for a fifth of both summer and winter overnight stays. The high incidence of second-home ownership (estimated at 3 million) and their wide distribution throughout the country are reminders that most city-dwellers have rural roots. However, improvements in transport have resulted in the growth of a second-home belt within a 100–150 kilometres radius of the major cities.

Outbound tourism

Around 20 per cent of French holidays are taken abroad, mainly in Spain or Italy. This represents a growth in foreign tourism since 1945 that is rooted in the changing social and economic circumstances of France. Spending abroad by French nationals is low compared to receipts from inbound tourists and France therefore runs a surplus on its travel account. Inclusive tour holidays account for a smaller percentage of French travellers abroad than is the case in Britain or Germany, and most foreign travel is by car. However, long-haul tourism has shown consistent growth, with the USA and French-speaking destinations tending to be the most popular. The French travel trade is mainly concerned with outbound tourism and, in contrast to the UK, is made up of many small and medium-sized enterprises. For example, the top ten operators in France generate one third of the total turnover in this sector, compared to Britain where the equivalent figure is well over two-thirds. The most well known tour operators are Nouvelles Frontieres for package holidays, and Club Mediterranée which pioneered the all-inclusive concept in tourism, and has over a hundred holiday villages worldwide. Other companies are less innovative, and technological development is less advanced than in the UK, with most of the business still being done by post.

Inbound tourism

In the late 1990s France ranked as the world's most popular international tourist destination, helped by developments such as the Channel tunnel and Disneyland Paris, as well as a number of sports events that attracted worldwide television coverage. The majority of visitors are from Western Europe, although new generators, such as Eastern Europe are growing in significance. Germany, Belgium, the Netherlands and the UK account for most of the visits to France, attracted by the ease of road and ferry access and the range of French tourism resources. Most British tourists travel independently by car and tend to fall into two distinct types:

● day visitors to the Channel ports such as Calais, where shopping in the hypermarkets for wine and beer is the main objective

● those on a touring holiday who are attracted by the cultural differences between the two countries as expressed by specialist shops – such as the *charcuterie*, the bistros and the cafés.

The geographical position of France does mean that it attracts a large number of day excursionists, as noted above. Also, a large percentage of international tourists arrive in June, July or August to exacerbate the already acute concentration of French domestic holidays. However, winter holidays and the German trend to take second holidays in France in the off-peak season may help to alleviate the problem.

France has always been popular for conventions and sales meetings and a government-run conference bureau co-ordinates the promotion and development of conference activities. Business travel is an important sector of French tourism, typically concentrated in major urban centres and using higher category hotels:

● Paris has for long been the world's leading conference centre, offering a range of venues, with the added incentive of a short-break holiday before or after the business trip.
● Nice now boasts Europe's largest conference venue with its 'Acropolis Centre'.
● Other important conference cities are Lyons, Marseilles, Cannes and Strasbourg.

Event attractions have also played an important role as a 'pull factor' for foreign tourists. They include:

● the 1989 celebrations for the Bicentenary of the French Revolution
● the 1992 Winter Olympics at Albertville in the French Alps
● the 1994 celebrations of the fiftieth anniversary of the D-Day landings in Normandy
● the 1998 football World Cup.

The supply of tourism in France

Tourism is a fragmented industry in France, comprising many small, often family-run, enterprises. It is therefore difficult to gauge levels of employment in the industry. Official figures estimate 500 000 jobs in hotels and catering, official tourist offices, and agencies, but this figure clearly falls short of the real total. A further 1 million jobs are attributed as an indirect result or 'spin off' from tourism.

Accommodation

The bed-stock in France is concentrated both in Paris and on the French coasts, and is comprehensive in terms of both self-catering and serviced accommodation:

1 There is an increasing trend among holidaymakers toward self-catering. In total, self-catering accounts for about 3 million bed-spaces, mainly concentrated in the southern and western parts of France:
   (a) Camping and caravanning are popular both among foreign and domestic tourists, and the number of sites – especially at the top end of the market – has increased. Most campgrounds are located on or near the coast, where demand can exceed supply at the height of the summer season – particularly on the Côte d'Azur.
   (b) British holidaymakers have shown an interest in *gites*, which combine the advantages of self-catering with living in a small rural community. Typically these holiday homes are converted farm buildings which are surplus to their original purpose. In the past, *gites* were subsidized by the state as part of a campaign to stem rural depopulation; nowadays, they are self-financing but still subject to controls by the local authorities and the non-profit-making National Federation of Gites de France. Some of the ferry operators and the British motoring organizations have been active in marketing this type of tourism.
   (c) In addition, large numbers of British, Dutch and German holidaymakers own second homes, partic-ularly in Provence, the Dordogne and the Ardèche regions.
2 In terms of serviced accommodation, only a small percentage of domestic nights are spent in hotels, so these increasingly rely on business travellers and foreign tourists. Despite this, hotel-building, especially in the two-star and budget categories, has continued – both to attract the foreign market and also under social tourism schemes. Hotel capacity is concentrated in Paris, the Rhône–Alps region, and in Provence–Côte d'Azur. The hotel sector is less dominated by international chains than in most European countries, although the French-owned Accor is one of the world's leading hotel groups. The hotel stock includes a large number of small, budget-priced hotels (*logis de France*), inns (*auberges*) and converted chateaus (*relais-chateaux*).

Transport

Transport by car dominates tourism in France, accounting for two-thirds of inbound tourists and almost 80 per cent of domestic holidays. This reflects the demand for self-catering and informal holidays, as well as the asset of a road system that ranks among the best in Europe, including 9000 kilometres of motorway and 28 500 kilometres of *routes nationales* (first-class highways). There are few long-distance bus services in France, so the rail system handles a high proportion of inter-city travel, competing effectively with the private car and domestic air services. The state-owned railway authority (SNCF) has invested in the electrification of main line services and in high-speed trains

– the famous TGVs. These run mainly on dedicated track at speeds of 270 kilometres per hour, linking Paris to Lyons, Lille, Nantes, Bordeaux and Nice. The rail network continues to be focused on Paris, so that it is usually necessary to transfer between termini to make inter-regional connections. However, an overnight through-train runs between Calais and the French Riviera all year round, and between Calais and Languedoc in summer.

International air connections are comprehensive, with three airports serving Paris, while Air France is one of the world's leading airlines. Domestic services from Paris are provided by Air Inter to over forty destinations. Although opposed by the French, the air transport sector has undergone deregulation as part of the European Commission's liberalization of air transport.

Cross-Channel ferries are the preferred transport mode for tourists from Britain. The present wide choice of routes is, however, diminishing as the car-carrying Le Shuttle train service through the Channel tunnel becomes an established alternative, having overcome widely publicized safety and operational problems. Similarly the airlines' share of the lucrative business travel market is being reduced through competition from the Eurostar train service between London and Lille/Paris. Trans-Mediterranean ferry connections to Corsica, Sardinia and North Africa are provided by SNCM (Societe Nationale Maritime Corse-Mediterranee) from the ports of Marseilles, Toulon and Nice. The 9000 kilometres of inland waterway are now mainly used for recreation and have become a tourist attraction in their own right, the most well known being the Canal du Midi between Toulouse and Sete, built in the reign of Louis XIV to link the Atlantic and the Mediterranean. Converted barges – *peniches* – and hotel-boats provide an interesting way of viewing the French countryside.

Tourism organization in France

Tourism in France is strongly controlled by central government in Paris through the Direction du Tourisme ministry, and the ministry's promotional and marketing agency – La Maison du France. In 1982 the twenty-two regions were given scope for economic development, although at local level, the ninety-five *departements* into which France has been divided for administrative purposes since the Revolution have much less importance for determining policy than the counties of the UK. Tourism illustrates the importance of the 'mixed economy' in France, with the public and private sectors co-operating at regional level on the regional boards and at local level in the *syndicates d'initiatives* – which in most French towns provide information for travellers (there are over 5000 offices nation-wide). Where resorts have development potential but lack private initiative, a government-run *office du tourisme* can be set up to carry out promotion and development. At national level some degree of co-ordination between the various government departments and agencies involved in tourism is achieved by the Commission Interministerielle D'amenagement Du Territoire (the Inter-Ministerial Commission for Land Development).

Since the time of Louis XIV, there has been a tradition of state intervention in the economy of France, with a tendency to favour large-scale projects. The re-planning of Paris by Haussmann and Napoleon III and the public works carried out by President Mitterand, are the best known examples. The Languedoc-Roussillon project is a good example of the state taking direct responsibility for large-scale tourism development. In 1963 the government set up an inter-ministerial commission to co-ordinate the work of various public agencies and local chambers of commerce in developing seven new resorts on the western Mediterranean coast. The objectives were to:

- take pressure off the congested Côte d'Azur
- divert holidaymakers who might otherwise go to Spain – in other words, to act as an intervening opportunity.

The state financed the necessary land acquisition and preparation for development, including mosquito eradication from the coastal marshes, as well as a new motorway to improve access. Mixed economy companies – bringing together the private and public sectors – carried out the infrastructure works for each resort. Private developers then provided the accommodation and other facilities under the direction of an architect charged with giving each resort 'unity' and 'style'. Although Languedoc-Roussillon is one of the world's most ambitious tourism projects, many of the jobs created are seasonal, and there is a danger that the region could become as overdependent on tourism as it previously had been on agriculture.

Similarly on the Aquitaine coast a management plan was inaugurated in 1967, with the aim of maximum use of the dune, lagoon and forest resources of the area for recreation. Nine 'tourist unities' were to be created, based primarily on existing resorts, to provide 760 000 bed-spaces in hotels, guesthouses, campsites and marinas. However, this project has not achieved the success of Languedoc-Roussillon due to insufficient public funding, lack of enthusiasm from some of the communities affected and opposition from environmentalists. Since the 1980s tourism policy has moved from large-scale initiatives towards smaller, local projects where environmental considerations are taken into account. These initiatives are spearheaded by the regional councils with financial support from central government.

Tourism plays an important role in regional development, enabling the economic regeneration of stagnating rural areas such as those of the Massif Central. Government grants, loans and subsidies not only encourage the upgrading of accommodation in spas and seaside resorts throughout France, but provide much of the funding for conservation. The government showed little concern for countryside conservation until 1960, when the first national park was designated. This was due to the country's low population density, compared with, say, the UK, so that the need for protection was seen as less pressing, and also the French passion for field sports. The majority of France's most scenic areas now have protected status as national parks or regional nature parks, under the overall control of the Ministry of the Environment and the Quality of Life.

The national parks are managed by a state agency with the primary objective of conserving the natural flora and fauna, and the impact of visitors is controlled by a system of zoning:

● Tourism is encouraged in the outer zone with information points, accommodation and recreational facilities – for example, there are a number of ski resorts in the Vanoise National Park.
● A second zone supports traditional rural activities, subject to regulations on field sports and activities that might be detrimental to the natural environment.
● The inner zone severely restricts entry to give maximum protection to individual species and ecosystems.

With the exception of the Port-Cros marine park off the Mediterranean coast, and the Parc des Cevennes in the Massif Central, the six national parks are situated in the Alps and the Pyrenees. The Vanoise is linked with the Gran Paradiso National Park in Italy, while the Parc des Pyrenees adjoins Spain's Ordesa National Park.

The regional nature parks generally consist of landscapes that have been greatly modified by human intervention and where multiple use management of resources is necessary. Unlike the national parks, the twenty-five regional nature parks are widely distributed throughout France, and are more accessible from the major cities. Examples include St Amand Reismes near Lille, the Camargue, and the Parc d'Armorique in Brittany. The Corsican regional nature park has the triple aims of nature conservation, providing for tourism, and preserving rural life and traditions, in an attempt to stem the movement of population from the mountainous interior to the coastal resorts.

Conservation of the built heritage has a longer history in France, although there is no real equivalent to the English National Trust. The French tend to take a more robust approach to the conservation of historic buildings, with an emphasis on full-scale restoration. Notable examples include:

● the chateaux of the Loire, ransacked during the French Revolution
● the medieval city of Carcassonne – which is actually a nineteenth-century reconstruction
● the port of St Malo, destroyed in the Second World War and subsequently rebuilt complete with the medieval fortifications.

Tourist regions of France

Tourism in France is more evenly distributed than in most European countries, with the interior sharing the benefits to a greater extent than is the case in Spain, for example. This is because the French countryside and the many historic towns are significant tourism resources, ideally suited to touring holidays. Nevertheless, there are important differences between the regions of the south and west, which attract a large international as well as domestic market, and the climatically less-favoured regions of the north, where the resorts along the Channel coast have suffered a decline since the Second World War.

Northern France

As far as the majority of sun-seeking tourists from northern Europe are concerned, most of northern France is a zone of passage on the routes south to the Riviera, Italy and Spain, while its heritage attractions and gentle landscapes are overshadowed by the more dramatic scenery of the south and west. A major exception is the Paris region, known historically as the Ile de France, which is in fact the part of the country most visited by foreign tourists, for the following reasons:

1 The city of Paris offers a complete range of cultural attractions, many of which are world famous – such as the Eiffel Tower, Notre Dame, the Arc de Triomphe and the Louvre. Then there are the romantic associations evoked by the River Seine and its bridges, and the city's reputation as a centre of high fashion and stylish entertainment. Compared to most world capitals, the townscapes of central Paris within the *peripherique* (ring road) consist of low-rise buildings, and broad tree-lined boulevards forming a harmonious whole. Many of the historic *quartiers* (districts) have preserved their specific character – although areas like Montmartre have become commercialized as a result of tourism. Nevertheless a considerable amount of urban renewal has taken place since the 1970s, including such exciting examples of modern architecture as the Louvre extension, the Beaubourg Centre, the Bastille Opera and La Defense. The Musee de'Orsay is an example of an old building with an obsolescent function (railway station) revitalized as an impressive art gallery. For many years Paris has been the most popular city-break destination and this is likely to continue, given its improved accessibility as a result of the Channel tunnel to the UK. However, its share of the market has declined during the 1990s largely due to competition from the 'newcomers' in Eastern Europe such as Prague.
2 The French capital offers the opportunity of excursions to the former royal palaces at Versailles and Fontainebleau, or to the historic towns of Orléans, Chartres and Beauvais.

3 The tourism industry of Paris was boosted in 1992 by the opening of the largest theme park in Europe – Disneyland Paris (formerly Eurodisney) to the east of the city. This is an interesting example of co-operation between the public sector and a foreign-owned private corporation, with the French government providing the dedicated rail link from Roissy-Charles de Gaulle Airport. After initial teething troubles, due in part to the wide cultural gap between French and North American tastes and expectations, Disneyland Paris has established itself as the leading theme park in France, with just over half of its visitors from overseas. Much more than a theme park, it is a resort in its own right, adding 10 000 beds to the accommodation stock in the Paris region. Faced with this competition, the Asterix Park to the south of Paris has managed to retain its share of the market, basing its appeal on traditional French themes.

4 Paris is also a major destination for business travellers, and this is reflected in the availability of modern conference facilities and top quality hotels (half of the 'de-luxe' class of French hotels are located in the capital).

The North

Consisting of the historic provinces of Artois and Picardy, this region contains Calais, the major gateway to France for British tourists travelling by car, coach or train. Dunkirk also handles a significant volume of ferry traffic, but Boulogne has lost its ferry link, and like Dover across the Channel, has had to diversify, investing heavily in the Nausicaa marine-life attraction. (Similar projects have been proposed for Cherbourg and Brest, faced with the decline of their traditional maritime industries.) Inland, parts of the region have been adversely affected by nineteenth-century heavy industry, but Lille has become a major transport hub and business centre thanks largely to the Channel tunnel. Lille's cultural attractions, along with those of historic towns such as Arras and Douai, are now more widely appreciated for short break holidays. The 'Opal Coast' south of Boulogne, particularly the attractive resort of Le Touquet, was fashionable with British holidaymakers before the Second World War. It continues to be popular with Parisians and golf is providing the impetus for rejuvenation.

Normandy

Normandy's history has been closely linked with that of England, as shown by the Bayeux tapestry commemorating the Norman conquest in 1066 and the battlefields of the Hundred Years War. In more recent times, the Normandy beaches at Arromanches were the launch pad for the Allied campaign to liberate Europe in the Second World War. Visitors are drawn to its attractive countryside and a number of historic towns such as Caen and Rouen, but in summer the seaside resorts provide the main appeal. The Côte Fleurie between Caen and the Seine estuary remains popular with domestic holidaymakers. A creation of the late nineteenth century *belle époque*, Deauville continues to be visited by fashion-conscious Parisians, although it has invested heavily in a marina and other modern facilities. Other resorts such as Trouville are more family oriented and suffer from competition from self-catering complexes, a surplus of hotel accommodation, and changing holiday tastes. Normandy also boasts one of France's most unique and most visited heritage attractions – the medieval abbey of Mont St Michel, which is daily separated from the mainland by some of the world's strongest tides.

Brittany

With its Celtic language, strong cultural traditions and maritime outlook, the peninsula of Brittany, with its deeply indented coastline has long been peripheral to the mainstream of French economic and social life. Yet these characteristics have considerable tourism potential, especially to the growing British market. The main holiday area focuses on the part of the north coast – the Côte Emeraude – which includes the resort of Dinard and the historic seaport of St Malo. Efforts are being made to disperse tourism away from these established centres to the more rugged coastal areas of western Brittany and the neglected interior, which, unlike Normandy, is a poor area agriculturally.

Western France

Consisting of the regions of La Vendée, Poitou-Charentes and Aquitaine, western France has a mild but sunny Atlantic climate, some of the best beaches in Europe, and is regarded by the French themselves as the land of gastronomy and good living. On the coast there are old-established resorts such as Biarritz and Arcachon, which have adapted to modern trends such as surfing and camping. The Aquitaine coast also boasts the highest sand dunes in Europe and extensive lagoons backed by pine forests. North of the Gironde estuary there are a number of offshore islands where the number of summer visitors greatly outnumbers the local inhabitants. The interior is also well endowed with scenic and cultural attractions which include:

1 The Loire Valley, one of the best known touring areas, where the main attractions are the chateaux and palaces associated with French royalty in Renaissance times, notably Chenonceaux, where history is brought to life by *son et lumière* performances during the summer months.

2 The caves of the Dordogne, which contain outstanding examples of Ice Age art. The most famous of these – Lascaux – was not discovered until 1940. A replica cave has been opened to protect the original paintings, which

otherwise would have deteriorated from the impact of visitors.

3 The wine-producing area around Bordeaux, a city which is also famous for its eighteenth-century Grand Theatre.

4 Futuroscope near Poitiers, a science theme park showcasing the film industry.

The Massif Central

This mountain and plateau region in south central France offers scope for a wide variety of recreational activities, including hang-gliding, mountain-biking and whitewater rafting. The landscapes include deep limestone gorges, extensive forests and the strange remnants of extinct volcanoes known as *puys*. Geothermal activity is evident today in the large number of mineral springs – as a result the Massif Central contains more than a third of French spas. Agrotourism has been encouraged to stem depopulation from one of France's poorest farming regions, by integrating holiday villages and second homes with rural communities. There has also been some development of winter sports tourism for the domestic market.

Vichy is probably the best known of French spas, although it now attracts fewer wealthy foreign clients than in the era prior to the Second World War. The hotels, bathing establishments, casino and opera house are grouped around the Parc des Sources, which is the major focus of the resort. Like other European spas, Vichy has adapted to changing demands by:

● diversification of the product from health tourism into conferences, exhibitions and festivals
● modernization of spa treatments to appeal to today's busy executives rather than the traditional three week *cure*
● the provision of sports facilities to attract young tourists.

Eastern France

The vast swathe of France extending from the Ardennes to the Jura mountains has for centuries been a zone of passage for trade and invading armies and is now well suited for touring holidays. Resources include:

● the rolling countryside of the Champagne region which includes Rheims, historically important as the religious capital of France
● Lorraine, although more industrialized, boasts one of the best examples of eighteenth-century town planning in the city of Nancy
● German-speaking Alsace has more to offer the visitor, with its picturesque half-timbered villages and an important wine route based on Colmar
● its regional capital – Strasbourg – which has acquired a major international role as a seat of the European Parliament and other EU agencies.

Burgundy, lying astride the routeways connecting the Rhine to the Rhône, and thus linking northern Europe to the Mediterranean, played a major role in European history in the Middle Ages. Its rich cultural heritage includes the Romanesque abbeys of Citeaux and Cluny, and the historic cities of Dijon and Beaune, although Burgundy is best known for the wines of the Côte d'Or and Beaujolais districts.

The South of France

For the tourist travelling overland, the Rhône Valley south of Lyon provides the introduction to the region known by the French as Le Midi. The South of France is distinguished by its Mediterranean climate, but more tangibly by the colourful landscapes and the quality of its light, which have attracted many world famous artists. Regional lifestyles also differ from those of northern France, while the popularity of bull fights in Nîmes, Perpignan and Arles, and the use of the Catalan language in Roussillon, reflect the influence of Spain. The South includes two major tourist regions – the Languedoc-Roussillon coast, that we mentioned earlier as an example of large-scale planning, and the French Riviera, the subject of a case study at the end of this chapter.

1 In Languedoc-Roussillon the coastal resorts have tended to draw tourists away from the interior, which includes such scenically attractive areas as the Corbieres and the Cevennes. During the summer months the new resorts such as Cap d'Agde with its Mediterranean village ambience, and La Grand Motte, distinguished by its pyramid-shaped apartment blocks – are full of activity. They provide a contrast to the historic cities of the interior, notably Montpellier with its university, Carcassonne, and Nîmes, which has one of the best preserved Roman arenas.

2 In Provence the rural areas have been more successful in attracting tourists and second-home owners. The cities of the region are also important tourist centres, with a wealth of heritage attractions dating back to Roman times, and a calendar of cultural events such as music festivals. The best known are Aix en Provence, which is a major artistic centre, Arles and Avignon – where the Palace of the Popes is a reminder of the city's former importance as a political and religious centre. However tourism is of secondary importance in Marseilles, which is by far the biggest city of the Midi, due to the dominance of industry and commerce and its reputation for crime. Provence can also offer a number of contrasting natural attractions such as the wetlands of the Camargue and the gorges of Verdon.

Corsica

Known to the French as 'the island of beauty', Corsica offers some of the most spectacular scenery in the western

Mediterranean. From the deeply indented western coast rise high mountains covered with forests of pine and chestnut and sweet-smelling maquis. Tourism has underlined the differences between the coastal towns, which have always been more outward-looking, and the remote interior, where traditional lifestyles prevailed until recent times. The main resorts – Calvi, Ile Rousse and Porto Vecchio lie on the west coast and offer facilities for water sports such as sailing and diving, while the island's capital – Ajaccio – has capitalized on its fame as the birthplace of Napoleon. Development plans for the island seek to redress the imbalance between the coast and the interior, although continuing to recognize the key role of tourism which provides a quarter of employment. Attention is focused on the flatter east coast, where development is taking place in a more orderly way than in the past. Improved transport links to the mainland, and the growth of inclusive tours, will ensure a greater role for tourism in Corsica. However, tourism must be seen to benefit the local population, who are keen to preserve their cultural identity.

The French Alps

The traditional economy of this mountain region was based on pastoralism, with the livestock being moved to the high pastures above the tree line in summer and back to the villages in autumn. The economy is now dependent on tourism, including winter sports and in summer, lakes and mountains holidays. Most of the development has taken place in the north, where the mountains are higher, yet more accessible. Mountain-climbing has been a major activity at Chamonix since the early nineteenth century, due to its proximity to Mont Blanc and the spectacular glacier known as the Mer de Glace. It has now become a major ski resort. Villages at lower altitudes – in the so-called Pre-Alps – are less used for skiing due to the unreliable snow cover, but are much in demand for second home development, while Aix les Bains and Evian rank among Frances' most noted spas.

Full-scale development for winter sports tourism began in the 1960s involving public sector investment under the *Plan Neige*. Purpose-built resorts were planned at high altitudes above the tree line, where glacial cirques provided maximum snow cover. These were to be veritable ski-factories of a uniform design appealing to sports-minded tourists, with apartment blocks sited to give direct access to the lift system. Resorts such as Tignes have been criticized for their lack of human scale, severely functional design and their impact on the fragile alpine environment. Overall, the majority of the development has been in the northern Alps, where the fifteen major resorts account for over three-quarters of the industry's turnover. In the 1990s there has been something of a reaction favouring smaller resorts of a more traditional design.

The French Alps have become Europe's most popular winter sports destination, attracting domestic and foreign skiers alike, for the following reasons:

1 Proximity to the areas generating the demand. Thanks to the Channel tunnel, British skiers have a wide choice of routes and modes of transport to the resorts. In addition to airports at Nice (serving the southern resort of Isola 2000), Lyons, Grenoble, Chambery and Geneva, there are Eurostar ski-trains, and 'ski-drive' arrangements are available for motorists using the excellent road network.
2 Good infrastructure, with over 300 'ski centres' boasting the most extensive lift system in Europe.
3 Suitability for a wide range of markets, from family holidaymakers to young singles and snowboarders.
4 An extensive range of accommodation, from first-class hotels to family-run *auberges*, serviced chalets and self-catering studio apartments.

The French Pyrenees

Winter sports play a less important role in the Pyrenees than in the Alps, and the region attracts fewer foreign skiers. Although the mountain peaks are not as high, remoteness from Paris and transport problems retarded the development of tourism. Nevertheless, a number of spas function as ski centres during the winter months. In summer, visitors are attracted by the unspoiled scenery – notably the Cirque de Gavarnie, a spectacular natural amphitheatre resulting from glacial erosion – and the opportunities for eco-tourism and adventure sports. The major tourist centre of the region – Lourdes – is in fact one of the world's leading attractions and deserves special consideration, because:

1 This small town with only 20 000 inhabitants annually hosts 5 million visitors (compared to 2 million in the 1950s). With over 400 hotels and a number of campsites on the outskirts, Lourdes can accommodate more than 100 000 visitors at peak times.
2 Its fame as a tourist centre is based not on a tangible physical resource, but on the visions of St Bernadette. The Grotto of Massabielle, where these occurred in 1858, subsequently became the focus of pilgrimage. Miraculous cures were attributed to the spring water in the grotto and, although a Medical Bureau scrutinizes these claims, Lourdes is not a spa in the conventional sense.
3 Lourdes was the first pilgrimage centre to be created by modern means of transport and communication, which explains its rapid growth, and it has become a role model for similar developments in other countries.
4 One-third of the visitors to Lourdes can be described as true pilgrims. More than 500 organized group pilgrimages take place every year, brought in by charter flights, coaches and special trains equipped by SNCF to carry the large numbers of sick and disabled. This involves considerable organization, in which volunteer carers play a major role.
5 The distinction between the religious and secular aspects of pilgrimage is not always clear, but in Lourdes there is some geographical separation of the two. Religious

activity is centred on the Domain of the Sanctuaries covering an area of 20 hectares. This includes the esplanade – a vast open space for processions – and a number of large churches grouped around the entrance to the Grotto. The devotion of the pilgrims provides a stark contrast to the commercialism of the town centre, with its array of shops displaying tawdry souvenirs.

Summary

Changing economic and social conditions in France since the Second World War have encouraged participation in tourism. The majority of French tourism is domestic, characterized by long-stay holidays concentrated into the peak summer months. Domestic holidays are widely distributed throughout France, and tend to be organized independently, although social tourism is important. The majority of French holidays abroad are to Spain and Italy, although long-haul destinations are becoming more popular, spearheaded to some extent by Club Mediterranée. Incoming tourism is more significant, and France is the world's most popular destination.

The tourism industry in France is fragmented, comprising many small businesses. A wide choice of accommodation is available, with self-catering the preferred option for holidaymakers, leaving the hotel sector largely dependent on business and foreign travel markets. Tourism benefits from comprehensive air, rail and road networks. Tourism tends to be strongly centralized at government level, with the state also initiating major development projects, although both regional and local organizations are now playing a more important role.

France can offer a great diversity of tourism resources and products, based on its countryside, coastal resorts and cultural heritage, and ranging from winter sports and adventure tourism in the Alps to sightseeing in Paris and the Loire Valley. Each region can offer different attractions, although tourism tends to play a more significant role in the coastal and mountain areas.

Case study

The French Riviera: fashion as an influence on resort development

Introduction

One of the world's best known and most fashionable resort areas, the French Riviera is the name given to the stretch of Mediterranean coast extending almost 200 kilometres from Toulon to the Italian border, while the Côte d'Azur is usually defined as the section east of Cannes. It is a spectacularly beautiful coastline – east of Nice the mountains of the Maritime Alps almost reach the sea. Three scenic highways, known as *corniches*, hug the contours of the cliffs. The mountains also shelter this south-facing coast from the blustery Mistral. Well endowed with natural attractions the Riviera is easily accessible by road, rail and air communications and offers a full range of amenities. The region has experienced several stages of development in response to changing fashions in tourism, namely:

1 *Exclusive winter health tourism* From the mid-nineteenth century to the outbreak of the First World War, the Riviera was exclusively a winter destination. Wealthy British tourists began the vogue for winter holidays on the Mediterranean coast, a fact commemorated by the Promenade des Anglais (sea front promenade) at Nice. In 1886 a French poet named the coastline the Côte d'Azur – an early example of resort promotion. By this time the coast between Cannes and Menton was already well established as a destination for the rich, well connected and famous throughout Europe, including Russian aristocrats, whose legacy is still evident in Nice. Queen Victoria made several visits, confirming the Riviera's exclusive status. Grand hotels such as the Carlton in Cannes, and the Negresco in Nice were built to accommodate these visitors, while casinos and racecourses were provided to keep them entertained. The world famous casino in Monte Carlo opened in 1863, an initiative which almost overnight made the fortunes of the principality of Monaco and its ruling Grimaldi family.

2 *Exclusive summer beach tourism* Until the 1920s, the élite had shunned the Mediterranean in the summer months. This changed when celebrities such as the French fashion designer Coco Chanel and the American writer Scott Fitzgerald made sunbathing fashionable. Juan-les-Pins was the Riviera's first summer resort, attracting a new moneyed clientele of writers, artists and entertainers who were quite different from the European aristocracy, whose fortunes had declined as a result of wars and revolutions. The region's accessibility improved with the construction of a new coastal highway – the *moyenne corniche* – and the inauguration of the *Train Bleu* (the Calais-Mediterranean express) which provided luxury travel to the resorts. The coast's mediocre beaches were also improved, sometimes by importing sand from elsewhere.

3 *Popular tourism* After the 1950s, the Riviera considerably widened its appeal, catering for a much larger domestic market. This had been foreshadowed by the French government's decision in 1936 to introduce holidays with pay and encourage cheap rail travel to the resorts, but the Second World War set

back the process of democratization. Campgrounds and a sprawl of holiday villas developed along the western Riviera, while many luxury hotels were converted into apartments. On the other hand, new resorts – such as the former fishing village of St Tropez – strove to maintain exclusivity along with some of the established centres. Fashion innovations such as the bikini ensured that the Riviera remained the focus of international attention.

Attractions

The Riviera offers a diversity of tourism products, and has to a large extent adapted to changing fashions. It retains its stylish image as a result of pricing and the types of facilities offered – marinas, often combined with luxury accommodation, as in the purpose-built resort of Port Grimaud, beach clubs, casinos and grand hotels. The resorts also vary considerably in character, from the exclusive hideaways of the very rich – Cap Ferrat near Nice is a good example – to unpretentious places catering for the French family market such as Saint Maxime and Saint Raphael. Market segmentation was evident as early as the 1920s, when an advertising slogan for Cannes claimed that 'Menton's dowdy, Monte's brass, Nice is rowdy, Cannes is class'. This had an element of truth in that Menton had a reputation for attracting elderly invalids, whereas Monte Carlo appealed to the *nouveaux riches*. Nowadays, Menton, with its pink stucco villas set amid lemon groves, is the most old-fashioned of the resorts. Most of its visitors still tend to be elderly, in contrast to Juan-les-Pins, which attracts hordes of young French holidaymakers to its bars and discotheques. The main resorts and tourist areas of the Riviera are described below.

Monte Carlo

Monte Carlo has always gone for the big money. However, the principality of Monaco is less dependent on gambling revenues than in the past, having diversified into hosting international sports events and exhibitions as well as the business sector – many of its 27 000 residents are wealthy tax exiles. With an area of only 195 hectares, space in this tiny state is at a premium, resulting in a mini-Manhattan of high rise buildings. Nevertheless, the old town of Monaco perched above the yacht harbour retains some of its traditional atmosphere in contrast to Monte Carlo, which developed around the Casino. The principality's attractions include:

- the Oceanographical Museum – associated with the undersea explorer Jacques Cousteau
- the Jardin Exotique – a world famous collection of cacti, made possible by the favourable micro-climate.

Nice

Nice is less of a resort and more a large commercial city and major port, with a population approaching 500 000. It has a range of accommodation to suit most budgets, while its airport handles not only a large volume of holiday traffic – much of it on 'no frills' airlines – but also a substantial amount of business travel attracted by the growing information technology industries which have developed in this part of France. Nice is a major cultural centre, with a history going back to the times of ancient Greece and a recent association with some of the greatest modern artists; as a result, it boasts almost as many museums and art galleries as Paris.

Cannes

Cannes has retained its style and exclusive image to a greater extent than the other major resorts of the Côte d'Azur. The crescent-shaped Croisette beach of imported golden sand is backed by a promenade lined with palms and grand hotels. Designer boutiques line the streets of the new town, which contrasts with the old quarter overlooking the harbour. The Film Festival is the most well known of the event attractions that bring in considerable revenue.

The Western Riviera

The Western Riviera between Cannes and Hyères is generally less exclusive than the Côte d'Azur and less heavily developed. Hotel and restaurant prices are lower (except in St Tropez), while the beaches on the other hand are more attractive and in many cases open to the public. Inland, the Esterel and Maures uplands are less spectacular than the Maritime Alps, but give rise to some striking scenery. St Tropez is the leading resort of the Western Riviera, with a setting on a beautiful bay, a fashion scene that attracts celebrities, and a multitude wishing 'to see and be seen'. As a result, more than 10 000 cars arrive each day in St Tropez during the tourist season, stretching the town's resources to the limit.

Provence

The hinterland of Provence offers a contrast to the sophisticated resorts of the Riviera, but this is changing since the rural villages are increasingly drawn into the tourism industry, providing accommodation, for example, as pressures on the coast increase. The cultivation of flowers for the perfume industry at Grasse, and of fruit and early vegetables for the Paris markets still remain important to the local economy. The numerous hilltop villages – the so called *villes perchés* – are a reminder of former times when the coast was menaced by Saracen pirates rather than tourists. Some of these – notably Eze and Saint Paul de Vence – have become artist's colonies and specialize in a variety of craft industries aimed primarily at the tourist market.

The impacts of tourism

The Riviera's popularity as a tourist destination has resulted in a number of problems, including:

1 *Seasonality* The reluctance of the French to stagger their holidays leads to overcrowding in the peak months of July and August. Traffic congestion is acute, hotels increase their tariffs by 40 per cent, while spaces in campsites are at a premium. Water shortages are also a major problem due to excessive demands on supplies.
2 *Appropriation of land for development* Of the 5500 kilometres of French coastline, 1000 kilometres are said to be densely urbanized and another 2000 kilometres are characterized by 'dispersed development'. Pressures are greatest on the Côte d'Azur where 90 per cent of the coastline is already built-up. These pressures result from a rapidly growing population combined with the burgeoning demand for second or retirement homes. Not only is there an almost continuous linear development of apartments and villas along the coast, but dispersed development in the hinterland threatens to engulf the rural communities.
3 *Pollution and environmental degradation* Pollution from industrial effluents and untreated sewage has closed beaches, while fires – many started deliberately to clear land for development – have devastated large areas of pine forest and *maquis*.
4 *Crime* Drug-related crime, emanating from Marseilles and Nice, is an increasing threat to tourist security on the Riviera.
5 *An outdated image* The Riviera is also finding it difficult to adjust to new forms of holidaymaking that have an emphasis on self-catering, and is vulnerable to competition from Spain and Italy.

(Web site at http://www.maison-de-la-France.com)

Spain and Portugal

After reading this chapter you should be able to:

1 Describe the major physical features and climates of the Iberian Peninsula and the Spanish and Portuguese islands, and understand their significance for tourism.
2 Trace the development of Spanish tourism and understand the reasons for Spain's success as a tourist destination.
3 Appreciate the nature of tourism demand in Spain and Portugal.
4 Appreciate the cultural differences between Spain and Portugal, and contrast the nature of tourism development in the two countries.
5 Outline the major features of the tourism infrastructure in Spain, Portugal and Gibraltar.
6 Outline the main features of tourism administration in Spain and Portugal.
7 Demonstrate a knowledge of the tourist regions, resorts, business centres and tourist attractions of Spain, Portugal and Gibraltar.

Introduction

The Iberian Peninsula and the Spanish and Portuguese islands have been favourite holiday destinations for north Europeans since the availability of inclusive tours in the 1960s. By the late 1990s tourist arrivals in Spain and Portugal had exceeded 50 million. Spain was one of the first countries in the world to enter the mass inclusive tour market, taking advantage of its long Mediterranean coastline, and a sunny climate much desired by, and within easy reach of, north Europeans. To an extent, Spain has attempted for many years to promote products other than beach tourism, but this is proving difficult for the following reasons:

● Most of the tourism development is well established on the Costas – the resort areas of the Mediterranean coast of Spain – or in the islands.
● Spain's image of 'sun, sand and sangria' is firmly engrained in the popular culture of northern Europe.

Portugal, on the other hand, entered the international tourism scene later than Spain. It not only made a determined effort to avoid some of the worst excesses of tourism development made over the border, but also attempted both to control tourism's impact on the country and to attract the more affluent tourist from the outset.

Spain

Introduction

In area, Spain is the second largest country of Western Europe after France, and accounts for 80 per cent of the Iberian Peninsula. You should bear this in mind when planning a holiday itinerary, as it is almost 1000 kilometres by road from Bilbao or Santander on the north coast, to Malaga in the south. The dominant feature of the Iberian Peninsula is a high plateau – the Meseta – separated by rugged mountain ranges or *sierras*, from the narrow coastal strips where most of the tourism development has taken place. Because of this, only the Balearic islands and the south and east of Spain have a typically Mediterranean climate. The northern coast from Vigo to San Sebastian is not called 'Green Spain' without reason; summers are cooler and rainier and it enjoys less sunshine than the Mediterranean coast. The Meseta experiences a more extreme climate, with cold winters and hot summers.

The rugged nature of much of the Iberian Peninsula has helped to isolate Spain from the rest of Europe – often referred to as the 'Continent' by Spaniards. Even today, the Pyrenees are crossed by very few roads and railways. In the south, only a narrow stretch of water separates Spain from North Africa and its Islamic culture. In fact most of Spain – with the exception of Asturias and Galicia – was at one time under the domination of the North Africans (called Moors by the Spaniards). This heritage is evident today, particularly in the architecture and folklore of Andalucia, where Moorish rule lasted for eight centuries (from 711 to 1492). The religious fervour and devotion to the Roman Catholic Church that still characterizes much of Spain was forged in the long struggle to oust the Moslems from the Peninsula. Despite the impressive economic development, and social changes (in the role of women for example) that have taken place since the 1960s, Spain has retained its traditions perhaps to a greater extent than any other West European country. This is shown by:

1 The persistence of craft industries, notably ceramics and Toledo metalwork.
2 The *fiestas* which play such an important role in the life of most communities. These provide an opportunity to display Spain's rich heritage of regional dances and colourful costumes.
3 The revival of languages other than Castilian Spanish, especially in Catalonia and the Basque Country since the 1970s, reflecting the great cultural diversity of Spain.

Spain has achieved outstanding success as one of the world's top five destinations, and can offer over 1 million bed spaces in serviced accommodation alone. There is no doubt that tourism has contributed greatly to transformation of the Spanish economy from that of a developing country to one of Europe's major industrial nations since the 1950s. By the 1990s, tourism supported 1.5 million jobs, and contributed one-third of the country's export earnings. However, this success has been achieved at a cost to society and the environment, for example:

1 Spanish culture has been affected, due to the demands of the tourism industry on family life. A commercialized version of *flamenco* for tourist consumption has been substituted for local folklore in the resorts.
2 Uncontrolled resort developments mar part of the Mediterranean coastline and bring pollution.
3 Tourism has sharpened regional contrasts, particularly between the developed coastal areas and the interior.

Yet the Spanish beach product is still guaranteed a loyal repeat market, and tourism is likely to continue as a vital sector of the economy. Spain's success in tourism is due to a variety of factors, namely:

1 There was a growth in demand for holidays in the sun from countries in northern Europe once they had recovered from the effects of the Second World War.
2 Spain was well placed to benefit from the development of civil aviation and changes in the structure of the travel industry, especially the introduction of low-cost air inclusive tours.
3 Spain's relatively late entry into the European tourism market allowed it to evaluate the competition and offer lower prices than those of established destinations such as Italy and the French Riviera.
4 The Spanish government responded positively to the opportunities tourism offered, by:
   (a) Abolishing visa requirements for most European tourists in the late 1950s.
   (b) Maintaining a favourable rate of exchange for the tourist by successive devaluations of the peseta.
   (c) Providing advantageous credit terms to developers.
   (d) Regulating the industry to protect the consumer.
   (e) Creating a new Ministry of Tourism in 1962 to provide more effective co-ordination and promotion.

Arguably, the tourism industry was able to benefit from the long period of political stability under the authoritarian rule of General Franco (1939–75), as industrial unrest was outlawed. The views of local communities on tourism development were also frequently ignored in the interest of economic expediency. However, although the Franco regime tried to isolate Spain from the social changes taking place in Western Europe, tourism, through the demonstration effect, played a major role in bringing about the liberalization of Spanish society.

The demand for tourism

Domestic and outbound tourism

Before the 1960s only a relatively small minority of the Spanish population could afford to take holidays away from home. The middle and upper classes escaped the summer heat of the cities by visiting spas in the mountains, the beaches of the east coast or the northern coastal resorts such as Santander and San Sebastian. The economic progress which took place after 1960 increased personal incomes and boosted car ownership, so that participation in holiday-taking increased to a propensity of 60 per cent. The pattern of holiday taking by Spaniards contrasts with that of foreign visitors. Although the coasts are popular with both, many Spaniards visit the rural areas of the interior, often retracing their family roots. Domestic tourism in Spain has the following characteristics:

- Almost 80 per cent of trips are by private car.
- Only 20 per cent of overnight stays involve hotel accommodation, as two-thirds of domestic tourists stay with friends or relatives, or in second homes.
- The most popular month is August, when one in four Spaniards is on holiday.

Although 90 per cent of holidays taken by Spaniards are domestic, the number of foreign holidays taken has gradually increased to approach 13 million trips in the late 1990s. It is only in the 1990s that Spaniards have begun to view a foreign holiday as an annual event and forecasts are that trips will more than double by 2005. The most visited destinations are neighbouring France and Portugal, although touring holidays in Northern Europe, Morocco, and long-haul destinations are becoming popular. Spending per capita by Spanish tourists abroad is higher than the European average, demonstrating the country's new found prosperity. History, culture and education are important features sought by the Spanish abroad, with guidebooks stressing the culinary attractions of a destination. Day-trip volumes to neighbouring Portugal, France and Andorra are significant and estimated to be in the region of 25 million trips annually.

Inbound tourism

Spain was a relative latecomer to the international tourism scene. It did not usually feature on the Grand Tour, since the generally poor state of the roads and the inns tended to deter all but the more adventurous travellers. A major improvement in the situation took place after 1928, when the government-sponsored Patronato Nacional de Turismo began to set up a chain of state-run *albergues* (inns) and *paradores* offering a high standard of accommodation. The small numbers of foreign visitors to Spain before the Civil War (1936–39) were attracted by the country's picturesque traditions and not by sun, sand and sea, unlike most of today's tourists. For example, the American writer Hemingway was largely responsible for publicizing bullfighting and Pamplona's Fiesta de San Fermin, which attract a wide international following. The most spectacular expansion of tourism began in the 1950s with the influx of French tourists to the Costa Brava, a wave that soon spread to the Balearic Islands and the other Costas. By the early 1970s Spain had become the leading holiday destination for most of the North European tourist-generating countries. However this has left Spanish tourism vulnerable to the effects of recession in these countries, with the result that demand stagnated during the 1980s and early 1990s. This prompted the search for new markets – such as the USA and Japan – and volumes recovered in the mid to late 1990s to exceed 40 million staying visitors and 20 million excursionists (the latter including cruise passengers and day visitors from France and Portugal). The most important tourist-generating countries continue to be the UK, Germany, France, the Benelux countries and Italy. Surprisingly, although you might expect the Latin American countries, which contain over 200 million Spanish-speakers, to be a major source of tourists, in fact they account for less than 2 per cent of all foreign arrivals.

Despite the efforts of both national and regional governments, tourism in Spain is highly concentrated both seasonally and geographically. Well over half of foreign visitors arrive between June and September, coinciding with domestic holiday demand, and creating congestion in the resorts. The Canaries do not have this problem because of their subtropical climate, but other areas – notably the Costa Daurada and Costa Brava – are overwhelmingly dependent on summer visitors. Seasonality creates a problem for businesses as many find it uneconomic to remain open out of season, whereas those that do stay open reduce their staff and add to seasonal unemployment in the community. The public sector, too, is affected as services – such as water and power supplies – must have the extra capacity to cope with the peak demand, but are underutilized at other times of the year. One solution to the problem is to encourage third-age tourism in which Spanish senior citizens stay in resort hotels at reduced rates outside the peak season.

Geographically the distribution of tourism is very uneven. Over two-thirds of Spain's hotel capacity is concentrated in just four of the autonomous regions, namely the Balearic Islands, Catalonia, Andalucia and Valencia, which contain the most popular coastal areas. At the other extreme the interior regions of La Rioja (famous for its wine industry), Navarra and Extremadura, each have less than 1 per cent of hotel capacity, and the ratio between tourists and residents here is very low compared with the coastal resorts and islands. This means that the benefits of tourism are not spread widely throughout the country, and it has led to a migration of labour from the less developed areas to the resorts. Tourism could therefore be said to have contributed to the massive exodus from Spain's rural areas, where many villages are now virtually deserted. Agrotourism has grown in popularity in recent years and may help to stem further rural depopulation, but this in turn leads to another problem – loss of cultural identity – if villages simply become second homes for north European expatriates seeking 'the good life'.

Also the very nature of tourism demand to Spain has reduced the economic benefits. Spanish tourism is dominated by the demands of the large north European tour operators who provide high volumes of visitors yet demand low-priced accommodation. This encourages low-cost, high rise hotel and apartment development in the coastal resorts and reduces the contribution of each tourist to the economy. The anti-social behaviour of some of the youth element in mass tourism has also caused problems. This is concentrated for a few weeks in July and August in resorts dominated by the British or Germans, such as Magalluf and Arenal in Mallorca, Playa de las Americas in Tenerife, and San Antonio in Ibiza. Here, the phenomenon is referred to by some Spanish commentators as *turismo de basura* ('rubbish tourism'). This is because these visitors, who mainly belong to the lower socioeconomic groups, contribute little to the economy in relation to the nuisance they cause, and they tend to deter other tourists from staying in these resorts. The problem is not confined to Spain, but has spread to other Mediterranean destinations and even beyond, thanks to cut-price charter flights. You might discuss whether this type of tourist behaviour is a symptom of deeper problems in the post-industrial societies of Northern Europe.

The organization of tourism

Transport

Around two-thirds of all visitors to Spain arrive by surface transport, especially by road through the eastern Pyrenees. The inclusive tour market ensures a constant supply of tourists arriving mainly on charter airlines, owned in most cases by the major north European tour operators. Independent travellers and those touring Spain on fly-drive arrangements are more likely to use scheduled services. The national carrier Iberia plays a major role, with its subsidiaries BINTER and AVIACO, each specializing in different markets for air travel. Although Madrid and Barcelona are major international gateways, most North European holidaymakers fly to one of the regional airports serving a particular holiday area, namely:

● Gerona or Barcelona for the Costa Brava
● Reus or Barcelona for the Costa Daurada
● Alicante or Valencia for the Costa Blanca
● Málaga for the Costa del Sol
● Palma, Ibiza and Mahon for the Balearic Islands
● Las Palmas, Tenerife Sur and Arrecife for the Canary Islands.

Touring Spain by car has become much more convenient than in the past due to the massive improvement of the road network that has taken place since the 1980s, including some 6000 kilometres of motorways. One of the most important of these is the Autopista de Levante (east coast motorway) which is being extended to Cartagena. There are also plans to link Madrid with Seville, Valencia and Zaragoza. The rail system under Spanish State Railways (RENFE) is tightly focused on Madrid and therefore touring is less convenient. The break of gauge at the borders with France and Portugal also affects most international train services. However, plans are now well advanced to integrate Spain with the rest of the European rail network, and high-speed trains link Madrid with Seville, Barcelona and San Sebastian. The 'golden age' of rail travel is recalled by the luxury Al Andalus Express, which allows the visitor to see the countryside and cities of southern Spain in style.

Accommodation

Spain offers a variety of accommodation to suit most budgets from luxury resort hotels to simple *hostales* (pensions). Hotel classification is based on the facilities provided, rather than the quality of service. The private sector is increasingly dominated by large hotel groups, usually Spanish-owned, of which Melia and Sol are the best known internationally. In addition there are some 100 state-owned *paradores*, situated away from the main tourist centres and providing accommodation in traditional Spanish style (often in converted castles, palaces or monasteries). As such, they are favoured by independent travellers touring the 'real Spain' (as distinct from the Costas) by car. Self-catering accommodation, in the form of apartments and holiday villas is mainly found in the resort areas of eastern and southern Spain. Campsites are concentrated in those locations that are most accessible from France, such as the Costa Brava and the Valencia region.

Tourism administration

Spain's organization of tourism has attracted attention from countries around the world and many have adopted the Spanish model. Tourism became the responsibility of a cabinet minister in 1951 and the national tourism plans since 1953 have set the institutional and public service framework for Spain's growth and continued presence in the world tourism market. At national level, the Ministry of Trade, Tourism and Small and Medium-Sized Businesses is responsible for tourism policy and promotion. Generally the government is anxious to provide an environment within which tourism can flourish and a variety of grants and incentives are available for developers, in addition to the government's direct investment. There are also two specialist national agencies, one to promote conferences, and the other to manage state-owned accommodation, restaurants, hunting reserves and tourist routes.

Until 1978 tourism was firmly administered by central government from Madrid. The Spanish Constitution of that year gave the new autonomous regions (*communidades autonomas*), based on the cultural and historic regions of Spain, wide powers as part of the post-Franco democratization of the country. Tourism is therefore administered by seventeen regional governments who have the power to approve developments and determine policy. At the local level, the *municipios* (town councils) also take on the responsibility for some aspects of tourism and can impose taxes to finance projects in their area. This may well mean that tourism receives more favourable treatment in some areas than others. In the largest resorts there are associations of business people (*centros de iniciativas*) who promote their destination and local facilities – as in other areas of Spanish politics much depends on the personality and connections of those in power.

Although the authorities are aware that the mass inclusive tour market for beach tourism still represents the majority of demand, attempts are being made to develop new holiday styles in order to reduce seasonality, spread tourism more evenly throughout the country and encourage higher-spending visitors. The market continues to become more sophisticated and independent travel is increasing. Changes in the pattern of demand may mean that as much as 10 per cent of the accommodation stock needs to be taken off the cheaper end of the market, especially in Mallorca. The main objectives of the Spanish Tourist Office are to:

- increase awareness of the less well-known areas, mainly from the cultural viewpoint
- upgrade standards for those seeking beach holidays on the Costas and islands.

In line with this policy, conferences and activity holidays are being promoted. Many Mediterranean resorts are now well equipped with marinas for the high-spending yachting enthusiasts, and some have invested in aqua-parks to attract the family market. Winter sports facilities have been developed in the Pyrenees and Sierra Nevada, although as yet these cater mainly for domestic demand. The remaining coastal areas are being opened up for international tourism, although under more stringent environmental controls than was the case in the 1960s.

Tourism resources

Northern Spain

Dominated by the Cantabrian Mountains and overlooking the Atlantic Ocean to the west and the Bay of Biscay to the north, the coastlands of northern Spain are characterized by a green countryside of meadows, woodlands and orchards. Appropriately enough, the attractions of coast, countryside and mountains have been promoted by the regions of Galicia, Asturias, Cantabria and the Basque Country under the banner of *España Verde* (Green Spain). For an increasing number of foreign visitors, usually travelling independently by car, the appeal lies in this 'real Spain' of unspoiled scenery, rich folk traditions and distinctive regional cuisines, in contrast to the bland international food and artificial attractions of the Mediterranean beach resorts. Away from the coast with its many fishing villages, there is in Asturias and the Basque Country a less attractive hinterland, where declining 'smokestack industries' provide the impetus to expand tourism as a means of regenerating the area.

Galicia

Starting with the west, the region of Galicia has much in common with other areas on the 'Celtic fringe' of Europe. Although the Galicians speak a language similar to Portuguese, the folk traditions and misty landscapes are reminiscent of Ireland. This is one of the poorest areas of the Iberian Peninsula as the pocket-sized farms cannot provide a decent livelihood, so that in the past large numbers of Galicians have emigrated, particularly to South America. There is an important fishing industry based on ports such as Vigo and Corunna, where the *rias* (drowned river estuaries) provide excellent harbours. Although there are many fine beaches facing the Atlantic, major seaside resorts have not developed, and the region's most important tourist centre – Santiago de Compostela – lies some distance inland.

Asturias and Cantabria

The scenery becomes more rugged in Asturias and Cantabria, culminating in the spectacular Picos de Europe National Park. The area is ideal for activity holidays such as hiking and canoeing, and a number of spas and picturesque seaside resorts have developed along the fine beaches fronting the Bay of Biscay, including Laredo and Castro Urdiales. By far the best known is Santander, with its festival attractions, and growing in importance, along with Bilbao, as a gateway to Spain for British tourists arriving by ferry from Plymouth or Portsmouth.

The Basque Country

The Basque Country, known locally as Euskadi, lies between Bilbao and the western end of the Pyrenees. It is marked off from the rest of Spain by its people, who speak a language unrelated to any other in Europe, and by its regional pastimes – notably *jai alai* or *pelota*, an exciting ball game which has gained an international following in the Americas. Many Basques are not content with autonomy, and have given support to the ETA separatist movement. Despite this, there are two tourist centres of international standing, namely:

1 San Sebastian (Donostia) with its wide sweep of beach between two protecting headlands, festivals and fashionable shops, is the premier resort of northern Spain, although it is no longer the summer capital of the country.
2 Bilbao in contrast is primarily a port and industrial centre, which until recently had little to recommend it for tourists. This has now changed, thanks to the ultramodern Guggenheim Museum, showcasing international art, which has transformed the waterfront area.

El Camino de Santiago

The various regions of northern Spain are linked by one of Europe's most important tourist routes – the Pilgrims' Way to Santiago de Compostela – which attracts millions of visitors from all over Western Europe to the shrine of St

James. True pilgrims must have made a substantial part of the journey on foot or horseback, as in medieval times, although cyclists are also deemed worthy of the honour. The route is marked by numerous hostels providing accommodation, and some of Spain's finest examples of Romanesque and Gothic architecture.

Eastern and southern Spain

The majority of foreign tourists to Spain are less culturally inclined, and head straight for the Mediterranean coastal resorts where summer sunshine is guaranteed. For this reason the numerous cultural attractions of the regions of Catalonia, Valencia, Murcia and Andalucia, tend to be overshadowed by the pull of the beaches – Barcelona, Seville and Granada being the most notable exceptions.

The Costa Brava

The Costa Brava, the rugged coastline between Blanes and Port Bou on the French border was the first area to be developed for mass tourism in the 1950s and 1960s. Prior to this the scenic beauty of the coast – the pine-covered hills, red cliffs and sheltered coves – had attracted artists and fashionable holidaymakers to picturesque Tossa and the resort of S'Agaro, purpose-built for tourism in the 1920s. Some resorts – notably Lloret de Mar – have been given over to the package holiday market and their natural assets buried under concrete, whereas other stretches of coastline – as at Bagur and Cadaques – remain unspoiled.

The Costa Daurada

The Costa Daurada takes its name from its long beaches of golden sand and extends beyond Barcelona as far as the Ebro Delta. It is scenically less attractive, due to the proximity of industry in places. Sitges is the most attractive resort and one that is popular with Spaniards, but like others on this coast it is moribund out of season. Salou is the most popular resort with foreign holidaymakers, and has experienced a revival in its fortunes following the opening of the Port Aventura theme park nearby in 1993.

Barcelona

The Costa Brava and Costa Daurada form part of the region of Catalonia, which has its own language, culture and a strong sense of national identity. Historically the Catalans have been more outward-looking and progressive than other Spaniards and they have made their capital, Barcelona, one of Europe's great seaports and centres of industry and commerce. Barcelona has also attracted avant-garde artists and architects and is pre-eminent in fashion design. The 1992 Summer Olympics focused world attention on the host

city and gave the impetus for many civic improvements, notably the regeneration of the run-down waterfront area. Major sightseeing attractions in the city include:

- the street life and floral displays of the Ramblas
- the Pueblo Español (Spanish Village) showcasing architectural styles and regional crafts from all over the Peninsula
- the Cathedral and its quaint medieval district – the Barrio Gotico
- the Basilica of the Sagrada Familia, Gaudi's unfinished masterpiece.

Barcelona is also a good centre for touring other places of interest in the hinterland of Catalonia, notably Montserrat – an impressively sited monastery and place of pilgrimage, and the picturesque medieval city of Gerona.

Valencia

Likewise tourism plays an important but not exclusive part in the economy of the Valencia region. Despite its dry climate, the narrow coastal plain is one of the great agricultural regions of Spain, thanks to sophisticated irrigation techniques. Although it has some good beaches nearby, the city of Valencia is primarily a seaport and industrial centre. Valencia's tourism appeal lies not so much in its historic buildings but in its most well-known culinary product – paella, and the spectacular festival known as Las Fallas, culminating in the burning of elaborate papier-mâché effigies. The city's go ahead outlook is represented by a new science park commemorating the millennium and a model civic tourism administration. Resort developments to the north and south of Valencia along the Costa de Azahar are on a small scale.

The Costa Blanca

The Costa Blanca, however, between Denia and Alicante is one of Spain's most popular holiday areas. The main resort is cosmopolitan Benidorm; in 1960 this was a mere fishing village but rapidly became a high-rise mega-resort catering for over 4 million visitors a year, of which 250 000 arrive during the first two weeks of August. Benidorm's success is due to its sheltered position, two fine sandy beaches, proximity to Alicante airport, and entertainment geared primarily to the north European market. A forward-looking municipal government has attempted to rectify the mistakes of the boom years of the 1970s by a programme of improvements to meet the changing tastes and requirements of today's tourists. Elsewhere on the Costa Blanca, particularly around Javea and Denia extensive *urbanizaciones* of holiday villas have developed, often dominated by one particular national group. Here tourism is in direct competition with the important citrus industry for land, labour and water supplies.

The dry south-east

The south-eastern part of Spain, consisting of the Murcia region and the province of Almería, is the driest part of Europe. The arid, eroded landscapes have made this area a favourite location for the producers of budget western films. Yet even this coastline has been exploited for tourism as the 'Costa Calida' and the Costa de Almeria, with development for golf and water sports around the lagoon known as the Mar Menor, and at the picturesque town of Mójacar.

The Costa del Sol

The Costa del Sol is the name given to the 300-kilometre stretch of Mediterranean coast between Gibraltar and Adra, which forms part of the region of Andalucia. It is the holiday area that has shown the most spectacular growth since the 1960s, with resorts such as Torremolinos having experienced the various stages in the tourist area life cycle from 'discovery' to 'decline'. The location of the Costa del Sol in the extreme south of Spain is advantageous for the following reasons:

1 The Sierra Nevada and other mountain ranges protect this south-facing coast, guaranteeing warmer temperatures and more sunshine in winter than elsewhere in Western Europe, and making it possible to cultivate sugar cane and other subtropical crops.
2 The Costa del Sol can offer the tourist an exceptionally wide range of outdoor activities, including golf, tennis, horse-riding and sailing, while skiing can be enjoyed in the Sierra Nevada, where the snow cover lasts from December to May.
3 The coastal resorts provide easy access to the extensive hinterland of Andalucia, which contains many of Spain's greatest cultural attractions.
4 Morocco is also within reach, via the ferry services linking Málaga to Melilla, or from Algeciras to Tangier and Ceuta. It is worth noting that the North African cities of Melilla and Ceuta are administratively part of Spain, and enjoy duty-free port status.

This part of Andalucia has long been a winter destination for wealthy tourists, starting with Málaga in the nineteenth century, while the picturesque mountain town of Ronda served as a summer retreat for British officers stationed in Gibraltar. However, the development of the Costa del Sol for mass tourism did not get under way until after the opening of Málaga airport in 1962. The completion of the E340 coastal road improved access to the resorts, but soon acquired a reputation as the 'highway of death', as high-rise ribbon development extended from Málaga to Estepona. Tourism has largely replaced fishing and farming as a source of employment for local people, and has greatly improved living standards. However, in some of the villages – Mijas is a notable example – expatriates from the countries of northern Europe now make up almost half the population.

The section of the Costa del Sol to the east of Málaga contains fewer resorts and most of the development consists of holiday villas designed to blend in with the local landscape. Most of the hotel accommodation is found in the large resorts to the west of Málaga, which include:

1 *Torremolinos* which has become a byword for the ills of mass tourism and speculative development. However, this former fishing village was an upmarket, fashionable resort with a handful of luxury hotels in the late 1950s and early 1960s. This was followed in the 1970s by a massive expansion of accommodation in the form of high-rise hotels and apartments, initially encouraged by the Spanish government and, using cheap materials such as concrete and breeze blocks, to cater for an ever-growing demand from the mass-market tour operators of northern Europe. Nevertheless, Torremolinos, along with its neighbours Benalmadena and Fuengirola, has a vital role in concentrating vast numbers of holidaymakers in a small area, providing them with familiar food and entertainment, and thereby saving the villages of Andalucia from some of the negative impacts of mass tourism.
2 *Marbella* first became fashionable in the 1920s, and has been more successful than the other resorts on the Costa del Sol in retaining an image of sophistication, based on a large number of five-star hotels, a wealthy expatriate community, yacht marinas such as Puerto Banus, golf and cultural activities. But even Marbella experienced a period of stagnation, if not decline, in the 1980s, caused by its association with sleaze and drug-related crime. Under energetic leadership, the resort has invested in improved facilities on its beach front, more efficient policing to ensure visitor security, and the diversification of its product to attract conferences and foreign business enterprise based on high-tech industries to the 'California of Europe'.
3 *Málaga* differs from the other tourist centres of the Costa del Sol in being primarily a working seaport and commercial city. It has been shunned by the hordes of package holidaymakers heading straight from the airport to the beach resorts, but has the potential to attract tourists seeking a genuine Spanish ambience. Málaga has done much to renovate its waterfront and city centre, as well as restoring such important examples of Moorish heritage as the Alcazaba citadel. The city also hopes to promote its cultural appeal as the birthplace of Picasso.

Costa de la Luz

Andalucia also boasts an extensive Atlantic coastline with some of the best beaches in Spain, known as the Costa de la Luz. This is a popular holiday area for the Spanish but has attracted little attention so far from foreign tour operators. Most of the development has been grafted on to existing seaports. Cadiz – once the leading commercial city of Spain in the days of empire and now famous for its carnival, is a tourist centre of growing significance, while Tarifa is noted for windsurfing. North of Sanlucar, mass tourism is in conflict with conservation in one of Europe's most unique wetland environments – the Coto Doñana National Park where the ecosystems depend on the maintenance of the water table. This is already under intense pressure from large-scale agrobusiness and mining activity to the north, causing pollution. Further expansion of the resort of Matalascanas would tip the balance still further. The national park has attracted opposition for its strict management policies, which have allowed local communities little share in decision-making or the profits to be made from eco-tourism.

Andalucia

Away from the coast, the region of Andalucia for many people epitomizes Spain, with its warm sunny climate, colourful folklore, the music of *flamenco* and *sevillanas*, and the traditional architecture. Yet this region has had more than its fair share of social and economic problems, as much of the land is dominated by large estates given over to olive production, unemployment is high and the gypsies, who have inspired much of the popular culture, remain a marginalized element in society. Andalucia's major tourist centres include:

1 *Seville*, the regional capital has historic links with the Americas and achieved international acclaim as the host city for the 1992 World Expo. Tourists arrive in great numbers each spring for the awe-inspiring spectacle of the Holy Week processions, followed a few weeks later by the colour and excitement of the April *Feria*.
2 *Cordoba* contains one of the most outstanding relics of Spain's Moslem past – the Mezquita – and is also famous for its colourful patios.
3 *Granada* is world famous for an exquisite example of Moorish architecture – the Alhambra Palace. The adjoining gardens of the Generalife, with the often snow-capped mountains of the Sierra Nevada in the background, provide an incomparable setting for festivals of music and dance.
4 *Jerez* is the centre for the production of one of Spain's most well-known exports, the fortified wine known throughout the English-speaking world as sherry. The city is also renowned throughout Spain as a showcase for equestrian skills in a region devoted to horse-riding and the bullfight.
5 *The pueblos blancos* – the many picturesque towns and villages which are accessible but culturally a world apart from the bustling resorts of the Costa del Sol. For this reason Andalucia is ideal touring country.

The Spanish heartlands

The mountains and mesetas (plateaus) of central and northern Spain present a harsh landscape, quite different from the average tourist's perception of Spain. The Northern Meseta gave rise in the early Middle Ages to the warlike Kingdom of Castile, which strove for centuries to dominate the Peninsula, and whose language became modern Spanish. Here the rich cultural heritage is evident in the numerous castles and historic towns. However, with the notable exception of Madrid, few of these heritage attractions feature in short break or extended touring holidays, possibly because there is less cultural awareness among north Europeans of Spanish history and contribution to the arts, compared with that of France or Italy. This may change, in much the same way as the wines of La Rioja and the Rueda Valley have achieved a high international profile in recent years. The Spanish tourism authorities, for their part, have promoted a number of tourist routes linking the major cultural attractions. These include:

- the Pilgrim Route to Santiago we mentioned earlier, which includes the historic cities of Pamplona, Burgos and Leon
- the 'Silver Route' linking northern and southern Spain. This crosses the region of Extremadura, land of the *conquistadors* – who colonized the Americas, and includes Salamanca, one of the great university cities of Europe
- the 'Don Quixote Route' which crosses the region of La Mancha south of Toledo, famous for its windmills and associations with Spain's best known literary creation.

The region of Aragon to the east of the meseta also played a major role in Spanish history, where for centuries, Moors and Christians coexisted to produce the Mudejar style of architecture. Its capital Zaragoza is one of the great cathedral cities of Spain.

The Spanish Pyrenees and Andorra

The Pyrenees mountains along the French border include a number of national parks – Ordesa being the most important – spas and winter sports developments, notably in the Aran Valley. Wildlife and traditional lifestyles, for long protected by isolation, are now threatened by road and power projects, as well as the growth of summer recreation.

Tourism has been most successful in Andorra, a tiny nation largely dependent on revenue from duty-free shopping; this attracts over 12 million visitors annually from France and Spain, few of whom spend more than a few hours in the capital Andorra-la-Vella. Andorra's budget prices attract skiers in the winter months to resorts such as Pas de la Casa.

The Spanish islands

The two groups of Spanish islands – the Balearics in the western Mediterranean and the Canaries in the Atlantic – are different in many respects from peninsular Spain, so that we are justified in regarding them as separate holiday destinations.

The Balearic Islands

The Balearic Islands, consisting of Mallorca (Majorca), Menorca, Ibiza and Formentera, account for one-quarter of all tourism to Spain – Mallorca alone has more hotel beds than Portugal, and tourism is estimated to account for almost 60 per cent of the economy in the islands. The islands are of limestone formation with few surface streams, but they are generally well cultivated, mainly with tree crops such as almonds, olives and citrus. Agriculture has to compete for supplies of ground water with the tourism industry, which has to cater for a massive influx of summer visitors, and is now by far the main source of income and employment. Each island has distinctive landscapes, architecture and even dialects.

1 *Ibiza* is relatively small in terms of area and population, and it is here that the impact of tourism has perhaps been greatest. The island was also much poorer economically in the pre-tourism era than Mallorca or Menorca. Ibiza has passed through several stages of tourism development, namely:
   (a) The initial period of 'discovery' by hippy-style travellers in the early 1960s, who were attracted by the island lifestyle that was perceived to be more tolerant than the rest of Spain at that time. Some of these visitors later became permanent residents, and Ibiza remains something of an artists' community.
   (b) The introduction of direct charter flights to Ibiza airport shortly after this led to the growth of the inclusive tour market, mainly from Britain, catering for family beach holidays.
   (c) Since the 1980s there has been a growing emphasis on the international youth market and the all-night club scene. The rowdy behaviour of some north European tourists has attracted unfavourable publicity in the media, which in turn has deterred holidaymakers from the older age groups from visiting Ibiza.
   In fact, the worst excesses of mass tourism are mainly confined to San Antonio, which is a noisy high-rise 'tourist ghetto' catering for the lower end of the market. The island's capital Eivissa (Ibiza Town) has managed to retain some of its character as a historic Mediterranean seaport and offers nightlife that is more reputable and expensive. However, Ibiza's best beaches are often located at a distance from the resorts. There is concern that the traditional way of life based on agriculture has all but disappeared, while the island is reaching saturation point as far as tourism is concerned due to problems of water supply.

2 *Formentera* is the smallest of the Balearics. It is comparatively barren, sparsely populated and scenically low key. It does however have some good beaches, and because it is featured by few tour operators, and can only be reached by ferry from Ibiza, attracts holidaymakers seeking relative seclusion.

3 *Menorca* is scenically and culturally much more diverse, and its economy is less dependent on tourism. The island authorities have managed to secure greater control over tourism development than was the case in Ibiza, with well-planned holiday villages at Binibeca and Fornells catering for up-market tourists. The island's main tourism resource is its fine harbours which provide an ideal environment for yachting. The largest of these – Mahon – was an important base for the British navy in the eighteenth century, when it replaced the old city of Ciudadela as the island's capital. Due to its windy climate, Menorca is rarely featured as a winter sun destination, unlike Mallorca.

4 *Mallorca* is much the largest of the Balearic Islands, with a coastline 550 kilometres in length and mountains rising to over 1000 metres in the north-west. Between these and a lower range in the east lies a fertile plain meeting the sea in a number of fine bays. Most of the high-rise hotels and apartments are concentrated in the south-facing coastal strip extending from Paguera to Arenal, within easy reach of Palma airport, which in summer is one of Europe's busiest. Even here, the worst excesses of sun, sea and sand tourism are confined to Magalluf–Palma Nova, with its 500 or so pubs, fast-food outlets, discos and souvenir shops. The rugged west coast is little developed for tourism although it was the beauty of this area which attracted writers, the rich and the famous to Deya and Formentor in the 1930s, when it took the best part of three day's travel to reach Mallorca from Britain. The east coast, indented with numerous small coves is given over mainly to villa developments. Mallorca has much to offer the sightseer, including:
   (a) The Caves of Drach, a natural attraction which has been exploited with flair and imagination.
   (b) The islands' industries, notably the manufacture of artificial pearls – although the matter of presentation for the foreign visitor could be improved.
   (c) Palma, the regional capital, is one of the leading seaports of the Mediterranean, with ferry services to the mainland and the other islands. It boasts an imposing cathedral and castle among its heritage attractions, and except for one small district, has been relatively unaffected by mass tourism.

Since the early 1990s the Balearic regional government has followed a policy of sustainable tourism; a third of the islands' area has been designated for conservation, while steps have been taken to improve the environment of the most overcrowded resorts. However, you might discuss whether the further development of golf courses is truly 'green' tourism in view of their demands on water supplies, while the buying up of rural properties, mainly by Germans, has implications for the social balance of the Mallorcan countryside.

The Canary Islands

While the Balearics are essentially summer sun destinations, the Canaries have the advantage of a subtropical climate, which favours beach tourism throughout the year. Winters are pleasantly warm, while the cool ocean current moderates summer temperatures; however, sea temperatures are too cold for bathing for much of the year. The islands are of volcanic origin and contain some magnificent scenery, but this does mean that there are relatively few fine beaches. Situated some 1000 kilometres to the south-west of Cadiz, they are much closer geographically to Morocco and the Western Sahara than to mainland Spain. The location of the islands, on important shipping routes, resulted in the 'discovery' of Tenerife and Gran Canaria as winter destinations by wealthy British travellers and returning colonial officials in the nineteenth century. Large numbers of cruise ships still call at the ports of Santa Cruz and Las Palmas, which offer duty-free shopping as their main attractions. Since the 1960s the great majority of visitors have arrived on charter flights and are drawn from a wider range of countries and social classes. Most north European tourists still arrive during the winter months, whereas Spanish holidaymakers are more evident in summer.

1 *Tenerife* is the largest of the islands and offers the greatest variety of scenery and climate, due to the effect of the spectacular peak of Teide on the prevailing trade winds. The strange volcanic landscapes of Las Cañadas National Park in the centre of the island contrast with the desert-like south and the fertile valley of Orotava, with its woods and banana plantations to the north. In this part of the island, Puerto de la Cruz is a well-established resort catering primarily for the older age groups. This is because its position on the windward slopes of Teide means that sunshine cannot be guaranteed, and its lack of beaches is only partly compensated by a magnificent lido. The south coast has the climatic advantage, where hotels and timeshare apartments line beaches within easy reach of the international airport. Playa de Las Americas – a creation of the tourist boom of the 1970s – is now the most popular resort on the island.

2 *Gran Canaria* has, on balance, more to offer mass tourism than Tenerife, particularly in the fine sandy beaches of its southern coast. This supports a tourist concentration second in size only to Benidorm, consisting of the resorts of Playa del Inglés, San Agustin and Maspalomas, attracting mainly German and lesser contingents of British, Scandinavian and Spanish holidaymakers. Some of the human-made attractions – 'wild west shows' for example – have no Spanish connection, the emphasis being purely on international-style entertainment. Away from the resorts, the interior of Gran Canaria has been described as 'a continent in miniature' offering spectacular contrasts in scenery.

3 *Lanzarote* is still volcanically active, and the craters of Monte del Fuego in the Timanfaya National Park are a major attraction. Development has been carefully planned by the architect Cesar Manrique to enhance a landscape of lava spreads dotted with white villages. Upmarket tourists are catered for at Costa de Teguise and sports enthusiasts at La Santa, while Puerto del Carmen is the most popular resort.

4 *Fuerteventura* is the driest of the Canary Islands, due to its closeness to the Western Sahara, and is the most sparsely populated. Persistent trade winds provide ideal conditions for windsurfing, while the vast beaches attract jeep safaris and are popular mainly with German tourists.

5 *Gomera*, *La Palma* and *Hierro*, the three western islands, have remained relatively untouched by mass tourism due to their relative isolation, lack of good beaches and the rugged topography. The prospects for tourism are most promising in La Palma which is linked by charter flights to Germany. The main natural attraction is the beautiful mountain scenery, culminating in one of the world's largest volcanic craters – the Caldera de Taburiente. There is also the appeal of a more traditional lifestyle, based on agriculture and crafts such as cigar-making rather than tourism.

Gibraltar

We have included Gibraltar, one of Britain's few remaining colonies, because it is physically attached to Spain, although its people are a mixture of Mediterranean cultures and are equally fluent in English and Spanish. Britain's interest in Gibraltar was primarily due to its strategic location guarding the entrance to the Mediterranean. Nowadays its military role is less significant, and the Royal Navy dockyard has closed forcing the colony to develop other roles as an offshore financial centre and tourist destination.

Gibraltar is a small territory, only 6 square kilometres in area, dominated by the great limestone mass of the Rock, which towers 400 metres above the densely packed town and busy harbour on its western flank. Since 1985, when the frontier with Spain was reopened, Gibraltar has attracted millions of Spanish excursionists, as well as cruise passengers and much smaller numbers of staying tourists, mostly from Britain. The Spanish are motivated by curiosity and the lure of shopping bargains, while the British, many of whom are first time visitors overseas, are reassured by the familiar language, food, currency, British-style 'bobbies' and pubs, combined with Mediterranean sunshine. Apart from these, the colony's main attractions include:

- the world-famous Rock, which is honeycombed with caves and 'galleries' constructed for military purposes – it also provides a habitat for Europe's only ape colony
- the duty free shopping in Main Street
- the historical associations with the British army and navy
- Gibraltar's Moorish heritage which is promoted, but less attention is paid to the period of Spanish rule
- the facilities for water sports, including a yacht marina; the beaches, however, are few and small
- its proximity to Morocco, using the hydrofoil and ferry service to Tangier
- its proximity to the holiday resorts of the Costa del Sol. Prior to the 1960s, Gibraltar was the gateway to this part of Spain, and since 1985, growing numbers of British visitors have again been using it as a base for touring Andalucia.

However, the expansion of tourism in Gibraltar faces a number of problems, namely:

- the lack of space for development, with much land remaining in military ownership
- the threat posed by rockfalls, a symptom of the erosion of the Rock, caused by massive tunnelling in the past
- the accommodation stock consists of a small number of hotels, guesthouses and self-catering complexes that need to be upgraded and extended
- the restricted site of the airport that lies on 'neutral territory' with its runway on land reclaimed from the Bay of Gibraltar. To the south the airport is hemmed in by the sheer face of the Rock, while the Spanish frontier lies immediately to the north; which brings us to the most deep-seated problem –
- the continuing political difficulties with Spain.

Although Gibraltar has been British since 1703, Spain has never relinquished its claim to sovereignty. During the last major dispute, which lasted from 1969 to 1985, telecommunications were cut, the land border was closed and the ferry service to Algeciras was severed by the Spanish government. Cut off from its natural hinterland, Gibraltar was forced to develop its own tourist attractions and recruit labour from Morocco. Another bone of contention is Gibraltar's alleged role in smuggling contraband from North Africa to Spain. The response of the Spanish authorities has been to subject motorists crossing the border at La Linea to lengthy delays.

Portugal

Introduction

Portugal is a much smaller country than Spain, both in population and land area. Due to its long Atlantic coastline, Portugal's climate is milder and more humid, and the landscape generally greener, than is the case in most of Spain. In culture and temperament, the Portuguese differ from the Spanish in a number of ways; for example, the music form – *fado* – is full of the melancholy or *saudade* which is part of the national character and the Portuguese bullfight is an altogether gentler affair than the Spanish *corrida*. Portugal's contacts with its former colonies, particularly in Asia are reflected in its cuisine and the ornate decoration of its churches and country houses.

The demand for tourism

Although agriculture, fishing and textiles still dominate the Portuguese economy, tourism has made a major contribution, supporting 6 per cent of jobs and 8 per cent of the gross domestic product. Nonetheless, Portugal has one of the lowest standards of living in the EU, a fact reflected in the holiday propensities of the Portuguese that are lower than the Spanish. However, propensities have increased over the late 1990s partly boosted by the Expo '98 exhibition and now around 60 per cent of the Portuguese take a holiday. Inbound tourism on the other hand, has grown steadily since the 1960s, with the exception of a downturn in the mid-1970s following the April Revolution which introduced democracy and industrial unrest. This affected the hotel industry, which also had to cope with a massive influx of refugees from Angola and Mozambique. The early 1990s were a second period when international arrivals were depressed, partly as a result of overpricing. This prompted a fierce debate as to a future strategy for Portugal and resulted in major changes in the organization and approach to tourism, as outlined later in this chapter. This new strategy was successful and by the late 1990s arrivals of foreign tourists exceeded 11 million – mainly for holiday purposes. However, day visitors make up over twice this number – Spaniards crossing into Portugal for shopping, or cruise passengers visiting Funchal and Lisbon on shore excursions. Spain is by far Portugal's largest market; they account for most of the visitors arriving by road, but are usually short stay. For Portugal's other main markets – Britain, Germany and France:

- air inclusive tours are the norm
- there is a marked summer peak in demand
- tourists stay longer than Spanish visitors
- spending per tourists is higher than is the case with Spanish visitors.

The organization of tourism

Transport

Portugal's location in the south-west corner of Europe necessitates a long journey if road or rail are used as travel modes. This has prompted a major road upgrading programme and also explains why air transport is the dominant mode for tourists arriving from northern Europe, and the importance of fly-drive arrangements for those staying in self-catering accommodation in the Algarve. The national airline, TAP is undergoing a programme of privatization to take it into the millennium and the major scheduled and charter airlines operate flights into Lisbon, Faro (for the Algarve) and Oporto on the Portuguese mainland and to the island of Madeira.

Accommodation

As in Spain, villas used as second homes or retirement properties have created a long-stay market, particularly in the Algarve and Madeira. Around two-thirds of visitors to Portugal use hotel accommodation, although an increased preference for cheaper forms of accommodation has become evident as more Spaniards visit Portugal and use campsites or stay with friends. Nonetheless, Portugal's accommodation stock is well developed, with a concentration of larger hotels in the Algarve, at Estoril and on Madeira (both catering for inclusive-tour clients), and in Lisbon, where business travel is important. The government owns a chain of hotels – *pousadas* – similar in concept to the Spanish *parador*. Camping and caravanning is important on the Algarve, especially around Faro, and attracts German, French and Spanish visitors, while the many sites around Lisbon are a popular and cheaper alternative to the capital's hotels. The British and Dutch patronize apartments, again mainly in the Algarve.

Tourism administration

The Portuguese economy is very reliant on the success of the tourism industry, supporting 500 000 jobs and providing a safety net against changes in demand for Portugal's traditional products in agriculture, fisheries and textiles. The importance of tourism is reflected in the government's response to depressed arrivals figures in the 1990s. The organization of tourism was changed by merging government departments to create Investimentos Comercio e Turismo de Portugal (ICEP) in 1992. This new body has put into a place a successful new tourism strategy to:

- diversify source markets
- introduce quality controls
- reduce bureaucracy

- establish a new image for Portugal stressing historic and cultural resources
- use the *fundo de turismo* (tourism fund) to create new products and upgrade existing ones.

In addition, Portugal is anxious to control the impacts of tourism on both the environment and Portuguese society. There are a number of national nature reserves and management plans exist for national parks, as well as the estuaries and coasts in the more popular recreational and tourist areas. Impacts are also reduced by Portugal's emphasis on the upper and middle sectors of the tourism market, in contrast to Spain's domination by mass-market tourism, and this is reflected in the generally higher quality of the Portuguese tourism product compared with that of Spain. Portugal is also attempting to spread the load of tourism more evenly, both seasonally and geographically (well over half of foreign arrivals are between June and September). The Algarve is already nearing saturation in terms of tourist development, and contrasts with the more remote interior provinces – such as Tras-os-Montes – which see few tourists. Counter-attractions are being developed in the Porto-Espinho area in the north and at Setubal, south of Lisbon. Finally, Portugal is diversifying its tourist product by encouraging activity holidays and conference tourism.

Tourism resources

Algarve

The most popular holiday region is the Algarve, in the extreme south, which has an exceptionally sunny climate, fine sandy beaches, rocky coves and picturesque fishing villages. Tourism did not develop until the mid-1960s when Faro airport was opened and the April 25 Bridge across the Tagus from Lisbon greatly reduced travel times by road to what had been a remote region. In the late 1990s, a second bridge – the Vasco da Gama – opened and is set to boost tourism south of Lisbon. Many of the resort developments (for example, near Lagos, Albufeira and Portimao) are in the form of self-contained holiday villages. Sports facilities (above all, golf courses) have been important in attracting investment from northern Europe. However, not all the development has been of a high standard – the haphazard growth of Quarteira compares unfavourably with nearby Vilamoura, planned around its yacht marina. Tourist development is extending westwards towards Cape St Vincent following upgrading of the coastal road and a museum celebrating Portuguese achievements in maritime exploration, planned for Sagres. Inland, popular excursions from the Algarve include:

- the hills and spa at Monchique
- the medieval walled town of Silves
- the markets, as at Loule.

Central Portugal and Lisbon

Tourism in central Portugal around Lisbon has been established for much longer, and there is a wealth of attractions available for the cultural tourist as well as the sun-seeker. Lisbon, on the wide Tagus estuary, is one of Europe's major seaports, while Portela airport is a hub for international flights to Europe, South America and Africa. The capital is rich in reminders of Portugal's maritime history, notably the Tower of Belem and Jeronimos Monastery, and tourism received a boost with Expo '98. Around Lisbon tourist resources include:

1 The strip of coast to the west of Lisbon – known as the Costa de Estoril, after its most well-known resort – has good beaches, hotels, a casino, and facilities for sport and entertainment, especially at Cascais.
2 South of the Tagus, the coastline around Setubal underwent considerable development during the 1980s with much self-catering accommodation.
3 North of Lisbon, and extending from Peniche almost to Oporto, the Costa de Prata is mainly popular with Portuguese holidaymakers. Its long sandy beaches are, for the most part, exposed to the Atlantic surf. The most important resorts are Nazare (famous for its traditional fishing industry) and Figueira da Foz.
4 Away from the coast, this part of Portugal boasts many places of interest, readily accessible from Lisbon. They include:
  (a) Sintra, in a scenically beautiful location overlooking the capital, was once favoured as a health resort by Portuguese royalty and wealthy foreigners.
  (b) Caldas da Rainha – a spa noted for its ceramics.
  (c) Obidos – a picturesque medieval town.
  (d) Fatima – a world-famous shrine, particularly in May when vast numbers of pilgrims are attracted to the basilica for candle-lit processions.
  (e) Coimbra, noted for its university.

The north

Tourism development is being encouraged in northern Portugal, assisted by regional development schemes and upgraded road transport. Resources include:

1 Aveiro, known as the 'Venice of Portugal' with its large sheltered lagoons, famous for wildlife and ideal for water sports.
2 Oporto (Porto) at the mouth of the river Douro is Portugal's second city, its major commercial centre and gateway to the northern region. Oporto's main claim to fame is its association with the port wine industry, although the actual vineyards are located 150 kilometres upstream and the picturesque barges are no longer used to transport the wine.
3 Stretching from Oporto north to the Spanish border lies the Costa Verde, which is attracting increasing numbers of foreign visitors, travelling independently by car rather than using inclusive tours. Espinho, Povoa de Varzim and Viana do Castelo are the chief resorts in this area.
4 The Peneda Geres National Park on the Spanish border offers wild granite mountain scenery, while the small historic towns of the region are interesting places to visit, notably Braga, the religious centre of Portugal with its spectacular Bom Jesus shrine.

The Portuguese islands

In addition to mainland Portugal, there are two groups of islands in the Atlantic that we can treat as separate destinations – Madeira and the Azores. They are both of volcanic origin and since 1975 they have enjoyed a degree of autonomy from Lisbon. In view of the limited resource base of the islands, and with fewer opportunities than in the past for the islanders to emigrate to the Americas or South Africa, tourism should play an important role in the economy. However, tourism has been much more successful in Madeira than in the Azores, and this is largely due to differences in accessibility.

1 *Madeira* is situated 800 kilometres south-west of Lisbon and slightly nearer to Casablanca. Of greater significance is the position of the harbour of Funchal on the main shipping routes from Europe to South America and South Africa. It was largely for this reason that Madeira became a fashionable winter destination for well-to-do British travellers in Victorian times. The island was able to broaden its appeal after 1964 when the international airport was opened east of Funchal, and the number of visitors increased fivefold between 1970 and 1990. However, mass tourism in the way it has occurred in the Canary Islands is ruled out by:
  (a) The impossibility of extending the airport, which is not capable of handling wide-bodied jets.
  (b) The lack of land for development generally on this mountainous but densely populated island.
  (c) The absence of beaches, except on the small and otherwise barren island of Porto Santo some 50 kilometres from Funchal.
  The regional government of Madeira has therefore aimed at promoting quality tourism. Foreign visitors are attracted by the beautiful scenery of mountains, coastal cliffs, subtropical vegetation and the almost ideal climate – winter is still the peak season for the British, Germans and Scandinavians. Hiking trails follow the intricate network of *levadas* (irrigation channels) which carry water from the mountains to the pocket-sized farms. The road network is being improved to make the interior more accessible, sports

facilities are being developed to attract a younger market and traditional craft industries such as embroidery are encouraged.

2 *The Azores* are situated 1500 kilometres west of Lisbon and 3500 kilometres east of New York. Their mid-Atlantic location was important in the early years of transatlantic flight when Faial and Santa Maria were staging points, but with the introduction of longer-range aircraft the islands have been bypassed. Although the Azores have three international airports – Santa Maria, Lajes (on the island of Terceira) and Ponta Delgada (on Sao Miguel) – no foreign airlines as yet operate scheduled services, and charter flights from Europe are discouraged by the Portuguese government. The islands are dispersed over 800 kilometres of ocean, making it difficult to organize multicentre holidays. Unlike Madeira, the Azores are not regarded as a winter sun destination because, although the climate allows the cultivation of subtropical produce such as tea and pineapples, sunshine amounts compare unfavourably with the Mediterranean. There are few beaches and the islands' main appeal is the spectacular volcanic scenery, the best known examples being the crater lakes, hot springs and geysers on Sao Miguel. Yachting, whale-watching (replacing the traditional whaling industry), and sea fishing also offer prospects for the growth of tourism.

Summary

The Iberian Peninsula and the Spanish and Portuguese holiday islands are among the world's major tourist destination areas. This is partly due to Spain's early entry into mass tourism in the 1960s based upon its holiday resources of an extensive Mediterranean coastline and proximity to northern Europe. Portugal was a later entrant into the tourism market and is attempting to avoid mass tourism, focusing instead upon more affluent markets.

Tourist accommodation is concentrated at the coast, on the islands, and in the major cities. The major resort areas are served by a well-developed transport infrastructure. However, in Spain uncontrolled resort development has caused environmental damage, deepened regional contrasts and affected Spanish lifestyles to such an extent that many other countries – including Portugal – have been anxious to avoid these negative effects of tourism. The attractions of both countries are mainly based on the coastline and there are major resort concentrations on the islands, the Spanish Mediterranean Costas, and the Algarve. Other attractions include winter sports in the Pyrenees and the Sierra Nevada, the cultural attractions of the cities of Spain and Portugal, and the natural appeal of the landscapes of the Iberian Peninsula and the islands, although eco-tourism has some way to go.

Case study

Madrid as a centre for cultural tourism

Few package holidaymakers based in the coastal resorts have either the desire, still less the opportunity, to visit the capital of Spain. This is mainly because Madrid is situated at the geographic centre of Spain, as far from the Mediterranean beaches as it is possible to get. In the 1990s, the capital accounted for only 5 per cent of overnight stays spent by foreign visitors in Spain, and only 5 per cent of the nation's hotel capacity. This is in contrast to the situation in most European countries, where the capital tends to take a much greater share of the international tourism market.

Tourism could be said to have begun in 1560, when Philip II chose the small provincial town of Madrid, because of its central location, as the capital of what was then the world's greatest empire. It was the policy of virtually all Spanish governments, until the Constitution of 1978 devolved power to the regions, to concentrate political power in Madrid, much to the annoyance of Barcelona. However, unlike most European capitals, Madrid developed few industries (other than the luxury trades serving the court and the governing élite). For most of the nineteenth and twentieth centuries, Barcelona was culturally and economically much more dynamic than Madrid. The situation began to change in the 1950s, when the Franco regime promoted an industrialization programme which attracted vast numbers of immigrants from all over Spain; as a result the population trebled between 1950 and 1990 to reach 3 million. Since 1975 Madrid has also experienced a cultural revival, making it one of Europe's leading centres for fashion and creative design. Although the city has become more cosmopolitan as a result, it is still very Spanish in its appearance and lifestyle.

Madrid is now firmly established as a short-break destination. Tourism is set to grow as this market expands in Northern Europe with the tendency to take second holidays, and as Madrid's cultural attractions become more widely known. Madrid is highly accessible, as it is the focus for road, rail and air communications to all parts of the Iberian Peninsula. Barajas airport is also the gateway to Europe for many visitors from the Americas, particularly the Spanish-speaking countries. The city has good infrastructure and support services, including an efficient Metro system, hotels of international standard, restaurants offering the best of Spain's regional cuisine, theatres, modern sports facilities and speciality shopping. The city is also well equipped to handle conferences and exhibitions. The following features give Madrid special appeal as a destination:

1 The altitude of 700 metres makes it Europe's highest capital, giving it clear skies most of the year, mountain breezes and strong contrasts in temperature.

2 A cultural appeal, based not on historic monuments – Madrid is a newcomer compared to most Spanish cities – but on its unique artistic heritage. This is concentrated in the 'Golden Triangle of Art' consisting of three of Europe's finest art collections – The Prado Museum, the Reina Sofia Art Centre and the Villahermosa Palace. Of these, the Prado is the best known, as it contains masterpieces by the Spanish painters Velazquez and Goya with their realistic portrayals of Spanish life in the seventeenth and eighteenth centuries.

3 A vibrant entertainment scene appealing to a wide range of age groups and tastes. Madrid is 'the city that never sleeps' – renowned for its hectic nightlife – *la movida* – a constant movement of people doing the rounds of tapas bars and discos. Much of the action takes place in the historic core of the city between the Plaza Mayor – a picturesque arcaded square built in the seventeenth century – and the Puerta del Sol, the recognized hub of Madrid.

4 Its central location making Madrid an ideal base for touring Central Spain. There is a great contrast between the sophisticated capital and the timeless quality of the historic towns and villages of the Castilian heartland. The following internationally renowned world heritage sites are within a two and a half hour journey by bus or train from the city centre:
(a) Toledo – the ancient capital of Spain and its religious centre, which has preserved its medieval character.
(b) Segovia – famous for its well-preserved Roman aqueduct and picturesque castle – the Alcazar.
(c) Avila – the birth place of the great visionary St Theresa. The town still retains its medieval city walls making it a favourite location for film makers.
(d) El Escorial – the austere and awe inspiring monastery-palace built by Philip II as the nerve centre of the Spanish Empire. Equally sombre is the monument to the Spanish Civil War – La Valle de los Caidos – situated nearby.
(e) Cuenca – noted for the picturesque 'hanging houses' overlooking the River Jucar and its reputation as an artists' resort.

5 Other places are also popular with the people of Madrid who are less concerned with sightseeing than having an enjoyable day out with the family:
(a) Aranjuez – the former summer palace of the Bourbon Kings of Spain, with its gardens and fountains.
(b) Chinchon – a town that has preserved its traditional character, with a picturesque plaza.

The variety of attractions offered by Madrid means that it can appeal to the more affluent tourists coming from a significantly wider range of countries than is the case for the Spanish coastal resorts and islands. This has the following advantages for its tourism industry:

1 It is much less dependent upon the economic situation in the tourist-generating countries of northern Europe.
2 It attracts high-spending visitors.
3 It is less affected by seasonality of demand.

16

Italy

16

LEARNING OBJECTIVES

After reading this chapter you should be able to:

1 Explain the special appeal of Italy as a tourist destination.
2 Describe the major physical features of Italy and understand their importance for tourism.
3 Appreciate the nature of the demand for inbound, outbound and domestic tourism.
4 Outline the major features of tourism infrastructure, especially the differences between North and South Italy.
5 Appreciate the public sector organization of tourism in Italy.
6 Demonstrate a knowledge of the tourist regions, resorts, business centres and tourist attractions of Italy.

Introduction

As a tourist destination, Italy for many people means sunshine, good food, music and, perhaps, romance. Others are attracted by the style and quality of Italian fashion and engineering products. Tourism in Italy has a long pedigree. Domestic tourism was certainly flourishing at the time of the Roman Empire, when the wealthier citizens of Rome had holiday villas in resorts such as Baia on the Bay of Naples. As far as international tourism is concerned, during the Middle Ages, Rome was the destination for hordes of pilgrims from all over Europe. They were followed as a result of the Renaissance, by what we might call cultural tourists, attracted to Italian cities such as Florence and Venice, then at their zenith as the 'cutting edge' of European civilization. Shakespeare was strongly influenced by Italian culture and a host of writers and artists from northern Europe – among them Milton, Goethe and Shelley – visited Italy for inspiration. It became the custom for wealthy young men (and very occasionally women) to go on the 'Grand Tour', which involved a stay of at least a few months in Italy. Here they completed their education – in more ways than one – buying classical sculptures (not all genuine) and paintings as souvenirs of their travels, while on their return, they renovated their country houses in the style of Italian architects such as Palladio. In a sense, the expansion of the railways allowed entrepreneurs such as Thomas Cook to popularize the idea of a European tour, bringing Italy within the reach of the expanding middle class of Victorian Britain.

Even today, most tourism to Italy is to an extent cultural, and the country is among the world's top five tourism destinations. It is likely to retain this position because of the appeal and variety of its tourism products, although the marketing and organization of these could in many cases be improved. These products include:

- short city breaks and longer touring holidays, appealing mainly to art lovers
- music festivals, usually associated with a particular composer's hometown, such as Pesaro (Rossini) and Torre del Lago (Puccini); Italy originated opera as an art form and here it enjoys widespread popular support
- seaside holidays
- summer lakes and mountains holidays in the Alps
- winter-skiing holidays in the Alps
- health tourism, based on Italy's abundant geothermal resources – spas such as Ischia, Montecatini Terme and Abano have an excellent international reputation

- religious pilgrimages to the shrines of Rome, Assisi, Loreto and Padua
- rural tourism including stays on rural farms and villas that vary in size from the modest to the magnificent; the government agency, Agriturist, has done much to promote rural tourism as a means of stemming the depopulation of the countryside
- trade fairs and exhibitions; notably Milan, Genoa, Bologna and Turin
- sports tourism
- activity holidays, for example, hiking and climbing in the Dolomites.

With some notable exceptions – the Gran Paradiso National Park in the Western Alps being one – Italy's environmental record has been relatively poor compared with the countries of northern and central Europe, and eco-tourism is not well developed. Conservation of the nation's cultural heritage is also a major problem, given the vast number of art treasures and historic sites, and the inadequate public funding available.

Physical features

Italy is separated from Northern Europe by the high mountain barrier of the Alps and has a long coastline facing both the Adriatic and the western Mediterranean. Another chain of mountains – the Apennines – forms a rugged spine down the boot-shaped Italian Peninsula, and is a formidable obstacle to east–west communications. Between these mountains and the Alps lies an extensive area of fertile lowland – the North Italian Plain – that includes most of the regions of Piedmont, Lombardy, Veneto and Emilia-Romagna. This area contains some of Europe's largest and most prosperous industrial centres. Central and southern Italy are hilly or mountainous, and geologically unstable – as witness the 1997 Assisi earthquake, the frequent landslides in the Apennines and the volcanic activity evident in the Naples area and Sicily. The landscape becomes drier and more neglected south of Rome, and it is here in the Mezzogiorno that we find some of the poorest regions of Europe.

Social and cultural features

The Italian lifestyle has always been an attraction for visitors from the more reserved countries of northern Europe. The people enjoy public displays, as you can see in the evening *passegiata* or parade in every town. With a population of over 58 million, Italy now has one of the lowest birth-rates in Europe due to the economic and social changes that have taken place since the Second World War; however it is still true that family ties are very strong. The Roman Catholic Church continues to play an important role, although it is no longer the all-powerful patron of the arts it was in Renaissance times. Italian culture is characterized by great regional variety, as expressed, for example, in food specialities, handicrafts and dialects. This is due largely to the fact that Italy became a united country only in the nineteenth century – before that it was a collection of small states largely under foreign domination. Italians continue to have stronger loyalties to their city or region than to the state as a whole. One of the biggest obstacles to national unity is the long-standing negative attitude of North Italians toward the South, which they regard as socially backward and a burden on the economy.

The organization and supply of tourism

Government organization

There is a clear demarcation between public sector tourism support at the national and the regional level.

National level

Italian governments since the Second World War have been weak coalitions lasting less than a year, making it difficult to implement clear policy objectives on, for example, tourism development. In contrast to a flourishing private sector, much of the public sector is characterized by inefficiency and widespread political corruption. The Italian State Tourist Office (Ente Nazionale Industrie Turistiche – ENIT), which was set up as long ago as 1919, has tried to remedy this situation. However, in 1993, the Ministry of Tourism and Performing Arts was disbanded and replaced by a small department of tourism located in the Prime Minister's Office. The Italian State Tourist Office's main purpose is promotion and research, and it is particularly attempting to diversify Italy's tourism product away from beach holidays and the 'big three' historic cities – Rome, Florence and Venice – towards other forms of tourism. At the same time ENIT is hoping to achieve a more balanced spread of visitors by including less well-known cities in the classical tours, promoting the ski resorts in the Eastern Alps, and by developing tourism in the Mezzogiorno – aided by INSUD, the public sector agency promoting tourism to the South. With reduced public sector commitment to tourism ENIT is involved in co-operative marketing with the private sector – such as airlines.

Regional level

Each of Italy's twenty regional governments has responsibility for tourism, although some – notably the autonomous regions of Sicily, Sardinia, Valle d'Aosta and Trentino-Alto Adige – have been more active than others in planning, development and promotion. Nonetheless, it is at the regional level where the most activity is occurring, with funding based on the number of inhabitants in the region, rather than the number of tourists visiting.

Accommodation

Most hotels are small family concerns, and large hotel chains are less of a feature in the resort scene than elsewhere in Europe. Pensions and *locande* (inns) are also favoured by Italian tourists. There is a trend toward greater use of self-catering accommodation, and campgrounds are numerous, especially along the Adriatic coast. Holiday villas are owned or rented by the more affluent. A number of holiday villages are also available, run on similar lines to Club Mediterranée by the Italian tour operator Valtur.

Transport

Domestic and international tourist travel is mainly by surface transport.

Roads

Italy has an excellent road network, including over 6500 kilometres of autostrada (motorways). This is effectively linked to the wider European system, despite the bottlenecks (caused mainly by excessive numbers of trucks) which do occur on the approaches to the Brenner Pass and other routes through the Alps. It is possible to drive at high average speeds from Flensburg in North Germany all the way south to Reggio, which is separated from Sicily only by a narrow stretch of water. The most important link in this network is the Autostrada di Sole from Milan to Reggio used, not surprisingly, by hordes of sun-seeking tourists from Germany and the countries of northern Europe. The engineering problems involved in building the autostrada in mountainous terrain are shown, for example, in Liguria, where there are more than 100 tunnels, and almost the same number of viaducts in a distance of less than 100 kilometres.

Rail

The rail network is also extensive and generally offers travellers an efficient service with some of the lowest fares in Europe, although it does suffer from overcrowding in the summer. Italian State Railways (FS) own most of the network, apart from a few narrow-gauge lines. A number of high-speed trains are in service between the major cities, including the *Direttissima* from Florence to Rome. Although the system is in state ownership, most of the funding for these high-speed rail projects comes from the private sector. Italian State Railways also own the major tour operator, CIT, and by catering for both holiday and business tourists, have done much to revive the demand for rail travel.

Sea

Italy's long coastline and location in mid-Mediterranean has encouraged a long seafaring tradition. Genoa, the birthplace of Columbus, is one of the most important ports in the Mediterranean. Although few tourists arrive by sea, cruise ships operating in the Mediterranean usually call in at Italian ports, such as Venice or Naples. A number of Italian ports such as Fiumicino (serving Rome), Ancona and Brindisi, are essential nodes in a network of coastal shipping services and international ferries linking various parts of the Mediterranean, not just neighbouring Corsica, Tunisia, Croatia and Greece, but as far afield as Turkey, Egypt and Israel. High-speed hydrofoils operate on the short sea crossings between the mainland and the smaller islands such as Capri; they are also used for sightseeing excursions on the lakes of northern Italy.

Air

Italy is well served by international airports, the most important being Leonardo da Vinci (Rome) and Linate (Milan), which rank among Europe's busiest. Alitalia, the national airline, is active in tourism promotion, working closely with CIT and the national tourism organization. Alitalia and its subsidiary ATI provide a network of domestic flights to over thirty destinations, while a number of charter airlines link the islands and resort areas to the tourist-generating areas.

Tourism demand

Inbound tourism

Italy receives more international visitor arrivals than any other European country, but this is misleading, as less than half are staying visitors as distinct from cruise passengers and other excursionists. In fact, during the late 1980s and much of the 1990s the tourism industry stagnated, due to unfavourable publicity regarding:

● overcrowding and environmental conditions in the main resorts
● high prices
● high crime rates, terrorist bombings and Mafia trials
● obsolescent hotel stock, where facilities compared unfavourably with those in other Mediterranean countries such as Spain.

Although there is a considerable volume of business travel to cities such as Milan and Turin, holidays are the main reason for visiting Italy. Germany is an important market on account of the good road access (most German tourists arrive in their own cars) and the strength of the mark against the Italian lira, which is generally one of Europe's weaker currencies. The most popular destinations for German tourists are:

● Venice
● the Alto Adige region (which is German-speaking) for skiing

- Campania for camping
- Sicily for beach holidays.

Other important markets are neighbouring France, Switzerland and Austria, the USA and Britain. The French, Swiss and Austrians typically arrive by car and visit the beach resorts and historic cities. In contrast, British tourists are less inclined to be independent travellers, with over half arriving by air, although the proportion using charter airlines is less than for other Mediterranean destinations such as Spain and Greece. For British visitors, Venice, Tuscany, Campania (particularly the Sorrento Peninsula) and Emilia-Romagna (especially Rimini and Cattolica) remain the most popular destinations – a pattern that has changed little since the 1960s. Important long-haul markets are the USA and Japan. Visitors from the USA are commonly touring Europe and consequently spend only a short time in Italy, which is just one of the countries visited. The main attractions for North Americans are the well-known art cities. Not surprisingly, most of Italy's luxury hotels are concentrated in Rome, Florence and Venice. For Jubilee Year (2000) record numbers of visitors had to be accommodated.

Domestic and outbound tourism

Despite Italy's appeal to the foreign visitor, it is the large domestic market which dominates and sustains the tourism industry, accounting for about two-thirds of all overnight stays. Italians have a legal entitlement to at least four weeks' annual leave, and well over half the population take at least one holiday away from home. The domestic market is highly seasonal with three-quarters of trips in July and August and average lengths of stay are falling as the three- or four-week vacation becomes less popular. Domestic tourism is more evenly spread geographically than is the case with foreign tourists, who tend to be concentrated in a few cities, resorts and regions, although seasonality is a problem. Although participation in winter sports and activity holidays is growing, summer beach holidays remain the most popular type of domestic tourism. Whereas some of the resorts of the Adriatic coast and Liguria favoured by Italians are also very much part of the international tourism scene, many of the small seaside resorts of Tuscany, Lazio and the South rarely see a foreign holidaymaker.

An increasing number of Italians are travelling abroad, especially to long-haul destinations, and in fact, Italy is among the top ten tourist-generating countries in the world. However, it is only relatively recently that the country has become sufficiently affluent to generate a massive demand for foreign travel, and since there is a wealth of holiday attractions nearer home, the Italian domestic market remains important. In consequence, Italy has a surplus on its travel account.

Tourist attractions and resources

Italy's tourist attractions are so diverse and numerous that it is impossible to provide more than a shortlist of those we consider to be of major importance or to be unique in some way. As this is a large country by European standards, we have divided it for convenience into the following areas:

- northern Italy – including Liguria, the Italian Alps, Milan, Venice and Emilia-Romagna
- central Italy – including Tuscany, Umbria and Rome
- southern Italy – including Naples
- the islands of Sardinia and Sicily.

Northern Italy

The Alps

The Italian Alps are generally sunnier than the mountains of Austria and Switzerland, but this does mean that the ski season tends to be shorter. We can divide the Alps for convenience into central, western and eastern sections.

The *central Alps* are dissected by long transverse valleys that end in a number of large lakes of glacial origin. The Italian Lakes region is sheltered from northerly winds and has a milder, sunnier climate than the plains further south. Because of this and the magnificent scenery, it is well established as one of Europe's major holiday areas and is the subject of a case study. The central Alps also include a number of skiing resorts, such as Bormio, Livigno, and Madessimo which are popular with price-conscious foreign skiers and accessible from airports at Milan and Bergamo.

The *western Alps* include the highest mountain peaks in the system, and are popular with foreign, as well as Italian skiers. The most important resorts in the area are located within easy reach of Turin, such as Sauze d'Oulx and Sestriere. The Valle d'Aosta region has a French-speaking population and its government has done much to promote tourism in an effort to stem rural depopulation. Cervinia on the slopes of the Matterhorn (Monte Cervino) is an important resort in this area along with Courmayeur near Mont Blanc. Both resorts form part of international ski circuits – Cervinia with Zermatt in Switzerland, and Courmayeur with Chamonix and Megeve in the French Alps.

Much the same can be said of the *eastern Alps*, although here, the scenery, and to a greater extent, the cultural features, are different. Although the Dolomites are by no means the highest part of the Alps, the limestone rock has been sculptured by erosion with a breathtaking array of spectacular landforms. This area is a paradise for walkers and skiers alike, with one of Europe's longest ski circuits – the Val Gardena, and one of its most stylish resorts – Cortina d'Ampezzo. The nearest airports are at Venice and Verona. The eastern Alps include the German-speaking South Tyrol (Alto Adige in Italian), where the villages and folklore are reminders that this area formed part of the Habsburg Empire for more than six centuries, before becoming part of Italy after the First World War.

The North Italian Plain

In comparison with the Alps, the North Italian Plain stretching from Turin to the Adriatic Sea is scenically unattractive. It has a continental, rather than a Mediterranean climate, with cold, often foggy winters and hot rainy summers. Its main river, the Po, has changed course many times over the centuries, and is held in check by an extensive system of artificial embankments. Rice fields are a feature of the landscape in some areas, and this is Italy's main food-producing region. The main tourist attractions lie in the many historic towns, where, despite industrialization, the art treasures and buildings of medieval times have been preserved. Apart from Venice, which is truly unique and the subject of a case study, the most important of these are:

1 *Milan* Italy's second largest city and main business centre, world famous for its fashion industry. More important in terms of employment are the car industry and engineering, and the skyline is dominated by office buildings. Nevertheless, this brash, bustling city has much to attract cultural tourists, including its magnificent multispired cathedral and the Teatro Alla Scala, home of the world's greatest opera company.
2 *Turin* is also a centre of the car industry, including the Fiat empire. The cathedral is a focus for pilgrimages due to 'The Shroud', venerated as a relic of Christ.
3 *Verona* has one of the world's best preserved Roman arenas. Capable of seating 20 000 spectators, this forms an atmospheric setting during the summer for one of Europe's most popular opera festivals. However, as many tourists are attracted to this beautiful city because of its association with the legendary Romeo and Juliet.
4 *Bologna*, along with the other cities of Emilia-Romagna, has been overshadowed by the cultural centres of Venice and Tuscany. It is better known as a focus of Italy's railway system and for its food industries. Nevertheless it has much to offer the tourist including its medieval shopping arcades and leaning towers to rival those of Pisa!
5 *Ravenna* is famous for its Byzantine art treasures, a reminder that this city served as capital of the Roman Empire during its death throes.

The Adriatic Coast

For less culturally inclined holidaymakers, the extensive sandy beaches of the Adriatic coast offer safe bathing and a wide range of facilities appealing to families as well as the young. Scenically, most of the coastline from Trieste to Cattolica is flat. The type of development is also not particularly attractive, consisting of high-rise apartments

and hotels, separated by extensive camping areas. Rimini, with more hotel beds than any other Italian tourist centre, is the gateway and chief resort of the 'Adriatic Riviera'. Along with Cattolica and Lido di Jesolo, it is popular with foreign holidaymakers on package tours, while Riccione is more upmarket. To the south of Cattolica, in the Marche region, the coastline becomes more attractive, with the Apennines in the background. Of the many hill towns in the area, San Marino is the most visited, mainly because of its curiosity value as an independent mini-state. As in Italy as a whole, most beaches are privately owned and well maintained, with catering concessions in the hands of family businesses.

The Italian Riviera

The coast of Liguria, sometimes known as 'the Italian Riviera' is very different in character. Mountains to the north offer protection from the weather and it was the mild climate that initially attracted foreign as well as domestic tourists in the nineteenth century. It is generally divided into two sections:

- the Riviera de Ponente between Genoa and the French border, which has the better beaches
- the Riviera di Levante lying to the south east of Genoa, which is for the most part rocky.

Of the many resorts along this coast, San Remo is probably the best known and remains highly fashionable, with an important yacht marina. Portofino, once a small picturesque fishing village has become a very exclusive (and expensive) yachting centre due to its location on the most attractive stretch of the Riviera di Levante. Most of the other resorts such as Alassio, have seen better days and are suffering from overdevelopment and overcrowding in summer, now that much of the coast is highly accessible by motorway as well as by rail from the industrial cities of northern Italy.

Central Italy

South of the Apennines the landscape changes and is scenically much more attractive than the plains of Lombardy and Emilia-Romagna. It is characterized by small farms, vineyards, olive groves and rolling hills crowned by a small town or village which on first impressions, appears to have changed little since medieval times. The picturesque countryside largely explains the appeal of Tuscany, and to a lesser extent, Umbria and the Marche region, for rural tourism. In fact, the area of Tuscany near Siena has attracted so many British second home-owners that it has been nicknamed 'Chiantishire' after the well-known local wines. The rather flat coastline of Tuscany gets less attention from foreign holidaymakers despite the fine beaches, with the exceptions of the lively resort of Viareggio, and the island of Elba, famous for its associations with Napoleon. However, it is the cities, rather than coast or countryside, which have made central Italy, and especially Tuscany, one of Europe's most popular destinations. Cities that have received wide international recognition for their tourist attractions include:

1 *Florence* This city on the River Arno is the capital of Tuscany and since medieval times has been one of Italy's leading cultural centres. Thanks to its wealth and the power of its ruling family – the Medicis – during the Renaissance, Florence was able to attract the leading artists of the day, including Leonardo da Vinci, Michelangelo and Botticelli. As a result, the city can boast three of Europe's finest art collections. The skyline is dominated by the dome of the cathedral, which was a major architectural achievement for that era. Other attractions include the famous covered bridge known as the Ponte Vecchio. The city is also famous for its luxury trades, notably high-quality leather and jewellery. Unfortunately, Florence has suffered from pollution and overcrowding due to its popularity as a tourist destination.

2 *Pisa* It is doubtful if this city would be included on the international touring circuit were it not for the world famous 'Leaning Tower', actually one of a number of medieval buildings around the cathedral square. Pisa's international airport is the gateway to Tuscany.

3 *Siena* on the other hand, is a fascinating medieval city, whose narrow streets open out onto the Piazza del Campo, where the Palio horse race in medieval costume is held every August. Facing the Campo are two spectacular buildings – the cathedral, beautifully designed in black and white marble, and the medieval city hall.

4 *San Gimignano* is a small hilltop town famous for its towers, built by rival families in the Middle Ages and a reminder of the strife that characterized Tuscany in those times. It is a favourite location for film-makers and music festivals.

5 *Assisi* is the most visited town in Umbria, with pilgrims expected to reach record numbers in Jubilee year. Assisi's fame is due to its association with two great religious leaders – St Francis (nowadays widely regarded as the patron of ecology) and St Clare. The magnificent Basilica of San Francesco is actually two churches on one site.

6 *Rome* is known as the 'Eternal City' because it has been a centre of civilization for the past 3000 years. With the new millennium, exceptional numbers of tourists were anticipated from all over the world for the Holy Jubilee. This is mainly because Rome includes Vatican City, a tiny independent state ruled over by the Pope, who is the spiritual head of the world's 900 million Roman Catholics. The main gathering place for pilgrims is St Peter's Square, which provides a magnificent approach to the world's largest church – St Peter's Cathedral – which contains the celebrated Sistine Chapel with its paintings by Michelangelo. Rome was given a makeover in the seventeenth century by the architect and sculptor Bernini,

and many of the city's monuments, fountains, public squares and historic buildings date from that period. Traces of the ancient city, however, can still be seen, as reminders of the grandeur of the Roman Empire. They include:

(a) The Colosseum, where the populace spent much of their leisure time watching fights to the death between gladiators and other 'Roman Games'.
(b) The Forum which was the 'nerve-centre' of the empire.
(c) The Baths of Caracalla which are a reminder of the importance of public bathing as recreation in ancient Rome.
(d) The Pantheon that is the best preserved Roman temple, largely because it was converted early on into a Christian church.

With so much history, it is easy to overlook the fact that Rome is no museum piece, but a bustling modern capital, with acute traffic problems.

The South

The Mezzogiorno or 'land of the noonday sun' tends to be more traditional than the North in its outlook and way of life, with a much larger proportion of its people dependent upon agriculture. Because of widespread poverty and lack of resources, the region has experienced two great waves of emigration:

● to the New World – mainly the USA and Argentina in the early 1900s
● mainly to northern Italy during the economic boom of the 1950s and 1960s

The Italian government after 1950 made great efforts to redress the economic disparity between north and south through the Cassa de Mezzogiorno, which initiated development projects and improved transport infrastructure. Funding was made available for hotel building and upgrading along with other tourist facilities. In 1984 the role of the Cassa was largely taken over by the seven regional governments, which include Sicily and Sardinia. The South is now largely dependent on financial assistance from the EU, INSUD and private investors. Yet, despite the efforts of the agencies concerned, the South has not attracted foreign tourists on a large scale, with the exception of well-established areas such as the Neapolitan Riviera. Also the stranglehold of the secret societies on local businesses and politicians, particularly in Naples and western Sicily, has tended to discourage long-term investment in tourism as well as other industries.

Nonetheless, southern Italy can offer the tourist large stretches of almost empty beaches, combined with spectacular mountain scenery in Calabria – 'the toe of Italy' – and many historic towns that remain 'undiscovered'. There are also curiosities such as the *trulli* – strange beehive shaped dwellings in the villages of Apulia, 'the heel of Italy'. The Abruzzi National Park contains some of the finest scenery in the Apennines.

Campania

Campania is popular because it includes the Neapolitan Riviera, the name given to the coastline and islands of the Bay of Naples, and as the most visited region of southern Italy, deserves closer study. As mentioned earlier, the area is subject to volcanic activity and near Pozzuoli, there is an area known as the Phlegrean Fields, with numerous hot springs, steam jets and emissions of sulphurous gases. In 79 AD the towns of Herculaneum and Pompeii were destroyed by an eruption of Vesuvius. The excavated buildings provide a fascinating glimpse of many aspects of life in Roman times and Pompeii is very much on the tourist circuit.

Most of the resorts are situated in the Sorrento Peninsula that forms the south side of the Bay of Naples. Beaches are in short supply and the main attractions, especially to the older foreign visitor are:

- the superb scenery of the coastal road from Sorrento to Amalfi
- the picturesque resorts of Positano and Ravello
- the easy-going lifestyle.

Excursions are also available from Sorrento to the island of Capri – world famous for its Blue Grotto, and Ischia, which is renowned for its therapeutic radioactive springs. Both Capri and Ischia attract fashion-conscious Italians as well as large numbers of excursionists.

Although Sorrento is the largest holiday resort, Naples is the gateway to the region. Unfortunately, as Italy's third largest city and busiest port, Naples has a reputation that tends to deter visitors rather than attract them. Once the capital of an independent kingdom, the city has had more than its fair share of problems, notably chronic unemployment. Naples deserves to be better known for its contributions to Italian culture. These include:

- the street life of the Santa Lucia district, inspiration for the sentimental popular music which to many tourists, epitomizes Italy
- the Teatro San Carlo, the nation's oldest opera house
- one of Europe's best archaeological museums
- numerous Baroque churches.

The islands

The Italian islands, because they are widely scattered, are less important in the tourism scene than those of Greece, Croatia or Spain. With the exception of Capri, Ischia and Elba, most of the smaller islands rarely see foreign tourists. One example is Ponza, with its spectacular rock formations, despite its location on the coastal shipping route between Fiumicino and Sorrento. The two larger islands – Sicily and Sardinia are each almost the size of Belgium.

Sicily

Although Sicily is separated from the mainland by only a narrow stretch of water – the Straits of Messina – it is very much a region apart from the rest of Italy. This is due to the island's closeness to North Africa and its extraordinary history under the domination of many different civilisations. Although Sicily's former overlords left a rich architectural heritage, the natural environment has suffered from centuries of exploitation, resulting in widespread deforestation. Many of the tightly packed hill towns and villages of the interior rise out of a parched landscape and they depend upon one industry – agriculture. They have a neglected, somewhat forbidding appearance – Corleone (of 'Godfather' fame) is a typical example. Tourism has made more headway on the coast, where a number of fishing villages have become beach resorts.

Sicily has much to offer the tourist. The climate is generally warm and dry, although the heat of summer is often oppressive when the Sirocco wind blows from North Africa. The rich cultural mix, which includes Spanish, Arab and Greek contributions as well as Italian, is evident in the Sicilian dialect, food specialities, handicrafts and folklore, and the religious intensity of Holy Week. The two major cities are not particularly attractive to tourists, although they are ports of call for cruise ships:

- Palermo is the gateway to the western half of Sicily.
- Catania is the gateway for the east.

Ferries serve the island from Genoa, Livorno and Naples, as an alternative to Reggio, so shortening the long road journey down the Italian Peninsula. Sicily will become even more accessible once the long-awaited bridge linking Messina to Reggio becomes a reality.

Sicily's natural attractions include Mount Etna, one of the worlds' largest active volcanoes; you can approach the crater rim by road or by cable car. The Lipari Islands off the north coast are also volcanic and offer interesting scenery as well as opportunities for scuba diving; Stromboli is the most impressive of the group. Sicily's heritage attractions include:

1 An array of temples and theatres built by the ancient Greeks, which rival anything to be found in Greece itself. The most outstanding example is the Valley of Temples at Agrigento. Other important sites from this period (*c.* 300 BC) can be seen at Syracuse, Segesta and Selinunte.
2 The cathedral at Monreale near Palermo, which is a blend of Norman and Arab styles.
3 Taormina, in a spectacular setting with Mount Etna as a backdrop, is Sicily's most sophisticated and fashionable

resort. Many cultural events are staged in the beautiful theatre overlooking the sea, which was built by the ancient Greeks and added to by the Romans.

4 Cefalu caters more for families and is favoured by foreign tour operators, as it has an asset that Taormina lacks – a fine beach. It also boasts an impressive Norman cathedral and picturesque fishing port.

Sardinia

Tourism is an important part of Sardinia's economy. Because of its relative isolation, tour operators feature the island as a separate destination; certainly a greater number of foreign tour operators feature Sardinia for beach holidays than Sicily. Until the 1960s the island was a remote backwater outside the mainstream of Italian culture, while the sparsely populated interior had a reputation for lawlessness. Nowadays, four-wheel drive wildlife safaris are available in the mountains, and rural tourism is well developed, including a scheme run by a women's co-operative movement. Most of the development however, has taken advantage of the white sandy beaches. One of the first areas to be developed was the Costa Smeralda, north of Olbia, which includes some of the most expensive hotels and holiday homes to be found anywhere in the Mediterranean, and yet blending perfectly with the natural scenery. Most of Sardinia is much less exclusive, and Alghero in particular caters for package holidays. Sardinia is well connected by charter flights to northern Europe and by ferry services to the mainland of Italy, Corsica and mainland France.

Summary

Italy has a long pedigree as a tourism destination, with a dominantly cultural tourism product, based on the country's past civilizations and contemporary lifestyle. Physically, Italy is characterized by two mountain chains – the Alps and the Apennines, with extensive lowland plains and long Mediterranean coastlines. Public sector support for tourism has waned in the 1990s, and most of the activity takes place at the regional level. Small family hotels dominate the accommodation supply, and surface transport is the most important means of travel both to and within the country. Italy's tourism market is dominated by domestic travel, although more Italians are travelling abroad. Inbound tourism is heavily dependent upon the European market.

Italy's attractions and tourist resources are varied and of international importance. In northern Italy, the Alps are a region for winter sports and summer touring holidays, while the North Italian Plain comprises a number of towns, such as Milan and Venice, which are important for both cultural and business tourism. The northern Italian coasts have a number of important resorts such as Rimini. Central Italy has both rural tourism and city tourism products. For the latter, Florence and Rome are world-ranked tourism cities. In the South, efforts are being made to develop tourism to counterbalance the economic dominance of the North. Here coastal resorts complement the volcanic landscapes of the Bay of Naples. The Italian Islands of Sicily and Sardinia are tourism destinations in their own right.

Case study

Venice: heritage in danger

The tourist city

Venice is truly unique, an irreplaceable resource. Here we see a city without the problems of the motor car; this is due largely to the city's location on a cluster of low-lying islands in the middle of an extensive shallow lagoon. Venice has few rivals in its wealth of historic buildings and art treasures. However, it is not so much individual attractions that define this city's appeal, as its waterland setting and townscape which have changed remarkably little over the centuries. We need to remember that Venice is not just this historic island-city, but also includes a sprawl of industrial suburbs on the mainland, and it is here that most Venetians actually live and work (see Figure 16.1).

Attractions

The best known tourist attractions of Venice are to be found in and around the Piazza di San Marco (St Marks Square), one of Europe's finest meeting places. Like the rest of this city it has evolved over the centuries without planning, but somehow seems of a piece. Here you can see the Basilica of St Marks, which is architecturally quite unlike any other cathedral, and the Doge's Palace, which was the seat of government for the powerful Venetian Republic. The palace is lavishly decorated with paintings by Titian and other famous artists, and is connected by 'The Bridge of Sighs' to the former prisons. Venice's other well-known bridge is the Rialto that dates from medieval times. Many of the 200 or so palaces lining the Grand Canal were built by rich merchants between the thirteenth and sixteenth centuries, when Venice controlled the Eastern Mediterranean and the trade in luxuries from Asia. By the eighteenth century Venice had declined as a business centre, but had found a new role as a resort for gamblers and pleasure-seekers from all over Europe. The Venice Carnival, when people dress up in elaborate masks and costumes, is a reminder of this period. It is during carnival that the timeless quality of this city can best be appreciated, long after the hordes of summer tourists have departed.

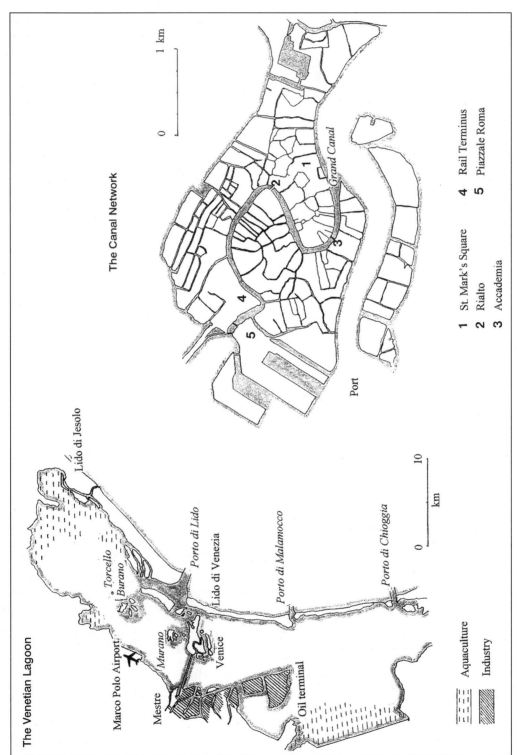

The Venetian Lagoon

Lido di Jesolo

Marco Polo Airport

Mestre

Torcello

Burano

Murano

Venice

Porto di Lido

Lido di Venezia

Oil terminal

Porto di Malamocco

Porto di Chioggia

Aquaculture

Industry

0   10

km

The Canal Network

Grand Canal

Port

0   1 km

1   St. Mark's Square

2   Rialto

3   Accademia

4   Rail Terminus

5   Piazzale Roma

Figure 16.1 Venice

To escape the crowds you can visit the other islands in the Lagoon. These include:

- Murano – famous for its glass industry based on traditional craftsmanship and exclusive design
- Burano – noted for lace making
- Lido di Venezia (Venice Lido) – Venice's own beach resort, built on a sandspit (lido) separating the Lagoon from the Adriatic Sea. Venice Lido is famous for its casino and international film festival.

Transport

Between Mestre and Treviso, Venice has its international airport, named after Marco Polo, the famous Venetian merchant-adventurer. Relatively few tourists arrive by sea, other than cruise passengers, although Venice ranks as Italy's fifth largest port. You can also reach the city by road or rail. The most stylish way to arrive is by the Orient Express, where the standards of service and the décor of the carriages recall the 'golden age of travel' before the Second World War. But whatever your mode of transport, once you have crossed the causeway linking the island-city to the mainland, and arrived at the bus terminal or car park in the Piazzale Roma, or the Santa Lucia rail terminus, all onward travel to your destination must be on foot or by boat. Confronting you is a maze of narrow streets and alleys, superimposed on an intricate network of canals (see Figure 16.1). The S-shaped Grand Canal, 4 kilometres in length, is the main artery of Venice, bisecting the city and crossed by only three bridges. The *vaporetto* (waterbus) and water taxi provide transport. The traditional gondola is expensive and nowadays used by Venetians only on special occasions. However, gondoliers are very much part of the city's image, and their expertise as guides is appreciated by tourists.

Accommodation

Accommodation is expensive everywhere in Venice, so that many visitors prefer to stay at Lido di Jesolo, the principal resort of the 'Venetian Riviera', 30 kilometres to the north.

The problems

As a destination Venice has many strengths but it also has weaknesses. Opportunities for developing the tourist product are strictly limited, and the unique qualities of the resource are under threat for a number of reasons.

The social impact of tourism

- *The issue* Venice's popularity is itself a major problem. More than 50 000 visitors arrive in the historic city

each day during the summer. The great majority are excursionists or tourists on a tight budget, whose contribution to the city's economy may be minimal while adding to its costs in litter disposal, policing, etc. Venice is in danger of becoming a 'museum-city' for tourists. Venetians allege that the regional culture is being neglected in favour of Neapolitan music which foreign tourists regard as more 'typically Italian'. The resident population of the historic city is now less than 70 000, half what it was in the 1950s, and the decline is accelerating as Venice's environmental problems increase. The social composition of the population is also becoming less balanced. Middle-income families continue to move to Mestre on the mainland, where most of the job opportunities outside tourism are to be found. This leaves the historic city to the wealthy, who can afford the upkeep of expensive palazzo-apartments, the elderly and those on low incomes, who are unable to leave.
- *The solution* In 1989, the City Council tried to ban backpackers from sleeping rough in the city's few public open spaces, but later revoked the law when it proved unworkable. They have also seriously considered imposing a quota on the number of day visitors.

The threat of flooding and subsidence

- *The issue* You should appreciate that Venice is built on foundations consisting of billions of timber pilings driven many centuries ago into the mud of the lagoon – these pilings are slowly eroding. Venice has always been subject to flooding, but the problem is getting worse due to the rise in sea level brought about by global warming. The combination of high tides and storm surges in the Adriatic has led to St Marks Square being flooded much more frequently than was the case earlier in the twentieth century.
- *The solution* Although Venetians have coped with the flood risk by, in effect, abandoning the lower floors of their dwellings, great damage has already been done to the fabric of many buildings, which are slowly sinking into the Lagoon. The 1966 flood disaster alerted the world to the possibility that the city would have to be abandoned. The Venice in Peril Fund was set up to co-ordinate international efforts in the work of restoration and salvage, and to galvanize the authorities into action. The Italian government's response has been to propose the construction of huge movable floodgates across the three entrances to the Lagoon, saving Venice by closing it off from the Adriatic. This has attracted widespread criticism as a 'quick-fix' solution because:
  - The project is not cost-effective, as the savings in the costs of flood damage do not justify the vast expense.

– It would disrupt navigation into the port of Venice. Considerable investment has taken place to improve port facilities, including the dredging of a deep-water channel for oil tankers (which itself has upset the balance between salt and fresh water in the Lagoon). The scheme would accelerate the silting up of the shipping channels.
– It would aggravate the build-up of pollution in the Lagoon.

The impact of pollution on the Lagoon ecosystem

The Lagoon is a fragile ecosystem. It is a patchwork of marshes, small islands, slow-flowing rivers and sand-banks, acting as a sponge-like barrier between the city and the Adriatic Sea. Pollution is the most deadly and insidious threat to Venice. Venetians have, for centuries, been aware of the need to protect their water resources and the Magisterio alla Acqua, financed by the city government, is probably the world's oldest environmental protection agency, with regulatory powers over the canal system and the lagoon. The scale of the problem is probably much greater now than in the past with pollution coming from the following sources:

● *Source* Waste from the city's households, hotels and restaurants. Venice has no sewers and domestic sewage is simply dumped in the canals.
● *Solution* Regulations that hotels and restaurants should install biological water treatment works have been largely ignored. Sewage treatment works around the lagoon have themselves contributed to the problem and a city-wide system of sewage disposal is required.
● *Source* Discharges of effluents from industrial plant on the mainland at Porto Marghera. Factories were built here in the early 1900s to solve Venice's unemployment problem, but they were sited in the wrong place, far from the cleansing action of the tides. Pollutants include concentrations of heavy metals and ammonia.
● *Solution* Limits for discharges are set by the Magisterio alla Acqua, but penalties for non-compliance are limited to a fine. Industrialists prefer to pay this rather than install waste treatment facilities; in effect a polluter's charter. This is true of Murano's glassworks that emit arsenic; here the individual enterprises are much smaller than on the mainland and financially unable to carry out the treatment required.
● *Source* The drainage into the Lagoon of pesticides and fertilizer from agriculture, much of it taking place on reclaimed land. An excess of nitrates and phosphates has contaminated fish and shellfish resources, to the extent that fishing is now prohibited over wide areas of the Lagoon. These conditions favour the spread of algae, which in turn decompose, giving off a foul stench in the process. With the absence of natural predators, swarms of chironomides (insects similar to a mosquito) have become a plague, at times even threatening to disrupt air and rail communications.
● *Solution* No effective solution has been implemented, partly because it is difficult to track down the polluters. A long-term solution would be for farmland to revert to marsh, restoring the original ecosystem.

The future

These problems are not just the concern of the environmentalists, but clearly threaten the viability of Venice as a tourist destination, unless both the private and public sectors can agree on drastic anti-pollution measures. In the public sector, closer co-operation is needed between the three levels of government – the city of Venice, the region of Veneto, and the Italian state, to formulate a policy of sustainable development for the area.

Case study

The Italian Lakes

The Italian Lakes are one of the great holiday destinations of Europe. Their appeal is due, not just to the breathtaking mountain scenery, but also the human-made attractions, above all, the villas and gardens for which the region is famous. The lakes are highly accessible and can offer many amenities for the visitor. Long before the region became a holiday destination the mountain valleys containing the lakes were trade routes, linking central Europe with the cities of northern Italy. Even today, many visitors are simply 'passing through' on their way south to the Mediterranean, although some, seeing the lakes as an 'intervening opportunity', may be persuaded to stay longer.

Tourism to the Italian Lakes has a history going back to the early nineteenth century, when it was 'discovered' by the Romantic writers and composers. They made it a fashionable destination for the wealthy, and some of the former exclusiveness is still evident in the luxury hotels of the resorts and the villas dotting the lakeshores. Nowadays the Italian Lakes have a much wider appeal, attracting the following types of visitor:

● Holidaymakers from northern Europe on 'lakes and mountains' package tours. They tend to be mainly in the over forty-year-old age groups.
● Independent travellers visiting the area as part of a wider Italian or European tour.

- Day-trippers from the industrial cities of northern Italy seeking recreation; Milan for example, is only 60 kilometres from Lake Como.
- Cross-border day-trippers, usually from Switzerland seeking shopping bargains in Italy.
- Participants in a wide variety of activity holidays, including hiking, riding, cycling and mountain-climbing, as well as water sports. These come mainly from Italy and neighbouring countries, and tend to be in the twenty-five to forty-year age group
- conference delegates – the larger resorts, such as Riva del Garda, Stresa, Lugano and Locarno, have conference facilities of international standard, and feature event attractions such as music festivals.

Much of the region suffers from the impacts of mass tourism especially with overcrowding in July and August. However, efforts have been made to maintain water quality and pollution of the lakes themselves is not a serious problem. Nonetheless, overdevelopment of the ski resorts in the upper valleys leading into Lake Como is having an environmental impact, by increasing the risk of landslides and floods.

The lakes owe their elongated shape, and their great depth, to glaciation of the mountain valleys during the most recent Ice Age (Lake Como, for example, is over 400 metres deep, which means its lowest point is 300 metres below sea level). The southern ends of the lakes (Garda is the best example) open out into relatively flat countryside, while the northern sections, which are also deeper, are hemmed in by mountains. The vast quantities of water stored in the lakes has an important effect on the local climate, making winters milder and summers cooler than in the Lombardy Plain to the south. As a result you would notice many Mediterranean features in the landscape, for example, palms and lemon orchards. Travellers from northern Europe appreciate the contrast most in early spring, when they emerge from the cold and gloomy weather prevailing north of the St Gotthard Tunnel into the warm sunshine of the Ticino Valley and Lake Lugano. The mountain topography does have the following effects, causing:

- the weather to be more unpredictable than on the Mediterranean coast
- considerable variations in sunshine between different parts of the lakeshore
- the funnelling of airflow through the valleys. The result is the *tramuntana* wind blowing south down the valleys and from north to south across the lakes in the mornings, and the *ora* wind blowing in the reverse direction in the afternoons. These local winds are greatly appreciated by windsurfers for their regularity, but unlike the *Mistral* of Southern France, they are rarely a nuisance to campers and bathers on the lakeshore.

The most important lakes for tourism are, from east to west, Garda, Como, Lugano and Maggiore. Each has specific attractions.

Lake Garda

Lake Garda is the largest of the lakes and the most visited. Apart from its many scenic attractions, it is close to three of the major art cities of northern Italy – Verona, Trento and Mantua, while the Dolomites are within easy reach of the resort of Riva del Garda. Some 40 per cent of visitors to Lake Garda are foreign tourists, and of these, almost two-thirds are German. About one-quarter of the accommodation stock is in hotels, with pensions, self-catering and campsites making up the remainder. The western side of the lake is studded with so many resorts offering high-class accommodation that it has been described as a 'lakeshore riviera', offering a range of sophisticated entertainment and recreational facilities. Riva del Garda enjoys a particularly mild climate due to its south-facing location protected by mountains. Malcesine is the most attractive resort on the eastern shore, with access by cableway to Monte Baldo, an important ski area in winter. The best beaches are to be found on the southern shore of the lake. Here Sirmione is the best known resort, with its spa and medieval castle.

Lake Como

Lake Como has been affected by industrial development spreading out from Milan to the southern fringes of the lake, particularly around Lecco. Although the city of Como is used by visitors as a base for excursions, tourism here is probably less important than the silk industry. Bellagio, because of its scenic location between the two arms of the lake, is the most stylish of the resorts (with the accolade of being chosen as the theme for the most luxurious hotel in Las Vegas). Most tours of Lake Como feature a visit to the villas built by wealthy landowners in the seventeenth and eighteenth centuries (such as the Villa Carlotta in Tremezzo) which are admired by garden-lovers worldwide. Resorts such as Menaggio featured by tour operators, offer less expensive accommodation than Bellagio. Within easy reach for excursions is the picturesque medieval city of Bergamo.

Lake Lugano

Two-thirds of this lake is actually Swiss territory, forming part of the Italian-speaking canton of Ticino. The resorts on the Italian side are little more than villages, with the exceptions of Porlezza and the enclave of Campione with its casino. The most important resort by far is the Swiss city of Lugano at the foot of Mount San Salvatore, which is noted for its parks and gardens.

Lake Maggiore

The northern tip of this lake also lies in Switzerland, and includes the cultural attractions of Locarno and Ascona. Most of the development on the Italian side is on the western shore of the lake, where Stresa and Verbania are the most important resorts. Growth was rapid after the opening of the Simplon Tunnel in 1906 greatly improved accessibility to the area. Stresa remains a fashionable centre, catering mainly for the older age groups. The highlight of a tour of Lake Maggiore is a boat excursion to the Borromean Islands, named after a wealthy local family who transformed them into an extravaganza of luxuriant gardens, villas and grottoes.

Malta, Greece and Cyprus

After reading this chapter you should be able to:

1 Explain the special appeal of Greece and the Greek Islands.
2 Appreciate the cultural and economic ties that link Cyprus and Malta to other countries.
3 Describe the major physical features and climate of these countries and understand their importance for tourism.
4 Appreciate the tradition of tourism in Greece and the more recent entry of Malta and Cyprus into the holiday market.
5 Appreciate the role of shipping and air services in the development of tourism in Greece, Malta and Cyprus.
6 Understand the nature of tourism demand to the region.
7 Appreciate the administration of tourism in the region.
8 Demonstrate a knowledge of the tourist regions, resorts, business centres and tourist attractions of Greece, Malta and Cyprus.

Introduction

Apart from their location in the eastern half of the Mediterranean, we think there is justification for including Malta, Greece and Cyprus in the same chapter. Although Greece is not an island-nation like the other two countries, most of its popular tourist areas are islands and the country has a strong maritime outlook. All three countries have developed tourism industries based on Mediterranean beach holidays, serving the north European market. Cultural tourism is also important, and part of their attraction to visitors is a heritage that is a blend of Western and Middle Eastern influences. During the period of Turkish expansion, Malta, the Greek Islands and Cyprus were often in the front line in the struggle waged by the Republic of Venice and the Knights of St John in the defence of Christian Europe. There are also cultural ties linking Greece to Cyprus that go back thousands of years. In more recent times, there is the connection between Britain and its former colonies of Malta and Cyprus – both countries remain members of the Commonwealth and their people are to a large extent English-speaking.

Malta

The Maltese islands, small in size and poor in natural resources, are strategically important because of their location, midway between the Straits of Gibraltar and the Suez Canal, and between Europe and Africa. The main island – Malta itself – was a valuable prize for foreign invaders, the last being Britain, which used the Grand Harbour at Valletta as a base for the Royal Navy. The smaller island of Gozo was neglected and remains something of a backwater compared to Malta, although it is greener and scenically more attractive. The first impression of Malta is an apparently barren landscape of small terraced fields, separated by drystone walls and dotted with villages built from the honey-coloured rock. Because of the limestone formation of the islands and the rather dry climate, water supply is a major problem and tourism has to compete with other uses for this scarce resource.

Before independence from Britain in 1964, Malta was not a major tourist destination. The departure of the British armed forces meant that the government had to transform the country's economic base, by concentrating on the service sector, including tourism. Tourism to Malta rapidly expanded in the 1970s, reaching 700 000 by 1980. In the first half of the 1980s visitor numbers declined, but have grown steadily to reach just over 1 million arrivals in the 1990s. The tourist authorities are concerned at Malta's dependence on a few markets – the UK represents almost half of all arrivals, while Germany, Italy and France are also generators. The national carrier, Air Malta, also operates services to Libya and Egypt, demonstrating the importance of the Arab market in business travel. The capital Valletta has been successfully promoted as an international conference venue and financial centre, yet despite this the majority of arrivals to Malta are holidaymakers. About one-quarter of Malta's visitors are cruise passengers, spending up to twenty-four hours on the island, with much smaller numbers – mainly Italians – arriving on ferries from Sicily and Naples. However, Luqa Airport is the main gateway, with large numbers of holidaymakers arriving on charter flights operated by North European tour operators. Most of these are on package holidays, but other passengers are 'flight only' visiting their second or retirement homes on the island.

Malta's main appeal for holidaymakers lies in its warm sunny climate, with sheltered, unpolluted bays and harbours providing an ideal environment for sailing, windsurfing and scuba diving. However, sandy beaches are mainly restricted to the north-west of the island, where a number of resorts have developed, such as Bugibba – St Paul's Bay and Mellieha. Malta has a large stock of hotel and self-catering accommodation, with the lower end of the package holiday market being concentrated in Sliema and a number of new resort developments by international companies responding to the government's upgrading strategy. In contrast, Gozo's tourism industry is much less developed since it is highly dependent on day visitors, using the ferry services linking it to the main island.

Malta's unique heritage also attracts cultural tourists. Although the Maltese people are service-orientated, used to dealing with foreigners, they have retained their traditional culture that has some Middle Eastern influences as well as being characterized by a strong devotion to the Roman Catholic Church. Each village has its *festa* (festival) and elaborately decorated church. The main attractions include:

1 Valletta and the Three Cities built by the Knights of St John to defend the finest natural harbour in the Mediterranean from the Ottoman Turks. Some of the Renaissance palaces have found a new role as conference centres or luxury hotels, while St Johns Co-Cathedral is outstanding for its works of art. The *dghajsas* used to ferry tourists across the Grand Harbour are similar to Venetian gondolas.
2 The prehistoric temples at Tarxien built by a mysterious early civilization.

3 The medieval walled town of Medina, the former capital, known as the 'Silent City' in contrast to the bustle of Valletta.

Government commitment to tourism is evidenced by the fact that the Parliamentary Secretariat for Tourism has three major departments dealing with marketing, planning and product upgrading, and education/training. The authorities are anxious to maintain Malta as a competitively priced destination, but they face a number of problems. These include:

● water shortages – desalinization is an expensive solution
● the social and economic imbalance between Malta and Gozo; to encourage tourism and employment prospects for young Gozitans, inter-island ferry services need improvement
● traffic congestion on the island's road system
● development pressures on an island that already has one of the world's highest population densities
● poor standards of accommodation.

These problems have led to restrictions on further development in St Paul's Bay, Sliema, and in the south-east of the island. There is also the realization that, if Malta has reached saturation point in terms of tourism development, then the only way the industry can expand is to use the spare capacity in the off-peak months and to attract higher spending clientele.

Greece

Introduction

The location of Greece on the periphery of the EU, and its weak economy compared with those of its partners, has tended to obscure the unique contribution that this small country has made to European culture. This includes:

1 Greece as the birthplace of European civilization. The Minoan culture of Crete flourished at the same time as ancient Egypt (*c*.2000 BC) and was in some respects more advanced. It was followed by the more warlike Mycenean culture on the mainland, which formed the basis of legends such as the Iliad, the Odyssey and the Argonauts. Greece as 'the land of gods and heroes' has inspired a good deal of European art and literature.
2 Later (after 500 BC), Classical Greece under the leadership of Athens, developed many of the ideas and institutions which became central to the Western heritage, such as democracy and the Olympic Games. Architectural achievements, such as the Parthenon, continue to provide inspiration, and the dramas of Sophocles are still performed for modern audiences in the original open-air

theatres as at Epidauros. Hellenic culture was spread far beyond Greece by Alexander the Great, and later strongly influenced the Romans.

3 After the fall of the Roman Empire in the West, the torch of civilization was carried on by the Greek-speaking Byzantine Empire, based in Constantinople (now Istanbul). The Greek Orthodox Church spread to much of Eastern Europe and Russia, strongly influencing religious art (for example, the use of ikons) and architecture.

Geographically, Greece forms part of the Balkan Peninsula, and has a cultural outlook different from Western Europe. It shares with other countries in the region:

● Orthodox Christianity, rather than Roman Catholicism
● the Cyrillic rather than Roman alphabet
● a history of centuries of domination by the Ottoman Empire.

Greece is also situated at the threshold of the Middle East, and Greek communities have long been a feature of the Levant – the eastern shore of the Mediterranean – from Alexandria to Asia Minor. Middle Eastern influences are evident in many aspects of modern Greek culture, including food and music. However, relations with Turkey have often been strained, with emotional responses based on historical grievances getting in the way of international co-operation that would benefit tourism in both countries. The geographical proximity of Greece to some of the world's 'trouble-spots' in the Balkans and the Middle East has also had a negative impact on the country's tourism industry. For example, the Western media have alleged lack of security at Athens airport on several occasions.

The country's geography also explains why Greece has a maritime outlook extending well beyond the Mediterranean. The 16 000 kilometre-long coastline is deeply indented and has many islands, while the interior is, for the most part, mountainous – in Greece the sea and the mountains are never far away. The landscape in many areas has been devastated by soil erosion (largely due to deforestation) and good agricultural land is scarce. Not surprisingly, Greeks have been seafarers throughout their history, and Greece today has one of the world's largest shipping fleets. Due to the lack of economic opportunity there has been a great deal of emigration, particularly from the Aegean islands, to countries such as Australia or the USA. In fact, the Greeks of this overseas diaspora far outnumber the population of Greece itself. As far as tourism is concerned, the multiplicity of islands and harbours provides an ideal environment for sailing holidays and cruising, while the clear water of the Aegean favours diving.

Cultural tourism has a long history in Greece, and although the country was not included in the Grand Tour, it was visited by writers like Lord Byron, who did much to promote the cause of Greek independence in the early nineteenth century. However, organized tourism did not take

place on any scale until the 1950s. Along with other Mediterranean destinations, Greece developed rapidly during the 1970s largely on the basis of price and the attractions of the Greek islands. By the mid-1990s, arrivals for the country as a whole were exceeding 11 million a year. The majority of tourists to Greece nowadays are visiting for recreational rather than cultural reasons – in search of sun, sand, sea, the nightlife of the taverna and disco, and for a substantial number of visitors, the so-called 'Shirley Valentines' – romance. The Greek tradition of hospitality known as *philoxenia* (literally love of strangers) has probably been an asset in developing a vast service sector dominated by small family-run enterprises. Britain and Germany each supply about 25 per cent of the total number of visitors, most of whom arrive on inclusive tours. Italy, the Netherlands, Austria and the Scandinavian countries are also major generators of tourism to Greece. Large numbers of tourists also come from the USA, attracted mainly by the heritage of Classical Greece.

Three-quarters of visitors to Greece arrive by air. The most important gateways are Athens, serving southern and central Greece, and Thessaloniki for the north. The national carrier Olympic Airways and its associate Olympic Aviation operates a network of domestic air services based on Athens throughout this fragmented country, although it no longer holds the monopoly. Quite a few Greek islands can be reached by direct charter flights from the cities of northern Europe, the most significant being Corfu (Kerkira), Cephallonia, Zante (Zakynthos), Crete (Iraklion and Chania), Mykonos, Rhodes and Kos. Greece receives 5 per cent of its visitors from cruise ships plying the eastern Mediterranean. Overland travel by road or rail is also available, but it is time-consuming as it involves:

● ferry crossings from Ancona or Brindisi to Patras if the visitor is arriving via Italy, or
● lengthy delays at border crossings if the visitor is travelling through the republics of the former Yugoslavia. Before the break-up of that country and the subsequent wars in Croatia and Bosnia (1991–4) this was the preferred route, but it remains potentially unsafe given the likelihood of a further crisis in the Balkans.

The rail network within Greece, operated by Hellenic Railways (OSL) has suffered from chronic underfunding and many of the lines are single-track, reducing speed. However, fast inter-city services do link Athens to Thessaloniki and Patras. Much of the road system is also poor by EU standards, especially on the islands where the accident rate among moped-users, for example, is unacceptably high. On the other hand, Greece has one of the world's most extensive networks of coastal shipping services. However, the system is not ideal from a tourism viewpoint, as most ferries operate from Piraeus, the port of Athens, inter-island connections can be infrequent, and shipping companies are reluctant to provide an integrated service. 'Island-hopping' is part of the attraction of Greece for many tourists, but it requires patience and an element of planning. Ferries are subject to delays and even cancellations, especially in the Aegean, when the *meltemi* wind blows during the summer months. In good weather, the more remote islands can be reached by *caiques* (converted fishing boats).

Tourism is vital to the Greek economy, since it accounts for about 8 per cent of gross domectic product and nearly half of the international trade deficit. Around 10 per cent of the workforce are employed in the industry during the peak summer months, according to official figures. However, the contribution of tourism to job creation is even higher if we consider the 'black economy' of unregistered businesses, which is a fact of life in Greece as in other south European countries. Tourism is also responsible for facilitating economic and social development in areas where other opportunities for wealth-creation are lacking. For example, it has stemmed the tide of emigration from the Aegean islands, and there is now a reverse flow including entrepreneurs from the mainland (which is not always to the advantage of the island economy).

The accommodation and catering sectors are well represented in Greece, and consist mainly of small and medium-sized enterprises (SMEs). The official stock of hotels and self-catering villas, apartments and studios is considerable, but it is exceeded by unregistered accommodation known collectively as *parahoteleria*, amounting to perhaps one million bed spaces. Most of the establishments offering rooms to let to visitors arriving in the Greek islands fall into this category. A large number of campsites are also available.

The importance of tourism is recognized by the government. The Ministry of Tourism shares responsibilities with the Greek National Tourism Organization (GNTO) for promotion, planning, the implementation of policies at both national and regional levels and co-ordination of the public and private sectors in tourism development. Government involvement currently is less than in the 1970s when it took a direct role in encouraging tourism, itself building facilities on a considerable scale, and offering a wide range of incentives to private developers. Tourism is included in the five-year plans for economic and social development, supplemented by EU funding.

The GNTO faces a number of problems brought about by both the nature of tourism to Greece and the sensitivity of many of the country's resources. They include the following:

Seasonality

The emphasis on 'summer sun' tourism does mean that there is a major problem, as 75 per cent of tourist arrivals are concentrated in the months May to September. This forces those employed in the tourism sector to work excessively long hours, to the detriment of the traditional family values characteristic of the Greek way of life.

Geographical concentration

Tourism development is mainly restricted to Athens, the coastal resorts and some of the islands. This makes it difficult to spread the benefits of tourism more evenly throughout the country, and to provide adequate accommodation and other facilities to cope with demand.

The negative social impact of mass tourism

During the off-season, the islands are almost crime free, but health and police services are stretched to the limit in some popular resorts during the peak summer months – to cope with the effects of alcohol and drug abuse by some north European holidaymakers. This type of behaviour is offensive to the host community but is tolerated because tourism brings in much needed income.

Overdependence on foreign tour operators

Attempts by hoteliers to introduce higher standards and prices mean that the mass market no longer sees Greece as an inexpensive destination, while high-spending tourists are deterred from visiting the popular resorts.

Environmental degradation

The development of tourism has often been characterized by unplanned, haphazard building that has blighted the landscape. The rapid development of tourism and its concentration in the dry summer season, has placed severe pressure on water supply systems. Marine pollution has been caused by inadequate sewage treatment and waste disposal. Noise pollution is a feature of the popular resorts, and has contributed for example, to the decline of endangered species of turtle on the island of Zakynthos. It is estimated that two-thirds of the forest fires that afflict Greece each summer are deliberately carried out to clear land for development.

These issues do mean that, while Greece is endowed with superb tourism resources, the country's tourism does not always fulfil its potential (see the first case study at the end of this chapter).

Tourism resources

We can divide Greece for tourism purposes into:

1 The Greek mainland, which consists of a number of regions, the most important being the Peloponnese, Sterea Hellas (central Greece, including Athens), and Macedonia in the northern part of the country.
2 The Greek islands, which includes Crete and a number of separate groups or archipelagos. The most popular of these are the Ionian Islands lying to the west of the mainland, the Cyclades in the central Aegean, and the Dodecanese to the south-east.

Mainland Greece

The mainland of Greece is divided into two by the Corinth Canal, itself a major engineering achievement. To the south is the Peloponnese, where mass tourism has as yet made little impact, largely due to the absence of good beaches. Tolon and Naplion are significant holiday resorts, within easy reach of Athens. The government has encouraged the revitalization of traditional communities such as the Mani in the extreme south, famous for its fortified villages. This formerly remote area has been opened up for walking and special interest holidays, which include Mystra, an important city in the Byzantine era. The Peloponnese contains some of Greece's most important archaeological sites. Some of these are included in classical tours based on Athens, such as:

● Olympia – site of the original Olympic Games (entry was restricted to Greek citizens and women were barred)
● Mycenae – associated with the legends of the Trojan War
● the well-preserved theatre at Epidauros, dating from the fourth century BC that is still used for cultural events.

Tourism in Athens has declined significantly since the 1970s, when it was still the centre par excellence for sightseers. This has come about partly as a result of the growth in popularity of the Greek islands, at the expense of cultural tourism. Ugly urban sprawl and severe air pollution resulting from motor vehicles and factory emissions have also diminished the sightseeing experience. (Athens accounts for about 90 per cent of the country's manufacturing industries.) The local authorities now regularly ban private vehicles from the city centre, usually on a rota basis, in an attempt to reduce the *nefos* (smog) which endangers both health and historic monuments.

The capital's main attractions include:

● The Acropolis, the fortified hill which was the core of ancient Athens, containing a number of important temples such as the Parthenon, as reminders of the glory of Ancient Greece.
● The agora, once the marketplace of Athens in Classical and Roman times, which has only partly been excavated. There are plans to unite all these sites as one archaeological park.
● To the east of the city lie a number of beach resorts – the so called 'Apollo Coast' which are mainly visited by domestic tourists and day-trippers.
● To the south of Piraeus are the Argo-Saronic islands, the most popular being Aegina, while Spetses is perhaps the most attractive, providing a welcome relief from the extreme summer heat and congestion of Athens.
● To the north-west is the classical site of Delphi in its beautiful mountain setting – this was an important place of pilgrimage in ancient times.

In northern Greece, the well-wooded Halkidiki Peninsula with its fine beaches has been developed for recreational tourism, with yacht marinas, golf courses and holiday villages. The area is close to Thessaloniki, which is second in importance only to Athens as a business centre. Elsewhere, the emphasis has been on selective tourism to:

● stem rural depopulation
● revive traditional village industries
● conserve the region's natural and cultural heritage.

Attempts to develop winter sports tourism in the Pindus Mountains as a means of reducing seasonality have not been particularly successful, and northern Greece is mainly visited for its national parks – the Vikos gorge is outstanding – and its cultural attractions – such as the spectacular monasteries of Meteora.

The Greek Islands

Of the hundreds of Greek islands, less than eighty are served by regular ferry or hydrofoil services, and relatively few have been developed for international tourism. Each of these islands offers a unique product on the basis of its scenery and cultural heritage, rather than the quality of its beaches.

Crete

Crete is the largest by far of the islands, with a mountainous interior where the traditional lifestyle has persisted to a greater extent than elsewhere in Greece, contrasting with the well-developed international tourism scene along the north coast. Mallia has borne the brunt of mass tourism, while Aghios Nikalaos, with its attractive harbour, has remained more up-market. Crete has much more to offer than most Greek islands to those tourists looking for more than beaches and nightlife.

The two major attractions are:

1 The Samaria Gorge, one of the most impressive examples of its kind in Europe. Unfortunately, its very popularity with hikers has caused ecological damage to this national park and disruption to its wildlife.
2 The impressive remains of the Minoan civilization at Knossos; this, too, is popular with tourists on day excursions from the nearby resorts. Phaestos on the less visited south coast is an uncrowded alternative.

The Cyclades

The Cyclades are generally rather barren in appearance, and the small island communities are characterized by their white cube-shaped buildings, interspersed with tiny blue and white chapels. On these and other Aegean islands, we can usually identify two types of tourist centre, which are complementary in terms of the facilities they provide – the port, and the *chora*, the traditional focus of island life – often situated some distance inland. The most popular islands in the group are:

- Mykonos perhaps most closely resembles the tourist stereotype of a Greek island, but it is in fact a sophisticated resort, with expensive bars and boutiques.
- Paros at the hub of the Aegean ferry network is ideal for the independent traveller.
- Ios likewise attracts swarms of young backpackers during July and August, on account of its fine beaches and non-stop nightlife.
- Naxos contains more scenic variety and is the most fertile of the islands. Until the completion of a new airport with EU funding in 1990, tourism took second place to agriculture and is still relatively low-impact in nature.
- Santorini (Thira) is undoubtedly the most spectacular of the Greek islands. It features prominently on cruise itineraries, thanks to its unique volcanic scenery – the harbour is the centre of a huge caldera – and the remains of the Minoan city of Akrotiri, buried by a volcanic eruption circa 1500 BC.

The Sporades

- Skiathos is the most popular island in the group known as the Sporades in the north-west Aegean, thanks to a combination of pine-covered landscapes and fine beaches.
- Skyros, in contrast, has developed a niche market in 'holistic community' holidays as a solution to the stress of modern life.

The north-east Aegean

The islands of the north-east Aegean are notably Lesbos, Samos and Chios. Here, agriculture and shipping continue to be the mainstays of the local economy, rather than tourism, which is dominated by the domestic market.

The Dodecanese

The Dodecanese are a chain of twelve islands situated far from the Greek mainland and close to the coast of Turkey. Their cultural heritage is different from other Greek islands in that they were ruled successively by the Crusaders known as the Knights of St John, the Ottoman Empire until 1912, and by Italy until the Second World War. For the most part, they are relatively undeveloped for tourism, with the exceptions of Kos and Rhodes where mass tourism, based on the beaches rather than any cultural attractions, has made a major impact (see the second case study at the end of this chapter).

The Ionian islands

The Ionian islands actually include three popular destinations – Corfu, Cephallonia and Zante (Zakynthos). They are mountainous but fertile, with a softer climate than the Aegean islands and a greener landscape. Their cultural heritage reflects a long period of rule by the Republic of Venice, and also British occupation (from 1815 until 1864).

- *Corfu* has for long been a favourite with British holidaymakers, and a large number of resorts have developed, particularly along the east coast, although the west coast has the best beaches. Mass tourism has had an adverse effect on Corfu, particularly in Ipsos and Benitses that have become mass-market resorts, while Kavos is very much an enclave for the youth market, attracted by its throbbing nightlife. In contrast, Corfu Town has a number of cultural attractions.
- *Cephallonia* and *Zante* have less to offer in this respect, as they were badly affected by an earthquake in 1956 and underwent subsequent rebuilding. Zante is the more popular of the two and much of the development for the package holiday market has been insensitive, especially in the resort of Laganas. The island is a good example of the struggle between environmentalists, who want part of the coast to be designated as a marine national park, and local hotel developers and boat operators eager to boost profits.

Cyprus

Cyprus is the third largest of the Mediterranean islands, offering a great variety of coastal and mountain scenery and the heritage of many civilizations. Yet it is a divided island, occupied by two different ethnic groups – the Greeks and the Turks – separated by language, religion, history and, since 1974, by a military/political frontier – the Green Line – which also divides the capital, Nicosia. The Greek-speaking Republic of Cyprus occupies two-thirds of the island, contains 75 per cent of its population, and accounts for perhaps 95 per cent of its tourism industry – mainly because the Turkish Republic of North Cyprus (TRNC) is ostracized by the international community. The location of Cyprus, only 200 kilometres from Beirut, has meant that tourism is affected not only by the long-running dispute between Greece and Turkey over the island itself, but also by the uncertain political situation in the nearby Middle East. In the 1990–1 Gulf War, for example, tourism suffered badly.

Before Cyprus gained independence from Britain in 1960, few tourists visited the island. In the late 1960s it was 'discovered' by British tour operators, since Cyprus (along with Gibraltar and Malta) was part of the 'sterling area' and not subject to the strict currency exchange controls imposed by the British government at that time. After the invasion and occupation of the northern part of the island by the Turkish army in 1974, there was a drastic decline in tourist numbers, as most of the hotel stock was destroyed in the conflict. However, a major investment in tourism facilities in southern Cyprus followed, including the opening of a new airport at Larnaca to replace Nicosia, and the rapid development of Ayia Napa as a resort for the mass market. In the 1990s international tourist arrivals grew to around 2 million, three times the Greek Cypriot population of the island.

The British inclusive tour market remains important to the island's tourist industry, using charter flights to the airports at Larnaca and Paphos. There are also substantial numbers of independent British visitors travelling to their holiday villas and retirement homes on the island. As is the case in Greece, the Cyprus government discourages seat-only charters.

Tourism is represented at ministerial level as it is so important to the economy (almost three-quarters of the economy is dependent upon tourism). This overdependence on tourism also causes concern in terms of the industry's use of scarce resources and the impact of tourism across the island's environment and communities. The Cyprus Tourist Organization (CTO) has promotion, development and licensing responsibilities. In this respect, the CTO is very concerned about the risks of overdevelopment of the coastline – already evident in resorts such as Limassol and Ayia Napa – and is aiming for high-quality, high-spending tourism by upgrading the tourist offering. It has successfully promoted the island as an all-year destination and as a result, the Scandinavian countries and Germany have become important generators of tourism to Cyprus. The CTO is also actively seeking new markets, notably Russia, Israel and the Arab states of the Middle East. It is also worth mentioning that there is a considerable internal domestic demand for the island's recreational resources, generated not just by the Cypriots themselves, but also by the United Nations peacekeeping force in Nicosia, and the British armed forces stationed at the Sovereign Base of Akrotiri.

Before the 1974 invasion, Famagusta (now Magusa) and Kyrenia (Girne) in northern Cyprus, were the major resorts of the island. They are moribund today as few Western tour operators are prepared to risk retaliation from the Greek or Greek Cypriot authorities by including the TRNC in their programmes. Nevertheless, the best beaches of Cyprus are in the Turkish occupied zone, and there is also scope for cultural tourism, as the mountains near Kyrenia contain a number of monasteries and castles dating from the time of the Crusades. Apart from Turkish visitors from the mainland, a small but growing number of British and other West European tourists are attracted to the TRNC, arriving on Turkish Airways flights at Erkan airport via Istanbul or Izmir.

The Republic of Cyprus has a more varied resource base for tourism, supported by a good infrastructure and a considerable stock of accommodation of international standard, although there are relatively few first-class hotels to attract the top end of the market.

We can summarize the main tourism products as:

1 Beach tourism is based on major resort developments at Paphos, Limassol, Larnaca and Ayia Napa. The trend is to go up-market with the provision of golf courses and yacht marinas, although Ayia Napa is likely to appeal mainly to the mass market, particularly young tourists.
2 Conferences and incentive travel are catered for by the larger resort hotels, and a conference centre in Nicosia.
3 Agro-tourism in the rural villages which are being carefully restored to attract visitors to the 'traditional Cyprus'.
4 Eco-tourism, specifically bird-watching in the Akamas National Park, the one remaining undeveloped stretch of coastline in the south-west of Cyprus.
5 Skiing during the winter months in the pine-covered Troodos Mountains. During the summer, resorts such as Platres continue to be visited by Cypriots escaping the intense summer heat of the plains around Nicosia. There are a number of small country hotels.
6 Business tourism in Limassol and Larnaca (which is being positioned as a hub for air services to the Middle East). Tourism in Nicosia is discouraged by the political situation, but it has nevertheless become an important communications and financial centre for a large part of the Middle East.
7 Cultural tourism based on the heritage of Cyprus includes Ancient Greek theatres at Kourion (now used for music festivals) and Amathus, Byzantine monasteries, Crusader castles, and Islamic monuments from the Ottoman Empire.
8 Cruises to the Greek Islands, Israel and Egypt from the port of Limassol.

Summary

Greece has a long tradition of tourism, while Malta and Cyprus are comparative latecomers to the industry. All three countries have benefited from their proximity to the tourist-generating countries and the demand for 'sun, sand and sea' holidays, but large-scale tourism had to await the introduction of air-inclusive tours in the 1960s. Outbound and domestic tourism are much less significant than incoming tourism.

The primary resources are the attractive island and coastal environments, while the Mediterranean climate is ideal for recreational tourism. The islands in particular have a rich cultural heritage, blending West European and Middle Eastern influences; however, cultural tourism takes second place to beach holidays. Cultural attractions include well-preserved archaeological sites, religious buildings, castles and festivals. Malta, Greece and Cyprus have a long maritime history, and as a result their people are service orientated and used to dealing with foreign visitors. The tourism sector is well developed, and characterized by small family enterprises so that the benefits of tourism are spread widely through the economy.

One of the main problems facing tourism is a pronounced summer peak in demand, especially in Greece. Attempts to develop winter tourism have met with little success, except in Cyprus. The domination of the industry by foreign tour operators makes it difficult for local entrepreneurs to respond with new quality products as the markets are price sensitive. After a long period of neglect, there is a growing awareness by the authorities in each country of the need to protect the coastal environment and the cultural heritage from the impacts of mass tourism.

Case study

A SWOT analysis of Greek tourism

Introduction

There is no doubt that Greece is one of the leading destinations in the world, and has a long pedigree in the tourism sector based upon its unique heritage, natural resources and unparalleled hospitality since ancient times. At the same time, however, the country is also suffering from a range of factors relating to tourism which may act to prevent the Greek tourism sector fulfilling its true potential and thus contributing more fully to national welfare. In particular these issues focus upon the country's lack of co-ordination, poor planning and thus an inability to deliver the type and quality of tourism products that will be demanded in the next millennium. This case study provides a strengths, weaknesses, opportunities and threats analysis of Greek tourism in order to demonstrate these issues.

Strengths

As noted above, Greece has unparalleled tourism resources and a tradition of hospitality. In addition it has:

- a long involvement in tourism
- excellent heritage, natural and cultural products
- a flexible private sector able to design and deliver tourism products tailored to customers' needs
- a high level of entrepreneurial involvement in tourism with strong labour loyalty and low labour turnover, partly due to the many family-run enterprises
- a broad tourism sector with the ability to support a wide range of tourism products and activities
- the strong local flavour of Greek hospitality and products.

Weaknesses

However, Greece does suffer from a number of weaknesses inherent in a traditional tourism sector with a long pedigree:

- amateur tourism enterprises in terms of strategy, finance and marketing; in addition these enterprises are not reinvesting in their businesses
- domination by small enterprises run by families with little formal training in tourism; this leads to poor levels of management and marketing in the creation and delivery of tourism products
- domination by foreign tour operators who pay low prices for services and products
- inconsistent and uncoordinated political intervention by government based upon emotional and subjective judgements
- lack of visibility in global distribution systems which leads to both overdependence on tour operators to supply the Greek market, and also to an overall reduction in the arrival of independent, higher spending tourists
- infrastructure and tourism plant of poor quality, which fails to satisfy higher spending and emergent market sectors and, therefore, handicaps attempts to diversify markets; lack of co-ordinated tourism planning
- inadequate levels of education/training in tourism
- poor levels of information technology understanding
- seasonality, particularly for coastal tourism
- the peripheral coastal areas and islands have to import many of their goods to supply tourism
- poor levels of quality assurance and regulation of the tourism sector
- lack of information and interpretation of the cultural product for the visitor
- inadequate research in the tourism sector.

Opportunities

Fortunately, it is possible to identify a range of real opportunities which could allow Greece to overcome these weaknesses:

- European Union support for Greek tourism, particularly in terms of cultural products, environmental improvements, information technology and aid to small businesses; infrastructure will also benefit from European assistance
- growth of demand for Greece combined with trends in demand that will support the Greek cultural and environmental product
- emergence of a new breed of tourism enterprise utilising contemporary management approaches,

run by professionals and setting a benchmark for future operations; in part this has been caused by consolidation of companies in the domestic sector

- new organizational focus on quality by agencies such as the Association of Greek Tourism Enterprises
- emergence of co-operation at regional and local levels to co-ordinate tourism
- increasing penetration of the use of the Internet and other information technology in the operation and marketing of tourism enterprises
- emergence of a new professional breed of human resources in the sector as a result of formal tourism education both in Greece and overseas, which will allow Greece to capitalize upon good practice in the tourism sector globally.

Threats

But Greece must be vigilant if it is to counter a range of threats to its tourism sector:

- concentration of tourism initiatives into larger companies through globalization, which could marginalize smaller enterprises in the distribution channel
- environmental degradation of the Greek product, through poor environmental management, leading to reduced demand
- oversupply in the tourism sector is increasing, leading to price competition
- overdependence upon traditional beach products
- the Single European Market opening up Greek enterprises to takeovers from larger European firms
- low-priced exotic long-haul products in the inclusive tour market
- geographical proximity to regions where war and terrorism may impact upon demand (Balkans, Middle East).

The way forward

Buhalis (1998) sums up the implications of these issues:

> As a result, Greece fails to attract the desired *high quality, high expenditure* tourists as it is increasingly unable to satisfy their requirements. The deterioration of the tourism product and the image leads to a lower willingness to pay by consumers which consequently, leads to a further drop in quality, as the industry attempts to attract customers with lower prices.

Clearly the issues identified above demonstrate the need to closely link tourism products with demand, and in particular to safeguard the unique environmen-tal and cultural assets which form the basis of the tourism sector in Greece. What is needed is a co-ordinated public/private sector strategy that addresses these problems and recognizes that the tourism marketplace is changing. This approach would allow the Greek tourism sector to take advantage of its unique environmental and cultural resources, as well as its unparalleled heritage.

This case study is based upon the work of Dimitrios Buhalis. See Buhalis (1998).

Case study

Rhodes

Introduction

Far from the coast of mainland Greece and close to the Turkish coastline lies the chain of islands known as the Dodecanese. Of these islands, the largest one is Rhodes, which has become an important tourism destination with its attractions of beaches and the heritage left by successive occupations. The island's Mediterranean climate and landscapes have led to major resort developments in the north of the island where the beaches offer a range of water-sports. The island's history, however, provides a wealth of unique attractions. Rhodes' strategic position led to it becoming a major commercial centre from the fifth to the third centuries BC. Later the island became part of the Roman and Byzantine empires. By the fourteenth century AD the Knights of St John were established in Rhodes, leaving a rich legacy of buildings. In the ensuing centuries Rhodes was part of both the Ottoman and Italian empires before returning to Greece in 1948.

Demand

International tourism demand for Rhodes grew slowly following the Second World War. Although Rhodes was always part of the geographical entity known as Greece, it did not become part of the modern Greek state until 1948. Domestic tourism before then would have been from Italy, rather than Greece. In the late 1950s, international tourism grew to equal and overtake domestic tourism, partly helped by the number of cruise passengers visiting the island. In this postwar period a large number of US service personnel visited the island. However, over recent decades, the number of American visitors has reduced and the island's market has become dependent upon northern Europe, particularly Germany, the UK and Scandinavia. In the 1970s, growth of international tourism to Rhodes was rapid, surpassing that of mainland Greece and reaching a total of over 500 000 visitors by 1980. Rhodes, in common with many Mediterranean destinations, saw the arrival of mass tourism and a doubling of arrivals over the decade, leaving domestic demand trailing with only a 10 per cent share of arrivals to Rhodes. The growth rate stabilized in the subsequent two decades, although demand for the island proved to be vulnerable to external events such as the Gulf War and recessions in the generating countries. Length of stay has remained stable at between nine and ten days, with international visitors staying on average twice as long as domestic visitors. Demand for tourism to Rhodes is seasonal, with the bulk of arrivals by air between April and September.

Attractions

Rhodes has a combination of both natural and heritage-based attractions, as well as a number of cultural events, sound and light shows and festivals.

Rhodes Town

The old town retains its medieval walls built by the Knights of St John, and the visitor is confronted by a maze of streets and alleyways. It opens onto the harbour where two bronze statues of deer stand, probably in the same area as the Colossus of Rhodes, one of the original 'seven wonders' of the world but destroyed by an earthquake many centuries ago. Throughout the town is the architectural heritage left by the Knights of St John – such as the Knights' Hospital and the Knights' Castle. Close to the town are the remains of the ancient city including an acropolis and stadium, with many artefacts in the town's museums.

East Coast

The main touring circuit is down the east coast to Lindos, a picturesque small town built under the hill of an ancient acropolis. Lindos retains the traditional architecture and many of the houses are preserved. En-route to Lindos from Rhodes Town, the coastline has a number of resorts including Kalithea, Faliraki and new developments south of Lindos. Other attractions include the Prassonissi peninsula on the southern tip of the island.

West Coast

South-west of Rhodes Town lie major hotel developments stretching to Ialissos. Along the coast, attractions include the ancient sites at Ialissos, Polias Athena and the ruins of ancient Kamiros, while the butterfly valley of Petaloudes is an important natural attraction.

Inland

Parts of Rhodes are military zones as the island lies close to the Turkish coastline. Elsewhere there are mountain villages such as Koskinou and Afandou, the monastery at Profitas Ilias, the pine-shaded 'seven springs' and the castles as at Katavia.

Accommodation

In the early days of tourism accommodation was concentrated in Rhodes Town, but over time developers focused the accommodation initially on to the north-west coast and then the north-east coast of the island and in Rhodes Town itself. Recent developments have seen accommodation developments south of Lindos between Pefkos and Genadi. By the late 1990s, Rhodes had almost 400 establishments with 50 000 bedspaces, and two campsites, representing around 10 per cent of the total bed stock for Greece and nearly three-quarters of the bed stock for the Dodecanese. In addition, there are a large number of unofficial bedspaces and rented rooms with local inhabitants that could total as many as 25 000 bedspaces. In Lindos almost all of the accommodation comprises rented rooms with local families.

Transport

Rhodes International Airport is 16 kilometres from Rhodes Town in the north-west of the island. There is international access on scheduled services via Athens, or direct charter flights for the generating markets. For domestic services Rhodes has a series of flights linking it to the other islands and to the mainland. Rhodes is also accessible by sea from the mainland port of Piraeus, and there are both hydrofoil and ferry services to the other islands. Ferries also operate from Rhodes to Crete, Cyprus and Israel. The road network is well developed allowing the development of touring circuits into the Ataviros mountains, along the coasts and to the major historic sites such as Lindos and Kamiros.

Issues

It is clear that the sustainable future of tourism on Rhodes will depend upon the island's ability to diversify its markets to reduce dependence on package tourists. This should allow a reduction of seasonality and also improve the earnings from tourism. This approach will demand that the island carefully analyses the attractions that draw visitors and develop appropriate support services:

1 Rhodes has a unique heritage of historic sites and buildings that need to be carefully developed and sensitively interpreted and managed. In addition there is a need for the sensitive conservation of the island's culture, heritage, natural history and cuisine.

2 In terms of support services there is also an issue of previous poor planning, particularly of coastal accommodation. Some hotels claim private beaches and there has been a general lack of any overall development plan. At the same time, developments have taken advantage of government investment incentives that have encouraged hotel building, but have failed to place any planning restrictions upon the developments. There is a clear need for quality accommodation provision at all levels.

(*Source*: Richter Papaconstantinou, 1992)

Eastern Europe and the CIS

LEARNING OBJECTIVES

After reading this chapter, you should be able to:

1 Describe the major physical features and climates of the region and understand their significance for tourism.
2 Understand the role of communism in promoting social and economic change in Eastern Europe and the former Soviet Union.
3 Be aware of the possible consequences of the demise of communism as a system of government on the organization of tourism and on tourist flows.
4 Recognize the importance and social character of domestic tourism in these countries.
5 Understand that outbound tourism has been mainly directed toward other destinations within the region, but that with the collapse of communism travellers are venturing further afield.
6 Appreciate the role of inbound tourism in boosting national economies.
7 Recognize the problem of pollution in many areas due to reliance on outdated heavy industry.
8 Appreciate that, with the collapse of the communist system, the cultural differences between the various countries are now more important than the similarities.
9 Demonstrate a knowledge of the tourist regions, resorts, business centres and tourist attractions of Eastern Europe and the CIS.

Introduction

Eastern Europe is the name given to the great tract of land, over 1 million square kilometres in area, extending from the Baltic to the Black Sea. It has acquired a special identity mainly for political reasons since 1945, but its historical background puts it definitely in the mainstream of European culture. Russia, on the other hand, includes vast Asian territories and most of the former USSR lies outside Europe. In such an extensive region there is great scenic and climatic variety. However, it is generally the case that, except in a few favoured coastal areas, the climate is definitely continental, with much colder winters than are experienced in the same latitudes in Western Europe.

Between 1945 and 1989 the countries of Eastern Europe could be said to form a political and economic region sharply differentiated from those on the western side of the 'Iron Curtain'. With the exception of Albania and the former Yugoslavia, these countries were closely associated with the Soviet Union (USSR). However, this impression of unity was, to a large extent, imposed by the Soviet Union following the Second World War and concealed the deep-seated differences between the many and varied ethnic groups which make up the population of the region. In the long historical perspective, the countries of Eastern Europe had found their progress towards nationhood, stability and economic prosperity retarded by their location in the path of invading armies, many originating in the steppes of Central Asia. Most countries had substantial ethnic minorities at variance with the majority culture, and all had experienced periods of foreign rule, forming part of various empires with their centres outside the region. The Ottoman Empire, based in Istanbul, imposed its cultural stamp on the countries of the Balkan Peninsula. These came to be less advanced in their economic and social development than the lands to the west of the Dinaric Alps and the Carpathians, which fell under the sway of the Habsburg Empire based in Vienna, or even those of the Russian Empire to the north-east. Thus a case can be made for dividing 'Eastern Europe' and the former Soviet Union into three subregions:

1 The Czech Republic, Slovakia, Hungary, Poland and the Baltic States are the most advanced economically and have long had a strong cultural orientation towards the West, and the same is true of Slovenia and Croatia in the former Yugoslavia.
2 The countries of the Balkan Peninsula where the influence of the Greek Orthodox Church and Islam have been dominant in the past, namely Romania, Bulgaria, Albania, Serbia and the other republics of the former Yugoslavia.
3 The third group extends well beyond Europe to the Pacific Ocean in northern Asia – this includes Russia and the other countries of the former USSR.

Nevertheless, the adoption of communism as the political and economic model, first by Russia after 1917 and then by the countries of Eastern Europe after 1945, has had a profound effect on tourism in the region. Communism, which entails the state ownership of the means of production and distribution, influenced both the nature of the demand for tourism and recreation and the type of facilities that were on offer. Governments in the so-called 'socialist' or 'people's republics' had virtual monopoly control over all aspects of tourism from strategic planning to owning and managing accommodation. Public institutions were closely involved in 'social tourism' or 'trade union tourism' by subsidizing workers' holidays and providing tourist facilities. The type of holidays on offer differed fundamentally from commercial mass tourism as it developed in the West. Generally, the role of the private sector was limited to very small enterprises, and advertising scarcely existed.

Some East European countries had well-developed tourist industries before 1939, but, with the notable exception of Czechoslovakia, the majority of the population were too poor to afford holidays. Following the communist takeover, the luxury hotels in spas, seaside resorts, and cities were nationalized and put to other uses. Concern for leisure and tourism revived in the 1960s when the economic restructuring was well under way, and considerations of housing, education and health care were less pressing. The rights of all citizens to recreational opportunities had been recognized in the constitutions drawn up by the new republics. Pressure for longer holidays and two-day weekends coincided with the growing move from the rural areas to the industrial cities. Demand also grew for the introduction of leisure goods, including cars,

although long waiting lists meant that ownership levels remained at only a fraction of those in the West. Domestic holidays were customarily spent at the seaside or in spas, where rather spartan accommodation was provided, often in the form of holiday villages or workers' sanatoria, provided by the government-controlled trade unions. However, the *nomenklatura* – the Communist Party élite and other favoured groups – had access to more luxurious facilities, including, in some cases, private beaches and hunting reserves. In the cities, the government provided generous subsidies to the arts and cultural attractions that to some extent compensated for the restrictions and consumer shortages that made everyday life drab for most citizens. The rich folklore of the various ethnic groups was also encouraged as a tourist attraction.

Demand for international tourism grew slowly, despite currency and visa restrictions. Inevitably, most outbound travel was to other socialist countries and its volume was regulated by bilateral agreements between the governments of the region. Inbound tourism from the West was initially viewed with suspicion, but in most countries was actively sought from the 1960s, as it earned hard currency to purchase much needed imports from outside the Council for Mutual Economic Assistance (Comecon) trading bloc. Indeed, Western visitors had privileges denied to most of the population, as they could buy goods from so-called 'dollar shops', which accepted only hard currencies. Giving preference to group travel, which could be carefully supervised, was one way of ensuring favourable publicity for 'socialist achievements'. However, low standards of service, outdated infrastructure and bureaucratic controls inhibited the growth of international tourism, while the simple lack of bed-spaces held back domestic tourism.

The dramatic political changes which have taken place in Eastern Europe and the former Soviet Union since 1989 are undoubtedly having a profound effect, as yet not fully determined, on the pattern of tourism development. The state tourist organizations, which were, in effect, tour operators and travel agencies, have lost their monopoly position. Changes have been most rapid in those countries such as the Czech Republic, Poland and Hungary, which had a flourishing tourism industry before 1939 and where there is a strong entrepreneurial tradition. Many pensions and small family-run hotels have appeared, while joint ventures with Western hotel consortia are increasingly sought to increase the stock of accommodation for business travellers. (For a more in-depth analysis see the case study at the end of this chapter.)

On the other hand, the switch to a market economy has had a damaging effect on social tourism. It is likely that domestic tourists will be priced out of international hotels, where previously they had been charged very preferential rates, as tariffs reflect what the market will bear. The introduction of democracy has given the peoples of Eastern Europe and the former Soviet Union much greater freedom to travel to the West, but low wages, inflation and continuing restrictions on the purchase of hard currency are major constraints on outbound travel.

Nevertheless, East Europeans and Russians are now frequent visitors to the Mediterranean coastal resorts and the ski slopes of the French Alps. The Poles and Czechs arrive by car, coach or charter flights and use budget self-catering accommodation. Most of the Russian tourists on the other hand, are high-spending members of the former *nomenklatura* or new business class.

The surge in car ownership has necessitated massive investment in road improvement schemes to meet West European standards, while public transport has been relatively neglected. However, the economies of most East European countries are still suffering from the impact of high energy costs brought about by the loss of cheap Russian petroleum with the collapse of Comecon. The economic crisis makes governments less able to deal effectively with the region's numerous environmental problems, such as those caused by the smokestack industries of Silesia and Transylvania. There is also concern over nuclear power plants in Bulgaria and elsewhere, highlighted by the 1986 Chernobyl disaster in the Ukraine. Unless these problems can be addressed, the recent rapid growth in popularity of some of the East European destinations with Western tourists will not be sustained.

Tourism resources of Eastern Europe

Eastern Europe is rich in tourism resources, although these are of a kind more likely to attract visitors with cultural or special interests than the mass market. Beach tourism is well established on the Adriatic, Black Sea and Baltic coasts. The mountain ranges, such as the Carpathians, provide opportunities for winter sports, although facilities rarely attain the standard of the ski resorts of the Alps. With the growing interest in health tourism, the numerous spas of Eastern Europe are due for a revival. All the countries of the region have designated national parks or reserves, but considerable land-use conflicts need to be resolved if the wildlife resources are to be adequately protected. The region's great rivers offer scope for recreational tourism, especially the Danube. However, the main attraction of most countries is likely to be the heritage of past cultures, exemplified in historic cities such as Dubrovnik and Krakow, and the colourful peasant folklore of the rural areas. Cities and countryside alike reflect the strong national differences to be found within Eastern Europe.

We will now look at the resources and the type of development that has taken place in each of the countries of the region, starting with the Czech Republic, Slovakia and Hungary – countries that consider themselves to be part of Central, rather than Eastern, Europe, and where German is the second language.

The Czech Republic

In January 1993 the Federal Republic of Czechoslovakia was dissolved with the Czech Republic and Slovakia electing to go their separate ways. The Czechs of Bohemia and Moravia differ from the Slovaks not only in language but also in cultural traditions. Before Czechoslovakia was established in 1918 the Czech lands were part of the Austrian Empire, whereas Hungary had for many centuries ruled Slovakia. The Czech Republic is not only much larger than Slovakia, with twice the population, but is also disproportionately wealthier. Since the 'Velvet Revolution' of 1989 it has attracted considerable foreign investment as a result of its drive to a free market economy, and is in the forefront of those countries seeking membership of the EU.

Although the Czech Ministry of Economics does not have a strong tourism policy, the Czech Republic has a well-established tourism industry and has long been famous for its therapeutic springs and spas. Karlovy Vary (Carlsbad) and Marianske Lazne (Marienbad) in Bohemia were the favourite meeting places for the statesmen and the wealthy of Europe in the early 1900s. Under communism the luxury hotels were taken over by labour unions and fell into neglect, but since 1990 there has been something of a revival. Spearheaded by Cedok, the former state tourism organization and now the largest hotel and travel company, a wide range of products are available to today's foreign visitor, including city breaks, spa treatments, sporting holidays, stays in lake and mountain resorts and touring holidays.

Since the 1989 revolution, tourist numbers have greatly increased, especially from the West and particularly to Prague, the capital of the Czech Republic – over the decade of the 1990s the volume of international tourists has more than doubled to approach 20 million. However, the majority of these were on day excursions, mainly from neighbouring Germany and Austria. The recent economic changes have not benefited all sections of the Czech population, and one of the less acceptable results is the growth of sex tourism on the main highways leading from Prague to the German border.

The country's new found popularity has highlighted the shortage of accommodation, especially the three- and four-star hotels, favoured by Western tour groups, and the need to upgrade standards. Until recently, most of the demand has come from other East European countries where expectations are lower, and this has resulted in a proliferation of low-cost camping sites. The situation should improve as a result of joint ventures by Cedok with Western corporations for the larger hotels and privatization (already well advanced) for the smaller hotels and pensions.

In the sphere of domestic tourism an advanced industrial economy has given most Czechs comparative affluence by East European standards. Sport and an interest in physical fitness and outdoor life had been fostered by the *Sokol* movement even before 1918. This has resulted in a growing demand for a wide range of outdoor recreation activities and for second homes in the countryside.

The Czech Republic offers scenic variety and a physical environment that is generally favourable for tourism. The large number of rivers and small lakes make up to some extent for the lack of a coastline. Forests cover 20 per cent of the country and are particularly extensive in the mountain ranges along the national borders. These forests are managed as a recreational resource, with nature reserves, waymarked trails and areas set aside for hunting – an important earner of foreign currency. Skiing is popular during the winter months, and Cedok is promoting the resorts of Harrachov in the Giant Mountains and Spicak in the Sumava Mountains. Southern Bohemia and Moravia also boast spectacular limestone caves among their natural attractions.

A rich natural and cultural heritage is given a considerable degree of environmental protection, with the establishment of a 400-kilometre long 'green corridor' linking Prague to Vienna, designed for hiking, riding and cycling holidays, or leisurely touring by car. This tourist route includes some of the historic towns of Southern Bohemia – notably Cesky Krumlov, with its unique Baroque theatre – and a number of castles. Cedok has converted some of these to luxury hotels, while others are being restored to their former aristocratic owners after a long period of neglect under communism. Despite these initiatives, the Czech Republic has its share of conservation problems. These include:

- serious pollution from smokestack industries using lignite, in North Bohemia and North Moravia–Silesia
- lack of government funding often means that historic buildings continue to fall into disrepair, while art treasures illegally acquired from the country's churches, find their way on to the international market.

Of the cities of the Czech republic, only Prague has achieved worldwide significance as a tourist centre (see case study at the end of this chapter). The others are mainly important as centres for business travel, namely:

- Plzen (Pilsen) and Ceske Budejovice (Budweis) are famous for their brewing industries
- Brno, the capital of Moravia is noted for its engineering industries, and is an important venue for trade fairs.

Slovakia (The Slovak Republic)

Slovakia has made less progress with free market reforms than the Czech Republic. Before the Second World War, it had a predominantly agrarian economy, and it is now suffering from the effects of overdependence on the less competitive heavy industries introduced under communism.

Slovakia is a country with great tourism potential, and has benefited from the share-out of federal assets following its 'divorce settlement' with the Czech Republic. Although it now has both its own national airline and national tourist organization – created from the old Cedok agency and renamed the Slovak Agency for Tourism (SATUR) – the CSA airline continues to play an important role in promoting the country's attractions.

The main appeal of Slovakia for foreign visitors lies in its beautiful mountain scenery rather than the attractions of the capital, Bratislava. Unlike the Czech Republic this is a wine rather than beer-drinking nation, with some cultural similarities to neighbouring Hungary; for example, gypsy folk music is an important part of the entertainment on offer to foreign tourists in both countries. Slovaks take even greater pride in their rural peasant traditions than the Czechs, and a considerable variety of village architecture has been preserved. Other heritage attractions include medieval mining towns, the castles of the former Hungarian nobility and, in eastern Slovakia, Orthodox churches show the influence of the Ukraine.

However, tourism is mainly focused on the following areas:

1 The High Tatras on the border with Poland, which contain the highest peaks of the Carpathians. Apart from the superb lake and mountain scenery, the area can provide some of the best skiing to be found in Eastern Europe.
2 The karst limestone region of eastern Slovakia, which boasts the spectacular Dobsina ice cave, waterfalls and rock formations.
3 The spas of western Slovakia, the most important being Piestany, which attracts large numbers of wealthy Arab and German tourists.
4 Bratislava and southern Slovakia, which forms part of the Danube Plain. Bratislava is known primarily as a modern industrial city and its cultural attractions have been overshadowed by those of Prague. It is now a major port, thanks to the controversial power project on the Danube at Gabcikovo which, in taming the river, also threatens to destroy the wetland environment of the area.

Hungary

Hungary is a small landlocked country in the centre of Europe, marked off from its neighbours by the complex Magyar language, history and spicy cuisine. The bulk of the country consists of a great plain in the middle of the Carpathian Basin, crossed by the rivers Danube and Tisza; only in the north and west are there highlands rising to, at most, 900 metres. Winters are cold and cloudy, but summers approach Mediterranean conditions in heat and sunshine.

Tourism has become an important part of the economy, due partly to the successful marketing of Hungary's two main attractions, namely the capital Budapest and Lake

Balaton; together these account for the majority of foreign visitors. From the 1960s, Western tourists were encouraged by the removal of restrictions, and a limited amount of foreign investment in hotels was permitted by the Kadar regime. During the 1980s the number of visitors from the West almost trebled, whereas those from other socialist countries actually declined. This was largely due to the low value of the Hungarian forint relative to Western currencies, whereas it was overvalued compared to the non-convertible currencies of the Soviet bloc. Hungary's success in attracting international tourists continued in the 1990s and volumes approached 20 million by the end of the decade.

The majority of tourists arrive by car and are short-stay, particularly the Austrians, who cross the border on shopping forays to towns such as Sopron and Szombathely. The gateway for air travellers is Budapest's Terihegy airport, while large numbers of excursionists use the hydrofoil service on the Danube from Vienna. A high proportion of the accommodation stock is in camp sites or private homes. There is a shortage of hotels, especially in Budapest, and this has held back the development of tourism and reflects the undercapitalization of the industry. Before 1989 the state-owned Ibusz company handled both inbound and outbound tourism, but it has since been reorganized as part of the new government's policy of economic liberalization, and faces competition from a multiplicity of independent travel agencies.

Even before the parliamentary elections that introduced democracy to Hungary, its citizens were freer than those of most socialist countries to travel to the West. Although visa and currency restrictions have been relaxed, the severe economic crisis facing the country means that relatively few Hungarians can afford to travel abroad. Most travel to the former socialist countries and to neighbouring Austria. Although annual holiday entitlement averages twenty days, effective demand for domestic tourism is reduced by the widespread practice of 'moonlighting' at several jobs to make ends meet.

Hungary's tourism resources include:

1 Numerous spas based on the thermal springs that underlie the Carpathian Basin. These not only provide rest and recuperation for Hungarian workers, but also attract much needed hard currency from long-stay Western visitors.
2 Excellent facilities for activity holidays, such as horse-riding, cycling and water sports.
3 Cultural attractions appealing more to the older tourist. These include the traditional peasant dances and crafts – notably embroidery – of the villages of the Great Hungarian Plain, but the country's art treasures are mainly found in the capital.
4 Budapest – Budapest is one of Europe's most attractive capitals. Formed from what were two separate cities – Buda, picturesquely situated on the hills above the Danube, and Pest, the commercial centre on the river's left bank – it contains many reminders of its pre-1918 role as the joint capital of the Austro-Hungarian Empire. These include:
  (a) The magnificent neo-Gothic Parliament Building in Pest and the Fisherman's Bastion in Buda are the city's two major landmarks.
  (b) The Hungarian State Opera is a reminder that Budapest vies with Vienna as a centre of art and music.
  (c) The shopping boulevards, café society and vibrant nightlife, which even in the Soviet era, earned it the title of 'Paris of the East'.
  (d) Spa establishments such as the Hotel Gellert, and the Szechenyi Baths, with year-round open-air bathing.
  (e) Business opportunities in the new climate of economic liberalism. Since 1990, Budapest has attracted an international business community and the city is growing in importance as a conference venue.

Budapest is close to the other main tourist areas of Hungary, namely:

1 The Danube Bend where the great river changes its course between mountain ranges is a popular excursion zone. It contains some of Hungary's most historic towns including Szentendre, with its *skansen* or museum of Hungarian rural life.
2 Lake Balaton is one of Europe's largest at 77 kilometres in length, but averaging only 3 metres in depth. Its shores are fringed by beaches, modern hotels and campsites, while a number of areas have been designated as nature reserves. Demand for accommodation in summer frequently exceeds supply and the threat of pollution from intensive agriculture has to be constantly monitored.
3 Heviz is the most well known of a number of spas in the vicinity of Lake Balaton, due to its unique thermal lake.
4 The Great Hungarian Plain, where the *pusztas* or vast, treeless pasturelands east of the Danube, provide Hungary with many of its characteristic landscapes and traditions, such as the *csikos* (cattle herders), whose displays of horsemanship are a tourist attraction. Many of the *csardas* (country inns) feature the traditional folk music and dances that inspired Liszt and other Hungarian composers. In the Hortobagy National Park near Debrecen aspects of the traditional culture and the steppe ecosystem have been carefully preserved.

Poland

Poland is one of the largest countries of Europe, with a population of almost 40 million. Its exposed situation on the North European Plain between Germany and Russia has resulted in a history of invasion, fluctuating boundaries, and periods of foreign domination. The Roman Catholic Church has long been identified with Polish nationhood and resistance, particularly to the communist regime. Largely as a result, less than 20 per cent of Poland's farms were collectivised after 1945. At the same time, massive industrialization brought about the Solidarity Trade Union movement that did so much to inspire opposition to communism during the 1980s. In some respects, Poland was better placed than most East European countries to make the transition to a market economy after 1989.

Until the early 1990s, tourism played only a minor role in the Polish economy. The majority of visitors originated from the former socialist countries and tended to be short-stay. This market has declined in importance now that more appealing destinations are available to the Russians, Czechs and East Germans. However, to a greater extent than other East European countries, Poland can attract a large ethnic market in North America, the UK and other countries of Western Europe. Most of the tourism from these countries has been for VFR or business purposes, but increasing numbers are visiting Poland on inclusive tours or on tailor-made holiday arrangements, primarily for cultural reasons. As a result, inbound tourism volumes of between 19 and 20 million contributed about US$9 billion annually to the Polish economy during the late 1990s. The recovery of Poland from the economic crisis of the early part of the decade has also led to considerable growth in domestic and, to a lesser extent, outbound tourism.

A much greater choice of accommodation is now available to Polish holidaymakers than was the case in the past. Tourism's higher profile has led to a change in government policy, with the State Sport and Tourism Administrations' responsibilities in marketing being taken over by the new Tourism Development Agency in 1999. This organization is staffed by tourism industry professionals and is funded by the government and the regional administrations. It aims to stimulate further investment and growth in the sector, in line with the government's National Development Strategy, and is involved in tourism training initiatives with West European countries. Orbis, the national tourism organization, has been privatized, although it remains one of Poland's major tour operators and hotel companies.

The main tourist areas of Poland are situated near its southern and northern borders, and a fair distance from Warsaw, the capital and gateway for air travellers. The tourist areas include:

1 *The Baltic Coast* is by far the most popular area accounting for one-third of all holiday overnights. On offer are 500 kilometres of sandy beaches and coastal lagoons, backed by pine forests, but the climate is often cloudy and windy, with temperatures rarely getting much above 20°C. From Miedzyzdroje at the mouth of the Oder to Hel and the Amber coast along the Gulf of Gdansk, a string of resorts attract Swedish as well as domestic holidaymakers. Sopot is a popular and relatively sophisticated resort adjoining the historic seaport of Gdansk (Danzig). Two of Poland's most important recreational resources lie a short distance inland from the Baltic coast, namely:

(a) The lake country of Pomorze (Pomerania) which includes the medieval fortress of Malbork (Marienburg) built by the Teutonic Knights, a reminder of the former German domination of this region.

(b) The Mazurian Lake District, an area of forests, lakes and low hills of glacial drift, which is popular for sailing, canoeing and camping.

2 *Southern Poland* The border country of southern Poland offers more interesting scenery and facilities for winter sports. To the west lie the Sudeten Mountains, adjoining Bohemia, where a number of spas have long been established. Further east, the Carpathian Mountains, culminating in the Tatry and Beskid ranges adjoining Slovakia, rise to over 2000 metres and account for one-fifth of all holiday overnights in Poland. Zakopane in the Tatry Mountains is a well-developed resort with a year-round season. In addition to skiing, organized walking tours and rafting through the gorge of the Dunajec River are available. Tourism has greatly benefited the economy of this formerly remote and poverty-stricken mountain region.

3 *Central and western Poland* The flatlands of central and western Poland are scenically less attractive, but the countryside does provide opportunities for fishing and riding holidays, often based on the manor houses of the former Polish aristocracy. On the eastern border with Belarus the Bialowieza National Park provides a refuge for rare animals such as the European bison.

4 *Cultural attractions* Poland's cultural attractions are mainly to be found in the cities, although most of these suffered wholesale destruction in the Second World War. The historic cores have generally been meticulously restored, and provide a welcome contrast to the bleak industrial suburbs. The most important cities from the viewpoint of tourism are Warsaw and Krakow, whereas others such as Poznan and Wroclaw are primarily business centres.

5 *Warsaw* is one of the world's most impressive examples of urban reconstruction. The old city was painstakingly rebuilt *as it was* in Baroque style, on the basis of old paintings, photographs and plans, as hardly a building was left standing at the close of the Second World War. As a short-break destination, the Polish capital is popular with art and music lovers – especially Chopin enthusiasts. One of Warsaw's most impressive – if not best loved – landmarks is the Palace of Culture and Science built during the Stalinist era.

6 *Krakow* Warsaw is surpassed as a tourist centre by Krakow, Poland's former royal capital and religious centre, which has been designated as a World Heritage Site and European City of Culture. The city, which largely

escaped wartime destruction, has retained its medieval atmosphere, and has attracted worldwide interest due to its association with Pope John Paul II. The major attractions include the impressive Market Square, the Cloth Hall and Wawel Castle. Unfortunately, the restoration programme has difficulty in keeping pace with the ravages of pollution from the steelworks at Nowa Huta nearby. Krakow is conveniently near the ski resorts and scenic attractions of the Carpathian Mountains. In addition, a tour based on the city might include:

(a) The salt mines of Wielisza, which have been worked for thousands of years.
(b) The shrine of the Black Madonna at Czestochowa, which is Poland's most important pilgrimage centre.
(c) The former concentration camp at Oswiecim (better known by its German name of Auschwitz) – one of many established in Poland during the Nazi occupation. It is regarded by the Jewish community as the main site of the Holocaust and as a place of national martyrdom by the Poles.

The Baltic States

Like most of Poland, the three small countries of Lithuania, Latvia, and Estonia on the eastern shore of the Baltic Sea formed part of the Russian Empire from the eighteenth century to 1918. Between the two world wars they enjoyed a brief period of independence before being annexed by the Soviet Union in 1940. With a combined population of only 8 million, the Baltic States have much closer cultural ties with Scandinavia and Germany than with Russia, and since regaining their independence in 1991 they have sought economic association with those countries and see tourism as an important source of foreign currency. In 1993, all three states agreed to co-operate in the sphere of tourism policy and promotion.

The scenery is low-key, the highest point reaching only 300 metres above sea level, but is made attractive by the combination of pastureland, forest and myriad lakes. The sandy beaches of the Baltic have been adversely affected by pollution in this shallow, largely enclosed tideless sea, into which flow the industrial wastes of eastern Germany, Poland and Russia.

During the period of Soviet rule the coastal resorts were popular with Russian tourists, and Intourist developed some of its best hotels in the area. The Baltic States are now attempting to attract Western tourists, and direct flights link the capitals Vilnius, Riga and Tallinn with cities in Western Europe. Outbound tourism from the states has increased dramatically since 1990 and Estonia has benefited from improved ferry services to Finland. All three countries are noted for their music festivals and folklore, in which national identity was nurtured during the long period of foreign domination.

Lithuania

Lithuania was united with Poland for much of its history and is likewise staunchly Roman Catholic. The impressive 'Hill of Crosses' on the outskirts of Siauliai is the country's most famous religious site. The capital Vilnius (Vilna) is a major cultural centre with many fine Renaissance buildings, and has a famous university. Trakai, with its medieval lakeside fortress was the ancient capital. Lithuania has a much shorter coastline than its neighbours but boasts fine beaches along the Neringa, a 100-kilometre sand-spit separating the Kursia Marios lagoon from the Baltic Sea.

Latvia

In Latvia the former German influence is particularly evident in the seaports of Courland in the western part of the country. The capital, Riga, is the industrial hub of the Baltic States and an important cultural centre. The city's elegant Art Nouveau buildings are a reminder of the period before 1914 when Riga was the leading port of the Russian Empire. Similarly, Jurmala on the Gulf of Riga was then a fashionable resort, but facilities will need upgrading for it to become once more the 'Baltic Riviera'. The Gauja National Park in eastern Latvia is an important area for winter sports.

Estonia

Estonia shows many reminders of Swedish and Danish rule and has close affinities with Finland. The capital, Tallinn, a former Hanseatic port, is one of the best preserved medieval cities of northern Europe. It is also a major yachting centre, stemming from its role in the 1980 Olympic Games. To the west, Saaremaa is the largest of Estonia's many offshore islands. The Lahemaa National Park in the east of the country is noted for its lakes and waterfalls. Estonia would prefer to reduce its dependence on the Finnish day-visitor market – mainly attracted by cheap alcohol – by promoting itself as a cultural destination for British and other West European tourists.

The Balkan countries

Compared to Poland and the Baltic States, the Balkan countries of south-eastern Europe are well endowed with tourism resources. However, they have suffered from a long history of misgovernment that has inhibited economic progress. During the era of Soviet domination, the Black Sea beaches of Romania and Bulgaria were, in some respects, Eastern Europe's equivalent of the Spanish Costas, attracting sun-seeking tourists from the more developed socialist countries of Poland, East Germany and Czechoslovakia.

Romania

Romania is the largest country in the region, with a population of 23 million. The Romanian people regard themselves as different – Latins surrounded by Slavs – but although in language and temperament they are akin to Italians, their religion is Orthodox and the climate is definitely continental rather than Mediterranean. The forested Carpathian Mountains divide the country in a great horseshoe-shaped arc, separating picturesque Transylvania from the broad plains of Wallachia to the south and the rolling plateau of Moldavia to the east. Whereas Wallachia and Moldavia were separate principalities on the fringes of the Ottoman Empire until 1858, Transylvania was part of Hungary until 1918. As a result, Transylvania has substantial Magyar and German minorities who differ in religion as well as language from the Romanians. There are also perhaps 2 million gypsies who form a marginalized group in society (as elsewhere in Eastern Europe) but who play an important role in Romanian folklore.

After the communist takeover in 1947, Romania experienced considerable industrialization and urbanization. Nevertheless, traditional peasant lifestyles persist, despite the attempts by Ceaucescu in the 1980s to create a 'new socialist man' by replacing villages with apartment blocks. Domestic tourism is said to have increased tenfold between 1965 and 1987, although it is probable that much of this was group travel, including youth organizations. Second-home ownership was low by East European standards, and, despite the fact that the country is rich in petroleum, chronic petrol shortages have limited the range of domestic travel to day excursions.

During the 1960s the Romanian government embarked on a major investment programme for the Black Sea coast, creating a number of new holiday resorts. In 1971 a Ministry of Tourism and Sport was established and the state tourism organization, ONT, and its subsidiary, Carpati, set out to increase numbers of visitors from the West as well as from other socialist countries. During the 1970s they were successful in attracting Western tour operators. However, after 1979 the economic situation in Romania deteriorated and the Ceaucescu regime became increasingly repressive. Although Western tourists in their resorts were spared the worst of the shortages, standards of service declined. As a result, tourism receipts fell by 40 per cent between 1981 and 1986. The violent overthrow of Ceaucescu in December 1989 was not followed by economic reforms. Although Romanians are now free to travel abroad, and Western tourists can stay in private homes (forbidden under Ceaucescu), hotel accommodation has to be prebooked and there is a flourishing black market. However, in a bid to improve the situation the Romanian Ministry of Tourism has implemented a 'master plan for tourism', encompassing each of the key elements of Romanian tourism. These mainly focus on two contrasting areas – the Black Sea coast, and the Carpathian Mountains in the north west of the country.

The Black Sea coast

The flat Black Sea coast is scenically the least interesting part of Romania, but with its broad gently shelving beaches and a holiday season lasting from mid-May to September it has become the main destination for foreign holidaymakers and accounts for the majority of all bed-spaces. Mamaia is the largest resort, situated on a sand spit between the sea and an extensive lagoon. Like the tourist complexes of Aurora, Jupiter, Neptune, Venus and Saturn, it offers a variety of accommodation and sports facilities. The older resort of Eforie with its mud-bathing establishments is well known for health tourism. Further north, the Danube Delta is a wetland environment over 4000 square kilometres in extent, teeming with wildlife and now protected as a nature reserve.

The Carpathian Mountains

The spas and mountain resorts of the Carpathians have not received as much investment as those of the Black Sea. Neither as high nor as rugged as the Alps, they form a number of separate massifs, of which the most impressive are the Bucegi and Retezat Mountains, noted for their lakes and glaciated landforms. Exploitation of the region's forest resources has gone hand in hand with tourism, and there are a large number of dispersed mountain chalets to supplement hotels and camp site accommodation in the resorts. Before the Second World War Sinaia attracted Romanian royalty, but nowadays the main resort is Poiana Brasov, purpose-built for winter sports, but also a centre for hiking and adventure holidays. Between the mountain ranges lies the fertile Transylvanian Plateau, where the rural communities preserve much of their traditional culture. The historic towns have a strong German influence in their architecture. The 'Gothic' ambience of towns such as Sibiu and the castle of Bran, in its picturesque mountain setting, are inevitably associated with the Dracula legend.

Moldavia

Moldavia's main tourist attractions are the unique painted monasteries of the Bucovina region; amazingly the exterior frescos have survived since the fifteenth century.

Bucharest

Romania's capital lies in the rather less appealing plains of Wallachia bordering the Danube. The city, with its spacious boulevards, was known before the Second World War as 'the Paris of the East' but it has little to offer the tourist nowadays. This is due to the destruction of many churches during the Ceaucescu era to make way for the dictator's grandiose projects such as the 'House of the Republic'. The Herastrau Village Museum, however, is one of the best of its kind.

Bulgaria

Bulgaria is a small country in the heart of the Balkan Peninsula, which is best known in Western Europe for budget-priced beach and skiing holidays. It does, however, offer a great variety of scenery and is rich in the remains of many civilizations. The country is traversed from east to west by several thickly forested mountain ranges, rising to over 2000 metres, which attract heavy snowfalls in winter. Between the mountains lie fertile valleys enjoying a warm sunny climate which have given Bulgaria its reputation as 'the market garden of Eastern Europe', producing fine tobacco and the famous perfume known as 'attar of roses'. Before the violent break-up of Yugoslavia, the country received a good deal of transit tourism due to its location on the E5 route from Belgrade to Istanbul. Proximity to Turkey in the past was a disadvantage, resulting in Bulgaria being submerged in the Ottoman Empire for several centuries. It regained its independence, with Russian help, in 1878 – a fact commemorated by the elaborate Alexander Nevsky Cathedral in Sofia. Despite the presence of Turkish and Pomak (native Moslem) minorities, the Islamic contribution to the cultural heritage has been neglected. Restoration projects have focused instead on the 'museum towns' such as Veliki Turnovo, which played a major role in the medieval period or in the National Revival leading to independence.

The country was one of Europe's poorest and most underdeveloped before the Second World War, with over 80 per cent of the population employed in agriculture. The development of an industrial economy since the 1950s has greatly improved living standards, while the introduction of the two-day weekend encouraged the ownership of second homes, which are situated mainly around the capital Sofia and on the Black Sea coast. As in other East European countries, spas play an important role, the most popular being Sandanski, Kustendil, Hissarya and Velingrad. However, throughout the 1990s the country has suffered a severe economic crisis, which has depressed the demand for domestic as well as outbound tourism

Bulgaria recognized the importance of tourism as a source of hard currency in the 1960s and concluded agreements with a number of Western tour operators. Balkantourist was the state agency responsible for international tourism, owning most of the large stock of hotel accommodation, particularly on the Black Sea coast. Nevertheless, most Western visitors are on low-budget inclusive packages and the rate of return per individual tourist is small. In addition, many areas need improving if the Bulgarian tourism product is to remain competitive. These improvements include upgrading the facilities at Sofia airport, the road and rail networks, improvement of catering services, and more effective marketing. Since the collapse of the Zhivkov regime in 1989 Bulgaria has moved towards a free-market economy, encouraging joint ventures with Western hotels and banking enterprises, while small businesses have proliferated.

Bulgaria can offer the visitor the Black Sea coast, the mountains and special-interest tourism.

The Black Sea coast

The Black Sea coast of Bulgaria is scenically more varied than that of Romania. It has a long season from May to October, and fine beaches that are ideal for family holidays. Resort development has centred around Varna in the north – Golden Sands, Albena and Drouzhba are the main resorts – and Bourgas in the south, where Sunny Beach is the most popular centre. Most of these resorts offer international entertainment and are rather characterless; however, the holiday village of Dyuni has been developed in a more traditional style.

The mountains

Bulgaria is also a winter-sports destination with major resorts at Borovets and Bansko in the Pirin Mountains, Aleko on Mount Vitosha which caters for large numbers of weekend skiers from nearby Sofia, and Pamporovo in the Rhodope Massif. However, facilities, although improving, are not as sophisticated as those of the Alps, and the Balkans cannot offer the high-altitude skiing favoured by Western tour operators.

Special interest tourism

There is more scope for future development in promoting special-interest holidays. These include spas, wine tours, musical folklore (the country is noted for its fine choirs), archaeology (the Thracian civilization is probably the oldest in Europe) and caving. Bulgaria is also noted for its monasteries, often situated in remote mountain settings where the Orthodox Church preserved the national identity during the centuries of Ottoman rule. The most famous of these are those of Rila to the south of Sofia and Boyana on the outskirts of the capital. For such cultural tourism to be successful, more attention needs to be paid to improving accessibility and visitor-management facilities to a standard appropriate for Western tourists.

The republics of the former Yugoslavia

The pre-1991 Yugoslavia has been described as an experiment to unite many peoples of widely differing languages (including two alphabets), religions and historical backgrounds. It was a federation of six republics – Serbia, Croatia, Slovenia, Bosnia-Herzegovina, Macedonia and Montenegro – and two autonomous regions – Kosovo and Vojvodina. This complex arrangement was made to work largely through the authority of Marshal Tito, who ruled the country from 1945 to 1979. While accepting aid from the West in recognition of his country's role during the Cold War as a buffer against Soviet communism, Tito imposed his own brand of socialism, known as 'workers self-management', and allowed a high degree of local and regional control over tourism development. At the same time, a national system of economic planning tried to even out disparities in wealth between the republics and guaranteed internal markets for their products.

Furthermore, Yugoslavia set out earlier to attract foreign investment and was far more successful than Bulgaria or Romania in attracting package holidaymakers from Western Europe. In 1960 Yugotours was set up to market the country and in 1965 restrictions on the movement of foreign visitors were removed. In the same year the Adriatic Highway was completed with Western aid, permitting the development of resort facilities along the coast from Istria to Montenegro. By 1988 Yugoslavia was attracting 9 million foreign visitors annually, but these were highly concentrated geographically on the Adriatic coast, while the former West Germany accounted for one-third of the total visitors. Although domestic tourism was mainly accommodated in low-cost holiday villages away from the main Adriatic resorts, Yugoslavs were not discouraged from contact with Western tourists at home and had greater freedom than other East Europeans to travel to Western countries.

However, the system of worker's control in practice caused problems in hotel administration and marketing, and did little to encourage private enterprise. The ending of the Cold War also brought about the revival of nationalism and ethnic rivalries, initiated by Serbia. This caused the break-up of the federation, swiftly followed by a series of wars that have lasted throughout most of the 1990s. Needless to say, this has been disastrous for the tourism industries of the former Yugoslavia, although the republics of Croatia and Slovenia have recovered some of their former popularity. As the following sections show, tourism resources are far from evenly distributed throughout the region.

Croatia

In contrast to the other republics, Croatia can offer the visitor a wealth of natural and cultural attractions and a well-established tourism industry. The country is fortunate in occupying some 1500 kilometres of Adriatic coast, including the greater part of the Istrian Peninsula and the scenic, island-studded Dalmatian region. The coast is protected from the cold winters experienced in the capital, Zagreb, by the parallel ranges of the Dinaric Alps, so that it enjoys a typically Mediterranean climate. However, where there are gaps in the mountains, the blustery *Bora* wind can be disruptive in spring and autumn. Croatia accounted for over 80 per cent of tourist nights in registered accommodation in the former Yugoslavia during the late 1980s. With the ending of the war in Bosnia in 1995 the country seemed poised to regain its position as a major holiday destination.

However, the Kosovo crisis of 1999 has set these hopes back and a return to growth will depend very much on a permanent peace settlement in the Balkans.

Tourism has particularly benefited the economy of the Dalmatian islands and stemmed outmigration, which was a problem in the early part of the twentieth century. Some islands – such as Brioni – are protected as national parks, while others – notably Hvar, Korcula and Rab – have been developed as holiday resorts. A network of shipping and hydrofoil services provides access to the mainland, where most of the major resorts are located. Some of these have a long history. For example, Opatija, which has good road and rail links to Central Europe, was a favoured resort for the Austrian and Hungarian élites before the First World War. Most of the development, however, has taken place since the 1960s, much of it in the form of self-contained hotel complexes, as for example, on the Babin Kuk peninsula near the historic city of Dubrovnik. Makarska is Croatia's nearest equivalent to a typical Mediterranean resort, with big hotels and a range of entertainment. The numerous sheltered deep-water harbours have encouraged cruising and sailing, while the clear unpolluted sea is ideal for diving and bathing. A disadvantage for family holidays is the lack of good sandy beaches. Croatia since the 1960s has been more liberal than most Mediterranean destinations in its attitude towards naturism, which continues to be favoured by German holidaymakers.

The coast can offer a rich cultural heritage, including:

1 Important Roman remains, such as the arena at Pula, and the impressive palace of the Emperor Diocletian at Split.
2 The architecture of the coastal towns and islands, showing the influence of Venice, which was a major power hereabouts in medieval times.
3 Dubrovnik, an almost perfect example of a medieval seaport, complete with city walls and pedestrianized streets and squares. Most of the buildings damaged by the Serbian bombardment of 1991–2 have been meticulously restored while the international summer festival continues to be a major attraction.

The interior of Croatia consists of the plains of Slavonia – similar to those of neighbouring Hungary – to the east, and mountains in the west. These contain some of the best examples of karst limestone scenery in Europe, culminating in the lakes and waterfalls of Plitvice National Park. The capital, Zagreb is an attractive historic city as well as being an important business centre, hosting international trade fairs and sports events.

Slovenia

With a small area of 20 000 square kilometres and a population of only 2 million, Slovenia has nevertheless a broad tourism appeal. The country was economically advanced compared to most of the former Yugoslavia, and its state carrier, Adria Airways, has energetically promoted business travel from Western Europe to replace the loss of Yugoslav markets for its products.

Austrian influence is particularly evident in the attractive capital, Ljubljana, and in the mountain villages of the Julian Alps, which resemble those of the Tyrol. Winter sports facilities have long been established at Kranjska Gora, Bovec and Rogla, while the lake resorts of Bled and Bohinj provide a range of summer activities. Although Slovenia has only a short stretch of Adriatic coastline this includes the popular resort of Portoroz and the seaports of Piran and Koper with their Venetian-style architecture. Other attractions include the spectacular and much visited network of caves at Postojna and the equestrian centre at Lipica.

The Yugoslav Federation

Montenegro and Serbia are the only republics remaining in the Yugoslav Federation. As their respective governments in Podgorica and Belgrade do not always see eye to eye, we feel justified in treating them as separate countries.

Montenegro

Montenegro has one of the finest stretches of Adriatic coast, including some good beaches and the magnificent fjord-like Gulf of Kotor. International-style resorts were developed in the 1960s at Budva, and Sveti Stefan – which is unique in being a one-time fishing village converted to a luxury hotel complex. The interior of Montenegro, with its stony mountains, deep gorges, and 'eagle's nest' villages, is very different from the lush greenery of the coast. The former capital, Cetinje, is a reminder that Montenegro was an independent kingdom before the First World War, and this small city, approached by a spectacular road, is one of the curiosities of the Balkans. Inbound tourism has suffered from the effects of the sanctions directed at the regime in Belgrade and the Kosovo refugee crisis in 1999.

Serbia

Serbia's tourism industry has been handicapped by its landlocked situation, and throughout the 1990s, by international ostracism, economic sanctions and NATO bombings in 1999. Previously, Belgrade was a major business and conference centre, and Serbia received a large volume of transit traffic en route to Greece or Turkey. Winter sports facilities were developed at Kopaonik and Zlatibor, but these attracted little attention from foreign tour operators. Serbia's cultural heritage includes a number of medieval Orthodox monasteries – Studenica and Sopocani are World Heritage Sites – but again these are little appreciated in the West compared to the art treasures of Croatia.

Macedonia

Provisionally known as FYRM – the former Yugoslav Republic of Macedonia – in deference to Greece, this small country was the poorest region of Yugoslavia before independence. The reopening of the Greek border should allow Macedonia to develop its trade and fledgling tourism industry, depending on the impact of the 1999 Kosovo crisis on the country. Tourism is based not so much on Skopje the capital, which was rebuilt after a major earthquake in 1963, but on Ohrid, which is scenically located on the deepest lake in Europe.

Bosnia-Herzegovina

Bosnia's war-ravaged economy and refugee crises have allowed even less scope for tourism than the other republics. The 1995 Dayton Agreement secured an uneasy peace on the basis of power-sharing between the three principal ethnic groups – the Moslems, the Croats and the Serbs, but in effect the country has become a United Nations (UN) protectorate. In the former Yugoslavia, Bosnia's diversity of cultures and religions was no small part of its appeal for foreign visitors, most of whom were based in Dubrovnik and other holiday resorts on the Adriatic coast. Tourists were particularly attracted to the old Turkish quarter of Sarajevo, and the picturesque Turkish bridge over the River Neretva at Mostar. The federal government also invested heavily in Sarajevo as the venue for the 1980 Winter Olympics, as part of its policy to spread the benefits of tourism from the coast to the mountainous interior. In the late 1990s the hotels and ski facilities are used almost exclusively by the considerable number of UN personnel who are based in Bosnia. The only type of tourism that has flourished, despite a lack of government encouragement, are the pilgrimages to Medjugorje. Since 1981 this obscure Croat village in Herzegovina has attracted over 30 million Roman Catholics, making it a shrine of worldwide significance.

Albania

A small mountainous country, known to its people as Shqipri (land of the eagles), Albania is different in language and culture from its Greek and Slav neighbours. It is also the poorest and least developed of the East European states. In 1991 the government envisaged ambitious plans for tourism development, under a new Ministry of Construction and Tourism. There is little doubt that the country has considerable potential, including an extensive and as yet unspoiled Mediterranean coastline, as well as spectacular lake and mountain scenery. However, Western-style tourism has been held back throughout the 1990s for the following reasons:

1 The historical legacy of the hard-line communist regime established by Enver Hoxha between 1945 and 1989, which imposed a policy of economic self-sufficiency, closed mosques and churches, and isolated the Albanian people from contacts with foreigners.
2 Inadequate infrastructure. The road network is poorly developed, with horse-drawn vehicles impeding the traffic flow. Many mountain villages remain inaccessible by road. External transport links by road, air and ferry are limited.
3 Lack of investment due to the poor state of the economy. The collapse of get-rich-quick 'pyramid' investment schemes discredited government attempts to introduce a free market economy.
4 Political instability. In the northern part of Albania there has been a recrudescence of the tribal feuding that characterized much of the country's pre-1945 history, and visitor safety cannot be guaranteed.

The European Bank for Reconstruction and Development (EBRD) is closely involved with the funding of facilities suitable for Western tourists, such as hotels, holiday villages and camping grounds. Most of the development will be on the coast, particularly south of Vlore. The EBRD would like developers to concentrate on a relatively few upmarket projects. However, the Albanian government desperately needs the foreign exchange earnings from tourism to modernize the country's infrastructure, and some observers fear that this will put pressure on Albania's unique ecological and cultural resources. These include:

1 The archaeological sites at Apolonia and Butrint – the 'lost city' of the ancient Illyrian civilization, and one of the best-preserved classical sites in the Mediterranean. Because of its accessibility from the beach resort of Ksamil and Corfu, Butrint may have to cope with visitor numbers well beyond its present capacity.
2 The mountains of the interior. These contain a number of medieval fortress-towns which played a major role in the Albanian struggle for freedom against the Ottoman Empire – of these Berat, Gijrokastro and Kruje are the most important.
3 The lakes on the Albanian border, where a limited amount of resort development has taken place.

The changes that have taken place in Albania since the fall of Communism are mainly evident in the capital, Tirana. Under Hoxha the city was effectively a car-free zone, but it now has traffic problems, while the private sector, often with Italian financial backing, is providing hotels and restaurants in competition with Albturist, the state travel organization.

The Commonwealth of Independent States (CIS)

It is difficult to imagine the vastness of the CIS – the Russian Federation alone is twice the size of the USA and spans eleven time zones. In other words, a difference of half a day separates Kaliningrad on the Baltic coast, from Petropavlovsk on the Bering Sea, 12 000 kilometres to the east. As you might expect, there is a great range of climatic conditions in a landmass that also extends across more than 40° of latitude, and we can broadly distinguish the following life zones, starting in the north:

1 Treeless boggy tundra bordering the Arctic Ocean from the Kola Peninsula in the west to the Bering Straits in the east, very sparsely occupied by groups of reindeer herders.
2 The wide zone of the *taiga* – the world's largest forest – covering 8 million square kilometres of northern Russia, including the greater part of Siberia. Due to the harsh subarctic climate and poor soils this is almost entirely dominated by a few tree species such as birch, firs and larch.
3 A belt of mixed forest, typifying the more varied landscapes of central Russia and Belarus.
4 A zone of treeless grassland or steppe extending from the Ukraine to the Mongolian border in the east. Much of this zone has very fertile 'black earth' soils and was the 'bread-basket' of the USSR, but it is often prone to devastating droughts.
5 A zone of deserts in southern Central Asia, where summer temperatures exceed 40°C, but can drop to –20°C in the winter months.
6 A series of high mountains along the southern fringes of the CIS, namely the Caucasus, Pamirs, Tian Shan and Altai ranges.
7 Landscapes and climates comparable to those of the Mediterranean are found only in sheltered pockets on the coastlands bordering the Black Sea and the southern valleys of the Caucasus.

The continental climate that characterizes almost the whole of Russia and most of the other republics is a major constraint on tourism development. Winters are severe – for example, snow lies on average for 80 days in Kiev and 160 days in St Petersburg. Some 7 million square kilometres of northern Russia are affected by permafrost, which in parts of Arctic Siberia reaches a depth of 1000 metres or more.

The cultural diversity of the CIS is greater than the variety of its landscapes. The population of almost 300 million is a mosaic of as many as 400 ethnic groups, although Russian Slavs account for half the total. Within the Russian Federation itself, there are twenty-one autonomous republics that represent the more numerous non-Russian minorities. As a result of *glasnost* (the policy of open government), religion and nationalist feeling, previously suppressed under Soviet communism, have come to the fore. There has been some revival of the Russian Orthodox Church, but the greatest growth has been among Moslems who account for over 20 per cent of the population of the CIS, particularly in the Central Asian republics, among the Tatars of Kazan on the River Volga, and in the Caucasus, where the Chechens were in revolt against the Russian government throughout most of the 1990s. Although Moslem fundamentalism is not widespread, the threat of ethnic strife is a deterrent to tourism in some parts of Central Asia and the Caucasus.

Transport

The sheer size of the CIS, the difficult climate and terrain of most of the region, and the undeveloped nature of surface transport means that aviation has long played a major role. Many communities in Siberia are only really accessible by air, since they lie more than 1600 kilometres from the nearest railhead, the dirt roads are impassable during the spring thaw and the autumn rains, while the rivers are ice-free only in the brief summer.

In the former USSR the state-owned Aeroflot had a monopoly of domestic air services, making it the world's biggest airline. With the break-up of the Soviet Union it was likewise divided up between the various republics and separate national airlines emerged. Aeroflot-Russian International Airlines, reorganized as a joint-stock company in 1992, now provides two-thirds of Russia's international air services, with a worldwide network like its Soviet predecessor. However, its network within the CIS is a far cry from the 1980s, with flights to only 40 or so cities now compared to 3600 destinations then. Aeroflot also faces competition from a number of private airlines, notably Transaero. Air fares throughout the CIS remain relatively low, even for foreign tourists paying in US dollars. On the other hand, flights can be irregular due to recurrent fuel shortages, staff morale is affected by low pay, and some say that safety standards are below those considered acceptable in the West.

We mentioned in Chapter 5 that Russia has the world's longest railway – the Trans-Siberian – that provides the major west to east transport link. Although the journey from Moscow to Vladivostok – a distance of almost 10 000 kilometres – takes over a week, and the trains make no concessions to tourism, the Trans-Siberian has become one of Russia's most sought-after travel experiences. On the other hand, the Bolshoi Express, with carriages designed for the Soviet ruling élite, is a luxury product aimed at high-spending foreign tourists. Most rail services are cheap by Western standards but also slow, and security on the trains is a problem. Road transport is even less efficient, and the standard of road maintenance, even between major cities in European Russia, is well below Western standards. On the other hand, Russia and the Ukraine have a very extensive network of inland waterways. These link the great rivers Dnieper, Don and Volga (which have played a major role in Russian history), to the Baltic, White and Black Seas. In the summer months, fleets of hydrofoils ply the waterways with large numbers of domestic passengers, and Russian expertise in the field of hydrofoil design may yet see a new role for this type of vessel elsewhere. River cruises on more conventional ships are becoming increasingly popular with Western tourists, especially those linking St Petersburg to Moscow via Europe's largest lakes – Ladoga and Onega, which provide a leisurely way of absorbing the timeless quality of Russia's countryside. We mentioned in Chapter 4 that the Arctic is also attracting tourists. With the Cold War now a distant memory and desperate for foreign currency, Russia is prepared to open up its strategic Arctic sea route north of Siberia, as a summer cruise destination, using Russian nuclear-powered ice-breakers.

Demand for tourism

Internal demand

Domestic tourism under the Soviet system was mainly the responsibility of the state-controlled trade unions. Health care and rest from labour was provided in a network of sanatoria and purpose-built holiday centres which provided workers from various state industries with a subsidized, if somewhat regimented, two-week vacation. Only a small proportion of this *kurort* (health resort) accommodation, amounting to 2 million beds in 1988, was allocated to families, while children had their own Young Pioneer camps.

The transition to a market economy since 1990 has dealt the system of subsidized domestic tourism a severe blow. *Perestroika* (the restructuring of the economy) has been accompanied by rampant inflation and devaluation of the rouble. The consequent rise in the prices of food and other essentials has drastically reduced the amount of discretionary income available to the average citizen. Most of the sanatoria on the Black Sea coast are now in an independent Ukraine or Georgia, and therefore less accessible to Russians. Most of the Young Pioneer camps have closed down as funding is not available from government ministries, factories or trade unions; those that remain, now called 'children's health camps' have been reorganized on less regimented lines than under communism. With *glasnost* has also come rising expectations, fuelling a demand for independent holidays on the Western model. Activity holidays have grown in popularity, especially canoeing on the many rivers, which is usually combined with camping in the forests. Russian tourists touring the CIS prefer to use *tubaza* (tourist bungalows) which provide a cheap but basic alternative accommodation, as they are paid for in the local currency, rather than US dollars, which is the case with Western-style hotels. Although half the workforce are entitled to paid holidays of twenty-four days, most Russian city-dwellers have to be content with a stay nearer home, in a *dacha* (country cottage) in one of the villages on the outskirts, which they may own themselves, part-own through a garden co-operative or else rent. The trend for independent holidays will increase as car ownership levels rise – at present these are low by Western standards.

Inbound tourism

In the past, inbound tourism contributed only a small proportion of the Soviet Union's foreign exchange earnings, and attitudes towards foreign visitors have been ambivalent since the times of the tsars. Bureaucracy, an obsession with state security and travel restrictions characterized Russia even before 1917 and seems likely to persist after the demise of communism. Large areas were officially closed to foreign visitors until the early 1990s. Although tourists no longer have to keep to approved itineraries, and stay only in officially designated accommodation as in the Soviet era, the independent traveller is at a disadvantage compared to those on an inclusive tour. Tour itineraries still need to be prebooked and paid for in hard currency. The Soviet authorities saw tourism as a means of promoting the achievements of the world's first socialist state, and in 1929, Intourist was founded as an all-purpose agency to serve foreign visitors. As such, it became the model for the tourism organizations set up by the countries of Eastern Europe after the Second World War.

With the demise of Soviet power Intourist no longer has a state monopoly. Now reorganized as a joint stock company, it nevertheless has the advantage over its competitors in having offices in fourteen countries outside the CIS, as well as an established network of agencies in all the countries of the former Soviet Union. It still owns and manages hotels and restaurants, arranges surface transportation for clients, organizes excursions and tickets for cultural events, and supplies guides and interpreters. In 1957 international youth travel to the USSR became the responsibility of the Sputnik organization, part of the Komsomol (League of Young Communists) with a network of camps and low-budget hotels. In 1991 it too was privatized and is now a commercial company in which Aeroflot is a major shareholder.

Until the 1960s facilities for foreign visitors were limited, but from 1966 onwards, the Soviet government's Five-Year Plan invested in tourism infrastructure and staff training. Additional impetus was given by the choice of Moscow as the host city for the 1980 Olympic Games, and by 1986 the number of foreign visitors stood at 6 million. During the Soviet era, most tourists were travelling for cultural rather than ideological reasons. However official itineraries stressed the achievements of socialism since the 1917 October Revolution, by including visits to factories and collective farms.

Since the late 1980s the appeal of Russia and the other countries of the CIS has broadened, both tourist arrivals and receipts have increased, and a diversity of products are available for foreign visitors. By the late 1990s international arrivals exceeded 15 million. Trading on Cold War nostalgia, Western tourists can participate in a James Bond theme, or operate Soviet military hardware. Sochi, the Russian Black Sea resort, which in the 1980s attracted 6 million Soviet tourists annually to its beaches, is now planning to attract Western tourists by emulating Benidorm. Other options include wildlife safaris, river cruises, conference tourism, adventure holidays and home-stays with Russian families. We can summarize the main problems affecting the expansion of Western-style tourism in the CIS as:

1 The language barrier.
2 The lack of nightlife – although casinos are springing up in many cities throughout the CIS they are not always reputable.
3 A continuing shortage of accommodation, particularly in the major centres, where hotels are prebooked by the travel companies prior to departure.
4 Foreign investment in the tourism industry, as in the economy generally, is deterred by the absence of a reliable banking system, bureaucratic inertia and corruption, and uncertainty over the laws relating to private property.
5 The prevalent low standards of services in hotels and restaurants.

On the other hand, the younger generation in the work-force is well educated and eager to adopt Western-style methods.

Tourism resources of the CIS

Russia

Russia is officially known as the Russian Federation and is by far the largest country – in area, population and resources – of the loose grouping of former Soviet republics, known as the Commonwealth of Independent States, which replaced the USSR in 1991. Only 20 per cent of Russia is geographically within Europe, together with Belarus, the Ukraine, Moldova and the republics of Transcaucasia. In the public sector, tourism is closely linked to physical culture and sports, and regulated by the 1996 Tourism Law. There is a strong organization for tourism at city level that recognizes the fact that most Western tourists to the CIS spend at least part of their stay in the cities of St Petersburg and Moscow, located in the central part of European Russia:

1 *St Petersburg* is probably the most beautiful city in Russia, and occupies a special place in the country's history for these reasons:
   (a) It was founded as the capital of the Russian Empire in 1703 by the modernizing Tsar Peter the Great as Russia's 'window on the west'. No expense was

spared to import the best European architects of the time to design a city on classical lines, with broad streets, canals and impressive public buildings.

(b) The attack on the Winter Palace in October 1917 brought Lenin and the Communist Party to power in Russia (for this reason the city was renamed Leningrad during the Soviet era).

(c) The epic siege of the city from 1941 to 1943, epitomizing the almost unimaginable sacrifices made by the Russian people during the Second World War.

Because of its northerly latitude St Petersburg is best visited during the season of the 'white nights' (from May to July). Among its many cultural attractions, the following are of special significance:

(a) The Hermitage is one of the world's largest art collections, which includes the Winter Palace of the Tsars.

(b) The Maryinsky Theatre, home of the renowned Kirov Ballet.

(c) The former palaces of the Tsars on the outskirts of the city, which were restored by the Soviet government at enormous cost after the Second World War.

St Petersburg is also convenient for excursions to the well-preserved medieval city of Novgorod and the island-monasteries in Lakes Ladoga and Onega.

2 *Moscow* is a much older city, which has grown to a sprawling metropolis of almost 10 million people. The historic nucleus is the Kremlin – the walled inner city of the tsars, and later the seat of power of the rulers of the USSR and the Russian Federation. It is adjoined by Red Square and Russia's most well-known building – St Basil's Cathedral with its distinctive onion domes. Under Stalin, the city acquired its Metro system – with ornately decorated stations – and 'wedding-cake' skyscrapers, one of which accommodates the University of Moscow. Since the fall of communism, a dynamic mayor has embellished the capital with some impressive new projects, including the reconstructed Cathedral of Christ the Saviour – symbolic of the revival of the Russian Orthodox Church after seventy years of official atheism. Other attractions include:

(a) The Bolshoi Theatre, world famous for its touring ballet company.

(b) The Moscow State Circus with some 16 000 performers.

(c) The Pushkin and Tretyakov art collections.

(d) The Exhibition of Economic Achievements, showcasing technology.

(e) The Izmaylovo market where the tourist can buy antique samovars, icons and Soviet memorabilia.

Moscow also has one of the world's largest hotels – the Rossiya – and conference centres – the Palace of Congresses in the Kremlin. The international airport at Sheremetyevo was expanded for the 1980 Olympics Games but has since acquired an unenviable reputation among foreign business travellers for bureaucratic delays, indifferent service and not least the taxi touts controlled by the Russian Mafia, who have flourished under the new regime.

Moscow is a good base for excursions to other places of interest in Central Russia including:

(a) The Golden Ring of historic towns such as Vladimir, Sergiev Posad and Suzdal that have preserved much of the Old Russia of wooden churches, colourful Byzantine-style monasteries, traditional craft industries and *troika* rides.

(b) The country houses of Tchaikovsky at Klin, and Tolstoy at Yasnaya Polyana, which are a 'must' for lovers of Russian music and literature.

(c) Star City, the centre of Russia's space programme.

The other tourist attractions of Russia are more widely scattered. They include:

1 The River Volga, which is a major tourist route. Along its banks lie:

(a) Kazan – a mixture of mosques and Orthodox churches.

(b) Ulyanovsk – famous as the birthplace of Lenin.

(c) Volgograd (formerly Stalingrad), scene of one of the most important battles of the Second World War.

2 Archangel is the base for exploring northern Russia, including the island monasteries of Solovetsky in the White Sea and the nature reserve of Belomorie.

In the extreme south, Russia retains a section of Black Sea coast – including the important resorts of Sochi and Dagomys, and the northern slopes of the Caucasus Mountains where a number of spas have developed. However, these are uncomfortably close to the republic of Chechenya, one of the major areas of ethnic tension in the CIS.

Siberia is the name given to the vast expanse of the Russian Federation lying to the east of the Urals. It has long been regarded as a storehouse of mineral resources and a land of opportunity for immigrants from European Russia, although it recently had another more fearsome reputation as a place of exile. Until the end of the 1980s the territory was closed to Western tourists, with the exception of a few cities along the Trans-Siberian Railway. Siberia now offers possibilities for special interest tourism undreamed of in the pre-*glasnost* Soviet Union, including:

● whitewater rafting and eco-tourism in the Altai Mountains, a vast area of unspoiled wilderness

● visits to the sites of the former *gulags*, the notorious labour camps of the Stalin era, where untold millions died of privation

● cruises in the Arctic Ocean, to view the wildlife of the region

● river cruises on the Ob, Yenisei and Lena.

Some areas of Siberia have benefited economically from the collapse of Soviet communism, notably the Far East region, including the port of Vladivostok and the island of Sakhalin which are free enterprise zones, open to foreign, mainly Japanese, business investment. However, this has a downside in that the region's monsoon forests and unique wildlife – including the rare Siberian tiger – are under threat due to exploitation of its timber resources. The mining communities of northern Siberia, notably Norilsk – the world's most northerly industrial city – face an uncertain future as the government can no long afford to subsidize transport and other services. The native peoples of Siberia – the Evenki reindeer herders and the Yakuts, for example – have an age-old way of life that is better adapted to the severe environment, and may yet enjoy a cultural renaissance as a result of tourism.

Two of Siberia's natural attractions deserve special mention because of their unique character, namely:

1 Lake Baikal, which is the world's biggest natural reservoir of fresh water, due to its size, purity and extraordinary depth. The lake also supports a remarkable variety of species that makes it a fascinating area for eco-tourists. As early as 1916 Russia's first nature reserve was established here, and it was the birthplace of the fledgling environmentalist movement in the 1960s. Baikal's ecology continues to be threatened by effluent from pulp mills, fertilizers and by acid rain.
2 Kamchatka, despite its raw, foggy climate and poor communications, has considerable tourism potential due to its proximity to Alaska on the other side of the Bering Sea, which gives it access to the growing market for eco-tourism in the USA. It contains no less than thirty-three active volcanoes and large numbers of geysers and hot springs. The region is also known for its salmon fisheries and abundant wildlife.

The cities of Siberia are of less interest to tourists, except for those that have preserved the traditional wooden buildings of the pre-Soviet era, such as Tobolsk and Irkutsk. Others worth mentioning include:

● Ekaterinburg in the Urals is visited mainly because it was here that the last of the Romanov tsars, Nicholas II, was murdered
● Novosibirsk with its modern industries is the business capital of Siberia
● Academgorok nearby is a centre for space research.

The western republics of the CIS

The three new nations of Ukraine, Belarus and Moldova are finding it difficult to forge a new identity distinct from that of Russia, to which their economies continue to be closely linked.

1 *Ukraine* Kiev, the attractive capital of the Ukraine, was also historically the nucleus of the first Russian state before Moscow came on the scene. The surviving medieval heritage includes the Caves Monastery and the Cathedral of Saint Vladimir. On the other hand Lvov, the chief city of the western Ukraine, has many Baroque buildings which are reminders of its long association with Poland and the Austro-Hungarian Empire. The main tourist area is undoubtedly the Crimea, where the warm climate and beautiful coastal scenery – in contrast to the uniformity of the Ukrainian steppes – made it a favourite for the Russian nobility before the 1917 Revolution. Resorts such as Yalta were later made available to all Soviet citizens and, following the collapse of the Soviet Union, to foreign tourists with hard currency to spend. The elegant city of Odessa is the home port of the CTC cruise fleet.
2 *Belarus* Belarus contains extensive beech forests and marshes and is popular with cross-country skiers in winter. Its capital Minsk is also one of the major business centres of the CIS.
3 *Moldova* Moldova is closely associated by language and culture with neighbouring Romania, and is one of the major wine-producing areas for the CIS.

Transcaucasia

The three nations to the south of the Caucasus Mountains have more in common with the Mediterranean countries or the Middle East than with Russia. Few other areas of the CIS have such potential – a favourable climate, spectacular scenery, a rich cultural heritage going back to ancient times, and a people with a tradition of hospitality and business enterprise. Yet this potential has been blighted since the late 1980s by intercommunal violence between Armenians and Azaris, and Abkazians and Georgians.

1 *Georgia* Georgia once attracted vast numbers of Soviet citizens to its Black Sea resorts of Sukhumi, Gagri and Pitsunda. The country is also noted for its vineyards and tea plantations, and has a strong culinary tradition (in contrast to the mediocre catering which is characteristic of most of the former USSR). The capital Tblisi has a lively Mediterranean atmosphere, and is well placed for excursions to the spectacular scenery and ski resorts of the High Caucasus.
2 *Armenia* Armenia is mainly a high plateau, separated by mountain barriers from its neighbours – also there are no rail, road or air links with Turkey or Azerbaijan due to international tensions. The country was also badly affected by a major earthquake in 1988. Armenia is famous for its ancient churches and monasteries set amid spectacular lake and mountain scenery. However, tourism is in its infancy and the country is largely dependent on remittances from the millions of ethnic Armenians, living mainly in the USA.

3 *Azerbaijan* Azerbijan is a predominantly Moslem nation, and the old quarter of Baku has a strong Middle Eastern ambience. In the early 1900s Baku was famous for its oilfields, and foreign business travellers are now poised to exploit the revival of the petroleum industry. For the leisure tourist, Azerbaijan can offer scenic variety – the subtropical coastlands of the Caspian Sea, snow-capped mountains, and deserts.

Central Asia

In the five Central Asian republics of the CIS east of the Caspian Sea, Russian rule came relatively late, and was imposed on civilizations that had developed over thousands of years. The Moslem religion and heritage are dominant throughout the region, and the Russian influence is relatively slight, except in Kazakhstan and the modern cities of Tashkent and Almaty, which were massively industrialized during the Soviet era. The Soviet authorities were responsible for most of the environmental problems in the region. The best known example is the shrinkage of the Aral Sea, which was brought about by vast irrigation projects for cotton cultivation in the desert. This has resulted in a deterioration of the local climate, with salt and sand-laden winds blowing in from the dried-up lake bed.

There are important differences between the individual republics and these are reflected in the extent of tourism development:

1 *Uzbekistan* Uzbekistan has the richest heritage in the region, and has a well-developed tourism industry, but one that still discourages independent travel. Its capital, Tashkent, is the major air hub of Central Asia and an important conference venue. However, tourism is mainly concentrated in the oasis cities of Khiva, Samarkand and Bokhara, which served as staging points on the 'Silk Road' – the ancient overland trade route between the Mediterranean and China. Of these:
   (a) Samarkand is the best known as it boasts one of the world's most striking Islamic monuments – the Registan, resplendently decorated in blue tiles and gold leaf
   (b) Khiva is a perfectly preserved 'museum city'.
   (c) Bokhara is a hive of activity, with bazaars similar to those of the Middle East.
2 *Kazakhstan* Kazakhstan is a vast expanse of steppe and desert, except where it includes parts of the Tian Shan and Altai mountain ranges. Tourism possibilities include whitewater rafting on the River Ili and trekking in the mountains. The capital Almaty (Alma-Ata) is the second largest city of Central Asia, with direct air links to Western Europe. The nearby resort of Medeo is an important centre for skiing and ice-skating.
3 *Kyrgystan* Kyrgystan is dominated by the glaciated Tian Shan mountains, and has as its main attraction the lake of Issik Kul, which is a centre for health tourism.

4 *Tajikstan* Tajikistan is the smallest, the most mountainous, and throughout the 1990s the most politically unstable of the Central Asian republics, which has held back development of its tourism industry. Unlike the other countries in the region, it has looked to Iran, rather than Turkey, as a role model.
5 *Turkmenistan* Turkmenistan includes some of the hottest and driest locations in Central Asia. It is noted for its traditional carpet weaving industry and the city of Mary (Merv) is one of the oldest in the region, but tourism is still at an early stage of development.

Summary

A long period of state control over tourism, amounting to forty years in Eastern Europe and seventy years in the former Soviet Union, has left a legacy which strongly differentiates these countries from those of Western Europe. Since 1989 this has been followed by a strong liberalizing trend, characterized by economic restructuring, privatization and the encouragement of local initiative. Western involvement in the development of tourism has greatly increased. Entry, exit and currency restrictions were severe under the communist regimes but have eased with their demise. However, the flow of tourists still remains predominantly from the Western countries. This unequal pattern is due to the continuing difficulty which outbound tourists from the region face in obtaining hard currency, against an adverse economic situation. Domestic tourism was state-subsidized, mainly through the trade union and youth organizations under communism, but now increasingly has to meet market forces and adapt to change.

In the transition period, East European citizens may see little benefit to their living standards. On the other hand, the removal of communism has improved the image of the region in Western eyes. This needs to be reinforced by each country emphasizing its individual attractions. The differences between countries were previously concealed by the grey uniformity of communism and are now much more evident. There is increasing scope for innovation in tourism products and niche marketing. Some countries, notably the Czech Republic, have made much more progress than others.

However, the encouragement of mass tourism might well result in the region becoming a cheap playground for West Europeans. This is particularly true of Romania and Bulgaria, who have long depended on a captive regional market that is now free to travel to other 'sun-lust' destinations. Environmental problems are already widespread, and eco-tourism is in its infancy. Transport systems need to be improved, to cope with rising car ownership levels and the expectations of Western tourists. Future growth in tourism could also be severely constrained by these negative factors:

- political instability and ethnic strife
- rising crime levels
- poor standards of service, and mediocre products – once the novelty of visiting a previously 'forbidden' destination has faded.

Case study

Tourism as an agent of economic restructuring

Introduction

In the former communist countries of Eastern Europe tourism is seen to be central to the process of economic restructuring as it cuts across a variety of economic sectors and is primarily comprised of small and medium-sized enterprises (SMEs). The transformation of economic, political and social frameworks in the region, allied to the curiosity factor and deregulation of international travel constraints have actively encouraged tourist development. However, there are very real practical difficulties and issues surrounding the use of tourism as a medium of change since the political events of 1988–9 moved the region towards a market economy. In particular there is a need to ensure that tourism developments are sustainable and do not threaten the already vulnerable environmental resources in the region. Also, there is the need to win hearts and minds in the host population by motivating enthusiastic entrepreneurs and explaining the relevance of 'Western' concepts of business management – the progress towards a market economy is as much a political process as an economic one. The incorporation of the region into the international tourism industry has not therefore been easy. For example, the European Commission has identified twenty-five key issues that the industry is faced with if tourism is to be successful in the region (Table 18.1).

We can examine the role of tourism as an agent of change under four key headings:

- economic restructuring
- tourism administration
- environmental concerns
- tourism infrastructure.

Economic restructuring

Communism as the political and economic model has had a profound effect on tourism in the region. Following the political events of the late 1980s, the

Table 18.1   Development obstacles to tourism in Eastern Europe

Insufficient buying power in domestic tourism markets
Difficult political environment to operate in
Lack of understanding of the nature of tourism
Lack of economic incentives for tourism development
Lack of clearly defined tourism image
Lack of funds for tourism promotion
Lack of regional tourist boards
Lack of local tourist boards
Overcrowded honey-pots such as Prague
Insufficient transport facilities
Insufficient accommodation at some levels
Unreliable catering standards
Poor entertainment facilities
Inadequate tourism services – such as information and interpretation
Poor telecommunications
Poor facilities for currency exchange
Difficult border crossings and lack of good border facilitation
Slow privatization process
War, terrorism and organized crime in some parts of the region
Lack of tourism product innovation
Lack of tourism market research
Insufficient knowledge of tourism marketing
Insufficient sources of funds for local tourism investment

Source: Adapted from the European Commission (1992).

former countries of Eastern Europe are moving from a centralized to a market economy, and from a totalitarian, one-party system towards a pluralist democracy. In the case of countries such as Hungary, this transition is proceeding relatively smoothly. Elsewhere in the region, the change is more complex, particularly in those countries where the regimes had developed a highly centralized economy. For these countries, the economy is going through a series of stages:

1 The 'hiatus' period rejects the past and institutions and structures seriously debilitated by past misuse begin to recover.
2 The transition stage, where tourism is seen as playing an important role in the process.
3 A market economy.

Tourism contributes to this process in a variety of ways:

- privatization of state monopolies exposes organizations to competition and efficiency measures

- private sector entrepreneurs are encouraged as tourism is often used to demonstrate 'Western' business practice
- exposure to international tourism competition often demands the imposition of universally recognized standards – such as hotel classification.

Tourism administration

These economic and political changes have had a profound effect on tourism administration. In the past, the state tourist organizations, which were in effect tour operators and travel agencies operating at national, regional and local level, had a monopoly position. Many were set up on the lines of Intourist, and their inflexibility, standardization of approach and lack of competition meant that they were unable to respond to the demands of Western tourists. The old state agencies have now lost their monopolies and a range of new organizations are emerging which range from the purely private, through co-operatives, to state-run concerns. Here, tourism is acting as a medium for a change of attitudes in the public sector, towards, for example, concepts such as marketing.

Environmental concerns

Economic problems in the region render governments less able to deal effectively with the environmental problems and degradation that is the legacy of communist rule. However, unless these problems are tackled the growth of tourism experienced in the 1990s will not be sustained. A particular concern is the lack of understanding of these issues by those involved in tourism:

1 For example, hunting is still common in some countries, yet this is a practice which demands sensitive handling – some tourists will be attracted by the activity, while others will be deterred.
2 Also, in countries dominated by almost fifty years of centralization, the idea of 'bottom-up' planning and the involvement of host communities in decision-taking still requires some adjustment of attitudes.
3 Encouragement of SMEs may also be problematic, as this is not a sector that traditionally has the will, the expertise or the resources to respond to environmental initiatives.

Already tourist sites are suffering. In Hungary for example, there are high levels of pollution in many leading tourist centres; the historic buildings in Budapest are eroding; and Lake Balaton is heavily polluted. Clearly tourism must act as an agent of change in terms of both environmental attitudes and the demonstration of good environmental practice.

Tourism infrastructure

The low and variable quality of tourist attractions, facilities and service in the past have created a poor image of tourism. Training of tourism staff is under way to adapt the workforce to new approaches and the priorities of customer service. Initiatives to upgrade the industry include assistance with catering, computerization and ticketing, through to the redevelopment of transport systems.

Transport systems are struggling to cope with a market orientation as public subsidies are removed and investment fails to keep pace with increased tourist numbers. The ability of international carriers in the region to compete with the rest of the world is also in question, particularly as the region is experiencing increased demand from the West and Vienna emerges as the regional hub.

Accommodation is in short supply in some categories. In the budget category of accommodation, the emergent class of entrepreneurs now acts as providers, but in the four- and five-star categories there is a need for partnerships with international companies. Joint ventures are a useful way to stimulate the accommodation industry, not only by exposing the region to international good practice but also by putting into place the quality mechanisms needed (and expected by Western tourists) and to act as a catalyst for other businesses to adopt these practices in a competitive market environment. However, over-reliance on foreign investment and joint ventures may lead to reduced economic benefits for the host country. Elsewhere in the accommodation sector state-run hotel chains have been sold, franchise agreements and management contracts are operating, and loan agreements are making capital available in the sector.

Case study

Prague

The cities of the Czech Republic contain many heritage attractions, but only Prague has achieved worldwide recognition as a major tourist centre. The city's cultural appeal is due to:

- a strong musical heritage, including associations with Mozart and the Czech composers Smetana and Dvorak
- a unique architectural heritage, with outstanding examples of buildings in the Gothic, Baroque and Art Nouveau styles. In contrast to other European cities, Prague escaped widespread damage in the Second World War, and subsequent redevelopment of its historic centre

● a vibrant contemporary arts scene that has attracted a large expatriate community from other countries, particularly the USA, who are also encouraged by a favourable exchange rate.

As Prague has more than one historic centre, tourist attractions tend to be clustered in three distinct areas, namely:

1 *Hradcany* – the original fortress-capital on a hill overlooking the River Vltava. This contains Prague Castle – seat of Bohemian kings, Holy Roman emperors and Czech presidents, St Vitus Cathedral, and the picturesque street known as Golden Lane.
2 The *Old Town* on the east bank of the river, which is linked to Hradcany by the highly decorative Charles Bridge. Two of the finest masterpieces of Gothic architecture in the Old Town are Tyn Church and the clock tower in Old Town Square.
3 The *New Town* – which was actually planned as early as the fourteenth century but rebuilt in the nineteenth century. It is centred around Wenceslas Square, the setting for some of the key events in Czech history, nowadays lined with hotels, apartment buildings, restaurants and shops. Many of these are decorated in the Art Nouveau style associated with the great Czech artist Alfons Mucha (who is better known for his French poster designs).

Tourism has brought economic benefits to Prague, including international funding of much-needed restoration work. However, the enormous influx of visitors, especially of tour groups and young backpackers from all over the world, is threatening to turn the city into another Florence. This has the following effects:

1 The commercialization of the historic city – as a result of the upsurge in land prices, neighbourhood shops have been replaced by those catering for tourists. Historic buildings have been altered in inappropriate ways and defaced with advertisements. Local residents can no longer afford the high rents for their apartments, or the prices in bars and restaurants, and have been forced to move to the suburbs.
2 Wear and tear on the most popular historic attractions such as Charles Bridge, which is constantly thronged with buskers, street traders and hordes of tourists.
3 A predatory attitude by the city's taxi operators toward Western tourists.

It remains to be seen whether the civic authorities can achieve a balance between the encouragement of business enterprise and the need to preserve Prague's historic townscape. This is threatened by the growth of car ownership and the commercial pressures brought about by the free market economy and the international leisure industry.

The Middle East

After reading this chapter, you should be able to:

1 Describe the major physical features and climates of the Middle East and understand their importance for tourism.
2 Account for the fact that the region's tourism potential is largely unfulfilled despite its closeness to the tourist-generating markets of Northern Europe.
3 Appreciate the continuing importance of religion in the everyday culture of the region, and the impact of religious fundamentalism on the political stability of many of these countries and the safety of foreign tourists.
4 Appreciate that inbound tourism to the region encompasses beach holidays, cultural tourism and business travel.
5 Recognize that the Middle East is an important generator of international tourism.
6 Identify the major features of tourism infrastructure in the region.
7 Demonstrate a knowledge of the tourist regions, resorts, business centres and tourist attractions of the Middle East.

Introduction

Vast petroleum resources and the Arab–Israeli conflict have brought the region generally known as the Middle East under the international spotlight since the Second World War, culminating in the Gulf War of 1990–1. However, this is but a recent episode in a history of trade, migration and conquest, which goes back thousands of years. The Middle East is strategically located at the crossroads of trade routes linking the Mediterranean to the Indian Ocean – and at the interface of three continents – Europe, Asia and Africa. The component countries share many physical and cultural features. Similarities in religion, language, architecture, food specialities and other aspects of lifestyle, plus a shared historical experience link almost all of the countries in the region, together with those of North Africa (which we will look at in the next chapter).

Cultural features

As far as cultural similarities are concerned, you should be aware that:

● all but three of the countries in the region (Israel, Iran and Turkey) are Arabic-speaking
● all the countries (except for Iran), at one time formed part of the Ottoman Empire based in Constantinople (now Istanbul); during much of the twentieth century, most of these countries have experienced various forms of control by European powers such as Britain, and to a lesser extent, France.
● although there are substantial religious as well as ethnic minorities in many of the countries of the Middle East, all except Israel and Lebanon are predominantly Moslem.

Western perceptions of Islam have been strongly influenced on the one hand, by historical memories of the Crusades and the threat posed to Europe by the Ottoman Empire and, on the other, by highly romanticized images of the region created by European writers and artists in the nineteenth century. More recently, unfavourable publicity in the Western media has been a reaction to the growth of Moslem fundamentalism.

Although it is true to say that, in this secular age, religion plays a greater role in everyday life than in most other parts of the world, the influence of Islam does, in fact, vary greatly in strength from country to country. Only a minority of these countries, for example, practices *sharia law* based on the Koran, rather than adopting Western legal practice. Attitudes towards the status of women and towards foreign tourists also vary from the strict (for example, Saudi Arabia) to the relatively liberal (Jordan, Lebanon and Turkey). We should take into account the following aspects of Islam as they influence the tourist experience:

1 The obligation of Moslems to pray five times a day with special emphasis on Friday (the Moslem Sabbath). This is the basis for the mosque with its distinctive architecture, especially the tall minaret forming a dominant feature in the skyline.
2 As figurative art is discouraged by the Koran, the decoration of mosques and other traditional buildings, in contrast to the churches and temples of most other faiths, tends to be limited to abstract patterns or inscriptions in Arabic.
3 Moslems are required to fast between sunrise and sunset during the month of Ramadan. This is based on a lunar calendar, so that the timing of Ramadan varies from year to year. This has an effect on business practice.
4 At least once in a lifetime, Moslems are supposed to make the pilgrimage or *haj* to the holy city of Mecca, the birthplace of Mohammed. As a result, the pilgrim routes extending to all parts of the Moslem world became important for trade, and were therefore, well supplied with inns or caravanserais. Some of these traditional types of accommodation still survive (although the camel caravan has long since been replaced by motorized transport).

Another important cultural feature of the region is the contrast between the cities and the countryside, where settled and nomadic lifestyles appear to have changed little since Biblical times. Even in the cities, the older districts retain their seemingly chaotic street pattern while the colourful *souks* and bazaars retain many traditional features. These are essentially covered markets with whole sections devoted exclusively to a particular trade or type of merchandise. Traditional domestic architecture is characterized by rooms opening off an enclosed courtyard, allowing privacy for the extended family and protection from the sun. The major cities have well laid-out, modern districts similar to those of Europe – Tel Aviv is a good example here – very different in character from the adjoining Arab town of Jaffa with its maze of twisting, narrow streets.

Physical features

There is no clear physical break (the Suez Canal and Red Sea hardly count) and as we have seen, no distinct cultural boundary between Africa and Asia. Most of the Middle East region forms part of the arid climate zone, and irrigation is essential. Agriculturally, productive land is restricted to a few areas that in turn have attracted the great majority of the population, which is concentrated in these areas at densities similar or exceeding those of Western Europe. They comprise:

- the coastal plains adjoining the Mediterranean, Aegean and Black Seas which enjoy relatively good rainfall
- a narrow strip along the river Nile in Egypt
- the alluvial plains of the rivers Tigris and Euphrates, which link up with the Mediterranean coastal plain in Syria to form the so-called 'Fertile Crescent'.

To the east of the coastal strip, mountain ranges and high plateaus prevent rain-bearing winds from penetrating further into the interior. Often the dividing line between the desert 'wilderness' and the cultivated area is very distinct. Not surprisingly, water supply and distribution is a major problem in the Middle East, and this precious resource is the subject of local and even international disputes.

Most of the region is characterized by extremes of heat in summer, and even the Mediterranean coast can be oppressive. In winter, the weather is usually mild or pleasantly warm, with the important exception of some mountain areas that experience heavy snowfalls. Conditions are particularly severe in Kurdistan, where temperatures are comparable to those of Russia. Cold, overcast weather is not uncommon – even as far south as Amman and Jerusalem which are situated at quite high altitudes – in contrast to the subtropical warmth and sunshine of the Red Sea coast.

Tourism in the Middle East

The countries of the Middle East are close enough to the inclusive tour markets of north-west Europe to have developed a tourism industry based on sun, sea and sand. In fact, this is a logical extension of the coastal resort developments of Mediterranean Europe, facilitated by improvements in air transport. However, the response to this opportunity has been uneven. Most countries with the potential to enter the market have only done so since the 1980s – Turkey is a notable example. Long before the expansion of mass tourism, Israel and Egypt had based their tourism industries on the attractions of the Holy Land and the relics of ancient civilizations. More recently, the oil-based prosperity of Saudi Arabia and the Gulf States has attracted a large business travel market. There is also a considerable volume of intra-regional travel, particularly between various Arab countries, involving business tourism, returning migrant workers, visiting relatives and health tourism.

Contrary to popular belief in the West, only some of the countries in the Middle East have become affluent on oil resources. Tourism's foreign exchange earnings are needed to even out regional imbalances. The population, as in most developing countries, contains a high percentage of young people and tourism is seen as a means of providing much needed employment. Both foreign investment and that of host governments have produced an extensive tourism infrastructure, including good roads and a large number of airports of international standard as well as a good deal of hotel development in the major cities and coastal resorts. External transport links are good as the region is a crossroads between Europe, Africa and Asia and its airports are important as staging points for business on the long-haul routes between Western Europe and the East Asia Pacific region. Although most tourists visiting the Middle East arrive by air, movements within the region are predominantly by road. The main exception is the Arabian Peninsula, due to the vast distances and difficult terrain. Throughout the Middle East, rail networks are poorly developed and there are few international services. Given the abundance of cheap oil, an ever-growing demand for car ownership, even in the poorer countries, and a lack of environmental awareness, this situation is not likely to change.

The Middle East has many strengths as a destination region, with opportunities for further development, but these are constrained by a number of serious problems. We can summarize the tourist resources of the region as:

1 A wealth of cultural attractions, due to the fact that this region gave rise to the world's earliest civilizations and three major world religions – Judaism, Christianity and Islam. Successive invaders, including the Greeks and Romans in ancient times, followed by Crusaders from Western Europe defending the pilgrim routes to the Holy Land, have all left their mark. Some of the best known of these sites can be visited on a Mediterranean cruise. However, land-based cultural tours, taking in several countries, have not developed to the same extent as in Europe, due to the political situation in the region.
2 A generally favourable climate for beach tourism. A growing number of tourists now visit the region purely for the sake of recreation and relaxation. A number of resorts have developed to meet their needs, but with the exception of Turkey and Israel, facilities are not to the same standard as those of the western Mediterranean.
3 There are opportunities for winter sports in some of the mountain ranges of the region. At present, resorts have developed to meet the needs of the small domestic market and are generally not well equipped by international standards. Many mountain areas, such as Kurdistan, are relatively inaccessible.
4 There is also scope for adventure holidays in the more accessible mountain and desert areas. Eco-tourism has made little progress, except in Israel and Jordan.

The main threats to tourism are twofold:

1 The political situation has been a major factor in preventing the region realizing its tourism potential.

Since the peace initiatives in 1994, tourism has ebbed and flowed to the region depending upon the optimism or otherwise for peace. The region is still torn by internal unrest, often provoked by religious fundamentalism Terrorism by groups such as Hamas in the Israeli-occupied territories and the PKK (Kurdistan Workers Party) in south-east Turkey has resulted in much negative publicity. Some governments in the region have done little to encourage tourism by their attitude to human rights. In consequence, tourism has suffered, despite the region's accessibility and its wealth of natural and man-made attractions. The Gulf War of 1990–1 for example, not only disrupted tourism throughout the Middle East, but disturbed world tourism flows, although the actual hostilities were highly localized.
2 The unique attraction of the region lies in its antiquities and cultural sites. These sites need careful management and have a limited capacity to receive visitors. This implies that there is a limit to the numbers of tourists that the region can absorb if these unique resources are to remain available for future generations.

Egypt

In many ways, Egypt typifies the contrasts found in the Middle East. It is a meeting place of East and West; it is mysterious and yet highly accessible. Cairo is the hub of the air routes between Europe, Asia and Africa, while the Suez Canal is one of the world's most important shipping routes. Egypt is the most populous of the Arab countries and a cultural centre for the Arabic-speaking world. However, the people themselves are not of Arab origin, and in many respects, the way of life of the *fellahin* (peasant farmers) along the Nile has changed little since the time of the Pharaohs. The Nile is also a reminder that Egypt has strong connections with Africa to the south.

The bulk of Egypt's territory is desert, but we should make a distinction between the dune-covered expanses of the Western Desert extending into Libya, and the rugged scenery of the Eastern Desert and Sinai Peninsula. In between, lies the narrow green ribbon of cultivated land along the Nile, widening in the north as the Nile Delta. Just as in ancient times, Egypt is 'the gift of the Nile', highly dependent on the river's vagaries. Although it is the most highly industrialized of the Arab countries, Egypt is not self-sufficient in petroleum and its economy cannot provide enough jobs for a population approaching 70 million. In this context, the contribution made by tourism is crucial, as it filters down to the lowest levels of society. The government recognizes this and has had a long involvement in tourism. The first formal tourist authority was established in 1935, and the present Ministry of Tourism dates from 1967. The Ministry has three main departments:

- the Tourist Development Authority
- the Tourist Authority for Promoting Tourism
- the General Authority of Conferences.

In addition, the Supreme Council for Tourism, chaired by the Prime Minister acts to co-ordinate public sector actions in tourism.

Travellers from the West have visited the Pyramids at least since Roman times, although modern tourism did not begin until the late nineteenth century. To a large extent this was due to the British travel company – Thomas Cook – who inaugurated steamship services on the Nile and the development of Luxor as a winter resort. Since the 1960s tourists from other Arab countries, visiting primarily for recreational rather than cultural reasons, have formed a growing share of the Egyptian market. Arab visitors tend to stay during the summer months, when the Mediterranean coast around Alexandria is cool by comparison with the stifling heat of the Arabian Peninsula. Most Western sightseers arrive during the winter season, which is pleasantly warm and much drier than other Mediterranean destinations.

Egypt is the dominant destination for international tourists in the Middle East. In the 1950s there were fewer visitors but they stayed for an average of one month, and even in the 1980s, the main reason for visiting was for the cultural sites. In the 1990s, however, recreational tourism is increasingly important. International arrivals have risen steadily despite the setbacks of terrorist attacks and the Gulf War, and approached 4 million by the end of the decade, comprising both Western and Arab markets. Although there are few charter services, most tourists arrive by air in Cairo. Domestic tourism is also significant with both social tourism and travel by the more affluent population.

Most of Egypt's hotel rooms are found in the capital or, and to a lesser extent, in Alexandria and Luxor. The government encourages investment in the accommodation stock by both Egyptian and foreign companies, and tourism is given priority at the highest levels of government. The Tourism Development Authority was set up to identify potential areas for growth. Egypt is therefore attempting to widen its resource base by encouraging conferences and special interest tourism. The objective is to tempt tourists away from the Nile Valley, where the tourism industry is competing with other economic sectors for scarce water, power and land resources. This is problematic as ancient Egypt – notably the Pyramids and the Valley of the Kings – is the subject of worldwide interest, probably to a greater extent than any other civilization of a bygone era.

Most Western tourists stay firmly on the cultural circuit, the highlights of which are:

- the Pyramids of Giza just outside Cairo – these are the unique survivors of the 'seven wonders' of the ancient world

- the temples and other antiquities near Luxor, which is the main centre for touring Upper Egypt. These include the world-famous Valley of the Kings
- the temple at Abu Simbel near Aswan, which UNESCO campaigns saved from inundation by the Aswan High Dam project.

Although the very dry climate of the Nile Valley has ensured the survival of artefacts for over 4000 years, safeguarding the monuments from pollution for future generations is a matter of concern. Tourist pressure on the Pyramids has led the government to implement drastic conservation measures, including attempts to curb the activities of unauthorized guides and entrepreneurs. A popular way of visiting the sites in Upper Egypt is by a river cruise on the Nile, as an alternative to road transport or domestic air services from Cairo (see the first case study at the end of this chapter).

The emphasis on the relics of the Pharaohs has obscured the fact that Egypt has a more recent heritage and many other attractions. This is particularly true of Cairo, although the congestion in this city of over 15 million people can be a traumatic experience. In addition to early Islamic buildings such as the Citadel of Saladin, there are Coptic churches, a reminder that this early form of Christianity was in existence in Egypt centuries before Islam. But for most tourists, the main attraction is shopping in the bazaars for an assortment of souvenirs. Other tourist resources include:

- the Fayyum oasis, 100 kilometres to the west of the Nile Valley is culturally interesting and a good deal less hectic than Cairo; A number of hotels have been built in this area
- sailing a traditional *fellucca* on the Nile offers a more authentic experience of rural Egypt than a luxury cruise in a 'floating hotel'
- trekking in the Sinai Desert, including a visit to St Catherine's monastery with its biblical associations.

The greatest potential for attracting a wider market lies in the development of Egypt's coastal resorts where a year-round season is possible, and there are good facilities for water sports.

1 *The Mediterranean coast* west of Alexandria has long attracted well-off domestic tourists. Egypt's second city is a cosmopolitan seaport with Greek and French cultural influences, but much of its former elegance faded after the 1952 revolution. Almost nothing remains of the ancient city, although there are exciting proposals for the world's first 'marine archaeological park' in the harbour, centring on the long-lost palace of Cleopatra.
2 *The Red Sea coast* has clear waters where diving holidays are being developed, based on the new resorts of Hurghada, Nuweiba and Sharm al Sheikh.

However, tourism has to overcome a number of problems, not the least of which is Egypt's infrastructure, particularly overloaded water and power supplies, and an inadequate road system. Environmental considerations are also important, especially along the Red Sea coast where there is concern for the ecology of the coral reefs. But perhaps the main problem is the uncertain political climate of the region, which causes severe fluctuations in tourist arrivals, especially from the USA. Although the government is pro-Western and was the first Arab state to normalize relations with Israel, Egypt suffers from acute social and economic tensions. This has contributed to the rise of fundamentalism among the poorer classes in society, which is causing concern for the future stability of the country and the future of its tourism industry.

Israel

Israel has a significance out of all proportion to its size. Within an area less than that of Belgium, you can find a great variety of scenery and climate, from quite high mountains in the Galilee region, to the lunar landscapes of the Dead Sea, 400 metres below sea level. People's perceptions of the country are largely coloured by their religious background:

1 To Jews, Israel is the homeland for a people dispersed in exile since Roman times, and Jewish religious practice plays an important role in everyday life.
2 To Christians, Israel is the Holy Land, attracting large numbers of pilgrims to sites associated with the Bible. The new millennium has posed a major security problem for the Israeli authorities, as some Christian fundamentalists as well as Jews and Moslems regard Jerusalem as their holy city.
3 To Moslems many of the sites associated with the Bible are also of great significance.
4 To the Palestinian Arabs (both Moslems and Christians) this is also their homeland, and there have been constant disputes with Jewish communities over land rights.

Since the founding of the independent Jewish state in 1948, the tourist potential of the country has been severely affected by strife with its Arab neighbours as well as unrest from the Palestinians of the occupied territories. Since the late 1990s the Palestinians of the Gaza Strip and communities such as Bethlehem, have been given limited autonomy, including some control over tourism development and an international airport (with very restricted services) at Gaza. Israel faces other major problems, such as the absorption of large numbers of immigrants from the former USSR. The special relationship with the USA is therefore crucial in reducing the economic burden.

Israel has attracted between 1 million and 2 million international tourists annually in the 1990s, with neighbour-ing Jordan and Lebanon dominating arrivals. The USA is also an important generator of tourists to Israel. European countries, including Britain, have become important markets since the liberalization of charter flights in 1976. The Israeli Ministry of Tourism endeavours to develop new markets, such as Japan, in close co-operation with the national carrier El Al – indeed, the majority of arrivals are by air. Israelis are avid travellers both domestically and internationally, to the extent that Israel has a deficit on its international travel account.

Israel can offer a great variety of tourist products including:

1 Summer holiday resorts along the Mediterranean coast at Herzliya and Netanya north of Tel Aviv, and at Ashkelon to the south.
2 Eilat, Israel's outlet to the Red Sea has become a popular winter sun destination, with facilities for underwater photography, diving and water-skiing.
3 Health tourism has been developed around the picturesque Sea of Galilee, and in a more spectacular setting on the shores of the Dead Sea, utilizing the unique resource provided by the mineral-rich lake and its microclimate.
4 Working holidays on a *kibbutz*, the uniquely Israeli experiment in communal living – however, some kibbutzim have departed from their socialist ideals by providing guesthouse accommodation to paying tourists.
5 The attraction of seeing a nation in the making, composed of immigrants from all over the world. Israel's achievements in making the Negev Desert productive are particularly interesting.
6 Adventure holidays, including desert trekking.
7 Cultural tourism based on the large number of archaeological sites, many of which are mentioned in the Bible. Galilee in particular attracts large numbers of Christian pilgrims as well as sightseers with no particular religious conviction. Herod the Great's fortress at Masada is a must-see attraction because of its unique significance as a shrine to the Jewish struggle for freedom.

Business travel gravitates to the three major cities, namely:

1 *Tel Aviv* is the business and financial centre of the country. The city is very much a creation of the twentieth century, with a good deal of nightlife.
2 *Haifa* is Israel's largest seaport, catering for tourists arriving by ferry from Greece, Cyprus and Turkey as well as cruise passengers.
3 *Jerusalem*, the ancient and modern capital, is an important venue for conferences. It is also a world-class tourist attraction as the meeting place for three major religions. Some allege that the Israeli authorities have insensitively handled hotel expansion into the Arab quarters of the old city. Major points of interest for the visitor include:

(a) Yad Vashem – Israel's major memorial to the Jewish Holocaust of the Second World War.

(b) The sites associated with the events leading to the crucifixion of Jesus, including the Mount of Olives, the pilgrim route known as the Via Dolorosa, and the Church of the Holy Sepulchre.

(c) The Temple Mount, an area sacred to Christians, Jews and Moslems alike. The mosque known as the Dome of the Rock is the holiest site in Islam after Mecca and Medina. The Western Wall is all that remains of the Jewish Temple after its destruction by the Romans in 70 AD.

(d) The nearby Arab town of Bethlehem is a major centre for pilgrims, attracted to the Church of the Nativity. Palestinians claim that the run-down tourist facilities here can offer little competition in the Millennium to the new hotels designated for the Jewish settlement of Har Homa.

Jordan

Without significant oil resources and consisting largely of semi-arid plateaus and desert, Jordan is a small and relatively poor Arab country. The population includes two very different communities – the Palestinian refugees, mainly concentrated in the capital Amman, and the Bedouin tribes of the desert. However, the country has remained politically stable thanks to the statesmanship of King Hussein who ruled from 1953 to 1999.

Tourism plays an important role in the economy, with around 1 million international arrivals annually. However, over-reliance on the attractions of East Jerusalem, Bethlehem and Jericho meant that most of Jordan's appeal, as well as its hotel stock were lost when Israel occupied those territories (the West Bank) in 1967. Jordan had then to redevelop tourism east of the River Jordan, on a less promising resource base. The major attractions now include:

● Petra – an ancient city in a unique setting, concealed in a deep valley; this accounts for a substantial part of Jordan's tourism revenue, and has encouraged hotel development in the area
● the desert scenery of Wadi Rum, where eco-tourism is being developed
● the Dead Sea and its coast where spa and health tourism is being developed
● the Crusader castle at Kerak
● the well-preserved Roman city of Jerash with its annual festival
● the pilgrim sites on the east bank of the River Jordan
● the beaches and water sports of Aqaba on the Red Sea coast, developed as a rival to Eilat.

Tourism has been restricted by the lack of infrastructure and good hotels, although the Middle East peace initiatives have encouraged hotel investment, particularly in Amman, Aqaba and on the Dead Sea coast. Most hotels are located in Amman although a network of formerly government-run 'rest houses' (now privatized) provides accommodation in the areas likely to be visited by tourists. The normalization of relations with Israel since 1994 should enable Jordan to benefit fully from the millennium tourist boom by easing access between the two countries. The Ministry of Tourism and Antiquities has encouraged sustainable tourism and community tourism projects, as at the award-winning Taybeh-Zaman tourist village close to Petra where visitors can see local craft skills in action and stay in traditional rural village houses.

Syria

Unlike Jordan, the Baathist regime that has ruled Syria since 1971, has done little to encourage foreign investment or Western tourism, although since the Gulf War, it is no longer shunned by the international community as a 'pariah state'. Relations with the USA have improved, if not with Israel. Roughly the size of England and Wales, Syria comprises a large section of the Fertile Crescent, contrasting with the stony Syrian Desert in the south-east. Poor infrastructure, such as intermittent power supplies, is a major constraint on tourism development. Nevertheless the country has major tourism potential with international arrivals in the late 1990s approaching 1 million (mainly from Lebanon and Jordan). The economic potential of tourism is taken seriously by the Ministry of Tourism, and the Prime Minister chairs the co-ordinating 'High Council of Tourism'. Most of the limited development has taken place in the western part of the country, although the Euphrates Valley in eastern Syria contains a number of important archaeological sites. There are beach resorts on the Mediterranean coast north of Lattakia as well as mountain resorts taking advantage of the cooler climate of the Anti-Lebanon Range, but as yet these are visited almost exclusively by domestic tourists. Of greater appeal to Western sightseers is Syria's cultural heritage, represented by:

● the capital Damascus, reputedly the world's oldest city. It is famed for its association with St Paul and contains the Ommayad Mosque and numerous bazaars
● the ruins of the ancient trading city of Palmyra in the Syrian Desert
● the Krak des Chevaliers, the most spectacular of the castles built by the Crusaders.

Most of Syria's hotel stock is geared to the business market, being concentrated in the major cities of Damascus, Aleppo and Lattakia. Few tour groups from European countries visit Syria (Spain is one exception) due to the negative image given by the Western media. Although Damascus airport is an important regional gateway, most visitors arrive overland from neighbouring Arab countries and their length of stay tends to be short. There seems little scope for expanding holiday tourism until the international situation in the Middle East improves.

Lebanon

Although the Lebanon is a mountainous country only half the size of Wales, its people have been involved in overseas trade since the time of the Phoenicians, and Lebanese communities are found all over the world. By the 1960s Beirut was not only the financial capital for a large part of the Arab world, but also its main entertainment centre. Arab tourists came to Lebanon not only for relief from the intense summer heat of their own countries, but also to escape the restrictions imposed by a strict interpretation of Islam. Tourism received a severe setback as a result of the civil war between the two main communities – the ruling Maronite Christians and the Moslems – which lasted from 1975 to 1991, turning once elegant Beirut into a battleground. Since the mid-1990s European tour operators have slowly added Lebanon to their stock of destinations, and MEA, the national airline, has staged a comeback. Arrivals have grown steadily since 1992 with the main sources being Jordan, France and Saudi Arabia. Beirut and the country's infrastructure are being reconstructed with a new airport and railway system. Aside from Beirut, the country's tourist attractions include:

1 Mount Lebanon, where a number of ski resorts have developed only a short drive from the beach resorts of the coast. They are mainly frequented by domestic tourists and those from other Arab countries. Unfortunately the cedar forests which once covered the mountains have largely disappeared.
2 The fertile valley of the Bekaa and the ancient temples of Baalbek which provide an ideal setting for cultural events.

Accommodation in the Lebanon tends to be expensive. As in Syria most of the beaches are polluted, and the country is not yet prepared for family holidays. The three Arab countries of Jordan, Lebanon and Syria have much in common from a tourism point of view and regional promotion would be sensible. However, although Syria and Jordan do co-operate on an economic basis, Lebanon's participation is unlikely, given its government's minimal involvement in tourism.

Turkey

In many ways distinct from its Arab neighbours to the south, Turkey has affinities with both Europe and Asia, acting as a physical and cultural 'bridge' between East and West. It controls the Dardanelles and the Bosphorus, the strategic waterways linking the Aegean to the Black Sea. As we mentioned earlier, Turkey under the Ottoman Sultans dominated not only the Middle East but also most of North Africa, the eastern Mediterranean and the Balkan Peninsula. The heritage of that empire, and of the earlier civilizations that flourished here in Anatolia before the arrival of the Turks from central Asia, is part of the fascination the country holds for foreign visitors. Turkish traditions, particularly in cuisine, craft industries such as carpet weaving, and entertainment, help to give the country a clearly defined tourist image.

Turkey is a large country by any standards, with the natural advantage of having an extensive, and for the most part, picturesque coastline along three seas – the Mediterranean, the Aegean and the Black Sea. The heartland of Turkey is less attractive, consisting of the semi-arid steppes of the Anatolian Plateau. This is separated from the fertile coastlands by a ring of mountain ranges. The climate is generally favourable for tourism, except in the mountainous north-east, which suffers from winters of almost Siberian intensity. The Black Sea coast receives a good deal of rain throughout the year, in contrast to the rest of the country.

Turkey also has the advantages of relative political stability, and an economy that is strong enough, despite rampant inflation, for its application for EU membership to be taken seriously. This is due in no small measure to the reforms carried out by Kamal Ataturk after the abolition of the sultanate in 1923. He imposed Western institutions, the Roman alphabet and Western dress. As a result, the influence of Islam is less evident than elsewhere in the Middle East, particularly in the cities of western Turkey. However, as in other developing countries, the population is growing faster than job creation and the provision of public services. This explains the large number of Turks working in Western Europe and the growth of shantytowns (known as *gekekondu*) around Istanbul and Ankara to accommodate the vast numbers of immigrants from the rural areas.

Despite having much to offer the tourist, Turkey did not participate in the boom in Mediterranean beach tourism that characterized the 1970s because:

● Turkey was expensive to reach
● Turkey was poorly promoted
● Turkey did not seek to enter the inclusive-tour market.

This situation changed when tourism was included in the government's Five-Year Plans. Charter flights were permitted, and the country was 'discovered' by the major European tour operators. As a result, the numbers of visitors trebled during the 1980s but growth subsequently slowed as a result both of the Gulf War and also the adverse publicity about the poor standard of some accommodation in the Aegean holiday resorts of Bodrum and Kusadasi. In the 1990s Turkey attracted between 2 and 3 million international visitors annually.

Germany is by far the most important generator of tourism for Turkey, followed by the UK, Russia and the Central Asian Republics. Britain was a latecomer on the scene but, despite predictions to the contrary, Turkey's popularity with the British market as a value for money destination shows no sign of waning. In the 1980s most visitors arrived by surface transport. However, the 1990s have seen a change, with the majority of visitors arriving by air, due to the fact that border crossings have been adversely affected by political turmoil in neighbouring countries, and new regional airports have been developed to serve the tourist areas. Istanbul, as the country's leading cultural and business centre, is the busiest gateway, while Ataturk's new capital at Ankara ranks far behind in terms of international traffic. Business and conference tourism is being encouraged by new convention centres in both Istanbul and Ankara. Western European holidaymakers, most of whom are on inclusive tours to the resorts of south-west Turkey, are much more likely to use the airports at Izmir, Bodrum, Dalaman and Antalya. Relatively few visitors arrive by sea, through ports such as Izmir, although these do attract substantial numbers of cruise passengers and day excursionists from the Greek Islands. There is also a large and growing domestic market, but Turks prefer to stay with relatives rather than use the country's considerable stock of hotel and self-catering accommodation.

Holiday tourism is both highly seasonal and concentrated in a small part of the country, namely the south-west coastal strip. This concentration of tourism is largely the result of short-sighted planning in the 1980s when the Ministry of Tourism envisaged coastal development on a massive scale. A number of resorts in the area have already experienced most stages in the tourism life-cycle, from initial discovery by wealthy Turkish families, yachtsmen and women, and a few backpackers, through development by small specialist tour operators, to consolidation by large companies serving the mass market. In some resorts the environmental impact of tourism has been considerable, but elsewhere, as at Olu Deniz, famed for its beautiful beach and lagoon, development has been confined to the hills overlooking the coast. In a rare instance, development was halted altogether at the Dalyan delta following protests by environmentalists. This shows that the Turkish government is willing to forgo short-term profit in the cause of conservation, and to learn belatedly from the mistakes made by other Mediterranean destinations.

South-west Turkey can be divided into the following holiday areas:

1 *The Northern Aegean*, north of Izmir. This area caters mainly for domestic tourists.
2 *The Southern Aegean*, between Izmir and Dalaman. The environmental and cultural impacts of mass tourism have been most evident in Marmaris, where overdevelopment and brash commercialism are rife, and at Gumbet on the Bodrum Peninsula, now easily accessible from the new airport. Although a lively resort, Bodrum itself has preserved more of its Turkish ambience, due largely to its superb setting on a bay dominated by a Crusader castle.
3 *The Turquoise Coast* or 'Turkish Riviera' around the Gulf of Antalya is backed by the pine-covered Lycian and Taurus mountain ranges. The resorts of Antalya, Alanya and Side contain many large up-market hotels, but other resorts, such as Kalkan, lack suitable beaches and are small and less sophisticated.

Apart from the standard beach holiday, south-west Turkey can also offer a choice of cultural, special interest, and activity tourism products, including:

1 *Sailing holidays*. The coastline, with its many harbours, secluded coves inaccessible by road, and warm sunny climate with reliable afternoon breezes is ideal for sailing. Bareboat yacht charter is available, but most holidaymakers prefer a *gulet* cruise – on a traditional wooden motor yacht, with Turkish skipper, crew and full-board arrangements.
2 *Golf*. The purpose-built resort of Belek on the Gulf of Antalya claims to be Turkey's answer to the Costa Del Sol.
3 *Spa tourism*. The unique natural resource provided by the calcified springs at Pammukkale has been known since Roman times.
4 *Activity and adventure holidays*. In the mountains close to the coastal holiday resorts, the lifestyle of the villagers has been little affected by the twentieth century. Trekking, jeep safaris and whitewater rafting are offered by a number of specialist tour operators.
5 *Cultural tourism*. Here the emphasis is on the ancient civilizations that flourished in this coastal region. Many of the most important sites are within a short drive of the coastal resorts:
   (a) Ephesus, one of the greatest cities of the Roman Empire, with its well-preserved theatre and library, is a 'must-see' attraction, but there are many other sites that are less well known, and as a result, much less crowded.
   (b) Troy and Pergamum (Bergama) are also firmly on the tourism circuit.
   (c) Other sites are less easily reached as they are widely dispersed across the Anatolian Plateau, necessitating a lengthy coach tour or internal flight to Ankara, Kayseri or Erzurum. We think the following deserve special mention:
      (i) The strange lunar landscapes of Cappadocia where the soft volcanic rock provided a refuge for early Christian communities, complete with underground churches and cave dwellings.
      (ii) The Armenian monasteries around Lake Van in eastern Turkey.

(iii) The ancient monuments at Nemrut Dagh, a World Heritage Site. Even in this remote area, visitor management and conservation are major issues.

The major cultural attractions for most visitors to Turkey, however, lie in Istanbul, the former capital of the Byzantine and Ottoman Empires. This city of 12 million people has become a popular short-break destination for the following reasons:

1 It is a major meeting point of East and West, with two bridges across the Bosphorus literally linking Asia to Europe.
2 It contains the finest achievement of Byzantine architecture – Aya Sofya (Holy Wisdom), once the largest church in Christendom.
3 The Blue Mosque, with its six minarets, is one of the most outstanding examples of Islamic architecture.
4 The Grand Bazaar is a 'must-see' for bargain-hunters, with over 4000 shops under one roof.
5 The Topkapi Palace evokes the splendour and mystery of the Sultans, particularly the *harem* or women's quarters.
6 The Cagaloglu Hamman provides the experience of a Turkish bath, another traditional institution of the Moslem world, with separate sections for men and women.

Most of Turkey still remains largely undeveloped for tourism, notably the eastern part of the Anatolia Plateau, with its harsh climate and earthquake-prone, rugged terrain. The unrest among the Kurds who inhabit the region (and adjacent parts of Iraq, Syria and Iran) has certainly been a contributory factor in discouraging tourism. The Black Sea coast, picturesque and well wooded, is mainly frequented by domestic tourists; the same also applies to the ski resorts in the mountains nearby. The south-eastern part of Turkey centring on Adana is one of the few substantial stretches of Mediterranean coastline still awaiting development, probably because agriculture and industry have been given priority.

The Arabian Peninsula

Extending between the Red Sea and the Persian Gulf, the Arabian Peninsula offers some of the most extreme contrasts to be found in the Middle East. It mostly consists of desert landscapes, although there are mountain ranges along its western and south-eastern edges that attract some rainfall, and support a greater variety of vegetation. Saudi Arabia dominates the interior and contains most of the region's population, while the Gulf States of Kuwait, Qatar, Bahrain, the United Arab Emirates and Oman are maritime in their location and outlook. To the south Yemen remains largely undeveloped for tourism.

The rapid development of the vast oil reserves of the countries around the Persian Gulf has led to a tremendous growth in demand for all kinds of goods and services from a population which, a generation ago, were largely nomads and peasant farmers. It has also attracted many temporary immigrants, comprising skilled professionals from Western countries, and a large number of labourers and domestic servants from Third World countries such as Pakistan and the Philippines, as well as from the poorer Arab countries such as Jordan. In some of the Gulf States, expatriate workers form a large percentage of the population. The whole region has become an important generator of international travel, led by Saudi Arabia, and per capita expenditure on foreign travel is among the highest in the world. The major outbound flows are to the UK and France, although Egypt and Cyprus are also significant destinations. Outbound travel is concentrated between June and September when the summer heat is intense.

Spending by residents of the region abroad is estimated to be almost twice that of inbound foreign visitors, who come mainly for business reasons. Before the 1980s, there was little in the region to attract holiday tourism from the West, and outsiders were distrusted by a traditional society strictly adhering to the teachings of Islam. However, a small but growing number of sophisticated, culturally aware European tourists are attracted to the United Arab Emirates, particularly to Dubai and Sharjah in the winter months, and both business travellers and expatriates take advantage of their stay to explore the region. Tourists can benefit from the slight decline in the business travel market that occurred after the boom in the 1970s, as the region's airlines – Gulf Air and Emirates – are anxious to fill aircraft seats, while the luxury hotels of the Gulf states also need to increase occupancy levels.

Most internal and external travel is by air, and a comprehensive network of services has developed to link the cities. Ports such as Dubai and Aden have been important in communications between the Mediterranean and the Indian Ocean for centuries. The airports at Bahrain and Dubai are important as stopovers on intercontinental flights between Europe and the Far East. The duty-free shopping in Dubai – especially the gold souks – is attractive to passengers on these routes, while both states are important as trading and banking centres for the region.

The Gulf States

The Gulf States have less to offer the cultural tourist, with the exception of Oman. Much of the traditional architecture, with its picturesque wind towers (a device to cool buildings by evaporation) has disappeared, and cities such as Abu Dhabi are thoroughly modern in appearance. The Gulf States are well aware that the oil resource will soon be exhausted. Dubai in particular is successfully attracting tourism to diversify its economic base, led by the Dubai

Commerce and Tourism Promotion Board. It is using its oil wealth to create golf courses in the desert, to become a cruise destination. 'Wadi-bashing' – four-wheel drive expeditions into the desert – appeals to many visitors, along with the opportunity to observe the more traditional lifestyle of the Bedouin. The coasts of the Persian Gulf provide a number of good beaches and opportunities for water sports. So far, the oil industry does not appear to have made a serious impact on the ecology of this shallow sea, but circumstances could change. Oman, with its long seafaring traditions, has perhaps the most tourist potential. The mountains contain a number of archaeological sites and resorts based on mineral springs, while Muscat is an interesting seaport.

Saudi Arabia

Saudi Arabia is solely a destination for business travellers as far as the West is concerned. It is however, the destination for well over a million Moslems each year from outside Arabia, performing the *haj* or pilgrimage to the holy cities of Mecca and Medina. The *haj* is concentrated within a few weeks during the last month of the Moslem calendar and involves a major logistical exercise with a huge charter airlift. Saudi Arabia has no official tourism agency at national level, but regional authorities have assumed the role where needed. The Saudi government has spent a substantial part of its oil revenues on highway construction and the expansion of terminal facilities at Jeddah airport, as the majority of pilgrims now arrive by air rather than use the slow and perhaps dangerous land and sea routes.

Yemen

Unlike the other countries of the Arabian Peninsula, Yemen is poor and tribal traditions persist to a much greater degree, so that the government is often ineffective. Tourism is in its infancy, and there are no holiday resorts, while negative publicity has followed a spate of kidnappings of Western tourists by tribesmen in the interior highlands. Yet Yemen has much to interest the more adventurous tourist, notably the unique tower houses of the capital Sana'a, and the remains of the Sabaean (Sheba) civilization that grew rich on the incense trade in biblical times. Yemen is also the subject of the second case study at the end of this chapter.

Iran and Iraq

Two of the most important countries in the Middle East – Iran and Iraq – have strongly influenced the development of tourism elsewhere in the region, while tourists have been deterred from visiting by unfavourable publicity in the Western media.

Iraq

The major part of Iraq is made up of the fertile plains of the Tigris and Euphrates, historically known as Mesopotamia, where a number of civilizations developed in ancient times. During the 1970s the government began to develop a tourist industry, based on projects such as the Habbaniya Tourist Village near Baghdad, which catered mainly for wealthy foreign visitors as well as Iraqis. A number of archaeological sites were also restored, such as Nineveh, capital of ancient Assyria and, more controversially, Babylon. Development was halted by the Gulf War, and the economic sanctions that followed. Few tourists other than business travellers visit Baghdad, and little remains of the city that inspired the *Arabian Nights* over 1000 years ago.

Iran

Formerly known as Persia, Iran is different in language and culture from its Arab neighbours. Before the 1979 revolution, which overthrew the pro-Western Shah and installed a fundamentalist Islamic regime under Ayatollah Khomeini, Iran attracted a significant volume of tourism. After the revolution, Western hotel chains were expelled and tourism is now under the authority of the Ministry for Cultural and Islamic Guidance – which implies the importance of culture in the Iranian tourist product. Tourists are now returning and international arrivals have increased tenfold in the 1990s, mainly from neighbouring countries. Iranians are proud of their heritage, which goes back to the time of the Persian Empire, long before the Arabs introduced Islam to the Middle East. Iran is a large country, consisting mainly of an arid central plateau surrounded by high mountain ranges. Tourist resources include:

1 Some of the finest examples of Islamic architecture are found in the cities, particularly Isfahan.
2 A number of ski centres exist in the Elburz Mountains within reach of Tehran.
3 There are resorts along the Caspian Sea, the Gulf coast and on Kish Island in the Persian Gulf, with segregated beaches for male and female bathers. These resorts cater for the domestic market, however, the Caspian Sea coast is scenically and climatically much more attractive than the Gulf Coast. Only the Caspian resorts are within easy reach of the majority of the population.
4 Teheran is an overgrown metropolis of some 8 million people with little to recommend it to tourists.
5 The historic cities of Isfahan and Shiraz are much more attractive as potential tourist centres. Shiraz is also situated near the impressive ruins of Persepolis, capital of the ancient Persian Empire.

The position of tourism in Iran mirrors the situation in the Middle East generally. Further growth will depend upon the extent to which modernizers can prevail over hard-line fundamentalists, and on an improvement in relations with the USA.

Summary

The countries of the Middle East are close enough to the tourist generating markets of northern Europe to have developed a sizeable tourism industry. Yet only Turkey has developed beach tourism on a scale comparable with other Mediterranean destinations. Cultural tourism is more significant in the region, but only Israel, Egypt and Turkey have attracted cultural tourists in large numbers. Saudi Arabia and the Gulf States receive a considerable volume of business tourists, and this part of the Middle East is also a major generator of outbound international tourism. Domestic tourism is also significant in most countries of the region, but is mainly VFR, rather than hotel based.

The region's tourism products are varied, including summer and winter sun beach holidays, spas and ski resorts in the mountains, adventure holidays in the desert, religious pilgrimages and cultural tours. The Middle East can offer many natural and human-made attractions, some of which are unique. The region's history as the setting for many civilizations over thousands of years is important, while religion continues to play an important role in everyday life.

Historically, the Middle East lies at a crossroads in world communications, where Europe, Africa and Asia meet. Transport to and within most of the region is good, and highways and airports have been provided to meet the increased demand for international travel.

There are many problems affecting the further growth of tourism. The prevailing warm dry climate, allied to demographic and economic pressures has put a severe strain on the region's scarce water supplies. Governments need to pay more attention to the conservation of the cultural as well as the natural resources on which tourism depends. However, the greatest threat is the political instability of most countries in the region, fuelled by religious fundamentalism, social and ethnic tensions, such as the unresolved conflict between Palestinians and Jews – and the legacy of the Gulf War.

Case study

Tourism in the Republic of Yemen

Introduction

Yemen is a fascinating, yet complex country, classified by the United Nations as among the world's poorest forty countries. Tourism has the potential to make a significant contribution to the economy and quality of life of Yemen, yet religious and cultural constraints are problematic and the kidnappings and deaths of tourists in the late 1990s were a major setback for the fledgling tourism industry. In part, the attraction of the country is that it still retains the lifestyles of centuries ago and a feeling of isolation from the rest of the world. The country was formerly divided – South and North Yemen – and two distinct approaches are still identifiable in the approach to tourism development:

1 The *People's Republic of South Yemen* came into being when British colonial rule, based in Aden, ended in 1967. The politics of South Yemen were hard-line Marxist-Leninist.
2 In the north, the *Yemen Arab Republic* was a despotic tribal country, fiercely religious and true to the Islamic faith.

In 1990 the two former Yemens joined to create the Republic of Yemen with a population approaching 12 million. This merger brought together two very different political and economic systems and led to civil war in 1994. It was not until the ending of the civil war and the return to a more stable environment that tourism could be seriously considered.

Tourism is in the very early stages of development in Yemen – a good example of the involvement stage of the tourism area life cycle. The majority of visitors either arrive in organized parties to see the antiquities and lifestyle of the Yemeni people, or are on oil-related business trips. Although tourism to Yemen was stimulated by British colonial rule, with Aden's role as an entrepôt and sea port on the British P&O route to India, organized international tourism began as recently as the 1970s. Two international hotels were built in the 1980s; yet even in the 1990s volumes of tourism remain small, fluctuating considerably according to the levels of security and the political situation.

Tourism demand

While there is real potential for tourism in Yemen, the kidnappings and violence in the late 1990s discouraged large numbers from visiting. Tourism was still on a very small scale – reaching around 60 000 international visitors with a spend of US$39 million, before the problems of 1998 and 1999. The gateways are the international airports at Sana'a and Aden. For leisure visits:

1 The focus is on north Yemen, based on the capital Sana'a where touring circuits for the antiquities have been developed.
2 Visitors stay on average four or five days.
3 Europeans dominate the market.

4 Most visits are with organized groups.

5 Demand is highly seasonal, concentrated in the cooler months of December to March.

Domestic tourism is important – both for visits to friends and relatives and adventurous visits to the desert – contributing between one-half and two-thirds of bed-nights in Yemen. Here there is a contrast with international tourism as domestic visits are less seasonal and tend to focus on the south of the country.

Tourism supply

Tourism resources

The tourism resources of Yemen are based upon the culture and lifestyle of the people, and the antiquities of the country. In addition. Yemen offers the potential for snorkelling, trekking and diving, although cultural traditions mean that beach tourism is not really an option.

The culture and lifestyle of the people is all-pervasive in Yemen, yet it is strangely difficult to access for the international visitor. In contrast, the architecture is accessible and of international significance – as for example in the central area of the capital Sana'a, a World Heritage Site. The local architecture of tall buildings with stained-glass windows provides a medieval feel to many of the towns and villages.

The archaeological resources are found mainly in the north and focused around the Marib and Baraqish region north-west of Sana'a. However, lack of care has meant that many are in poor repair and some are being lost. For the antiquities, the main tourism circuits have been designed by the many ground handlers in Yemen, although two companies dominate the market. In addition, unification of the country has allowed operators to provide more extensive circuits. The circuits are mainly in the triangle between Sana'a, Hudaydah and Ta'izz. However, the infrastructure to support tours is primitive, the roads are dusty and in poor repair, and this has led the tour operators to invest in their facilities en route, such as hotels.

Organization of tourism

Overall, the Ministry of Tourism co-ordinates tourism, with the General Tourist Authority (GTA) as the implementing agency. These public bodies are assisted by:

● the Higher Tourism Council with an oversight of strategy and policy
● the Yemen Tourism Promotion Board.

Tourism priorities for Yemen are as follows:

1 Develop sustainable tourism for the benefit of the community.

2 Enhance and preserve Yemeni cultural, historic and natural assets.

3 Promoting the unified Yemen internationally.

4 Facilitating tourism and removing constraints.

5 Assisting in the construction and upgrading of the accommodation sector.

6 Improving the level and output of tourism training.

In addition to these priorities, there is a need to address the imbalance of tourism between north and south Yemen – the north receives the bulk of international tourism. In part international assistance will achieve these aims through two master plans carried out since unification. However, tourists' fears regarding their safety and security may render these plans meaningless.

Accommodation

In the past, the state has intervened in the accommodation sector – in the former South Yemen the government owned and operated hotels, whereas in the former North Yemen government incentives were provided. A number of projects demonstrated how historic buildings could be converted and managed as hotels. Since unification, the government has leased its own hotels to the private sector. This means that the accommodation sector remains dominated by locally owned small hotels and *funduks* (local hotels and inns, often with outdoor sleeping quarters for the very hot summers) at the lower end of the market. However, this situation is slowly being addressed as a number of international chains have expressed interest in investing in the sector to complement those already there (Movenpick, Sheraton and Taj). By the mid-1990s there were around 12 000 bed-spaces in Yemen, but expansion will depend on the political stability of the country.

(Burns and Cooper, 1997)

Case study

Nile cruise tourism

Introduction

The Nile is the world's longest river at 6700 kilometres, and Nile cruises are probably Egypt's best known tourism product. A cruise is a romantic way of seeing many of Egypt's best known 'antiquities' – the sites of its ancient civilizations – which include the temples at Luxor and Karnak, the Colossi of Memnon, Tutankhamun's Tomb and the Valley of Kings. Cruising has the advantage of providing an accommodation base in a floating hotel, avoiding the often arduous journeys by road or rail otherwise involved in sightseeing.

The Nile is synonymous with Egypt and for thousands of years it has been a vital resource and the transport lifeline between the north and south of the country. Until recently, the river used to flood extensive areas regularly between July and October, following the rains at its source in the highlands of Ethiopia. These floods renewed the fertility of the soil by depositing a layer of silt on the fields. With the construction of the Aswan High Dam in 1971, a gain of 20 per cent in the area of cultivatable land and a boost to power supplies has been offset by ecological changes and a reduction in water levels, which has impeded cruise operations. When Thomas Cook inaugurated steamship services on the Nile in the 1870s, thus opening up Egypt to modern tourism, the entire length of the river was navigable to Aswan throughout the year. Since the early 1990s, cruises no longer operate on the lower Nile between Cairo and Luxor, as silt has built up in the river, aggravating the problem of low water levels during the winter months.

The development of Nile cruises

Since the days of Thomas Cook, tourism on the Nile has grown steadily. Initially, small groups of independent, adventurous tourists were attracted, and the Agatha Christie novel 'Death on the Nile' exemplified the upper class, predominantly British, image of Nile cruising before the Second World War. More recently, larger groups on inclusive tours, drawn from a wider range of countries and socioeconomic groups have become the norm. Many Nile cruisers are young couples in their twenties, although the over fifty age group is also well represented. All-inclusive packages are now common, bringing the price of a Nile cruise within reach of budget travellers. The international hotel chains have entered the cruise market; Hilton, for example, began operating five-star cruise vessels in 1988, while Sheraton and Marriott soon followed. The number of vessels grew

Table 19.1 Floating hotels on the Nile, 1995

Rating	Units	Cabins	Beds
5-star	82	5 186	10 312
4-star	40	1 831	3 642
3-star	20	607	1 209
2-star	13	249	488
Under classification	51	2 659	5 267
Total	206	10 532	20 918

considerably during the early 1990s from a total of fifty-five in 1990, to over 200 by 1995. This probably represents the Nile cruise industry at its peak (see Table 19.1). Since then, terrorism by Moslem fundamentalists has drastically reduced both the numbers of visitors to Egypt and the number of cruise operators.

Table 19.1 clearly shows that on average the higher-quality 'floating hotels' are much larger than the two-star vessels, with three times as many cabins. The majority of cabins have two berths, indicating the importance of the 'couples' market. Most of the vessels have air conditioning and water purification systems. Onboard facilities for those in the higher price range include a sundeck with bar, games area and small swimming pool, entertainment lounge, restaurant and boutiques.

Characteristics of Nile cruises

1 Nile cruises are a unique product, using shallow-draft four-deck vessels. Most are of a standardized 'shoe-box' design, but some have been modelled on the paddle steamers used in Cook's time. The emphasis is on comfort and sightseeing rather than speed. The newest vessels can cruise at 16 kilometres per hour upstream against the Nile current, and 22 kilometres per hour downstream.

2 The major cruising stretch of the Nile is between the Valley of the Kings, the site of ancient Thebes, Luxor and Karnak in the north, and Aswan to the south. En route passengers visit the temples at Edfu before arriving at Aswan to see the 3-kilometre long High Dam and the Temple of Philae.

3 To the south of Aswan, another cruising area has been opened up as a result of the High Dam, on the 500-kilometre long Lake Nasser. Known locally as the 'Nubian Sea' its attractions are less well known, with the exception of the temples of Abu Simbel, which were rescued from inundation by UNESCO.

4 Most cruises last between three and eleven nights. In the shorter version clients cruise from Luxor to Aswan in one direction only, with domestic flights based on Cairo forming the other 'legs' of the trip. Longer cruises allow more quality time for sightseeing with short excursions on both banks of the Nile. Sometimes, tour operators offer 'cruise and stay' arrangements with one or more nights in a hotel at Luxor and/or Aswan, adding an extra dimension to the holiday.

5 The high season for cruising is from October to April when the climate is ideal for sightseeing. The vessels also operate in the low season, when the heat can be extreme, at considerably reduced prices.

6 Crews tend to be recruited locally, with the length of training varying from a few weeks to a few months according to the job description.

7 Ground-handling of cruise passengers at the sites tends to be organized by Egyptian travel agencies who

provide transport and guides for the visiting groups, often under contract to the larger inbound tour operators.

8 The base for the Nile cruise industry is at Luxor, which has a long history as an international tourist centre. It was made world famous by Howard Carter's discovery of the tomb and treasures of the boy – Pharaoh Tutankhamun in 1922. Until recently Luxor was difficult to reach except by boat. The construction of a new road to the Valley of the Kings in 1995, followed by a bridge linking Luxor to the west bank of the Nile two years later has improved access considerably. The floating hotels moored on the east bank complement other accommodation in and around Luxor.

The issues

Overcrowding

The Nile cruise industry is poorly organized and visits to the sites when a vessel has berthed can be chaotic with guides, taxi drivers and traders vying for tourists' attention. At Luxor, for example, most guided tours are arranged to meet tour buses and the arrival of cruise ships at certain times of the day, resulting in considerable congestion as visitors and vehicles converge. There is a case for phased visits and good visitor management as the focused visitor pressure is threatening the integrity of the sites. Some idea of the pressures can be gauged from the average daily numbers of visitors at the key sites in December, shown in Table 19.2.

Table 19.2 Average daily numbers of visitors at the key sites in the Nile Valley in December

Valley of the Kings	9297
Karnak Temple	2647
Luxor Temple	2426
Deir El Bahri	1074
Tomb of Tutankhamun	848
Valley of the Queens	743

Source: Supreme Council of Antiquities, Luxor.

Terrorism

The Egyptian government has stepped up security in the Luxor area, since the terrorist attacks in November 1997 at the Temple of Hatshepset received wide international publicity. This led to a severe downturn in the number of visitors, particularly from European countries, with hotel occupancy rates in Luxor falling to 25 per cent during most of 1998. In response, the Egyptian government has launched an initiative to encourage Egyptians to visit the antiquities in greater numbers – however, the success of this campaign adds to congestion at the sites.

Port facilities

The main overnight berthing points for cruise vessels are Luxor, Esna, Kom Ombo and Aswan, where docks and other facilities are of a poor standard. Travel agents and cruise operators are developing their own quays in the absence of official provision. For example, at any one time there can be between thirty and eighty vessels moored at the dock on the east bank at Luxor, with as many as seven moored side by side. This means that passengers have to cross from vessel to vessel to reach the shore, at some risk and inconvenience to themselves.

Pollution

The vessels are mainly diesel powered, causing pollution in the Nile and corrosive fumes at the sites.

Low water levels

Low water levels in the Nile can disrupt cruise schedules at certain times of the year. This is nowadays due to controls by the authorities on the amount of water leaving Lake Nasser through the Aswan High Dam. A more insidious problem is the run-off of the fertilizers that farmers are forced to use, now that the annual cycle of Nile floods has been disrupted. This encourages the growth of algae and weeds that not only upsets the ecological balance of the river, but causes damage to the propellers of the vessels.

(Pakkala, 1990; Rivers, 1998; web site at www.idsc.gov.eg)

20

Africa and the islands of the Indian Ocean

After reading this chapter, you should be able to:

1 Describe the major physical regions and climates of Africa and understand their importance for tourism.
2 Appreciate the social and economic factors behind the development of tourism in the most important African destinations.
3 Recognize that aside from development in North Africa and South Africa, the continent's tourism potential is largely unfulfilled.
4 Appreciate the nature of the demand, especially safaris, for inbound tourism to Africa south of the Sahara.
5 Describe the major international gateways and the relevant features of internal transport in Africa's major tourist regions.
6 Outline the organization of tourism in the major tourist destinations of Africa.
7 Demonstrate a knowledge of the tourist regions, resorts, business centres and tourist attractions of Africa.

Introduction

We mentioned in Chapter 19 that the countries of North Africa share many characteristics with those of the Middle East region. There are indeed major cultural and physical differences between North Africa and the rest of the continent. Physically, Morocco, Algeria and Tunisia consist largely of fold mountains that are geologically similar to those of southern Europe. Much of the scenery, with the

exception of the desert zone, resembles that of Greece, Spain or southern Italy and its peoples are predominantly Arabs or Berbers. In contrast, most of Africa south of the Sahara consists of plateaus and block mountains, with only a narrow coastal plain separated from the interior by high escarpments. In terms of their ethnicity and culture, the nations of 'Black Africa' are different from the Arab states of the north. They have only recently emerged from a period of colonial rule by Europeans. However, this is an experience that is also shared with North Africans, who are represented in the Organization of African Unity (OAU). Although the Sahara Desert acted as a formidable physical barrier between the countries of North Africa and those to the south, it was frequently crossed by camel caravans, allowing an exchange of goods and ideas.

The sheer size of Africa is at once an asset and a hindrance to developing a tourism industry. On the one hand, most of the continent is sparsely populated, offering wide open spaces, an almost unique wealth of wildlife, spectacular scenery, and tribal cultures that have fascinated travellers for centuries. Yet apart from North Africa, which has taken advantage of its proximity to Europe, and South Africa, with its well-developed infrastructure, the continent's tourism potential is largely untapped. This is due to the following factors:

1 *Accessibility* Before the advent of air travel, much of the interior of Africa was virtually inaccessible. Even today, air services are poor by world standards and many experts consider this is holding back the development of tourism. The same is true of surface transport. There are very few harbours along the coast, and even penetration up the largest rivers – the Congo or Zambezi for example – is blocked by rapids and waterfalls. Road and rail infrastructure is generally inadequate in most African countries, so that touring holidays can be a major undertaking.

In the absence of adequate public transport, improvised alternatives, such as the 'bush taxis' of the Gambia and the *matatus* of Kenya can be used by the more adventurous independent travellers.

2 *A low level of economic development* Most African countries fall in the 'least developed' category with only a few having reached the intermediate level of development. They tend to be rural in character, although the populations of the national capitals are expanding faster than the provision of jobs or public services. Levels of poverty and illiteracy generally mean that outbound travel is restricted to an élite, while the volume of domestic tourism is insignificant compared with that of Western countries. Although some countries do see tourism as an important source of foreign currency and a stimulus to the economy, many governments give tourism a low priority for investment compared with other economic sectors.

3 *Poor organization* There is a generally poor level of organization, particularly at the regional level. Some governments also place bureaucratic obstacles in the way of tourists, making intra-regional travel difficult. In addition, education and training for the tourism sector are of a poor standard and marketing budgets are inadequate.

4 *Political instability* Many of the world's 'trouble-spots' are located in Africa, fuelled by tribal unrest, ethnic rivalries or boundary disputes (few African countries are nation-states in the European sense). This has led to concern in the Western media over the physical security of tourists, and has also discouraged Western investment in the tourism industry.

5 *Perceived health and safety risks* The high incidence of AIDS, as well as insect-borne diseases such as malaria and yellow fever, is due in large measure to the inadequate infrastructure of public health services in most of Africa.

6 *Sceptical investment environment* Investors are often reluctant to invest in tourism in countries where the political climate is changeable and where a return on their investment is not guaranteed, and price inflation is not under control.

All these constraints and structural weaknesses have frustrated Africa's ability to capitalize on the growing long-haul market, and it is clear that tourism is still a fledgling industry. This is borne out by the statistics – for the whole of the continent international tourist arrivals scarcely exceeded 20 million in the second half of the 1990s – less than international arrivals to the UK in an average year. Indeed, for a continent that contains 15 per cent of the world's population, it receives only a small share of the tourist market, amounting to 4 per cent. Out of more than fifty countries considered in the region, less than half have developed significant tourism industries. In the remaining countries, hotel accommodation is rarely found outside the national capitals. However, there are a number of positive factors that will boost African tourism as we enter the new millennium:

● interest in African peoples and cultures
● increasing pace and variety of tourism development
● Africa will be attractive to segments of the population in the generating markets who have both the time and the income to travel
● growing importance of ethnic ties between Africa and Europe
● pursuit of free market economic policies in many African countries
● improved air access.

North Africa

In contrast to most of sub-Saharan Africa, the North African countries, with the significant exception of Libya, have developed a sizeable tourism industry, based on beach holidays and inclusive tours for the north European market. This in fact, is an extension of the resort developments around the Mediterranean coast of Europe, although the cultural setting is quite different. This region now accounts for over a third of foreign tourist arrivals to the African continent, with more than half arriving from countries across the Mediterranean, namely France, Spain and Italy. Morocco was the first country to enter the market in the 1950s and both Tunisia and Algeria soon followed.

We can divide most of North Africa into three main zones:

1 The fertile coastal plains, which have a Mediterranean climate.
2 The Atlas mountains, which reach their greatest extent in Morocco. In relation to their resources, these highlands are quite densely populated. There are frequent snowfalls during the winter months.
3 The deserts of the south where productive land is restricted to the oases. The Sahara and its peoples provide the region with its best known tourist image, but in reality, nomadic tribes now make up only a small minority of the population, while the camel caravan has been superseded by motorized transport.

Morocco, Algeria, Tunisia and Libya, have formed an important part of the Moslem world since their conquest by Arabs from the Middle East in the eighth century AD. Arabic is the official language of all four countries, and Arabs form the majority of the population, especially in the cities. However, the earlier inhabitants – the Berbers – still carry on their traditional way of life in the more remote areas. During the first half of the twentieth century, France ruled Algeria, Tunisia and the greater part of Morocco. As a result, French is the second language and some French cultural characteristics have been adopted by the educated classes of the cities. The French were also responsible for constructing a good highway system, and well-planned European-style cities. To a lesser extent, the Spanish in their zone of Morocco, and the Italians in Libya, left a similar legacy. However, the influence of the Middle East remains predominant, as evidenced by the mosques and the souks, along with the crowded *medinas* and *kasbahs* (the old Arab districts) of the cities. Traditional handicrafts – notably leather, metalwork and pottery – are important in the local economy and have been stimulated by the growth of tourism – often with government encouragement.

The main problem facing the Maghreb countries (Morocco, Algeria and Tunisia) is the 'demographic time-bomb', causing acute pressure on land and water resources – half the population of about 70 million is under twenty-one years of age. Poverty, illiteracy and unemployment are widespread, both in the cities – which are surrounded by *bidonvilles* (shantytowns) – and in the countryside. The national economies cannot produce enough jobs to meet expectations, even for those with a Western-style education. This situation has contributed to the rise of Moslem fundamentalism in Algeria, which has so far been checked in Morocco and Tunisia. Not surprisingly, Western tourists with their relative wealth are also seen as an obvious target for exploitation by unlicensed guides, vendors and touts of every description – Tangier in Morocco is a notorious example here.

Morocco

The timeless, almost biblical scenes that can be found in Morocco have a particular appeal. For the adventurous tourist travelling overland, it is the gateway to Africa. Its markets assault the senses with a medley of sights and pungent aromas, resulting in 'culture shock' for Western visitors. Its cities also contain some of the most exquisite examples of Islamic architecture. Yet this most 'oriental' of North African countries extends further west geographically than any part of the European continent, and can be reached by a three-hour flight from the cities of Western Europe. Morocco is also unique among North African countries in having been an independent kingdom for many centuries, whose power at one time extended over most of Spain and the western Sahara. It experienced only one period of foreign domination (from 1912 to 1956) when it was divided into French and Spanish protectorates. Under the rule of King Hassan II it has remained politically stable, with the government steering a course between traditional Islam and modernization. However, the unresolved conflict with the Polisario guerrillas over the issue of independence for the Western Sahara (formerly Spanish territory) has held up tourism development in southern Morocco.

The heartland of Morocco is a fertile plateau separated by rugged mountain ranges from the Sahara Desert to the south and east, and the Mediterranean coast to the north. The High Atlas, rising to 4000 metres near Marrakesh, is the most spectacular of these mountain ramparts. Morocco is fortunate in having an extensive coastline on both the Atlantic and the Mediterranean. The climate of the Atlantic coast is particularly favourable for tourism, due to the influence of the cool Canaries Current, which ensures that the summers are usually free of the excessive heat and dust-laden winds, found elsewhere in North Africa. Winters are much warmer, drier and sunnier in southern Morocco than in the north, which explains why Agadir is promoted as a winter sun destination rather than Tangier.

Of the 3 million or so annual tourist arrivals during the 1990s one-third are Europeans, mainly from France, Spain, Britain and Germany. This is not surprising given the development of air-inclusive tours to Morocco and the convenient ferry links from Spain and Gibraltar. Neighbouring Algeria is an increasingly important source of visitors. Moroccan expatriates working in Western Europe and returning for their annual holiday form a large proportion of the remaining arrivals, along with tourists from other Arab states. However, this is not reciprocated, as those Moroccans who can afford foreign travel prefer to visit Europe. Morocco has one of the best transport systems in Africa, with tarmac highways penetrating mountains and desert, and a network of inter-city bus services, supplemented by *grands-taxis*. The national carrier, Royal Air Maroc operates an efficient domestic air network. Two-thirds of Morocco's accommodation is in hotels and the rest in self-catering. The French tour operator Club Méditerranée pioneered all-inclusive holiday villages on the Mediterranean coast and at Ouarzazate in the Sahara.

In the past, the Moroccan government invested heavily in tourism development, particularly in middle category and luxury hotels, so that tourism employs over 500 000 people. The Ministry of Tourism has the overall responsibility for the financing and development of tourism projects as well as promotion. Following depressed arrivals in the first half of the 1990s, the government seriously revised its approach to tourism. This involved changing the promotion of Morocco with a new image of landscapes and culture, and the development of new products – (such as desert tourism around Ouarzazate), quality assurance across the sector, and the search for new markets. The government is now emphasizing the role of the private sector, by offering attractive incentives to developers, but ensuing that projects should be in keeping with local traditions. Two examples illustrate this policy:

1 Agadir is Morocco's most popular international beach resort. The old town was destroyed by an earthquake in 1960, and a modern resort of high-rise hotels and apartment blocks soon took its place to meet the demand for accommodation. Later expansion has been more sensitively designed, in the form of low-rise developments in the traditional Moorish style.

2 As part of its conservation strategy, the government has also encouraged the use of historic buildings as hotels, as shown by projects in Essaouira, formerly an important trading centre known as Mogador.

As you may have already gathered, Morocco is far more than just a beach destination. The country's resource base is varied and includes the following products:

1 Two-centre holidays, combining a stay at a beach resort with sightseeing in the major cities and excursions into the countryside. For example, Agadir is the gateway to Southern Morocco, and is often combined with Marrakesh, perhaps the most fascinating of all Moroccan cities.
2 More in-depth cultural tours, such as the 'Imperial Cities' circuit with combines Fez, Meknes, Rabat and Marrakesh – all of which at one time have served as the capital of Morocco.
3 Short city breaks in Fez and Marrakesh.
4 Business and conference tourism, with facilities of international standard in the modern city of Casablanca, which is Morocco's financial and commercial centre, complementing the capital Rabat.
5 Special-interest holidays, including golf, painting and photography, and sport fishing off the Atlantic coast;
6 For trekking the main area of interest is the High Atlas, which contains spectacular mountain scenery and Berber villages, apparently unchanged over the centuries. To the south of these mountains is the very different climate and landscapes of Southern Morocco, where the desert is never far away. Major attractions include the oasis towns of Zagora and Ouarzazate, the gorges of the Todra and the Dades, and the strange fortress villages, built of red sun-dried clay by the local Berbers, known as *ksour* or *kasbahs*.
7 For skiing the main resorts are Ifrane in the Middle Atlas near Fez, which was originally developed by the French as a summer health resort, and Oukamaiden in the High Atlas near Marrakesh. Both cater almost exclusively for the domestic market and French skiers.
8 Surfing on the largely undeveloped Atlantic coast south of Casablanca.

In contrast to Agadir and the popular beach resorts around Casablanca, the other major tourist centres of Morocco cater more for sightseeing. They include:

1 *Tangier* This is a popular beach resort as well as being a major gateway. For many visitors arriving by ferry or cruise ship, the medina of Tangier is their first impression of Morocco and a stressful one – due to the hordes of hustlers. The city's reputation as a centre for gay tourism is partly a legacy of its pre-1956 status as an International Zone. Near Tangier is the fishing port of Asilah, now an artist's colony, and the picturesque towns of Tetouan and Chefchaouen, which retain some of the cultural influence of Spain. The Rif Mountains are less accessible, due to their role in the international drug trade.
2 *Fez* Although its extensive medina is a World Heritage Site, Fez is not as well known as Marrakesh and has been less affected by tourism. Its main attractions are the Attarine Medrassa (one of a number of Moslem colleges) the Karaouine Mosque and the spice market. Those interested in Moroccan leather can visit the dyeworks and tanneries where medieval industrial methods are still carried on.
3 *Marrakesh* The city has been fashionable as a winter sun destination since the 1930s but is now mainly famous for its souks and the colourful market square known as the Djemaa el Fna, which is ideal for people-watching. Here crowds gather around entertainers such as storytellers, snake charmers, acrobats and musicians. Berber folklore features in the event attractions known as *fantasias*, which feature impressive displays of horsemanship by local tribesmen. One of the most attractive features of Marrakesh is the gardens which provide a refuge from the extreme summer heat; those of the Mamounia Hotel are world famous.

Tunisia

With a long history of contact with other parts of the Mediterranean, Tunisia is one of the most tolerant of the Arab states. This has been a factor in the development of the country as a holiday playground for Europeans seeking sun, sea and sand. Tunisia not only has the advantages of superb beaches and, especially in the south, a favourable winter climate, but tourism development has been encouraged and carefully managed. Compared to most other Arab states, Tunisia is politically stable, while the government has consistently applied liberal social and economic policies. Tourism caters mainly for the mass market, and this is shown by the fact that about half of the 4 million annual arrivals are mostly package holidaymakers from France, Germany and Britain, concentrated during the summer months. However, Tunisia has been successfully promoted as a winter sun destination and this has boosted arrivals between October and March. Nevertheless the country's dependence on the European market leaves it vulnerable to recession in the generating countries and also to the international political situation. For example, although it is geographically far from the Middle East, tourism was adversely affected by the Gulf War crisis of 1990–1.

As you would expect in a country dependent on the mass market, the majority of visitors arrive by air. Tunis airport mainly handles scheduled services, but most holidaymakers on inclusive tours arrive at Monastir, which was specially built to handle charter flights. La Goulette and Bizerta are the ports of arrival for cruise passengers. Tunisia's professional approach to tourism includes upgrading the welcome facilities for travellers at the major gateways.

Hotel accommodation on the coast is mostly in low-rise developments, physically separate from the local communities, designed in the traditional style and blending with the local environment. Other forms of accommodation include youth hostels and campsites. The French tour operator Club Méditerranée chose Tunisia as the location for several of its all-inclusive holiday villages.

Tourism is an important sector of the economy and government involvement is extensive. The National Ministry of the Economy formulates the policy context tourism but its day-to-day implementation is carried out by the Tunisian National Tourism Office (ONTT). Since the 1980s Tunisia has diversified the tourism product away from the sea, sun and sand image, by promoting:

- an upmarket marina and sports complex at Port El Kantaoui north of Sousse
- a number of golf courses of world-class standard
- the Tabarka area in the north west – the 'Coral Coast' – as a scuba-diving destination
- Saharan tourism in the desert south, where a number of luxury hotels are available in oasis towns such as Tozeur
- the rich cultural heritage of the country, particularly relating to the time when Tunisia was the granary of the Roman Empire.

Most tourists prefer to spend their time on the beaches and holiday complexes of the coast, the most important being Hammamet, Monastir and Sousse. In the south, the island of Djerba with its myriad palm trees is an important winter sun destination, while the Kerkenneh islands offer a less sophisticated holiday product.

Tunisia is a relatively compact country, giving the holidaymaker based on the coast a wide choice of excursions, including:

1 The city of Tunis, with its spacious modern boulevards, contrasting with the medieval Arab medina. The Bardo Museum has a world-renowned collection of finds from nearby Carthage, one of the great trading centres of ancient times.
2 The remains of the Roman cities of Dougga and El Djem – the amphitheatre here was almost as large as the Colosseum in Rome.
3 The holy city of Kairouan, famous for its Great Mosque and traditional crafts, such as saddle-making and carpet-weaving.
4 The troglodite community of Matmata and the oases of southern Tunisia. Although very few Tunisians are Saharan nomads, tour operators have exploited Western visitors' perceptions of the country by staging 'Bedouin feasts' that are really pseudo-events. Excursions by jeep or camel, from oasis towns such as Douz, provide a more genuine desert experience.

Algeria

In some respects Algeria is the most Westernized of the North African countries. It experienced a much longer period of French rule, and was in fact treated as part of metropolitan France. After the wars of independence that ended in 1962, the FLN government established a secular, socialist-leaning state, using Algeria's considerable oil revenues to industrialize the country, expand education and redistribute wealth. Tourism was not given a high priority, and the number of arrivals was much smaller than in neighbouring Morocco and Tunisia. The situation worsened after 1991, as a result of the vicious struggle between Moslem fundamentalists and the Algerian army. In these circumstances, it has been impossible to guarantee visitor security in much of the country, including the capital.

Much of Algeria's 500 000 inbound arrivals is VFR, as there are large numbers of Algerians working abroad, particularly in France, who return home for their annual summer holidays. French tourists visiting Algeria, and even more so Algerians visiting France, have been subjected to visa restrictions, as a result of the controversy over Algerian immigration. The majority of international tourists arrive by air, with the exception of Tunisians who use road or rail transport. Algeria has five international airports and scheduled flights are operated by the major European airlines as well as Air Algerie, which also serves the extensive domestic network. Air transport is important in a country more than four times the size of France, and allows access to remote desert and mountain areas. The country has good ferry links to Marseilles in France (operated by the French Societe Nationale Maritime Mediterranee (SCNM) and the Algerian state-owned shipping line). There is a very extensive road network and excellent bus services allow visitors in less troubled times to travel throughout the country and into Tunisia. Rail transport is less efficient and surface transport links with Morocco have been adversely affected by the dispute over the Western Sahara.

Even in good times, Algeria's tourism industry has suffered from an acute shortage of accommodation. This has been made worse by the need of many foreign companies to accommodate their employees in hotels, owing to the shortage of housing. At the same time, service standards are poor. The difficulty is at its worst in Algiers, where accommodating delegates attending conferences is a continual problem. Most hotel beds are located in the purpose-built tourist centres on the coast and in some of the Saharan oases.

Like other sectors of the economy, tourism is closely controlled by the state. Policy is decided by the Ministry of Tourism which also oversees the Office Nationale Algerien Tourisme (ONAT) – responsible for promotion and development; the Enterprise des Trevaux Touristiques (ETT) responsible for implementing development schemes; and there are other agencies concerned with running most of Algeria's hotels, campsites and health spas.

Algeria's vastness offers a diversity of natural and cultural resources to the tourist. In the extreme north, the Mediterranean coast is largely unspoilt, consisting of 1200 kilometres of small bays backed by cliffs, and scenically not very different from the Côte d'Azur. During the 1970s a number of beach resorts (Tipasa, Zeralda and Sidi Ferruch) were developed on the coast to cater for European tour operators. These were planned as self-contained towns in Arabic style, complete with well-designed souks, entertainment and sports facilities. However, the coastal lowlands – the Tell – contain 84 per cent of Algeria's population and the bulk of its industry so marine pollution is a serious problem. Algiers itself – a metropolis of over 5 million people – is famous for its Kasbah, the fortified old town built during the Turkish occupation. Despite having been declared a World Heritage Site, conservation has been neglected and its buildings are grossly overcrowded.

A series of mountain ramparts separating the coast from the Sahara have potential for skiing during the winter months. However, much of the area, particularly the Aures Massif and Kabylie, is off limits to tourists. The area between the two main Atlas ranges is known as the Plateau of the Shotts because of the large number of salt lakes. The true desert – and the date palms for which Algeria is famous – are reached at Laghouat, some 400 kilometres from Algiers. From here, the Trans-Saharan Highway, the most important of the desert routes, runs a further 2400 kilometres to Kano in northern Nigeria. Apart from the areas of sand dunes known as *erg*, the Algerian Sahara is scenically quite varied, including the volcanic rock formations of the Hoggar rising to 3000 metres, and eroded badlands, criss-crossed by a network of wadis. Each oasis town has a distinct character, the most interesting being those of the M'zab region, while Tamanrasset is the main centre of the 'people of the veil' – the Tuareg nomads. Prehistoric rock paintings at Ain Sefra and in the Tassili Mountains show that the Sahara once enjoyed a much wetter climate.

Libya

In contrast to Tunisia, few tourists visit its neighbour Libya, largely because the Western media accuse the Islamic socialist regime of supporting terrorist movements throughout the Middle East. Although 95 per cent of the country is desert, Libya is a wealthy country by African standards, but the economy is very narrowly based – 99 per cent of export earnings is derived from petroleum. With the fall in oil prices during the 1990s, Libya has had to seriously rethink its policy of isolation from the West. There are the following opportunities for tourism development:

● the expansion of business travel in Tripoli and Benghazi
● the longest stretch of pristine Mediterranean coastline (although most of it is backed by desert)

● important Roman remains at Leptis Magna and Sabratha (near Tripoli) and Cyrene (near Benghazi)
● the oasis towns of Ghadames and Ghat on the former caravan routes across the Sahara.

However, the success of any tourism project will depend on the lifting of UN sanctions which prohibit direct flights from Europe to Libya.

East Africa

Tour operators regard the countries of Kenya, Tanzania, and Uganda as constituting East Africa. Their tourism resources are similar, and before independence they had a measure of unity under British rule. The wider geographical region also includes the Sudan, and the countries of the 'Horn of Africa' – Ethiopia, Somalia, Eritrea and Djibouti – where tourism is still in its infancy. The Swahili language is widely understood throughout East Africa, while the heritage of Islam and Arab traders is evident throughout the coastal belt.

Contrasts of scenery, climate and culture are particularly evident in East Africa. Most of the region consists of an undulating plateau over 1000 metres in altitude, but it also contains the most spectacular scenery to be found anywhere on the continent. Part of the Rift Valley – a deep gash in the earth's surface extending from the Dead Sea to Lake Malawi – cuts through the region as two branches. The western branch contains Lakes Albert, Edward and Tanganyika, while the eastern branch is bounded by a high escarpment in western Kenya. The earth movements which formed the rift also raised the high mountains of volcanic origin on either side, notably Mounts Elgon, Kenya and Kilimanjaro. The valley floor is littered with a number of craters (the most famous being Ngorongoro, which is a spectacular wildlife sanctuary) and there are numerous lakes. Some of these, like Naivasha, contain fresh water and are rich in fish, whereas others – Nakuru, Magadi and Natron – have deposits of salt and soda which have attracted the attention of mineral developers as well as of conservationists who wish to protect the millions of flamingos which breed there.

Most of East Africa has a tropical wet-dry climate but, because of its position astride the Equator, the region has two dry seasons and two rainy ones. The coast is also influenced by the seasonal shift in wind direction caused by the monsoon over the Indian Ocean. Altitude, too, has an important effect. Conditions in Nairobi at 1800 metres are ideal for Europeans with daytime temperatures between 20°C and 25°C all year round. The main tourist seasons for East Africa's big-game areas are December to early March and July to early October as these correspond to the dry seasons when the animals are concentrated around the water-holes and the grass is short, aiding visibility. Travel is also easier then, whereas the dirt roads are often impassable at the height of the rains.

East Africa contains a large variety of habitats for wildlife, ranging from the semi-deserts of Northern Kenya and Somalia which support herds of antelope and gazelle to the dense rain forests of the Ruwenzori on the Uganda–Congo border which shelter the chimpanzee and gorilla. The dominant type of vegetation is thorny scrub in the drier areas, alternating with open plains or savanna where the tall grasses dotted with umbrella-shaped acacia trees support large herds of grazing animals and the great predators such as the lion.

Wildlife is the basis of East Africa's tourism industry. The organization of big-game hunting safaris began at the end of the nineteenth century, although the first national parks were not designated until the 1940s. Since independence, Kenya, Tanzania and Uganda have devoted large areas to wildlife conservation, either by designation as national parks, where the protection given to animal life and vegetation is absolute, or as game reserves. In some of these reserves, the local nomadic tribes, notably the Masai on the Kenya–Tanzania border, have the right to continue using the land for grazing their cattle. In other cases local communities have lost their traditional rights to these lands while their crops remain at risk. The wildlife is under threat for the following reasons:

1 Poaching for skins, ivory and rhinoceros horn (greatly valued in Yemen and the Far East, for different reasons).
2 Poaching receives wide publicity in the Western media; but a more serious long-term problem is the encroachment of the human population (growing at the rate of 3 per cent annually) on wildlife habitats by land-hungry Africans. Most of the best land has already been given over to the production of cash crops for export and not to food staples.

The term 'safari' has come to include the following types of products:

1 Budget-priced minibus tours of the most accessible national parks such as Amboseli and Masai-Mara, based on Nairobi or one of the coastal resorts. Drivers often approach the game too closely so that tourists can get a better view. Tourists also spend most of their time looking for the 'big five' – lion, leopard, elephant, rhino and buffalo, causing bottlenecks in the process.
2 In the higher price bracket, tour operators include stays in one of the government-run game lodges in the national parks. These are designed to blend in with the local environment, the most famous being 'Treetops' in the Aberdare Mountains, and Seronera in the Serengeti National Park. They offer five-star service and, to an extent, tourists are cut off from the realities of life in the African bush.

3 Camping safaris, for example in the Tsavo National Park, are a much more authentic and sustainable alternative.
4 Balloon safaris provide an ideal way to view game. However it is said that the noise from the burners frightens away game, while the back-up vehicles damage the terrain in the wet season.
5 Other options include camel safaris in the remoter parts of northern Kenya; fishing expeditions to Lake Turkana; trekking and mountain climbing on Mount Kenya or Kilimanjaro; and escorted expeditions to privately owned game reserves and game ranches.

The negative impacts of safari tourism can be minimized by:

1 Visitor management, ensuring that tourist numbers do not exceed the carrying capacity of the area; in other words, low-volume, high-spending, low-impact 'eco tourism' rather than mass tourism.
2 Involvement of the local community, so that they derive tangible benefits from wildlife conservation.

Kenya

Kenya is the most developed of the East African countries. Prior to independence it had a large number of white European settlers and an Asian middle class, which generated a sizeable demand for domestic tourism. Since independence in 1963 it has been politically stable and has encouraged foreign investment in its tourism industry. The Kenyan Ministry of Tourism and Wildlife reflects the importance placed on both conservation and tourism as the major source of foreign exchange, and it enjoys private sector support from the Kenya Tourist Board which has responsibility for promotion. Although it has pursued a policy of 'Kenyanisation' replacing foreign nationals by Africans, the government in other respects has had a *laissez-faire* attitude toward the private sector and foreign tour operators. This is changing in response to the impact of mass tourism in the more accessible national parks and on the coast. The tourism authorities are also faced with a decline in tourism numbers as fears of safety and political unrest have grown. Such is the problem that neighbouring countries are set to challenge Kenya's crown as the leading tourism destination in the region. This is a serious issue as tourism represents over 10 per cent of Kenya's economy. Since the early 1990s eco-tourism has been encouraged by the government's Kenya Wildlife Service (KWS), while the government's development plan has the following aims:

1 To diversify the tourism product.
2 To attract high-income, low-volume tourism. Here, privately owned game ranches play an important role, as they integrate tourism, wildlife and cattle farming. Tourists can participate in activities on the ranch, while local communities benefit, with the enterprise providing jobs and funding for schools.

Kenya became one of Africa's most popular destinations (with 0.7 million arrivals in the mid-1990s), because it has a wealth of tourism resources, including some of the best known game reserves, such as the Masai-Mara, Amboseli and Tsavo, and an attractive coastline along the Indian Ocean. The capital, Nairobi, is a modern city, with facilities for shopping and entertainment, and good communications by air, road and rail to most of the region, making it the recognized gateway to East Africa. Most foreign tourists spend one or two nights in Nairobi, and the Kenyatta Conference Centre is a major venue for business travellers.

The old city of Mombasa, with its modern port facilities at Kilindini, and extended international airport, is the gateway to the Kenya coast. In the old port, Arab *dhows* can still be seen and the markets sell tourist curios such as Masai beadwork, wood and soapstone carvings and animal trophies. The modern resort developments near Mombasa and at Malindi attract large numbers of winter sun package holidaymakers, mainly from Germany, Britain, Switzerland and Italy. In fact, beach tourism is expanding in Kenya, while visits to game reserves (except by Americans) are declining. The long white sandy beaches, and lagoons protected by an offshore coral reef, provide safe conditions for diving and other water sports. Although the underwater wildlife is protected by marine national parks at Malindi and Watamu, excessive numbers of glass-bottomed boats, and illegal shell-collecting for the lucrative souvenir trade, have caused extensive damage to the reef. Western visitors have also caused offence to a traditional Moslem society by their dress and behaviour, and social mores are changing to the extent that sex tourism is a problem. The island of Lamu has minimized these environmental and social impacts by carefully controlling tourism. The income is used for conservation projects, so that the Swahili-Arabic heritage of this attractive resort has been retained.

Tanzania

Tanzania has a less well developed tourism industry than Kenya. In part, this is due to history – until 1989 government policy encouraged African-style socialism with the state taking a major shareholding in tourism enterprises. Western-style tourism did not fit easily into this scheme and foreign companies were reluctant to invest. However, since 1990 the government has adopted a more pragmatic approach, liberalizing the tourism sector and ambitious to become a leader in this field. This has been aided by the decline in tourism in neighbouring Kenya. The Tanzania Tourist Board, created in 1992, has revitalized the sector so that it supports 27 000 jobs and generates one-quarter of the country's foreign exchange. By the mid-1990s healthy growth put international arrivals at over 330 000.

Tanzania's most well-known attractions lie close to the Kenyan border and this has made the task of promotion more difficult. They include:

- Africa's highest mountain – Mount Kilimanjaro
- the world-famous Serengeti National Park, with its spectacular seasonal migrations of animals in search of water and grazing
- the Ngorongoro Reserve, an extinct volcanic caldera, with excellent game-viewing from the crater rim.

Ironically, it is easier to reach these attractions from Nairobi than from Tanzania's former capital, Dar-es-Salaam – on the coast. This induced the government to build an airport near Arusha (Kilimanjaro International) and invest heavily in hotel complexes in that city. The enormous game reserves of southern Tanzania are underutilized as they lie off the tourism circuit and are usually reached by fly-in safaris.

Tanzania's other focus of tourist attention is the coast, particularly the islands of Zanzibar, Pemba and Mafia, where game-fishing and diving are the main attractions. Zanzibar is also of major cultural interest for its heritage from the times of the Arab Sultans, when it was Africa's leading centre for the trade in spices.

Uganda

Uganda, in contrast to Tanzania, had a flourishing tourism industry before the Amin regime brought disorder and maladministration to the country in the 1970s. Political stability in the 1990s has led to the growth of eco-tourism, based on the country's rain forest resources, which have the highest biodiversity in East Africa. Another major attraction is Murchison (Kabegera) Falls near the headwaters of the River Nile. However, the main area of tourist interest – the Queen Elizabeth National Park and the Ruwenzori Mountains – lie close to the Congolese border, and are threatened by the turmoil prevalent in Central Africa. Entebbe is the main gateway for international tourists, with ferry services across Lake Victoria linking it to Kenya and Tanzania.

The other countries of East Africa

Tourism development in the Sudan and the countries of the 'Horn of Africa' has been adversely affected for many years by drought and political strife.

The Sudan

The Sudan, the largest country in Africa, is deeply divided along religious and cultural lines between the Arab-speaking, Islamic north and the black African, largely Christian south. The northern Sudan, which is largely desert, has close cultural links with Egypt and the Middle East. The Sudanese section of the River Nile is not used to any extent as a tourist route, and accommodation is severely limited outside the capital Khartoum. There are, however, opportunities for diving along the Red Sea coast. Other attractions include the Dinder National Park, a major wildlife reserve near the Ethiopian border, and the volcanic highlands of Jebel Marra in the western Sudan, which provide a refuge from the extreme heat of summer.

Ethiopia

Ethiopia has huge tourism potential and is of particular interest to cultural tourists. The heartland is a high plateau where an ancient Christian civilization has survived, isolated by mountains, deserts and often hostile Moslem neighbours. The main tourist circuit links Addis Ababa to the art treasures of Axoum, Gondar and Lalibela. There are few hotels outside the capital, which was developed as a conference venue for Africa by the last Emperor, Haile Selassie. To the east of Addis Ababa lie the game reserves of the Rift Valley and the historic Moslem city of Harar. Tourism is co-ordinated by the Ethiopian Tourism Commission and arrivals were stable at around 100 000 in the 1990s.

Eritrea

Eritrea broke away from Ethopia in 1993 after a long and bitter civil war. It offers two contrasting environments – the arid but sweltering Red Sea coast, and the cool fertile highlands, where Asmara, the Italian-style capital, is situated. The country has a Ministry of Tourism and has been the subject of tourism planning exercises in the 1990s.

Somalia

Somalia has the advantages of a long coastline with fine beaches and some of the best fishing in Africa; also there are no ethnic minorities to create divisions, as in other African states. However bitter clan rivalries have effectively caused the breakdown of government authority outside the capital Mogadishu.

Djibouti

With few other resources, this small ex-French colony has exploited its deepwater harbour at the entrance to the Red Sea with the view to becoming a major trading centre between Africa and the Middle East.

Southern Africa

Most of the countries of Southern Africa have also realized the importance of wildlife conservation as a major part of their tourism appeal. Even in war-torn Angola and Mozambique, there are a number of national parks recognized by the International Union for the Conservation of Nature (IUCN). To counter the threats of drought, poaching and development pressures to wildlife, a number of cross-border parks have been proposed. These would allow the animals to migrate freely within their natural ecosystems. In 1993 the first of these international 'peace parks' came into effect, joining the Kalahari-Gemsbok in South Africa to Botswana's much larger Gemsbok National Park.

Most countries in the region have strong economic and cultural ties with Britain, and have succeeded in attracting visitors from the main generating markets. International air services to Southern Africa have improved considerably during the 1990s. There is scope for more regional co-operation in reducing border formalities to encourage travel between the various countries, and in overseas promotion, by expanding membership of the Southern Africa Regional Tourism Council (SARTOC). However the future growth of tourism will depend to a great extent on the continuance of political and economic stability in South Africa, which is by far the leading country in the region, accounting for 85 per cent of its gross domestic product.

South Africa

Under white rule, South Africa – particularly the Cape area with its Mediterranean climate – was often perceived as an outpost of Europe. Since the coming to power of the ANC government in 1994 attitudes have changed; the country is no longer isolated by world opinion as it was in the era of *apartheid* (the policy of racial segregation), and it is now taking a larger share in the development of the African continent. South Africa can be regarded as a developed country rather than part of the Third World for the following reasons:

1 It has an advanced economy, with only 14 per cent of its workforce employed in agriculture (compared with 80 per cent in Kenya, for example). South Africa also accounts for over half the electricity generated in the continent.
2 Literacy levels are generally quite high.
3 It has a well-developed infrastructure, with good air, road and rail systems.
4 There are fewer health risks than in other parts of Africa, with malaria confined to the Lowveld region on the eastern border.

This prosperity has been built primarily on the basis of its vast mineral resources. On the other hand, South Africa is characterized by great disparities of wealth, to the extent that large sections of the population continue to live in conditions of Third World poverty, without basic services, as in the tribal homelands or the townships adjoining Cape Town and Johannesburg. Although there has been much more social mobility since the ending of apartheid, with the growth of a black middle class, most of the Bantu (Black African) majority are too poor to generate a demand for tourism, in contrast to the whites and Asians. One of the great challenges facing the ANC government is to balance the economic aspirations of black Africans with the need to retain white expertise and attract foreign investment, and here tourism is playing a role.

Whereas under the old regime, much of the inbound tourism from Britain and other European countries had been for VFR or business purposes, in the 1990s there has been a substantial growth of interest in South Africa as a holiday destination by tour operators. The depreciation of the rand has made it a competitively priced long-haul destination. However, the low value of their currency has made it much more difficult for South Africans to travel abroad.

Demand for domestic tourism is far more important in South Africa than inbound tourism in terms of bed-nights. During the 1990s up to 4.6 million arrivals a year were recorded, of which many came from other African countries, notably Zimbabwe. The other major sources of overseas visitors are the UK, Germany and the USA. The Netherlands accounts for only a small percentage of overseas visits, which is perhaps surprising in view of the strong historical links with the first white settlers – the Afrikaaners, who speak a language derived from Dutch.

The great majority of overseas visitors arrive on scheduled air services, as the South African government discourages charters. Johannesburg, at the hub of a network of intercontinental and regional services, is the major gateway to South Africa. Cape Town, although it has direct flights to the UK, is of less importance than in the 1970s, when it was a major port of call for passenger liners. South African Airways operate most of the scheduled domestic services, with several flights a day linking the main cities. Another convenient way of seeing the country is by South African Railways. The luxury 'Blue Train' is one of the country's most famous tourist products, linking Pretoria and Cape Town and passing through some magnificent scenery on its descent from the Karoo Plateau to the coast. A large number of tours by coach or minibus are also available.

South Africa's tourism industry is effectively organized and marketed, within the legal framework of the 1993 Tourism Act. The legacy of segregation is reflected in the politics of tourism in South Africa with different political parties and ethnic groups having their own agendas for the sector. Policy is largely the responsibility of the Tourism Minister and the South African Tourist Board (SATOUR) which is responsible for maintaining standards of accommodation and services, promotion and developing new products. A wide range of accommodation is available, from luxury hotels to *rondavels* (African-style huts, with modern facilities) in the game reserves. SATOUR has helped to promote a wide range of special-interest tourism, including for example, botanical tours and wine-tasting in the Western Cape; steam locomotives; mining heritage at Kimberley in the Northern Cape; and the battlefields of the Zulu and Boer Wars in Natal-Kwazulu.

Generally, South Africa has a warm temperate climate, which is almost ideal for Europeans, with sunshine hours exceeding most Mediterranean resorts. With the exception of the Western Cape, most of the rainfall occurs in the summer

months (October to April). There are however important differences in climate and scenery between the coastal areas and the high interior plateaus – the Karoo and the Highveld, where night-time temperatures frequently fall below 0°C during the winter months. In the Drakensberg Mountains of the Eastern Cape, there is sufficient snow for a modest winter sports industry to have developed at Tiffindell, near the border with Lesotho. This caters for the small but growing domestic demand, whereas beach tourism and other types of outdoor recreation are far more significant. The Atlantic Coast north of Table Bay is less suitable for sea bathing as it is cooled by the cold Benguela current. In contrast, the Indian Ocean coasts from False Bay eastwards are influenced by the warm Mozambique Current that brings high temperatures and greater humidity. Although the climate is suitable for tourism for most of the year, the timing of school holidays in the Christmas period and April, results in a seasonal peaking of demand, which places pressure on accommodation, particularly on the Natal coast.

Although the early settlers wiped out much of the game they encountered, the remaining wildlife habitats have long been given a high degree of protection by the South African government. There are eleven national parks and many game reserves, most of which are small in area compared with other countries in Southern Africa. The exception – and the most popular – is the Kruger National Park located in the Lowveld along the Mozambique border, which is served by an extensive all-weather road network and well-supplied with self-catering accommodation. Prior reservation is necessary for foreign visitors, due to the heavy domestic demand. Other notable reserves – Hluhluwe and Umfolozi – are situated in Kwazulu. There are also a large number of private game reserves – such as the Sabi-Sabi adjoining the Kruger National Park – which permit hunting and the viewing of wildlife on foot as well as in open vehicles. They provide luxury chalet accommodation and most have their own airstrips.

The main holiday area for South Africans, especially for Afrikaaners from the interior provinces, is the coast of Natal-Kwazulu, where conditions are ideal for swimming, sunbathing and surfing. Durban is the largest holiday resort, as well as being a busy cosmopolitan port. To the south lies the 'Hibiscus Coast', a string of resorts along magnificent beaches. To the north of the Tugela River, the coastline is less developed, and here the main attractions are the game reserves and the villages of the Zulu, the best known of the Bantu peoples, who have retained many of their warrior traditions. West of Durban, the Drakensberg Mountains are visited by large numbers of people from the coast during the hot humid summers, with Pietermaritzburg, Estcourt and Ladysmith as the most important resorts. Areas increasingly sought out by tourists from Europe, sometimes with a view to purchasing second homes include:

1 The Cape Peninsula and the hinterland of Cape Town, often considered to be the most beautiful part of South

Africa. Contrasts of climate have created an extraordinary range of habitats for wildlife, and the coasts are ideal for whale-watching. Cape Town, situated on one of the few good harbours in South Africa, is the oldest European settlement, the second largest city in South Africa, and its legislative capital. The waterfront has been redeveloped as an international focus for retailing and restaurants. The best known landmark is Table Mountain, while to the east along False Bay, there are extensive beaches. Inland lie the vineyards of the Hex River Valley and many old farmhouses in the distinctive 'Cape Dutch' style of architecture.

2 The Garden Route – the stretch of coast between Port Elizabeth and East London – offers rugged but attractive scenery, with forest-covered mountains alternating with fertile valleys and small sandy bays.

On the central plateau the main centres are the cities of Johannesburg, Pretoria and Bloemfontein:

1 *Johannesburg* is South Africa's largest and most prosperous city, largely due to the gold mines of the Witwatersrand nearby. Not surprisingly, one of its major attractions is the Gold Reef City theme park which interprets this mining heritage. Johannesburg has become a regional centre for financial services, comparable with the great cities of Europe and North America.

2 *Pretoria*, the administrative capital of South Africa, and *Bloemfontein*, its judicial capital, are centres of Afrikaaner culture, and as such form a contrast to the cosmopolitan brashness and bustle of Johannesburg.

3 *Sun City* was developed in the apartheid era as a gambling centre to rival Las Vegas in what was then the quasi-independent state of Bophutatswana, as gambling and multiracial entertainment were illegal in the republic itself. In the new South Africa it continues to be a major resort, offering casinos and cabarets attracting international stars, golf courses and other sports facilities, and 'the Lost City' theme park developed by a South African entrepreneur.

The future of tourism in South Africa will depend on the maintenance of political and economic stability, and the extent to which the new multiracial 'Rainbow Nation' can offer social and economic opportunities to all ethnic groups. Throughout the 1990s levels of crime increased to become among the world's highest, especially in Johannesburg, and the resulting insecurity is one of the biggest problems facing the country and its tourism industry.

The other countries of Southern Africa

Most of the other countries in Southern Africa are landlocked, so that their external surface transport links (and to an extent their economic fortunes) are vulnerable to the political situation in South Africa and Mozambique. The small kingdoms of Lesotho and Swaziland are particularly dependent on South Africa. Most of their visitors are South Africans, who tend to be short-stay and interested primarily in gambling in the hotel casinos of Maseru and Mbabane. But these countries have more to offer, namely:

1 *Lesotho* (known as 'the Roof of Africa' or 'The Kingdom in the Sky') is situated high in the Drakensberg Mountains. Apart from the impressive scenery, there are facilities for pony-trekking, and even skiing (although the season is restricted to July and August). Four-wheel drive vehicles are necessary for travel because of the rugged terrain.

2 *Swaziland* (or Ngwane) is not quite as mountainous, and includes a section of the game-rich Lowveld along its boundary with Mozambique. The country's tribal traditions are among the best preserved in Africa.

3 *Namibia* and *Botswana* likewise have strong economic ties with South Africa, but with the advantage of direct air services from Europe to the capitals of Windhoek and Gaborone, they have been more successful in attracting overseas visitors. They are mostly made up of desert landscapes, but the Kalahari is not as arid as the Sahara and supports a surprising variety of game. Because of the vast distances and sparse population, fly-in safaris are a major element in their tourism industries.

(a) Botswana has deliberately pursued a policy of restricting tourism in the interests of conservation by keeping prices high and limiting the supply of accommodation. The main focus of tourism is the Okavango Delta, a unique wetland, created by annual flooding, which is one of Africa's most fertile habitats for wildlife.

(b) Namibia differs from its neighbour in having a long Atlantic coastline, and a large white minority of mainly German or Afrikaaner origin. A newcomer to international tourism, it can offer a large number of game reserves and some of Africa's most interesting attractions, including:

(i) The Etosha Pan, which attracts great concentrations of wildlife during the dry season.

(ii) The Fish River Canyon, a spectacular geological feature.

(iii) The Waterberg Plateau, famous for its rock paintings – created by the nomadic San (more widely known as 'Bushmen') who were the original inhabitants of Southern Africa.

(iv) The 'Skeleton Coast' – where the Namib Desert meets the Atlantic Ocean. Fogs from the cold Benguela Current offshore sustain some unique plants and animals although the climate is virtually rainless. This coastal area also boasts some of the world's highest sand dunes.

In contrast to Namibia, the countries of Zimbabwe, Zambia and Malawi usually receive an adequate rainfall, and since they mainly consist of highlands and plateaus rising over 1000 metres above sea level, they have a climate which is cooler than you might expect for the tropics. Under British rule the three countries were briefly united as the 'Central African Federation of Rhodesia and Nyasaland', but since then they have gone their separate ways.

Zimbabwe

Before 1980 Zimbabwe (then known as Rhodesia) had a tourism industry serving the domestic market – made up of the white settlers – and South Africans; overseas visitors were few due to the country's political isolation. With the coming to power of the ZANU government, Zimbabwe was recognized by the international community as an independent state. As a result, overseas visitor numbers grew rapidly (to exceed 1.3 million in the 1990s), aided by political stability under the new government and good infrastructure. The Zimbabwe Tourist Authority was formed in 1996 with promotion and development responsibilities.

One of the country's main problems is overcommercialization of its major attraction – Victoria Falls on the border with Zambia, compared with underexploitation of some of its game reserves and the scenic attractions of the Eastern Highlands. Below the Falls, the River Zambezi attracts a fleet of rafts and kayaks, while above, the visitor can experience bungee-jumping. In comparison, Lake Kariba – a vast inland sea created by the great Kariba Dam in 1959 – offers few facilities. Zimbabwe's two major cities – Harare and Bulawayo – have hosted events such as international conferences, trade fairs and the All Africa Games. The Matapo Hills south of Bulawayo – an area of dramatic granite scenery – is a barely exploited resource, with the burial place of Cecil Rhodes as the attraction offered to Western tourists. A less controversial heritage attraction is the mysterious ruined city of Great Zimbabwe, a reminder of African achievement centuries before the colonial era. Zimbabwe's experience of wildlife management has implications for other African countries (see the case study at the end of this chapter), and the future would seem to lie in the growth of eco-tourism.

Zambia

Zambia since 1980 has enjoyed good relations with its neighbour to the south, facilitating international tourism. However its economy is precariously dependent on the export of copper and other minerals, and tourism is increasingly seen as a more reliable way of earning foreign exchange. The government has put a high priority on conservation – almost one-third of its area is devoted to national parks and game reserves, although facilities are generally not as well developed as in Zimbabwe. In the most popular national parks – Kafue and the South

Luangwa – accommodation is in thatched lodges blending in with the local habitats. The main tourist centres are Livingstone – situated close to Victoria Falls, and the capital, Lusaka, which has good conference facilities.

Malawi

Malawi's main attraction is the lake of the same name, the third largest in Africa, with some of the world's best fishing, and attractive beaches along its 600 kilometre shoreline. There are good facilities for water-skiing, sailing and windsurfing at the resorts of Salima and Monkey Bay. Compared with some other countries in Southern Africa, it is not rich in big game. However its undulating green plateaus and mountains are ideal for riding and trekking holidays. Since the mid-1990s a new government has liberalized the tourism sector, created a Ministry of Tourism and there has been healthy growth in international arrivals.

Angola and Mozambique

Angola and Mozambique are Portuguese-speaking and their cities still retain some of the heritage of centuries of colonial rule although Independence in 1975 was followed by an exodus of well over 1 million Portuguese settlers. Since the early 1990s the socialist governments of both countries have adopted a more pragmatic approach to economic development, although tourism has to cope with the legacy of two decades of civil war.

1 Mozambique had a small tourism industry before 1975, catering mainly for South Africans. This was concentrated in its capital Maputo (then called Lourenco Marques) with its extensive beaches. With the ending of the civil war, there has been some development of inclusive tours, especially to the Bazaruto Islands that offer resort facilities and sport fishing.
2 Angola has the advantage of a healthier climate than Mozambique, although its Atlantic coastline is less suitable for beach tourism. The country has great mineral wealth but it has been siphoned off to fuel a civil war, which shows no real prospect of ending. The hotels of the capital Luanda cater almost exclusively to business travellers.

The islands of the western Indian Ocean

To the east of the African continent lie several island groups, which are very different from the mainland in geology, flora and fauna, and where the cultures have been strongly influenced by France and Asia. All island ecosystems are vulnerable to the changes brought about by tourism and other types of development, and the wildlife resources of the Indian Ocean islands are particularly at risk:

1 Pressures are most severe in Madagascar, habitat of the lemur and other unique animals.
2 In Mauritius only 1 per cent of the original forest still survives and up to 50 per cent of the fringing coral is dead or dying.
3 In the Seychelles much of the coral reef around the island of Mahe was destroyed to make way for the international airport.

Madagascar, the Comores and Reunion were formerly French colonies, whereas Mauritius and the Seychelles, although originally colonized by the French, experienced a long period of British rule.

Madagascar

Madagascar (the Malagasy Republic) stands in a class of its own – it is the world's fourth largest island, with an area greater than France and a coastline 5000 kilometres in length. A central spine of mountains dominates the country, separating the dry savannas of the west from the lush vegetation of the east coast. Population growth and inefficient agricultural methods have caused extensive deforestation, in turn, threatening destruction of the wildlife that is Madagascar's most important tourist resource. Culturally, too, the island is interesting with its mix of Indonesian, African and Arab ethnic groups; as in South-East Asia, rice fields are a common feature of the landscape. Other distinctive features are the elaborate tombs and funeral ceremonies. The capital Antananarivo located high on the central plateau contains the palaces of the Merina monarchs who ruled the country before it came under French control. However, this diversity of resources has not been paralleled by a thriving tourism industry. The island is expensive to reach, and once there, surface transport is poor. The two major resorts, situated on the offshore islands of Nosy Be and Nosy Boraha (Ile Ste Marie), can only be reached by domestic air services. Since independence the government has given tourism a low priority, but this is changing now that relations with France and South Africa – its largest potential markets – have improved.

The Comores

The Comores comprise four volcanic islands lying between Madagascar and Mozambique. The people are Moslems and Arabic influences are dominant in the culture. While the other islands have opted for independence, Mayotte has retained its links with France and is the most prosperous of the group. Anjouan is the most picturesque, but Grand Comore contains the international airport and most of the few hotels. Diving and sport fishing provide the main appeal for foreign tourists, mainly wealthy Americans and

Europeans, although South Africa has provided much of the investment in hotels.

Reunion

Reunion is another volcanic island, situated to the east of Madagascar. It has perhaps the most impressive scenery of any tropical island, with high mountains rising to 3000 metres within a short distance of the coast, and boasting spectacular calderas, an active volcano – the Piton de la Fournaise, and sheer lava cliffs enclosing deep canyons. There are hiking trails between the craters and good surfing off the west coast. The island's close relationship to France (it is an overseas *departement*) has benefited the infrastructure and allows French tourists to take advantage of cheaper flights from Paris to St Denis. Tourism is handicapped by the proximity of Mauritius, which has much better beaches.

Mauritius

Mauritius is more accessible with direct flights from Britain and South Africa. It is encircled, except to the south, by a coral reef that is responsible for the island's greatest assets – 150 kilometres of attractive coastline with calm seas ideal for water sports and white sand beaches. Mauritius is a good example of how tourism, properly handled, can benefit a small developing country. In the 1960s the island was faced with a decline for sugar, its principal export, and a seemingly inexorable pressure on resources from a rapidly growing population. Tourism (along with light industry) was seen as a solution to the grave economic situation, but the government was determined from the outset that Mauritius should be an up-market destination. This has been achieved by:

● a ban on charter flights
● the resort hotels are built to high standards of design and landscaping, taking maximum advantage of the beach and lagoon setting
● the hotels use local resources, so that profits have stayed within Mauritius
● a professional Ministry of Tourism, aided by the Mauritius Tourism Promotion Authority (created in 1996)
● standards of service and cuisine that bear comparison with the best in Europe, North America and Asia.

By the 1990s Mauritius was attracting 500 000 international visitors, of which approximately one-half came from Europe. Mauritius has the advantage, of a highly skilled workforce (15 000 are employed in tourism), where the different ethnic communities – Hindus, Moslems, Chinese, Creoles (of African origin) and Europeans – live in apparent harmony. Beach resorts such as Grand Baie are the main attraction, but with the achievement of economic success, the government is giving conservation a higher priority, in a bid to attract eco-tourists. Compared with other Indian Ocean islands, the scenery of the interior is unspectacular, although there are numerous waterfalls where the central plateau of Mauritius meets the coastal plains. Away from the beaches, the main tourist centres are the multicultural capital St Louis with its markets and festivals around the calendar, Curepipe with its casino and textile shops, and the Royal Botanical Gardens at Pamplemousses. The possible disadvantages of Mauritius as a winter sun destination for North Europeans are:

● distance
● high humidity and occasional cyclones from December to April
● little nightlife compared with other destinations such as the Caribbean islands.

The Seychelles

The Seychelles are strategically located on the major shipping routes for oil tankers from the Gulf, about halfway between East Africa, India and Madagascar. The country has a small population and land area compared to Mauritius, but lays claim to over 1 million square kilometres of Indian Ocean. The islands are ecologically interesting because they contain many species of birds and plants which are unique to the Seychelles. The islands fall into two main groups:

1 The main islands of Mahe, Praslin, La Digue and Silhouette are of granite formation, the possible remnants of a 'lost continent'. The combination of picturesque coves, rock formations, palm-fringed beaches and rugged mountains gives these islands a rare beauty.
2 The outer islands are low-lying coral atolls. Fresh water is scarce and the islands are mostly uninhabited. The largest, Aldabra is also the most remote and is world famous for its giant turtles.

The construction of the international airport at Mahe brought an isolated destination within reach of the main tourist generating markets of Western Europe and South Africa, with the result that tourist arrivals increased from less than a thousand in 1970 to 80 000 annually in the 1980s. While foreign investment in tourism is encouraged, and charter flights are permitted, the government has given conservation a high priority, so that only a few localities – mainly on Mahe – have been developed with low-rise hotels. However, tourism has not made the islands less vulnerable to recession in Europe than their previous dependence on agricultural exports such as cinnamon. Standards of service and facilities in the Seychelles compare unfavourably with those of Mauritius, as tourism was grafted on to a less developed economy and social system. As in other small developing countries tourism has caused or aggravated a number of problems namely:

1 The industry is dominated by foreign tour operators and foreign-owned hotels, so that the bulk of tourist spend does not benefit the country.
2 The tourism sector has attracted workers away from agriculture, to the extent that the islands are now dependent on food imports from Europe and South Africa to meet local as well as tourist demands.
3 The need to train Seychellois workers in the skills and attitudes necessary to serve affluent foreign visitors has undermined the government's efforts at socialism and nation-building based on the Creole language and lifestyle. Those involved with tourism tend to be upwardly mobile, imitating Western lifestyles – the so-called 'demonstration effect'.

West Africa

We can think of West Africa as being two distinct regions:

1 A southern tier of states occupying the forested coastal belt from the Gambia to Gabon.
2 A northern tier – the Sahel states – extending from Mauritania to Chad along the southern edge of the Sahara Desert. This region is characterized by extreme summer heat and drought, the dry season getting progressively longer as we travel further from the Equator, so that savanna grassland gradually merges into semi-desert.

Tourism and business travel in West Africa gravitate to the coast where commercial export-based agriculture is well developed. The climate here is characterized by sultry heat, except during the dry season – usually from December to March – when the 'Harmattan' wind blows from the Sahara, drastically lowering the humidity. In Victorian times, the unhealthy reputation of the region earned it the name 'White Man's Grave'. However, conditions are by no means uniform – the coasts of Ghana and Togo, for example, are much drier than Liberia or Equatorial Guinea.

Most of West Africa has failed to develop significant tourism industries, due to the chronic political instability affecting most countries in the region and inadequate infrastructure. Yet these countries are just within reach of the markets of Western Europe for winter sun beach holidays. The Gambia, for example, is only six hours' flying time from London, and unlike the Caribbean, it has the advantage of being in the same time zone. The Gambia's dry and sunny winter climate allows it to compete with the Canary Islands as a beach destination for the British and Scandinavians – with an extra ingredient – the chance to experience African markets and village life. Similarly, French tourists are attracted to their former colonies, especially to the beaches of Senegal, the Ivory Coast and Togo. Apart from beach tourism West Africa can offer:

1 *'Ethnic' tourism* There is a large potential market for tourism among the black populations of Brazil, the Caribbean and the USA, who are mainly the descendants of West Africans brought over as slaves. The attempt by the Gambian government in the 1980s to attract Black Americans to Alex Haley's ancestral homeland met with some success. More tangible reminders of the slave trade can be seen in Senegal, Benin and Ghana.
2 *Cultural/special-interest tourism* The contribution of West African woodcarving, textile design and dance rhythms to Western art and music is increasingly recognized. The more adventurous tourists seek out countries like Ghana, Mali and Senegal for this reason.
3 *Eco-tourism* West Africa offers a considerable diversity of wildlife habitats. Gambia attracts birdwatchers to its Abuko reserve, while a rainforest project in Ghana's Kakum National Park has won acclaim from environmentalists. Game parks exist in several countries but safari tourism has not developed on any scale, because the attractions are not as well publicized as those of East and Southern Africa, and are less accessible.
4 *Adventure tourism* Adventure tourism is based on four-wheel-drive expeditions, to areas such as the Niger Valley.

There has been some degree of co-operation among West African countries to promote tourism to the region. In 1976 the Economic Community of West African States (ECOWAS) was formed to bring together French-and English-speaking countries. The Francophone states constitute the majority and, with few exceptions, chose to retain close links with France after independence. Several countries (Côte d'Ivoire, Burkina Faso, Niger, Togo, and Benin) are also united by the Conseil de l'Entente whose tourism committee aims for the harmonization of entry requirements and greater uniformity in the standard of hotels. A number of West African countries have state-run hotel corporations. However, their main purpose is to attract business travellers rather than tourists, and hotel rooms are often unavailable in the major cities such as Accra due to block booking for regional conferences.

Lagos, Abidjan, and Dakar are the focus of air routes into West Africa, the most important carriers being Air Nigeria, Air Afrique (which is joint-owned by several Francophone states) and the French airline UTA. The winter sun destinations of the Gambia, Sierra Leone and Côte d'Ivoire are encouraging charter flights to counter the high fares of scheduled airlines. Road and rail transport is geared to the commercial objectives laid down in colonial times, so that routes lead from the interior to the seaports. This inhibits travel between the countries of West Africa, but does, to some extent, allow excursions from the coastal resorts to the hinterland.

The Gambia

Of the five English-speaking states, only the Gambia has attracted much attention from British tour operators. No larger than Yorkshire in area, the country consists of little more than a narrow strip of territory along the River Gambia, and a short stretch of Atlantic coastline where the resort facilities are concentrated. Tourism is encouraged by the government to reduce the country's dependence on groundnut exports. With the help of the World Bank, Yundum airport has been extended, the infrastructure improved, and a hotel training school established. Yet relatively few tourists venture far beyond the beaches on excursions up the river Gambia, one of the finest waterways in West Africa. Almost all the hotels are foreign-owned and many of the economic benefits of tourism are not retained, while there is concern in this traditional Moslem society about some of its social manifestations such as beach hustling. The military coup in 1994 severely affected tourism to the Gambia with estimates of up to a 40 per cent reduction in volume of foreign tourists. However, by the late 1990s volumes were approaching 100 000 visits annually.

Senegal

Senegal is the oldest of France's former colonies, and is a mixture of French sophistication and African traditions, best exemplified by the capital, Dakar. Near Dakar is the island of Gorée with its historic associations with the slave trade, and picturesque villages. In Senegal, we can observe two contrasting approaches to tourism:

1 French expatriates staff the Club Mediterranée village at Cap Skirring, and there is little contact with the local population.
2 In the *campements rurales integrales* near Ziguinchor, the tourist shares the life of an African village, the accommodation being provided by a co-operative of the villagers with government support.

The Côte d'Ivoire

The Côte d'Ivoire (Ivory Coast) has been more successful than most West African countries in developing its tourism industry and its economy in general. This has been due in part to a long period of stability since independence and very substantial foreign (primarily French) investment. State-owned hotels and travel companies are involved in the provision of tourist facilities, mainly along the coast east of Abidjan, where the beaches are protected by a series of lagoons from the heavy surf of the Atlantic. However, the resorts of the 'African Riviera' are expensive and beyond the reach of all but a privileged minority of the Ivorians themselves. In the interior there are a number of game parks, and the new administrative capital of Yamassoukro which boasts a cathedral second in size only to St Peter's in Rome. Abidjan remains the commercial centre of the country with good conference facilities.

Togo

Togo's capital, Lomé, has also become a leading conference destination as well as attracting tourists (many of them from other West African countries) to its beaches and entertainment facilities.

Nigeria

Nigeria is essentially a business travel destination. It is the most populous nation in Africa, with well over 100 million inhabitants, and as the world's fifth largest oil producer, it should be one of the wealthiest. Income from petroleum has created an enormous demand for Western consumer goods and costly development projects. However, the collapse in oil prices and mismanagement of the country's resources have led to a situation in which shortages of basic commodities and power failures are a fact of everyday life. There is also a shortage of hotels, especially in Lagos, which remains Nigeria's main commercial centre, although the federal capital was moved to Abuja nearer the geographical centre of the country. This was done to satisfy the four main ethnic groups – the Fulani and Hausa, who are Moslem – in the less developed north, and the mainly Christian and more business-minded Yoruba and Ibo in the south-west and south. Responsibility for tourism development is shared between the Nigerian Tourist Board, funded by the federal government, and the various state governments. For the independent traveller, the main interest of the country lies in the traditional lifestyle of Kano and other cities of northern Nigeria, while the Yoruba city of Benin is noted for its skills in metalworking.

Cameroon

Nigeria's eastern neighbour, Cameroon, offers even more scenic variety and has been described as 'Africa in miniature'. In the Korup National Park part of the equatorial rain forest has been protected, in contrast to the unrestricted commercial logging prevalent in Gabon and the Ivory Coast. Volcanic Mount Cameroon nearby is the highest mountain in West Africa. The drier northern part of the country includes extensive savannas where a number of game reserves have been designated, the most important being the Waza National Park. Yaoundé, the administrative capital, and Douala, the country's commercial centre, attract a substantial volume of business travel, while the beaches of Kribi on the Gulf of Guinea are increasingly popular with tourists. More than most African countries, Cameroon is a mosaic of tribal groups, but has the advantage that both French and English are the official languages.

Elsewhere in West Africa tourism is in its infancy, or has even declined since the 1980s.

1 In French-speaking *Guinea* and *Benin*, along with *Guinea-Bissau* (an ex-Portuguese colony) tourism was for many years after independence given a low priority by governments, apparently for ideological reasons; and these countries have only recently encouraged private enterprise.
2 Oil-rich *Gabon* has seen little need to attract tourists.
3 The former Spanish colony of *Equatorial Guinea* lacks the basic infrastructure for tourism development; although it can offer the beautiful volcanic island of Bioko and scheduled air services link Madrid to its capital Malabo.
4 Both *Liberia* and *Sierra Leone* had tourism industries on a small scale before the outbreak of civil war in the 1990s:
    (a) Liberia had strong cultural and economic ties with the USA, and its capital, Monrovia, was one of West Africa's leading conference venues.
    (b) The former British colony of Sierra Leone, whose capital, Freetown, has one of Africa's finest harbours, attracted tour operators to the fine white sand beaches of the Freetown Peninsula. The unrest in both countries is due to the tensions between the Westernized élites of the coast and the strongly tribal societies of the interior.
5 *Ghana* on the other hand made an economic recovery during the 1990s. The Ghana Tourist Board has focused attention on the 'castles' of the Gold Coast, such as Christiansborg and Elmina, where slaves were held before being transported on the infamous 'Middle Passage' to the plantations of the New World. Other attractions for the independent traveller include the rainforests of the south, the markets of Accra and the Ashanti heritage of the interior.
6 In the Sahel states, tourism is handicapped for the following reasons:
    (a) Their landlocked situation, (with the exception of Mauritania).
    (b) The low level of economic development and poor infrastructure.
    (c) There are few hotels outside the national capitals.
    (d) Political instability and ethnic strife. In most of these countries there is a north–south divide between the Saharan nomads of the north (Moors, Tuareg and Arabs) and the Black African farming communities of the south. This is particularly evident in *Chad*, whereas in Mauritania the Moors are clearly the dominant group.
    Yet this region has seen the rise of great African civilizations in the past. *Mali* can boast the legendary trading centre of Timbuktu and the great mosque at

Djenné, which is a superb example of Sudanese architecture.

- Similarly in the *Niger Republic* the ancient Tuareg city of Agades attracts many tourists due to its location on the main Trans-Saharan Route. Compared to the Nile, the great River Niger is underutilized as a commercial waterway and tourist route.
- There has been some development of safari tourism in *Burkina Faso*, focusing on the 'W' National Park where the country borders on Benin and Niger.

Central Africa

This region is essentially landlocked with only a short section of coastline near the mouth of the River Congo. It includes Africa's most extensive river system and its largest area of rainforest. Most of this area is virtually inaccessible, especially during the rainy season, which prevails for most of the year near the Equator. Hotels of international standard are few, and those in the major cities – Kinshasa, Kisangani, Bangui and Brazzaville – cater primarily for business travellers. Before the outbreaks of ethnic strife between the Hutu and Watussi that characterized the 1990s, tourism was best developed in the two small countries of Rwanda and Burundi, once called the 'Switzerland of Africa' on account of their lake and mountain scenery. The dense forests of the Kagera and Volcanoes National Parks provided a refuge for gorillas, and attracted Western tour groups for this reason. Population pressures and the devastation caused by civil war have put this resource at severe risk. The situation is equally serious in the neighbouring Democratic Republic of the Congo (DRC) (formerly Zaire) which is by far the largest country in the region. In the colonial era the Belgian Congo had been a pioneer in wildlife conservation, and as a legacy 12 per cent of the territory of the DRC is, in theory at least, designated as protected areas. The most important of these are:

- the Virunga National Park which shares with neighbouring Uganda the spectacular Ruwenzori Mountains with its strange high-altitude vegetation
- the Ituri Forest – home of the Pygmies
- two of Africa's largest lakes.

Transport on the River Congo and its tributaries is confined to small-scale local commerce, and many improvements will need to be made, to both vessels and port facilities, before this network of inland waterways is viable for international tourism.

The Atlantic islands

To the west of the African continent lie several groups of volcanic islands in the Atlantic Ocean. They are isolated from the mainstream of international trade, and tourism is handicapped by the difficulty and expense of reaching them. They include three British territories, namely:

1. *St Helena* does not have an airport, and is served only by infrequent shipping services linking Europe to South Africa. Known mainly for its associations with Napoleon, the island has potential for tourists interested in dolphin-watching, game-fishing and the colonial heritage.
2. *Ascension* has a military airport, acting as a staging point between Britain and the Falkland Islands, but this barren island has little to attract visitors.
3. *Tristan da Cunha* is storm-swept, rugged and harbourless, and must rank as one of the world's most remote communities.

Prospects for tourism seem brighter in the former Portuguese colonies of Saõ Tomé and the Cape Verde Islands, which are linked by scheduled air services to Lisbon:

1. *Saõ Tomé* and its smaller neighbour Principe are situated on the Equator. Their main assets are the fine beaches backed by a lush setting of forests and plantations.
2. *The Cape Verde Islands* lie to the west of Senegal, and are climatically not very different from the Canaries. Sal has an international airport, built to serve South African Airways when that airline was prohibited for political reasons from overflying the African continent. Sal is rather barren however, and the other islands offer more attractive scenery. Mindelo on São Vicente is the most cosmopolitan town on the islands, with a cultural scene that resembles Brazil rather than West Africa. Sailing, windsurfing, diving, and trekking in the mountains of São Antonio and São Tiago, are the activities offered to visitors. It is hoped earnings from tourism will help the islands' economy, which is dependent on remittances from Cape Verdeans working overseas.

Summary

Africa is the second largest of the continents and is rich in both natural and cultural tourist resources. Aside from a sizeable North African tourist industry serving the mass inclusive-tour markets of Europe, Africa's tourist potential is largely unfulfilled. This can be attributed to a rudimentary transport network, the generally poor organizational framework, and the low level of industrial development of most African countries. Yet in such a vast continent generalizations are inappropriate; South Africa, for example has an advanced economy, a high standard of tourist organization and infrastructure, and also generates international tourists. Some African countries have identified tourism as an area for expansion to attract foreign currency and enhance their economic position. This has been most evident in Southern Africa, and the islands of the Indian Ocean but most of the countries of West and Central Africa have been less successful. The tourist resources of North Africa are based on both winter and summer beach resorts with the added ingredient of a taste of Arab culture and excursions to the Sahara. East Africa's tourist resources primarily comprise the national parks and game reserves, but developments at the coast allow combined beach and safari tourism. South Africa's attractions include beaches and wildlife, as well as spectacular scenery and a warm temperate climate. In West Africa, beach tourism is important, but here, as in all African countries, holidaymakers can sample the colourful everyday life of African towns and cities.

Case study

Local community involvement in safari tourism: the CAMPFIRE project in Zimbabwe

The Communal Areas Management Programme for Indigenous Resources (CAMPFIRE) was founded in the 1980s in Zimbabwe and has since spread to other countries in Southern Africa. It involves the management of wildlife resources by local African communities to earn money from tourism. Wildlife conservation is no longer an end in itself – it must be seen to pay its way.

The rural areas of Zimbabwe, as elsewhere in Africa, are experiencing the following problems:

- a demographic crisis, with the population in some areas doubling every twenty years
- a fall in real incomes
- a decline in investment
- climatic change, with droughts becoming more frequent – this particularly hits subsistence farmers who make up more than 80 per cent of the population.

At the same time wildlife habitats are dwindling. This causes:

- environmental degradation in the existing game reserves through overgrazing
- damage to African farms outside the reserves – for example, by elephants trampling crops, or predators killing livestock.

Traditionally, wildlife in Zimbabwe had been utilized by the African tribes as a community resource controlled by the chief and his council. Under British colonial rule, wildlife was declared the property of the state and hunting was outlawed. The best agricultural lands were reserved for the white settlers. The designation of the Hwange and Gonorezhou National Parks in the 1950s and 1960s involved the eviction of thousands of Shangaan tribespeople from their lands without compensation. When Independence brought no improvement to their situation, the Shangaan reacted with a poaching campaign directed against the national park system. The government responded by transferring ownership of wildlife from the state to the local community. The CAMPFIRE programme is a partnership between local councils and the public and private sectors in tourism.

Although a few CAMPFIRE communities are involved with whitewater rafting companies operating on the Zambezi, and in managing luxury camps for ecotourists, the bulk of their income is from hunting safaris, as follows:

- Safari companies pay rent for the use of communal lands, and employ local people as trackers, for example. Hunters pay hunting and trophy fees, amounting to approximately $10 000 for a mature elephant, the most sought after game. While the hunter retains the trophies, the meat is shared out among the villagers, whose everyday diet lacks protein.

The district council decides on an annual quota of animals to be killed, with the advice of the World Wide Fund for Nature as to sustainability. The revenue is distributed to the local villages, each of which has a CAMPFIRE committee that decides how the money should be spent.

From an African viewpoint CAMPFIRE is justified for the following reasons:

1 It encourages high-income, low-volume tourism. Although fees are high there is no shortage of wealthy clients.
2 Big-game hunting is beneficial for the conservation of wildlife, as numbers are kept within the ecological capacity of the area by selective culling. Elephant numbers have actually increased in CAMPFIRE managed areas, as poachers no longer gain support from the local community.
3 Hides and ivory are valuable wildlife resources in marginal areas where little else can be produced. The lifting of the 1989 ban on the export of ivory by CITES (The UN Convention on International Trade in Endangered Species) would earn Zimbabwe as much as $50 million a year in revenue from countries like Japan. This ivory would be from legally culled elephants.
4 Hunting benefits the local community, bringing in revenue for much needed schools, clinics and infrastructure. It encourages enterprise and involvement

by local people. The revenue from sport hunting is four times more profitable per hectare than raising cattle on the same land. Not surprisingly, one-third of all land in Zimbabwe is now given over to wildlife conservation, including privately owned game reserves and game ranches.

Opposition to the CAMPFIRE programme has come mainly from environmentalists in the USA. The powerful animal-rights lobby – the Humane Society – oppose hunting in principle. The future of this type of tourism hangs in the balance because the CAMPFIRE project is funded as part of the package of foreign aid that has to be approved each year by the US Congress.

The issue here for discussion is whether the Western world is justified in imposing its own value systems regarding hunting on a different culture, thereby denying the people an opportunity of becoming more self-reliant on the basis of their own resources.

21

South Asia

After reading this chapter you should be able to:

1 Describe the major physical features and climates of the Indian subcontinent and understand their importance for tourism.
2 Understand the importance of religion in everyday life and its effect on tourism in the region.
3 Recognize the great economic and social contrasts within the region.
4 Show that inbound tourism is being encouraged by most of the countries in the region to provide foreign exchange and employment
5 Recognize that the tourist appeal of the Indian subcontinent for the West lies in the exotic cultures of its peoples, as well as the familiar resources of beach tourism.
6 Recognize the growing importance of the Himalayas as a tourism resource, and the potential for conflict between tourism development and conservation.
7 Demonstrate a knowledge of the tourist regions, resorts, business centres and tourist attractions of South Asia.

Introduction

We mentioned in Chapter 3 that Asia is the world's largest continent, so we need to divide it into regions of more manageable size, made up of countries which are broadly similar in cultural terms. Three regions which are geographically part of Asia – the Middle East, the Central Asian

republics and Siberia – we described in Chapters 18 and 19. This leaves South Asia, which the World Tourism Organization (WTO) regards as a separate world region, likewise South-East Asia and the Far East, which the WTO includes as part of the East Asia-Pacific region.

The governments of most Asian countries realize the importance of tourism, and many have joined organizations such as the Pacific Asia Travel Association (PATA) to promote travel to the region more effectively. From the viewpoint of the Western tourist, these countries offer interesting contrasts in landscapes and cultures, living costs are generally low and hotel service is more personalized than in the West. On the other hand, the provision of infrastructure outside the main tourist areas is often inadequate. Until recently the Asian countries themselves generated few tourists, and those that did travel abroad tended to do so within the region. As the economies of Asian countries develop, so does demand for tourism, particularly in the business sector.

Physical features of South Asia

South Asia is better known as the Indian subcontinent, which consists of three major physical divisions:

1 *The northern mountain rampart*, which separates the subcontinent from the bulk of the Asian landmass. This includes the Himalayas to the east, and the Pamirs, Hindu Kush and Karakoram mountains to the west. These mountains rise to over 6000 metres and boast the world's highest summits. They also have the following important characteristics:
   (a) They act as a barrier to the movement of the very cold air masses building up over Central Asia in winter, so that the lowlands to the south enjoy a warm climate throughout the year.

(b) They also act as a barrier to north–south communications. Few roads cross the high mountain passes, and unlike the Alps, no railways penetrate the ranges. Even the pattern of air routes is affected to some extent.

(c) Because of their altitude, the mountains themselves have a much cooler climate than the lowlands, and support a number of contrasting life zones based on differences in rainfall as well as temperature. The western Himalayas for example are much drier than those to the east – where Cherrapunji in the Assam foothills has the unenviable distinction of being one of the world's wettest places.

(d) In relation to their resources the mountain valleys are often densely populated. The growth of tourism poses a threat to local communities already under pressure, as well as providing economic opportunity.

(e) In the past the mountains contained a number of independent kingdoms, which were protected from outside influences by their remoteness and rugged terrain. At the present time only Bhutan, and to a lesser extent Nepal, have managed to preserve their cultural as well as political integrity. Sikkim and Ladakh have been absorbed by India, while Tibet has been forcibly integrated into China. On the other hand, some of the ethnic groups remain essentially nomadic, ignoring the modern frontiers.

2 *The Northern Plains*, through which flow the great rivers Indus, Ganges and Brahmaputra. These lowlands contain most of the historic cities and business centres of South Asia. The western part of the region has an arid climate, as shown by the Thar Desert on the India–Pakistan border. Elsewhere winter tends to be the dry season, with a large daily range of temperature. Stifling heat (with temperatures frequently exceeding 40°C) can be expected from April to June before the onset of the monsoon. The arrival of the rains provides some initial relief, but is soon followed by months of sweltering weather, as the high humidity negates any cooling effect the slightly lower temperatures might have.

3 *Peninsular India and the islands* This part of South Asia is dominated by the great plateau of volcanic rocks known as the Deccan, which is separated from the coastal plains by the mountains known as the Western and Eastern Ghats. The region has a more moderate tropical climate than the northern plains, making it a suitable winter sun destination for tourists from Europe. Coastal locations such as Goa and Kerala, as well as the island states of Sri Lanka and the Maldives in the Indian Ocean have developed tourism industries based primarily on their beach resources.

Cultural features of South Asia

Despite the attractions of beaches and spectacular mountain scenery, the tourist appeal of South Asia is to a large extent cultural. The street life, bustling markets, colourful festivals and distinctive foods are fascinating for Western tourists, who also experience a degree of 'culture shock' on arrival. Religion has a major impact on everyday life, and the best of the cultural heritage is to be found in temples and shrines rather than secular buildings. The perceived *other-worldliness* of countries like India and Nepal attracts many Western tourists alienated by materialism, some of whom seek spiritual guidance in religious communities or *ashrams*.

At this point we feel some explanation of the major religions is necessary:

1 *Hinduism*, with over 700 million believers is the majority religion in India, and its rituals have profoundly influenced Indian civilization for at least 3000 years – far longer than Christianity in the West or Islam in the Middle East. The Hindu belief in *Karma* and reincarnation often results in a fatalistic attitude to life that most Westerners find difficult to accept. Hindu temples are dedicated to a particular god or goddess (Brahma, Vishnu and Shiva are the most important), and are sumptuously decorated with polychrome sculptures.

2 *Buddhism* also originated in northern India, but is now much more widespread in Sri Lanka, the Himalayan kingdoms, South-East Asia and the Far East. Common to all Buddhists is a belief in the importance of meditation as the path to *Nirvana* (enlightenment). Buddhist temples usually contain stylized images of the religion's founder – Gautama Siddhartha who is venerated as the Buddha (enlightened one). However, styles of architecture vary widely – temples in Sri Lanka and Burma are quite different from those in Bhutan for example.

3 *Islam* is the predominant religion in Afghanistan, Pakistan, Bangladesh and the Maldives. The Mogul Emperors imposed Islam on northern India in the sixteenth century, and were responsible for some of the world's finest Moslem architecture, including the Taj Mahal.

4 *Sikhism* originally arose as a resistance to the Moslem domination of northern India. Sikhs differ from Hindus in being monotheistic, placing much less emphasis on ritual, and rejecting the rigid social distinctions or castes that have characterized traditional Indian culture. Although they number only some 18 million, based mainly in the Punjab, they play an important role in commerce and the professions.

Religious tensions also threaten the political stability of most countries in the region, and thus reduce their appeal to tourists. Differences between Moslems and Hindus in British India led to its partition into two separate countries on independence in 1947. However, this left unresolved the status of Kashmir, causing a long-running dispute between the Republic of India and Pakistan and disrupting communications between the two countries. In the late 1990s the rise of Hindu fundamentalism in the Republic of India poses a threat to the government's policy of secularism and religious toleration. Moslem fundamentalism has already influenced social attitudes in Afghanistan and Pakistan, where religion and politics are less clearly separated than they are in India.

Western cultural influence was largely due to the British, although the Portuguese arrived in the region much earlier. In fact, almost the whole of the Indian subcontinent was under British rule or protection during the nineteenth and early twentieth centuries, with the exception of a few small Portuguese and French enclaves such as Goa, Diu and Pondicherry. The legacy of the British Raj remains after independence in the widespread use of the English language and administrative framework, sporting and military traditions, an extensive railway network and a supply of mountain resorts known as hillstations. These had provided British officials and their families, in the days before air conditioning, with a refuge from the summer heat of the plains. These places still retain much of their colonial architecture, although they are now resorts for middle-class domestic tourists. They include:

● Murree in Pakistan
● Simla in the Himalayas (the summer capital of British India)
● Ootacamund in the Nilgiri Highlands of southern India
● Nuwara Eliya in Sri Lanka.

An overview of tourism in South Asia

South Asia as a whole accounts for less than 4 per cent of international world tourism arrivals. Over half of all tourist arrivals, and over three-quarters of receipts are accounted for by the largest of the nine component countries of South Asia – the Republic of India. Elsewhere in much of the region tourism is of little significance, notably for Afghanistan due to political unrest rendering the country unsafe for travellers, and for Bangladesh, where tourism development is overshadowed by more pressing economic concerns. Most countries have encouraged inbound tourism, and most have a positive balance on their tourism account, with the notable exception of Pakistan, where outbound travel is much greater in terms of expenditure.

We can see a variety of approaches to tourism within the region including:

● stringent restriction on visitor numbers in the case of Bhutan – in contrast to neighbouring Nepal
● a policy of tourist segregation from the local communities in the Lakshadweep and the Maldive Islands
● promotion of Western-style beach holidays in Goa.

India

India demands our attention for a number of reasons:

1 In extent and cultural variety it is the equivalent of Europe, but with a much older civilization. There are at least eighteen major languages, although Hindi is the most widely spoken. The country is a mosaic of different religions, ethnic groups and castes.
2 With a population approaching 1 billion, India is second only to China. It has 15 per cent of the world's population on just 3 per cent of the world's land area, so that demographic pressures on the resource base are severe.
3 Over half of India's population is under twenty-five years of age, 50 per cent are illiterate and the majority are living at subsistence level. Although India is a predominantly rural country, it also contains three major world cities – Delhi, Bombay and Calcutta – each with well over 10 million inhabitants, and increasing at the rate of 500 000 a year. Not surprisingly, in such a large country there are also very many wealthy people who travel extensively.
4 Despite these pressures and many other socioeconomic problems, India has retained a democratic form of government since independence, although the Congress Party has been dominant in politics for most of that time. The cultural diversity of the country is recognized in the federal system of government, in which each of the twenty-five states has a large degree of control over its internal affairs, including tourism development.
5 India is one of Asia's leading industrial nations, with technological expertise as part of its vast human resources. Bangalore for example is one of the world's leading computer centres. India also has a well-developed communications infrastructure compared to most Third World countries. On the other hand, bureaucratic controls and inertia inhibit progress.

The demand for tourism

Domestic and outbound tourism

A substantial middle class, estimated to be between 15 to 20 per cent of the population – or over 150 million people – has the means to participate in domestic tourism in India and the volumes are impressive, exceeding 200 million trips per year. Traditionally a good deal of domestic travel has been undertaken for religious reasons, as all the major faiths encourage pilgrimages to shrines or holy places. The best known of these is the Hindu centre of Varanasi (Benares) on the River Ganges, where the *ghats* – the steps leading down to the water's edge are the focus for ritual bathing, readings from the sacred texts by gurus and cremations. However, there are many other shrines, often in remote locations in the Himalayas and Kashmir. Often these pilgrimages entail an arduous journey, partly on foot, and embrace all classes of society, including large numbers of wandering *sadhus* (holymen). Bodhgaya is the main pilgrimage centre for Buddhists, while the Golden Temple at Amritsar is the holy place of the Sikhs. Leisure travel for other motives, visits to beach and mountain resorts for example, is expected to increase as incomes rise among a Western educated middle class.

Outbound tourism is much smaller in volume, but nevertheless accounted for 4 million departures a year in the late 1990s, mainly to neighbouring countries such as Nepal. Business travel accounts for 25 per cent of these journeys. Leisure travel to countries outside South Asia should grow with the relaxation of strict foreign exchange controls imposed by the Indian government. For many years Britain has been the most popular European destination, reflecting the cultural ties between the two countries.

Inbound tourism

Despite having vast tourism potential, India received only a very small share of world tourist arrivals during the 1990s, amounting to some 2 million visitors a year. Even so, tourism is India's third largest earner of foreign exchange, and the sector is responsible for employing at least 8 million people. The impact is much greater if we consider the informal sector of the economy, and the very large numbers engaged in the handicraft industries. However, a number of factors are holding back the expansion of tourism in India:

1 Inadequate infrastructure, especially water and power supplies.
2 Negative publicity in the Western media. For example, outbreaks of disease and intercommunal strife, in reality confined to specific areas, are seen as affecting the whole country.
3 Promotion of this enormous and complex country as one destination, whereas India consists of many quite different destinations and tourism products. There is a need to market specific destinations and target specific types of tourist.
4 The seasonal concentration of visits in the final quarter of the year, creating occupancy problems for India's hotels.
5 A shortage of medium-priced accommodation, particularly in Delhi.
6 Other negative factors include air pollution in the cities during the dry season, noise, poor hygiene, and harassment by beggars and street vendors.

The main generating markets for India are its neighbours, Britain, Germany, France, the USA, the Middle East and Japan. Many arrivals from the Middle East and Britain are in fact returning expatriates, who tend to stay with friends or relatives and make little use of tourist facilities. The average length of stay of tourists to India – 28 days – is among the world's highest. Backpackers, for example, from Europe, Australia and North America, who are including India as part of an Asian tour, spend at least three weeks in the country. The role of these young budget travellers has been important in opening up new destinations to conventional tourism. However, the typical backpackers of the 1990s are different from their predecessors of the 1970s in that they are:

● usually following an established route pattern, staying at hostels and cheap hotels patronized by other Western budget travellers
● less concerned with a search for 'spiritual values'. Nowadays, an extended visit to India is seen more as an interesting way of filling the 'gap year' between college and a career.

The most popular time to visit India is from October to December when the weather is at its best, but there is a steady flow of business travellers throughout the year.

The supply of tourism

Transport

The vast majority of foreign visitors to India (other than those from neighbouring Bangladesh and Pakistan) arrive by air. Delhi and Mumbai (Bombay) are the most important gateways, and have invested heavily in improving facilities for air travellers. Calcutta and Chennai (Madras) serve the eastern and southern parts of the country. The Indian government has responded to the growth in air travel by adopting a liberal *open skies* policy, which allows foreign charter airlines to fly direct from Europe to resort areas such as Goa. Moreover the national carrier Air India has a code-sharing agreement with the American airline Continental Airways.

Only a small minority of Western tourists travel overland to India, due to the political situation in Afghanistan which has closed the historic route through the Khyber Pass, while the long-standing dispute between India and Pakistan over Kashmir places another obstacle in the way of travellers. Internal transport is less fraught with difficulties. Indian Airlines operate domestic services to over seventy destinations within the country as well as neighbouring states. India inherited from Britain the most extensive railway network in Asia, amounting to over 70 000 kilometres of track. This provides a cheaper and more interesting way of touring than by air, with express services linking all the main cities. As the system is heavily used, foreign tourists need to purchase Indrail passes or make prior reservations to ensure travelling in comfort and without hassle. In some areas steam locomotives are still used, as for example on the narrow-gauge Darjeeling–Himalaya railway, which is a major tourist attraction in its own right. Luxury rail products such as the 'Palace on Wheels' and the 'Royal Orient' are promoted by the India Tourist Office as a way of touring the classical sites in the north-west of the country.

India also boasts over 1 million kilometres of passable roads, which provide access to even remote mountain areas; however, accident levels are very high by Western standards, livestock on the road are a frequent hazard, and travel even by express bus can be a noisy and exhausting experience.

Accommodation

India's accommodation stock is extensive ranging from luxury hotels to basic hostels used by backpackers more concerned about price than say fire safety. Modern Western-style hotels catering for both business and leisure tourists are found in all large cities and the popular tourist centres. This sector is dominated by Indian-owned chains, namely Taj, Oberoi and the state-owned India Tourism Development Corporation (ITDC). More unusual types of accommodation include:

1 The luxury houseboats moored on Lake Dal at Srinagar, a heritage of British and Mogul rule in Kashmir.
2 The former palaces of the Indian princes or maharajas who were semi-independent under the British Raj. These have now been converted into 'heritage hotels', the most famous being the Lake Palace Hotel at Udaipur in Rajahstan, in a highly romantic setting.
3 *Dak* bungalows, used primarily by government officials as rest houses, are sometimes available for overnight stays by tourists in remote areas.
4 Hostels provided by religious organizations.
5 Tourist bungalows providing self-catering facilities and private guesthouses are available in resort areas. Camping grounds have also been developed along the main overland routes and forest lodges are available in wildlife reserves such as the Kanha National Park.

Tourism organization

In the 1960s tourism development began to form part of the government's Five-Year Plans (whose primary objective is to raise living standards) and more recently tourism has been the subject of specific 'action plans'. Since 1967 the Ministry of Civil Aviation and Tourism has been responsible for formulating policy at cabinet level and was responsible for shaping tourism in the 1970s and 1980s. The Ministry is supported by a number of other agencies including:

1 The *India Tourism Development Corporation* (ITDC) This was set up by the government in 1965 to develop infrastructure in those areas where the private sector was reluctant to invest. Apart from hotels the ITDC also owned resorts, restaurants and transport operations, some of which have since been privatized.

2 The *Tourism Finance Corporation of India* established to assist with tourism financing.
3 The *Indian Insititute of Travel and Tourism Management* (IITTM) established to set up high-quality training and education in tourism.

As well as supporting many projects through the ITDC, the government also provides financial incentives to domestic and foreign companies in the private sector. At the regional and local levels the various state and city authorities have a regulatory role, and some have set up development corporations to carry out tourism projects. In recent years, however, the public sector has not been particularly active in encouraging tourism. It is perhaps not surprising that in a country with so many pressing social and economic problems, the development of tourist facilities, which the majority of the Indian population cannot afford, is seen as a low priority.

Tourism resources

India offers a unique blend of ancient civilizations, religious monuments, spectacular scenery, beaches, mountain resorts and wildlife reserves. We can summarize the main tourism products as:

1 *Cultural tourism* – usually focusing on a particular region, and taking the form of a tour circuit linking a number of sites to a gateway city.
2 *Beach tourism* At present this is mainly found in the states of Goa, Kerala and Tamil Nadu, and little of India's 7500-kilometres long coastline has been developed for tourism.
3 *Adventure tourism*, including trekking, mountain climbing and river-running is mainly focused on the more accessible parts of the Himalaya region.
4 Eco-tourism. India is second only to Africa in the variety of its wildlife resources. This is perhaps surprising given the demographic pressures and the threats of increasing pollution and deforestation (only 13 per cent of the land has any type of forest cover). The first national park – Jim Corbett to the north of Delhi – was established under British rule in 1911 due to the efforts of a hunter turned conservationist. There are now some seventy national parks and 330 wildlife sanctuaries, although most of these are restricted in area compared with those of Africa. The federal government has effected a number of conservation measures; the most widely publicised is 'Project Tiger' which seeks to protect India's best known animal. Kanha National Park in Madhya Pradesh, the setting for Kipling's *Jungle Book*, is the best known of these game reserves. Much of the responsibility for wildlife management has devolved to the individual states. Limited funding is a problem, and issues of economic development often conflict with conservation.

Due to its extent India is usually treated as four regions, based on the gateways of Delhi, Mumbai, Chennai and Calcutta.

Northern India

This region has played a major role in the history of India, and contains the best known cultural attractions. The so-called 'Classic Triangle', a tour circuit linking the cities of Delhi, Agra and Jaipur, is the most popular route for foreign visitors.

1 Delhi actually consists of two cities – the old and the new. Old Delhi was the capital of the Mogul Empire, a maze of narrow streets, chaotic traffic and bustling bazaars. Among its Islamic monuments are the Jama Masjid Mosque and the Red Fort, once a royal palace. New Delhi was planned by the British as the capital of India in the closing decades of the Raj. The most important of its broad ceremonial avenues is the Rajpath linking India Gate to the Presidents' Palace.
2 Agra is mainly visited for the Taj Mahal, the white marble mausoleum commemorating Shah Jehan's love for his wife Mumtaz. This beautiful building is under threat from:
    (a) Tourist pressure, leaving in its wake, litter in the gardens and even graffiti on the monument itself.
    (b) Pollution. Although tourism provides a livelihood for many thousands employed in the craft and service sectors, Agra is also a major industrial city. Sulphur dioxide emissions have caused a massive deterioration in the stonework.

Within easy reach of Agra are other relics of bygone India:

● Fatehpur Sikri, the remains of a short lived capital of the Mogul Empire
● Orchha, which has undergone less restoration and is not as commercialized
● the temples at Khajuraho with their erotic sculptures are also a well-established part of the tour circuit.

1 Jaipur is the gateway to Rajahstan, a state which to many epitomizes India, with its colourful costumes, ethnic crafts, and the palaces of the former maharajas. It also exemplifies the problems brought about by tourism in an arid region where there are few other sources of income. Some allege that conventional organized tourism does not benefit local communities as profits mainly go to the owners of 'heritage hotels', who furthermore prefer to employ immigrant Nepalis, who are prepared to accept even lower wages than the locals. On the other hand, backpackers have also been criticized for showing little respect for Hindu traditions, while the Pushkar camel market has become a commercialized tourist event. Of the tourist centres, Jaipur itself is famous for its markets and the 'Palace of the Winds', but suffers from chronic pollution and lack of investment.
2 Jodhpur, which gave polo to the British, is noted for its *son et lumière* performances re-creating the warrior traditions of the Rajput princes.
3 Udaipur is the best preserved of the Rajput cities, with a beautiful setting on Lake Pichola.
4 Jaisalmer, once a major trading centre for camel caravans crossing the Thar Desert, but now a picturesque stop on the tourist itinerary. Income from tourism enabled the authorities to provide a piped water supply, but this together with vastly increased water consumption, has caused widespread subsidence, as the town's open drains cannot cope. As a result, many of the *havelis* (merchant houses) are in urgent need of repair.
5 Kashmir with its beautiful mountain scenery and cool climate was the favourite resort area for the Mogul rulers of India, who designed the famous Shalimar Gardens in Srinagar. The chronic dispute with Pakistan, with most of this largely Moslem state under military occupation, has not encouraged Western visitors, although Gulmarg was developed in the 1970s as the premier skiing and golf resort of India. On the other hand, Ladakh has become a trekking destination, offering spectacular, if barren, high mountain landscapes and a largely unspoiled Tibetan culture.

Eastern India

The eastern India region is centred on Calcutta, now the capital of West Bengal. The former capital of British India is better known for its overcrowding and Mother Teresa's work among the destitute than for its cultural attractions which outshine those of Delhi. Although rickshaws still feature in the traffic, Calcutta boasts India's only metro system, and its technological achievements are showcased in 'Science City'. Within easy reach are the beach resorts of the Bay of Bengal, including Puri, which is also a major religious centre for Hindus. It is one of a number of temple-cities in the state of Orissa, the others being Konarak and Bhubaneswar. Calcutta is also the gateway to the eastern Himalayas, particularly the mountain resorts of Darjeeling and Shillong, which are noted for their tea plantations. Large areas of this sensitive frontier region are, however, tribal territories under military control, and access is restricted.

Southern India

The Dravidian peoples of southern India are culturally distinct, and overseas trade has played an important role in the history of the region. The port of Cochin, for example, was noted for its trade in pepper and other spices in ancient times, and in the picturesque fishing villages, Hinduism has coexisted peacefully with Christianity and other religions.

With its favourable climate, lush scenery and fine beaches, the state of Kerala is set to rival Goa as a holiday destination. A unique asset is provided by the 'backwaters', a system of canals adapted from transporting agricultural produce to recreational use. With the introduction of charter flights in 1995, Kovalam has become a major beach resort, particularly for British holidaymakers. However, this has failed to benefit the local community to the same extent as the small-scale informal tourism of earlier years, and stands in apparent contradiction to the socialist leanings of the state government. Most of the Coromandel Coast is less attractive for tourism development, due to the heavy surf. Nevertheless, Madras has fine beaches as well as being a major cultural centre. It is a good base for exploring the temples of Madurai and Kanchipuram, which are spectacular examples of Hindu architecture.

Western India

Beach tourism has developed to a greater extent in western India along the Malabar coast. The region is dominated by Bombay, India's major port and business centre, while Goa is the leading holiday destination.

1 Bombay is a new city by Indian standards, with many reminders of the British Raj when it was the 'gateway to India'. It is seen as a city of opportunity by rural immigrants, who pour in at the rate of a thousand a day. With little room for expansion on a narrow peninsula, the city's congestion is acute, and the contrasts between skyscrapers and grand hotels on the one hand, and the *bustees* (slums) on the other, are extreme. This may explain the dominant role of 'Bollywood' – Bombay's booming film industry – in popular culture. Apart from shopping, the city's attractions include Chowpatty Beach, with its snake charmers and other performers, the 'hanging gardens' of exclusive Malabar Hill, the Gandhi Memorial and the art collections of the Prince of Wales Museum. The ancient history of India is brought to life at the Elephanta Caves, while Bombay is a good base for visiting the temples of Ajanta (Buddhist) and Ellora (Hindu).
2 Goa's small area offers scenic variety, over 100 kilometres of fine beaches, and a relaxed lifestyle. Culturally it is unique – a blend of Indian and 'Latin' influences. Carnival and both Catholic and Hindu festivals are celebrated here, while alcohol is freely available – unlike the situation elsewhere in India. Portugal ruled Goa for almost five centuries until it was ousted by the Indian Army in 1961, and the Portuguese influence is evident in the architecture, music and the cuisine. The immense Baroque church of Bom Jesu in Old Goa – the former capital – contains the tomb of St Francis Xavier, the greatest of Jesuit missionaries to the East.

Western tourists are not attracted to Goa primarily for cultural or religious reasons however; since the arrival of the 'hippies' in the 1960s the focus has been on beach tourism. Nevertheless we can distinguish between different categories of visitor and a range of accommodation and services has developed to meet their needs:

(a) Low-budget backpackers, mainly from Europe and Australia, who are stopping off in Goa as part of an extended Asian tour. They stay in cheap guesthouses in the Anjuna area, 'discovered' by the hippies of a previous generation.
(b) Indian domestic tourists taking seaside holidays, cultural tours and business trips, who stay at hotels in Panaji, the state capital or other towns.
(c) High-income Western tourists and returning Goan expatriates, staying at luxury resort hotels on tailor-made itineraries.
(d) Package holidaymakers from the UK, Germany and other West European countries arriving during the winter season on direct charter flights to Goa's Dabolim Airport. They stay in three-star hotels contracted to particular tour operators. Due to the rapid growth of charters since 1987, fishing villages such as Calangute have become commercialized resorts.
(e) Middle-class West European holidaymakers who take advantage of the cheap charter fares but who prefer to use locally owned small hotels and guesthouses.

Tourism has arguably brought economic benefits to Goa, but the state government's policy of encouraging upmarket tourism has been opposed by local non-governmental organizations (NGOs) concerned with the social and environmental issues associated with tourism development. These include:

(a) The diversion of scarce resources, such as water and power from agriculture to the hotel sector. It is claimed, for example, that one five-star hotel consumes as much water as five villages.
(b) Unlike the guesthouses and small hotels that are locally owned, the luxury hotels are linked with multinational chains or owned by Indians from outside Goa. The state government's attempts to control the beach shacks selling food and beverages is seen as favouring the hotels at the expense of local people's livelihood.
(c) The expansion of tourism has resulted in a decline of traditional occupations such as fishing and cashew nut farming.
(d) Many Goans are offended by the association of tourism in some resort areas with Western sex and drug culture.

Goa has reached the stage in the resort life cycle where it is facing growing competition as tour operators discover more unspoiled beach locations. Backpackers for example, are increasingly attracted to the island of Diu, another former Portuguese territory, which is much closer to the tourist attractions of Rajahstan.

The islands of India

India's island territories as yet remain largely untouched by Western style tourism, although they attract a growing number of domestic visitors. They include:

1 The Lakshadweep (Laccadives) archipelago in the Indian Ocean, composed of small coral atolls similar to the Maldives further south. Bangaram is the only island open to Western tourists for diving holidays.
2 The Andaman and Nicobar Islands in the Bay of Bengal are rugged and largely forest covered. There is potential for eco-tourism and diving, but development is restricted by lack of infrastructure and the sensitive nature of relationships between mainland India and the indigenous tribes, an example of a 'Fourth World' culture which is increasingly under threat.

Pakistan

Pakistan has been less successful than India in attracting Western tourists and the sector accounts for less than 1 per cent of gross domestic product. In part, this is due to the strength of Islamic fundamentalism, security concerns, poor infrastructure and the restrictions on cross-border travel. Most of the country consists of mountain and desert landscapes, and some of the world's most difficult terrain separates Pakistan from its neighbours to the west and north. During the 1990s tourist arrivals were less than 500 000 a year, the most important generating countries being the UK and the USA. In addition, domestic tourism is significant, and set to grow, with an estimated 40 million trips per year.

The Pakistan Tourist Development Corporation offers a wide selection of hotels, motels, and rest houses (known as *musafir khanas*) and tours operated by its subsidiary Pakistan Tours Limited. The national airline Pakistan International Airlines (PIA) provides a network of international and domestic services.

Although Urdu is the official language, Pakistan is made up of a number of ethnic groups and the country has been less politically stable than India. In the northwest of the country, government control is only loosely exercised over the Pathans and other tribes. In the time of the Raj, this was the North West Frontier of British India, immortalized by Rudyard Kipling; nowadays it is an area awash with guns and refugees as a result of the continuing crisis in Afghanistan. For this reason, the Khyber Pass throughout the 1990s ceased to function as an overland tourist route, although the regional capital – Peshawar – is visited by the more adventurous travellers. The majority of Pakistan's population live in the irrigated valley of the River Indus, which also contains the major tourist centres:

1 Lahore is the religious and cultural centre of the country, conserving much of the heritage of the Mogul emperors of India, including its own Shalimar Gardens.
2 Multan is another historic walled city, situated close to the remains of a much older civilization which flourished at Mohenjo–Daro over 4000 years ago.
3 Karachi is Pakistan's largest city and major international gateway.
4 Islamabad, the new city deliberately planned as the capital of the Moslem state, and the old city of Rawalpindi nearby, are mainly centres for business travel.
5 In the north of Pakistan, Gilgit provides facilities for skiing, trekking and mountain climbing, while the adventurous can follow the Karakoram Highway. This spectacular feat of engineering threads its way between some of the world's highest mountains and glaciers into China.

Bangladesh

From 1947 to 1971 Bangladesh, formerly east Bengal, was a detached part of Pakistan, but strong cultural differences led to a war of independence. The new nation had to face severe economic and environmental problems, namely:

1 This country of 120 million people is densely populated even by Asian standards, relying on an economy dominated by agriculture, and with few industries other than textiles.
2 Most of the country is low lying and is effectively a 'waterland' after the monsoon rains. Unusually devastating floods occur when tropical cyclones from the Indian Ocean coincide with heavy monsoon rains in the eastern Himalayas.
3 The country's many rivers are an obstacle to an effective road network, with ferry links below Western standards.

Nevertheless, Bangladesh is no longer regarded as an economic 'basket case' by some Western experts, and business travel to the capital Dhaka is growing in importance. Small enterprises are expected to play a major role in any expansion of tourism. Aside from the capital, the main areas of interest for tourists are:

● the foothills of Sylhet in the northern part of the country
● the vast wetland environment of the Sundarbans, formed by the deltas of the Ganges and Brahmaputra, which provides a refuge for wildlife
● Cox's Bazaar which boasts one of the most extensive beaches in Asia, as yet little developed.

Afghanistan

Until the Soviet invasion of 1979, Afghanistan was a transit area for travellers on the overland route from the Middle East to India. Since then, civil war arising out of long-standing tribal feuds has devastated the country's economy and infrastructure, particularly in the capital, Kabul. The present Moslem fundamentalist regime has done nothing to encourage Western tourists. Even in good times, the country was difficult to visit – most of it consists of arid, rugged mountains, while the climate and culture have much in common with Central Asia. Some examples remain of the country's ancient Buddhist heritage, but these are increasingly under threat from neglect.

The Maldives

A group of small tropical islands in the Indian Ocean, the Maldives have little in common with the other Moslem countries of South Asia. The government has done much to encourage Western tourism, but on its own terms, as shown in the second case study at the end of this chapter.

Sri Lanka

Formerly known as Ceylon, Sri Lanka is a large island rich in tourism resources. Its capital Colombo is well placed in relation to the air and shipping routes crossing the Indian Ocean. In the past, the island's closeness to India and fabled wealth attracted Arab traders who were followed by the Portuguese, Dutch and British. This resulted in a mix of cultures and one of the country's highest mountains – Sri Padu (Adam's Peak) is sacred to all four major religions. However, there have long been tensions between the Sinhalese and the Tamil minority, who were originally brought in by the British from southern India to work in the tea plantations. During the 1980s these erupted into civil war, which has since rendered much of the north and east of the country off limits to tourists, and as a result, Sri Lanka has lost favour with Western tour operators and visitor numbers have fallen.

Until the 1970s Sri Lanka had been one of the more stable countries in South Asia and the prospects for tourism seemed bright. The Ceylon Tourist Board was established in 1966, when 19 000 visitors were received. By 1982 this had grown to over 400 000, most of whom were on air-inclusive holidays, organized by West European tour operators (the entrepreneur Freddie Laker was largely responsible for introducing Sri Lanka as a long-haul beach destination to the British market).

The government ministry responsible for tourism is the Ministry of Tourism and Rural Industrial Development while the Ceylon Tourist Board is responsible for promotion and market research. Although Sri Lanka has suffered from the lack of a clear tourism policy, a master plan commissioned in the 1990s has provided a framework for tourism in the country. In response to this, the Sri Lanka government, while encouraging foreign investment, wished to steer development to the coastal areas closer to Colombo in the west, and the port of Trincomalee in the east, in this way protecting the country's cultural and wildlife resources from the impact of tourism. The plan also stimulated a change in emphasis of tourism development to 'beach plus' products, in contrast to the sun, sand and sea formula of earlier years. Sri Lanka's tourist attractions include:

1 Extensive sandy beaches along the south and west coast, although sea conditions can be rough during the period of the south-west monsoon from May to July. Here the Ceylon Tourist Board has developed resort hotels of an international standard, particularly at Bentota. The beaches on the east coast are less developed, although they are more sheltered and enjoy a drier climate.
2 The 'cultural triangle' of the interior, based on the historic cities of Kandy, Anuradhapura and Polonnaruwa, each of which served at one time as capital of a powerful kingdom. The Rock Fortress at Sigiriya, rising above the northern plain is particularly impressive, as are the remains of ancient temples, palaces and complex irrigation systems. Traditional crafts and dances continue to flourish in Kandy, which contains the 'Temple of the Tooth', a world famous Buddhist shrine.
3 The wildlife resources, including the elephant orphanage at Pinnawela, and a number of national parks, such as Yala and Gal Oya in the south-east which offer bungalow accommodation to tourists.
4 Colombo is a major business and conference centre, as well as providing shopping opportunities, especially in jewellery, batik and wood-carving.

Nepal

Although the Gurkhas had long played a major role in the British Army, the Hindu Kingdom of Nepal was closed to the outside world until the 1950s. Since its discovery by 'hippies' and overland travellers in the 1960s the growth of tourism has been rapid, to achieve well over 300 000 international arrivals in the late 1990s. With an area only half that of Great Britain, Nepal can offer a great variety of climates and scenery. There are three main divisions running east to west, namely:

1 The Himalayas, which contain eight of the world's highest mountain peaks, including Everest and Annapurna, attracting trekkers, mountain climbers and adven-

ture-seekers from many different countries (see the first case study at the end of this chapter).

2 The foothills, including the valleys of Kathmandu and Pokhara, which contain the majority of the population. Cultural attractions abound in the form of Buddhist temples, as at Bhadgaon and Patan.

3 The subtropical lowlands, known as the Terai, which still contain areas of jungle, including the Royal Chitwan National Park and its famous 'Tiger Tops' game lodge. Buddhists from all over the world are attracted to Lumbini, the birthplace of Buddha.

The Ministry of Tourism and Civil Aviation along with the Department of National Parks and Wildlife is responsible for tourism organization, and the Nepal Tourist Board is a public/private sector partnership body. In practice, Nepal relies very much on foreign aid for tourism development, and on Indian tour operators to bring in the visitors. In the 1990s, air policy has undergone a degree of liberalization allowing in other carriers to supplement Royal Nepal Airlines.

Poor access, pollution, inadequate infrastructure and frequent shortages of power and water supplies are major constraints on the growth of the tourism sector. In addition, criticism from environmentalists about the pollution found on the mountains, and the lack of robust environmental policies (for example, timber-cutting to maintain tourist lodges) may also constrain tourism growth. Yet the government is now keen to develop tourism as a solution to both economic growth and employment.

Bhutan

This Buddhist kingdom is much smaller than Nepal in area and population as well as being more remote. The government is determined to preserve traditional lifestyles from the impact of tourism, which is therefore strictly controlled. Access is restricted to a small number of accredited tour operators offering special interest holidays to small groups of visitors, rather than trekking on the Nepalese model. Culturally, Bhutan is similar to Tibet, with numerous fortified monasteries known as *dzongs* dominating the countryside.

Summary

South Asia contains comes of the world's most densely populated countries, at various stages of economic development but nevertheless poor by Western standards. Most countries in the region are developing an inbound tourism industry to earn much needed foreign exchange and provide jobs for rapidly growing populations. The generally low level of incomes means that domestic tourism is less significant while volumes of outbound tourism are small;

however, both are set to increase due to the growth of a middle class, especially in India. Despite a wealth of resources, South Asia accounts for only a small percentage of world tourism.

The attractions of the region are based on the exotic cultures and landscapes, and a lifestyle in which religion plays a major role. Of particular note are the classic tour circuits in India, the beaches and gentle way of life of the Indian Ocean islands, and the spectacular scenery of the Himalayas.

Case study

Adventure tourism in Nepal: environmental and social impacts

Nepal offers an attractive environment for Western tourists seeking wilderness adventure. In fact, surprisingly little of this mountainous but quite densely populated country is uninhabited wilderness in the North American sense. Adventure tourism includes the following related activities:

1 *Mountain climbing* The expedition to climb Annapurna was the first group of Western visitors allowed into Nepal. It was followed three years later by Hillary and Tenzing's successful ascent of Mount Everest in 1953, which attracted worldwide attention. Climbing the Himalayas is exceptionally hazardous, because of the extreme weather conditions and the lack of oxygen at high altitudes; even the base of a mountain like Annapurna is at a higher level than any summit in the Alps. In view of these conditions, most expeditions have been organized on a lavish scale, involving teams of climbers, sophisticated equipment and a small army of Sherpa porters to provide logistical support. The accumulated waste left by successive expeditions, particularly on Everest has been an environmental disgrace, necessitating a major clean-up operation. However, more climbers are adopting the minimalist approach, pioneered by Reinhold Messner, who proved it was possible to climb peaks at over 8000 metres without the use of supplementary oxygen.

2 *River-running* Nepal's fast-flowing rivers, including the Trisuli, Sun Kosi and Karnali, offer ideal conditions for whitewater rafting and kayaking, particularly the first two which are more accessible from Kathmandu (see Figure 21.1).

3 *Mountain-biking* like river running, is often combined with trekking by younger Western tourists, and takes place at relatively low altitudes.

4 *Trekking*.

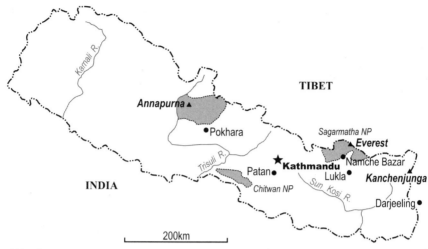

Figure 21.1 Map of Nepal

Trekking

Introduction

Trekking is the most popular tourist activity in the Himalayan zone of Nepal. During the late 1990s trekkers accounted for over one-quarter of all visitors. Trekking originally developed as a separate activity from climbing in the 1960s, and the treks were based on the approach routes used by the Everest and Annapurna expeditions. Trekking is a way of visiting locations 'off the beaten track', but differs from hiking in a number of ways. Trekkers usually walk in organized groups escorted by a *sirdar* (guide), with a backup team of cooks and porters who carry food supplies and equipment between the stopping places on the route. Although itineraries can be tailor-made to meet the requirements of small groups of clients, most treks differ little in organization from other types of inclusive tour. Western-based tour operators carry out the marketing, bring together the clients in their country of origin and arrange for the trekking permits, which for independent travellers involves a time-consuming hassle with Nepalese bureaucracy. Like other tour operators, they may opt for consolidation if there is not enough demand for a particular trek. Some also allege that trekking is not really a sustainable, alternative type of tourism and, as we shall see, there is some evidence to support this view.

The organization of trekking

Nepal offers a great variety of trekking opportunities including some of the world's most spectacular scenery,

the ethnic groups who have modified this landscape over the centuries, and a wide selection of routes and types of trek to suit most clients:

1 The longer treks, such as the Annapurna Circuit, take up to three weeks and involve tackling steep gradients at altitudes ranging from 1000 to over 5000 metres above sea level. These require a high standard of fitness, and *hypoxia* (altitude sickness) is a risk at the higher levels even for experienced hikers.
2 On the other hand, short treks lasting three days or so are available at lower altitudes on less rugged terrain.

The trails – based on established trading routes – are well maintained and trekkers are rarely far from a village. Moreover, large numbers of lodges providing overnight accommodation and tea houses offering basic catering facilities have sprung up along most routes to meet their needs.

However, trekking in Nepal shows a high degree of seasonality. Climatic conditions largely dictate that the majority of treks take place between October and December (when snow blocks the high mountain passes) and from March to May, prior to the monsoon rains.

Although new areas are being opened up to meet the demand, trekking also shows a high degree of concentration in particular areas of central and eastern Nepal, including:

1 The Annapurna region west of Pokhara, with its well-developed infrastructure of trails and lodges, is the most popular with trekkers and tour operators. It

includes among its attractions the Kali Gandaki Valley, reputed to be the world's deepest gorge, and the Annapurna Sanctuary. The region is particularly rich in plant and animal species, including more than 100 species of orchid and the endangered snow leopard.

2 The Everest route, from Lukla to the base camp at the foot of Mount Everest is more demanding for trekkers than the Annapurna circuit and acclimatization to high altitudes is even more essential. It includes the Khumba region with its Sherpa villages, the famous Thyangboche monastery, and the Khumbu glacier that marks the approach to the world's highest mountain. Most of the region has been designated as the Sagarmatha National Park.

Economic impacts of trekking

Trekking is estimated to provide about 24 000 full time jobs and another 20 000 on a part-time basis. In the Annapurna region, 60 per cent of the population rely on tourism for a livelihood. Here the Thakali ethnic group has been particularly successful in taking advantage of the trekking boom, since they run most of the lodges on the Annapurna Circuit. Nevertheless the local economy is too poorly developed to supply most of the goods and services needed by Western tourists, so these have to be imported, often from India. As a result, only an estimated 20 cents out of the US$3 spent daily by the average trekker actually contributes to the local village economies. In the Khumba region, one of the least fertile and highest areas of Nepal, the Sherpa lifestyle has changed within a generation, from subsistence pastoralism based on the yak – to a cash economy. With a long tradition as traders over the high mountain passes into Tibet, the Sherpas are very much in demand as guides and porters for at least part of the year. Others work in tea houses, shops selling local handicrafts and tourist lodges. Income from tourism allied to Sir Edmund Hillary's fundraising from international donors, has provided schools and basic infrastructure. These impacts are most apparent in Namche Bazar, once a small hamlet and now an important tourist centre, where almost every other building is a hotel or curio shop.

Social/cultural impacts

The economic opportunities presented by trekkers and mountaineering expeditions have stemmed the previously high rates of out-migration from Himalayan villages, while improved medical care and greater prosperity have encouraged a high rate of population growth. Nevertheless, as in other Third World countries, the contrasts between the lifestyles and attitudes of affluent Western tourists and the poverty of the village communities has resulted in a number of impacts, including:

1 The breakdown of traditional social structures due to the differentiation of earning power between those involved in the tourism sector as compared to agriculture.
2 The demonstration effect as younger Nepalis strive to emulate Western lifestyles.
3 The high incidence of begging from tourists, particularly by young children.
4 The loss of the cultural heritage. This can be direct, as in the desecration of religious artefacts that are stolen and sold on the international art market. Also, craftsmen adapt their designs to suit the preferences of Western tourists, for example, in the purchase of *thankas*, Buddhist temple scrolls, which are highly decorative.

Environmental impacts

Although national parks and other protected areas demonstrate Nepal's commitment to conservation, the country's forest resources were already dwindling before trekking arrived on the scene to make matters worse. In a country without cheap renewable sources of energy, firewood is used by villages for fuel and cooking. Forest clearance on steep slopes means accelerated soil erosion, resulting in devastating floods and landslides. Trekkers have contributed to Nepal's environmental problems in the following ways:

1 The lodges along the major trek routes demand firewood for heating, often from virgin rhododendron forest which is slow to regenerate at high altitudes.
2 Large quantities of litter are discarded by trekkers, including plastic water bottles and a trail of toilet paper.
3 Water sources are contaminated.

On the other hand, strict conservation measures, as applied in the Sagarmatha National Park, may put additional strains on traditional agricultural systems already under threat from tourism.

Trekking, perhaps more than other forms of tourism, is characterized by an insatiable demand for new 'unspoiled' locations, which may well be in countries other than Nepal. Despite tourism's impact on the culture and environment of the host community, there is little to show for it in economic terms, as Nepal remains one of the world's poorest countries.

The Annapurna Conservation Area Project

Measures involving local communities would appear to provide one solution to the problem, as in the Annapurna Conservation Area Project. This is a partnership between tour operators and local entrepreneurs to encourage sustainable development and prevent ecological disaster along Nepal's most popular trekking routes. The project covers an area of 2600 square kilometres. Its conservation strategy includes:

1 The levy of a permit fee on each visitor which goes toward conservation projects.
2 The substitution of solar power or kerosene as alternative fuels to firewood.
3 Reafforestation.
4 The raising of environmental awareness among visitors and the local communities.

Case study

The Maldives

Introduction

The Maldives is an independent republic located in the Indian Ocean, south-west of the Indian subcontinent. Geographically, the Maldives are a unique collection of twenty-six coral atolls, containing almost 1200 coral islands and hundreds of small sandbanks. The Maldives was formed by volcanic eruptions millions of years ago, leaving behind coral reefs as the volcanic cones subsided. All the islands are low lying, on average less than 2 metres above sea level, making them vulnerable to long-term changes in sea level. The islands are scattered over a large expanse of the Indian Ocean, more than 800 kilometres from north to south and 130 kilometres from east to west. This makes transfer to the tourist resorts a logistical problem – indeed, in the early days of tourism experts recommended that the distances involved made tourism development impossible. The climate is hot and humid, with a rainy season between May and October and sea temperatures between 25°C and 29°C, perfect for both beach tourism and the marine life.

Resorts have only been developed on islands not inhabited by the local people. This has the following advantages:

1 The privacy of visitors is assured.
2 It minimizes negative impacts on the culture of the islanders.
3 It minimizes competition for scarce resources between the tourism industry and other sectors.

The islands are strictly Islamic and no alcohol is allowed except in the resorts. Mosques are found on many islands and visitors are expected to respect the traditions of Islam in terms of modest dress when visiting the capital, Male. English is the second language to the local *Dhivehi* tongue.

Apart from tourism, the Maldives also have an important fishing industry. However, tourism is the driving force in the economy as it:

● supports 45 per cent of the jobs in the islands
● brings the islanders an enhanced quality of life
● provides amenities and facilities both for tourists and locals alike through the taxes levied on tourists (there is both a bed tax and an airport tax)
● contributes 56 per cent of the gross domestic product
● represents almost a quarter of capital investment.

Tourism demand

The Maldives receives around 300 000 international visitors annually, predominantly from Europe (Germany, Italy and the UK), but other important source markets are Japan, Australia, India and South Africa. The North American market is in its infancy for the Maldives but holds considerable potential. Growth of demand has been steady through the 1990s and is expected to increase in line with greater bed capacity to the year 2005.

Tourist resources

The marine environment

The prime tourism resource of the islands is the pristine marine environment where the quality of the coral reefs and marine life is unrivalled anywhere in the world. The majority of visitors arrive in the Maldives to experience this marine environment and also for water sports. Each of the resort islands (many of which are very small) has a diving base and the resort house reef is commonly within wading or swimming distance from the accommodation. Scuba, snorkelling, diving (night dives and drift dives are a speciality), fishing, underwater photography and a variety of water sports are popular, and many resorts have both indoor and outdoor sports facilities, swimming pools and other activities to supplement the attractions of the reef. However, this does raise the question as to whether air conditioning, swimming pools, gyms, etc. are compatible in terms of their energy use, with truly sustainable tourism.

Male

The capital, Male, is a small town with a few shops and restaurants, but little to attract the visitor, although it contains two-thirds of the Maldives population. However, it is the gateway to the islands through Hulhule International Airport.

Resorts and safari vessels

Tourism is a relatively recent development in the Maldives, with the first resort opening as recently as 1972. By the late 1990s tourism was developed on seventy-three islands. Tourists have the choice of either basing themselves on one of the resort islands or using safari vessels with 'floating beds'. In the late 1990s, the resorts had almost 12 000 bed-spaces, and the safari vessels a further 1500 bed-spaces.

The resort islands are self-contained, tending to import all the produce for visitors, although a few are experimenting with growing their own vegetables. Water is desalinated and each resort island has its own fleet of boats. Staff tend to work on the islands for short intensive periods before returning to Male for a few days to be with their families. This highlights the isolation of each of the resort islands – visitors are effectively trapped on the island of their choice for the duration of their stay unless they opt for an 'island-hopping' excursion for a day. There are two trends in the accommodation sector:

1 The growing popularity of 'all inclusive resorts'.
2 A number of international hotel companies are now active in this area (namely Hilton, Four Seasons, and Club Mediterranée), although most of the accommodation is leased by local resort operators from the government of the Maldives, which retains ownership of the islands.

Transport

As with all island destinations, air access is the key to success or failure. The Maldives are a difficult destination to reach. There are charter flights from Europe (the UK and Germany), and scheduled services include:

● Air Lanka
● Emirates
● Lauda Air
● Air Maldives (part government owned)
● Singapore Airlines.

However, scheduled services are routed through the respective hub of the airline, so that there are no direct scheduled flights to the Maldives from its main generating markets.

The main gateway to the islands is Hulhule International airport. The airport is a short speedboat or *dhoni* journey to Male. Each resort island or safari vessel has to be reached by transfer from the airport. These transfers are sometimes lengthy and thus expensive, as many resorts are over 120 kilometres from Male. Transfers are by:

● traditional sailboat or *dhoni* (slow and rarely used)
● speedboat (becoming less popular as some resorts are up to three hours from Hulhule by speedboat)
● seaplane (more commonly used today because of the distances involved).

In the early 1990s, Russian-built helicopters were used for transfers but safety issues led to them being withdrawn from service. Two companies – Maldivian Air Taxis and Hummingbird – operate seaplane transfers. However, seaplanes cannot land at night, so visitors arriving or departing on night flights have to spend one night in a hotel in Male before being transferred in daylight. For the more remote islands, regional airstrips are being developed to allow landing at night, as well as to stimulate investment.

Tourism policy and organization

It is imperative that tourism development in the Maldives does not threaten the marine environment. Although global warming and rising sea temperatures have affected the coral, these events are outside the control of the islands themselves. In the islands there are marine reserves and tourism codes of conduct. Tourism development is being used as a regional development tool for the remoter islands, although this does mean visitors have long transfers from Male.

The Ministry of Tourism oversees tourism development and regulates the tourist resorts. In the late 1990s the Maldives Tourism Promotion Board was created to market the islands internationally. The islands were the subject of a tourism master plan in the mid-1990s and also have rolling marketing plans. These plans and policies will determine the future direction of tourism in the Maldives:

1 *Marketing* The islands are attempting to position themselves as the premium eco-tourism destination in the world, and to diversify their markets.
2 *Development* For tourism development in the Maldives the key phrase is *the highly managed expansion of tourism*. The target is to have around 15 000 bed-spaces in resorts by the year 2005. This will be achieved on a geographical basis as follows:
  (a) The Central Region of Male and Ari atolls – consolidation and upgrading of accommodation.
  (b) Expansion of development to the north and to the south of Male and Ari atolls to add twenty or thirty new resorts.
  (c) In the Southern region the development of Vilingili Island.
  (d) In the more remote atolls development of regional airport gateways to stimulate investment.

East Asia

Introduction

East Asia consists of two distinct regions – South-East Asia, and the countries to the north, which Europeans refer to as the 'Far East' – although to an Australian, say, this would seem geographically inappropriate. Most countries in East Asia have experienced rapid growth since the 1970s and have adopted Western technology without sacrificing their cultural identity, which is based on older civilizations and religions than those of the West. Economic growth has fuelled the demand for business travel, and also encouraged a significant volume of outbound leisure tourism, despite the tax disincentives imposed by some governments in the region. The financial crisis of 1997–8 had severe consequences for most East Asian countries, including the so-called *tiger economies* that have threatened to overtake the West (see the second case study at the end of this chapter). However, Japan and the more developed countries in the region are resilient and growth can be expected to continue, although at a slower rate than in the late 1980s and early 1990s.

Domestic tourism has become increasingly significant as living standards rise, expressed in car ownership and the purchase of leisure equipment. The more traditional patterns of travel to religious shrines and mountain resorts are changing as a growing middle class emulates Western fashions. As a result, beach resorts and theme parks, combining American and Asian motifs, are growing in popularity. However, the family unit remains much stronger than in Western societies and individual freedom is less highly regarded, due to the influence of Confucian and Buddhist teachings. Those employed in the service sector may attempt to comply with unrealistic demands by Western tourists rather than lose face, leaving considerable scope for misunderstanding.

East Asia offers a wide variety of landscapes and attractions, although in most countries business and cultural tourism are more important than beach tourism. In the late 1990s international tourist arrivals stood at around 30 million annually for East Asia as a whole, while receipts from tourism accounted for 7 per cent of the world total.

Between 1987 and 1995 hotel capacity in the East Asia/Pacific region increased by 75 per cent, an indication of the dynamism of the tourism sector.

The growth of air traffic in the region is even more impressive. Demographic trends – the region already contains well over one-third of the world's population – the global economy, and the rise of China as an economic superpower, are responsible for a rate of passenger growth which is among the world's highest. Aircraft movements are expected to treble between 1995 and 2010 on the routes linking Europe and North America to the main East Asia hubs – Singapore, Tokyo, Osaka, Hong Kong, Seoul, Taipei and Bangkok. Many Asian airports are reaching the limits of their capacity, while only a few – notably Hong Kong's Chep Lap Kok, Singapore's Changi and Kuala Lumpur's Sepang – are equipped to handle the new breed of aircraft, seating up to 800 passengers, envisaged by the region's airlines. The airspace over the South China Sea is already one of the most congested in the world. In most countries – except for Japan, China and Vietnam – road transport plays a more important role in domestic tourism than the railway systems. However the Eastern Orient Express, linking Bangkok, Kuala Lumpur and Singapore, has shown there is a market among Western tourists for luxury train services.

South-East Asia

Introduction

The part of Asia extending from Burma to the Philippines was culturally influenced many centuries ago by India to the west and China to the north. Overseas Chinese communities play an important role in the economic life of many countries in the region, and indeed throughout the Pacific, but since the nineteenth century the influence of Western Europe and the USA has become increasingly important. The whole of South-East Asia – with the exception of Thailand – was under colonial rule during the first half of the twentieth century:

1 The British administered Burma, Singapore, Malaysia, Brunei and Hong Kong.
2 The French administered Indo-China (now Vietnam, Laos and Cambodia).
3 The Dutch administered the East Indies (now Indonesia).
4 The Portuguese administered East Timor and Macau.
5 The USA administered the Philippines, where they took over from the Spanish.

The Western powers were soon challenged by Japan, which although defeated militarily in the Second World War, has subsequently become the major economic influence in the region. After the Second World War most countries in South-East Asia suffered a good deal of political upheaval, that was part of the wider struggle between the West and the communist powers. This adversely affected the growth of tourism, which was also restricted or given a low priority by those countries with a socialist regime.

Most countries in the region have joined together to form ASEAN (Association of South East Asia Nations), which promotes co-operation in all spheres of economic activity. Although member countries compete for visitors, they each see the advantages of joint promotion aimed at the main tourist-generating markets. However, ASEAN has been less effective at coping with environmental issues, notably the severe pollution, caused by forest burning in Indonesia, which blighted many cities in 1997–8. This threatens to recur, unless more sustainable types of economic development can be implemented throughout the region.

There are wide disparities in wealth between the different countries of South-East Asia. The per capita incomes of Singapore and Brunei approach those of Western Europe, while Burma, Laos and Cambodia rank among the world's least developed nations. There are also great contrasts in economic and social development within many countries, particularly between the major cities on the one hand, and the impoverished rural communities on the other. The countries of South-East Asia also contain tribal societies, often regarded as primitive by the mainstream culture. These include:

- the hill tribes of northern Thailand
- the Montagnards of Vietnam
- the forest-dwellers of Malaysia
- the indigenous peoples of Irian Jaya (West New Guinea) in Indonesia.

Traditional cultures such as these fascinate Western tourists, but they are highly vulnerable to the negative impacts of tourism, as well as the exploitation of their environment by commercial logging and plantation agriculture.

Almost the whole of South-East Asia lies within the tropics, and experiences warm to hot weather throughout the year with frequent but brief torrential downpours. The northern parts of the region do have a clearly defined cool dry season, while the timing and duration of the rainy season in the coastal areas of West Malaysia, Southern Thailand and Indonesia depends on their exposure to the monsoon winds; this has important consequences for beach tourism. During the colonial era, mountain resorts, similar to the hillstations of British India, were established to provide relief from the heat and humidity for the expatriate community. These are now important for domestic tourism, although their development is often hampered by poor road access. Examples include:

- Maimyo in Burma
- Cameron Highlands in West Malaysia
- Dalat in Vietnam
- Bogor in Indonesia
- Baguio in the Philippines.

More important in vying for the international tourist market are the beach resort developments on the palm-fringed coasts of the region. These are either based on established seaports (as at Penang) or have been planned on a comprehensive scale (as in the Langkawi Islands), using two examples from West Malaysia. Often such development has aroused criticism not on visual grounds (they are usually low rise and well designed) but on account of their impact on local communities. This is particularly the case where golf courses have been included in the resort as they make excessive demands on land and water supplies. The economic crisis of 1997–8 has further underlined the importance of tourism as a source of much-needed foreign exchange, the main generating markets being Japan, Australia, Western Europe and the USA.

Singapore

Singapore is one of the most prosperous and stable countries in Asia, despite being a group of small islands lacking natural resources. It owes its importance to its strategic location on the shipping routes linking the Indian and Pacific oceans, which have made the city one of the world's largest seaports as well as the gateway to South-East Asia. The people are culturally diverse, with a Chinese majority, but united by the English language and a belief in technology and enterprise. Since independence, the government of the small island republic has encouraged foreign investment in a free market economy, but has also imposed a degree of social discipline that many Westerners would find draconian. As a result, Singapore is less plagued by squalor, car-dominated traffic and crime than most other urban societies throughout the world, and as such can offer Western tourists a sanitized glimpse of 'instant Asia'. The country's high-profile national carrier – Singapore Airlines – is the largest in the region in terms of passenger-kilometres, and it works closely with the Singapore Tourist Promotion Board. Singapore's Stock Exchange and World Trade Centre rank among the world's most important financial institutions – not surprisingly, it has become a major conference venue and business destination.

Singapore attracts a large volume of inbound tourists – over 7 million a year during the late 1990s – but with a short length of stay. The majority are from neighbouring countries, although Japan is the leading market. Duty-free shopping accounts for a large part of the tourist spend, particularly by Western visitors, who see the city primarily as a stopover rather than as a sole destination. In an attempt to attract longer-stay visitors, the government is emphasizing Singapore's cultural diversity, and safeguarding what remains of the old-style colonial heritage, once threatened with obliteration as a result of the drive to modernization. Such examples as the Raffles Hotel, the markets and outdoor food stalls, contrast markedly with the ultramodern shopping malls and high-rise office buildings. Singapore's attractions include:

- a number of zoos and wildlife parks
- the waterfront area of Clarke Quay, with its leisure and shopping developments
- the Suntec conference and exhibition centre
- the beach resort of Sentosa Island, which includes a number of Asian-style theme parks.

Singapore is compact, densely populated and low lying, and the lack of scenic variety, together with urban pressures, generate a large volume of outbound tourism. Most of this is to neighbouring Malaysia – easily reached by the causeway to Johor, or to the beach resorts of Bintam and Batan in Indonesia's Riau archipelago which are only a short distance away by hydrofoil.

Malaysia

Like Singapore, Malaysia is a multicultural nation, but here the Moslem Malays are the dominant ethnic group. The country is a federation of thirteen states but one party has dominated politics since independence and the nine hereditary sultans have little effective power. Malaysia also consists of two culturally distinct areas, separated by the South China Sea, namely:

- Peninsular or West Malaysia, known under British rule as Malaya, which is the southernmost peninsula of mainland Asia
- East Malaysia, consisting of the states of Sabah and Sarawak, which form part of the island of Borneo.

Unlike Singapore, Malaysia is rich in natural resources such as rubber, tin, petroleum and tropical hardwoods. These provided the basis for rapid industrialization after 1980, and a number of large-scale development projects. The 'Petronas Towers' dominating the skyline of Kuala Lumpur and the ultramodern shopping malls in the capital were the products of an economic prosperity that was badly affected by the 1997–8 financial crisis. Nevertheless, the choice of Kuala Lumpur as the venue for the 1998 Commonwealth Games and the opening of a new international airport at Sepang, underline the importance of tourism as an earner of foreign exchange. At present the great majority of visitors are from other Asian countries, and there has been considerable investment, particularly by the Japanese, in resort hotels and golf courses. The government has encouraged tourism, with the entrepreneurial Malaysian Tourist Development Corporation being responsible for promotion and development. The infrastructure for tourism is efficient, including a good highway network in Peninsular Malaysia and the air services operated by the Malaysian Airline System (MAS).

Malaysia can offer the following resources for tourism:

- the beaches of West Malaysia
- a variety of cultural attractions
- the wildlife resources of the interior mountains and rainforests.

Most of the tourism development has taken place in West Malaysia. Seasonality is not a major problem, thanks to the pattern of the monsoons, which bring heavy rain to the west coast of Peninsular Malaysia between June and September, and to the east coast from November to February. Much of the west coast is low lying, with extensive areas of mangrove swamp along the estuaries. The best beaches are found on the offshore islands that include:

1 Penang, which has retained its commercial importance as well as being a major destination for West European holidaymakers on inclusive air tours. Most of the resort development has taken place around Batu Feringhi on the island's north coast.
2 The Langkawi Islands, that provide an ideal environment for scuba-diving, but which offer much less in the way of nightlife, shopping and cultural attractions than Penang.
3 Pangkor and its small neighbour, Pangkor Laut.

Although boasting finer beaches and attractive scenery, the east coast is less developed, and the traditional Malay lifestyle is much more evident in the villages. Tioman Island and Cherating – where there is a Club Méditerranée village – are the main resort areas.

West Malaysia's attractions also include:

1 The Taman Negara National Park, covering much of the forest covered highlands of the interior. With a huge biodiversity of species, it attracts growing numbers of eco-tourists.
2 The Batu Caves, a major religious shrine for Hindus.
3 The old Portuguese trading centre of Malacca, with its colonial heritage providing a contrast to the modern capital of Kuala Lumpur.
4 The mountain resort of Genting Highlands, with its casino, golf course and funicular railway.

East Malaysia is much less developed, and caters mainly for adventure tourism, based on Kuching (Sarawak) and Kota Kinabalu (Sabah). From Kuching, tourists travel upriver to visit the villages of the Dyak tribes and perhaps stay in one of the traditional longhouses. The state of Sabah boasts the highest mountain in South-East Asia – Kinabalu – attracting climbing and trekking expeditions.

Brunei

Brunei, which is located in the same region, derives most of its considerable wealth from petroleum, and tourism development as yet is not a priority. Royal Brunei Airlines and the capital, Bandar Sara Begawan, cater mainly for business travellers.

Indonesia

In contrast to tiny Brunei, Indonesia is one of the largest countries in the world, and one of the most populous, with over 200 million inhabitants. It consists of a multitude of islands, of which 5000 are inhabited, and extends across three time zones, from Sumatra in the west, to New Guinea in the east. Yet, despite a great diversity of cultures and scenery, Indonesia is better known for its problems in East Timor and Irian Jaya (West New Guinea) than for its tourist attractions. In fact, many people in the West are unaware of the fact that Bali is part of Indonesia, and think of it as a separate destination (see the first case study at the end of this chapter).

Nevertheless, we need to look at Indonesia's socio-economic problems as they affect tourism. They include:

1 The political and economic dominance of Java, which contains almost two-thirds of the population and most of the country's industrial development. The government has attempted to relieve the acute pressures of over-population and rural poverty by a policy of transmigra-tion, settling Javanese in the more sparsely populated islands among people whose cultural background might be very different.
2 The effects of the 1997–8 financial crisis and the fall of the Suharto regime on the economic and political stability of Indonesia, bringing to the surface religious and ethnic tensions between the Moslem majority and minority groups, such as the Chinese, and the Christian community in the Moluccas.

During the 1980s and early 1990s, Indonesia experienced a very high rate of tourism growth. This was encouraged by the government which restructured its Directorate General of Tourism in a drive to attract conventions, exhibitions and incentive travel. Despite a government policy of spreading tourism throughout the islands, most of the growth in hotel capacity has taken place in Bintam/Batan and Bali (for leisure tourism) and in Java (mainly for business tourism, particularly in the major cities of Jakarta, Surabaya and Yogyakarta). International hotel chains dominate the sector, particularly in the mid-range and luxury categories. Although the government has moved toward a more liberal policy in aviation, the national carrier Garuda and its subsidiaries dominate air transport. We will now look at the tourism resources of the islands, including:

1 Java, which is dominated by a chain of high volcanic mountains, some of which are still active. Over many centuries, land has been brought under cultivation by an elaborate system of terracing and the island's fertility has supported a number of advanced civilizations. The most spectacular examples are the temple at Borobodur, which is the world's largest Buddhist edifice, and the lesser known Hindu temple at Prambunan nearby. Other major cultural attractions are the palaces of former sultans at Solo and Yogyakarta.
2 Sumatra has an important oil industry and tourism is less developed than in Java. Medan is a major business centre

and the island offers lake and mountain scenery and the distinctive folklore of the Menankabau people.

3 Sulawesi offers some of the best dive sites in Indonesia. The mountainous interior has been opened up for tourism, where the Toraja people, with their interesting architecture and funeral customs, provide the main attraction.

4 Many of the other islands increasingly feature on the back-packers' trail and some are visited by cruise ships. Eco-tourism is becoming increasingly important, for example in Komodo, famous for its so-called dragons.

The Philippines

Like Indonesia, the Philippines is a populous island-nation containing many ethnic groups and a landscape dominated by volcanic mountains. Culturally however, it is quite different from the other countries of South-East Asia. There are few impressive monuments from pre-colonial times, and the islands have been greatly influenced by their experience of three centuries of Spanish rule, followed by half a century of administration by the USA. The Spanish legacy of devout Roman Catholicism is evident in the churches and religious festivals, whereas the Americans introduced the English language and sports such as baseball; the result is a culture in which Western influences and attitudes are stronger than elsewhere in Asia.

Tourism received a major boost under the Marcos regime in the 1970s, which left Manila with a glut of luxury hotels. Since that time the emphasis by the Philippines Tourism Authority has been on planning resort clusters of international standard on a number of islands, which are linked to an international airport by boat and domestic air services. The main tourist markets are Japan, the USA, Taiwan, South Korea and overseas Filipinos – returning expatriates from other countries. Some aspects of tourism have given cause for concern, such as damage to coral reefs and the prevalence of sex tours, particularly in Manila and Olongapo. In many areas the transport infrastructure, including roads and domestic air services, falls short of Western standards of efficiency, although ferry links between the islands have greatly improved.

Tourism is concentrated mainly in the following areas:

1 South Luzon, particularly in and around Manila. The capital's attractions include:
   (a) The Malacanang Palace, former residence of the Marcos family.
   (b) The Nayong Pilipino – an exhibition village showcasing the country's regional cultures.
   (c) The highly decorated *jeepneys*, which play a vital role in the city's transport system.

A number of beach resorts, the Taal lake and volcano, and the Pagsanjan waterfalls are located within easy reach of Manila. However, one of the country's major attractions – the rice terraces at Banaue – can only be reached by a long road journey and are much less accessible.

2 The Visayas, a group of islands in the central Philippines served by the international airport at Cebu, which has direct flights to Hong Kong, Seoul, Taipei, Singapore and Tokyo. The island of Boracay is the best known, having evolved from discovery by backpackers in the 1970s to become an up-market destination.

3 Palawan, until recently one of the more remote islands, offers world-class diving facilities and a number of small up-market resorts that have escaped the pollution problems experienced by Boracay.

4 Mindanao, much of which is still forest covered. Beach tourism is being developed around the cities of Davao and Zamboanga.

Thailand

Although Thailand was the only country in South-East Asia not to experience Western colonial rule, it has been the one most affected by Western-style tourism. Growth has been phenomenal, from less than 500 000 international arrivals in 1970, to over 6 million in the late 1990s, with a corresponding increase in hotel capacity. Tourism has become the country's biggest earner of foreign exchange and a major employer, but it has also exacerbated Thailand's socioeconomic problems, notably the disparities in wealth between Bangkok and the rural areas of the north and east. Although largely ignored by the government and the Tourist Authority of Thailand, sex tourism has become a major industry in Bangkok and Pattaya, with damaging consequences to the country's image as a destination.

Although there is considerable cross-border traffic between Thailand and Malaysia, the majority of tourists arrive by air on inclusive tours. Less than 10 per cent are business travellers. Leisure tourists come from a wide range of generating countries, including Western Europe, North America, Japan and Australia. The 1997–8 financial crisis made Thailand the bargain basement of Asia, attracting even Russians to the fleshpots of Pattaya. Bangkok's Don Muang airport is the main gateway and is served by over forty scheduled airlines, while the north and south of the country are visited from Chiangmai and Phuket respectively. Thai International and its domestic arm, Thai Airways, operate an extensive network of air routes, while express bus and overnight rail services also link Bangkok to the major regional centres of the country. Thailand is a multidestination country, with different areas offering sightseeing tours, beach tourism and adventure holidays:

1 Bangkok is the primary destination. Despite acute traffic congestion, this sprawling city has a wide range of attractions, and its Western-style hotels enjoy high occupancy rates throughout the year. Many of the city's canals have been replaced by highways, but the Chao Praya River, with its long-tail boats and floating markets,

remains a major artery. As you might expect from a country steeped in Buddhist tradition, Bangkok is noted for its *wats* – temple-monasteries of a highly distinctive appearance. Shopping for Thai silk and other handicrafts is an important part of the city's appeal to Western tourists. Specific tourist attractions in Bangkok and the surrounding area include:

(a) The spectacular Grand Palace, which contains the Temple of the Emerald Buddha.
(b) The Rose Garden Country Resort, 33 kilometres west of the capital, features cultural shows for visitors, including traditional Thai dances and boxing.
(c) The nearby beach resort of Pattaya, which began as a 'rest and recreation' centre for American servicemen during the Vietnam War (1965–73). It is noisy and overcommercialized, despite attempts by the government to clean up the environment, curb the jet skiers and tone down the exuberant nightlife of the bars, discotheques and massage parlours.

2 Chiangmai has been developed as a counter-attraction to Bangkok in the northern part of the country, with the advantage of a cooler climate. Although the city is a major cultural centre, it is regarded by most backpackers and Western tourists as a convenient base for trekking tours among the hill tribes of the mountainous country bordering Burma and Laos. It is alleged that tourism does not benefit these local communities but merely exploits them as a curiosity.

3 The islands of the Andaman Sea, off the west coast of Thailand, and those of the Gulf of Siam to the east, cater in varying degrees for beach tourism, in response to the quest, first by backpackers, and later by tour operators, for 'unspoiled' holiday destinations:

(a) Phuket was the first to be developed, to the extent that mass tourism has now displaced the island's traditional mining and fishing industries.
(b) Koh Samui is less developed and more up-market.
(c) The Phi-Phi Islands are partly protected as a marine reserve, but environmentalists fear that development is inevitable as a result of the publicity for the film 'The Beach'.

4 Isan or Eastern Thailand is an economically poor region, but rich in local culture. The Tourism Authority of Thailand hopes that visitors will be attracted to a number of historical parks focusing on the heritage of past civilizations. The region is also conveniently located for excursions across the Mekong into Laos and Cambodia, where tourist accommodation is limited and expensive.

Laos, Cambodia and Vietnam

The countries of Indo-China remain on the margins of international tourism as a consequence of half a century of conflict, political isolation and instability. Until the 1990s, the socialist governments of the region gave tourism a low priority, restricting the numbers of foreign visitors and discouraging Western investment. Nevertheless, these countries have considerable potential for tourism, although infrastructure and facilities tend to be well below Western standards.

Laos

Laos is the least developed country in South-East Asia, due largely to its mountainous and landlocked character, and its involvement in the Vietnam War. The northern part of the country, along with the east of Burma, forms part of the famous 'Golden Triangle' of opium production. The cities of Vientiane and Luang Prabang are well endowed with Buddhist temples, and the traditional culture is one of the country's strengths as a tourist destination. However, these are largely outweighed by the weaknesses – a poor transport infrastructure, visa restrictions and the high cost of accommodation.

Cambodia

Cambodia is better known for the 'killing fields' of the Khmer Rouge regime than for its tourist attractions. These largely centre on the capital Phnom Penh, which attracts gamblers from other South-East Asian countries, and the world famous Hindu temple-city at Angkor. This was built by the powerful Khmer empire between the ninth and thirteenth centuries, but the temples were subsequently abandoned and covered in tropical jungle until their excavation by French archaeologists in the 1920s. By the late 1960s Angkor was attracting 45 000 visitors a year, and the nearby town of Siem Reap had a flourishing hotel and restaurant trade. Plans by Asian developers to revive tourism after decades of conflict and neglect, include *son et lumière* performances, and the provision of large modern hotels close to the monuments. Although the Cambodian government is eager to maximize foreign exchange earnings from Western tourists, these projects are regarded as inappropriate by conservationists.

Vietnam

Vietnam is best known for the battlefields of the Vietnam War, the Cu-Chi tunnels near Saigon that sheltered the Vietcong from American firepower, and China Beach near Danang. However, since the late 1980s the government has adopted a policy of economic liberalization, and in 1995 the USA lifted its trade embargo. Vietnam hopes to attract business travellers, the large numbers of overseas Vietnamese living in the USA, Canada, Australia and France, the 2.7 million American war veterans, Western adventure tourists and holidaymakers on cruises in the South China Sea. However, tourism development is hampered by poor infrastructure, such as an inadequate road system and power supplies, and a bureaucracy resistant to change. Tourism is concentrated in four major zones:

1 Hanoi and Haiphong in the north. This is close to the scenic wonderland of the Bay of Halong, studded with thousands of picturesque islands.
2 Danang and the former royal capital of Hue in the centre, with its many Buddhist pagodas.
3 Nha Trang with its beaches in the centre south.
4 Saigon (Ho-Chi Minh City) preserves much of its French colonial past, and is a much more vibrant city than the capital Hanoi. The entertainment scene for which the city was famous during the Vietnam War has revived to some extent, after a long period of banishment following the communist victory in 1975. In contrast, the nearby Mekong Delta attracts eco-tourists.

Burma (Myanmar)

Before achieving independence, Burma was ruled as part of British India, and the government's renaming of the country, its cities and physical features is part of a strategy to throw off the colonial heritage. For decades after independence, the country was isolated from the West by the government's policy of self-sufficiency; visas were difficult to obtain and tourists were restricted to a short period of stay. Security was also a major problem, with uprisings by dissident ethnic groups, such as the Shans and the Karens, in the mountainous border areas.

Since the early 1990s the military regime has encouraged foreign investment in the fledgling tourism industry, primarily from Japan. Tourist arrivals increased tenfold between 1992 and 1995, albeit from a low base. However, the way that tourism development has been carried out by the government, with apparent disregard for human rights, has raised the issue of ethical tourism. For example:

1 The use of unpaid 'volunteers' (in effect, forced labour) to build infrastructure necessary for hotel development, such as much needed roads and railway improvements, and the new airport at Bassein.
2 The relocation of villagers to make way for tourist facilities.
3 The exploitation of the more 'picturesque' tribes for tour groups.
4 Opponents of the regime, such as the democrat leader Aung San Kyi, claim that tourism revenue simply enriches those in government circles who have invested in the new hotels, and urge a Western boycott of the country. However, some tour operators take the view that tourism can be a powerful force for liberalization and change.

Although its coastline is bordered for the most part by mangrove swamps, Burma has much to offer the cultural tourist, including for example:

1 The Irrawaddy (Ayayarwady) River runs through the country's heartland, providing a major transport artery, as in Kipling's time, from Rangoon (Yangon) to Mandalay. River transport is now being revitalized after decades of neglect, including luxury cruises by Eastern and Orient Express.
2 Rangoon boasts one of the world's most impressive Buddhist temples – the Shwe Dagon Pagoda, which is covered in gold and precious stones.
3 Pagan (Bagan) is renowned for its hundreds of temples, a reminder of Burma's 'golden age' during the thirteenth century.
4 Mandalay was the royal capital prior to British rule. The palace has been restored as a tourist attraction.

The Far East

The lands around the East China Sea and the Sea of Japan include some of the world's largest modern cities, as well as some of its oldest civilizations. In contrast to the tropical conditions prevalent in South-East Asia, the climate is characterized by four well-defined seasons, not unlike those of Europe and North America. Spring and autumn are the best times for visiting, as winters can be cold and summers oppressively hot and humid. Japan and South Korea have long been important destinations for the business traveller and the cultural tourist, but during the 1990s, China has emerged as a formidable competitor for the world travel market.

Japan

Introduction

Japan is the leading industrial nation of Asia with an economy based on overseas trade. Despite suffering from a prolonged recession throughout the 1990s, it boasts a gross domestic product second only to the USA, and four times larger than the UK. As a result of the recession there has been a certain amount of industrial restructuring and deregulation, and the country has become more open to foreign investment. Japan is by far the largest generator of tourists in the East Asia/Pacific region, with a huge deficit on its international tourism account.

Japan consists of four main islands located off the eastern fringe of the continent – Honshu, Hokkaido, Kyushu and Shikoku – and groups of much smaller islands, such as the Ryukyus and Iwo Jima, lying to the south. The total area of the Japanese islands is only slightly greater than the British Isles, with more than twice the population. The pressure on land resources is even more acute when we consider that over 80 per cent of the country is mountainous. Geological instability has produced the beautiful mountain landscapes of Japan – Mount Fuji is the best known example – and the numerous hot springs, but it is also responsible for natural disasters such as the earthquakes which devastated Kobe in 1995.

As a nation Japan has the following characteristics:

1 It is remarkably homogenous, with one language, few social divisions and no large ethnic minorities.
2 It has enjoyed political stability since 1945.
3 Respect for tradition coexists with admiration for the new.
4 There is a readiness to adopt the latest technological innovations.
5 Society is bound by discipline and respect for authority.

Due to a low birth rate and high life expectancy, the Japanese population is ageing, with a higher proportion of people aged over 65 than in most European countries. There are also social trends toward a more relaxed and individualistic lifestyle, a greater emphasis on leisure and sport, and a greater readiness to adopt Western fashions. Even so, the concept of an annual holiday has only slowly been accepted in Japan, which is still largely a work-oriented society. Working hours are longer than in Europe or the USA and paid annual leave amounts to fifteen days; however, Japanese workers often take only nine days out of their full holiday entitlement out of loyalty to colleagues or to cover for illness. Holidays and leisure activities generally are frequently sponsored by large industrial corporations for their employees; however, this paternalism is not resented by most Japanese, who are prepared to accept a degree of regimentation that Westerners would find irksome.

Demand for tourism

1 *Domestic tourism* The domestic holiday market is significant, accounting for 90 per cent of all trips, with business and VFR accounting for the remainder. Pilgrimages to Shinto and Buddhist shrines continue to be popular with family groups, while *onsen* (hot spring resorts) appeal more to the stressed executive at weekends. The Western influence is evident in the rapid growth of skiing, golf, baseball, water sports and visits to theme parks. The scarcity of land particularly affects demand for skiing and golf:
   (a) Skiing is practised by some 15 million Japanese. The mountains of Northern Honshu and Hokkaido receive abundant snowfalls during the winter months, and this has encouraged the development of a large number of ski resorts. However, apart from Nagano in the Japanese Alps and Sapporo in Hokkaido which have both hosted the Winter Olympics, few resorts approach Western standards, and overcrowding on the slopes is a major problem.
   (b) Golf courses are few and far between and green fees are prohibitively expensive. Most would-be players are confined to multistorey driving ranges, and real golf can only be played on overseas trips. This goes far to explaining why the Japanese are active in purchasing tourist plant overseas, and in providing Third

World governments with aid for projects where golf is a major component.

2 *Outbound tourism* During the long period of Japan's self-imposed isolation from the West under the rule of the Tokugawa shoguns, outbound travel was strictly forbidden, and even after the Meiji Restoration in 1868 could only be undertaken for the purposes of business or study. After 1964 the restrictions on leisure travel were lifted, and in the late 1980s the government made a positive effort to encourage overseas travel through the 'Ten Million Programme', as a way of restructuring Japan's trade balance with the rest of the world and promoting mutual understanding. However, participation in outbound travel still accounts for only 7 per cent of the population, and with limited holiday time available the length of stay is short, averaging eight days. In many countries the Japanese are the largest source of tourists, and they tend to be the biggest spenders. Over half visit destinations in Asia, mainly Taiwan, South Korea and Hong Kong; around a third go to the USA, particularly to honeymoon in Hawaii and Guam; and the remainder travel to Europe or Australasia. Group travel is important, and so is *omiyake*, the customary purchase of gifts for friends, relatives and employers. Young unmarried women in their twenties – the so-called 'office ladies' constitute a major market, particularly for the countries of Western Europe.

3 *Inbound tourism* Inbound tourism stands at around one-fifth of the volume of outbound travel and the difference is even greater in terms of spend. This is due to Japan's relative isolation from the traditional generating markets of Western Europe and the USA, and the country's reputation for being expensive. One of the reasons that Japan has experienced less growth as a tourist destination than most other countries in the East Asia/Pacific region is inadequate marketing on the part of the Japan National Tourist Organization (JNTO). Business travellers account for about a third of incoming tourists, with the cities of Tokyo, Osaka and Nagoya as the major destinations. South Korea is the largest source of tourists, due to cultural and business ties with Japan. South East Asia accounts for half of all visitors, with a further 10 per cent coming from the USA.

The supply of tourism

1 *Transport* For domestic travel, road and rail is most commonly used. The northern island of Hokkaido is linked to Honshu by the world's longest rail tunnel, and bridges similarly integrate Kyushu and Shikoku with the main transport network, supplementing the ferry services. There is an extensive network of railways (20 000 kilometres), including the famous Shinkansen (bullet trains), linking Tokyo to Fukuoka, Niigata, and Morioka in northern Japan. For foreign visitors, train travel is preferable to driving due to the problems of road

congestion and inadequate signposting. Most foreign visitors arrive by air, the majority through Tokyo's Narita Airport. However, other airports are growing in importance, particularly Osaka's Kansai airport (built on an artificial island), which has the advantage of being much closer to downtown than Narita, which is 60 kilometres from central Tokyo. Tokyo's other airport, Haneda, handles domestic flights to a large number of destinations. The busiest air routes are from South-East Asia, Hawaii and the USA. The aviation sector is dominated by three airlines – Japan Airlines, ANA and Japan Air Systems – but with deregulation these face a growing challenge from newcomers.

2 *Accommodation* The hotel industry is driven by domestic demand, but occupancy rates for other than medium-priced hotels has declined as a result of the 1990s recession and the resulting cutbacks in corporate entertaining by Japanese business executives. Tourists can stay in Western-style hotels or in *ryokan* – Japanese inns where the food service, bathing facilities and furnishings of *tatami* matting follow native traditions, and these are becoming increasingly popular with Western visitors. Tokyo and Osaka are the main locations for major hotel projects, some of which are financed by international chains. These tend to be very expensive, but an alternative is available for the budget traveller in the so-called *capsule hotels* – stacks of cubicles, each consisting of little more than bed-space. Subsidized family travel villages and lodges are also available for the domestic market.

3 *Tourism organization* Responsibility for the industry lies with the Ministry of Tourism, which supervises the JNTO whose role is to promote 'a fair and realistic image of Japan' to increase international understanding of the country, particularly among the international business community. The Japan Convention Bureau (JCB) plays a leading role in developing facilities for the important conference market.

Tourism resources

Japan's tourism resources are a unique mix of the traditional, best seen in the rural areas, and modern technology, evident in the cities and theme parks such as Tokyo Disneyland. The highly distinctive Japanese art and architecture, miniaturized landscape gardening, the delicate skills of traditional handicrafts, the *Kabuki* theatre, even sumo wrestling – all these things have widespread appeal. Despite severe pollution problems, much has been done to preserve the country's coasts, mountains and forests, including the designation of twenty-seven national parks in the most scenic areas. However, unlike their counterparts in North America, these are scarcely wilderness areas, but contain hundreds of rural communities, such is the pressure on land and water resources. Western visitors are mainly drawn to southern Honshu – and to a lesser extent Kyushu – and to the cities which include:

1 Tokyo, which is above all a business centre, but also a city containing many temples and museums. The Ginza district includes the Stock Exchange, while leisure activities are concentrated in the Shinjuku district.
2 Kyoto was for centuries until 1868 the Imperial capital of Japan, and a cultural centre which preserves the country's traditions, with *geishas* in evidence, hundreds of shrines and temples, and gardens inspired by Zen Buddhism. However, this city of 1.5 million people is no museum piece, but a major industrial centre.
3 Nikko, Nara and Ise are also religious centres, preserving much of the feudal past of Japan.
4 The Inland Sea between western Honshu and Shikoku is probably the most scenic region of Japan, studded with picturesque islands and numerous Buddhist temples.
5 Kyushu offers a wide variety of attractions, including:
  (a) Theme parks such as Space World near Fukuoka.
  (b) Huis Ten Bosch, a reproduction of a seventeenth-century Dutch city, a reminder that Dutch merchants in nearby Nagasaki were Japan's only contact with Europe before 1853. It also provides the Japanese with a simulated European holiday experience without the trouble and expense of the real thing.
  (c) The Seagaia resort in Miyazaki which contains the world's largest artificial beach and all-weather water park.
  (d) Beppu, the most important of a number of spas based on the island's abundant geothermal resources.

Two other islands – Hokkaido and Okinawa – attract relatively few Western tourists:

1 Hokkaido, with its long bitterly cold winters and forested mountains, was settled by the Japanese in the nineteenth century. It offers space, lake and volcanic scenery, and native *Ainu* communities, now a small minority of the population. Sapporo is noted for its annual snow festival.
2 Okinawa in contrast has a subtropical climate, and is visited by large numbers of Taiwanese tourists.

Korea

The ancient land of Korea occupies a mountainous peninsula lying between China and Japan. Since the Second World War the country has been divided between the communist North, and South Korea, which has become a major industrial power under a free market economy. Since the Korean War (1950–3) an uneasy stand-off persists between North and South, long after the ending of the Cold War elsewhere.

South Korea

Like Japan, South Korea has experienced an 'economic miracle', but its tourism growth has been even more spectacular. The main impetus was initially business tourism, but the Seoul Olympics and the Asian Games in 1988 provided the country with the opportunity to showcase its achievements and leisure tourism followed. The demand for outbound tourism was suppressed for decades in the interests of building up the national economy. In 1989 the travel restrictions were removed, and the country soon became one of the major generators of tourism in the East Asia/Pacific region. Although the work ethic remains strong, domestic tourism is also growing in popularity. South Korea's prosperity received a major setback with the 1997–8 currency crisis, which particularly affected the banking sector.

The majority of foreign visitors are from Japan, due to cultural and business ties. The USA is a long way behind in second place, but the American connection has been important since the Korean War. A large number of American servicemen are still stationed in the country and there is a substantial VFR market of Korean expatriates in the USA. For Western tourists, South Korea is not as expensive or as crowded as Japan, while it is less of a culture shock than China, and offers similar cultural attractions to both.

Seoul is a modern capital which preserves some relics of its past, but tourists looking for ancient Buddhist temples and traditional ambience find that Kyongju, a former royal capital, has more to offer. Other attractions include:

- the beaches of Cheju Island in the extreme south
- the mountainous interior, where there are a number of national parks – Sorak is the best known – hot spring resorts, and ski centres that cater mainly for domestic demand.

North Korea

North Korea's hard-line regime has discouraged tourism, with the exception of invited groups who can be easily controlled. The country's chronic economic difficulties may eventually lead to a rapprochement with South Korea. This would have far-reaching consequences as the border between the two countries would reopen for overland travel.

Mongolia

In the thirteenth century the steppes of Mongolia gave rise to the empire of Genghis Khan, who conquered most of Asia and Russia. Since then the country has been overshadowed by its neighbours Russia and China, but its people still retain much of the nomadic way of life and warrior traditions, such as displays of horsemanship, archery and wrestling. In the absence of hotels outside the capital Ulan Bator, tourists are accommodated in *gers*, the portable structures of felted material traditionally used by the nomads. With the collapse of the Soviet Union, Mongolia has moved to a free market economy, and private tour companies compete with the state agency for the growing numbers of Western eco-tourists. The climate is extreme, with temperatures ranging from –40ºC in winter to +40ºC in summer, but the country can offer a variety of scenery, including the Gobi Desert, high mountains, grassy plains and the northern forests around Lake Hovsgol where the reindeer, rather than the horse, yak or camel, supports the local lifestyle.

China

Introduction

Few countries have the tourist potential of China, which is a unique destination for the following reasons:

1 The Chinese civilization is the world's oldest, with an alphabet, code of ethics and art traditions that have survived relatively unchanged for thousands of years. Much of the technology developed by the West had been invented centuries earlier by the Chinese.
2 China accounts for over a fifth of the world's population. In addition to the 1.25 billion inhabitants of the People's Republic of China (PRC) there are at least 55 million overseas Chinese, who constitute a large ethnic market for tourism.
3 The land mass of China is comparable in size to the USA. It contains some of the world's highest mountains and plateaus, one of the most inhospitable deserts – the Takla Makan – and the world's fourth longest river – the Yangtse.
4 During the twentieth century, China has experienced social and economic change on a vast scale, from an empire rooted in ancient tradition, to the totalitarian state of Mao Zedong, dedicated to revolutionary change. Since 1978, the government has rejected Mao's rigid socialist ideology and gradually moved toward a free market economy, although the Communist Party, backed up by the People's Liberation Army (PLA), remains firmly in control. Some commentators believe that China is on course to become the major power of the twenty-first century.

Demand for tourism

Tourism has been encouraged by the government since 1978 as part of the campaign to make the Chinese more receptive to Western ideas and technology, and also to generate the foreign exchange needed to modernize the economy. Growth has generally been rapid, although the adverse publicity following the suppression of the pro-democracy movement in Beijing's Tiananmen Square, brought about a downturn in Western visitors in the early 1990s.

Nevertheless, the 1997 PATA Conference was held in Beijing, highlighting the fact that China had become one of the world's leading tourist destinations, with over 5 million foreign tourist arrivals (plus much larger numbers of Chinese visitors from Hong Kong and Macau). The most important markets are Japan, Russia, the countries of South-East Asia, Western Europe and the USA. This success in tourism has not been achieved without growing pains. Pricing, poor service standards and a shortage of trained personnel remain problems, as does the adjustment of a centrally planned economy to one trying to accommodate enterprise and market forces. Positive changes have taken place in the following areas:

1 Improvements in the transport infrastructure.
2 A greater choice of destinations (in 1982 only thirty cities or areas could be visited without a travel permit – by 1994 this had increased to over 1000).
3 A greater choice of attractions within established destinations such as Beijing and Shanghai.
4 More competition between tour operators and travel agencies. In the past, group travel had been monopolized by the state-controlled China International Travel Service (CITS) which has had to improve its performance for Western tourists.
5 A great increase in hotel capacity and improvement in standards, although most Western-style accommodation is concentrated in the major cities, notably Beijing, Guangchou (Canton), Shanghai and the Shenzhen Special Enterprise Zone adjoining Hong Kong.

Outbound tourism is still not encouraged by the Chinese authorities, except for the purposes of business or study. This may change with the growth of a middle class, estimated to number 400 million consumers, who have the means to travel. However, the volume of domestic tourism is restricted by the low earning power of the average worker, and there are growing regional disparities between those cities that have benefited most from the market economy, and the outlying rural areas. Family visits to shrines, such as the sacred mountain of Tai Shan, are popular. Beach resorts such as Beidahe, within easy reach of Beijing, are favoured by growing numbers of holidaymakers.

Most travel in China is by rail or air, as the road network is rudimentary by Western standards. The rail network on the other hand, is the fifth largest in the world (52 000 kilometres), and offers two classes of accommodation – 'soft' – recommended for Western tourists, and 'hard', for those on a budget. China has an extensive system of domestic air services, but only a few airports are, as yet, capable of handling large volumes of international traffic. Air China and a number of regional airlines compete for the growing market for air travel. Since 1984 the China National Tourism Administration has been responsible for defining overall tourism policy and overseeing its implementation, but both provincial and local authorities are now allowed considerable initiative.

Tourism resources

In such a vast country, there are considerable contrasts in climate, scenery and lifestyles – including cuisine. The most notable differences are those between:

● North China, with its cold dry winters, and subtropical South China, which is Cantonese rather than Mandarin-speaking, and
● the Chinese heartland in the east and the sparsely populated western provinces of Tibet, Sinkiang and Inner Mongolia, where the people have quite a different cultural background to the Han Chinese.

China is mainly famous for its age-old craft industries, traditional styles of architecture, and distinctive landscapes. Since the 1980s Western fashions and styles of advertising have largely replaced the drab uniformity normally associated with communist regimes, and traffic jams are now commonplace in cities where bicycles and pedicabs used to be the only forms of transport. However, in the headlong rush to industrialize, great damage has been inflicted on the forest and wildlife resources of the mountain areas. Air and water pollution is also widespread in the cities of eastern China, and the country's environmental record and attitude to human rights – particularly in Tibet – has aroused international concern.

1 *North China* North China is the historic cradle of Chinese civilization, centring on the great river known as the Hwang Ho. With its treeless landscapes of wind-blown loess it is scenically low key, but it does contain a number of cultural attractions, namely:
(a) The burial place of the First Emperor at Xian, which yielded the famous terracotta warriors.
(b) The Great Wall of China – 6000 kilometres in length – built as a defence against the Mongol nomads to the north. The section most visited by tourists is at Badaling, reached by a 50 kilometre rail link from Beijing.
(c) Beijing (formerly Peking) contains a range of attractions:
   (i) The Forbidden City, the former palace compound of the emperors, which opens onto Tiananmen Square.
   (ii) The Great Hall of the People, symbolizing post-revolution China.
   (iii) The Ming Tombs.
   (iv) The Summer Palace.
   (v) The Temple of Heaven.

2 *East Central China* This part of China centres on the River Yangtze and the cities of Nanjing and Shanghai:

(a) Shanghai is China's largest city, and one largely created by overseas trade with the West. In the 1920s the city was renowned for its wealth and uninhibited nightlife. The new Pudong Special Enterprise Zone across the Huang Pu river from the famous Bund, underlines Shanghai's revival as one of the major business centres of Asia.

(b) To the west of Shanghai lie a group of historic cities along the Grand Canal – Hwangzhou, Wuxi – famous for its silk industry – and Suzhou, noted for its traditional Chinese gardens.

(c) Yangtze River cruises are a popular tourist route to the fertile but mountainous province of Szechwan, the highlight being the impressive Three Gorges near Ichang. However, the government's project to build a dam here as a flood control measure will have an adverse effect on the scenery, apart from the long-term environmental impact.

3 *The West* The western provinces consist mainly of mountain and desert landscapes quite unlike those of eastern China. Vast sums of money have been spent by the central government to improve communications, and millions of Han Chinese have moved into these areas, as part of a policy of integration. Tourism has been encouraged, with the opening of hotels in areas that were once virtually inaccessible, namely:

(a) Sinkiang where the oasis-towns along the Silk Road, the overland trade route which linked China to the Middle East centuries ago provide accommodation.

(b) Tibet, where Western tourists are attracted to the capital Lhasa. A number of monasteries have been restored, and the Potala, the former palace of the Dalai Lama, is the major attraction. In encouraging tourism, the Chinese government takes the risk that the Tibetans will be exposed to Western ideas.

4 *South China* South China offers considerable potential for eco-tourism, adventure holidays and beach tourism, particularly on the tropical island of Hainan. The major tourist centres include:

(a) Guilin, famous for the spectacular karst mountain scenery along the River Li.

(b) Kunming is the centre for trekking tours into the hill country of Yunnan, where some thirty tribal minorities preserve much of their original culture.

(c) Guangzhou (Canton) is a major business centre, hosting two annual trade fairs in the Palace of Exhibitions which provide a showcase for the Chinese economy. In contrast, the city's markets display exotic foods and health remedies that recall an older China.

Hong Kong and Macau

These deserve special mention because of their former status as European colonies – Hong Kong was British from 1841 to 1997, while Macau was ruled by Portugal from the mid-sixteenth century to 1999. They both consist of parts of the mainland of South China and a number of offshore islands. Hong Kong and Macau now have special status within the PRC under the government's 'one country, two systems' policy, which in effect means a hands-off approach to their free enterprise economies.

Hong Kong

Densely built up around its magnificent harbour, with The Peak in the background, the city of Hong Kong has one of the world's most famous skylines. As a Special Administrative Region (SAR) Hong Kong retains some of the features of British rule, including:

● free port status and a free-wheeling private enterprise economy
● border controls with the rest of China
● the Hong Kong dollar as its official currency
● English as an official language
● its own tourist authority for promotion and development – the Hong Kong Tourist Association (HKTA).

Most of Hong Kong's commercial growth has taken place since 1950, as the result of a massive influx of refugees from the PRC, liberal tax laws and its geographical location at the focus of air and shipping routes. The SAR consists of a dozen islands at the mouth of the Pearl River, the peninsula of Kowloon, and the New Territories on the mainland. These are linked by an efficient transport system, including ferries, road tunnels and the MRT, Hong Kong's underground railway network, which carries more passengers, more efficiently, than its London counterpart. Inbound tourism has been encouraged by the availability of charter flights, and a well-developed business travel market. This provides most of the revenue for Cathay Pacific, one of the leading airlines in the East Asia/Pacific region. The importance of Hong Kong has been enhanced by the new international airport at Chep Lap Kok, as its predecessor – Kai Tak – had been handicapped by a very restricted site. Rising educational and living standards, combined with urban pressures, make Hong Kong an important generator of tourism to the rest of the East Asia/Pacific region.

Some 40 per cent of the SAR is protected from development by country parks, providing a much needed recreation resource for the people of Hong Kong. However, most of the beaches, such as Repulse Bay are overcrowded on summer weekends. Air and marine pollution are serious problems, and a massive clean-up operation will be necessary for Hong Kong to merit its name, which means 'Fragrant Harbour'.

For the foreign visitor, Hong Kong is a unique blend of Western business culture and Eastern traditions, such as *feng shui* in hotel and office developments, and *tai chi* as a popular form of recreation. There are a great variety of attractions, which include:

- shopping for consumer goods and Chinese items such as jade
- the *sampans* and floating restaurants of Aberdeen
- themed attractions such as the Sung Dynasty Village and the Middle Kingdom (showcasing China's history), Ocean Park and the Space Museum
- the outlying islands with their temples and peaceful countryside, providing a relief from the hectic pace of urban Hong Kong.

Macau

Macau lies 120 kilometres to the west of Hong Kong and consists of the city of Macau and the tiny islands of Taipa and Coloane. Now with its own international airport, Macau hopes to reposition itself as a destination and reduce its dependence on gambling as a source of revenue, by promoting other attractions to Western tourists. The majority of visitors are short stay, arriving by fast ferry from Hong Kong. Macau's main appeal would seem to lie in its blend of Chinese and Mediterranean culture. Other attractions include the Grand Prix motor race (modelled on Monaco) and a maritime museum evoking the Portuguese heritage. As with Hong Kong the future prospects for tourism are uncertain, since they depend to an extent on the political situation in Beijing.

Taiwan

In 1949, following the communist victory on the mainland, the followers of the Nationalist government of Chiang Kai Shek retreated to the island of Taiwan (or Formosa) where they established the regime which regards itself as the legitimate Republic of China in opposition to the PRC in Beijing. Not surprisingly, relations with mainland China have tended to be difficult, but in the 1990s there were moves towards eventual reunification, including the restoration of air and sea links. Taiwan has become one of the most successful Asian economies, and despite having diplomatic relations with relatively few countries, it enjoys trading relations with many more, and business travel is of major importance. The country's political isolation has had little effect on the volume of outbound travel, resulting in a heavy deficit on the tourism account.

Taiwan's main tourist markets are Japan (for golfing holidays) and the USA. The capital Taipei is a major business destination, but has little appeal to the leisure tourist apart from shopping and a number of museums, displaying Chinese art treasures. Of more importance is the island's subtropical climate, and its mountain and coastal scenery, much of which is protected in a number of national parks. Major attractions include:

- the Taroko Gorge, on the East West Highway crossing the island
- Sun Moon Lake, a favourite resort for Taiwanese holidaymakers
- the beaches of the east coast and offshore islands.

Summary

East Asia contains some of the world's most populous countries, as well as countries at varying stages of development. The region is remote from the major tourist-generating countries of Europe and North America, but improved air transport is overcoming the friction of distance. Many countries are developing an inbound tourism industry as a source of foreign exchange and to provide jobs. Domestic tourism and recreation are now an important part of the lifestyle, due to the emergence of a middle class in the more prosperous countries. Outbound tourism is also growing, particularly from the established market of Japan. Business travel is important throughout the region.

Away from the more established tourist destinations, the infrastructure for tourism is of a comparatively low standard, though many countries are remedying the situation, mainly by improvements in airport facilities and the development of self-contained resort complexes.

Cultural tourism is of primary importance in the countries of the Far East, which have much to offer in the way of historic cities, temples and landscapes. It is less significant in the countries of South-East Asia where the climate favours beach tourism and where adventure travel and eco-tourism increasingly play a major role. However, more needs to be done to protect natural resources and wildlife from the pollution and excessive development that has occurred in China and some of the countries of South-East Asia. Other attractions include shopping, particularly in Singapore and Hong Kong. Much of the future development of tourism will depend on the extent of recovery from the 1997–8 financial crisis, the resolution of regional conflicts, and the policies undertaken by China, formerly the sleeping giant of the region, but now a major economic player on the world stage.

Case study

Bali and Lombok

Introduction

Bali and Lombok are the best known of the holiday islands of Indonesia. Bali is separated from Java to the west by only a narrow stretch of water, whereas Lombok to the east is more remote and less developed. Bali has a long-established reputation as a tropical paradise, where a seemingly gentle, artistic people live in harmony with their environment. However, with tourist arrivals exceeding 2 million a year in the late 1990s – compared to less than 30 000 in 1969 – it is becoming difficult to sustain this image. Unlike most of Indonesia, Bali was relatively unaffected by the turmoil that followed the Asian financial crisis of 1997–8. In fact, the fall of the rupiah against Western currencies meant that Bali became a value for money destination for many tourists. Lombok has benefited from Bali's popularity, and tourism development has been rapid since the mid-1980s.

Bali

Tourism resources

Bali is densely populated, with some 3 million people living in a small mountainous island only 5600 square kilometres in area. The northern part of the island is dominated by a chain of volcanoes – some still active – rising to over 2000 metres. Rich volcanic soils, monsoon rains and a complex irrigation system support the agricultural village communities that make up 80 per cent of the population. Bali's appeal is based on the photogenic quality of its land and people, with physical and cultural resources that include:

1 A favourable tropical climate, with a dry season lasting from May to October. This coincides with the winter months in Australia, which provides 22 per cent of Bali's tourists.
2 A spectacular landscape – featuring emerald-green rice terraces carved out of the hills, mountains clothed in lush vegetation, and crater lakes.
3 Balinese art and culture – throughout their history the Balinese have adopted cultural traits from other peoples – the Hindu religion and dance dramas from India for example – and made them part of their own distinctive lifestyle. Art and religious ritual are part of everyday life. Along with the strong sense of village community, this has helped to preserve Balinese culture in the face of a mass invasion by international tourists. Cultural attractions include:
   (a) The Balinese-Hindu temples – there are at least three in every village.
   (b) The colourful festivals, that integrate art, music, drama and dance. The graceful *legong* dancers have become the island's best known tourist image. The Balinese do not seem to mind the presence of outsiders at their religious ceremonies – even the elaborate cremations have become tourist attractions.
   (c) Balinese painting and sculpture first became a means of personal expression and a commercial

activity in the 1930s with the encouragement of Dutch and other Western expatriates, who introduced new techniques and a much greater range of styles. Tourism has led to the development of new art forms and the revival of some traditional handicrafts.

Recreational resources

The most well known of Bali's recreational resources are the surfing beaches and the coral reefs for offshore scuba-diving. Other activities have been introduced as a result of tourist demand. For example, golf courses have been developed, primarily for the Japanese, while adventure sports, such as bungee-jumping and rafting, appeal to the international youth market.

Accommodation and transport

Bali offers a range of accommodation – from luxury five-star hotels – concentrated in Nusa Dua – to simple beach bungalows. Small hotels and guesthouses, known as *losmen* or homestays provide inexpensive, informal accommodation throughout Bali for backpackers and independent tourists. Often built in the style of a traditional Balinese village compound, with rooms opening off an inner courtyard, they allow the visitor to sample the Balinese way of life. As they are usually run by local families, a much higher proportion of the visitor spend is retained within the local community than is the case with the larger hotels, owned by Javanese and foreign enterprises.

Most foreign visitors to Bali, and a high proportion of domestic tourists – from Jakarta, Yogyakarta and Surabaya – arrive by air. The opening of the Ngurah Rai International Airport at Denpasar (DPS) in 1968 was the catalyst for the large-scale expansion of tourism in Bali. Denpasar is served by scheduled and charter air services from Australia, Japan, Western Europe and the USA. Internal transport is by road, using a variety of vehicles such as *bemos* (minibuses) and pick-up trucks as well as cars, coaches and taxis.

The impacts of tourism

Although the Balinese have had little say in determining the Indonesian government's policy of developing tourism in their island, they have experienced some of its economic benefits. Tourism now provides jobs for more than 20 per cent of the adult population, provides a supplementary source of income for rice farmers who can let rooms to backpackers, and ensures a ready market for handicrafts, such as wood-carvings, as well as a textile industry geared to producing beachwear. As a result, average incomes are twice those of Java. The Balinese have been able to market their culture, which has proved remarkably resilient compared with that of other tropical islands. However the high rate of tourism growth, and the modernization this inevitably entails, is putting a heavy strain on limited land and water resources, and is threatening the integrity of Balinese cultural traditions. For example, the need to provide electricity for luxury hotels has led to a controversial decision to build a power station on a mountain held sacred by the Balinese. Negative impacts which have already resulted from tourism include:

1 The loss of 1000 hectares of rice fields to development annually.
2 Coastal erosion, due to sand-dredging and the drainage of mangrove swamps to make way for development.
3 Damage to coral reefs.
4 Untreated waste disposal, causing marine pollution.
5 Problems of water supply, with priority given to luxury hotels and golf course developments rather than local communities.
6 Air and noise pollution from cars and motorcycles.
7 Leakages of tourism income. As inclusive tours dominate the industry, most of the income goes to the international tour operators and hotel chains.
8 The packaging of Balinese traditional culture for Western consumption in the big international hotels.
9 A spatial imbalance in the distribution of the benefits of tourism. Most tourist activity is concentrated in the south of the island, although development is spreading to the interior and the north coast.

The tourist regions of Bali

1 *South Bali* Once a relatively poor area in agricultural terms, this part of Bali has experienced considerable economic and population growth since the 1960s as a result of the tourist boom. Denpasar, the island's capital, is now a major city with a population approaching 400 000. It offers a number of attractions including the Bali Museum, which showcase Balinese dance, paintings and handicrafts. The south includes the major resorts of the island, which have developed along some of Bali's best beaches within easy reach of the international airport. Each resort exemplifies a different approach to tourism:
(a) Sanur. This small fishing village attracted Western artists and intellectuals in the 1930s, giving it wide publicity that eventually resulted in large-scale development along the seafront in the 1960s. Sanur is a mix of large hotels and smaller bungalow developments, interspersed with shops and restaurants. It attracts visitors from Europe, Australia, Japan and the USA.

(b) Kuta Beach. Kuta has acquired a down-market image, having developed in the 1970s as a resort for Australian surfers, who were attracted by its broad sloping beach, breakers and offshore breezes. Some 18 000 bed-spaces are available, accounting for almost a third of Bali's capacity. Much of the accommodation is both informal and small in scale, resulting in a low-rise sprawl of bungalows, small hotels, restaurants and shops, which extends northwards to Legian. A variety of traders compete to provide goods and services, which include 'beach massage'. In some respects, Kuta is to Australians what some Spanish resorts are to young British holidaymakers – a tourism experience based on 'sun and fun', fast-food, bars and discotheques, rather than any appreciation of the local culture. Kuta also exemplifies the complex relationships between hosts and guests in a Third World country. Young Balinese have adopted Western 'surf culture', and the surfboard has become yet another art form. The Western 'sun-worshippers' have become an attraction – to domestic tourists from Java – whereas the Balinese were persuaded to 'cover up' by the Indonesian authorities in the name of progress, following independence from Dutch rule.
(c) Nusa Dua. Land in Sanur was in short supply by the late 1970s, leading to the development of a purpose-built resort on the Bukit Peninsula just south of the airport. The site had the following advantages:
  (i) It was of little value for agriculture and thinly populated.
  (ii) The cultural impact of tourism could be minimized by physical separation.
  (iii) The beaches are protected by a coral reef, so are suitable for bathing.
Nusa Dua was designed and built as a World Bank project and is managed by the Bali Tourist Development Corporation. It is a beautifully planned and landscaped resort area, with its own water filtration plant, and accommodation is restricted to luxury hotels. The development has aroused controversy – some say that it is an excellent example of enclave tourism, while others argue that little of the culture of Bali, or contact with local people, is to be found there – in other words, Nusa Dua is a 'tourist ghetto', like so many other luxury resorts in the Third World.

2 *Central Bali* The central region of Bali is well known for its cultural traditions, with villages specializing in particular handicrafts. They include:
(a) Batubulan – where traditional dancers perform for tourists and the Pura Puseh temple is found.
(b) Celuk – famous for gold and silver filigree.
(c) Sukawati – for its puppeteers.

(d) Batuan – famed for paintings and dancers.

(e) Mas – for its carvings.

(f) Ubud – often regarded as the cultural centre of Bali with its artist's colonies and the Puri Lukisan Museum, Neka Gallery and nearby monkey forest temple.

(g) Goa Gajah – the Elephant Cave.

3 *North and East Bali* North Bali has a different culture, architectural style and dialect to the south. Roads leading over the mountains of the island to the north were built by the Dutch as recently as the 1920s and pass a number of attractions:

(a) The volcanic Lake Batur a spectacular 20-kilometre wide caldera with the villages on the rim.

(b) Lake Bratan, a peaceful backwater.

(c) The wooden shrines at Mengwi.

(d) The monkey forest at Sangeh.

On the northern coast is the port of Singaraja and quiet beaches; however, tourism is dispersing away from the south, particularly to east Bali, where the resort of Candi Dasa is an up-market newly developed beach resort. East Bali is also a centre for weaving and has a number of significant temples and pavilions. The port of Padang Bai is the base for cruise ships and the Lombok ferry.

Lombok

Lombok has been the main beneficiary of recent government policy to spread tourism away from Bali. The two islands are roughly the same size and are superficially similar – indeed, Lombok is often regarded as a less developed version of Bali. However, there are a number of important differences, for example:

1 The climate is drier. This is a disadvantage for agriculture – Lombok is one of the poorest regions of Indonesia – but a 'plus' for tourism.

2 Lombok has better beaches than Bali. The scenery of the interior is less spectacular, although there are some high mountains – Rinjani for example – in the north of the island.

3 Their ecosystems are different, due to the barrier presented by the deep Lombok Strait. The Wallace Line, which separates Asian species of plants and animals from those typical of Australasia, runs between the two islands.

4 They are culturally distinct. The Sasak people of Lombok are Moslems, and so tend to be less tolerant of immodest behaviour by Western tourists.

5 Lombok has a less developed feel. There is less of the 'hard-sell' approach to tourism and merchandising evident in Bali.

6 Lombok has a policy for up-market tourism development, further differentiating its product from Bali.

Lombok is, therefore, focusing on five-star hotels and resorts, with associated infrastructure development, including a new international airport and improvements to ferry services, port facilities and the road network. The Lombok Tourism Development Corporation has purchased land fronting beaches in the south and west of the island, and is proposing joint ventures with the big accommodation developers. It is alleged that local SMEs, catering for backpackers and other lower-spending visitors, are being squeezed out, with the tourism industry becoming dominated by Javanese and foreign interests.

Much of the development has taken place on the west coast of Lombok, which has safe sandy beaches, excellent coral reefs for diving and facilities for sailing and other water sports. The main resort is Senggigi Beach, a few kilometres north of Mataram, the island's capital, while the Gili Islands are also attracting developers.

Although Lombok has a number of villages noted for handicrafts such as weaving, basketwork and pottery, there is less emphasis on the decorative arts and fewer cultural attractions than in Bali. Most of these are located near the capital and include:

● Cakranegara – the former royal capital, which contains the Pura Meru Temple

● the Narmada Gardens

● the Suranadi Temple.

Case study

The Asian currency crisis: the impact on tourism

Introduction

The East Asia and Pacific region has been one of the fastest growing regions for the development of tourism, and for both inbound and outbound international tourism (see Chapter 2). However, in the middle of 1997, investor confidence in many of Asia's economies fell, resulting in a crisis of confidence in their currencies. Over the next twelve months, the value of the currencies of a number of Asian countries fell dramatically against other currencies such as the US dollar and the pound sterling.

The countries that were affected severely were:

● Hong Kong

● Indonesia

● Japan

- Malaysia
- Singapore
- South Korea
- Thailand.

Only China, Vietnam and Taiwan appear to have escaped the financial fallout from the crisis.

A series of other events, some related to the economic crisis, others not, made the problem even worse deterring inbound tourists:

1 The region was affected by a heavily polluting haze caused by forest fires blotting out the sun.
2 The economic crisis prompted political instability and riots in countries such as Indonesia, threatening the safety of visitors.

In response to the crisis, the International Monetary Fund stepped in to assist these countries and put into place a series of economic measures. However, although the currencies had begun to recover and stabilize by the end of the 1990s, the impact upon tourism in the region has been serious. It has set back growth forecasts, and affected every aspect of tourism from demand through to all the elements of supply and the public sector organizations. Indeed the impact of the crisis is an excellent example of the interdependence of all the elements of tourism:

1 Reduced demand meant that the airlines had to reduce capacity, lower fares and prune their route networks.
2 Hotels and airlines reduced their business for travel agents and tour operators, fuelling a crisis of confidence in the sector.
3 This led to the cancellation or delay of major infrastructure and tourism projects.

4 This in turn hit tourism earnings and employment in national economies, leading to reduced budgets for their national tourism organizations.

This case study examines the major impacts of the Asian currency crisis upon tourism in the region.

The impact upon demand for tourism

As Table 22.1 shows, the effect of the crisis across the region was widespread, though uneven. Overall, arrivals to the East Asia and Pacific region fell by 1.2 per cent, but South-East Asia suffered the most, with some countries suffering heavy declines in 1998.

The table shows that:

1 The impact upon other countries and regions not directly involved in the crisis – Australia, for example, has a high dependence on demand from the region and as a consequence, tourism suffered with the drop in arrivals.
2 Thailand managed to maintain growth in arrivals, in part due to prompt action by the Tourist Authority of Thailand (TAT) and the attraction of a country with a weak currency.
3 The fall in the value of the currencies did mean that a number of countries – Indonesia (including Bali), Thailand, Malaysia – became bargain basement destinations. Inbound tourism volumes rose accordingly, but the value per tourist of these visits to the countries concerned was much reduced, despite the receipt of much needed foreign exchange (see for example Thailand in Table 22.1). European, North American, Australian, Indian, Chinese and Middle East markets took advantage of the situation and showed increased arrivals to the region – except for Singapore and Hong Kong.

Table 22.1   The effect of the Asian currency crisis on tourism

	1998 arrivals (millions)	% change 1997–8	1998 receipts, excluding transport (US$ millions)	% change 1997–8
Australia	4.0	–7.1	8.6	–5.0
Hong Kong	9.6	–7.7	7.1	–23.0
Indonesia	4.9	–5.5	5.1	–5.5
Japan	4.1	–2.8	4.1	–4.0
South Korea	4.2	+8.8	5.7	+11.4
Malaysia	6.8	+10.4	3.4	+24.6
Singapore	5.6	–14.3	6.5	–5.0
Thailand	7.7	+6.9	6.4	–9.3
East Asia and the Pacific	86.9	–1.2	73.7	–3.8

4 Within the region, the rapid decline of previously strong outbound markets had a major impact upon arrivals across South East Asia. For example, Japan's outbound spending was down 10.2 per cent in 1998 compared with 1997, for Singapore the decline was 12.9 per cent and for South Korea, 10.1 per cent.

5 Within the region, the crisis also severely altered consumer spending patterns, particularly among the middle class who were the core of travellers before the crisis. Tourism and other luxury items were reduced in priority, and a loss of confidence by individuals regarding their financial situation in the future impacted upon demand. The demand-side response is a familiar one involving:
 (a) Switching from international to domestic travel.
 (b) Trading down in terms of type of trip and accommodation (including staying with friends and relatives).
 (c) Last minute bookings.

The impact upon the supply of tourism

There is no doubt that the crisis has changed the way that the tourism industry operates in the region, with some changes occurring already, while others will happen over the medium to long term. Employment has been severely affected with an estimated loss of some 6–7 million jobs in the hotel and restaurant sector in Indonesia. Across the region, the short-term response has been to:

● reduce operating costs (by cutting marketing budgets and laying off staff)
● in a bid to take business from competitors, cutting prices and/or offering many added extras such as free transfers and upgrades.

Airlines

Experts say that the aviation sector has suffered the greatest impact from the crisis, with one regional airline going out of business (Indonesia's *Sempati*), and the international carriers serving the region from Europe and North America scaling back capacity and frequencies to destinations such as Seoul. International carriers based in the region, such as Philippine Airlines, Thai, Malaysia Airlines and Cathay Pacific, were badly affected and have had to implement rationalization of routes, delay payments on new aircraft or delay the delivery of aircraft, and make redundancies. In addition, airlines are reducing fares and providing many added extras for passengers in a bid to secure business. The crisis has raised the issue of protectionism in the region, as the regional airlines seek some degree of priority over routes to their own countries. In contrast, aggressive international carriers based elsewhere in the world will expect deregulation and open access to these routes.

Accommodation

Occupancy levels and room rates have fallen in the hardest hit countries – in Indonesia in 1998 occupancy levels fell to 35 per cent. Also, new accommodation developments have either been cancelled or delayed, while many of those already under construction have been frozen (e.g. The new Hyatt hotel in Saigon). The region was already suffering from over-capacity of hotel rooms and the crisis has exacerbated this situation. Room rates fell as hotels competed for business and lucrative conference and incentive travel markets from within the region fell away. The accommodation sector has had to change the way it does business, as what was a seller's market in many of the leading cities in the region, becomes a buyer's market.

Travel agents and tour operators

The crisis has triggered a series of business failures in the travel trade in the region – particularly in Japan and South Korea, where the fall in outbound travel and the reduction of airline capacity meant that businesses could not survive. In South Korea alone, it is estimated that the size of the travel agency/tour operator sector will be halved. Only those companies with a substantial share of inbound travel will survive. In addition, the reduction of the value of airfares, allied to airlines attempting to reduce commission levels in their own attempt to survive, have resulted in a crisis situation for the travel trade.

Infrastructure

The crisis in investor confidence has meant that many infrastructure projects – airports, roads and telecommunications – have been either cancelled or delayed. In many respects this adds to the problem, as the region will lose its competitive edge in international markets.

The impact upon the organization of tourism

National Tourism Organizations have been affected by the crisis in terms of:

1 Budget cuts at exactly the time when enhanced marketing budgets were needed. This has meant the closure of overseas offices in some cases, while investment in regional markets has failed to deliver the tourists that were forecast before the crisis.
2 The need to rebuild confidence in their generating markets.

3 The need to seek out new markets – Russia, Latin America, the Middle East and South Africa, for example.
4 The search for alliances and cost-sharing with the private sector – airlines and hotels for example – as well as regional groupings of countries to share the cost of international promotion.
5 The need to stimulate domestic tourism to absorb spare capacity in the tourism sector. This has been particularly the case for Indonesia, Malaysia and Thailand.

In addition, governments in the region:

● have imposed financial penalties to discourage outbound travel
● are looking to accelerate the privatization of tourism assets – such as airlines – to reduce public sector liability and risk
● are coming under pressure to reduce bureaucratic delays over visas and border crossings in a bid to attract international visitors.

The way forward

The World Travel and Tourism Council has identified seven policy priorities to strengthen the role of tourism in the recovery of Asian economies:

1 Ensure that economic policy adjustments take into account the long-term growth potential of tourism.
2 Enhance the investment climate by demonstrating regional solidarity and cohesion.
3 Continue to progressively liberate markets.
4 Invest in tourism export promotion at regional and national level.
5 Advance the virtuous circle of sustainable development, infrastructure provision, and job creation.
6 Break the vicious circle of red tape, high taxes, reduced demand and less jobs.
7 Build on the enormous and well-deserved reputation for service by upgrading human skills and targeting quality.

(Muqbil, 1998; World Trade Organization, 1998a)

23

North America

After reading this chapter you should be able to:

1 Describe the major physical features and climates of North America and understand their importance for tourism.
2 Appreciate the scale and characteristics of domestic tourism in the USA and Canada.
3 Understand the importance of the USA and Canada as tourist-generating countries.
4 Appreciate the significance of the conservation movement in North America and the importance of the national park system in particular to tourism.
5 Be aware of the cultural diversity of the USA and Canada.
6 Recognize the importance of transport in the development of the tourism industry.
7 Demonstrate a knowledge of the tourist regions, resorts, business centres and tourist attractions of North America.

Introduction

Although the World Tourism Organization treats the Americas – North and South – as one region, the two continents need to be investigated separately in view of their extent and the striking differences between North and South America, particularly in terms of ecology and culture. In our definition North America excludes Mexico, which we treat as part of Latin America in the next chapter.

Both the United States and Canada boast a wealth of natural resources in a vast physical setting. Although the contribution of the native peoples is increasingly recog-

nized, both countries are predominantly 'nations of immigrants', who have blended to produce a distinct North American culture. The English language is dominant, despite being challenged by Spanish in Florida and the southwestern USA, and by French in much of Canada. Both countries have developed democratic federal structures of government and legal systems largely inherited from Britain. They are informal and competitive in their outlook, and share similar attitudes to business enterprise and the freedom of the individual. This has favoured an innovatory approach to leisure activities and tourism, particularly as regards marketing and merchandising.

In the late 1990s North America received about 10 per cent of the world's international tourist arrivals and accounted for almost a quarter of the world's hotel capacity. From a visitor's point of view the size of the continent is important – extending over eight time zones and including most of the world's climates – but so is the rich variety of landforms and ecosystems. The western part of North America is dominated by high mountain chains, including the spectacular scenery of the Rockies and the Sierra Nevada. Near the eastern seaboard rise the forested Appalachians, much lower in altitude than the Rockies. Between these two mountain systems lie vast interior plains, drained by great rivers such as the Mississippi and its tributaries in the south, and by the St Lawrence, Athabasca and Mackenzie in the north.

The climate of North America is largely determined by relief and tends to be more extreme than similar latitudes in Western Europe, with warmer summers and colder winters. In winter, Arctic winds penetrate far to the south, and occasionally bring freezing temperatures to the Gulf coast and northern Florida. Yet in summer most of the continent is open to tropical airstreams originating in the Gulf of Mexico, so that humidity tends to be high in the eastern half of the United States. Along the western seaboard high mountain ranges intercept moisture-bearing winds from the

Pacific Ocean, bringing heavy rainfall to coastal areas, which also experience much milder temperatures than the interior and eastern seaboard. Most of the western USA however has a dry climate, due to its situation in the 'rain shadow' of the mountain barriers. The most important climatic divide is between the *frostbelt*, consisting of Canada and the northern states of the USA, and the *sunbelt* stretching from California to the Carolinas. This has far-reaching social and economic implications in that industry and population, as well as tourism, increasingly gravitates from the northern states – with their declining industries and cold winters – to more attractive environments in the south and west.

Compared to the rest of the world North Americans have been profligate in their use of natural resources, favoured by energy costs amounting to only a quarter of those in Europe. This has not encouraged sustainable forms of development, as shown by the dominance of the motor car and the prevalence of urban sprawl. Nevertheless the USA and Canada are very much involved with issues of environmental protection. Despite the fact that the great majority of the population live in cities, the unsettled wilderness is very much part of the national heritage in both countries, and determined efforts have been made to save areas of unique scenery from development. The United States was the first country in the world to designate a system of national parks, starting with Yellowstone in 1872; Banff in the Canadian Rockies followed in 1885. Such areas are owned and managed by the federal government with the objectives of conservation and providing access for outdoor recreation. The services required by tourists, who in the main arrive by car, are however operated by the private sector on a concession basis. The national parks are widely regarded as a major North American contribution to world tourism, and a role model for good practice in wildlife conservation and visitor management. However national parks tend to be resource-oriented and they are mostly located in areas distant from the major centres of population. This has led to the development of recreation areas that are more user-orientated, providing a range of facilities, such as the state parks in the USA and some of the provincial parks in Canada.

North America also offers a variety of man-made attractions celebrating its achievements in science, technology and the arts. Canada and the United States are 'young nations' compared to those of Europe, while their cities are undergoing a continual process of renewal and reinvention, so that historical buildings are few. Those that have survived tend to be associated with celebrities or important events in the process of nation-building. They have been carefully restored – or in some cases reconstructed – as heritage attractions, with costumed guides and craft workers interpreting the lifestyle of the past – Colonial Williamsburg in Virginia is an outstanding example. This, like many others, operates as a non-profit making trust. Theme parks on the other hand, along with a host of lesser attractions are part of the much larger private sector of the tourism industry.

Big cities play a major role in the cultural life of the USA and Canada, with museums, theatres and art galleries that compare favourably with the capitals of Europe. There are 35 such 'metropolitan areas' with populations exceeding one million in the USA, and another three in Canada. As population centres, they generate most of the demand for holiday travel, and as commercial centres, they attract a considerable amount of business travel. The *convention* (conference) industry plays an important role, with city governments striving to increase market share with ever-more impressive facilities. However from the viewpoint of tourists from Europe relatively few North American cities are attractive in themselves. The pattern of high-rise central business districts, commercial strip development along the highways, and low-density suburbs is repeated throughout the continent. A number of cities have attempted to regenerate their run-down inner city areas, with projects aimed at attracting the leisure shopper and tourist. Many visitors from Europe and Asia find the out-of-town shopping malls more appealing, although they are no longer as unique to North America as they were in the 1980s.

The United States

The period since 1918 has been called the 'American Century', during which the United States has consistently been one of the world's leading generators of international tourism, especially long-haul travel. With its wealth of natural resources and technical know-how, the USA boasts the world's largest economy, and since the collapse of the Soviet Union it has become the only superpower. Although there is a tendency toward cultural homogeneity, regional differences persist. Each of the 50 constituent states is self-governing to a large extent, and Americans retain a strong attachment to their home state. United States territory also extends beyond the North American continent to the islands of the Caribbean – specifically Puerto Rico and the US Virgin Islands – and to the Pacific – Hawaii, Guam and American Samoa (these are included in Chapters 24 and 25).

The USA is also one of the world's leading destinations, with tourism accounting for 6 per cent of the gross domestic product, and in many states it has become a leading employer. In contrast to some other sectors of the economy, the industry is made up largely of small and medium-sized enterprises, and these have contributed substantially to the high rate of economic growth and job creation that the country has enjoyed since its recovery from the 1980s recession. Nevertheless, the promotion of tourism has generally been weak at the federal level of government. This is primarily due to two factors:

● The belief in free enterprise with the minimum of government interference; and
● The division of responsibilities between the federal government in Washington and the state governments.

It was not until 1981 that the United States Travel and Tourism Administration (USTTA) was set up to coordinate federal government policies regarding tourism and to promote the country more effectively abroad. The demise of the USTTA means that the USA enters the new millennium without an overall tourism strategy or tourist information service for the whole country. However, the Tourism Industries Office in the Department of Commerce does provide a coordinating role. Most states and many large cities do have some kind of official body concerned with tourism, although these vary considerably in their effectiveness. This has led a number of state governments to combine their resources to promote a particular region on the international stage.

The demand for tourism

Inbound tourism has continued to grow steadily over the last two decades of the twentieth century, to approach 50 million arrivals in the late 1990s. Canadians make up half of the total, in addition to many more day-visitors. Other important markets are Mexico (high volume but low spend), Japan, and the countries of Western Europe. The number of tourists from Europe fluctuates with the strength of the dollar and the level of air fares. The UK is by far the most important generator of demand, followed by Germany and France. Japanese visitors are growing in number and tend to spend more per capita than Europeans, Canadians and Mexicans.

Looking now at the United States market for travel, we find that only around one fifth of trips are to foreign countries. Almost 85 per cent of Americans have never travelled outside their own continent and only a minority own passports (which they do not require for travel to Canada or Mexico). There is seemingly a huge untapped market for overseas travel. However, national tourism organizations in Europe and elsewhere are aware that the US market is lucrative but volatile, notoriously sensitive to any hint of unrest in a particular region.

Although overseas travel by Americans has grown steadily over recent decades, most of the outbound tourism is to Canada and Mexico, accounting for over 30 million trips in the late 1990s. Much of this is business travel, stimulated by the success of the North American Free Trade Area (NAFTA) to which the three countries belong. Trips to Canada tend to be short-stay and undertaken mainly by car, whereas visits to Mexico tend to be of longer duration and involve air travel to the destination. The Caribbean attracts a large number of leisure tourists, including a major share of the growing cruise market.

An important constraint on the demand for tourism is the limited leisure time available to most Americans of working age. The USA is an affluent but 'leisure poor' society compared to most European countries, and predictions made in the 1970s of a 'leisure boom' have not materi-

alized. Since 1979 productivity has trebled but the amount of leisure time has been reduced substantially over the same period. Thanks to 'downsizing' and the resulting job insecurity Americans are working harder than before. For example:

● The average working week in the USA is 43 hours, compared to 38 hours in the UK;
● Workers in the USA on average have 19 days of paid annual leave (including public holidays) compared to 24 days for their counterparts in Europe;
● In the USA leave is negotiated with the employer as part of the contract. Many employers have reduced leave entitlement or have encouraged flexitime;
● A third of American workers only take half or less of their full leave entitlement; and
● Two weeks paid holiday taken en bloc is often frowned upon by employers and the corporate culture at the workplace.

This means that although 70 per cent of American households still take a holiday away from home, for middle income families this tends increasingly to be in the form of short weekend breaks rather than a long summer vacation. There continues to be peak in demand for domestic holidays in the months of July and August, so that beaches are generally deserted before Memorial Day in late May and after Labor Day in early September. Thanksgiving in late November is the time when family reunions, often involving long-distance air and car travel, are almost obligatory.

The beach is less important as a motivation for travel than shopping, visits to theme parks, sporting venues and heritage attractions, and the opportunity to participate in a wide range of outdoor recreational activities, such as fishing, golf, sailing and skiing. There is also a growing demand for the purchase of second homes (often a lakeside cabin), camper caravans, and off-the-road recreational vehicles.

The supply of resources

In the public sector a number of organizations are involved with the supply of recreational resources at the federal level of government. These include:

● The National Park Service, the Fish and Wildlife Service, the Bureau of Land Management, and the Bureau of Reclamation which come under the jurisdiction of the Department of the Interior; and
● The United States Forest Service, which is part of the Department of Agriculture.

The National Park Service (NPS) was set up in 1916, taking responsibility for a range of protected areas, variously designated as national parks, National Recreation Areas and

National Monuments (which are usually specific sites rather than large areas). The number of visitors to the national parks trebled between 1960 and 1994, and this has caused the following problems:

- Popular attractions and campgrounds in the most visited parks regularly reach their capacity at peak holiday times;
- Traffic on access routes and on roads within the parks has also risen considerably; and
- Footpath erosion is severe in the most visited areas, while vegetation and wildlife have been disturbed by trail bikes, hiking off the designated trails and careless behaviour by campers.

The Forest Service is responsible for the National Forest system, where the emphasis is on multiple-use management, including grazing, watershed control and wildlife conservation as well as forestry and recreation. Some 17 per cent of National Forest land is classified as *wilderness areas* under a 1964 Act of Congress prohibiting road building and other development for the benefit of backpackers and canoeists seeking unspoiled nature and physical challenge.

The coastline of the United States provides a more accessible and popular resource, particularly the beaches of Southern California, the Gulf of Mexico, and the Eastern Seaboard from Cape Cod to Florida. Off the Atlantic coast is the world's longest series of *barrier islands*, acting as natural sand breakwaters, that form parallel to a low-lying coastal plain. Miami Beach and Atlantic City are the best known examples of resort development on such offshore islands. Unfortunately these resources are threatened by over-development and by rising sea levels, not to mention the occasional hurricane sweeping up from the Caribbean. Many coastal communities have built sea walls as protection from destructive waves, but these merely accelerate erosion elsewhere. Others like Miami Beach have called upon the United States Army Corps of Engineers to carry out beach re-nourishment, using sand dredged from other locations. However the best long-term solution is for the state governments to introduce land use management regulations in the coastal zone.

Transport

Transport in the USA is highly developed, as you might expect from a nation constantly on the move. The following characteristics are worth emphasizing:

- The private car is the dominant transport mode for all types of journeys;
- Domestic air services are much more widely used than in European countries; and
- Public transport, except in some major cities, is poorly developed.

The United States has the highest level of car ownership in the world, with the number of motor vehicles in some states exceeding the resident population! Well over 80 per cent of holiday trips are taken by car. Although the internal combustion engine was not an American invention, it was largely due to Henry Ford that ownership of an automobile was brought within reach of people on modest incomes. As a result by 1930 there were 23 million cars registered in the USA, whereas in Europe similar levels were not reached until the late 1950s. Demand from vehicle manufacturers and motorists led to much-needed road improvements, such as the legendary Route 66 from Chicago to Los Angeles. Scenic routes or *parkways*, such as the Skyline Drive in the Blue Ridge mountains of Virginia, were designed in the 1930s to encourage sightseeing by car. From the late 1950s onwards some of the older highways – including Route 66 – were superseded by the Interstate Highway system, financed very largely by the federal government. This provided a nationwide motorway network – 69,000 kilometres in length – linking most of the major cities, and resulted in a threefold increase in the mileage travelled by car between 1950 and 1980. Motoring in the USA is subject to fewer inconveniences than elsewhere in the world and fuel costs are low compared to Europe. However the American love affair with the car has had an adverse environmental impact, including pollution, visual blight – with large areas given over to parking lots – and urban sprawl – which in turn necessitates ever-lengthening journeys to work, shopping and recreational facilities. Since the early 1990s even cities as wedded to the car as Los Angeles and Miami have realized that road-building alone cannot solve traffic congestion, and they have invested heavily in rapid transit schemes.

Air transport accounts for some 10 per cent of holiday trips, and most medium-sized towns in the USA have an airport within easy reach by car. Air fares are much cheaper than those paid to cover equivalent distances in Europe, thanks largely to competition between the airlines. After 1978, when the civil aviation industry was deregulated, routes were organized on a 'hub and spoke' system, with a few major airports handling the bulk of the traffic. As a result of deregulation many small airlines came into service, but some old-established carriers failed to adjust to the new conditions. The biggest casualty was undoubtedly Pan-Am, which had largely pioneered intercontinental air services before World War II. The airlines that have clearly emerged as front-runners include United, American, Delta and Continental, while Denver, Chicago, Atlanta and Dallas have developed as major hubs. A large number of regional carriers, often code-sharing with one of the major airlines, provide feeder services.

Public transport by road and rail compares unfavourably with the situation in most other developed countries. The major bus companies – Greyhound and Continental Trailways – do provide an extensive network of intercity services, as well as inclusive tours and bargain fares for foreign tourists. Nevertheless coach travel accounts for less than 3 per cent of the domestic market. The train provides a more stylish alternative compared to the downmarket image of coach travel. To a large extent the railways made America, but in the 1950s passenger services declined as a result of competition from the airlines and the private car. They might have disappeared altogether from the long distance routes had not the federal government intervened in 1970 with the introduction of Amtrak, a semi-public corporation that operates passenger trains over the networks of a dozen private railroad companies. Amtrak has upgraded rolling stock, in some cases introducing double-decker 'superliners' for scenic viewing. Historic routes have been revived, such as the 'Empire Builder' which takes 44 hours to cover the distance from Chicago to Seattle. The introduction of high-speed trains is however inhibited by the cost of upgrading track. Amtrak has achieved most success in the densely populated 'north-east corridor' linking Newport News in Virginia with Boston via Washington, Philadelphia and New York City. This is by far the most important route, accounting for 50 per cent of Amtrak's revenue, and competing effectively with the airlines for the lucrative business market. Elsewhere in the USA train services, where they exist, tend to be infrequent. This situation may change as Americans become more aware of the safety and environmental issues posed by growing congestion on the highways, at airport terminals, and in the airways. However Congress is reluctant to further subsidise Amtrak's investment programme, as politicians are inclined to take the short-term view of reducing public spending.

Accommodation

The supply of accommodation is closely linked to patterns of transport. In the largest cities hotels are most numerous in the *downtown* areas or CBDs. Elsewhere the distribution tends to be peripheral, with hotels clustering around an airport or located in the commercial strip developments fanning out along the main highways. Here a multitude of restaurants and other businesses also vie for the motorist's attention with a welter of advertisements. The first motels developed in the 1930s as family enterprises offering fairly basic accommodation. From the 1950s, following the example of the Holiday Inns chain the trend was to go more upmarket, with facilities such as swimming pools and standardization of the product in terms of service and décor. Hotels themselves have become increasingly innovative, with such features as the atrium lobby pioneered by Regency Hyatt, and the concept of theming, which is best seen in Las Vegas, to appeal to niche markets. Bed and breakfast in private homes is a growing sector, although it has a more upmarket image than its British counterpart, particularly in New England where much of the accommodation is in restored colonial buildings. Campsites and trailer parks for recreational vehicles are a major part of the accommodation sector. About 30 million Americans taking camping holidays use camper-vans (motor caravans) and other types of recreational vehicles.

The regional setting for tourism

The North-east

The North-eastern states facing Europe constitute the most densely populated and one of the most visited parts of the country, including the four major gateway cities of Boston, New York, Philadelphia and Washington. The urbanized belt –'Megalopolis' extending from Boston to Washington contains over 45 million inhabitants and has excellent transport facilities in the form of road, rail and shuttle air services. In contrast, there are large areas of forested wilderness in the mountains of the northern Appalachians.

New England is the most interesting region of the north-east from a historical standpoint, a relatively small area consisting of six of the original thirteen states of the USA. In the seventeenth century it was occupied by English settlers who were Puritans seeking freedom to practise their religious beliefs. What came to be known as the 'Yankee' traits of hard work, thrift and ingenuity were forged in the struggle to wrest a livelihood from a harsh environment of cold winters and infertile soils. This explains the importance in the region's history of fishing, whaling, overseas trade and manufacturing industry. New England played a crucial role in the struggle for independence from British rule in the 1770s, notably the 'Boston Tea Party' and the battle of Lexington. The region has a strong cultural tradition, as shown by the international reputation of its universities – particularly Yale, Harvard and the Massachusetts Institute of Technology – and it has produced many famous writers. Since the mid-nineteenth century New England has become a multi-cultural society as a result of further immigration, particularly from Ireland and Italy.

The rural interior is noted for its forested mountains and picturesque villages of clapboard houses grouped around a wooden church; two of the most visited examples are Sturbridge and Pittsfield in western Massachusetts. Many of the farms have long been abandoned and are now used as weekend or summer retreats by city dwellers. In the fall (autumn) the displays of brilliant foliage attract crowds of weekend visitors, particularly to the state of Vermont. During the snowy winters skiing is a major activity, particularly at Bretton Woods and Mount Washington Valley in New Hampshire, and at Stowe in Vermont.

The coast is equally appealing. In the state of Maine it is rugged, deeply indented, and backed by a sparsely populated hinterland of rivers and forests; sailing, fishing and canoeing are popular activities. Further south there are many fine beaches and a number of historic seaports. Tourists are particularly attracted to the following areas:

- The Cap Cod peninsula, with its extensive sand dunes. Summer resorts such as Hyannisport cater for wealthy second-home owners, while ferries connect to the islands of Nantucket and Martha's Vineyard. At Plymouth there is a 'living museum' commemorating the original settlement of the Pilgrim Fathers in 1620.
- Newport, Rhode Island was once the exclusive summer resort for America's millionaires. It is now a major yachting centre and a popular venue for music festivals.
- Salem is mainly visited because of its association with the witch trials of 1692, an example of Puritan intolerance.
- New Bedford and Mystic are historic seaports associated with the nineteenth century whaling industry.
- Boston is a major North American city that has retained its compact character and mellow brick buildings, although these are often overshadowed by examples of modern architecture such as Government Center. The 'Freedom Trail' commemorates Boston's role in America's struggle for independence.

The **Middle Atlantic Region** is less easily defined. Even in colonial times it was settled by immigrants from a variety of origins, including English Quakers, Irish Catholics, Dutch, Germans and Scandinavians. The region's big cities contain the attractions of major interest to foreign tourists, especially New York, which is the subject of a case study. The mountainous interior, which forms part of the Appalachians, and the beach resorts of Long Island, New Jersey and the Delmarva Peninsula, are mainly visited by domestic tourists. The cities are major tourist attractions in themselves:

- **Philadelphia**, the fourth largest city in the United States, is regarded as the birthplace of the nation, witnessing the Declaration of Independence (1776) and the ratification of the US Constitution (1788). Independence Hall, The Liberty Bell and Congress Hall are reminders of the early history of America. It is a major sports venue and cultural centre, while Penn's Landing is a maritime heritage attraction.
- **Baltimore** is another large seaport whose Inner Harbor development provides an excellent example of a decayed waterfront area being transformed into a high class tourist attraction. However unlike Philadelphia it is a staging point rather than a tourist destination.
- **Washington DC** has a unique appeal, as the capital of the United States. It was planned as such at the beginning of the nineteenth century, with wide avenues lined with Neo-classical buildings and attractive parks. The most important feature is the Mall, extending from the Lincoln Memorial to the Capitol housing the American Congress;

grouped nearby are other important public buildings such as The White House, the Smithsonian museums, and the National Gallery of Art. The federal government and various international agencies such as the World Bank generate a considerable volume of business travel. The capital is served by two international airports – Dulles International and Washington-Baltimore. Washington lacks the skyscrapers and entertainment facilities of New York, but it is growing in importance as a major cultural centre, with venues such as the Kennedy Center for the Performing Arts. The district of Georgetown is noted for its boutiques and restaurants. However the American pattern of wide separation of home and workplace is evident, with relatively few government employees living in the central city – the District of Columbia – as compared to the sprawling suburbs in Maryland and Virginia.

- **The Northern Appalachians** constitute the rural hinterland of the big cities of the Eastern Seaboard. They are made up of forested mountain ridges, narrow river valleys and rolling hill country. In parts of West Virginia and Pennsylvania the landscape has been blighted by coal mining and heavy industry, leaving behind polluted rivers. However there are widespread opportunities for field sports, white-water rafting (mainly in West Virginia) and skiing during the winter months:
  - 'Upstate' New York boasts the most popular scenic attractions, including the Finger Lakes, the Catskills' and the Adirondack Mountains, which contain some wilderness areas as well as Lake Placid, venue for the 1980 Winter Olympics. The Hudson Valley, with its vineyards, historic mansions and wooded scenery, has been called 'the Rhineland of North America'. The state's most famous attraction – although half of it lies in Canada – is Niagara Falls. Since the nineteenth century a variety of facilities has been provided for viewing the spectacle, but some of the development, particularly on the American side, is excessively commercialized and inappropriate for the setting.
  - Pennsylvania offers the Pocono and Allegheny Mountains, the Civil War battlefield of Gettysburg, and Lancaster County, famous for its Amish communities of German origin who have rejected technological progress. The Amish have accepted tourism on their own terms, but it nevertheless poses a threat to their traditional way of life.

The coastal resorts. These include the Hamptons on Long Island, Atlantic City and Cape May in New Jersey, and Ocean City in Maryland. Although some resorts aimed for exclusivity, Atlantic City in particular was the creation of the railroad and developed to meet the needs of the growing numbers of industrial workers. In the 1920s the resort achieved fame for its event attractions, such as the Miss America beauty pageant. After the Second World War however fashions changed as alternative destinations such as Florida became more accessible, and Atlantic City entered a long period of stagnation. The resort's fortunes changed in the late 1970s, following the decision of the state government to legalise gambling. Its casinos now attract more visitors than those of Las Vegas, although their length of stay tends to be much shorter. Atlantic City's other main attraction is the elevated *boardwalk* (promenade) along the beach.

The South

The South is the most distinctive region of the USA, although its boundaries are difficult to define. Many regard the Ohio River and the Mason-Dixon Line separating Virginia from Pennsylvania as the northern limit. We can regard the South as having these features:

● A climate characterized by long sultry summers, short mild winters and abundant rainfall;
● The importance given by Southerners to the American Civil War (1861–1865), in which the Confederacy, made up of eleven slave-holding states was defeated in its attempts to secede from the USA;
● The presence of a large Black minority, who for a century after the Civil War continued to suffer from many forms of discrimination;
● A lifestyle which is more traditional, family-orientated, and religion-based than other regions of the USA. The strength of fundamentalist Christianity explains the use of the term 'Bible Belt' for much of the region; and
● An economy in which areas of dynamic growth and prosperity – the so-called 'New South' – contrast with pockets of rural poverty.

The heritage of the era before the Civil War, often highly romanticized, is an important part of the South's appeal for tourists, usually focusing on the plantation houses of the former slave-owners. Of wider significance is the contribution the region has made to literature and popular music, including jazz, country and western, rhythm and blues, gospel etc. The South is also well endowed with recreational resources which include:

● Large areas of forest, particularly in the Southern Appalachians;
● The wetlands of the coastal plains, such as the Okefenokee Swamp in southern Georgia, and the *bayous* of the Mississippi Delta, that provide a unique refuge for wildlife;
● A number of large man-made lakes providing facilities for water sports. These are a legacy of the hydro-electric power projects carried out by the federal government to boost the region's economy, following President Roosevelt's New Deal in the 1930s;
● The abundance of golf courses, particularly in the hilly, well-wooded Piedmont zone between the Appalachians

and the coastal plains. Pinehurst in North Carolina and Augusta in Georgia are the most popular golfing resorts; and
● The barrier islands of the Atlantic and Gulf coasts provide many fine beaches. Some have been developed as resorts – Hilton Head Island is one example – while others such as Cape Hatteras and Cumberland Island are preserved from development by federal and state governments.

We can divide the South for tourism purposes into a number of sub-regions, starting with Virginia.

Virginia was the first English colony in the New World. It played a major role in the struggle for independence – George Washington and Jefferson were both Virginians. During the American Civil War Richmond, less than 200 kilometres from Washington D C, was the capital of the Confederacy. Not surprisingly, heritage attractions play an important role. They include:

● George Washington's home at Mount Vernon;
● The Civil War battlefield site at Fredericksburg;
● 'The Historic Triangle', consisting of Jamestown – site of the first English settlement; Yorktown and Williamsburg, the capital of Virginia in colonial times. Of these Williamsburg is the most popular, and it has become a role model for similar attractions in other countries, due to its meticulous attention to detail; and
● The western part of the state includes the scenic Blue Ridge Mountains and the Shenandoah Valley National Park. All of these attractions are within easy reach of Washington.

The South-east consists of Georgia and the Carolinas, states which have shown remarkable economic growth since the 1950s.

● Atlanta is the main conference venue of the South-east with its modern hotels and excellent communications. As a major hub its airport is second only to Chicago in terms of domestic traffic and is growing in importance as an international gateway – one of the main reasons it was chosen as the venue for the 1996 Olympics. As a major centre for finance and broadcasting, Atlanta is a symbol of the 'New South'. The city also has important associations with Martin Luther King and the Civil Rights movement of the 1960s. Other attractions include:

– 'Underground Atlanta' – a project to revive the decaying inner city;
– the 'World of Coca Cola' museum celebrating the city's best-known product; and
– Stone Mountain – reputedly the world's largest granite monolith.

The seaports of Savannah and Charleston have based their tourism industries on the heritage of the Old South.

Charleston attracts a large number of foreign as well as domestic tourists to its well-preserved 'ante-bellum' (pre-Civil War) mansions, with garden tours being especially popular. Strict zoning regulations ensure that the tourist facilities are kept separate from the historic district of Old Charleston.

The Southern Appalachians, a series of forest covered ranges separated by deep valleys rise to the north of Georgia and to the west of North Carolina, accounting for most of Tennessee and Kentucky. In the more remote mountain valleys the persistence of craft industries is a legacy of the old pioneering days. Gatlinburg and Cherokee, on the fringes of the much-visited Smoky Mountains National Park, are examples of rural communities that have exploited this heritage with a proliferation of tasteless souvenir shops and inappropriate 'attractions'. To the west of the mountains lie the fertile Nashville Basin and the 'Bluegrass Country' of Kentucky – an area noted for its bourbon distilleries and equestrian sports. Kentucky also boasts the world's most extensive cave system in the Mammoth Cave National Park. In Tennessee, Nashville and Memphis rank among the most important tourist centres in the South:

● Nashville is widely regarded as the 'capital' of the country and western music industry. This is showcased in the Grand Old Opry auditorium and a number of theme parks in the area, but many find that the clubs and bars in 'Music Row' provide a more authentic experience.
● Memphis is particularly rich in musical traditions, focusing on the historic district of Beale Street, known as the 'birthplace of the blues'. However the most popular attraction is undoubtedly Graceland, visited by Elvis Presley fans from all over the world.

The Deep South usually refers to the states of Alabama, Mississippi and Louisiana, where Southern traditions are strongest. Tourism is of particular importance to Louisiana, where the economy has been affected by the fall in oil prices. The cultural heritage of French and Spanish rule is a major part of its appeal, especially the spicy cuisine.

● New Orleans is a major port on the Mississippi River and ranks among the five most popular cities visited by foreign as well as American tourists. Much of the city lies below river level, and is protected by high artificial banks or *levees*. Tourists are mainly attracted to the historic core of the city, known as the Vieux Carré or the French Quarter, focused on Bourbon Street and St Louis Cathedral. New Orleans has a long-established reputation for entertainment and gambling, but its tourism industry is also firmly based on conventions and sporting events. The city's fame as the birthplace of jazz appeals to many tourists, and the annual Mardi Gras carnival is one of the USA's most popular event attractions. The Mississippi's historical role as a major transport artery is

recalled in the sternwheeler steamboats that are now used for short river cruises.
● Other tourist centres include Lafayette for visiting 'Cajun country', Natchez, famed for its pre-Civil War plantation houses, and the beach resorts of Gulfport and Biloxi.

The Ozarks in Arkansas and southern Missouri are similar in many respects to the Appalachians. Tourism centres on the spa resort of Hot Springs and the small town of Branson, which boasts no less than 40 theatres featuring big-name performers in the music industry. This success is difficult to explain in resource terms, but it is clearly demand-led, with most of the 7 million annual visitors arriving from other parts of the South and the Mid-West.

Florida

Although the northern part of the state – particularly the 'Panhandle' west of Tallahassee is typically 'Southern', most of Florida is quite different from the rest of the South, in the following ways:

● The scale of its tourism industry, with a constant flow of visitors all year round;
● Retired people from the northern states make up a high percentage of its population; and
● The influx of Cuban immigrants to southern Florida since 1960, who have largely made Miami a Spanish-speaking city and effectively the financial centre of Latin America.

Florida is among the world's leading holiday destinations, with an annual income from tourism exceeding Spain's receipts from its foreign visitors. Orlando alone received over 35 million visitors a year during the late 1990s, as the world's 'theme park capital'. At the beginning of the twentieth century Florida was largely wilderness, one of the least developed and most sparsely populated regions of the USA. Tourism was to change all that, along with the development of large-scale agriculture, and the aerospace industry after the Second World War. The population grew from 2.7 million in 1950 to more than 12 million in the late 1990s. This growth has put enormous pressure on the water resources and fragile eco-systems of the Florida Peninsula, which is low-lying and of limestone formation.

The great majority of Florida's visitors are Americans, mainly from the states east of the Mississippi, and Canadians. Overseas tourists come mainly from Latin America countries and from Western Europe, where the UK is the leading market for air-inclusive holidays. Florida's success can be attributed to its subtropical climate, a coastline of white sandy beaches, and not least, to a major investment by the private sector in sports facilities, theme parks and other man-made attractions. Florida is readily accessible, with domestic air services to all parts of the USA and three international airports – Miami, Orlando and

Tampa. The main east coast highway (US 1) brings the Atlantic coast resorts within the reach of the family motorist living in the cities of the Eastern Seaboard.

Florida originated as a winter destination for wealthy Americans in the 1890s, with the opening of hotels in the old Spanish town of St Augustine. By the 1920s, with the extension of the railroad, Palm Beach – catering exclusively for the wealthy, and Miami Beach, for those a little less affluent – had been established on barrier islands off the Atlantic Coast. Since the 1950s, with the vast improvement in road and air transport, Florida has broadened its appeal to become a summer destination within reach of the majority of Americans. However the southern third of the state has retained its image as a winter haven for Northerners and Canadians, and this is reflected in lower hotel prices during the summer months.

In the south-east of Florida a string of resorts has developed, the most important being Palm Beach, Fort Lauderdale and Miami Beach. Of these:

- Fort Lauderdale is known as the 'Venice of Florida', with its extensive marina facilities. During the spring vacation the resort caters for an influx of fun-seeking college students.
- Miami Beach with its concentration of high-rise accommodation suffered from a period of stagnation in the 1960s and 1970s with an ageing clientele and falling property values. It has since restored its Art Deco hotels, reclaimed its beachfront and re-invented its image as a centre of fashion.
- The city of Miami – (as distinct from Miami Beach) is primarily a business centre with a population of well over 2 million. Miami Airport is the major gateway to the Caribbean islands and the countries of Central and South America, while the port of Miami is the base for most Caribbean cruises.
- The Florida Keys – a chain of coral islands to the south of Miami – provide ideal opportunities for scuba diving. Key West, with its Hemingway associations, is the most developed tourist centre.

The development of tourism on such a large scale has created problems. Many of the hotels and condominiums have been built so close to the sea that the beaches have been badly eroded, while a great deal of the best recreational land has been bought up as sites for private homes. The demand for water by large-scale agriculture and the residents of Greater Miami has endangered the unique wetland ecosystem of the Everglades.

The south-west of Florida along the Gulf coast is much less developed, with the exception of the Tampa Bay area. The most important resorts are St Petersburg – one of America's largest retirement centres, Sarasota, and Clearwater, each catering for different markets. Further south, Naples and Fort Myers provide less expensive self-catering accommodation.

The beaches of the northern Gulf coast cater for summer visitors from Alabama and Georgia rather than foreign tourists, with Panama City being the clear favourite. Another important recreational resource in this part of Florida are the hundreds of crystal-clear freshwater springs underlying the surface. Some of these have been developed as secondary attractions, a notable example being Weeki Wachee Springs with its 'mermaid show'.

Central Florida is the fastest growing area, thanks largely to the success of Disneyworld since its opening in 1971. By 1985 this theme park had already received 200 million visitors – a world record for any attraction. Like Disneyland in California, it consists of five themed areas, but the development is on a much larger scale. Disneyworld is a self-contained resort with its own hotels and transport system, and many see in it a model for tourism in the future. In 1983 it was joined by the Epcot Center and later by Disney MGM Studios. Unlike the old fairground-style attractions, the Disney theme parks provide a clean, safe – some would say sanitized – environment for families, aim for very high service standards, and they are at the cutting edge of the new technology. The advent of Disneyworld does not appear to have taken business away from pre-existing attractions, such as the Cypress Gardens water park, and in fact its success has encouraged other leisure projects. The main impact has been on Orlando – a medium-sized town noted only for its citrus industry prior to 1971, but now a major international gateway. The other major attraction in Central Florida is the NASA space research centre at Cape Canaveral.

The Mid-West

In contrast to Florida, this region, with its cold winters and hot humid summers, is a tourist-generating area and a zone of passage rather than a destination. Lying to the west of the Appalachians and south of the Great Lakes, the Mid-West is one of the world's most productive agricultural areas. From the air the landscape from Iowa to Ohio appears like a huge chessboard, with fields, roads and settlements laid out on a regular grid pattern. Further north in Wisconsin, Minnesota and Michigan, the scenery is much more diverse with innumerable lakes and landforms resulting from past glaciation, and large areas of forest. The Great Lakes themselves are a major attraction; there are fine beaches along the southern shores of Lakes Michigan and Huron, while Lake Superior, the largest and deepest, has a shoreline of spectacular cliffs. The state of Michigan has a well-established tourism industry based on these resources. The resorts cater mainly for the demand from the region's cities, notable examples being Lake Geneva 30 kilometres from Chicago and Kensington, which serves Detroit. In winter large areas of Minnesota and northern Wisconsin are set aside for snowmobile trails, while Upper Michigan provides facilities for skiing.

Some of the cities of the Mid-west are important cultural as well as business centres, including:

- Detroit – still the world's leading city for motor vehicle manufacturing, although it suffered severely from the recession in the 1980s and became a byword for urban decay. At nearby Dearborn Henry Ford revolutionized transport and tourism with the Model T, and later founded Greenfield Village as an open-air museum of small-town America prior to the advent of the automobile.
- Cleveland offers the Rock n' Roll Hall of Fame, mainly because this industrial city boasts some of the largest audiences for this type of music; an example of an attraction based on demand.
- Chicago can claim to be the transportation centre of the USA and is its second largest city. O'Hare Airport is the world's busiest, the city is a major rail terminal, and despite its distance from the sea it is also a port – thanks to the St Lawrence Seaway. Chicago is renowned for its architectural achievements – particularly those associated with Frank Lloyd Wright and Mies Van de Rohe. Its many cultural attractions include the Museum of Science and Industry and the Art Institute. As a commercial centre it has excellent facilities for conventions and trade fairs. The city is also a major sports venue and its recreational facilities include 24 kilometres of public beaches, yacht marinas and parks along the shores of Lake Michigan. The popular perception of Chicago however owes more to its reputation for gangsterism in the Prohibition era of the 1920s and early 1930s, an image which the city has tended to downplay although it appeals to many visitors.
- Indianapolis with its motor racing circuit, Milwaukee and its breweries, St Louis – 'the gateway to the West' – each has a particular appeal for tourists.

The West

The West is defined by American geographers as the part of the USA lying beyond the 100th meridian, where the climate becomes too dry in most years to support arable farming and ranching is more significant. Most of this vast region is sparsely populated and its appeal for tourism is based on the 'great outdoors', and the heritage of the frontier. This has been evoked in countless 'western' movies, which have also made the extraordinary landscapes of the region familiar to millions the world over. The West contains not only most of the national parks but also the great majority of the Indian reservations where the Native American way of life continues to flourish. Tourism ranks as the most important employer in four western states – Colorado, Nevada, New Mexico and Wyoming – and is in second place in five others. Because of its extent we need to divide the West into a number of sub-regions as follows:

- **The High Plains** stretching from Oklahoma to North Dakota. This was the setting of the 'dustbowl' of the 1930s and is often afflicted by extreme weather events such as tornadoes. It is for the most part relatively featureless. One major exception is the granite Black Hills of South Dakota that rise abruptly from the surrounding prairies. The famous sculptures of Mount Rushmore are located in this area, along with the Crazy Horse Memorial commemorating the Indian resistance led by the Sioux chief of that name. Another tourist attraction is the former mining town of Deadwood – notorious in 'Wild West' mythology. Further south in Nebraska the Scotts Bluff National Monument was one of the landmarks on the trail of the covered wagons that carried millions of pioneers westward during the nineteenth century.
- **The Rocky Mountains** form a barrier 2,000 kilometres in length, 500 kilometres wide, and reaching a height of 4,000 metres. They are in fact a series of ranges separated by a number of enclosed basins. Winters provide dry 'powder' snow for skiing in the mountains of Idaho – where Sun Valley was developed in the 1930s – and in Colorado, where Aspen, Vail and other resorts became established in the 1950s. These are easily reached from the gateway city of Denver. Aspen in particular has a fashionable reputation and hosts an all-year programme of cultural events. Wyoming boasts two world-class national parks – the Tetons with their glaciated landscapes, and the better-known Yellowstone which contains many remarkable geothermal features. A touring circuit 237 kilometres in length provides access to the popular sites – the Yellowstone Falls, Mammoth Hot Springs, and Old Faithful – the most famous of the 200 or so geysers. These parks also provide a refuge for wildlife, notably bears, buffalo, antelope, elk and beaver. The National Parks Service has aroused controversy by introducing wolves to Yellowstone, and using controlled forest fires to create a more balanced ecosystem. Further to the north, Montana is less visited. It contains a number of old mining towns, forests and ranchlands, and the lake and mountain scenery of the Glacier National Park.
- **The South-West** is distinguished by its cultural heritage as well as its climates and scenery. The whole of this region, along with Texas and California was once part of the Spanish Empire and passed briefly to Mexico before its acquisition by the United States in 1848. Most of the South-West is desert 'basin and range' country with a sparse cover of sage brush and mesquite vegetation, or consists of high plateaus dissected by deep gorges or canyons. The tourist appeal of the region is based on these features:
  - The warm, dry, sunny climate, that has long attracted winter visitors and a growing number of retired people to cities such as Phoenix and Tucson;
  - The facilities for water-based recreation, unusual in a desert region, in Lakes Powell, Mead and Havasu.

These were in fact created by the damming of the Colorado River in the 1930s for power generation and irrigation projects;

- *Dude ranches* providing the tourist with accommodation, riding expeditions, and the opportunity to sample the cowboy lifestyle. Many communities also hold rodeos, where professionals display the horsemanship and other traditional skills associated with cattle ranching; and

- A wealth of scenic attractions, including for example Monument Valley – a much photographed group of *mesas* – (flat topped landforms formed by erosion) and the lesser-known Bryce and Zion Canyons in Utah. However the most visited attraction is the world famous Grand Canyon in Arizona. Here the Colorado River has cut a gorge almost 2,000 metres deep in the sedimentary rocks of the Colorado Plateau. The vast majority of the Canyon's 5 million annual visitors, arriving by car, coach and train, do not stray far from the tourist facilities on the South Rim. Flightseeing tours give some idea of the immensity of the Canyon, but for a true appreciation it needs to be explored on foot or by mule, camping overnight. Another alternative is to take part in one of the white-water rafting expeditions organized by tour operators.

- The Indian heritage. Arizona and New Mexico have large communities of Native Americans, notably the Pueblo and the Navajo. Archaeological investigations at the Mesa Verde National Park provide evidence of an advanced culture in the form of cliff dwellings many centuries before the arrival of Spanish missionaries and colonizers. Indian handicrafts are much in demand and tourist accommodation is available on some reservations. Indian traditions have influenced white Americans seeking alternative, more holistic lifestyles. However tourism may prove to be a threat as well as an opportunity to communities already under pressure, with levels of unemployment and alcohol abuse well above the national average.

- The heritage of the 'Wild West'. In the late nineteenth century the region's rich mineral resources supported thriving mining communities, which have now become 'ghost towns'. Some of these have been restored, notably Tombstone in Arizona, scene of the shoot-out at the OK Corral.

- Las Vegas provides 'the total leisure experience'. The tourism industry of Nevada is a special case, thanks to this state's liberal attitudes to marriage and divorce and above all to gambling, which elsewhere in the USA was illegal for most of the twentieth century. At the same time, the state authorities have exercised some control over the gambling industry, which is often associated with sleaze and organized crime. There are two major centres – Reno, which is more accessible from San Francisco, and Las Vegas, by far the most popular, which is easily reached by car from Los Angeles. Its airport – McCarran International – is linked to all major cities in the USA and a growing number of foreign countries. Despite its desert location Las Vegas has developed rapidly since the 1940s, sustained by power generated from the Boulder Dam on the Colorado River. It is now a major city of half a million inhabitants attracting 28 million visitors each year, where activity is centred on The Strip, a 6 kilometre long boulevard flanked by casinos and large hotels. The enormous revenues from the casinos have made Las Vegas the 'world's entertainment capital'. Nevertheless since the 1990s Americans can gamble in many places outside Nevada, including Indian reservations and Mississippi riverboats. By then the city had already re-invented itself as a family resort, by massive investment in theme parks, shopping malls and museums, while also going upmarket with luxury hotels and golf courses. Some see in Las Vegas the tourism of the future, in which themed hotels provide a virtual risk-free substitute for a real destination or an imagined past. The first themed hotel was Caesar's Palace in the 1960s based on Ancient Rome (as interpreted by Hollywood). Since then, advances in technology have made it possible to replicate a volcanic eruption (The Mirage); a naval battle (Treasure Island); and a foreign destination (Venice).

Two other tourist centres in the South-West deserve specific mention, both very different in character from Las Vegas:

- Santa Fe is the historic capital of New Mexico, with a well-preserved Spanish-Indian heritage of adobe buildings and traditional handicrafts. Large numbers of artists have been attracted to the city and nearby Indian communities such as Taos; and

- Salt Lake City is both a business and religious centre, where the Mormon Church plays a dominant role (hence most of Utah is 'dry'). Visitors are attracted to the Mormon Tabernacle and the Family History Library, which contains the world's largest collection of genealogical records. The Wasatch Mountains provide first class ski facilities, explaining why Salt Lake City was chosen as the venue for the 2002 Winter Olympics. The Great Salt Lake has been used for attempts on the world land speed record.

Texas

For historical reasons, the 'Lone Star State' is as much part of the South as it is of the West, while its closeness to Mexico is reflected in its food, architecture and music. Texas has a booming economy that has generated a considerable volume of business travel to its major cities. Dallas is a major financial and distribution centre, while the neighbouring city of Fort Worth takes pride in its cattle industry heritage. Houston is noted for its oil and aero-space industries, where the major attractions are the Space Center, the Astrodome – the world's largest covered sports facility – and the Astroworld theme park. The fine beaches of the Gulf coast are within easy reach, notably those of Galveston and Padre Island. Other tourist centres include Austin, the state capital with an important music-recording industry, and San Antonio which celebrates its 'Latin' traditions. The city's main tourist attraction is the Alamo, the old Spanish mission that played a major role in the Texan struggle for independence from Mexico.

California and the Far West

The West Coast, particularly California is much more populated, cosmopolitan and dynamic in its outlook than the interior. It faces the other countries of the Pacific Rim and is at the cutting edge of the new technology – 'Silicon Valley' around San Jose and the Boeing plant outside Seattle are just two examples. Since 1849, when gold was discovered near Sacramento, Americans have regarded California as the land of opportunity. It has long been the richest state, with a population that is extraordinarily mobile even by American standards. The 'Golden State' is renowned for its warm, sunny climate and the remarkable variety of its scenery. This includes lush farmlands, forests of giant redwood and sequoia, strange volcanic landforms, and the high peaks of the Sierra Nevada – contrasting dramatically with Death Valley, one of the lowest, driest and hottest locations on Earth. All these, and a wealth of man-made attractions, explain why California is the primary holiday destination for American families, and one of the most popular states for foreign tourists. However tourism is less important to the Californian economy than the engineering industries and agriculture, unlike the situation in Florida, where tourism is the main source of income.

There are important differences in climate between the Pacific coast, which is cooled by the California Current, and the Central Valley east of the Coast Ranges where summer temperatures frequently exceed 40°C. Northern California also has a generally cooler and wetter climate than the south, where conditions are ideal for outdoor recreation. Nevertheless California has its share of environmental problems. These include:

- The earthquakes associated with the San Andreas Fault and other lines of weakness in the Earth's crust. These destroyed San Francisco in 1906 and threatened Los Angeles in 1998;
- The devastating fires that occur in summer in the dry *chaparral* scrub, and the equally destructive floods and landslides affecting slopes cleared for development;
- The severe air pollution in Los Angeles which occupies a valley hemmed in by mountains. This can only be brought under control by stringent regulations aimed at curbing motor vehicle emissions; and
- The demands for water that may not be sustainable in the long term.

Tourism in California is mainly concentrated in the following areas:

- **Los Angeles**. 'LA' is not so much a city as a sprawling conurbation covering an area of 2,000 square kilometres and consisting of no less than 82 separate local authorities and many ethnic communities. It is held together by the most extensive freeway network in the USA, and this provides the only practical way of visiting the dispersed attractions. Los Angeles has grown to prominence on the basis successively of the citrus industry, oil, motion pictures, aerospace and music recording. The city's tourism industry was given a major boost by the 1984 Olympic Games. With the San Bernardino Mountains and the Mojave Desert at its backdoor, and with an extensive shoreline along the Pacific, Los Angeles offers a wide range of recreational opportunities. Malibu and Venice Beach have acquired worldwide fame for their surf culture, epitomizing the Californian obsession with youth and physical fitness. Southern California can claim to be the birthplace of the American theme park, the best-known being Disneyland which opened in 1955, but in this respect it now suffers by comparison with Florida. The glamorous image of Hollywood is a major draw for visitors, and some of the film studios have been transformed into tourist attractions. Even the desert interior has been affected by tourism due to its closeness to Los Angeles, and in some areas trail bikes and '*dune buggies*' have had a severe environmental impact. One of the most important resorts of Southern California is Palm Springs, an oasis of golf courses in the midst of the Mojave Desert.
- **San Francisco**. The 'City on the Bay' is very different from Los Angeles. It is relatively compact, with a good public transport system, and is widely regarded as the most scenic and 'European' of all North American cities. San Francisco has also acquired a reputation for tolerance of lifestyles that do not conform to the mainstream culture; it played a prominent role in the 'hippy' movement of the 1960s – centred in the district of Haight-Ashbury, and it has attracted a large gay community. The city developed after the 1849 gold rush as a major seaport on one of the world's finest natural harbours. Much of the waterfront is now devoted to tourism, restaurants and entertainment, notably at Fisherman's Wharf. Other major attractions include the largest Chinese community in North America, the famous 'cable cars' (actually nineteenth century trams), a flourishing theatre and arts scene, and the Golden Gate Bridge spanning the entrance to the harbour. The cold current offshore deterred would-be escapers from Alcatraz Island, and results in San Francisco having the lowest summer temperatures of any major city in the USA, often accompanied by fog.

Within easy reach of San Francisco are:

- The exclusive beach resorts of Carmel and Monterey;
- The wine producing area of the Napa Valley, including the spa town of Calistoga;
- The ski resorts around Lake Tahoe and the Sierra Nevada mountains;
- The Yosemite National Park with its spectacular waterfalls and sheer granite cliffs. Yosemite Valley is crammed to capacity at summer weekends; and
- The redwood forests to the north of San Francisco, reached by a scenic coastal highway.

- **San Diego** is the third gateway city to California, lying close to the Mexican border. The city is primarily a naval port, but visitors are attracted by an ideal climate and the excellent beaches such as those of La Jolla, with facilities for sailing and sport fishing.
- **Santa Barbara** deserves special mention, out of the many beach resorts of Southern California, for its attractive Spanish-style architecture. The city originated – like so many others in California – as a Spanish mission. However its buildings are not relics from colonial times but the result of a deliberate planning initiative following an earthquake in 1925.

The North-west

The other states of the Far West – Oregon and Washington – have been less affected by tourism. In fact the environmentally-conscious state government of Oregon has severely limited development along its coastline. The unspoiled national scenery provides the main appeal for tourists. Outstanding attractions include:

- Crater Lake, a perfect example of a volcanic caldera;
- The Olympic National Park, an area of heavy rainfall that supports dense temperate rain forests; and
- The Mount Rainier National Park, which boasts large numbers of glaciers, lakes and waterfalls. This forms part of the Cascades Range, which includes a number of active volcanoes such as Mount St Helens.

Portland and Seattle are the gateway cities to the North-west. Seattle has the advantage of an attractive coastal setting. One of its main landmarks is the Space Needle, erected for the 1962 World Fair. Seattle is also the main gateway to Alaska for visitors by sea.

Alaska

Alaska is physically separated from the 'lower 48' states of the USA by some of Canada's most difficult mountain terrain, and only the narrow Bering Strait – ice covered in winter – divides it from Russian Siberia. Before 1867 this vast territory was part of the Russian Empire and a few Orthodox churches in Sitka and other coastal towns are part of that heritage. To most Americans Alaska is the 'last frontier' – a wilderness image that has persisted since the 1898 goldrush. The gruelling Iditarod dog sled rally from Anchorage to Nome is an annual reminder of those pioneering days. Nowadays air transport is crucial to this sparsely settled region, and Alaska's main external links are also by air. Its major city, Anchorage, lies on the transpolar route from Europe to Japan. However there are alternative ways of reaching Alaska, namely:

- The Alaska Highway, constructed during the Second World War, remains the only practical overland route from Canada; and
- The Alaska Marine Highway System operates year-round ferry services from Prince Rupert in Canada to the coastal communities of southern Alaska as far west as Dutch Harbor in the Aleutians.

The south-east of Alaska has the greatest tourism potential, offering spectacular fjords, rugged mountain scenery, and some of the largest glaciers in the Northern Hemisphere. The climate is relatively mild but excessively rainy. A sheltered coastal waterway – the 'Inside Passage' – provides a route as far north as Glacier Bay for summer cruises operating out of Long Beach, San Francisco and Seattle. However the rapid expansion of cruise tourism in the 1990s has brought problems to the small coastal towns in the form of marine pollution – a sensitive issue ever since the *Exxon Valdez* oil tanker disaster – and overcrowding. Throughout Alaska ecotourism and adventure tourism are growing in popularity, bringing some economic benefit to the native Indian and Inuit (Eskimo) communities. In the interior the Denali National Park – boasting North America's highest mountain – is already experiencing visitor pressure despite its remote location, rigourous subarctic climate and lack of tourist facilities.

Canada

One of the world's largest countries, Canada exceeds the United States in area but has only a tenth of its population. In fact the great majority of Canadians occupy a narrow belt of territory lying within 200 kilometres of the United States border. About 80 per cent of the country is classified as wilderness – mainly coniferous forest and tundra – and Canada boasts some of the world's largest lakes and 15 per cent of its freshwater resources.

In economic and cultural terms Canada tends to be overshadowed by its powerful neighbour, and this together with a more northerly location, has resulted in an image problem. Canadian separateness is demonstrated by its political institutions, strict gun control laws, and by a number of heritage attractions commemorating French and

British rule, including resistance to United States expansion in the early nineteenth century. However Canada's quest for national unity is made problematic by the existence of two official languages, representing two different cultural traditions.

The demand for tourism

Domestic and international tourism together account for 5 per cent of Canada's gross domestic product and 10 per cent of employment. As early as 1929 tourism was a major earner of foreign exchange, and in 1934 the Canadian Travel Bureau was established under the Department of Commerce to carry out promotion abroad. However it is only since the late 1960s that the federal government in Ottawa has become directly involved. Marketing is carried out by the Canadian Tourism Commission (CTC) which is a partnership between the federal government and the domestic travel industry. The governments of the ten provinces and the three territories are also involved in product development and overseas promotion.

The majority of foreign tourists to Canada come from the United States, and less than 10 per cent arrive from European countries. Americans also account for the large volume of excursionists whose numbers fluctuate according to differences in prices on either side of the border and the strength of the two currencies. This does leave Canadian tourism vulnerable to a downturn in the US economy. The great majority of American tourists arrive by car, return frequently, and are attracted mainly by the recreational facilities of the Canadian countryside. Canada's cities are also perceived to be safe compared to those of the USA, the language and culture are familiar, and crossing the world's longest undefended border is an easy matter for Americans. Overseas visitors tend to spend much more per head than the Americans, the leading markets being the UK, France, Germany and Japan. Most overseas visitors arrive by air at Toronto or Montréal, and almost half of these stay primarily with friends and relatives in the cities.

The Canadian winter partly explains why Canadians have a high propensity to travel outside their own country, with around one third of the population taking a trip abroad in any one year. This, combined with a high travel frequency, results in a massive deficit in Canada's international tourism account. The American border states of New York, Vermont, Michigan and Washington are the most visited destinations. Florida is also popular with Canadians, particularly in winter, with many retired people spending several months either there or in Hawaii. This exodus of 'snowbirds' may well increase with the general ageing of the population, while the open skies agreement between the US and Canadian governments will favour a greater use of the airlines rather than travel by private car. Other destinations include Mexico, the Caribbean islands, Europe and East Asia. Most of the expenditure on foreign travel, especially to Europe, is generated by the more prosperous and urbanized provinces, such as Ontario, British Columbia and Manitoba. As in the United States, domestic tourism is far larger than inbound or outbound tourism. British Columbia and Prince Edward Island are the destinations most favoured by Canadian holidaymakers.

Tourism resources

Canada does not have such a wide range of resources for recreation as the USA, since it lies entirely outside the warm climate zone. Foreign tourists are attracted to the country's mountains, lakes and forests rather than its extensive coastline. Most of the national parks are situated in the more scenic western part of Canada. The Canadian Pacific Railway (CPR) was largely instrumental in their creation specifically as tourist attractions – hence the luxury hotels at such locations as Banff and Lake Louise in the Rockies. Until the National Parks Act of 1930, resource exploitation – including mining in some instances – took precedence over conservation. The provincial parks are more widely distributed, and while some provide many recreational facilities, others are less developed than the national parks.

The severity and length of winter – even most of southern Canada is snow-covered for at least three months of the year – is a constraint on tourism development. Canadians themselves participate in a wide-range of snow-based activities. Snowmobile trails thread the countryside, and many ski resorts have developed to meet domestic demand within reach of all the major cities. Some of the resorts in the Canadian Rockies and the Laurentian Mountains of Québec attract a growing international market. Canadian cities are well-equipped to meet the challenges of winter, and in some, underground shopping centres provide full protection from the weather.

Summers, at least in southern and western Canada, are warm enough for a wide range of outdoor activities, including beach tourism and water sports. Transport and equipment for fishing and hunting trips is provided by specialist *outfitters* in even the most remote areas of Canada. Boating and canoeing are especially popular in the many lakes and rivers of the Canadian Shield – the vast expanse of forest lying to the north of the Great Lakes and the St Lawrence River. Canada's waterways played a crucial role in the early development of the country. Unlike the French *voyageurs* and the Hudson Bay fur traders, today's canoeists have the advantage of lightweight equipment. The old canoe trails form the basis for a system of *heritage rivers*. This is a good example of co-operation between the public and private sectors in resource management; stakeholders include the federal government, provincial or territorial governments, the local communities – especially those of the

'First Nations' or native Indians, and tour operators. The activities of the users – anglers, campers and ecotourists as well as canoeists – are carefully monitored to avoid environmental damage.

Transport

In such a vast country transport is a major problem, and road vehicles have to be 'winterized' to cope with low temperatures for much of the year. As in the USA, the railways played a major role in opening up the western part of the country to settlement, and the scenic mountain areas to tourism. After the 1950s they faced severe competition from domestic air services. In 1972 the passenger services of the CPR and the state-owned Canadian National Railways (CNR) were combined under the banner of VIA Rail, an independent Crown corporation that is subsidized by the federal government. By the late 1980s scheduled train services had been drastically reduced on most routes with the exception of the Toronto–Montréal corridor. VIA Rail still provides a trans-continental service, but at a frequency of only three trains a week in either direction; however sightseeing tours by train are available in the Rocky Mountains in the summer months. The great majority of domestic trips are now undertaken by private car. Most of the major cities, from Vancouver to Halifax, are linked by the world's longest national road – the Trans-Canada Highway.

The regional setting for tourism

Ontario

Ontario is the most visited province, containing Canada's largest English speaking city, and easily reached by road from New York in the south and Michigan to the west. It has a third of Canada's hotel capacity and offers a wide range of accommodation, including the popular holiday homes known as 'cabins' or 'cottages'. Many of these are located in the Muskoka Lakes area north of Toronto. Most of the population of Ontario is concentrated in the fertile peninsula lying between three of the Great Lakes – Huron, Erie and Ontario. Relatively few live in the Canadian Shield to the north of Lake Superior – a vast area of granite outcrops separated by lakes and *muskeg* (swamps), and covered with forests of spruce and fir.

- Toronto is Canada's most cosmopolitan city, with a vibrant nightlife and cultural scene – a far cry from its staid reputation in the 1950s, when it was known as 'Toronto the Good'. Attractions include Ontario Place – a major waterfront recreation area; the CN Tower; the Ontario Science Centre – one of the first inter-active museums; and the Hockey Hall of Fame, celebrating Canada's national game.

- Ottawa as the federal capital attracts sightseers to its impressive Gothic-style Parliament Buildings, the National Gallery of Canada and other important museums.
- The Niagara area includes not only the famous water-falls, but also the resort of Niagara-on-the-Lake, famous for its theatre festival, and a popular wine route.
- Georgian Bay and the Algonquin Provincial Park offer large areas of unspoiled lake and forest scenery on the southern edge of the Canadian Shield.

Québec

Québec Province is culturally distinct from the rest of Canada, an island of French speakers in an English-speaking continent. Until the 1960s it was predominantly rural and traditional in outlook, but since that time there has been rapid economic growth, based largely on the province's huge resources of hydro-electric power. The great majority of the population live in a relatively narrow strip bordering the St Lawrence River. Even in southern Québec winters are much harsher than in southern Ontario, with heavy snowfalls.

- Montréal is Canada's largest city and the world's second largest French-speaking metropolis, with restaurants and *boites* (nightclubs) to match those of Paris. It vies with Toronto as the gateway to Canada, with two international airports – Dorval and Mirabel – and is a port on the St Lawrence Seaway linking the Atlantic to the Great Lakes. This has made Montréal a major financial centre. The 1967 World Exposition and the 1976 Olympic Games did much to improve the city's transport and recreation facilities. This includes Le Souterrain – an underground shopping area served by an efficient metro system, centred on Place Ville-Marie.
- Québec City is less cosmopolitan than Montréal and its historic core has preserved the ambience of eighteenth century France. Most of the tourist attractions are in the fortified Upper town, which is dominated by the Chateau Frontenac, a *grand hotel* built by the Canadian Pacific Railway. Québec is also famous throughout Canada for its Winter Carnival. The influence of Catholicism remains strong, as shown by the popularity of pilgrimages to the nearby shrine of St Anne de Beaupré.
- Downstream from Québec City are two scenic areas – the fjord-like Saguenay River – increasingly popular for whale-watching – and the picturesque Gaspé peninsula with its fishing villages.
- Ski resorts in Québec Province include Mont Tremblant in the Laurentian Mountains and Mount Orford in the Notre Dame Range.

The Atlantic Provinces

The provinces along the Atlantic seaboard of Canada are relatively poor, due to the decline of traditional industries such as fishing. International tourism is handicapped by the region's peripheral location and an indifferent climate.

● **Newfoundland**, consisting of the island of that name and the coast of Labrador, typifies these conditions. The climate is influenced by the cold Labrador Current – the Atlantic coast is called 'Iceberg Alley' for a reason! This results in the late arrival of spring, frequent fogs, and a short, cool summer. Hundreds of small fishing villages cling to the rocky coastline, where ecotourism in the form of bird-watching and whale-watching may provide an alternative livelihood. Newfoundland is the nearest part of North America to Europe and this was significant in the early days of trans-Atlantic communications; in the pre-jet era Gander Airport near St Johns was an important staging point. Coastal shipping services continue to play a major role.

● **Prince Edward Island**, the smallest of the three Maritime Provinces, enjoys a warmer climate and a flourishing tourism industry, although this caters mainly for the domestic market. The island's resources include fine sandy beaches, attractive countryside, golf courses and its literary associations – the town of Cavendish is the setting for *Anne of Green Gables*. The island now has a fixed link to the mainland.

● **Nova Scotia** offers a variety of coastal scenery, and an interesting French and Scottish cultural heritage. Tourism is based on a number of touring routes such as the Evangeline Trail, but some communities might well benefit from a greater influx of long-stay visitors. The capital Halifax is a major seaport with a marine heritage that includes its association with the *Titanic*. Louisbourg on Cape Breton Island is a former French fortress that has been restored as a 'living history' attraction.

● **New Brunswick** is less orientated toward the sea, although the Bay of Fundy is famous for its tides. The extensive forests and rivers of the interior attract hunters, anglers and canoeists.

The Prairie Provinces

The heartland of Canada consists of two provinces – Manitoba and Saskatchewan – that are mainly known for their vast wheat-growing prairies. Winters are comparable with those of Siberia, but Lake Winnipeg is a major focus for water sports during the short hot summers. Further north the prairies give way to forests, where fly-in camps and lodges provide accommodation for anglers. Although the scenery may be low-key, the region is culturally diverse, with large communities of Ukrainians, Germans and Icelanders that have retained the traditions of their homelands. Winnipeg is the main business and cultural centre of the region, followed by Regina, home of that world famous national institution, the Royal Canadian Mounted Police. The isolated community of Churchill on Hudson Bay – it cannot be reached by road – receives a brief influx of tourists each year to view the polar bears and other wildlife from the safety of *'tundra buggies'* – vehicles adapted to the marshy terrain.

The West

The provinces of Alberta and British Columbia offer some of the most spectacular scenery and wildlife to be found in North America. The Rocky Mountains contain no less than seven of Canada's national parks. Most of the tourism development is on the Alberta side, including:

● Banff National Park is the most popular, attracting 4 million visitors a year, mainly in the months of July and August. It contains two world famous resorts – Banff and Lake Louise. Banff was originally developed as a spa by the CPR on the basis of its hot springs and attracted a wealthy international clientele in the early part of the twentieth century. With the development of skiing after the Second World War it became an all-year resort, with a winter sports season lasting from November to May. It is now a major urban centre with attractions, restaurants, golf courses, and other facilities that often seem inappropriate to the setting and the national park ethos. Banff is also a cultural centre, offering important art and film festivals.

● Jasper National Park lies close to the Yellowhead Pass, the route across the Rockies followed by the CNR. Major attractions include the Columbia Icefield and Maligne Lake, both superb examples of glacial scenery. Outside the park boundaries, heli-skiing and heli-hiking allow access to the most remote mountain areas.

● Calgary is the gateway to the Canadian Rockies. It is also the centre for the ranching industry of south-western Alberta, hence the significance of the 'Stampede' – a world famous event attraction celebrating the cowboy lifestyle. The winter climate of this area is often affected by warm, dry *chinook* winds – similar to the *föhn* of the Alps – that can raise temperatures by as much as 25°C. This would be disastrous for the ski resort operations were it not for the availability of computerised snow-making systems covering most of the pistes. As it turned out, Waterton Lakes near Calgary was the venue for the 1988 Winter Olympics.

● Edmonton has long been regarded as the gateway to the Canadian North. Its modern prosperity is largely based on the oil industry, and the city boasts the largest shopping mall in North America – Edmonton West – offering a range of themed attractions.

The coastal region of British Columbia offers many attractions, including:

● A climate characterized by the mildest winters of Canada – with temperatures 20°C higher than in Labrador at the same latitude – and in the south, warm summers with abundant sunshine;

- A spectacular coastline backed by mountains, deeply indented with fjords, and with many offshore islands;
- Diverse ecosystems, including the rainforests of Vancouver Island, and rivers teeming with salmon; and
- The Indian heritage. The abundance of natural resources allowed the Haida of the Queen Charlotte Islands and other coastal tribes to develop a sophisticated culture. This was severely disrupted by contact with Europeans, but the totem pole survives as the best-known example of native skills.

The main tourist centres are Vancouver and Victoria:

- Vancouver is Canada's third largest city and a major gateway to the East Asia–Pacific Region. This makes the city particularly appealing for visitors from Japan, Hong Kong and other Asian countries. The superb natural setting means that sailing, golf and skiing can be enjoyed on the same day.
- Victoria, on Vancouver Island is a major holiday resort and retirement area, with a strong English ambiance that makes it appealing to American tourists from the West Coast.

The interior of British Columbia comprises high mountain ranges, broad plateaux, and deep, canyon-like valleys. The climate is much drier than the coast, with cold winters but very warm summers. This is particularly true of the sheltered Okanagan Valley, where sailing and water skiing are popular at the lake resorts of Penticton and Kelowna. On the Fraser River visitors can experience white-water rafting or pan for gold near former mining towns. Excellent winter sports facilities are available in the Selkirk Mountains at Kimberley, and at Kamloops, heart of BC's cattle-ranching country.

The North

Although most Canadians regard all of Hudson Bay, Labrador and northern Québec as being part of the North, we define it as comprising the Yukon, the Northwest Territories and Nunavut, which lie north of 60° latitude. Nunavut presents special problems for tourism development, that are investigated in the case study, but these also exist to a lesser degree in the other two territories.

- **The Yukon Territory** is more accessible than other parts of the Canadian North. Its tourism industry is mainly based on the heritage of the 1898 gold rush, Canada's equivalent of the 'Wild West' – at Dawson City and Whitehorse. The Kluane National Park provides limited facilities for adventure tourism.
- **The Northwest Territories** (NWT) caters more for expeditions, although there is road access to Yellowknife and Inuvik. The problems caused by even a limited amount of tourism are becoming evident in the region's

main natural attraction – the Nahanni National Park Reserve. This World Heritage Site includes the spectacular Virginia Falls and an extensive karst limestone system – unusual in such high latitudes. Although this remote area is only accessible by air, it is already experiencing severe impacts, resulting from the growth of white-water rafting on the South Nahanni River.

Greenland (Kalaallit Nunaat)

A permanent ice cap thousands of metres thick covers 84 per cent of this huge Arctic island, so that the sparse, mainly Inuit population live in scattered communities along the western and south-eastern coasts. A self-governing Danish territory, Greenland is more closely linked to Denmark and Iceland by air and shipping services than it is to northern Canada, although this may change. It faces similar problems to Nunavut and the NWT, such as a rapidly growing population and economic dependence on a few primary products. Greenland's main tourism resource is the spectacular fjord and mountain scenery, with glaciers reaching the sea to spawn a myriad icebergs. There are opportunities for outdoor adventure, and the ruins of abandoned Viking settlements – evidence of climate change over the last millennium. Tourism is however limited by the extreme unreliability of the weather, even in summer, and the expense of transportation, which is mainly by helicopter services.

Summary

North America is a vast continent of scenic and climatic contrasts. With the exception of northern Canada and Greenland it is highly developed economically. Urban landscapes, lifestyles, transport systems, and tourist facilities are broadly similar throughout both the United States and Canada, and there is a considerable volume of travel between the two countries. The main problem for the overseas visitor is the great distances involved, but this has been largely overcome by excellent highways and an extensive network of air services, with rail transport now playing only a minor role. Tourist facilities have been developed mainly to serve the enormous domestic market, and it is only recently that federal, state and provincial governments have become directly involved in encouraging inbound tourism. North Americans spend heavily on travel abroad, with the result that Canada continues to have a large deficit on its international tourism account. Overseas visitors to the United States and Canada are attracted mainly to the cities for broadly cultural reasons, and there is a large VFR market. However Florida is regarded mainly as a beach and theme park destination. Both the United States and Canada have realized the importance of conservation and their state controlled national parks and forest reserves are probably the world's finest. The native peoples of North America, marginalized in the past, are now taking a more active share in tourism development. The private sector of tourism is very much larger than the state sector, and is responsible for all profit-making enterprises; sports facilities and theme parks are particularly important.

Case study

New York City

Introduction

New York City (NYC) is a major tourist destination on the world stage, attracting 34 million visitors a year in the late 1990s. Tourism is of major significance to the city's economy, generating $US20.6 billion in revenue and providing almost 250 000 jobs. In spite of not being the national capital – or even the capital of the state of New York (which is Albany) – New York is the country's primary city in many other respects. It is for example the USA's leading financial centre and conference venue, and it is also a major centre for fashion and the arts. Until the 1960s it was the unchallenged 'gateway to America' and the Statue of Liberty at the entrance to New York Harbour was for most immigrants and visitors their first sight of the New World. Nowadays, few visitors arrive by sea, but New York remains the leading point of entry for tourists from Europe. New York plays an international role as the seat of the United Nations Assembly, while events in Wall Street have an even greater impact on the world economy.

New York stands on one of the world's finest harbours, created by the confluence of the Hudson and East Rivers, which also divide the city into a number of peninsulas and islands. The essential links in the transport network are provided by tunnels, bridges and ferries; the best known of these are Brooklyn Bridge, the Staten Island Ferry and George Washington Bridge. The city, as distinct from the metropolitan area in New Jersey and New York State, consists of five boroughs, spread over almost 500 square kilometres and with a population of 7.4 million. The five boroughs are:

1 Manhattan – the island between the Hudson, Harlem and East Rivers, which is one of the most densely populated and ethnically mixed areas in the world. High land costs have resulted in the townscape of skyscrapers, particularly in the 'downtown' commercial area south of Central Park. Although Manhattan accounts for only 7 per cent of New York's land area, it is the main focus of tourist activity.

2 Brooklyn and Queens on Long Island also contain some well-defined ethnic neighbourhoods.
3 The Bronx is mainly known for its run-down urban areas but also contains Yankee Stadium – the home of baseball – and the New York Botanical Gardens.
4 Staten Island in contrast is a quiet residential area.

New York's appeal is due to its cultural diversity and its dynamism as 'the city that never sleeps'. The climate, however, is less attractive. Summers are notoriously hot and humid, with episodes of high air pollution, while winters are cold and Central Park is often blanketed with snow. More than most cities, New York has suffered from a negative image of urban decay, sleaze and violent crime. In fact, it is by no means the most dangerous city in the USA, and a policy of zero tolerance by the civic authorities has greatly reduced the incidence of crime on the subway and in the streets, making most of New York safe for tourists.

Attractions

New York has a great variety of attractions, many of which are of world calibre. They include such famous landmarks as the Statue of Liberty and the Empire State Building, major cultural attractions in the fields of science, art and music, and a host of shopping, sport and entertainment facilities. Various offers are available such as the Culture Pass and the City Pass, allowing multiple visits to certain attractions. We can categorize New York's attractions as follows:

1 Historic monuments, such as Castle Clinton, Federal Hall, The Statue of Liberty and the Arch in Washington Square.
2 Cultural attractions such as the Metropolitan Opera House in the Lincoln Centre, Carnegie Hall, and some 150 museums, many of which are located along Fifth Avenue's Museum Mile. A selection of museums would include:
   (a) The Museum of Modern Art.
   (b) The Solomon R. Guggenheim Museum.
   (c) The Metropolitan Museum of Art.
   (d) The New Museum of Contemporary Art.
   (e) Ellis Island Immigration Museum.
   (f) Intrepid Sea-Air Space Museum.
   (g) The Museum of the City of New York.
   (h) Museum of Jewish Heritage.
   (i) American Museum of Natural History.
   (j) New York Hall of Science.
   (k) American Museum of the Moving Image.
3 The financial district centred on Wall Street attracts leisure tourists as well as business travellers. Attractions include the American Stock Exchange, the New York Stock Exchange and the Museum of American Financial History.

4 Sports venues include the Yankee Stadium, Shea Stadium, Flushing Meadows – home of the US Tennis Open – and the Madison Square Garden.

5 Recreational areas include:
   (a) Central Park, a beautifully landscaped area of 340 hectares in the heart of Manhattan. The park provides a wide range of activities and includes a Wildlife Center (formerly Central Park Zoo).
   (b) Coney Island was in the early part of the twentieth century, the popular beach area for New Yorkers, with an amusement park and other entertainment. Nowadays, it is mainly visited for the New York Aquarium.
   (c) The Bronx Zoo (officially the Bronx Wildlife Conservation Society) attracts more than 2 million visitors annually.

6 Architectural landmarks such as:
   (a) The Empire State Building, perhaps the best known 1930s skyscraper.
   (b) The Chrysler Building – distinguished by its art deco spire.
   (c) The World Trade Centre – a 1960s skyscraper – worth visiting for the view from the Top of The World Observation Deck.
   (d) The Rockefeller Centre – which includes Radio City Music Hall and the NBC Studio Tour.
   (e) The United Nations Assembly Building.

7 City districts with a strong identity – some of these are ethnic enclaves – for example:
   (a) Chinatown.
   (b) Little Italy.
   (c) Harlem – famous for its contribution to the development of jazz in the 1920s.
   (d) Spanish Harlem – an area occupied by Puerto Ricans and Spanish-speaking immigrants.
   (e) Greenwich Village and Soho on the other hand, are historic neighbourhoods, defined by their associations with artists, writers and craft industries.
   (f) Times Square, Restaurant Row and Broadway constitute New York's theatre district.
   (g) South Street Seaport – a section of New York's waterfront that has undergone extensive restoration, featuring historic ships, a maritime museum, shops and restaurants among its attractions.

8 Shopping attractions – shopping weekends to New York's Fifth Avenue stores, such as Macys', Bloomingdales, Saks Fifth Avenue, and Tiffany's, are becoming popular with the European market, encouraged by competitive air fares.

9 Restaurant attractions – New York offers cuisine from all over the world, and also a large number of themed restaurants.

10 A range of event attractions, the best known being the St Patrick's Day Processions.

Transport and accommodation

The main international air gateways to New York are:

- La Guardia (LGA) 13 kilometres to the east of midtown Manhattan, used mainly for domestic flights but with some services to Canada and Mexico
- John F Kennedy (JFK) 20 kilometres south-east of midtown Manhattan
- Newark (EWR) 26 kilometres to the south-west in New Jersey.

Domestic and charter carriers also use:

- MacArthur Airport
- Stewart International Airport (only international for livestock)
- Teterboro Airport
- Westchester County Airport.

Transfer buses, taxis and limousines, part of the extensive network of internal transport within the city and overseen by the Metropolitan Transportation Authority (MTA), serve the airports. Bus companies such as Gray Line and New York Apple Tours offer hop-on hop-off sightseeing circuits, and companies such as Circle Line or New York Waterway offer sightseeing river cruises. In addition there are rapid transit overland services and the New York underground railway system – the subway. The Staten Island ferry runs from Battery Park in Manhattan to Staten Island and offers views of the Statue of Liberty and the Manhattan skyline. The city has a number of well-known transport terminals such as Penn Station, Grand Central Terminal and the Port Authority bus station. Visitors can purchase passes which allow multiple rides on the public transport systems, though many visitors opt to travel around the city in one of the 12 000 famous yellow taxi cabs. New York also has a number of companies offering tailor-made walking tours and personal greeters can be organized to show visitors around the city.

New York City has a hotel capacity of some 65 000 rooms, mainly concentrated in Manhattan. Hotels range from budget to luxury in price, from boutique (small upmarket hotels of character) to themed hotels (on a particular period for example) and from suites to selfcatering apartments. Accommodation is at a premium, particularly in Manhattan, where annual occupancy rates exceed 80 per cent and hotel tariffs are higher than average for the USA.

Organization

The main tourist organization for New York City is the New York Convention and Visitors Bureau (NYCVB). The NYCVB is the city's official tourism marketing agency and has been in existence since 1935. It is a private, non-profit-making organization with a large membership of tourism businesses. It is very much marketing focused and as is clear from the name, sees the business and convention market as an important area for the City. The bureau's mission is 'to enhance New York City's economy through tourism development by marketing the City on a world-wide basis'. In this respect, the 'I love New York' marketing campaign of the 1980s was remarkably successful in turning round the city's negative image and generating a greater volume of visitors.

Demand for tourism

Out of New York's total estimated 34 million visitors annually:

- 6 million are international visitors
- over a half are day visitors.

New York is the number one destination for foreign visitors to the USA, ahead of Los Angeles, Miami and Orlando. In terms of market share, NYC receives over 20 per cent of the USA's international visitors. Canadians represent the largest group visiting New York with around 1 million visits, however, many of these are day visitors. In terms of staying visitors, the UK contributes the most to New York (over 15 per cent), followed by Germany and Japan (each with around 8 per cent), France, Brazil and Italy. Of course, much of this travel is visiting friends and relatives, given the very diverse ethnic mix of New York.

(Web site: www.nycvisit .com)

Case study

Nunavut: tourism in the Canadian Arctic

Introduction

In 1999 the Canadian government created a new territory – Nunavut – out of the Northwest Territories (NWT), and settled land claims to some 350 000 square kilometres with the Inuit people. This is a remarkable experiment in native self-government that may provide guidelines for indigenous peoples in other parts of the world, who are struggling to protect their lands and culture from exploitation by outside interests.

Nunavut – which means 'our land' in the Inuktitut language – is a vast, thinly populated and challenging wilderness that includes most of Canada's Arctic archipelago, and the tundra region known as the 'Barren Lands' lying between Hudson Bay and the Arctic Ocean. It covers an area of 1.9 million square kilometres – as large as Alaska and California combined – and yet contains only 26 000 inhabitants, widely dispersed in twenty-eight isolated communities (see Figure 23.1). The Inuit make up 85 per cent of the population, most of the rest being incomers since the 1950s from southern Canada. As the majority, the Inuit will gain political control of the territory and its potential wealth in mineral resources. Tourism also offers prospects for development, and it is a sector in which Inuit guides and 'outfitters', with their unrivalled knowledge of the country and skills in improvization, are already playing an important role.

As we saw in the cases of Lapland and Svalbard in Chapter 11, the Arctic regions are nowadays perceived as unspoiled wilderness areas, and visits there are part of the growing eco-tourism movement. This contrasts with the earlier view of the Arctic as a 'white hell', a grim test of endurance for expeditions seeking the North West Passage to Asia, or a route to the North Pole. Explorers like Peary and Amundsen, who were prepared to learn survival skills from the Inuit and adapt to the environment, were invariably more successful than those who carried their cultural baggage around with them, like the ill-fated Franklin expedition.

Tourists can now retrace these journeys in comfort and in a matter of a few days rather than the months or years it took the explorers, thanks to:

1 The accessibility brought about by air transport, especially Twin Otter charter aircraft, which are capable of landing on either ice or gravel airstrips.
2 Advances in cold-weather technology applied to clothing, equipment and shelter.
3 The ending of the Cold War, which has opened up areas of the Arctic formerly closed by Russia or the Western powers for strategic reasons. For example, it is now possible for tourists to cruise through the North West Passage from the Atlantic in summer as far as Provediniya on the Russian side of the Bering Strait. The Russians are also eager to share their technical expertise in ice navigation with Western tour operators in exchange for hard currency.

Tourism should also help to revive the culture of the Inuit as well as their economic well-being. As late as the 1950s, their age-old way of life was still based on the hunting of caribou and sea mammals for subsistence, although they had become tied economically to the Hudson Bay Company, who traded goods such as guns, tobacco and tea, in exchange for Arctic fox furs. Changes in fashion and the subsequent collapse in fur prices have resulted in the Inuit becoming much more

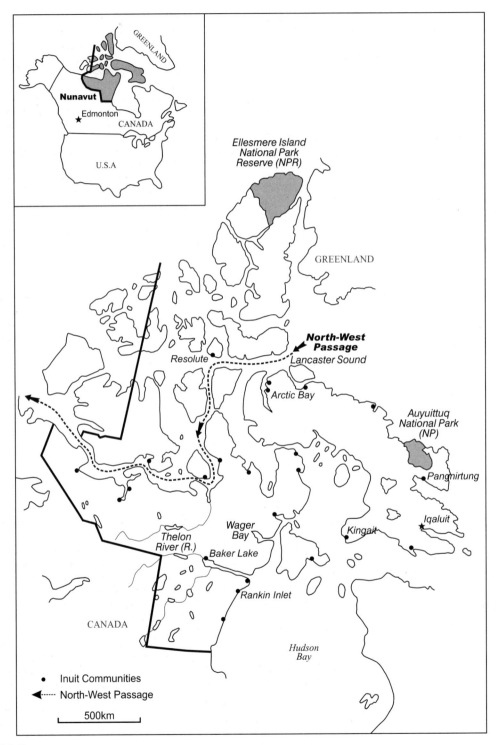

Figure 23.1 Nunavut

dependent on the social welfare programmes introduced by the Canadian government. Permanent settlements of 'identikit' wooden buildings replaced the skin tents used in summer, and the winter igloos. Dog teams have been largely superseded by 'skidoos' (supermobiles) that, in the words of one young Inuk 'are fast, don't eat meat, and don't stink' (quoted by Davis, 1998: 113). Nevertheless, the traditional image persists in the outside world, although the Inuit are no longer referred to as 'Eskimos' – the name given to them centuries ago by the Cree Indians, meaning 'eaters of raw meat' – now regarded as derogatory.

While the material improvements have made life less hazardous for the Inuit, they have suffered from a high degree of social dislocation due to the rapidity of the change from a nomadic Stone Age culture with a communal ethos, to one dominated by Western technology and value systems. The resulting social problems include a great deal of drug and alcohol abuse, and a suicide rate six times the Canadian average. A low level of education attainment also leaves Inuit communities vulnerable to manipulation by outside commercial interests. The birth rate is much higher than in southern Canada, posing a 'demographic time bomb' as more young people come on to the labour market with unrealistic expectations of what the new Nunavut can provide. All this has implications for the territory's economic development including its fledgling tourism industry.

Tourism resources

Although the Canadian explorer, Stefansson, described the Far North as the 'Friendly Arctic', Nunavut's rigorous climate, vast distances and forbidding terrain discourage independent travel. With seas, lakes and rivers frozen for eight months or more, and in the absence of any roads outside the main settlements, most tourist transport is by air. Overland transport by ATV (all-terrain vehicle) is much easier in late winter and spring, when the ground is snow covered, than in summer when the tundra becomes a mosquito-infested morass. Tourism development in Nunavut faces the following problems:

1 *High development costs* Building hotels on permafrost is expensive, as special provision has to be made for utilities and waste disposal. Businesses are also 60 per cent more expensive to operate than in southern Canada, due primarily to high transport costs. Since Nunavut has no agriculture or manufacturing industry, almost everything has to be brought in by supply ship during the brief Arctic summer, or airlifted at even greater expense.

2 *Limited accommodation* In 1998 there were only about 1400 bed-spaces in the entire territory, mainly in lodge-style accommodation. Even the capital

Iqaluit (Frobisher Bay), on Baffin Island, with less than 400 bed-spaces, had insufficient hotel capacity to accommodate guests for the inauguration ceremonies. More inexpensive bed and breakfast accommodation is in short supply, as most Inuit do not own their homes.

3 *Limited air transport* Although NWT Air and Canadian North operate scheduled services between the main communities in Nunavut and cities in southern Canada, interconnections between communities often involve a flight back to Iqaluit. This makes travel time-consuming and expensive. Airport delays are also frequent due to unpredictable weather throughout the year.

4 *Seasonality* Despite attempts to promote snow-based activities such as sledging, snow-mobiling and cross-country skiing in late winter and spring, most tourism takes place during the very short summer season.

5 *Cultural attitudes* The environmental sensibilities of Western tourists may be at variance with the attitudes of Inuit communities with their hunting traditions. In a society where nothing is wasted, what appear to be unsightly piles of garbage contain butchered carcasses and machine parts. The Inuit see hunting as an escape route from welfare dependency and a renewal of their close relationship with the land. This is generally accepted by the Canadian government, which has allocated hunting quotas to Inuit communities. What is more controversial is the fact that polar bear hunting tags are then sold to wealthy American tourists seeking trophies. In 1989, the Canadian government imposed a ban on seal hunting, following international pressure from environmentalists and animal lovers. One of the priorities of the new territorial government is to reverse this ban and find export markets for sealskin products in countries such as China.

We can summarize Nunavut's resource base for tourism as:

- a vast wilderness of tundra and glacial mountains, threaded by pristine lakes, rivers and fjords
- the wildlife of the tundra and the marine life – whales, narwal and walrus – of the Arctic seas
- the traditional culture of the Inuit, perfectly adapted to one of the world's harshest environments
- the heritage of polar exploration, particularly the quest for the North West Passage and the race for the North Pole.

Baffin Island

Baffin Island offers the largest share of the territory's attractions and amenities. It contains more than a third of Nunavut's inhabitants and the capital Iqaluit, which is set to grow as a regional hub for air services. Outfitters based in Iqaluit and other communities such as Pangnirtung and Arctic Bay, provide access to the following tourism resources:

1   The spectacular scenery of the eastern part of Baffin Island, with its serrated mountains, extensive glaciers and a rugged coastline deeply indented by fjords. This culminates in the Auyuittuq National Park, which attracts growing numbers of adventure-seeking tourists.
2   Other opportunities for adventure tourism include fishing for Arctic char in the island's lakes and rivers, and sea kayaking (the kayak was an Inuit invention). Wildlife tours focus on the coastal waters of Lancaster Sound, the summer habitat of vast numbers of migratory birds and whales.
3   Inuit communities such as Kingait (Cape Dorset) and Pangnirtung are centres for handicrafts such as soapstone carving and print making using local materials and traditional skills. These are marketed throughout Canada by a native-run co-operative, thus benefiting the local economy. The designs are popular with tourists, because they are inspired by Arctic wildlife and Inuit nostalgia for the past.

The Barren Lands of Keewatin

The Barren Lands of Keewatin, accessed from communities such as Rankin Inlet and Baker Lake, offer a different type of tourism experience. Here, the scenery is low key compared to eastern Baffin Island, but the effects of past glaciation are evident in a tundra landscape seamed with gravel-strewn eskers and pitted with countless lakes. Although the autumn migration of vast caribou herds is rarely seen nowadays, wildlife resources are abundant in the Thelon Game Sanctuary and around Wager Bay, where the Sila Lodge provides facilities for eco-tourism. The many rivers attract canoeists, although the risks are higher, with a season restricted to a few weeks of unpredictable weather, than in southern Canada.

The Ellesmere Island National Park Reserve

The Ellesmere Island National Park Reserve, situated in the northernmost part of Canada, some 800 kilometres from the North Pole, represents the extremely cold and dry climate conditions and glacial terrain characteristic of the High Arctic. Here, tourists number less than 100 annually, compared with the thousands visiting Baffin Island. This is mainly because access is limited to expensive charter flights from the airbase at Resolute Bay, the most northerly community on the scheduled air network, which lies 1100 kilometres to the south. Even a limited number of visitors may make a considerable impact on the fragile plant cover, which is extremely slow to regenerate, and on the animal life – including musk oxen and Arctic hare – which shows little fear of man in this remote location.

(Website at http://www.nunanet.com/nunatour)

24

Latin America and the Caribbean

LEARNING OBJECTIVES

After reading this chapter you should be able to:

1 Describe the major physical features and climates of Latin America and the Caribbean, and understand their importance for tourism.
2 Appreciate the significance of tourism to the economies of the Caribbean islands.
3 Appreciate the cultural heritage of Latin America and the Caribbean.
4 Assess the potential of South American countries as long-haul destinations.
5 Recognize the importance of adequate infrastructure and political stability in encouraging tourism development.
6 Recognize the potential for eco-tourism in many of the countries of the region.
7 Appreciate the importance of cruise tourism in the Caribbean.
8 Demonstrate a knowledge of the tourist regions, resorts, business centres and tourist attractions of Latin America and the Caribbean.

Introduction

Latin America is the collective name usually given to all the Spanish-, Portuguese- and French-speaking countries of the Western Hemisphere south of the USA/Mexico border. However this excludes the English- and Dutch-speaking countries, which share a similar environment and culture with their 'Latin' neighbours. In our definition Latin America refers to the mainland countries of Mexico, Central America and South America, as distinct from the island-states of the Caribbean.

Most of Latin America, and some of the Caribbean islands, were colonized by Europeans from the Iberian Peninsula in the sixteenth century, who imposed their language, religion and culture on the native Amerindians. As a result two-thirds of Latin America consists of sixteen Spanish-speaking republics, while Portuguese-speaking Brazil accounts for most of the remainder. The majority of the Caribbean islands, along with Belize and the Guianas, were colonized later, mainly by the British, the Dutch and the French. The European colonists imported slaves from West Africa to provide labour, and their descendants contribute a major ingredient to the cultural mix, particularly in Brazil and the Caribbean. The total population of Latin America and the Caribbean is well over 500 million and includes two of the world's mega-cities – Sao Paulo and Mexico City – each with about 20 million inhabitants. Most of the region is Roman Catholic, and religious festivals play an important role in the culture. However some of the Commonwealth Caribbean islands are strongly Protestant, while evangelical movements are challenging the dominance of the Roman Catholic Church in parts of Latin America.

Most Latin American and Caribbean countries are at the intermediate stage of economic development, with a few reaching the 'drive to maturity'. The 1990s have seen economic stability, halting the inflation that had characterized many countries in the region, and growing economic co-operation, in place of the protectionism of earlier decades. The most significant example is MERCOSUR, the common market of South America. Income growth has in turn encouraged business and leisure travel. Nevertheless most countries are still dependent on the export of minerals or cash crops, and economic growth has so far failed to benefit large sections of the population. There are usually great disparities in wealth between the major cities, that resemble those of Europe or North America, and the remoter rural areas where pre-industrial lifestyles persist. Rural poverty in turn has led to a massive exodus to the cities, which are often surrounded by shanty towns – such as the *favelas* of Rio de Janeiro and the *barriadas* of Lima; these are usually shunned by tourists and tour operators as 'no-go areas'.

In the late 1990s the region accounted for about 10 per cent of the world total of international tourist arrivals. Patterns of tourism do vary widely, with major differences between the countries of the mainland and the smaller Caribbean islands. Latin America includes four of the world's biggest spenders on international travel – Brazil, Mexico, Argentina and Venezuela – as well as some major destinations, while in other countries tourism is in its infancy. However we can make the following generalizations about tourism in most of the countries in the region:

1 The wealthier socioeconomic groups often prefer to travel abroad, particularly to the USA, rather than take holidays in their own countries.
2 Visitors from other countries in the region, usually short stay, make up the bulk of arrivals.
3 The USA provides the majority of tourists from outside the region to Mexico, Central America and the Caribbean, whereas South America attracts more of its tourists from Europe.
4 Tourism is much less significant as a source of foreign exchange in South America than it is to the Caribbean islands.

There is a great variety of tourism resources in a region which is greater in latitudinal extent than either North America or Africa. Products include beach tourism in the Caribbean islands and Mexico, adventure travel and eco-tourism in the mountains and forests of the interior, and cultural tourism in the Andes of South America and the 'Maya Route' of Central America.

The Caribbean Islands

Physical features

The islands of the Caribbean form a chain, extending for some 4000 kilometres from Florida to the northern coast of South America. The Caribbean Sea is almost enclosed, and has been called, with some justification, 'the American Mediterranean'. However it is warmer and less polluted than its Old World counterpart, with a greener coastline and finer beaches.

The islands are generally healthier than most tropical destinations. The north-east trade winds moderate the rather high temperatures and humidity, bringing heavy rainfall to the windward coasts; this means that locations on the sheltered side of a mountainous island, and low-lying islands generally, have a much drier climate, as evidenced by cacti and other drought-resistant vegetation. The best time for visiting the Caribbean is from December through to April when the weather is pleasantly warm, sunny and relatively dry. This has long been the high season for winter sun-seekers, arriving mainly from North America. Summer temperatures are appreciably higher and there is a greater probability of rain. Hotel prices are generally lower in summer, and this attracts a younger, less affluent type of holidaymaker, including many from Europe. In fact the Caribbean is no longer primarily a winter destination, as over 60 per cent of its visitors now arrive during the summer months. From July to November there is the risk of hurricanes occurring in some parts of the region, and these tropical storms can cause immense damage to the tourism infrastructure of the islands and the Caribbean coast of Central America.

While climatic conditions are fairly uniform throughout the region, there are considerable differences between the landscapes of the various islands. There are also great disparities in size – from tiny Saba, with little over 1000 inhabitants, to Cuba which is comparable in area and population to a medium-sized country in Europe. The Greater Antilles – Cuba, Hispaniola, Puerto Rico and Jamaica – could be described as 'continents in miniature'. The smaller islands or Lesser Antilles tend to fall into two categories:

1 The 'low islands' of limestone formation. These are scenically less interesting, but boast fine beaches of white coral sand.
2 The 'high islands' of volcanic origin in the eastern Caribbean. These are mountainous and often densely forested, but have fewer beaches and a wetter climate, while rugged terrain makes road-building and airport expansion difficult. There have been few volcanic eruptions in recent centuries – Mount Pelée in Martinique (1902) and Montserrat (1995–7) are notable exceptions – but there are significant geothermal resources in most of these islands.

Cultural features

The islands are a mosaic of different races, languages and religions, with a cultural heritage resulting from successive phases of European colonization namely:

1 *The age of discovery* The arrival of the Spanish under Columbus had a fatal impact on the native Americans, particularly the Arawak of the Greater Antilles, and few traces of their culture remain. The Caribs of the eastern Caribbean put up a longer resistance, and a small community still survive in Dominica.

2 *The age of piracy* The buccaneers of the seventeenth century used the smaller islands abandoned by the Spanish as bases for their expeditions, which were directed mainly against the Spanish treasure fleets from Mexico and South America.

3 *The plantation era* The plantation economy developed in the eighteenth century when sugar was a valuable commodity, and the islands a prize to be fought over by almost all the European powers. In the course of the next century slavery was abolished but the legacy of the plantation is still evident in the attitude of many Afro-Caribbeans towards tourism.

Tourism development

English is the most widely spoken language in the Caribbean, and this together with proximity to the USA has been a factor encouraging the development of tourism. The region is, however, highly fragmented politically. Even the Commonwealth Caribbean consists of no less than ten independent island-nations and five British colonies, but there is an increasing awareness of the advantages of co-operation in the fields of tourism planning and promotion (see the first case study at the end of this chapter). Most of the remaining islands retain close links with France, the Netherlands and the USA. Cuba, the Dominican Republic and Puerto Rico have strong cultural ties with Spain and the other Spanish-speaking countries of Latin America. There has been some progress toward economic integration through CARICOM (the Caribbean Economic Community), while the Caribbean Tourism Organization (CTO) carries out joint promotion with member countries in Europe and North America.

Most of the Caribbean islands are overpopulated in relation to their limited resources for economic development. Tourism is encouraged by most governments in the region who perceive that beaches, sunshine and scenery are more marketable assets than sugar or bananas. Since 1997 agriculture has become even less profitable, as the islands are no longer guaranteed a market for their produce in the EU, thanks to the ruling of the World Trade Organization. Tourism has the advantage of creating jobs in a region where unemployment is high, where emigration is no longer an alternative, and where manufacturing industry is generally not viable. Tourism is now the major earner of foreign exchange, the fastest growing sector of the economy and a major employer, accounting for over one-third of the workforce in many of the islands. Between 1985 and 1997 the Caribbean doubled its hotel capacity. However the region is highly dependant on the North American market, which supplies the majority of all staying visitors and over 90 per cent of cruise passengers, and is therefore vulnerable to the effects of recession in the USA. Most national currencies are tied to the US dollar, and resort accommodation is designed and priced to meet North American expectations. Foreign tour operators also tend to regard the islands as offering an interchangeable holiday product,

disregarding the considerable cultural differences that exist within the Caribbean and national aspirations.

An island's success as a tourist destination depends to a large extent on its accessibility to air and shipping services. Inter-island ferry services tend to be less reliable than air transport, making 'island-hopping' problematic. There are many small regional airlines in the Caribbean but only a few international airports with the capacity to handle a large volume of long-haul traffic. Barbados for example acts as a regional hub, providing services to the less developed islands such as St Vincent and Dominica. The vital air links to North America and Europe are dominated by airlines based outside the Caribbean, although BWIA (the national airline of Barbados) and Air Jamaica are gaining a larger share of the market.

Tourism in the Caribbean has had negative as well as positive impacts on host communities. This is particularly true of two holiday types which have been encouraged by most governments as a means of maximizing income from visitors, namely cruising and all-inclusives.

Cruising

The Caribbean has maintained its position as the world's most popular cruise destination, due largely to competitive pricing by the shipping lines, aimed particularly at middle-income groups in the USA. Cruising has shown a faster rate of growth than land-based tourism, from less than 1 million passengers in the early 1980s to about 4 million at the end of the twentieth century, while the ships boast a far higher occupancy rate than most resort hotels. In winter the Caribbean has unrivalled natural advantages, but in summer it faces strong competition from other destinations, leading some cruise lines to reposition their vessels in Alaskan or Mediterranean waters. Both the number of ships and their overall size is increasing, with the largest accommodating as many as 2500 passengers and 1000 crew. Size is an advantage for cruise operators in terms of yield, while stricter environmental and safety regulations also discourage the use of smaller, older vessels. Although providing terminal facilities is costly, an equivalent number of staying tourists would require a much greater investment in hotel-building. Nevertheless the economic benefits of attracting the multibillion-dollar cruise market have been disputed, and there are also negative environmental and cultural impacts (Pattullo, 1996). We can summarize the objections to cruising as follows:

1 Cruise lines offer unfair competition to Caribbean hoteliers, as they pay little in the way of taxes to island governments.

2 Cruise lines provide few employment and business opportunities to island communities. They source most of their food requirements from outside the Caribbean, claiming that local farmers cannot provide supplies to the quantity or quality required.

3 Cruising is high volume but low-spend tourism. With increasingly sophisticated onboard facilities for shopping, leisure and gambling, there is less incentive for passengers to spend in the ports of call. Duty-free goods – most of which have to be imported – account for half the spend ashore, which puts the smaller, less developed islands at a disadvantage. The sheer volume of passengers is difficult for some communities to handle, given the limited number of taxis and buses available.

4 Cruising is 'convenience travel'. In contrast to the Mediterranean and other cruise destinations, the Caribbean attracts 'sun and fun' holidaymakers rather than those interested in sightseeing, while the ship is often promoted as the primary attraction. With just a few hours ashore, passengers receive only a stereotyped impression of the Caribbean, and the commercialization of the ports of call can be demeaning to both the visitors and the host community.

5 Cruise ships generate an enormous amount of waste, and island governments are ill equipped to carry out clean-up operations on the scale required.

All-inclusives

Although Club Méditerranée pioneered the all-inclusive principle in their villages in the French islands of Martinique and Guadeloupe, the idea did not spread to the rest of the Caribbean until the late 1980s, following the example of the Sandals group in Jamaica. All-inclusives have the following advantages:

1 For tourists, they offer value for money holidays, as there is no need to budget for 'extras' such as drinks and the use of sports facilities.

2 For tour operators they boost profits by stimulating sales.

3 For the hotelier they improve occupancy rates, allowing more staff to be employed year-round.

However all-inclusives have been accused of widening social divisions between the tourists, who see little need to venture beyond the security of the hotels, and the host community. Also most are owned by multinationals, which reduces their benefits to the local economy.

Other forms of tourism allow more of the visitor spend to be retained locally, by encouraging linkages with suppliers in the islands. They include:

1 *Yachting* Whereas only a small number of harbours in the Caribbean can accommodate 100 000 tonne cruise ships, yachtsmen and women from Europe and North America have an almost unlimited choice of natural anchorages. Purpose-built marinas are available in many islands, providing facilities for both bareboat charter and crewed vessels. Nautical tourists are predominantly from the upper-income groups, but tend to be more informal in their dealings with local people than their counterparts in the luxury resort hotels.

2 *Diving* Some of the world's finest coral reefs fringe the Caribbean islands. The invention of the self-contained underwater breathing apparatus (scuba) in the 1950s revolutionized diving and opened up a new frontier for tourism. With an estimated 5 million practitioners in the USA alone, scuba-diving is one of the world's fastest growing sports, and divers are among those campaigning against the depletion of the reef ecosystem by overfishing and marine pollution. A number of resorts provide facilities for divers, but the best sites tend to be in areas which can only be accessed by *live-aboards* – boats specially designed and chartered for diving expeditions.

3 *Eco-tourism* Columbus was the first European visitor to describe the Caribbean islands, with their profusion of plant and bird life, as a 'paradise on earth'. Although the original forest cover has long since disappeared on most of the low islands, the Greater Antilles and volcanic Windward Islands retain much to attract nature lovers.

4 *Cultural and heritage tourism* Most Caribbean islands can offer an interesting colonial heritage and a vibrant contemporary culture, expressed particularly in music and dance (most 'Latin' rhythms are in fact Caribbean in origin), and to a lesser extent in the visual arts. The colourful Carnivals staged by many islanders, and other event attractions such as 'Reggae Sunsplash' in Jamaica, 'Junkanoo' in the Bahamas, 'Cropover' in Barbados, and 'Pirates Week' in the Cayman Islands – are showcases of national identity, giving tourists the opportunity to interact with the host community. We will now look at some of the islands in more detail, starting with the English-speaking countries of the Commonwealth Caribbean.

The Bahamas

Of the 700 islands that make up the Bahamas only fourteen are inhabited. Poor soils and a lack of surface water mean that only 5 per cent of the land is suitable for agriculture, forcing the islanders to find alternative sources of income. Nassau became fashionable as a winter destination for wealthy Americans in the late nineteenth century, but it was not until the 1960s, in the aftermath of the Cuban Revolution, that mass tourism developed. Proximity to Miami has ensured that the Bahamas are the most popular ports of call for cruise ships, including a number of private islands, where passengers are free of the unwelcome attentions of the beach vendors and hustlers prevalent in many Caribbean resorts. Most of the hotels and other facilities are concentrated on two islands:

1 New Providence contains the capital Nassau, and the resort areas of Paradise Island – which boasts casinos and the Atlantis theme park among its attractions – and Cable Beach, lined with expensive hotels.

2 Grand Bahama offers two purpose-built resorts – Freeport and Lucaya, based on golf, duty-free shopping and gambling.

The 'Family' or 'Out Islands' are less developed, but provide a range of outdoor activities. Abaco has a long established boat building industry and is a yachting centre; Eleuthera and Bimini are noted for game-fishing, while the exceptionally clear waters around Andros are ideal for scuba-diving.

The Turks and Caicos Islands

These islands lie to the south of the Bahamas and are flat and rather arid, but upmarket tourism has developed on Providenciales, which offers fine beaches and world-class diving.

Bermuda

We feel justified in including Bermuda as part of the Caribbean in view of the cultural and physical similarities. Nevertheless you should be aware that this small British colony is situated in the North Atlantic, much closer to North Carolina than to the Bahamas. A group of interlinked coral islands, Bermuda offers world-class beaches of pink sand, facilities for sailing and diving, as well as golf, cycling and riding among its attractions. Bermuda was originally developed as a winter resort for wealthy Americans from New York and Boston but, since beach tourism became fashionable, summer has been the preferred season. The islands have retained their exclusive appeal, primarily by careful resource management. For example:

1 Hotel capacity is limited to 10 000 bed-spaces.
2 Cruise arrivals are restricted, to protect the hotel sector from competition and Hamilton's shopping and port facilities from congestion.
3 The environment is safeguarded by a ban on rental cars and roadside advertising.

Jamaica

Jamaica is located in the centre of the Caribbean, and is the largest of the English-speaking islands, with a more diversified economy and a higher international profile than most countries in the region. Élite tourism was well established before the Second World War, with writers such as Ian Fleming taking up residence near Port Antonio. However large-scale development did not take place until the 1960s. Jamaica's image has since been damaged by internal political strife and drug-related crime. The government has countered the effect of negative publicity with infrastructural improvements, event attractions and currency devaluation to attract foreign visitors, while domestic tourism has also been encouraged. Outside Kingston, which

is a major business centre for the Caribbean, most of the hotel development is concentrated along the north coast, at Montego Bay, Ocho Rios – a major port of call for cruise ships – and Negril. Here the fine beaches are backed by forest-covered mountains, the best known attractions being Dunns River Falls near Ocho Rios and rafting on the Rio Grande near Port Antonio. Jamaica can offer excellent sports facilities, particularly at Negril which was developed in the 1970s to cater for the younger, more active type of holidaymaker. Much of the accommodation is in all-inclusives, but most of these are Jamaican-owned. Market segmentation is evident, with different hotels catering for young singles seeking a hedonistic lifestyle, couples, and families with young children. Jamaica can also offer the following alternatives to beach tourism:

1 Eco-tourism in the Blue Mountains and the karst limestone Cockpit Country based on small resorts such as Discovery Bay and Mandeville.
2 The colonial heritage, including the great houses built by wealthy plantation owners, the old pirate stronghold of Port Royal in Kingston harbour and the Seville Heritage Park.
3 Contemporary West Indian culture, particularly the musical legacy of Bob Marley.

The Cayman Islands

These small islands lying to the west of Jamaica are the best known of a number of Caribbean territories that provide offshore financial services to the international business community. Grand Cayman is also a developed up-market holiday destination, while the islands offer world-class diving, including the *'drop-off'* known as Bloody Bay Wall off Little Cayman.

The Eastern Caribbean

The islands of the eastern Caribbean fall into two major groups:

1 The Leeward Islands, clustering around Antigua.
2 The Windward Islands to the south, forming a chain from Dominica to Granada.

The two groups share a common currency – the East Caribbean dollar – and belong to the Organization of Eastern Caribbean States (OECS).

Leeward Islands

Antigua is the most developed of the Leeward Islands, with an international airport handling direct flights from London and North America as well as a network of regional services. Most of the island is low lying and suffers from chronic water shortages, and has few natural attractions other than a coastline indented with coves and harbours, and boasting may fine beaches. Tourism dominates the economy of this small island-nation and, with tourist arrivals greatly outnumbering the resident population, has been a mixed blessing. For example:

1 Most jobs in tourism are low status, with managerial posts usually filled by expatriates. Antiguans have been criticized for their attitude to service work.
2 Antiguan popular culture has been stereotyped to meet tourist expectations.
3 The island's ecosystems have been damaged by beach-front development.

Antigua does offer a major heritage attraction in English Harbour, an attractive yachting centre where Nelson's Dockyard is a reminder of the island's former importance to the British navy.

The other Leeward Islands can offer a greater variety of scenery than Antigua, and have not embraced mass tourism to the same extent, retaining a mix of small hotels, inns and guesthouses. *Anguilla*, with its pink and white sand beaches, *Nevis* and *Montserrat* are small-scale upmarket destinations reflecting a more traditional Caribbean lifestyle. *St Kitts* in its Frigate Bay development has sought the middle-income market, particularly from Canada, and the island is a venue for a number of cultural events such as music festivals.

Windward Islands

St Lucia is the most developed of the Windward Islands, and for many visitors it represents the ideal holiday destination. Fine beaches of coral sand, as at Marigot Bay, contrast with the mountainous interior. The twin peaks of volcanic origin known as the Pitons must rank among the most spectacular attractions of the Caribbean and provide St Lucia with a unique selling point (USP) which few other islands can offer. However the international airport is inconveniently located at the southern tip of the island in relation to the capital Castries. Tourism developed rapidly during the 1990s and most of the resort hotels are now all-inclusives.

Dominica was a latecomer to tourism, with its lack of beaches, rainy climate and relative inaccessibility. The island has set out to attract nature-loving tourists to its mountainous interior, which offers pristine rainforest, waterfalls, sulphur springs and a 'boiling lake' of volcanic origin. Accommodation is in small hotels and guesthouses that are locally owned and managed, with strong linkages to the island's farms and craft industries. However, tourism growth in the 1990s – including a tenfold increase in cruise passenger arrivals – has put the more accessible sites under severe pressure. Some would argue that cruise tourism on this scale is incompatible with eco-tourism, and that Dominica's unique appeal as the 'nature island of the Caribbean' is at risk.

Eco-tourism and adventure tourism have also been promoted by the governments of *St Vincent* and Grenada, on the basis of similar resources. *Grenada*, known as the 'Spice Island of the Caribbean', does have the attraction of white sand beaches, coral reefs and the fine harbour of St Georges, which is a major yachting centre. The chain of small coral islands known as the Grenadines are well developed for tourism, with a number of small resorts catering for divers and yachtsmen and women, while Mustique is famous as a hideaway for celebrities.

Barbados

Barbados is the easternmost of the Caribbean islands, with a long-established tourism industry. This is one of the few destinations in the region where British visitors outnumber those of North American origin, and the legacy of over three centuries of uninterrupted British rule is evident. The appeal of Barbados lies in its countryside – 'the garden of the West Indies', its sporting attractions, notably cricket, and the superb beaches. Most of the resort development is on the west coast near the capital Bridgetown, where land prices are among the highest in the world, fuelled by the influx of 'new money' and Concorde flights from London. The tourist authorities have tried to maintain the exclusive appeal of Barbados while at the same time encouraging middle-income holidaymakers on air-inclusive charters. The rugged east coast, exposed to the Atlantic surf, is protected from development, although this means that tourism has to compete with other land uses in this small densely populated island.

Trinidad and Tobago

The large island of Trinidad lies outside the hurricane belt close to the mainland of South America. It has a fairly developed economy based on petroleum, and a vibrant culture in which Asian as well as African and European influences are evident. The capital, Port of Spain, is an important regional gateway and business centre. The collapse of oil prices in the 1990s has induced the government to place more emphasis on tourism. Trinidad is famed for its steel bands, calypso singers and limbo dancers, and its Carnival must rank as one of the most spectacular event attractions in the Caribbean. The island also boasts a geological curiosity – Pitch Lake – and the Caroni Swamp with its wildlife resources. The much smaller island of Tobago offers a more relaxed lifestyle than Trinidad and an environment that is better suited to beach tourism and water sports.

The Virgin Islands

This cluster of islands is divided between Britain and the USA:

1 *The US Virgin Islands* have the advantage of free access to sources of investment in the USA and, in the case of St Thomas, frequent air and shipping services from the US mainland. The port of Charlotte Amalie is thronged with American cruise passengers seeking duty-free shopping bargains, seemingly oblivious to the reminders of former Danish colonial rule. St John's marine resources have been given national park status.

2 *The British Virgin Islands* (BVI) are much less well developed in terms of hotel capacity and, although Tortola and Virgin Gorda are on the cruise circuit, they receive far fewer visitors than St Thomas. The sheltered waters between the islands provide an ideal environment for flotilla sailing.

The French Antilles

The former French colonies of Martinique and Guadeloupe have opted for closer association with France, as overseas *départements*, instead of independence. This has advantages in guaranteeing a higher standard of living than their Commonwealth Caribbean neighbours, and frequent flights to and from Paris. The influence of French culture is apparent in the cuisine and architecture, and the islands cater mainly for French holidaymakers. Of the two main islands, *Martinique* is scenically the more attractive, with its volcanic peaks and lush vegetation, and Fort de France is one of the most sophisticated cities in the Caribbean. *Guadeloupe* is less popular as a destination, despite the fine beaches along its eastern coast. The outlying island of St Barts (St Barthélémy), at one time a Swedish colony, has become a 'jet-set' resort.

The Netherlands Antilles (NA) and Aruba

Six Caribbean islands are associated with the Netherlands and are regarded by the World Tourism Organization as separate destinations:

1 *Saba*, *St Eustatius* and *St Maarten* are situated among the Leeward Islands. Of these St Maarten (St Martin) is by far the most developed, and it is a major port of call for cruise ships. Part of the appeal lies in the fact that this small island is divided between the Netherlands and France, so that the visitor has the choice of shopping in Philipsburg or Marigot (on the French side).

2 The southern group, known as the 'ABC Islands' (*Aruba*, *Bonaire* and *Curacao*) lie close to the South American mainland and speak a language – Papamiento – which is a mixture of Dutch and Spanish. Their arid landscapes also mark them out from other Caribbean islands. The main tourism attraction lies in the excellent beaches, facilities for water sports and duty-free shopping. Aruba has set out to attract the mass market in the USA with casinos and non-stop entertainment, whereas Bonaire is mainly known for its diving resources. Curacao's capital

– Willemstad – offers picturesque canals and Dutch style buildings, and this island appeals to visitors from Europe and South America as well as the USA.

Cuba, Hispaniola and Puerto Rico

Three Caribbean countries – Cuba, the Dominican Republic and Puerto Rico – share a heritage from the time of the Spanish Empire in the Americas. During the twentieth century they have followed very different political paths, and this has affected the type of tourism that has developed.

Puerto Rico

Not yet a state, although a former US territory, Puerto Rico is associated with the USA as a self-governing commonwealth. With the advantage of ready access to markets and sources of finance in the USA, a large manufacturing and service sector has developed in an island that, prior to 1950, was one of the poorest in the Caribbean. The capital, San Juan, is a major business centre and one of the main gateways to the Caribbean. With a number of beaches within easy reach, it is also an important holiday destination with hotel accommodation geared to a clientele that is 80 per cent American. Another major source of visitors is the large number of Puerto Ricans resident on the US mainland, but these usually fall into the VFR category. Puerto Rico's major attractions include:

- Old San Juan, the fortified colonial city, showcasing the Spanish heritage
- El Yunque National Park, an area of rainforest in the eastern highlands
- Cultural events such as the Pablo Casals music festival.

Hispaniola

The large island of Hispaniola is divided on cultural as well as political lines between the Spanish-speaking Dominican Republic and French-Creole-speaking Haiti, where African influences are predominant. Between 1980 and 1995 the fledgling tourism industry of the two countries took a very different course; the Dominican Republic experienced a phenomenal rate of tourism growth, to become the most popular holiday destination in the Caribbean, while arrivals in Haiti declined considerably during the same period.

The Dominican Republic

The Dominican Republic has been much more successful in attracting foreign investment in a bid to become a low-cost beach destination catering primarily for West Europeans. The country is served by a large number of charter airlines, with international airports at Puerto Plata, Punta Cana and

Santo Domingo. Development is mainly in tourist enclaves on the 'Amber Coast' in the north and in the south-east, with all-inclusives dominating the accommodation sector. However tourism growth has tended to outstrip the provision of adequate infrastructure, and the country's vulnerability to the mass market was shown in 1997, when British tour operators dropped it from their programmes following a health scare. The Dominican Republic's cultural attractions are largely overlooked by most tourists, apart from an introduction to sensual *merengue* rhythms, but the country has much to offer besides fine beaches, golf and water sports. The Ministry of Tourism stresses the key role of the capital, Santo Domingo, in the Spanish conquest of the Americas; the city boasts the first cathedral in the New World and other early sixteenth-century buildings. This was given further emphasis in 1992, with the inauguration of the controversial Faro a Colón (Columbus Lighthouse) commemorating the great explorer's achievement. The interior offers scope for adventure tourism with a landscape that includes the highest mountain in the Caribbean, rainforest and desert. Although there are no less than ten national parks, conservation measures are largely ineffective, and there is a shortage of quality accommodation away from the coastal resorts.

Haiti

Haiti has suffered more than other Caribbean destinations from misgovernment, political instability and negative publicity – including an AIDS scare in the early 1980s and an ongoing reputation as the poorest country in the Western Hemisphere. Population pressures have resulted in ecological disaster, and only 2 per cent of the original forest cover now remains. All this has tended to overshadow the fact that Haiti was the first country in the region to win independence from colonial rule, and the skills of its people in painting and handicrafts. The rituals of voodoo – an alternative African religion – also attract the more intrepid type of tourist. However, hotel accommodation is in short supply outside the capital Port-au-Prince and Cap Haitien in the north. The latter is visited for the remarkable citadel built by Henri Cristophe, one of the leaders in the war of independence against the French. Cruise ships on the Western Caribbean circuit tend to use the private island of Labadee, with its fine beaches, in preference to calling at Port-au-Prince or Cap Haitien – yet another example of 'enclave tourism'.

Cuba

Only the 150-kilometre wide Florida Strait separates Cuba, with its centrally planned economy – unique in the Western Hemisphere – from the USA. This large island is far more than a beach destination and can appeal to a wider range of markets than most Caribbean countries. It has a vibrant Spanish and African cultural heritage, and Cuban dance

rhythms – notably salsa – have done much to promote the country's image in Europe. The ongoing US blockade has resulted in a '1950s time-warp' with American cars of that era still in use on the streets of Havana. At the same time Cuba has a high reputation for health care, and this attracts visitors seeking medical treatment.

Tourism has gone through the following stages of development, in response to political changes:

1 *Élite tourism* From 1902 until 1959 Cuba's economy was controlled by US interests. Tourism was concentrated, as it is today, in Havana and the beach resort of Varadero, which largely developed in the 1920s with American capital. Havana was renowned for its uninhibited nightlife and casinos, catering for a wealthy and predominantly American clientele. In the 1950s Cuba was the leading destination of the Caribbean.
2 *Socialist tourism* Following Castro's revolution in 1959, Cuba lost 80 per cent of its international tourist market as a result of the trade and travel embargo imposed by the US government. Castro turned to the USSR for economic aid, and tourism subsequently followed a similar pattern to that of the countries of Eastern Europe, with the state ownership of hotels, an emphasis on social tourism for the domestic market, and cultural exchanges with other members of the Soviet bloc. Visitors from the Western countries were largely restricted to group tours, organized by specialist tour operators who were broadly in sympathy with the regime and its achievements in education and health care.
3 *Incipient mass tourism* During the 1980s the government modified its attitude to international tourism. Joint ventures between Cubanacan, the state-owned tour operator and foreign companies, such as the Spanish Melia group were encouraged, with the aim of expanding and modernizing the hotel sector. Cuba became popular as a low-cost winter sun destination for Canadians. With the collapse of the Soviet Union, Cuba was deprived of cheap oil imports and a guaranteed market for its sugar, so that tourism was increasingly seen as a lifeline for the economy. Cuba is now offered as a package holiday destination by the leading tour operators of Western Europe, and the US dollar has become the only acceptable currency for most transactions involving tourists. Small business enterprises are allowed to participate in the tourism sector, such as the *paladares* (restaurants in private homes).

Tourist arrivals have grown from 30 000 in the late 1970s to over 1 million in the late 1990s. More than half of the arrivals come from Western Europe, with Italy and Spain as the leading markets. North America accounts for less than 20 per cent, mainly Canadians – although a surprising number of US citizens find ways of getting round the embargo. Foreign visitors are mainly concentrated in tourist enclaves such as Varadero – located on a sandpit with restricted access and which has its own international airport – and Cayo Largo, a beach resort that has been developed on a small offshore island. Tourism receipts now exceed those from sugar exports, but the net gain to the economy is much less, due to the need to import materials that Cuban industry and agriculture cannot provide, and the repatriation of profits by foreign investors. Tourism developers also have to cope with a deteriorating infrastructure – including power cuts, poor roads and inadequate public transport – and an inefficient bureaucracy. On the other hand, Cuba has one of the best educated workforces in Latin America.

Cuba's resource base includes extensive sandy beaches, coral islands for scuba-diving and picturesque mountain scenery. The best known scenic area is the Sierra Maestra in the south-east of the island. However the province of Pinar del Rio is closer to Havana and, as the main tobacco-growing area, supplies Cuba's best known export. Heritage attractions include the colonial cities of Trinidad and Santiago de Cuba. The latter is almost 1000 kilometres from Havana, and is best reached by air rather than the unreliable rail service.

However Havana has more to attract the tourist, as it is arguably the most sophisticated city in the Caribbean region. Old Havana is a World Heritage Site, although its colonial architecture is sadly neglected. The capital is a major cultural centre but the biggest attraction is the Tropicana floorshow, a relic of pre-Revolution Cuba that has been revived for tourists.

The future of tourism in Cuba depends to an extent on its relations with the USA. An intensification of the US embargo, by extending it to third parties – as threatened by the Helms-Burton Act – could discourage foreign investment. Even controlled Western-style tourism could undermine socialist principles, by creating divisions in Cuban society between those with access to dollars – in effect those in direct contact with tourists – and the 95 per cent of the population who are paid entirely in almost worthless Cuban pesos. Some say that sex tourism, which was rife in pre-1959 Havana, and prohibited after the revolution, is once more on the increase as a consequence.

Mexico

Although physically part of the continent of North America, culturally Mexico forms part of the region known to anthropologists as Meso-America, along with the countries of Central America. It boasts the largest economy in Latin America and is the world's most populous Spanish-speaking nation. Its heartland is a high plateau – the Meseta Central – separated by the mountain barriers of the Sierra Madre from the tropical coastlands. Although most of Mexico falls within the tropics, the variations in altitude result in striking differences in climate over quite short distances. Mexicans refer to three altitudinal life zones, each offering different habitats for plant and animal life, namely:

1 The *tierra caliente* or tropical zone up to 1000 metres.
2 The *tierra templada* or subtropical zone between 1000 and 2000 metres where warm-climate crops such as coffee and avocados are cultivated. Most of the health resorts favoured by better-off Mexicans are located in this zone.
3 The *tierra fria* or 'cold' zone above 2000 metres, where nights are chilly, especially during the dry season, although daytime temperatures are generally warm throughout the year. Some of the largest cities, including Mexico City are located in this zone.

Compared with most of Latin America, Mexico is politically stable. Although the thirty-two state governments also play a role, since the 1920s the federal government based in Mexico City has exercised firm control throughout the country, largely by means of the Revolutionary Party (PRI), which combines socialist and free enterprise policies. However, Mexico's impressive economic development scarcely keeps pace with rapid population growth, and there are regional disparities in wealth distribution. This has caused a massive flow of emigration – much of it illegal – to the USA, where the economic opportunities are so much greater. Mexico's membership of NAFTA (North American Free Trade Area) has opened up the economy to foreign investment, and stimulated business travel to and from the USA and Canada.

Mexico is one of the world's leading travel destinations, attracting 20 million foreign tourists in the late 1990s. Indeed the country ranks ninth in terms of foreign exchange earnings. However the tourism industry is highly dependent on the USA and Canadian markets; fewer than 5 per cent of visitors originate from other countries. Mexico's appeal to North Americans is partly based on its beaches and sunny winter climate, but the cultural contrasts which the country offers to the USA are equally important. Although the majority of Mexicans are *mestizos* (of mixed Spanish and Amerindian origins), the Indian heritage, as expressed in cuisine, folklore and handicrafts, is regarded as central to the national identity. There is a contradiction here, as the majority of present-day Indians are socially and geographically marginalized in the poorer southern states. The most significant features of this rich cultural heritage are:

1 The impressive remains of advanced Indian civilizations which flourished in Mexico before the Spanish conquest. The best known of these are Teotihuacán and Tula in central Mexico, and the cities of the Mayas in Yucatán and Chiapas in the south. These form part of the Ruta Maya tourist circuit, which also takes in neighbouring Belize, Honduras and Guatemala.
2 The legacy of the Spanish colonial period, particularly the numerous Baroque churches, and picturesque towns such as Queretaro, Morelia, San Miguel Allende and Guanajuato in central Mexico. These are associated with the Mexican struggle for independence, and have been

meticulously preserved. Most of the colonial *haciendas* (country estates) on the other hand were destroyed during the Mexican Revolution (1910–20). Other legacies of Spanish rule, such as the bullfight and the fiestas of the Catholic Church continue to flourish in the popular culture.

3 The artistic legacy of the Mexican Revolution, as expressed by painters such as Frida Kahlo (now a feminist icon), Diego Rivera and many others noted for their murals celebrating Mexican folk traditions, and the pre-conquest civilizations. Before the 1910 Revolution, France had inspired the culture of the Mexican élite, as can be seen in the fashionable districts of Mexico City.

While traditional Mexico provides the tourist image, modern Mexico – particularly the wealthier northern states – has adopted many aspects of the lifestyle of the USA. A substantial middle class generates a considerable demand for domestic tourism and for international travel – despite a number of economic crises that have resulted in the devaluation of the peso against foreign currencies. The majority of Mexicans do not have sufficient disposable income to take holiday trips. There is some development of social tourism, including holiday villages for industrial workers such as those employed by PEMEX, the state-owned petroleum corporation.

In an attempt to improve the economic situation the federal government has given tourism a prominent role in national planning since the 1950s. Foreign developers are encouraged to participate in large hotel projects that will stimulate job creation, especially in the less developed regions. There is a strong Ministry of Tourism (SETUR) that is responsible for policy-making. The federal government has also taken a direct role in tourism development through the FUNATUR funding agency. This has been responsible for a number of comprehensively planned resorts such as Ixtapa on the Pacific coast and Cancún.

With the exception of an antiquated rail network, Mexico has a good transport system especially compared with those of Central America. The major cities are linked by modern highways to the USA, but east–west communications are less adequate. Water supplies and sanitation are defective in many rural areas, falling far short of those considered acceptable in the USA.

The regional setting for tourism

The north

The north contains large areas of desert, similar to those across the US border in Arizona. The most visited tourist centres are the towns along the border, particularly Tijuana. Spending by US visitors in these border towns has accounted for over half of Mexico's receipts from tourism; such visitors are however cost-conscious and numbers vary according to the strength of the dollar against the peso. Also liberal attitudes to gambling and sex tourism are less alluring for young Americans now that such attractions are widely available nearer home. Monterrey is the major city of northern Mexico, rivalling the capital as a business centre.

1 The peninsula of 'Baja' (Lower California) in the north-west is largely desert, but the beaches and excellent game-fishing attract large numbers of Californians from north of the border, thanks to an excellent highway running the length of the peninsula. Ensenada and La Paz have become major tourist centres, while the federal government has developed purpose-built resorts at Loreto and Los Cabos.

2 The 'Mexican Riviera' further south has a tropical climate with a long dry season corresponding to winter in the USA. This has made this stretch of Pacific coast popular with North Americans as a winter sun destination and retirement area. Acapulco is the most important centre, with good air and road communications to Mexico City. The historic seaport is now overshadowed by a vast agglomeration of hotels and condominiums surrounding the famous bay. Other resorts have developed from fishing ports, such as Puerto Vallarta and Mazatlán.

3 The Gulf coast of Mexico, with its more humid climate, is less popular as a holiday area. Further east, facing the Caribbean, is the Yucatán peninsula, which offers a wealth of cultural attractions as well as fine beaches. Until the 1970s the region was somewhat isolated from the rest of the country, but the federal government made a heavy investment in improving the infrastructure and developing facilities, notably at Cancún. This part of Mexico can easily be included in a Caribbean cruise itinerary and also has the advantage of greater proximity by air to Miami and the cities of the eastern USA. Cancún itself could be described as an example of 'enclave tourism'. The hinterland with its ruined Mayan cities – notably those of Chichen Itza and Uxmal – is much more interesting.

Central Mexico

The area richest in cultural attractions is the southern part of the Meseta Central, which is dominated by volcanoes such as Popocatepetl. These include the archaeological sites and colonial cities mentioned earlier, and many others such as Puebla, noted for its folklore, and Taxco which grew rich on its silver mining industry. All of these are easily reached from the capital.

Mexico City is the world's fastest growing metropolis – from 1 million inhabitants in 1940 to 18 million sixty years later. This growth has been accompanied by severe air pollution and acute traffic congestion. Although no vestige remains of the Aztec city of Tenochtitlan, the central square or Zocalo, with the cathedral and Presidential Palace occupies the site of its most important temples. The capital's attractions include:

- the National Museum of Anthropology, celebrating the achievements of the Aztecs and other Indian civilizations
- the Basilica of Guadalupe, one of the world's most visited shrines
- the floating gardens of Xochimilco, popular for Sunday excursions.

Southern Mexico

Southern Mexico is also noted for its Indian heritage, particularly the states of Oaxaca and Chiapas. Along with the Yucatán Peninsula, Chiapas forms part of the *Mundo Maya* (World of the Maya) tourism development plan, which also includes four Central American countries – Belize, El Salvador, Guatemala and Honduras. This is an example of regional co-operation between governments, tour operators and the local communities, with the aim of achieving sustainable development.

Central America

Central America is the mountainous neck of land linking the continents of South and North America. It consists of three main physical divisions:

- the coastal lowlands along the Caribbean, often densely forested, and inhabited by ethnic minorities, including many English-speaking communities
- the central volcanic highlands, that contain the majority of the population
- the Pacific coast, which has better beaches and a drier climate than the Caribbean lowlands.

Central America consists of six Spanish-speaking republics, with the exception of English-speaking Belize which is culturally and economically part of the Commonwealth Caribbean. The other countries have as yet failed to achieve economic integration and co-operation for tourism promotion. Few air services link the region directly to Europe, and the majority of tourists – other than those from neighbouring countries – come from the USA. Most of these use air transport, especially from Miami, rather than the Pan-American highway system. Much of the region – notably Guatemala, El Salvador and Nicaragua – has only recently recovered from a long period of violent political strife. Conflict may attract a particular type of traveller who is motivated to seek out high-risk situations, but in general it has held back the development of tourism. During the 1990s Central America experienced a higher growth rate in tourist arrivals than either the Caribbean or South America, albeit from a very low base. Costa Rica and Belize have concentrated on the development of eco-tourism, while in Guatemala cultural tourism is dominant, but other countries in the region have been arguably less successful in defining their tourism product.

Guatemala

Guatemala has a legacy of ethnic division between the Ladinos (Spanish-speakers) who are the dominant group, and the Indian majority, who still live in traditional communities where the value systems are quite different. Guatemala has great scenic and cultural diversity for such a small country, and this is its strength as a tourist destination. Attractions include:

1 The colonial heritage. This is based mainly on Antigua, the former capital – which has become an important centre for Spanish-language tuition.
2 Traditional Indian culture. Each Indian community has its own distinctive costume, which makes their markets exceptionally colourful, the best known example being that of Chichicastenango in the northern highlands. Also ancient Mayan beliefs coexist with the Catholicism introduced by the Spanish.
3 The volcanic mountain scenery around Lake Atitlán.
4 The Tikal National Park in the Petén rainforest, protecting one of the most important Maya sites in Central America. This city, with its stepped pyramid-temples and ceremonial plazas was abandoned to the jungle centuries before the Spanish conquest, and was only rediscovered in the nineteenth century.

Belize

Belize can also claim large tracts of pristine forest, important Mayan sites and the world's second largest barrier reef. The policy of the government is to encourage 'community-based eco-tourism' but also to use it as a means of earning foreign exchange to finance economic development. In other words, Belize is an excellent example of how a country can use the notion of sustainability to promote the development of new types of tourism (Mowforth and Munt, 1998). Much of the tourism industry is owned by expatriates, mostly US citizens, and, although some reefs have been designated as marine reserves, others are likely to develop as exclusive resorts.

El Salvador

El Salvador has few ecological resources, as it is the most densely populated country in Latin America, and one of the most developed, with a large industrial sector. Its spas and beach resorts cater mainly for the domestic market.

Honduras

Honduras is primarily known for the banana plantations around San Pedro Sula than for tourism. The interior is rugged mountain country, making air transport almost essential. The country is one of the poorest in Latin America and its plans for economic development were dealt a heavy blow by Hurricane 'Mitch' in 1998. The Bay Islands offer diving facilities, while Copán is an important Maya site.

Nicaragua

Nicaragua came under the international spotlight in the 1980s, when the USA sought to bring down the left-wing Sandinista regime through economic sanctions and support for the 'Contra' rebels. The country no longer appeals as a 'cause' for politically motivated foreign visitors, but it does have much to interest the eco-tourist. Lake Nicaragua, studded with volcanic islands, and the San Juan River connecting it to the Caribbean is a unique ecosystem. There is some small-scale development for beach tourism along the Pacific coast.

Costa Rica

Costa Rica has a well-developed infrastructure and accom-modation sector and, unlike other countries in the region, has a long-established reputation for democracy and political stability. Since the 1960s the government has developed a system of national parks that cover about a quarter of the country, protecting its most precious natural asset – its forests. Despite serious under-funding, this is the resource base for a tourism industry that relies heavily on the country's biodiversity – including many species of orchids, birds and butterflies – and its scenic attractions. The accommodation sector is for the most part locally owned, and on a small scale, even in the capital San José. It caters to a large extent for the backpacker market. San José also attracts 'health tourists' from the USA – mainly from older age groups – with its low-cost medical services. There is also some beach tourism around the Gulf of Nicoya. However, the development of golf courses in this area has been criticized by environmentalists as being incompatible with Costa Rica's image as destination for eco-tourism and 'soft adventure'. The problem is that the government, like so many others throughout Latin America, needs a higher yield type of tourism to service the country's large foreign debt. The growth of cruise tourism to the Pacific port of Puntarenas is also likely to have an impact on some of the country's more accessible national parks; an arduous five-hour trek will become a one-hour journey by tour bus once road improvements are carried out.

Panama

Panama owes much of its importance as a tourist destination to the famous canal, which passed from US to Panamanian control at the end of 1999, along with the surrounding territory known as the Canal Zone. Some forty to fifty ships pass through the canal each day. The locks at Gatún, where the canal crosses the Continental Divide, must count as one of the world's major feats of engineering. The city of Panama, with its mixture of high-rise modern buildings and Asian bazaars is a major centre of international commerce, encouraged by the country's liberal banking laws and use of the dollar as the national currency. The free port of Colón,

at the western (Caribbean) end of the canal is another important trading centre. However Panama has yet to realize its full potential as 'the crossroads of the Americas', due to the jungles of Darien only 200 kilometres to the east. These pose a formidable barrier to the completion of the Pan-American highway system and any projected route must respect the land claims of the local Amerindian tribes.

Panama's holiday attractions mainly lie in the offshore islands. Of these the Pearl Islands have received the most attention from tour operators. The most important of these – Contadora – is a luxury resort and conference venue. The San Blas Islands are noted for game-fishing, but here the local Kuna Indians have kept development at arms length – tourism has to be on their terms.

It is likely that the former Canal Zone will be developed to yield maximum revenue, with marinas, hotels and time-share apartments. The canal itself is too restricted for the largest cruise ships, and a third set of locks will be needed to increase capacity – but this could have an adverse environmental impact, affecting water supplies to the city of Panama. In contrast eco-tourism is being encouraged in other parts of the country, along with projects to restore the old Spanish seaport of Portobelo – a reminder that the isthmus was important for trade centuries before the opening of the canal.

South America

South America receives less than 1 per cent of the world's international tourist arrivals. The high cost of airfares and the lack of charter flights partly explains why this continent remains a destination for the wealthy or adventurous traveller. There is also a shortage of suitable hotels for the inclusive-tour market. Long-term planning and investment in the tourism industry have been discouraged by political instability and inflation which have given South America unfavourable publicity.

Climatic conditions, dense vegetation and rugged ter-rain have been a great obstacle to road and railway construction in many areas. In the west, the Andes – the world's longest mountain range, and second only to the Himalayas in altitude – pose a formidable barrier. Most of South America lies within the tropics, and the continent includes the world's largest rainforest in the Amazon Basin. Water transport is still widely used wherever there are navigable rivers – such as the Amazon and the Paraná – but the shipping services are usually slow and uncom-fortable. Transport infrastructure is gradually improving with the expansion of the Pan-American highway network and the development of internal air services. Rail systems in South America tend to be rudimentary, but some of the world's most spectacular lines are to be found in the Andes, and these have become tourist attractions in their own right.

A number of countries in South America are undergoing rapid industrialization, with a resulting increase in business travel from Europe and the USA. As regards the holiday market, national tourist offices in South American countries are generally under-funded, so that overseas promotion has been left to the national airlines or to specialist tour operators in the tourist-generating countries. Closer international co-operation, as among the Andean Pact countries and those belonging to MERCOSUR, should facilitate travel within the region and bring about more effective tourism promotion.

Brazil

Brazil occupies almost half of South America and is a leading member of MERCOSUR. Unlike most Latin American countries, Brazil has a well-defined image, based on its beaches, the Rio de Janeiro carnival and the Amazon rainforest. The country is comparable in size to the USA – spanning three time zones – and ranks among the world's top ten economies. It is the world's sixth most populous country, with well over 150 million inhabitants, mainly concentrated along the Atlantic seaboard. Brazilians are essentially the result of a fusion of three cultures – Portuguese, African and native American. Since the nineteenth century the country has also attracted many millions of immigrants from all over the world, but it has arguably been more successful than the USA in blending different races and cultures.

Brazil's market potential for tourism is closely linked to the development of the economy, now the largest in Latin America. Growth has been particularly rapid during the 1990s as a result of currency reform and privatization initiatives, but it remains to be seen whether the 'boom and bust' cycle, so evident in the past, can be checked permanently. Most of the country's industrial wealth is concentrated in the Rio de Janeiro–Sao Paulo–Belo Horizonte triangle, while other regions, notably the North-east, remain poor and under-developed. Tourism development since the 1960s has been the responsibility of Embratur, a federal government agency that reports to the Ministry of Sport and Tourism, but this lacks the funding to carry out effective overseas promotion. Special incentives apply to the regional development areas in the North-east and Amazonia which are the responsibility of two other federal agencies – Sudene and Sudam respectively. There has been considerable investment by state governments and the private sector throughout the 1990s, in hotels, leisure complexes and theme parks. The federal government is investing in training for those employed in the tourism sector, along with improvements in infrastructure and more effective marketing.

The demand for tourism

Despite these efforts, tourism accounts for less than 1 per cent of the gross national product. A quarter of Brazil's foreign visitors come from European countries, compared to less than 15 per cent from the USA. About a third of these visitors come primarily for business reasons. The months of January and February see the greatest tourist activity, coinciding with the carnival season which also happens to be the hottest and most humid time of the year in most of Brazil.

Some 38 million domestic trips were undertaken in the late 1990s, but this is not particularly high given the population of Brazil. Under the country's labour laws employees are guaranteed a forty-eight hour week and an annual paid holiday of twenty days, but many are excluded from becoming tourists by low incomes, especially in the rural areas. However, recreational facilities are provided by the state governments in city areas, while the beaches are freely available to rich and poor alike. Domestic tourists tend to use small hotels and camping grounds, or stay with friends and relatives. Currently internal travel is very much road based (97 per cent of all journeys) due to the high cost of air transport. However, this may change as a result of competition between the airlines and domestic tour operators. Brazilians are far more interested in beach holidays than in trips to the Amazon, as the beach occupies a central place in the nation's hedonistic lifestyle. Television through the popular *tele-novelas* (soap operas) plays an important role in opening up new areas of Brazil for the domestic market. Brazil is among the world's leading generators of international travel, resulting in a considerable deficit on the country's tourism account. Successive governments have attempted to check the demand by requiring that Brazilians travelling abroad deposit a bond.

Transport

The vast size of Brazil poses a major problem for overland transport, especially during the rainy season from December to May. The Amazon and its tributaries provide 20000 kilometres of navigable waterways, but these are far from the major populated areas and port facilities are inadequate. The national transport strategy is to construct a number of major highways through the rainforest to improve access to the Amazon and eventually link up with the road system of neighbouring countries. However, the road network has not opened up the interior for development to the extent the government envisaged; rather it has facilitated rural out-migration, and contributed to the decline of Brazil's antiquated railway system. On the other hand Brazil's internal air network is well developed, with nine international airports and hundreds of airfields allowing access to even the most remote areas. Services are provided by the national airline, Varig, and its subsidiaries. Varig also plays a major role in overseas promotion. There is a frequent shuttle service between Sao Paulo and Rio de Janeiro for business travellers.

The regional setting for tourism

Brazil has five tourism regions, each offering a different appeal:

1 *Amazonia* forms the major part of the world's greatest river basin that covers 5 million square kilometres and contains 20 per cent of the planet's freshwater resources. The region's rainforests hold a fascination for foreign visitors as an ecological resource threatened with destruction. This is a good example of a change in perception, contrasting with the earlier view of the Amazon as the 'green hell' vividly described by Colonel Fawcett and other explorers. In Brazil itself there is a growing environmental movement, following the Rio Summit in 1992, to prevent further exploitation of the region for large-scale cattle-grazing, mining and road-building. Most tourists arrive by air at Manaos or Belem. Both cities have fine buildings dating from the rubber boom of the 1890s, particularly Manaos with its magnificent opera house. After a long period of decline, the city has been revitalized with its development as a free port. Santarem, at the confluence of the Amazon and the Tapajoz, is another important tourist centre. Eco-tourists seeking a closer encounter with the rainforest are accommodated in a number of lodges, some of which are built in the tree canopy, while others use 'floatels' moored at the river bank. Sustainable tourism is aimed for in the following ways:

(a) By restricting lodge capacity to a small number of guests.

(b) By keeping facilities simple, using solar power and local food supplies wherever possible, and dispensing with air conditioning.

(c) By maintaining remoteness, with the journey from say, Manaos being undertaken by boat and canoe rather than by air.

(d) Visits to Indian villages are controlled by FUNAI, the Indian Protection Agency. Tourists are taken to visit local families but no family is visited regularly, so minimizing impact. As a result of these policies the natural resources are protected and the quality of the experience for the visitor is also maintained.

2 *The North-east* consists of a fertile coastal belt and the semi-arid scrublands of the *sertao* or backlands, an area often described as the 'Triangle of Thirst'. This is a poverty-stricken region that has traditionally exported millions of rural migrants to the cities of southern Brazil. Unlike Amazonia, the coast is very popular with Brazilians, as it offers many fine beaches. Former fishing villages are 'discovered' and then cease to be fashionable in the never-ending quest for the 'perfect beach'. The coast is the subject of a tourism development programme, resulting from an agreement between the state governments of the region and the Inter-American Development Bank (IDB). International hotel groups have moved in, particularly along the 'Golden Coast' south of Recife, creating tourist enclaves. In contrast accommodation is in short supply and often substandard in the *sertao*, which has an important place in Brazilian folklore. Major tourism centres of the north-east include:

(a) Salvador de Bahia, one of the major cultural centres of Brazil, famed for its attractive colonial architecture, and as the birthplace of the samba, hosting a carnival that rivals Rio's.

(b) Fortaleza, noted for its fine beaches.

(c) Recife the international gateway to the region, known as the 'Venice of Brazil' on account of its many waterways.

3 *The Centre-west* is Brazil's underdeveloped heartland, although it received a major boost in the 1960s with the establishment of Brasilia as the new federal capital. Most of the region consists of savanna grassland, with extensive wetlands near the Paraguayan border. This area, known as the Pantanal, is rich in wildlife that had previously coexisted with cattle-ranching. This unique environment is now under threat from the activities of poachers, the expansion of agriculture, and projects to improve navigation on the Rivers Paraná and Paraguay. The government-sponsored National Environment Agency has designated a number of natural reserves in the region, but these are under-funded. In contrast, Brasilia is noted for its freeways and futuristic architecture, epitomized by the Palace of Congress.

4 *The South* is the only region of Brazil to experience a temperate climate, with occasional frosts during the winter months. The major attraction for foreign tourists is Iguacú Falls on the border with Paraguay and Argentina. This is actually a series of cataracts with many times the volume of Niagara. Walkways have been built in the Garganta de Diablo gorge at the edge of the biggest waterfall. The resort of Foz de Iguacú has good communications by air and is a major conference venue.

5 *The South-east* receives the most foreign tourists, largely because it contains Rio de Janeiro (see the second case study at the end of this chapter). The coastline between Rio and Santos, backed by the lush mountain scenery of the Serra do Mar, has been designated for major tourism development. A number of beach resorts are increasingly popular with foreign visitors, such as Buzios, Angra dos Reis and Sepetiba. However, development poses a threat to the Atlantic rainforests, already under severe pressure. The interior of this part of Brazil also has much to attract the cultural tourist, including the picturesque colonial town of Ouro Preto, which grew rich from the silver and diamond mining boom of the eighteenth century. Business travellers gravitate to the big modern cities of Belo Horizonte and Sao Paulo.

(a) Sao Paulo has diversified from coffee production to become one of the world's great manufacturing and financial centres during the twentieth century. The city typifies the contrast that exists in Brazil between private wealth and social deprivation; it has South America's highest car ownership and a major pollution problem.

Northern South America

We could include the northern countries of South America as part of the Caribbean region; in fact Venezuela and Surinam belong to the CTO while Guyana and Surinam are members of CARICOM. Colombia and Venezuela share an extensive coastline on the Caribbean, and the cities of Cartagena and Caracas feature prominently on some cruise itineraries. Guyana, Surinam and French Guiana have cultural similarities with the West Indies and retain close links with Britain, the Netherlands and France respectively. Moreover, the folklore of the tropical coastlands of Colombia, Venezuela and the Guianas is African rather than Amerindian in origin.

Colombia

Colombia is one of the leading tourist destinations of South America and the world's largest producer of coffee after Brazil. There has been considerable industrial development and its infrastructure compares favourably with neighbouring Ecuador. The national airline – Avianca – was among the first to pioneer domestic air services in the Western Hemisphere. However the country is better known for the long-running conflict between the army, paramilitaries and Marxist guerrillas that afflicts large areas of the country, and the drug-related crime prevalent in some of its major cities, such as Bogotá, Medellin and Cali. Colombia is compartmentalized by the triple chain of the Andes which provide formidable barriers to east–west communication.

Tourism development is the responsibility of the Corporación Nacional de Turismo (CNT) which has built a network of *paradors* along the main tourist routes. Most visitors arrive overland from Ecuador and Venezuela, attracted by shopping bargains. Promotion is mainly aimed at the US market, although growing numbers of tourists are coming from Germany and France.

Colombia's Pacific coastline has a humid climate and is relatively inaccessible. The Caribbean coastline is much more attractive with a long dry season. Tropical beaches are backed by the snow-capped mountains of the Sierra Nevada de Santa Marta. The most important tourist centres are the beach resort of Santa Marta and the historic seaport of Cartagena, the key fortress of 'the Spanish Main' in colonial times. The islands of San Andrés and Providencia offer duty-free shopping.

In the interior of Colombia the main tourist attractions are cities such as Popayán, located in beautiful mountain valleys, which still retain much of their Spanish colonial heritage. The capital Bogotá is noted for its Gold Museum, a collection of artefacts from the pre-conquest Indian civilizations, while San Agustín is one of the largest archaeological sites in the Americas.

Venezuela

As a major oil producer, Venezuela enjoyed the highest per capita income of any Latin American country prior to the fall in oil prices in the early 1990s. Middle-class Venezuelans travelled abroad in large numbers, particularly to Miami, leaving a substantial deficit in the international tourism account. The subsequent financial crisis has led the government to impose strict exchange controls and take a greater interest in encouraging inbound tourism. Venezuela has the reputation of being an expensive destination, despite the devaluation of the bolivar against foreign currencies. In contrast to the situation in other South American destinations, most of Venezuela's visitors do not come from neighbouring countries, but from Europe and the USA. About half are visiting for business reasons and 25 per cent are VFR tourists – the result of substantial immigration from Spain and Italy. The private car is the dominant mode of transport for domestic tourism, thanks to cheap petrol and an excellent highway network. Air transport is facilitated by a large number of airports throughout the country, and VIASA, the national carrier is one of South America's leading airlines.

Hotel capacity is mainly concentrated in the capital and the beach resorts of the Caribbean coast. Time-share apartments are an important part of the accommodation sector, particularly for domestic tourists. Venezuela's tourism resources include:

1 The capital Caracas, one of South America's great cities and a major gateway to the continent. It is primarily a business destination, but it does have historic significance as the birthplace of Simon Bolivar, who liberated much of South America from Spanish rule.
2 The beach resorts of the Caribbean, the most important being Porlamar on the island of Margarita, and Puerto La Cruz.
3 A section of the Andes, including the colonial city of Mérida, which also boasts the world's highest cableway.
4 The vast grasslands known as the Llanos in the south of the country offer many possibilities for eco-tourism. Fly-in camps in this remote, sparsely populated region provide a base for exploring the strange landscapes of the *tepuys* – sheer-sided, flat-topped mountains that inspired Conan Doyle's *Lost World* – and viewing the world's highest waterfall – Angel Falls.

The Guianas

In Guyana, Surinam and French Guiana tourism is in its infancy. Throughout the Guianas there is a contrast between the low-lying coast, with its plantation economy, and the forested interior, where Amerindian tribes maintain their traditional way of life. The majority of the population live on the coast and are mainly of African or Asian origin. The lack of beaches and poor infrastructure means that eco-tourism is often the only viable form of tourism. A coastal highway linking the three countries was only completed in 1998, while the rivers and internal air services provide the only access to the interior.

1 *Guyana* has some of South America's finest rivers and one of its highest waterfalls – Kaieteur – as yet unexploited as a tourist attraction. The few hotels are found mainly in Georgetown, and elsewhere forest lodges provide accommodation. The Rupununi region in the south-west of the country is an example of sustainable development, integrating eco-tourism and forest management for the benefit of the local Amerindian communities.
2 *Surinam* has the advantage of direct flights by KLM from Amsterdam to Paramaribo, but tourism has been handicapped by political instability.
3 *French Guiana* likewise benefits from direct flights between Paris and Cayenne, due to its status as an overseas *département* of France, and as the base for the European Space Agency's 'Ariane' programme. However the country is better known for its former role as a penal colony, including the infamous 'Devil's Island'.

The Andean republics

Peru, Ecuador and Bolivia share a similar physical environment, dominated by the Andes mountains, and a similar cultural heritage in which the Indian influence is more prominent than elsewhere in South America. The region consists of three major physical divisions:

● the Pacific coastal lowlands of Ecuador and Peru, where there is some development of beach tourism
● the 'Sierra' or High Andes, which is actually two mountain chains separated by a series of intermontane basins and high plateaus; here cultural tourism and, more recently, adventure tourism are important
● the forested lowlands to the east of the Andes, forming part of the vast Amazon Basin, where eco-tourism is being developed.

The majority of the attractions are to be found in the Sierra, where there is a great variety of climates and landscapes due to differences in altitude. The arrangement of zones is similar to that of Mexico, but there are also extensive areas above 4000 metres altitude, known as *puna* where the climate is bleak and dry, or as *páramo*, where it is cold and damp all year round. Although *soroche* (mountain sickness) is a distinct possibility due to the altitude, climbers from all over the world are attracted to the challenge of peaks such as Chimborazo, Huascaran and Ilimani, while the spectacular scenery attracts growing numbers of trekkers from Europe and North America. The Sierra also has much to interest the cultural tourist. Intricate cultivation terraces on steep mountainsides, and the remains of temples and fortresses bear witness to the achievements of the Incas who ruled this part of South America prior to the Spanish conquest. The Indian influence is also evident in the artistic heritage of the colonial period in cities such as Quito, Cuzco and Sucre, and in the folklore and plaintive music of the Sierra.

Due to the difficult terrain road transport in the Andean republics is inadequate. However, air travel within the region has been facilitated since the early 1990s under the terms of the Andean Pact. Accommodation varies widely in quality, standards of service and cost. There is a large informal sector of hostels, often with very basic facilities, that cater for the backpacker market.

Peru

Peru is the largest of the Andean republics and has the most well-developed tourism industry. Its capital, Lima, is the major gateway to the region. Since 1990 tourism has grown rapidly as a result of political and economic stability under the Fujimori regime and the demise of the 'Shining Path' terrorism movement. However, Peru continues to have many social problems, not least the marginalization of its Indian rural communities.

Tourists from Western Europe and the USA each account for about a quarter of all arrivals. Peru appeals both to the luxury tour market, which has proved resilient to the effects of recession, and to the young traveller on a budget who sees the country as an adventure destination. The Peruvian government has been involved in developing tourism through agencies such as Enturperu – now privatized – which runs a chain of hotels, and Copesco which is concerned with restoring historic sites. Tourism promotion is carried out by Promperu, with private sector backing. Most of the hotel capacity is concentrated in Lima and Cuzco – which is close to the major archaeological sites. The government's open skies policy has attracted foreign airlines, including European carriers. The rail system – primarily developed for conveying minerals from the Andes to coastal ports – is important for tourism, as it includes the highest narrow-gauge railway in the world (from Callao to Huancayo – reaching 4800 metres), and the line from Cuzco to Machupicchu – Peru's best known tourist attraction.

Most of the tourist attractions of Peru are located in the Sierra, although Lima is the usual starting point for cultural tours. The Peruvian capital is less appealing to foreign visitors than Cuzco, which is said to be the oldest continuously inhabited city in the Americas. Here Spanish buildings have been erected on Inca foundations. Cuzco and the 'sacred valley' of the Urubamba provide the best examples of the heritage of this advanced Indian civilization. These include:

1 The Inca fortresses of Sacsahuaman and Ollantaytambo, built of intricate masonry without the use of mortar or iron tools.

2 The 'lost city' of Machu Picchu, abandoned for centuries in the forest and rediscovered by an American archaeologist in 1911. During the late 1990s the site attracted 300 000 visitors a year, some arriving by helicopter, the majority making the journey by rail and road along the Urubamba Valley. Some 20 per cent of visitors followed the 'Inca Trail' – one of the world's most famous trekking routes. However, this has had a negative impact in the form of widespread erosion of a trail that was originally designed for barefoot Indian runners and llama pack-trains; discarded toilet paper and other refuse; and damage from illegal campfires. In 2000 the authorities closed the trail to all but authorized trekking companies employing local guides and porters. However, some argue that the ban on independent hikers, most of whom are environmentally aware, is indiscriminate. Another controversial project is the replacement of the buses that take tourists from the resort of Aguas Calientes to the site by a cableway with a capacity of 400 passengers per hour.

Alternative attractions to Cuzco and Machu Picchu include:

● the attractive city of Arequipa with its colonial architecture and the nearby Colca Canyon
● the Callejon de Huaylas in the north of the country with its spectacular mountain scenery
● Lake Titicaca – at almost 4000 metres altitude – the world's highest navigable body of water.

The Peruvian coast has a very dry climate, except during El Niño episodes that occur periodically at around Christmas time. There are a large number of beaches, but these are visited mainly by domestic tourists and, generally, tourism takes second place to the important fishing industry. A well-known attraction in the coastal desert is provided by the mysterious Nazca Lines, the relic of another advanced Indian civilization.

Ecuador

Ecuador has many natural advantages as a tourist destination, containing many attractions within a relatively compact area. However, the government has done little to develop and promote these assets effectively. Peru is better known for Indian handicrafts, and few people realize that 'Panama hats' are actually made in Ecuador. The Galapagos Islands, which we looked at as a case study in resource conservation in Chapter 3, has a higher international profile than mainland Ecuador. Eco-tourism is the largest growth market, and 17 per cent of the country has national park status. However, conservation is threatened by development pressures, under-funding and the lack of trained guides. During the 1990s visitor arrivals to Ecuador more than doubled, but many of these were low-spending backpackers

who perceive the country to be a safe destination compared with others in the region. Visitors from the USA far outnumber those from Europe.

Most of mainland Ecuador's attractions for foreign visitors are concentrated in the so-called 'Avenue of the Volcanoes', the series of valleys that lies between one of the world's greatest concentration of active volcanoes, notably Cotopaxi and Tungurahua. An attractive countryside, framed by mountains and eucalyptus trees, and picturesque Indian markets are part of the Sierra's appeal. The cities have a rich cultural heritage, especially the following:

1 Quito, known as 'the city of eternal spring' is recognized by UNESCO as a World Heritage Site on account of the number of Baroque churches and convents in its historic centre. However the capital is suffering from runaway growth, air pollution and the consequences of the economic crisis that has afflicted Ecuador since the early 1990s.
2 Cuenca, Ecuador's third largest city, has similar cultural attractions but fewer social and environmental problems.

Domestic tourists gravitate to spas such as Baños or to the beach resorts of the Pacific coast, which also attract large numbers of holidaymakers from Colombia and Peru. The coastal lowlands offer a very different environment to the Sierra, with a plantation economy geared to export markets. The important seaport of Guayaquil is Ecuador's main business centre.

Ecuador's section of the Amazon Basin is known as the Oriente, an area of rainforest that was undeveloped prior to the discovery of oil in the 1950s. Adventure tourism, including canoeing on the River Napo, is organized by tour operators based in Quito, who also promote the region for eco-tourism. However, much of this so-called eco-tourism is merely another form of exploitation that fails to benefit the local Indian communities. One exception is the Cuyabeno Reserve which is partly under the control of the Secoya tribe. Here tourist groups are limited in numbers, and sustainable forms of transport and accommodation are used. However, the region's ecosystems continue to be under threat from oil spillages and its native people from diseases against which they have little resistance.

Bolivia

Tourism in Bolivia is handicapped by the country's land-locked situation, inadequate communications and a poorly developed accommodation sector. Yet the country has as great a variety of landscapes as any in South America, including vast salt lakes in the south-west, lush subtropical valleys on the northern flanks of the Andes and tropical rainforests, swamps and savannas in the eastern part of the country. The Altiplano, at an average altitude of 4000 metres is Bolivia's heartland, a bleak plateau characterized by intense sunshine during the day and subzero temperatures for much of the year at night. The majority of the population are Indians, speaking the Quechua and Aymara languages rather than Spanish. The mysterious ruins of Tiahuanaco near Lake Titicaca are a reminder of an Indian civilization that flourished here many centuries before the Incas.

Mining was historically the basis for Bolivia's economy, as shown by the Baroque architecture of the city of Potosi. This was made possible by the rich mines of the mountain known as the Cerro Rico overlooking the city, and the backbreaking labour of untold millions of Indians. Bolivia also boasts the world's highest capital city and international airport, La Paz, and what surely must be the world's highest ski resort nearby. With its upper slopes at the breathtaking altitude of 5500 metres, Chacaltaya is suitable only for skiers who are fully acclimatized!

Temperate South America

Argentina, Chile, Uruguay and Paraguay occupy the southern third of South America lying outside the tropics. Due to its triangular shape, tapering toward Antarctica, this region is known as the 'Southern Cone' by Latin Americans. Distance from the main generating countries in both Europe and North America has been a major disadvantage for the development of international tourism. Nevertheless – with the exception of Paraguay – these countries share a relatively high level of economic development and educational attainment. Since the nineteenth century they have attracted large numbers of immigrants from Europe – particularly Italy and Germany, as well as Spain – and this has strongly influenced the culture, while the Indian population is much smaller than elsewhere in Latin America. Tourism industries are well established, and there is a substantial middle class providing a large domestic market.

Paraguay

Paraguay in contrast is one of the poorest and least developed countries in the Western Hemisphere. It is also the only nation in Latin America where an Indian language – *Guaraní* – has the same official status as Spanish. West of the River Paraguay lies the Gran Chaco, an expanse of scrubland characterized by drought, extreme summer heat and occasional winter cold associated with the *Pampero* winds from the south. Not surprisingly the great majority of the population live in the eastern part of the country that is also scenically much more attractive. An important part of Paraguay's appeal lies in the music and handicrafts of the Guaraní people, a legacy of the Jesuit missions that flourished here in colonial times. Paraguay's membership of MERCOSUR gives it access to funding from the wealthier South American countries for much needed infrastructural improvements. At present there are few hotels outside the capital Asunción and the border town of Ciudad del Este – which has developed largely as a result of the Itaipú dam project, and shopping bargains that lure Brazilian visitors.

Uruguay

Uruguay's position as a small country between two big neighbours – Argentine and Brazil – and its reputation for political stability, explains why it has become an important venue for international conferences. Almost half the population lives in the capital Montevideo, which is said to be the safest big city in Latin America – it also boasts one of the continent's largest football stadiums. The *estancias* or country estates in the interior are developing agro-tourism in response to the fall in beef and wool prices on the world market. Uruguay's main tourist asset, however, is 500 kilometres of fine beaches. Punta del Este is one of South America's most important holiday resorts, attracting the 'jet set' to its casinos, luxury hotels, boutiques and sports facilities. Other resorts along the Atlantic coast cater for large numbers of domestic tourists of modest means and Argentinians. The flow of tourists between Argentina and Uruguay should increase substantially with the opening of a fixed link across the Rio de la Plata between Buenos Aires and the historic town of Colonia.

Argentina

Argentina has a stereotyped tourist image, based on the *gaucho* (cattleman) of the Pampas and the tango music of Buenos Aires. In fact, the country boasts the second largest economy in Latin America and since 1994 it has become a leading player in the MERCOSUR free trade area. Traditionally Argentina has looked towards Europe rather than the rest of South America for trade and cultural inspiration. It is a country of vast natural resources, including cheap energy supplies and the fertile farmlands of the Pampas. These resources made Argentina one of the world's richest countries in the early part of the twentieth century, but much of this wealth was squandered as a result of the social and economic projects of the Perón regime and the decades of political instability that followed. One of the country's main problems is outdated infrastructure – most of the road and railway system was built in the early twentieth century; another is the imbalance between Buenos Aires, which contains a third of the population, and the provinces, which are deprived of political and financial influence despite a federal system of government.

Until the 1980s incoming tourism was of little importance to the country's economy and better-off Argentinians spent as much on travel abroad – particularly to neighbouring Chile, Uruguay and Brazil. Tourism is now the largest earner of foreign exchange and employs over 10 per cent of the workforce. Hotel accommodation is mainly concentrated in Buenos Aires and the second city of Argentina, Cordoba, but there is a tendency for new projects to be located in outlying regions such as the Andes. Domestic air services are improving as a result of privatization, but the same cannot be said of the Argentinian rail network, once one of the largest in the world. It now carries only a small volume of passenger traffic compared with road or air transport.

1 *The Pampas* is the heartland of Argentina, but these featureless grasslands are of little interest to foreign tourists. Some of the *estancias* do provide visitors with accommodation and the opportunity to sample an *asado* (barbecue) and the traditional skills of the *gauchos*. In contrast Buenos Aires is one of the world's great cosmopolitan cities and one with a decidedly European 'feel', with architectural styles derived from France, Spain, Italy and Britain. The beaches of Mar del Plata on the Atlantic coast provide relief from the city's humid summers.
2 *The north* has a semi-arid climate, with landscapes similar to those of neighbouring Bolivia. In the cities of Salta and Jujuy the colonial heritage of Spain is much more evident than in Buenos Aires.
3 *The west* includes the vineyards around Mendoza and the important ski resort of Las Leñas in the foothills of the Andes. The most popular area for domestic tourists is the Argentine Lake District around San Carlos de Bariloche, which is both a summer and winter resort.
4 *Patagonia* lies in the rain-shadow of the Andes and is mostly a windswept semi-desert. Here eco-tourism is growing in popularity based on the wildlife resources of the Valdez Paninsula and the mountain, lake and glacier scenery of Los Glaciares National Park. Tours by all-terrain vehicles are available as far south as Ushuaia, Argentina's gateway to Antarctica.

Argentina and Chile are separated by the southern Andes. The only major route across this barrier is between Mendoza and Santiago, over the Uspallata Pass with its famous statue of 'Christ of the Andes'. Nevertheless cross-border traffic forms a large percentage of the tourist arrivals in both countries. Further south these mountains offer attractive forest, lake and glacier scenery, and a number of national parks have been established on both sides of the border. The more accessible locations have been developed for winter sports, and the resorts in this area attract many skiers from the USA during the Northern Hemisphere summer.

Chile

Chile must rank as one of the world's most remote destinations. It consists of a narrow expanse of territory squeezed between the Pacific Ocean and the Andes, and further isolated by the world's driest desert – the Atacama – to the north. Nevertheless, Chile is one of the most successful economies in Latin America, and tourism is a major growth sector.

The latitudinal extent of the country results in striking differences in climate between the north and the south. Most of the population is concentrated in the central region, which enjoys a Mediterranean climate.

1 The desert north was the setting for an important mining industry for nitrates and copper before the Second World War, which brought prosperity to cities like Antofogasta. Many of the mining communities have since become 'ghost towns' amid a landscape of strange rock formations and sand dunes. There has been some development of beach tourism around ports such as Iquique, but fishing remains the most important activity on the coast.
2 Central Chile is scenically much more appealing. The region offers the vineyards of the Maipo Valley, adventure tourism and skiing in the Andes and fine beaches along the coast – although heavy surf and strong currents discourage bathing. Major tourist centres include:
  (a) Santiago – one of the great cities of South America, with a population of around 4 million. The capital has an attractive setting in the Central Valley of Chile, with the ski resorts of Portillo and Valle Nevado located nearby.
  (b) Valparaiso was one of the major seaports of the Pacific, with a setting similar to San Francisco.
  (c) Viña del Mar is Chile's premier beach resort and a major cultural centre.
3 The Lakes Region around Temuco boasts some of the world's most spectacular lake and mountain scenery, including the active volcano of Osorno. The rainy cool temperate climate supports extensive forests of Araucaria pine and many plant species that are unique to the region.
4 The Far South is one of South America's most challenging environments. It is a wilderness of fjords, evergreen beech forests and glaciers, with a cold, damp and windy climate. Nevertheless eco-tourism and adventure tourism are being developed in this region. Summer cruises navigate the more sheltered inner channels. This has led to a revival in the fortunes of Punta Arenas, which lost most of its former importance as a seaport on world shipping routes with the opening of the Panama Canal. The Torres del Paine National Park near Puerto Natales contains some of the most spectacular peaks in the Andes.

Chile also owns Easter Island in the Pacific and claims part of Antarctica (see Chapter 25).

The Falkland Islands

The Falklands are a group of islands in the South Atlantic some 500 kilometres east of Patagonia. Since 1833 they have been a British colony, but Argentina has a long-standing claim to the territory it calls 'Las Malvinas'. In scenery, climate and culture the islands more closely resemble the Scottish Hebrides than mainland South America. The wildlife – including penguins and sea mammals – is representative of the sub-Antarctic zone, and is of great interest to eco-tourists. The opening in 1985 of a modern airport near Port Stanley made the islands much more accessible to Europe, but they remain a remote and expensive destination.

Summary

The countries of the Western Hemisphere south of the US border form a cultural entity consisting of three distinct geographical regions. Of these the Caribbean is the most important from the viewpoint of inbound tourism and it is the world's premier cruise destination. The English language is widespread throughout the islands, while the Iberian culture and languages are dominant on the mainland. Broadly speaking, the Caribbean islands cater mainly for 'recreational' tourism, whereas the traditional lifestyles and historic sites of Mexico, Central America and South America appeal more to 'cultural' tourists. Eco-tourism is growing in importance, particularly in the more remote areas of Central and South America, but it has often failed to benefit the indigenous communities.

The USA dominates the market for Caribbean travel although the Dominican Republic, Jamaica and Barbados have achieved wider appeal as destinations due to their accessibility by air and shipping services. On the Latin American mainland Mexico is clearly the most visited destination, due again to its proximity to the USA. Despite having spectacular scenery Central and South America have been much less successful. This is partly due to political instability and the inadequacy of the infrastructure. However, countries such as Peru and Brazil are benefiting from the growing popularity of long-haul holidays. Business travel is also likely to increase to those countries which are undergoing rapid economic development such as Brazil and Argentina.

Although incomes are generally low throughout Latin America and the Caribbean, domestic tourism is significant and there is a considerable demand for outbound tourism to Europe and the USA from a growing middle class.

Case study

Tourism plans in the Caribbean

Introduction

The islands of the Caribbean vary significantly according to their geography, their tourism products, their stage of development, and their markets. In terms of tourism planning, Wilkinson (1997) has provided a useful review of plans in the Commonwealth Caribbean by examining islands at different stages of the tourism area life cycle. In addition, the Commonwealth Caribbean is a valid region to compare plans as the islands have retained a planning system based on the British model. There are two types of political entities in the Commonwealth Caribbean:

- independent nations (e.g. Barbados)
- colonies or dependent territories of Great Britain (e.g. British Virgin Islands).

Tourism plans

Wilkinson (1997) summarizes the key dimensions of the various policy recommendations in the tourism plans for the islands as follows:

Limits to growth

Small tropical islands are very vulnerable to environmental damage. Here the islands are realizing that tourism depends upon high levels of environmental quality and that management will be needed to conserve the resource. This implies that a capacity ceiling will be reached in terms of tourism – in other words there are limits to growth. The precise limit will depend upon the nature of the environment, economy, society and government of each island.

Increased professionalism

In an increasingly competitive market place, destinations which succeed will be those that have a highly professional and well-managed tourism sector. This will involve public and private sector partnerships, enlightened economic and tourism policy, good marketing underpinned by research, and staff training.

Modernization and upgrading of the accommodation sector

Here the issue is that the islands have a legacy of small-scale entrepreneurial accommodation units, locally owned and often not well managed. In addition there are the issues presented by larger-scale foreign-owned accommodation operators that do not always provide optimal benefits to the islands due to various 'leakages' (such as repatriated profits, imported supplies, etc.). The plans seek enlightened government policy towards the accommodation sector, to allow it to flourish, and where necessary provide development incentives.

Moving from incentives policies to the removal of constraints

This means creating a climate in which tourism can flourish. Many islands provide investment incentives to developers, yet there is little evidence that such incentives influence investment decisions. Rather, the islands should focus upon creating a positive climate for investment with stable political regimes, stable economic policies and a ready pool of trained staff. This involves removing constraints such as red tape, bureaucratic delays and inappropriate taxation.

Eco-tourism

Most of the islands are seeking to enter the eco-tourism market. However, if they are to be successful, more research is needed into the nature of demand for eco-tourism, the size of this market for the Caribbean, the nature of the environment and appropriate management approaches for eco-tourism operations.

Regional co-operation

In view of the small size of the countries, there is a powerful logic in promoting regional co-operation in tourism across the Caribbean. However, little success has been achieved, partly because island politics work against co-operation, but also because there are fears that regional promotion policies would exacerbate the problem of distinguishing between islands, each with their individual and unique products.

Wilkinson (1997) concludes that successful planning for the islands will need:

- a multipurpose approach, using many different methods and players to plan the economy, society and environment of the islands wherever tourism is involved
- consideration of a blend of different sectors and elements – such as the environment – in tourism plans
- to use tourism as a medium for social change (in terms of education and employment, for example)
- to involve all the stakeholders in the tourism planning process.

Case study

The regeneration of Rio de Janeiro

Introduction

Rio de Janeiro (or Rio) is one of the world's great tourist cities for the following reasons:

1 The spectacular beauty of its setting, between Guanabara Bay and the granite peaks of Sugar Loaf and Corcovado – (which is crowned by the famous statue of Christ the Redeemer).
2 The beaches of Copacabana and Ipanema, ideal for people-watching (but not for bathing due to the heavy Atlantic surf).
3 The uninhibited dance rhythms and extravagant costume parades of Carnival – one of the greatest shows on earth.

Yet in recent years Rio has reached the later stages of the tourism area life cycle and has begun to suffer from a number of problems. These problems are related to the fall in tourism demand for Rio, the changing nature of that demand and competition from other resorts. In response, Rio has embarked upon a major regeneration of both the resort and its marketing. This fits in well with the Brazilian government's aim of:

- creating a modern and efficient state
- reducing social and regional inequalities
- modernizing the economy
- enhancing competitiveness in world markets.

As part of this initiative tourism has been given high priority as a major job creation sector.

Rio de Janeiro is located in the heart of south-east Brazil and was founded in 1502 by Portuguese navigators. Rio has a population of 5.5 million inhabitants and is the capital of the state of Rio de Janeiro. However, until 1960 (when the capital was transferred to Brasilia) it was also the capital of Brazil. When it lost the status of national capital, Rio also lost political influence and many of the problems now experienced by the city stem from this. In terms of tourism, Rio lies in the largest economic and cultural region of Brazil and is in a good location with:

- a warm climate;
- 80 kilometres of good sandy beaches;
- 132 hotels;
- good conference facilities;
- two airports (Galeao and Santos Dumont);
- good highway and rail links to other parts of Brazil.

The development of tourism in Rio

The early days

Tourism began when the Portuguese royal family moved to Brazil in the nineteenth century and chose Rio as the place to live. However, it was not until the late 1950s that the resort began to attract visitors in large numbers based on the beaches and the climate.

Growth of tourism, 1960s and 1970s

Growth of both tourist volumes and facilities was rapid between 1960 and 1975, with international visitors beginning to complement the domestic market. In the early 1970s the international airport was built and from the mid-1970s onwards the resort grew with the addition of the major hotel chains.

The emergence of problems, 1980s and early 1990s

By the 1980s problems were emerging, based on the city's lack of planning and uncoordinated approach to tourism. In the period from 1985 to 1993 international arrivals to Rio fell from 621 000 to 378 000 and average hotel occupancies fell to around 50 per cent. The city began to have a reputation for crime, visitors were concerned about security, and price inflation began to reduce demand for tourism.

By this stage of Rio's development specific problems included:

● lack of integration between the private and public sectors
● lack of professionalism in the tourism sector
● lack of tourist information in key destinations
● few employees speak English or a language other than Portuguese
● minimal diversification away from beach tourism
● an expanding population competing with tourists for services and infrastructure
● beach pollution
● price inflation due to the unstable Brazilian currency
● crime against tourists.

The regeneration strategy, 1990s

It was at this time that the city decided that a concerted regeneration strategy was needed, both for the city itself and also for tourism.

The regeneration of Rio

Until 1993, Rio de Janeiro did not have any major planning initiatives for tourism. In 1993, the mayor, with the support of the private sector, embarked upon a strategic plan for the city – Plano Estategico da Cidade do Rio de Janeiro. The plan was city-wide and was approved in 1995.

However, because of the problems identified above, and the importance of tourism to the city's economy, it was also recognized that tourism needed its own strategic plan. This was drawn up in 1997 by the mayor, in co-operation with EMBRATUR and the private sector.

The plan is designed to run until 2006 with rolling reviews of the plan's five major programmes. The main objectives of the plan are to:

● increase receipts from tourism
● maintain Rio's leading competitive position in domestic tourism
● make Rio competitive in the international market
● reposition the image of Rio.

The five programmes of the plan are summarized below.

Programme 1: New product development to attract new and existing markets

There are four elements here:

1 Diversification of entertainment facilities.
2 Development of new products, such as eco-tourism in the city's forests, including Tijuca – a surviving example of coastal rainforest within the city limits.
3 Development of cultural and historical products.
4 Development of sports tourism.

Programme 2: Upgrading of current tourism products to both enhance quality and reposition the resort

Again there are four elements:

1 Conservation of existing features such as the famous Sugar Loaf.
2 Maximize accessibility and improve signposting.
3 Conservation of streetscapes and other features to enhance the quality of the visit.
4 Encourage private sector involvement in upgrading products.

Programme 3: Development of a database for tourism and the enhancement of tourism information in the city

There are two elements here:

1 Development of a statistical database for tourism.
2 Development of tourist information centres.

Programme 4: Implementation of a disciplined marketing approach for Rio

Here there are two key elements:

1 Create a new image of an attractive, culturally vibrant city – 'Incomparable Rio' and promote this new image to the travel trade, the media and the public.

2 Develop a public relations campaign targeted at the local population and media.

Programme 5: Development of a skilled and professional workforce for the tourism sector

There are two key elements here:

1 Development of a tourism education system in Rio.
2 Establishment of a quality management system for tourism in Rio.

Other initiatives include attempts to spread the benefits of tourism to the poor of Rio. So far tourism has done little to benefit the people of the *favelas*, the shanty-towns on the hillsides overlooking the city centre. However, Rocinha, the largest of these slums, is the subject of a private initiative to train local guides to show visitor the hidden side of Rio and help regenerate the area.

The regeneration strategy for Rio is attempting to reposition the resort's image away from sea, sun and sand and towards a city worth visiting for its modern cultural attractions – 'Incomparable Rio'. This is a good example of a disciplined and well-thought-out response to a problem in a tourist destination.

(Railson Costa de Souza, 1998; official tourist board web site at http:/www/embratur.gov.br/; Brazilinfo web site at http://www brazilinfo.com)

25

Australasia

LEARNING OBJECTIVES

After reading this chapter, you should be able to:

1 Describe the major physical features and climates of Australasia and understand their importance for tourism.
2 Appreciate that Australia and New Zealand are socially and economically part of the developed Western world, whereas most of the Pacific Islands are developing countries, and the influence these differences have on tourism patterns.
3 Recognize the importance of domestic tourism and outbound travel in Australia and New Zealand.
4 Appreciate the economic, social and environmental impacts of tourism on the native peoples and natural resources of the region.
5 Appreciate the effect of great distance from the major generating countries of the Northern Hemisphere on incoming tourism.
6 Be aware of the growing importance of eco-tourism in the region, and the potential of Antarctica as tourism's 'last frontier'.
7 Demonstrate a knowledge of the tourist regions, resorts, business centres and tourist attractions of Australia, New Zealand and the Pacific Islands.

Introduction

Australia, New Zealand, and the islands of the Pacific east of Indonesia and the Philippines form a separate geographical entity called Australasia. An alternative name – Oceania – is also appropriate as most of the constituent islands are insignificant in comparison with the vastness of the Pacific Ocean, which covers a quarter of the earth's surface and spans a distance of more than 12 000 kilometres from east to west at its widest extent. The only large landmasses are:

● Australia – often called the 'island-continent'
● New Guinea
● The two main islands of New Zealand.

The total population is small compared to that of neighbouring South-East Asia – well under 30 million – and there is generally less pressure on resources. Australia and New Zealand are economically, culturally and politically part of the developed Western world, but both countries play an important developmental role with regard to the other countries in the South Pacific region. In the northern Pacific, the islands of Hawaii are geographically part of Polynesia, although they became the fiftieth state of the USA in 1959. They provide a role model for tourism development elsewhere in the Pacific, and are the subject of a case study. The rest of Australasia is economically part of the developing world, consisting mainly of island mini-states with small populations and limited land resources. Most have become politically independent only since the 1960s, while some of the smaller islands are still governed by countries lying outside the region, notably France and the USA. With the ending of the Cold War, the islands are no longer supported by the defence industries of the Western powers and must become economically more self-sufficient. For this reason, tourism and the exploitation of the islands' potentially vast marine resources increasingly play a vital role.

The Pacific Asia Tourism Association (PATA) represents all the countries in the region. There are prospects for considerable growth in tourism, partly as a result of the publicity generated for the Millennium. More important, the region can offer generally favourable climates, unspoiled coastal and mountain scenery, and in the main, political stability. The market potential is certainly present. The Pacific Rim of Asia and North America is an area of impressive economic growth. Since 1970, Australia and New Zealand have loosened their ties to Britain and forged closer trade links with the USA and the countries of East Asia, especially Japan. This pattern of trade has resulted in a growing volume of air traffic across the Pacific, facilitated by long-range wide-bodied jets. Air transport now plays a vital role in the economy of all the countries in the region, and the peoples of Australasia are very aviation minded. However, these Pacific destinations are still a long way from the major tourist-generating countries – particularly those of Europe – and are therefore vulnerable to the impact of international crises, and competition from more accessible parts of the world that can offer similar attractions.

The native peoples of Australasia suffered severely as a result of Western colonization in the nineteenth century, losing most of their tribal lands and much of their culture in the process. This was particularly true of the Australian aborigines, who became a small, marginalized minority. Since the 1970s there has been a growing recognition of the value of indigenous arts, crafts and folklore as cultural resources, and native peoples not only take greater pride in their heritage, but increasingly take an active role in the tourism industry.

Australia

Introduction

For more than a century Australia, and New Zealand have been the destinations for large numbers of emigrants, chiefly from the British Isles, but more recently from Asian and Pacific countries. Until the 1980s Australia was not important as a holiday destination, the great majority of visitors being business or VFR travellers. In the 1980s and 1990s growth rates for inbound tourism accelerated, delivering arrivals of 4 million by the end of the 1990s. This has in part been due to the promotional efforts of both the Australian Tourist Commission (ATC) and the Australian state governments, especially fuelled by the publicity given to the Bicentennial in 1988, the Sydney Olympics in 2000, other media coverage and more competitive air fares. Tourism receipts are now Australia's number one export and tourism supports 500 000 jobs.

Australia is the only country occupying a whole continent, with an area of 7.6 million square kilometres – comparable in size to the USA. Not surprisingly, the country has a federal system of government, similar to Canada, in which the states and the two territories – Northern Territory and Australian Capital Territory – enjoy much freedom to manage their own affairs, including the development and regulation of domestic tourism. Each state has a tourism-marketing agency and

most states also have a government tourism department. At federal level, tourism began to be taken seriously in the early 1990s with a number of strategy initiatives and the appointment of a tourism minister to the cabinet. The federal Department of Tourism co-ordinates policy and action plans while the ATC is responsible for tourism marketing and is funded by the federal government with contributions from the tourism industry. Despite a very well-organized tourism sector at both regional and federal level, the organization of tourism is weak at the local level.

Physical features

Australia has great tourism potential, thanks to its warm sunny climates, unique wildlife and natural features, as well as a coastline – over 36 000 kilometres in length – which includes some of the world's finest beaches and the largest coral reef. However, most of the continent has been worn down by eons of erosion and as a result, is relatively low lying compared with other continents, with only a few mountain ranges and inselbergs – isolated rocky outcrops rising abruptly from the surrounding plains. The main exception is the mountain system – known as the Great Dividing Range – which runs for 3600 kilometres along the eastern margin of the continent, reaching its highest point – 2200 metres – at Mount Kosciuszko. These mountain ranges separate the fertile coastal belt – where most of the cities and tourist facilities are located – from the interior. Australia can also claim to be the world's driest continent. Most of the outback – the vast, thinly populated bush country extending west of the River Darling – is desert or semi-desert, where the lakes shown on the map are usually expanses of salt and the rivers merely a succession of pools or 'billabongs'.

The most interesting natural resources of Australia are the plants – mainly drought-resistant eucalyptus (or 'gums') – and the animals – marsupial species which are only native to the island-continent. Indeed, Australia has more than 2000 protected natural areas, including national parks, testament to the unique landscapes and the flora and fauna of the continent. Thirteen sites are on the UN's World Heritage list including:

- Kakadu National Park in the Northern Territory
- Uluru (Ayers Rock) also in the Northern Territory
- The Wet Tropics of north Queensland, an area of virgin rainforest
- The Great Barrier Reef off the Queensland coast
- Fraser Island – a sand island also off the coast of Queensland
- The Central Eastern Rainforest Reserves
- Willandra Lakes
- Lord Howe Island
- Tasmanian wilderness
- Shark Bay
- Australian fossil mammal sites.

These landscapes provide endless opportunities for tourism – tourists can prospect for gold or gemstones, go on whale- or dolphin-watching trips, take part in four-wheel-drive vehicle safaris that allow the more adventurous to visit remoter areas away from the all-weather roads, or try adventure sports such as abseiling and whitewater rafting. The Australians are leaders in minimizing the environmental impact of these recreational activities. The ATC has overall responsibility for monitoring the environmental impact of tourism and has initiated a number of state and federal eco-tourism strategies and awards for sustainable tourism practices.

The size of Australia and its geographical location means that it experiences a wide range of climatic conditions, but no real extremes. Most of Australia, with the exception of Tasmania, lies within tropical or subtropical latitudes, so that winter cold is rarely a problem. The desert interior has a more extreme climate; in winter pleasantly warm days are followed by nights with temperatures dropping below 0°C. The northernmost region of Australia, around Darwin, experiences a tropical monsoon type of climate with a rainy season between December and May, accompanied by high temperatures and humidity. The great majority of Australians live in the south-eastern part of the country and enjoy a warm temperate climate, which in general is ideal for outdoor recreation. However, summer temperatures frequently exceed 40°C due to winds from the desert interior, which bring the risk of bush fires to the cities. Snow is almost unknown except in Tasmania and the southern sections of the Great Dividing Range, where it provides good skiing conditions from June to September. Perhaps the best climate is around Perth in Western Australia where summers are dry but not excessively warm due to a constant sea breeze.

Demand for tourism

The population of Australia approached 19 million in the late 1990s and is concentrated into a few large cities – Sydney and Melbourne account for around 40 per cent of the population. Other major centres include Brisbane, Adelaide and Perth. Canberra is a relatively small city, though it is the federal capital. The urban character of Australia's population has an important influence on the patterns of tourism which have developed. A developed and diversified economy means that Australians enjoy a high standard of living. The ownership of motor vehicles, for example, approaches North American levels in Australia (9 million vehicles in the late 1990s) and the effects are seen in suburban sprawl around the major cities. Participation in outdoor activities is high by European standards. The most popular participant sports are tennis, swimming, sailing and surfing. Sports facilities are excellent, boosted by the Sydney Olympics in 2000, and spectator sports include football, cricket and horse-racing. Gambling is also popular, with casinos producing considerable revenue and attracting international visitors, particularly from Asia.

Each year Australians take, on average, at least two pleasure trips involving a stay away from home, and travel has become an important element of discretionary spending, increasing travel propensities. The domestic market is significant simply because of the wide range of experiences on offer in the continent, although only a small proportion of trips cross state boundaries, partly because of the distances involved. Deregulation of domestic airlines in the early 1990s led to a lowering of airfares and boosted the domestic industry. The majority of holidays are in December and January, mostly to the beach resorts between Sydney and north Queensland. During the winter months there is a smaller but much more concentrated migration to the semi-tropical beaches of Queensland and large numbers also head for the ski slopes of the Australian Alps, while others seek the unspoiled desert scenery around Alice Springs.

Australia is the largest generator of international tourism in the Southern Hemisphere, with almost 3 million trips taken in the late 1990s. Despite their distance from other destinations, Australians feel a strong need to explore other parts of the world. The majority of Australian tourists who travel abroad are residents of the two most prosperous states, New South Wales and Victoria, which between them contain almost two-thirds of the population. Despite the high costs involved, large numbers of Australians visit Europe on holidays extending over a few weeks, during which several countries may be visited. They include a high proportion of young people combining a European tour with work experience, some travelling overland from Singapore via India and the Middle East. Other popular destinations include the USA, New Zealand and the Pacific Islands such as Fiji, Vanuatu and New Caledonia. A glance at the map will show that Australia is in fact much closer to South-East Asia than it is to Europe or North America, with Indonesia being less than 1000 kilometres from Darwin. This accounts for the popularity of the beach resorts of Bali, Thailand and Malaysia. However, shopping trips to destinations such as Hong Kong and Singapore have declined.

The tourism industry in Australia caters in the main for the large domestic demand, and until the 1980s little attention was paid to the needs of foreign visitors. However, such has been the turnaround that Australia now runs a surplus on its tourism account and tropical destinations such as Cairns and the Whitsunday Islands are taking market share from places such as Fiji. Until quite recently, service standards were indifferent, partly because of the egalitarian attitudes prevalent in the country. Change has come about partly as a result of the influx of large numbers of immigrants from southern and eastern Europe and, to a lesser extent, from Asia. These *New Australians* have expanded the range of entertainments and restaurants on offer in their adopted cities and greatly improved standards in Australia's 5000-plus hotels.

Only a small percentage of foreign visitors to Australia come on inclusive tours and VFR tourism is decreasing in importance from Britain and Ireland as holiday tourism becomes more important. The main inbound markets for Australia are New Zealand, Japan, the USA and the UK/Ireland. The Japanese are predominantly in the younger age groups and are mainly attracted to the resorts of the Queensland coast. The Americans, on the other hand, are generally older with a high propensity to travel; they feel an affinity with the pioneering spirit of Australia and are most likely to take a touring holiday. A growing number of tourists come from Singapore, Hong Kong and other Asian countries, and many of these are in the student category. However, the Asian currency crisis in the late 1990s did reduce the numbers visiting Australia from Asian countries.

The great majority of foreign visitors to Australia arrive in Sydney or Melbourne and few travel beyond New South Wales or Queensland to take advantage of lower fares offered by the major domestic airlines. This is despite attempts to spread arrivals to other gateways (such as Perth), and the impact of deregulation of the domestic airlines in 1991 has meant that more services are on offer, and airfares have fallen – such that domestic air traffic stood at 18 million passengers in the late 1990s. Airports across Australia are also being privatized and upgraded. Providing adequate transport in such a vast, sparsely populated country is a problem. The journey across the continent from Perth to Sydney (3300 kilometres) involves a two-hour time change, a five-hour flight, or a journey by train or bus lasting three days. The 40 000 kilometre Australian rail system is not a viable alternative to flying as the network is incomplete and interrupted by changes of gauge at state boundaries. An exception is the Indian Pacific Express which allows direct travel from Sydney to Perth. Dedicated tourism rail services are also being developed and include the Great South Pacific Express between Sydney and Cairns.

The tourism resources of Australia

New South Wales

Tourism in New South Wales is dominated by its capital, Sydney. Sydney has arguably a better climate, a more spectacular setting, and a more varied nightlife than its rival Melbourne. The city has developed around one of the world's finest harbours and the beaches of the Pacific are within easy reach by hydrofoil or ferry. Sydney's attractions include:

1 The famous suspension bridge across the harbour, which can now be climbed by visitors.
2 Harbour-side attractions such as the Sydney Opera House, the ferry terminal at Circular Quay, shopping, restaurants and hotels on the harbour side and revitalized

areas such as The Rocks with art galleries and specialist shopping.
3 Darling Harbour has been revitalized with the Sydney Aquarium, an IMAX Cinema and theme parks.
4 Around the harbour are heritage sites and buildings such as Fort Dennison and the Quarantine Station where emigrants first landed, now converted into a hotel.
5 The city has many cultural attractions such as the Art Gallery of New South Wales and a range of museums.
6 Distinctive city areas such as Paddington and Kings Cross.

The best known of Sydney's beaches is Bondi, with its superb conditions for surfing, but since the strong tidal surges can be dangerous many families prefer the more sheltered beaches of Port Jackson or the small seaside resort of Manly with its Oceanworld attraction. Sydney's hosting of the 2000 Olympics gave tourism a major boost and involved the building of fourteen new hotels, improvement of the transport infrastructure and the provision of new sports facilities.

Recreational areas within easy reach of the city include:

● the Snowy Mountains with ski resorts such as Thredbo and Perisher;
● the gorges of the Hawkesbury River;
● the Hunter Valley vineyards;
● the Blue Mountains, a scenic area of forested ridges, caves and waterfalls; cable-cars and a funicular railway provide access from the resort of Katoomba to a variety of viewpoints.

Queensland

From Sydney a scenic coastal route leads northwards into Queensland, which is predominantly a destination for beach tourism. The route passes through resorts such as Newcastle, Coffs Harbour, Port Stephens, Port Macquarie, Byron Bay (a famous surfing beach) and the rainforest in the Dorrigo National Park. The area 50 kilometres south of Brisbane, known as the 'Gold Coast', is one of the most popular holiday regions for Australians, but also caters for international visitors, particularly the Japanese. The coast is a highly developed 70-kilometre strip of resorts with Surfer's Paradise at its heart. There is a good deal of badly planned, commercialized development with many high-rise hotels. The area is the site of both sporting events and a number of major theme parks, reminiscent of Florida:

● Seaworld
● Warner Brothers Movie World
● Dreamworld (A Disney-type park).

In the hinterland of the Gold Coast the Lamington National Park is well known for its bird life.

Brisbane, the state capital, received a boost to tourism in 1988 by hosting Expo, and the site has been redeveloped as the Southbank Parklands – a cultural and park area on the south bank of the Brisbane River. Brisbane has a spectacular setting on the river where CityCat catamarans ferry visitors and commuters. Brisbane has a range of cultural venues, museums and galleries.

Close to the coast near Brisbane are a number of islands – Fraser Island is the world's largest barrier island composed of sand deposits. Other islands off the coast are both recreational areas for Queenslanders and also good locations for dolphin- and whale-watching. To the north of Brisbane, the 'Sunshine Coast' has excellent beaches stretching from Caloundra to Rainbow Beach. One resort – Noosa Heads – has specialized in fine dining. In the hinterland are the Noosa and Cooloola national parks.

One of Australia's unique tourist attractions, the Great Barrier Reef, begins 350 kilometres north of Brisbane and extends northwards for 2000 kilometres to Cape York. The reef provides opportunities for scuba-diving that are unequalled elsewhere. Between the reef and the coast lies an enormous sheltered lagoon dotted with hundreds of islands. Some of these have been developed as exclusive holiday resorts with marinas, golf courses and other sports facilities, while others cater more for campers. Examples include:

- Hamilton Island on one of the seventy-four tropical Whitsunday Islands with its own jetport and is accessible by air from Brisbane
- Green Island specializes in eco-friendly tourism
- Bedarra specializes in honeymooners.

Pollution and overfishing are problems on the more popular islands with consequent danger to the reef ecosystem; to remedy this some areas have been designated as nature reserves. The ports of the Queensland coast, notably Cairns, Townsville and Port Douglas are the starting point of excursions to the reef and offshore islands by boat and helicopter. Cairns is now an important gateway, particularly for Japanese visitors, and is a booming resort city developing rapidly with new hotels and a casino. Inland, sugar plantations and the rainforests of the Daintree National Park and the Atherton Tableland provide the main interest away from the coastal resorts. The Kurunda Skyrail provides a 7.5-kilometre ride over the rainforest canopy, with Tjapukai Aboriginal Cultural Park at its foot. From Cairns northwards to Cape York there are the excellent and largely deserted white beaches of the 'Marlin Coast' and the tropical rainforest, designated as a World Heritage Site.

Victoria

Victoria experiences more variable weather conditions than other states of mainland Australia, with rural tourism playing a more important role. The capital of Victoria – Melbourne – rivals Sydney as the commercial capital of the

country, with a more conservative, less flamboyant lifestyle. Melbourne is set on the Yarra River and has an equally wide range of retailing, restaurants, cultural and sporting attractions, and is almost as cosmopolitan as Sydney with large Italian and Greek communities and its own seaside resort at St Kilda. Melbourne has a range of sporting venues such as the Melbourne Cricket Ground (MCG) and Albert Park, where the Australian Formula One Grand Prix is held. The city has retained its trams and is conveniently placed for touring the vineyards of the Yarra River. Other tourist resources accessible from Melbourne include:

- the Victorian Alps – a popular region for walking, skiing (in resorts such as Mount Buller) and whitewater rafting
- the Great Ocean Road drive along the picturesque Victoria coast with rock features such as the Twelve Apostles
- Phillip Island with its burrowing penguins
- the Gippsland Lake District
- reminders of Victoria's nineteenth-century mining heritage with living museums recreating the 1850s Gold Rush
- old-style steamboat trips on the Murray River, an important commercial waterway before the coming of the railways.

Australian Capital Territory

Canberra is the capital of Australia and is spaciously planned in a beautiful setting near the Snowy Mountains. It cannot compare in vitality to Sydney or Melbourne, but boasts major cultural attractions, including the National Gallery, national institutions such as the Australian Institute of Sport, as well as the Parliament House.

Tasmania

The small island-state of Tasmania lies 400 kilometres to the south of the mainland, across the Bass Strait and can be reached by ferry or fast catamaran from Melbourne, or by air to Launceston. With its mild oceanic climate and perpetually green countryside, Tasmania contrasts with the rest of Australia and has its own flora and fauna – such as the Tasmanian Devil. The small resorts along the north coast (such as Stanley) are not unlike those of England's West Country, and are particularly attractive for senior citizens escaping the summer heat and more hurried lifestyle on the mainland. Inland there is mountain and lake scenery in the Cradle Mountain – Lake St Clair National Park and the Cataract Gorge, a spectacular ravine popular for adventure sports. The south-west of the island receives the heaviest rainfall in Australia and is covered by barely explored rainforest. The Tasmanian Wilderness Railway – once used for transporting minerals – has been restored as a 30-kilometre journey through virgin wilderness. The island has a range of heritage attractions based on its past – such as the Port Arthur historic site, a reminder of Australia's most notorious penal settlement.

Western Australia

The largest and most thinly populated of the states, Western Australia suffers as a destination due to its great distance from the more popular tourist regions of the east coast, but is nevertheless developing markets based on eco-tourism, adventure tourism and its mining heritage. Perth is a green spacious city close to good surfing beaches (such as Scarborough and Margaret River) fronting the Indian Ocean, while Fremantle on the Swan River received wide publicity by hosting the America's Cup yacht race and now has a maritime museum. The city has a variety of attractions including the Perth Mint, Cultural Centre and gemstone shopping in the suburbs. Perth is also a good base for exploring the outback including:

- El Questro Station, one of a number of working cattle farms that provide facilities for tourists
- the Punululu/Bungle Bungle National Park with its multicoloured rock formations
- the even more remote Kimberley region, over 2000 kilometres north of Perth, a wilderness of sandstone gorges, transformed during the rainy season into a riot of vegetation and cascading waterfalls
- the gold mining towns of Kalgoorlie and Coolgardie.

Attractions along the coast include:

- Shark Bay which is renowned for its marine wildlife, including the dolphins of Monkey Mia that interact freely with visitors, but this situation could change if tourist numbers become excessive
- Exmouth on the Coral Coast is the base for exploring the Ningaloo Reef
- Broome, famous for its former pearl-diving industry, and now an upmarket beach resort.

South Australia

Most of South Australia is desert country, but in contrast, Adelaide, the festival city, has a very English feel to the architecture and has a parkland setting. Adelaide is close to the coastal resort of Glenelg, the vineyards of the Clare and Barossa Valleys and the scenic Flinders Mountains with the Flinders Chase National Park. Further afield is Kangaroo Island – subject of a case study, and the opal-mining town of Coober Pedy, deep in the outback where visitors can stay in the Desert Caves Hotel, built underground like most dwellings in this community to avoid the extreme desert heat.

Northern Territory

The Stuart Highway links Australia's southern city of Adelaide with the northern city of Darwin. Darwin is the largest city of the 'Top End' with a limited range of attractions but used as a base for exploring the region's tourist resources. These include Australia's tropical northlands with their game-rich grasslands and reserves on which the Australian aborigines continue their traditional lifestyle – the Tiwi islands off the coast allow visitors to interact with aborigines. There are a number of important areas accessible to Darwin:

1 The Kakadu National Park is probably the most popular attraction in this region. It was the setting for the *Crocodile Dundee* film and has rich wetland wildlife.
2 Litchfield National Park is closer to Darwin, famous for wildlife, aborigine rock art and the Gagudju Crocodile Hotel – so called because of its design.
3 Arnhemland is a large unspoilt wetland area under aborigine management where visitor numbers are strictly controlled by a permit system.

Further south lies the 'red heart' of Australia, an area of spinifex desert, salt lakes and strange rock formations such as the Olgas/Kata Tjuta and the more famous Ayers Rock/Uluru. The only town in the region, Alice Springs, offers a range of attractions such as:

- the Telegraph Station, a reminder of the city's pioneering role
- the Alice Springs Cultural Precinct showcasing the history of central Australia
- the School of the Air Outback Radio Service
- the base of the Flying Doctor Service.

However, Alice Springs owes its importance as a tourist centre more to its function as the gateway to the Uluru National Park and its prime attraction – Ayers Rock (or Uluru in the local aborigine language). This has achieved international recognition as an icon of Australia, due to its unique character as the world's largest monolith – it measures 9 kilometres in circumference and 300 metres in height – and the way the rock changes colour at sunrise and sunset. Ayers Rock became much more accessible with the opening of an airport and purpose-built resort at Yulara in the 1980s. This provides a range of accommodation from budget camping to the five-star Ayers Rock Resort Hotel. Guided tours of the Rock and the surrounding area interpret aborigine culture and legends of the 'Dreamtime', and visitors can sample 'bush tucker' – the natural foods of the outback. Nevertheless, the ever-growing number of visitors raises a number of issues regarding the future of tourism in the area, namely:

1 *Sustainability* Burgeoning demand may exhaust ground water supplies, already under pressure from the cattle

industry. Although the Yulara resort is built to an aesthetically high standard, it is difficult to justify air-conditioned swimming pools as being compatible with eco-tourism.

2   *The potential for conflict between tourists and the host community* Ayers Rock is a sacred site for the aboriginal people, but to most tourists, it is a photo opportunity and an objective to be climbed – albeit with difficulty. Many aborigines regard this as an act of desecration.

New Zealand

Although New Zealand shares cultural similarities with Australia, including a love of sport and the outdoor life, and a certain informality of outlook, it is different in many other respects. To begin with, the Tasman Sea separating the two countries is 1900 kilometres wide and often stormy. New Zealand is scenically very different from its big neighbour, boasting volcanoes, glaciers and fjords among its natural attractions. The native flora and fauna is quite unlike that of Australia. Much of this, including the unique flightless birds, was threatened with extinction as a result of the introduction of new species by Europeans in the process of clearing 'the bush' for farmland. New Zealand was among the first countries to establish national parks on the American model, to conserve what remained of the natural heritage. There continues to be a widespread interest in environmental issues, such as opposition to the French nuclear testing in the South Pacific. New Zealand's cultural heritage includes an export-orientated pastoral economy, and a nineteenth-century gold rush – in Westland – reminiscent of the Australian experience. However, New Zealand was colonized by the British with free settlers, in contrast to the convict origins of most of the Australian states. The indigenous Maori people had a highly developed, if warlike, culture derived from their homeland in Polynesia. They now account for some 12 per cent of the population and their cultural heritage, expressed in crafts and dances, forms an important ingredient in New Zealand's tourist appeal. The Maori have become more fully integrated into the mainstream culture than the native peoples of Australia, although the incidence of unemployment and other social problems in Maori communities is higher than the national average.

The demand for tourism

The New Zealand government was one of the first to recognize the importance of tourism, setting up an official tourist organization as far back as 1901. Tourism now accounts for 14 per cent of export earnings and foreign visitor arrivals in the late 1990s exceeded 1.5 million a year, compared to only 100 000 in 1970. This growth has been achieved, in spite of the remoteness of this small island nation from the world's major trade routes and centres of population, by successful promotion and development of the country's resources. The New Zealand Tourist Board works closely with the private sector to attract the more adventurous type of tourist who is interested in scenery, meeting people and the outdoor life. New Zealand can offer the unique resource of uncrowded countryside, with a population of only 3.3 million occupying an area comparable in size to the British Isles.

Most of New Zealand is hilly or mountainous and the country's greatest tourist asset is the beauty and variety of its scenery. The two large islands that make up the bulk of New Zealand offer quite different environments. Much of the North Island consists of a volcanic plateau, while the South Island is dominated by a range of high fold mountains, the Southern Alps, which contain glaciers, snowfields and a fjord coastline.

The climate of New Zealand favours the more active types of outdoor recreation, with its equable temperatures and pollution-free atmosphere. Although the islands enjoy more sunshine than the British Isles, sunshine is not guaranteed, and the range of latitude occupied by the islands means that while Auckland has a subtropical climate, at Invercargill 1600 kilometres further south the temperatures more closely resemble those experienced in the western islands of Scotland. This puts domestic tourism at a disadvantage compared with Australia's Gold Coast, Bali and the islands of the Pacific. The mountains in both the North and South Islands are high enough to receive heavy snowfalls, the skiing season lasting from July to October.

Two-thirds of New Zealand's population live in North Island and, of these, half are concentrated in the country's largest city, Auckland. The standard of living is high, with motor vehicle ownership approaching Australian levels, although cars and other consumer goods have to be imported. The economy is dependent on the export of primary products such as meat and wool, and a prolonged recession in the 1980s led to the drastic reduction in the role of the public sector and spending on social services. Nevertheless, despite the distances that must be covered, and the high cost of air fares, New Zealanders have a high propensity to travel abroad, and with much the same preferences regarding destinations as the Australians. About half of all overseas visits are to Australia, with the encouragement of cheap air fares.

A much greater number of New Zealanders take annual summer holidays in their own country, mostly during the six weeks from mid-December to the end of January. Since this coincides with the peak period of arrival for foreign visitors, there is considerable pressure on hotel rooms in most resort areas. Motels are the type of accommodation most favoured by domestic holidaymakers, although caravanning, camping and youth hostelling are also popular, and many families also own or share a second home at the coast.

Most tourism enterprises in New Zealand are small businesses catering mainly for domestic demand. However, foreign visitors are often attracted to remote and sparsely populated rural areas, where it has been uneconomic for the private sector to develop resort facilities of international standard. In the past, the government intervened by financing the Tourist Hotel Corporation to operate quality hotels in scenic locations. Since the 1980s the international hotel chains have developed large hotels in the main resorts, catering mainly for the inclusive tour market. Farm-stays are also available throughout New Zealand, providing welcome income to an agricultural sector that has been hit hard by recession.

Australia provides just under a third of incoming tourists, followed by North Americans, many of whom are interested in hunting and fishing holidays. Until the 1997–8 financial crisis East Asian countries such as Japan, South Korea and Taiwan were the fastest growing market. The Japanese are interested in New Zealand not only as a destination for skiing holidays, when the Northern Hemisphere season has ended, but also for other types of outdoor activities. The UK market has stayed fairly constant at around 10 per cent of arrivals since the 1950s but its composition has changed, with fewer British visitors falling into the VFR category, and an increasing number opting to purchase tailor-made holidays rather than inclusive tours.

New Zealand's transport system is well developed. The mountainous topography has encouraged the widespread use of domestic air services connecting the main cities – Auckland, Wellington, Christchurch and Dunedin – and the resort areas. Specially equipped light aircraft bring the Southern Alps within easy reach of tourists, while hiking trails and scenic mountain highways are used by the more adventurous. Other surface transport includes:

- the New Zealand Railways express service between the major cities from Auckland to Invercargill
- the vital ferry link across Cook Strait between Wellington and Picton
- the network of bus services to most parts of the country.

Auckland and Wellington serve as important gateways to the South Pacific region and are major centres for business travel.

Tourism resources

New Zealand has an extensive resource base for eco-tourism and adventure tourism, which includes some unusual, if not risky, pastimes such as jet-boating, parapenting and bungee-jumping, as well as sea-kayaking and whitewater rafting. Beach tourism, catering mainly for domestic demand, is well developed on the east coast of North Island, with resorts such as Hastings and Napier. Auckland, Rotorua and Wellington are the major tourist centres in North Island, catering for the bulk of the international demand.

1 Auckland, attractively sited between two harbours, is known as the 'city of sails', and venue of the 1999–2000 Americas Cup yacht race. Auckland is the centre for touring the subtropical north of the country with its *Kauri* forests, surfing beaches and opportunities for game-fishing.
2 Rotorua is situated in the volcanic plateau in the centre of North Island, which contains some of the world's most unusual scenery, including the Pohutu geyser, and Mount Tongariro which is still active. Rotorua became a resort in the late nineteenth century when it was fashionable to bathe in the hot springs. It is also the centre of traditional Maori culture as interpreted for tourists. Although tourism provides employment for Maori entertainers and craftsmen, most of the business enterprises are owned by *pakehas* (white New Zealanders), resulting in fewer economic benefits to local communities.
3 Wellington, the capital of New Zealand, has a harbour setting reminiscent of San Francisco and a range of cultural attractions. The city is convenient for visiting the vineyards of the Marlborough Sounds area of South Island, New Plymouth with its rugby football museum, and the beaches of Hawkes Bay, where Napier is noted for its art deco architecture – the legacy of reconstruction following the 1931 earthquake.

On South Island, the Mount Cook National Park boasts New Zealand's highest mountain and the Tasman Glacier, one of the largest in the Southern Hemisphere outside Antarctica. In the Westland National Park, glaciers flow almost to the sea amid dense evergreen forests. Eco-tourists are particularly attracted to Fiordland, a barely explored wilderness which is the nation's largest national park. One of its most spectacular features is Milford Sound that can be reached by boat, or overland on a popular hiking trail. Another important centre for eco-tourism is Kaikoura, a Maori community not far from Christchurch, which has become world famous for whale-watching. In contrast to Rotorua, tourism enterprises are operated by local people, who claim exclusive use of marine resources, in a bid to discourage competition by white New Zealanders. Other important tourist centres include:

1 Christchurch – the international gateway to South Island and a garden city with a reputation as the most English city in New Zealand. It is now attempting to diversify this image by promoting the scenic attractions and ski resorts of the Southern Alps, which are within easy reach. The city's Canterbury Museum focuses on Antarctica, a reminder that Christchurch has been the port of departure for many expeditions to the 'white continent'.
2 Queenstown on Lake Wakatipu has two tourist seasons, as a ski resort in winter, and as a centre for mountain-climbing, hiking and a whole range of activity holidays in summer. Queenstown's entertainment scene is also extensive, attracting young people from all over New Zealand.

The Pacific islands

The South Sea Islands image of blue lagoons, palm-fringed coral beaches, lush scenery and hospitable islanders has a powerful appeal to would-be escapists from the industrialized societies of the West. So far, the great distances separating the Pacific islands from the tourist-generating countries has prevented the development of mass tourism, based on sun, sand and sea. The exceptions are Hawaii and, to a lesser extent, Fiji. Except in Hawaii, there is little demand for domestic or outbound tourism, and most of the arrivals at airports in many of the islands are returning emigrants visiting their families.

Most of the Pacific islands have a tropical humid climate, characterized by abundant rainfall and strong solar radiation, with air and sea temperatures averaging well above 20°C, throughout the year. Sea breezes mitigate the heat and humidity, especially in Polynesia, but tropical storms are frequent during the rainy season and can cause widespread damage. The larger islands are generally of volcanic origin, mountainous and covered with luxuriant vegetation, with fringing coral reefs along the coast. The smaller islands are mostly coral atolls, low lying and consisting of little more than a narrow strip of sand, almost enclosing what may be an extensive lagoon.

Inter-island distances are great compared to the Caribbean, making it difficult to visit more than a few countries in one itinerary, while the absence of inter-line agreements between the various national airlines adds to the cost of travel. In the past, shipping services connected the islands, but these have long been in decline. However, most governments in the region recognize that, given their limited financial resources, some degree of international co-operation is necessary. The Tourism Council of the South Pacific, funded by the EU, plays an important role in promoting most countries in the region. Investment for the development of facilities has to come mainly from external sources of capital not only in the West but, increasingly, in Asian countries such as Japan and South Korea. Hotel accommodation is generally of a high standard, designed in sympathy with the environment and local building traditions. The main problems are a lack of infrastructure, especially poor roads, and an insufficiently skilled local workforce.

As with the Caribbean, it is a mistake to stereotype the Pacific islands as offering similar tourism products. In fact, we need to distinguish three culturally distinct regions, namely:

● Micronesia in the western Pacific, lying to the east of the Philippines
● Melanesia, with its darker-skinned peoples, in the south-west Pacific
● Polynesia, roughly forming a triangle drawn between Hawaii, Fiji and Easter Island, and covering a vast expanse in the centre of the Pacific Ocean.

Micronesia

The thousands of small islands that make up Micronesia total less than 3000 square kilometres in area, scattered over 8 million square kilometres of ocean. With the exception of the Marianas, which are volcanic and mountainous, most of the islands are coral atolls, with the former British colony of Kiribati claiming the world's largest atoll – Christmas Island. Following Japan's defeat in the Second World War, most of the region was ruled by the USA, until the islands gained independence in the early 1990s as four separate republics, namely:

● the Northern Marianas, including Saipan
● Palau
● the Federal Republic of Micronesia (formerly the Caroline Islands)
● the Marshall Islands, including Majuro.
● Guam – which was acquired by the USA from Spain in 1898 – continues to be administered as a US territory and, offering more attractions and facilities than the other islands, receives a large number of tourists.

There are important American military bases on some of the other islands, and US aid is crucial in the development of infrastructure projects such as airports and harbours. As a result, tourism grew rapidly during the 1990s, although as yet it has made little impact on the more remote islands. The USA, Japan and South Korea provide the majority of tourists, some of whom are ex-service personnel and their families revisiting the battlefields of the Second World War. Micronesia's main tourism resources are the beaches and lagoons that are ideal for sailing and diving. Palau boasts some of the world's best dive sites, including the Truk Lagoon, scene of a major naval battle in the Second World War. Here the wrecks of numerous Japanese ships and aircraft have been transmuted into colourful artificial reefs.

Melanesia

Melanesia mainly consists of fairly large, mountainous and densely forested islands. In fact, commercial logging has become a major earner of foreign exchange, but the rapid depletion of the forest cover could have a serious effect on the islands' wildlife, water supplies and offshore coral reefs. Melanesia includes the following destinations:

1 *Papua-New Guinea* – the second largest country of Australasia, boasting its highest mountains, its largest area of rain forest and a great variety of wildlife, including the bird of paradise. Pidgin-English, as elsewhere in the western Pacific, has become the means of communication in a country where there are no less than 400 different tribes. With surface transport poor or nonexistent, domestic air services play an essential role,

and most tribes, especially those in the central highlands, have moved from the Stone Age to the Jet Age within a generation. Outside the capital, tourist facilities are few, but a number of tour circuits have been established based on Port Moresby and Mount Hagen in the central highlands.

2 *New Caledonia* offers more sophisticated facilities and an attractive coastline, protected by a barrier reef. The capital of this French territory, Noumea, has been styled with some exaggeration, as the 'Paris of the Pacific'. Although tourism suffered a setback during the 1980s as a result of ethnic tensions between the French settlers and the indigenous Kanakas, the island attracts substantial numbers of tourists from Australia and Japan.

3 *Vanuatu* comprises the volcanic islands known prior to independence as the New Hebrides, when they were ruled jointly by Britain and France. This unique arrangement did little to encourage the development of the country, although the legacy of bilingualism has probably been an advantage for tourism. Vanuatu also earns considerable revenue from its status as a tax haven and flag of convenience. Tourist facilities have developed based on water sports and 'safaris' to native villages. Pentecost Island is celebrated for the ritual in which young tribesmen leap from towers with a jungle vine securing their ankles. It may be that bungee-jumping, developed as a commercial activity in New Zealand, originated in Vanuatu.

4 *The Solomon Islands* receive relatively few tourists and there is a lack of facilities outside Guadalcanal and the capital Honiara. However, the islands do offer some of the world's best dive sites.

Polynesia

Polynesia arguably contains the most attractive islands of the Pacific, offering a climate in which malaria and other tropical diseases are largely absent, lush scenery, and a culture in which music, dance and seafaring play major roles. The various island groups are separated by vast expanses of ocean, but the *Maohi* (Polynesians) long ago developed the double-hulled outrigger canoe and the navigation skills to make long voyages.

Tourism has developed most on those islands acting as staging points on the trans-Pacific air and shipping routes. This is particularly true of Hawaii and Fiji and to a lesser extent, of Tahiti and Samoa. At the other extreme the most remote islands – such as Pitcairn (of 'Mutiny on the Bounty' fame) lack airports and, moreover, are served by very infrequent shipping services. Cruise ships call at an increasing number of Pacific islands, but this can be a mixed blessing. As in the Caribbean, the economic benefits of cruising compared to long-stay hotel tourism have been questioned, while the arrival of 1000 Western visitors can cause considerable disruption to a small, unsophisticated island community. The more important destinations of Polynesia include:

1 *French Polynesia*, often referred to as Tahiti, after the most important island which contains the capital, Papeete, and, along with its neighbour Mooréa, the bulk of the tourist accommodation. However, there are actually five separate archipelagos, spread out over 4 million square kilometres of ocean. Since their discovery by Europeans in the eighteenth century, the islands have captured the Western imagination, inspiring artists such as Gauguin, writers and film-makers. Islands such as Mooréa and Bora Bora are exceptionally beautiful, and essentially unspoiled compared to Tahiti itself, offering a landscape of mountain peaks, waterfalls, forests and sheltered lagoons. Much of the development is in the form of *fare*, Polynesian-style bungalows built on stilts over the waters of a lagoon. The Tahiti Tourist Development Office has been successful in attracting large numbers of Americans, Japanese and Australian visitors, while Club Méditerranée operate villages on Mooréa and Bora Bora. Although the beach and water sports are the main attraction, horse-riding and mountain-trekking are also encouraged. Tourism has helped to revive the traditional dances and handicrafts such as pareo-weaving, but at the same time has undermined the integrity of the native culture. Although French Polynesia is a very expensive destination to visit, few hotels are profitable due to high labour costs. Most supplies are imported, and the economy is heavily dependent on huge subsidies from France – referred to locally as 'atomic rent' on account of the French government's nuclear tests in the Tuamotu Islands.

2 *Fiji*, as an ex-British colony, has a different appeal. The country consists of over 100 inhabited islands and contains two distinct ethnic groups – the native Fijians, and the descendants of Hindu immigrants from India brought in under British rule to work the sugar plantations. Although ethnic tensions contributed to the 1987 coup which caused a temporary downturn in tourism, multiculturalism is also one of Fiji's assets as a destination. Most of the population live on the large volcanic island of Viti Levu, which contains the capital, Suva – also the hub for domestic air services and a major port for cruise ships – and the international airport at Nandi. Fiji's national airline, Air Pacific, provides an extensive network of services throughout the region, with direct flights to Los Angeles, Tokyo and a number of cities in Australia and New Zealand. Resort development has mainly taken place along the drier west coast and the 'Coral Coast' to the south, which offers fine beaches and water-sports facilities. Entertainment is mainly geared to Australians and New Zealanders, who are the most important tourist markets. Fiji's cultural attractions, which include fire-walking and war dances, are of secondary importance to the beaches and duty-free shopping.

3 *Western Samoa* offers a more traditional lifestyle, with much of the tourist accommodation in the form of beach *fales* with an open verandah and thatched roof, operated by local families and located in village communities. Most of the tourist attractions, including waterfalls and the former home of the great writer Robert Louis Stevenson, are located on the island of Upolu.

4 *Tonga* is also traditional in character, and is the only Pacific island group to have retained a native monarchy. Most of the visitors arrive by cruise ship but, since the expansion of the airport in the early 1990s, the numbers of long-stay tourists have been steadily increasing. Tonga provides opportunities for surfing and other water sports, and a mix of accommodation that includes resort villages and guesthouses.

5 *The Cook Islands* have encouraged tourism to the extent that it now dominates the economy and the native culture, particularly on the main island – Rarotonga – which is often visited by cruise ships.

6 *Easter Island* is geographically the most remote of all Pacific destinations. However, scheduled air services cross the 4000 kilometres of ocean separating the island from mainland Chile and provide a link to Tahiti, which lies an equivalent distance to the west. Visitors are attracted by the mysterious giant statues or *moai* that stand as mute reminders of a vanished civilization. It is now thought that the people of Rapa Nui who built these monuments some centuries ago, exploited the resources of the island to the point of ecological collapse. The legacy is a treeless landscape that is very different from other Pacific islands.

Tourism, along with other aspects of Western consumer society, has been a mixed blessing to the Pacific islands. Most islanders have lost their skills for self-sufficiency in agriculture and fishing and have come to rely heavily on imported foods, with a negative effect on dietary standards. The native culture had in any case been under severe pressure for two centuries from Western missionaries, traders and administrators imposing their own value systems. Governments in the region see tourism as almost their only chance of raising living standards and reducing the dependence of the islands on world markets for their exports of copra and other products. Tourism has helped to revive the folklore of the islanders and provide new markets for their traditional handicrafts. However, much of the spending by tourists fails to benefit the local economy as it does not stay in the islands. Most of the hotels are owned by foreign companies, and considerable imports of food and drink have to be made to meet tourist requirements. Unless the development of tourism is carefully planned with regard to carrying capacity, further damage is likely to be inflicted on the traditional culture of the islands and the fragile marine environment that is their primary resource. The latter is already under threat from the effects of climate change, mentioned in Chapter 4.

Global warming might well result in a massive die-off of corals over large areas of the Pacific and the inundation of low-lying atolls through rising sea levels and storm surges, while ozone depletion could affect the food chain of the oceans, with disastrous consequences.

Antarctica

Australia and New Zealand have been foremost among the countries engaged in the exploration of Antarctica, the world's largest remaining wilderness. A generation ago, the 'white continent' was tourism's last frontier; now there are guidebooks to the Antarctic and the number of tourists arriving during the summer months of January and February exceeds the resident population of scientists and support personnel at the research stations. Tourists are attracted by the unique wildlife, awe-inspiring glacial scenery and the heritage of polar exploration, yet, aside from space, Antarctica is probably the most hostile environment known to mankind. Over 99 per cent of its 14 million square kilometres of land surface (larger than Australia or Europe) is permanently ice covered. Because of its high altitude, the interior of Antarctica is extremely cold and very dry, while the coast is swept by pitiless winds. As a tourist destination Antarctica differs from the northlands surrounding the Arctic Ocean in the following ways:

1 It is much less accessible. No international air routes cross the southern polar regions. Antarctica is separated from the nearest populated lands in the Southern Hemisphere by vast expanses of stormy ocean in the latitudes known as the 'Roaring Forties', the 'Furious Fifties' and the 'Screaming Sixties', and is moreover ringed by a barrier of pack-ice for most of the year. Travel from the major tourist generating countries is expensive and time-consuming, involving up to two days' air travel, plus a sea voyage lasting from two to ten days from the nearest ports in South America, South Africa, Australia and New Zealand.

2 Unlike the Arctic, which is divided among a number of countries, Antarctica is effectively a 'no-man's land'. Under the terms of the 1959 Antarctic Treaty, the various territorial claims made by seven of the signatory governments are in abeyance, so that the continent provides scope for international co-operation in scientific research. Environmental protection is given priority, and this includes a moratorium on mineral exploitation.

3 In contrast to the Arctic lands, the interior of Antarctica is devoid of all but the most primitive forms of life. The adjoining seas provide the food source for a few hardy species of birds, the largest being the Emperor penguin.

4 It is apparently the only large landmass never to have been visited by man until its discovery by Europeans in the early nineteenth century. Permanent scientific bases have only been established since the 1940s.

Antarctica is now thought to be two geologically distinct landmasses beneath the 2500-metre thick icecap, separated by the Trans-Antarctic Mountains:

- West Antarctica includes the most accessible part of the continent – the Antarctic Peninsula – which is only 1000 kilometres from Cape Horn in South America
- East Antarctica includes the 'Far Side' of the continent which is remote even from Australia and New Zealand.

The sub-Antarctic islands of the Southern Ocean are also included as part of the region, although the milder conditions allow a much greater variety of plant and animal life than in Antarctica itself. South Georgia and Macquarie Island frequently feature on cruise itineraries, whereas the French islands of Kerguelen and the Crozets are little visited.

Tourism, as distinct from government-sponsored expeditions, began in the late 1950s with the first Lindblad cruise and the first charter flights from Chile and New Zealand. However, it was not until 1977 that it received attention at the Antarctic Treaty Conference. Throughout the 1990s tourism grew rapidly, exceeding 10 000 arrivals a year by the close of the decade. This growth is due largely to the following factors:

1 Increased competition between tour operators offering cruises to Antarctica.
2 Since the collapse of the Soviet Union, Russia's scientific institutes have been eager to lease their ice-breaker ships at bargain rates to Western tour operators. This has opened up previously inaccessible areas, such as the Ross Sea, to cruising, and made it possible to circumnavigate Antarctica in a single season.
3 Advances in cold-weather technology have also made it possible to promote the interior of Antarctica as well as the coastal fringe for adventure tourism, including such activities as mountain-climbing, kite-skiing, snowmobiling and even sky-diving at the South Pole!

Tourism in Antarctica can be categorized as land based, air based or sea based.

Land-based tourism

Compared with the Arctic regions of North America, land-based tourism is in its infancy, due to the lack of ground facilities for commercial aircraft. Although the research stations are served by an elaborate infrastructure of aircraft, supply ships and fuel depots, this is very costly to maintain, and most governments are reluctant to support tourism ventures because of the health and safety issues involved, and the possible disruption to scientific programmes. However, Chile as long ago as 1983 and, more recently, Russia, have encouraged tourism development at their bases

on King George Island in the South Shetlands. Russia needs the hard currency, while Chile is using tourism to bolster its long-standing territorial claims to the Antarctic Peninsula – a policy likely to be followed by its rival Argentina.

Air-based tourism

In the 1970s overflying Antarctica was popular in New Zealand, until an Air New Zealand Boeing 747 crashed on Mount Erebus, killing all on board. In 1993 flightseeing tours resumed in Australia, and by the end of 1997 had carried 10 000 passengers to the Mawson Base in the Australian Antarctic Territory. For the adventurous tourist, a British tour operator operates DC4 aircraft to take climbers to the Vinson Massif in West Antarctica. Blue ice landing strips are used where the icecap has been swept clear of snow, and skidoos provide ground transportation.

Sea-based tourism

This includes expeditions by private yacht, which account for relatively few visitors to Antarctica, and commercial cruise ships, which carry the great majority of tourists. The west coast of the Antarctic Peninsula and its offshore islands is the most visited area, since it is relatively close to the ports of departure – Punta Arenas and Ushuaia in South America – and has a milder climate than other parts of Antarctica. During the cruise, visits are made by zodiac landing craft to penguin rookeries, geological curiosities such as Deception Island (a volcanic caldera), historic whaling sites and present-day research stations (the British Antarctic Survey Faraday Base currently limits cruise visits to four a year).

A smaller number of cruises originate in Australia and New Zealand, undertaking the much longer voyage to the Ross Sea. Here, the attractions include:

- Cape Evans – with its relics of Scott's ill-fated expedition to the South Pole
- the US Mc.Murdo Base (the largest in Antarctica)
- the Mount Erebus volcano
- the Ross Ice Barrier.

The ice-free 'Dry Valleys' of the interior – said to be the nearest thing on Earth to the landscape of Mars – can be reached by onboard helicopters.

The impacts of tourism

Cruise operators to Antarctica generally subscribe to codes of conduct based on the 1991 Environmental Protocol to the Antarctic Treaty. Passengers ashore are kept under constant surveillance, for their own safety and to minimize disturbance to wildlife. However, despite the enormous size of the continent, tourists follow established routes and are concentrated in a relatively few sites – mainly in the Antarctic

Peninsula – during the short summer season, and this is bound to have some effect on the breeding patterns of seals and penguins. Emissions from the outboard motors of the zodiacs pollute the water, while not all cruise ships dispose of waste in accordance with environmental guidelines. Nevertheless, land-based tourism represents a much greater threat to the environment, if we consider the impact already made by the permanent scientific bases. Tourism currently accounts for less than 1 per cent of all person days logged in Antarctica compared to more than 99 per cent for base personnel, who arguably do much more damage. Ironically it was the negative publicity generated by returning cruise passengers about the garbage at one American base that forced the authorities to clean up their act.

It is not just the growth in the numbers of tourists that threatens the environment, but the changing nature of the demand. The typical Antarctic cruise passenger is predominantly from the older age groups and is content with a passive role, seeing Antarctica from a distance and responding positively to the restrictions imposed by tour operators. The future is likely to see a growth in land-based adventure tourism, attracting younger visitors who may be less environmentally aware.

Summary

Australasia is located mainly in the Southern Hemisphere, and consists of Australia, New Zealand and a large number of relatively small islands separated by wide expanses of ocean. Isolation from the rest of the world is now being overcome by the development of air transport, but the distance from the major tourist-generating countries of the Northern Hemisphere has prevented the region from becoming a major holiday destination.

Australia, New Zealand and Hawaii clearly belong to the affluent West, while most of the Pacific islands have more in common with the developing countries of the Third World. The tourism industries of Australia and New Zealand have primarily developed to satisfy demand from their own populations, and incoming tourism is not nearly as significant or as vital to the economy as it is to the smaller, poorer islands of the Pacific.

Australasia is primarily a destination area for those travelling for recreational rather than cultural reasons, although eco-tourism is of growing importance in most of these countries and in the new destination of Antarctica. The climates of Australasia are generally favourable, and there is less population pressure on available resources than is the case elsewhere. Environments such as the Australian Outback, the Great Barrier Reef, the Southern Alps of New Zealand and the atolls of the South Pacific, offer a range of opportunities for adventure holidays. Another factor favouring the development of tourism is the political stability of the region that creates good conditions for investment.

Case study

Kangaroo Island

Introduction

Kangaroo Island is the third largest of Australia's offshore islands, and, as an important wildlife site, tourist destination and home to local communities, it has become a classic case study in the debate about the future development of tourism.

Kangaroo Island is situated off the coast of South Australia, 150 kilometres from the capital Adelaide. Its main feature is a low plateau rising 300 metres resulting in a spectacular coastline. It is thinly populated even by Australian standards with only 4000 inhabitants occupying an area of 4350 square kilometres. Most of these live in the coastal towns of Kingscote and Penneshaw, and inland around Parndana. During the 1990s, visitor arrivals steadily increased, so that the island has become a significant tourist destination in South Australia, second only to Adelaide. Tourism has diversified the island's economy, which was based on sheep and cattle-raising, and the local farmers have benefited from the additional income gained by developing farm-stays, bed and breakfast and camping.

Attractions

Kangaroo Island's tourist appeal is based upon its rural lifestyle and the fact that, although the island gives the impression of isolation, it provides easier access to Australia's wildlife resources than the outback. The attractions include:

- Flinders Chase National Park
- Seal Bay Conservation Park – the most popular destination on Kangaroo Island receiving at least three-quarters of all visits
- dramatic coastal scenery
- Kingscote – the main commercial centre
- nature retreats and wilderness areas for wildlife watching
- natural bushland – for bush walking
- unique natural attractions such as Remarkable Rocks, Cape de Coudic, and Seal Bay
- wildlife – notably seals and penguins
- heritage and historic sites
- events – horse races and local markets.

Transport and accommodation

1 Kangaroo Island is easily accessible from Adelaide by fast ferry.

2 Kangaroo Island is also served by a vehicle ferry from Cape Jervis, the nearest point on the South Australia mainland.
3 Small plane services are available.

Touring on the island is mainly by coach, or more tailor-made tours using four-wheel-drive vehicles.

Accommodation is mainly in the form of apartments, small motels and hotels, and ranges from informal camping sites, through farm-stays and holiday houses, to low impact holiday villages and heritage house accommodation in the Flinders Chase National Park. In many cases the accommodation stock is in need of rejuvenation, requiring upgrades and new development. In part this is due to the small-scale nature of the sector and the lack of appropriate management expertise, but it has become a constraint for the development of high-yield tours.

Demand

Most visitors arrive in the summer months and during school holidays. Many are day-trippers as the island is accessible from Adelaide and the main touring circuits can be completed in one day. By the mid-1990s, it was estimated that Kangaroo Island received 150 000 visits, having experienced rapid growth in visitation in the first half of the decade. The majority of visitors come from Adelaide (two-thirds) and while growing rapidly, international visitors make up a relatively small percentage (10 per cent of visitors, 8 per cent of overnight stays). The domestic market is more attracted to the recreational activities on the island while the international market is attracted to the viewing of wildlife and scenery, and experiencing a rural area in Australia.

Organization

There are a number of agencies involved in managing tourism on Kangaroo Island:

1 Local level
  (a) Local Councils on Kangaroo Island.
  (b) Tourism Kangaroo Island.
  (c) Economic Development Board.

2 State level
  (a) South Australia Tourism Commission.
  (b) Department of Environment and Natural Resources.

The nature of Kangaroo Island as a significant natural resource and also a living community has given rise to debate and conflict over the island's future, particularly in terms of tourism. In response a range of planning and management initiatives have been implemented:

1 In 1991 a tourism policy for the island was implemented dividing Kangaroo Island into eleven tourism zones, identifying the resources in each of the zones and the potential for future development. This stimulated considerable debate and community consultation that eventually culminated in a Sustainable Development Strategy for the island in 1995.
2 In 1995 the Kangaroo Island Sustainable Development Strategy was launched. The mission of this strategy was that 'Kangaroo Island will be one of the world's pre-eminent nature-based tourist destinations with a strong rural industry selling its products to tourist, mainland and overseas markets, a high quality of life for residents and well managed natural resources'.

In order to achieve this strategy an innovative approach to monitoring the island's tourism was developed, known as the tourism optimization model (tomm). Tomm involves extensive consultation as to the future of the island, identification of key indicators and benchmarks to monitor progress towards future conditions, and a system of monitoring to ensure the island is on track to achieve these conditions.

Kangaroo Island is therefore an excellent example of a disciplined and professional community-based approach to the management of tourism in a sensitive area.
(Mandis Roberts Consultants, 1996; Manuel, McElroy and Smith, 1996)

Case study

Hawaii

Introduction

Many millions of people the world over, who have never visited the islands, have a clear perception of Hawaii. The image of a 'tropical South Pacific paradise', exotic but safe, was largely created by the American media – particularly the Hollywood film industry in the 1930s. This image has spawned a multibillion dollar industry and attracted over 7 million visitors a year to the islands during the late 1990s. Hawaii's location in mid-Pacific sets it apart as a destination from the rest of the USA, but its popularity is mainly due to the American connection.

Hawaii actually consists of a chain of volcanic islands, originating as a geological hot spot in the ocean floor of the North Pacific. The largest island is also called Hawaii or the 'Big Island', and there are six others that are inhabited:

- Oahu
- Maui
- Kauai
- Molokai
- Lanai
- Niihau.

The islands are geographically isolated – 4000 kilometres from the American mainland but an even greater distance from Asia and the rest of Polynesia. Hawaii was first settled by Polynesians from Tahiti and the Marquesas Islands between 500 and 800 AD. However, it was not until 1795, shortly after Captain Cook had discovered the islands, that the various tribes were united by Kamehameha the Great, founder of the Hawaiian monarchy. In the course of the nineteenth century, Hawaii came increasingly under American influence through the activities of whalers, missionaries and traders, some of whom became plantation owners after acquiring tribal lands. Labour was imported from China, Japan and other countries to work the plantations, eventually resulting in the multicultural society that now characterizes the islands. However, these developments had a number of environmental and social impacts including:

1 Most of the native plants and animals, that had previously been protected by isolation, were displaced by introduced species, and are now found only in remote mountain areas.
2 The native Hawaiians became a marginalized minority in their own country, with their traditional culture in danger of disappearing.

Tourism development

Although the first tourist facility on the islands – the Hawaiian Hotel in Honolulu – opened as early as 1872, this catered mainly for business travel. Leisure tourism did not really develop until after Hawaii became a territory of the USA in 1898. In 1901 the Moana Hotel opened, the first of many resort hotels along Waikiki Beach, but catering strictly for a moneyed clientele. In the early part of the twentieth century the Hawaiian islands were expensive to reach, involving a voyage lasting four to six days, by luxury liner out of San Francisco or Long Beach. A rapid expansion of tourism took place from the 1950s as a result of:

- economic prosperity on the mainland following the Second World War, during which large numbers of American service personnel had been stationed on the islands
- the introduction of cheaper and more frequent air services, using jet aircraft, which ended the islands' comparative isolation

- the achievement of statehood, which integrated Hawaii more fully into the mainstream of American life.

Tourism stemmed out-migration from the islands and provided an alternative source of employment to a declining agricultural sector based on sugar and pineapple production. By the 1970s, inclusive air tours had brought Hawaii within reach of Americans on modest incomes and the age of mass tourism had arrived. Between 1950 and 1980 the number of visitors grew from 46 000 to 4 million, a rate of increase almost without parallel in any other destination.

Most tourism development has been concentrated on Oahu, the third largest of the islands in area, but the most important in other respects, as it contains 75 per cent of the population, the bulk of the tourist accommodation and the capital, Honolulu. Although the majority of tourists staying in Oahu visit one or more of the 'neighbour islands', such visits tend to be brief.

There is little doubt that mass tourism has had an undesirable impact on Oahu, particularly at Waikiki where development has been largely unplanned. The state government has therefore encouraged projects on the other islands, which are generally of a higher standard. On Maui for example, most of the development consists of condominiums, with some apartments owned on a time-share basis, catering mainly for wealthy Americans. However, these projects have been criticized for contributing even less to the community than the large high-rise hotels that characterize Waikiki. The Japanese have invested heavily in Hawaii, not just in hotel developments, but in golf courses, travel agencies and real estate.

Although Hawaii is not lacking in cultural and other attractions, the bulk of the demand is for beach tourism, and is generated from the following countries:

1 *The USA and Canada* – the US mainland accounts for two-thirds of all visitors to Hawaii. Thanks to cheap domestic air fares and competitive tour pricing, visitors from cities in the Middle Atlantic and Mid-Western states can reach the islands almost as easily as those from California.
2 *Japan* – the Japanese market is smaller in volume than that of the USA, but on average contributes four times as much per visitor in expenditure. Young Japanese are particularly attracted to the islands as a honeymoon destination. Honolulu is a major hub on the network of trans-Pacific air services, bringing Tokyo as close to Hawaii as many cities in the USA.
3 *Australia and New Zealand* are important markets, due to increased accessibility.
4 *Western Europe* generates less demand due to the greater distance and higher cost of air travel, with relatively few tourists visiting islands other than

Oahu. All travel between the islands and to the mainland is by air, except for cruises based on Honolulu, and there is virtually no public transport on the islands.

Tourism resources

Hawaii's appeal as a tourist destination is due to a combination of factors – a favourable climate, beautiful coastal and mountain scenery, the opportunities for surfing and a wide range of outdoor activities – and, not least, the Polynesian culture. We will now look at some of these resources in more detail.

Climate

The Hawaiian islands lie in the path of the prevailing north-east trade winds, which strongly influence the climate, moderating the heat and humidity of these tropical latitudes. However, from time to time, the trades are interrupted by *kona* winds blowing from the south or south-west that bring spells of more humid weather and have an important effect on surf levels off the beaches. As the islands are mountainous, there are also striking differences in climate and vegetation between the leeward and windward slopes. Most of the resort developments are on the more sheltered south and west coasts of the islands and enjoy a dry climate with abundant sunshine.

Surfing beaches

Hawaii can claim to be the home of surfing, and offers some of the most powerful waves in the world. These often originate as a result of winter storms in the Aleutian Islands, 4000 kilometres to the north. There is no intervening landmass to diffuse the ocean swells, and no continental shelf to reduce their impact before they reach the beaches. The northern coast of Maui and the better known North Shore of Oahu are the favoured locations for experienced surfers seeking the big waves in the winter months. At Pipeline surfers 'ride the tube', challenging waves shaped into hollow cylinders by a combination of a powerful swell and a shallow reef. Summer is the best time for surfing at Waikiki, where white American settlers adopted the sport from the native Hawaiians and introduced it to California and Australia in the 1920s. Since the Second World War, light fibreglass boards, undergoing constant improvements in design, have replaced the heavy long-boards made from native hardwoods, while the film, music and clothing industries and a professional competition circuit have spawned an international surf culture. A recent development is power surfing, using jet skis as tow-in craft to tackle the really big waves – needless to say this is decried by purists.

Hawaiian culture

Islanders of part-native Hawaiian descent form the largest ethnic group on Hawaii, accounting for 40 per cent of the population. There is some resentment of the *haole* (white American) domination of the economy, but race relations have generally been better than in mainland USA. This has contributed to a revival of the native Hawaiian culture since the 1980s, with islanders from all ethnic groups taking pride in what they now regard as their heritage. A less authentic and more commercialized version of these cultural traditions is promoted as part of the tourist image, including:

1 The *lei* or garland of welcome presented to visitors at the airport on arrival, symbolizing *Aloha*, the islanders' tradition of hospitality.
2 The *luau* or banquet staged in the hotels, featuring a pig baked in an earth oven, recalling the harvest festivals.
3 Hawaiian music and dance, of which the *hula* is the best known. This originally served a religious purpose, recounting the history and legends of the people through facial expressions, hip movements and hand gestures.

Hawaiian music and dance has changed since Captain Cook's time, adopting elements from other cultures such as the ukulele (a Portuguese introduction), the muumuu costume (imposed on the islanders by nineteenth-century missionaries), and even the grass skirt was introduced by the American entertainment industry from Micronesia in the 1930s. However, many native Hawaiians feel that as presented for tourist consumption, the traditional culture has lost its original meaning.

The marine environment

The seas around the Hawaiian Islands provide opportunities for a range of activities including:

1 Diving, based on the coral reefs along the leeward coasts of the islands. Since the 1980s it has also become possible to explore the underwater world in safety and comfort using submersible craft.
2 Yachting and windsurfing, particularly off Maui.
3 Whale-watching, especially off Maui where it is a major business. However, this very popularity may threaten the survival of the humpback whale as a species.

The national parks

The US National Park Service protects outstanding examples of the natural heritage of the islands, the best known being the Volcanoes National Park on the 'Big Island' of Hawaii.

Hiking tours and eco-tourism are beginning to develop in the interior of the islands, providing an alternative to the high-consumption tourist lifestyle based on the beach and the shopping mall that is typical of the resorts.

Although certain features are common to all the islands, such as surfing beaches, waterfalls and volcanic scenery, each of the major islands has a distinct character:

1 *Oahu* Aptly known as the 'Gathering Place', Oahu is the most visited of the islands, but even the famed Waikiki Beach is not as crowded as some Mediterranean resorts, nor its seafront as commercialized. Honolulu is like any other major American city, but it does have two outstanding attractions, namely:
   (a) The Bishop Museum – one of the world's finest collection of Pacific arts and crafts.
   (b) The Iolani Palace, with its reminders of the Hawaiian monarchy.
   The naval base at Pearl Harbor, of Second World War fame, is situated nearby. Another of Oahu's tourist sites is the Polynesian Cultural Centre at Lae, which combines education with entertainment as a living showcase for the folklore of the seven Polynesian nations of the Pacific.
2 *Maui* – the green 'Valley Island', contains a number of exclusive resorts such as Kapalua and Kaunapaali – which is now integrated with the former whaling port of Lahaina. Major attractions include the Haleakala Crater, one of the world's largest, and the Seven Pools of Hana.
3 *Kauai* – the 'Garden Island' is particularly renowned for its lush scenery, exemplified by:
   (a) The Fern Grotto at Wailua.
   (b) The Waimea Canyon.
   (c) The beaches of Hanalei – world famous as the location for 'Bali Hai' in the film *South Pacific*.
   Much of the island is only accessible by helicopter, boat or hiking trail. Kauai was badly affected by the Iniki hurricane disaster of 1992, which caused the island authorities to revise their tourism policy to favour small locally owned enterprises and native Hawaiian communities.

4 *Hawaii* – the 'Big Island' offers the greatest contrasts in climate, due to the high volcanic peaks of Mauna Loa and Mauna Kea. Kilauea is one of the world's most active volcanoes, and its frequent eruptions have created a lunar landscape of firepits, craters and lava caves in the south-eastern part of the island, and the characteristic beaches of black and green sand. Elsewhere cattle ranches, coffee plantations and rainforests add variety to the landscape.
5 *Molokai, Lanai* and *Niihau* have as yet been little influenced by tourism. The main attraction of Molokai – the 'Friendly Isle' – is the rugged coastal scenery of the Kaleapapa National Park, site of a former leper colony. Lanai until recently depended on its pineapple plantations but has now diversified into up-market tourism.

The impacts of tourism

Tourism has provided economic benefits to Hawaii, but at a cost to the environment and the island lifestyle. The dominance of the tourism sector is particularly opposed by native Hawaiian activists, who see it as threatening their agricultural lands, sacred sites, water supplies and fishing grounds, as well as trivializing their cultural traditions. Golf courses not only make enormous demands on water resources but also are a major source of pollution due to the constant applications of fertilizer and weed killer that are needed. The owners of large hotels have been accused of denying locals access to public beaches. Tourism has also been blamed for a rising crime rate, family breakdown and rising land prices that deny local people access to the housing market. Nevertheless since the 1980s, efforts have been made to introduce conservation measures and curb inappropriate tourism developments. The biggest long-term threat may not be from the growth of tourism as such, but from population growth, caused by immigration from the mainland of the USA.

(Web sites at http://www.gohawaii.com/ and http://www.state.hi.us/dbedt/tourism.html)

The future geography of travel and tourism

After reading this chapter, you should be able to:

1 Appreciate the role of technology in shaping the future geography of travel and tourism.
2 Understand the changing behaviour of tourists.
3 Recognize the importance of the environmental movement in tourism.
4 Understand the changing nature of tourism destinations.
5 Appreciate the changing global economic and political map in shaping the future geography of travel and tourism.
6 Recognize the trend towards the globalization of the tourism sector.

Introduction

The dawn of a new millennium has prompted a range of forecasting and visioning exercises as we anticipate the shape of tourism over the next 100 years. Identifying the drivers of future trends is difficult as, whilst some forces of change such as technology are already clearly evident, others have yet to emerge. This chapter therefore attempts to identify the key trends and issues that will reshape the geography of travel and tourism in the twenty first century by using the following headings:

● changing markets
● changing destinations
● the globalizing tourism sector
● the new political and economic world order.

Cutting through each of these headings are a range of other agents of change such as technology, the search for an acceptable, sustainable tourism sector and changes in consumer behaviour. Of course, these trends are interlinked and are combining to accelerate the pace of change. For example, the increasingly knowledgeable and sophisticated tourist can now be catered for by a tourism sector which is firmly embracing the marketing concept, facilitated by technological developments such as computer reservation systems (CRS) and database marketing. At the same time, the sector is becoming truly global as larger organizations operate across different cultures and time zones. In combination with continued shifts in the economic and political map of the world these trends are instrumental in changing tourism flows as new generators of international tourism and new destinations emerge. Cutting across this is the pressure for sustainable development to ensure that destinations will be better planned and managed, and show more concern for their environment and host community, than did their earlier counterparts – a trend supported by global gatherings such as the Earth Summit in Rio.

Markets

Patterns of demand

There is no doubt that in the second half of the twentieth century a wave of leisure and travel has broken across the globe, pushing the frontier of tourism further outward as more and more people have enjoyed access to travel. This trend will continue as demand for both domestic and international tourism expands in the twenty-first century. Indeed, as early as the year 2010 international arrivals will exceed 1 billion. However, forecasters also suggest that both demand and supply side constraints may slow the growth of tourism:

1 On the demand side, some countries are reaching ceilings of capacity and available leisure time that will constrain further growth. The WTO study on leisure time for example, has shown that leisure time is being squeezed by changing work practices, technology and competition.
2 On the supply side, problems of terrorism, disease and capacity ceilings in transport infrastructure may also discourage tourism growth in some areas.

There is no doubt that the distribution of tourism by the year 2020 will therefore differ in some respects from the position in the 1990s. Chapter 2 identified that the countries of the East Asia and Pacific (EAP) region are emerging as important generators of tourism and as major tourist destinations. While the currency crisis of the late 1990s has depressed growth in the region, forecasters predict that this will not have a long-term impact. Early in the twenty-first century, the EAP region will rival Europe and North America in its significance for tourism. To some extent, the success of the EAP region is at the expense of traditional regions such as Europe. Europe's share of international tourism will continue to erode as more long-haul destinations grow in popularity. The principal long-term factors affecting demand for tourism are demographic changes, the amount of leisure and holiday time available, consumer preferences and the economic performance of the main generating countries. In the short term, factors such as relative prices and exchange rates, cost of travel, marketing and promotion, legal commitments and political factors (wars, terrorism) will also be important. Although forecasters say that long-haul travel will continue to increase, short-haul travel – especially to neighbouring countries – will still account for a very high proportion of international trips. Business travel will remain an important segment of the market but there is a view that developments in communications – such as teleconferencing and video-phones – may reduce the need for business travel. The evidence here is inconclusive, suggesting that unless travel becomes prohibitively expensive, face-to-face meetings will remain an important reason for business travel.

Changing market demands

While there is no doubt that social and economic trends will encourage the growth of tourism, the nature of the market will change with consequent implications for destination development. The consumer of tourism is becoming knowledgeable, discerning, seeking quality and participation and, in the developed world, increasingly drawn from an older age group. Of course, demographics can be forecast, but it is more difficult to track the influence of changing values among the travelling public. For example,

motivations for travel are moving away from passive sun-lust towards active participation, with educational and curiosity motives becoming important. At the same time, travel will not only be facilitated by flexible working practices, sabbaticals, study leave and early retirement, but also will be tailor-made to suit particular groups in society such as single parents. Here, marketing research allied to technology will increasingly allow sophisticated segmentation of tourists so that product development and delivery can be closely linked to consumer preferences in order to ensure customer satisfaction. Use of CRS and the World Wide Web will allow modularization of the elements of travel packages so that consumers will be able to assemble their own vacations and trade direct with suppliers: an innovation with significant implications for the traditional way that travel is distributed. The trend is clearly away from mass passive tourism and towards more tailor-made, individual consumption of active tourism.

Destinations

Hand in hand with market changes are the forces impacting upon the development of the destination of the future. A clearly identifiable current trend is the pressure to deliver sustainable tourism destinations as the maturing of tourism markets, allied to the environmentalist movement and media exposure of bad practices, has seen changing attitudes on the part of both consumers and suppliers. This has been publicized through high-profile conferences such as the Earth Summit in Rio, and by initiatives from industry representative bodies such as the World Travel and Tourism Council (WTTC). In particular, the realization of the negative impacts of tourism upon host environments, societies and developing economies has prompted the search for alternative forms of tourism – such as eco-tourism – and a critical attitude towards mass tourism. Sustainable tourism ensures that the tourism sector is sympathetic to host environments and societies. An increasing number of public agencies are drawing up guidelines for the reduction of tourism impacts and there is no doubt that the consumer of the future will shun destinations that are not 'environmentally sound'. In essence, we are seeing a move towards the responsible development and consumption of tourism through:

- more local control of tourism development, as recommended by the Agenda 21 initiatives of the Rio Earth Summit
- adoption of the principles of sustainability across all forms of tourism
- adoption of professional approaches to the management of visitors, traffic and resources at tourist destinations
- use of marketing and information management to influence the behaviour of visitors at destinations
- an enhanced awareness and understanding of the impacts of tourism.

It is perhaps inevitable that these ideas will find more fertile ground in the developed world than in most developing countries, where the short-term imperatives of obtaining foreign exchange and job creation will still dominate and may eclipse the longer-term objectives of sustainable development.

Destinations are responding to these demands in a variety of ways:

1 Resource-based destinations, i.e. those based on elements of the natural or cultural heritage, are adopting sophisticated planning, management and interpretative techniques to provide both a welcome and a rewarding experience for the tourist, while at the same time ensuring protection of the resource itself. It is felt that once tourists understand why a destination is significant they will want to protect it. Protection here may be not only in terms of changed behaviour but also through such schemes as 'visitor payback' where visitors become financial supporters of a site. Good planning and management of the destination lies at the root of providing the tourism consumer of the future with a high-quality experience. To achieve this, it may be that tourists of the future will have to accept increasingly restricted viewing times at popular sites, comply with destination 'codes of conduct' and even be content with replicas of the 'real thing', or a virtual substitute using computer technology.

2 We will see an increased emphasis on human-made, 'artificial' destinations and attractions. The trend to more frequent trips taken closer to home will demand 'synthetic' destinations such as artificial ski slopes and destinations which combine leisure, entertainment, retailing, accommodation, food and beverages in a single setting. The emergence of totally enclosed and controlled tourist environments such as theme parks, cruise ships and vacation islands will be promoted as a 'market-orientated' alternative to the real, and increasingly fragile, 'resource-based', non-reproducible attractions of natural, historic or cultural destinations. Such settings have many advantages and can provide the safe and secure environment sought by most tourists – already destinations such as Las Vegas are bringing these trends to life.

In the future, destinations will be affected by climate change, with rising sea levels creating problems for coastal resorts, the erosion of the ozone layer driving a change in tourism products away from sun-bathing and beach tourism, and the generally more volatile weather experienced in many parts of the world affecting the profitability of the sector. As the frontiers of tourism expand ever outwards, destinations will be created under the oceans, or in cyberspace or even outer space:

1 Space travel is already taking bookings for suborbital flights and attracting the attention of the media. Space travel will involve extensive education, physical training and orientation of the tourist. It will not only include travel in space (orbiting hotels, space stations and shuttle flights, but also a range of other activities such as space sports and entertainment, earth-based visits to space facilities and the use of simulators (see the case study at the end of this chapter).

2 Virtual reality (VR) sparks extreme differences in opinion between futurists – some argue that it will never replace the real experience of travel, while others foresee the home becoming the centre for all leisure activities – a total immersive cave-experience chamber – with VR discs available for leading tourism destinations. In some respects, this is the perfect form of tourism – the destination receives a royalty for the disc, but receives none of the negative impacts of tourists actually on site: similarly the tourist receives the experience of the destination but without the risk of skin cancer, disease or crime. Crude versions of virtual destinations already exist – Stonehenge, for example – and clearly the diversion of visitor pressure away from the real thing is important. Of course we are then faced with the question: 'Is VR tourism in the true sense?'

The tourism sector

As the tourism market matures, the sector is striving for acceptability not only in terms of environmental practices such as auditing and total quality management, but also business ethics and social responsibility as short-term, profit-driven operations become less acceptable. Rather, there will be consideration for all stakeholders involved in the business, including the well-being of the destination and its residents. For example, it makes increasing commercial sense for tour operators to invest in destinations and their facilities, while industry representatives such as the WTTC are effective advocates for the industry.

Globalization has become an all-embracing term for the trends that are impacting upon the tourism sector. The term applies to the increasing interdependence of markets and production in different countries. Smeral (1998) has identified the key drivers of globalization in tourism as:

1 Adoption of free trade agreements, removing barriers to international transactions.
2 Computer and communications technology encouraging 'e-business'.
3 Worldwide-acting suppliers utilizing CRS and global distribution systems (GDS). Examples here include global-acting airlines, hotel chains and tour operators, as well as their strategic alliance partners both backwards and forwards in the supply chain.
4 Decreasing costs of international travel allowing access to most markets in the world.

5 Increasing income and wealth in the generating countries, allied to the 'new tourist' who is experienced and discerning.
6 Newly emerging destinations, and the increased demand for international travel in turn fuel these trends.

The consequences of globalization for the tourism sector include:

- standard procedures and quality control
- increased competition
- head office decisions on marketing and technology in the larger companies
- forging of strategic alliances
- adoption of global brands
- changing management approaches
- adoption of new ways of doing business, such as use of e-mail and the Internet
- adoption of global distribution systems and yield management
- more difficult trading conditions for small and medium-sized enterprises.

On this latter point, there is scope in tourism for both the large organization and also the small, where niche markets can be identified; however, the medium-sized enterprises have neither the power of the large firms, nor the niche opportunities of the small, and will therefore struggle to survive in a globalizing sector.

In response to these trends, the tourist sector is rapidly becoming more professional and embracing developments in technology. This has allowed the industry to move towards a marketing philosophy of anticipating consumer needs and ensuring that they can be supplied. Technology facilitates this through 'database marketing' allowing direct contact with the consumer.

Computer reservation systems developments are particularly important here. In the past, CRS have provided the larger tourist companies with a competitive advantage, while small and medium-sized enterprises in tourism have been unable to gain access to these systems. However, the development of new systems at the destination level will redress this balance. Nonetheless, the dominance of larger corporations in tourism will continue through their strict quality control and global branding which is designed to reduce the perceived risk of a tourism purchase. This has implications for tourism destinations that may become increasingly dependent upon decisions made by such corporations.

At the same time, CRS, combined with a more knowledgeable tourist market, will see the emergence of a growing number of independent travellers and the bypassing of intermediaries – especially travel agents – in the tourism distribution chain. Suppliers will target their products more closely to the desires of their customers and, increasingly, new tourist destinations will be created.

Technology and changing business practices will have a major impact upon the transport sector. For example, in the twenty-first century intercontinental airline operations will be characterized by the use of larger aircraft and more non-stop, very long flights – aided by the development of Concorde's hypersonic successor. For short-haul operations the use of VTOL (vertical take-off and landing) aircraft will provide added flexibility. Although it is generally accepted that total deregulation of the international airline industry is not practical, the trend towards deregulation will continue across the world. In the USA and Europe deregulation has led to domination by a small number of larger airlines and the forging of strategic alliances – a trend which is emerging in other sectors of the tourism industry. In such a deregulating environment for air transport, competitive advantage will not come from government protection. Instead, factors such as the quality of service on flights and the increased emphasis on hub-and-spoke operations will provide competitive advantage. Hub-and-spoke operations are characterized by airlines realigning schedules at their hub, and timing schedules on the spokes so they connect at the hub. This gives the hub airline a potentially strong competitive position and leads to a system of 'fortress' hubs, keeping out newcomers. These airports need well co-ordinated flights, a prime geographical location and good terminal facilities. In addition, new airports continue to be built, despite the protests of environmentalists.

Forecasts of international transport predict that technological developments, increased airline efficiency, and labour productivity savings will offset any rises in aviation fuel prices and thus, in real terms, fares will continue to fall. This will support the continued trend towards long-haul travel and longer journey lengths. However, if energy costs do rise significantly, then a shift towards surface transport and shorter journey lengths can be expected. While the use of the car for inter-city travel has declined in the USA there seems little prospect for a similar decline elsewhere in the world where the market is nowhere near reaching saturation. Continued developments of highway networks, developments of car technology to make driving more comfortable and environmentally acceptable, satellite navigation systems, and improved fuel efficiency will all make motoring cheaper and more attractive. New infrastructure developments – such as the Channel tunnel – will also continue to encourage touring holidays by car.

On the other hand, as the twenty-first century unfolds, it is likely that a shift in transport away from the car may occur. This will be influenced by:

1 The development of high-speed rail links, encouraged by the success of the French TGV. This means that short-haul journeys by train may be preferred over those by air to avoid road and air traffic control congestion. This will be influenced by the following factors:

(a) The train is perceived as a 'greener' form of travel.

(b) A range of new rail-based leisure and business tourism products will be developed.

(c) Faster trains using technology, such as 'flying' trains above a rail at 480 kilometres per hour using magnetic levitation or repulsion.

2 Within cities the growth of rapid transit systems will reduce road congestion and also lead to an inter-modal switch from the car to public transport. The new systems being constructed in Kuala Lumpur and Bangkok are examples here.

The new world order

The future of tourism cannot be divorced from political events and trends. Initiatives at different geographical scales are changing the world order and will impact upon tourism. For example, at the international level, tourism in the future will be facilitated by the free trade agreements under the umbrella of the General Agreement on Trade in Services (GATS) signed in 1994. This agreement is based on the principle that free market forces are the best means of providing consumers with the best products at the best prices. The General Agreement on Trade in Services has a controversial background in tourism:

1 On the one hand, supporters of GATS point to the elimination of barriers to tourism growth, removing restrictions on hiring staff from other countries, establishment of management operations and franchises in other countries, easier transfers of currency and other payments.

2 On the other hand, opponents of GATS maintain that freedom for companies to operate where they wish, to hire non-local staff and to franchise their products flies in the face of the development of sustainable tourism as there will be few controls on the activities of companies in the tourism sector.

An opposing trend to GATS is the formation of a number of trading blocs across the globe as country groupings come together in economic alliances. Notable here are the North American Free Trade Agreement, the creation of the EU under the 1992 initiative and the Association of South East Asian Nations. In terms of Europe, the prime initiative for creation of the 1992 initiative was to allow Europe to compete with the world economic powers – the USA and Japan – by forming 'an area without internal frontiers in which free movement of goods, persons and services is ensured'. The initiative has adopted the 'Euro' as the EU currency and in the twenty-first century it is likely that this will replace sovereign currencies, facilitating tourism and reducing barriers to travel and trade within Europe.

At the national level, the final decade of the twentieth century was marked by the emergence of market economies in Eastern Europe and the opening of borders, symbolized by the demolition of the Berlin Wall. This has paved the way for Eastern European countries to participate more fully in travel movements in the new millennium.

An opposing trend to that of GATS and the formation of trading blocs is noticeable in the politics of regions and nations. As well as the rise of alliances of nations into blocs and the GATS agreement that attempts to remove such blocs, there is also the rise of regionalism and a search for cultural identity – particularly among ethnic minorities. In some parts of the world this has led to conflict (as in the regions of Yugoslavia) but elsewhere the trend is less sinister. In the midst of this contradiction 'city-states' are emerging as major tourist destinations, whether it be as cultural centres, hosting major events or simply promoting themselves as significant tourist destinations and vying to stage mega-events such as the Olympic Games or the soccer World Cup.

Discussion

A number of commentators have attempted to synthesize the trends identified above. Poon (in Cooper, 1989) suggests that the future of tourism will be one of flexible, segmented, customized and diagonally integrated tourism rather than the mass, rigid, standardized, and packaged tourism of the 1970s (Figure 26.1).

Poon sees the key trends leading to this new tourism as:

● the diffusion of a system of new information technologies in the tourism industry
● deregulation of the airline industry and financial services
● the negative impact of mass tourism on host countries
● the movement away from sun-lust to sun-plus tourism
● environmental pressures
● technology
● competition
● changing consumer tastes (Poon, in Cooper, 1989: 92).

There is no doubt that the maturing and changing tourist market will have major implications for the geography of travel and tourism. This will manifest itself in changing patterns of tourism around the world as new destinations emerge and older ones decline. The type of tourism will also change tourism's impact at the destination and tourism planners will respond more positively to visitors. Above all, the challenge for the new century will be the balancing of environmental and social impacts of tourism against its perceived economic gains. It is here that geography can play a valuable role in helping us to understand the impact of

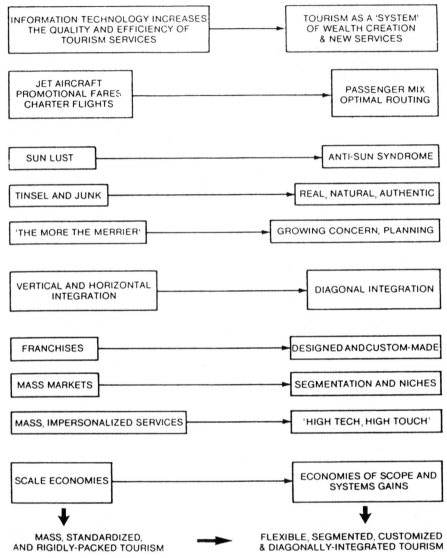

Figure 26.1 International tourism in metamorphosis
Source: Poon, in Cooper (1989).

tourism and thus the planning and management approaches needed to develop low impact tourism.

Summary

The future geography of travel and tourism will be influenced by a number of interrelated trends. These can be summarized as the changing tourism marketplace, new trends at the destination, the changing economic and political map of the world and the globalizing tourism sector. Cutting across these drivers of change are other influences such as technology, consumer behaviour and the rise of environmental awareness. Technology is forcing the pace of change in terms of transportation, database marketing and both CRS and the growth of the Internet. This is linked to changing consumer behaviour, particularly in the ageing markets of the developed world. Here knowledgeable, discerning tourists are looking to travel independently and to participate in, and learn about, the destination. Destinations will respond through positive planning, concern for the environment and host community, and provision of a quality experience. Finally, the world is changing and tourism will be affected by the developing economies of the EAP region, the continued opening up of Eastern Europe, the growth of signatories to GATS and the expansion of the tourism frontier into space. There is no doubt that geographers' skills and understanding of these global issues will be valuable in the management of the tourism sector in the twenty-first century.

Case study

Space: the final tourism frontier?

Introduction

This case study analyses the future activity of space tourism by using life-cycle analysis and Leiper's tourism system (see Chapter 1). We can define space tourism as 'The taking of short pleasure trips in low earth orbit by members of the public' (Collins and Ashford, 1998).

Space tourism became a possibility in the 1960s following the pioneering Russian Sputnik launch in 1957 and the success of NASA's (National Aeronautics and Space Administration) programmes and Apollo missions into space. Space tourism will mean that the tourism frontier is limitless and no longer bounded by the earth. According to the Space Tourism Society (STS) space travel is an emerging type of tourism that not only includes travel beyond Earth, but also Earth-bound simulations, tours, entertainment and, of course, cyberspace tourism experiences. The goal of the STS is 'to conduct the research, build public desire, and acquire the financial and political power to make space tourism available to as many people as possible as soon as possible'.

But if space tourism has attracted so much attention – and is technically feasible – why does it remain unrealized? We can identify a number of key reasons for this:

1 *Cost* Space tourism will be prohibitively expensive for the traveller well into the twenty-first century because of the high cost of launches and the fact that space vehicles are not yet truly 'reusable'.
2 *Investment* Space tourism launch vehicles are also very expensive and, to date, they would not provide investors with payback or a profit. Launch vehicles are also destroyed each time they are used. Reusable vehicles would keep costs down, but would need significant demand to make them profitable. Here reduced costs would be facilitated by the use of available Russian technology, but this is being pre-

vented by a lack of co-operation between NASA and the Russians.
3 *Health, safety and noise* NASA was developing space voyages for civilians until the *Challenger* disaster in the late 1980s. Safety will continue to be a real issue for space tourism, both in terms of consumer perceptions, and also in terms of the willingness of insurance companies to become involved. Health issues in space also act as a constraint, as does the noise associated with the launch.

The life cycle of space tourism

The life cycle of space tourism is expected to demonstrate four broad phases of development in the next century:

1 *Pioneer phase* Here the price per trip ranges from US$100 000 to US$1 million, with few travellers who can afford it. Comfort levels will not be high, with spartan accommodation making the trip more like 'adventure tourism' than 'luxury tourism'. Elaborate facilities will not be required or developed in this phase.
2 *Exclusive phase* By this phase the price has fallen to US$10 000–100 000 per trip, which will begin to attract a wider market. The trips will be available on a regular basis, with greater levels of comfort and attention to issues such as the quality of the experience. Facilities will be more extensive and accommodation could be in clusters of prefabricated modules.
3 *Mature phase* The price has fallen to US$2,000–10 000, with significant growth in the market, fuelled by price competition between the various suppliers. Facilities would be available on a large scale with accommodation constructed in orbit for hundreds of guests.
4 *Mass market phase* This phase is reached when space tourism becomes the equivalent of the air inclusive tour of the late twentieth century, with tens of millions of passengers every year.

The components of a mature space tourism system

Using Leiper's tourism system we can analyse space tourism in terms of the generating region, the destination region and the transit zone.

The generating region for space tourism

The actual volume of demand for space tourism will depend upon price, the length of stay in space and the associated facilities. Also, medical advances, such as anti-nausea drugs will affect the popularity of space tourism. On Earth, demand will be stimulated by the development of space-tourism centres where prospective travellers can experience simulated space travel. In the last quarter of the twentieth century prospective travellers have already paid thousands of dollars as a deposit for the first trip to space in the twenty-first century.

The destination region for space tourism

Accommodation will grow from orbiting hotels for a few hundred guests, to orbiting theme parks with accommodation for thousands of guests. These will have stunning views of earth and space with games and recreation designed to make use of zero gravity. Other accommodation options include space cruisers. Attractions will include:

- Earth-viewing
- astronomy

- low-gravity sports such as swimming, gymnastics, flying and ball games
- extra-vehicular space walks
- exotic worlds – simulated planet surfaces and low-gravity vegetation of large exotic plants.

The transit zone

By the mature phase of space tourism, transportation will involve shuttle ferries to take passengers to the orbiting accommodation, as well as cargo vehicles for launching the accommodation. By this stage, ferries will be 'airline style' with proven vehicles operated in substantial numbers. The experience will be designed to provide moderate acceleration during boost and re-entry, and the capability to operate from conventional airports.

(Collins and Ashford, 1998)

Sources

Since the first two editions of *The Geography of Travel and Tourism* the volume of tourism literature has expanded rapidly, not only in terms of academic texts, journals and case studies but also media coverage of tourism destinations now provides a rich source of material. This media coverage is in the form of television and video, newspaper supplements and dedicated travel magazines.

But perhaps the greatest innovation in source material has come from the World Wide Web. The web is now a major source of information about tourism and destinations. Of course, the web is disorganized and lacks any form of information quality control, but the official tourism sites in particular provide instant access to countries, cities and resorts unparalleled five years ago. Because we feel that this is such a valuable source for everyone reading this new edition, *Worldwide Destinations: The Geography of Travel and Tourism*, we have provided a complete list of the web site addresses of national tourist organizations of the major tourism countries in the world.

This section is not intended to be comprehensive, but simply aims to provide a listing of the key sources available in the subject area on a systematic basis. We have organized the section to cover the following key sources:

- books relevant to the chapters in *Worldwide Destinations: The Geography of Travel and Tourism*
- reports, dictionaries, yearbooks and encyclopedias
- abstracting services
- statistical sources
- tourism journals
- web site addresses of national tourism organizations.

Books: Part One The Elements of the Geography of Travel and Tourism

Chapter 1 Introduction to the geography of tourism

Ashworth, G. (1984). *Recreation and Tourism*. Bell & Hyman.

Bull, A. (1995). *The Economics of Travel and Tourism*. Longman.

Burkhart, A. J. and Medlik, S. (1991). *Tourism, Past, Present and Future*. Heinemann.

Callaghan, P. (ed.) (1989). *Travel and Tourism*. Business Educational.

Coltman, M. (1989). *Introduction to Travel and Tourism*. Van Nostrand Reinhold.

Cooper, C. P., Fletcher, J., Gilbert, D. and Wanhill, S. (1998). *Tourism Principles and Practice*. Addison Wesley Longman.

Dumazedier, J. (1967). *Towards a Society of Leisure*. Free Press.

Foster, D. (1985). *Travel and Tourism Management*. Macmillan.

Fridgen, J. (1991). *Dimensions of Tourism*. AH&MA.

Gee, C. Y., Choy, D. J. L. and Makens, J. C. (1989). *The Travel Industry*. Van Nostrand Reinhold.

Glyptis, S. (ed.) (1993). *Leisure and the Environment*. Wiley.

Holloway, C. (1994). *The Business of Tourism*. Addison Wesley Longman.

Howell, D. W. (1993). *Passport: An Introduction to the Travel and Tourism Industry*. South Western.

Hudman, L. E. (1980). *Tourism: A Shrinking World*. Wiley.

Ioannides, D. and Debbage, K. G. (1998). *The Economic Geography of the Tourist Industry*. Routledge.

Kelly, J. R. (1990). *Leisure*. Prentice Hall.

Leiper, N. (1990). *The Tourism System*. Massey University Press.

Likorish, L. and Jenkins, C. L. (1997). *An Introduction to Tourism*. Butterworth-Heinemann.

Lundberg, D. E. (1975). *The Tourist Business*. Van Nostrand Reinhold.

Lundberg, D. E., Stavenga, M. H. and Krishanmoorthy, M. (1995). *Tourism Economics*. Wiley.

Matley, I. M. (1976). *The Geography of International Tourism*. Association of American Geographers Resource Paper 76 1, Washington, DC.

Mcintosh, R., Goeldner, C. and Ritchie, J. R. B. (1995). *Tourism: Principles, Practices, Philosophies*. Wiley.

Medlik, S. (1995). *Managing Tourism*. Butterworth-Heinemann.

Mercer, D. (1980). *In Pursuit of Leisure*. Sorret.

Mill, R. C. (1990). *Tourism: The International Business*. Prentice Hall.

Mill, R. C. and Morrison, A. (1992). *The Tourism System: An Introductory Text*. Prentice Hall.

Poon, A. (1993). *Tourism, Technology and Competitive Strategies*. CAB.

Robinson, H. A. (1976). *Geography of Tourism*. Macdonald and Evans.

Ryan, C. (1991). *Recreational Tourism: A Social Science Perspective*. Routledge.

Sharpley, R. (1994). *Tourism, Tourists and Society*. Elm.

Shaw, G. and Williams, A. (1994). *Critical Issues in Tourism*. Blackwell.

Theobald, W. F. (1994). *Global Tourism: The Next Decade*. Butterworth-Heinemann.

Tribe, J. (1995). *The Economics of Leisure and Tourism: Environments, Markets and Impacts*. Butterworth-Heinemann.

Vellas, F. and Becherel, L. (1995). *International Tourism*. Macmillan.

Wahab, S. (1993). *Tourism Management*. Tourism International Press.

Williams, S. (1998). *Tourism Geography*. Routledge.

Witt, S., Brooke, M. Z. and Buckley, P. J. (1995). *The Management of International Tourism*. Unwin Hyman.

Chapter 2 The geography of demand for tourism

Baron, R. (1989). *Travel and Tourism Data: A Comprehensive Research Handbook*. Euromonitor.

Butler, R. W. and Pearce, D. G. (eds) (1993). *Tourism Research*. Routledge.

Crotts, J. C. and Van Raaij, W. F. (eds) (1993). *Economic Psychology of Travel and Tourism*. Haworth Press.

Davidson, R. (1994). *Business Travel*. Addison Wesley Longman.

Frechtling, D. (1996). *Practical Tourism Forecasting*. Butterworth-Heinemann.

Ioannides, D. and Debbage, K. G. (1998). *The Economic Geography of the Tourist Industry*. Routledge.

Iso-Ahola, S. E. (1980). *The Social Psychology of Leisure and Recreation*. W. C. Brown.

MacCannell, D. (1976). *The Tourist: A New Theory of the Leisure Class*. Macmillan.

Pearce, D. and Butler, R. (eds) (1993). *Tourism Research: Critiques and Challenges*. Routledge.

Pearce, P. L. (1982). *The Social Psychology of Tourist Behaviour*. Pergamon.

Poon, A. (1993). *Tourism, Technology and Competitive Strategies*. CAB.

Ritchie, J. R. B. and Goeldner, C. R. (1994). *Travel, Tourism and Hospitality Research: A Handbook for Managers and Researchers*. Wiley.

Ross, G. F. (1996). *The Psychology of Tourism*. Hospitality Press.

Ryan, C. (1995). *Researching Tourist Satisfaction: Issues, Concepts and Problems*. Routledge.

Ryan, C. (1997). *The Tourist Experience: A New Introduction*. Cassell.

Smith, S. L. J. (1983). *Recreation Geography*. Longman.

Smith, S. L. J. (1996). *Tourism Analysis: A Handbook*. Addison Wesley Longman.

Witt, S. and Witt, C. (1991). *Modelling and Forecasting Demand in Tourism*. Academic Press.

Chapter 3 The geography of resources for tourism

Ashworth, G. and Dietvorst, A. (1995). *Tourism and Spatial Transformations: Implications for Policy and Planning*. CAB.

Ashworth, G. and Goodall, B. (eds) (1990). *Marketing Tourism Places*. Routledge.

Ashworth, G. J. and Tunbridge, J. E. (1990). *The Tourist-Historic City*. Belhaven.

Boissevain, J. (1996). *Coping with Tourists: European Reaction to Mass Tourism*. Berghahn Books.

Boniface, P. and Fowler, P. (1993). *Heritage and Tourism in the Global Village*. Routledge.

Boo, E. (1990). *Ecotourism: The Potentials and Pitfalls*. World Wildlife Fund.

Bramwell, W. and Lane, B. (eds) (1994). *Rural Tourism and Sustainable Rural Development*. Channel View Publications.

Bramwell, W., Henry, I., Jackson, G., Prat, A., Richards, G. and Van Der Straaten, J. (1996). *Sustainable Tourism Management: Principles and Practice*. Tilburg University Press.

Briguglio, L. (ed.) (1995). *Sustainable Tourism*. Cassell.

Burns, P. M. and Holden, A. (1995). *Tourism: A New Perspective*. Prentice Hall.

Butler, R. and Hinch, T. (1996). *Tourism and Indigenous Peoples*. International Thomson Business Press.

Butler, R., Hall, C. M. and Jenkins, J. (eds) (1998). *Tourism and Recreation in Rural Areas*. Wiley.

Cater, E. and Lowman, G. (1994). *Ecotourism*. Wiley.

Coccosis, H. and Nijcamp, P. (1995). *Sustainable Tourism Development*. Avebury.

Cooper, C. and Wanhill, S. (1997). *Tourism Development: Environmental and Community Issues*. Wiley.

Craig-Smith, S. (1994). *Learning to Live with Tourism*. Addison Wesley Longman.

Croall, J. (1995). *Preserve or Destroy: Tourism and the Environment*. Calousie Gulbenkian/Tourism Concern.

Davidson, R. and Maitland, R. (1997). *Tourism Destinations*. Hodder & Stoughton.

De Kadt, E. (1979). *Tourism: Passport to Development*. Oxford University Press.

Eber, S. (ed.) (1995). *Beyond the Green Horizon: Principles of Sustainable Tourism*. Tourism Concern.

Edington, J. M. and Edington, M. A. (1990). *Ecology, Recreation and Tourism*. Cambridge University Press.

Farrell, B. H. (1987). *Tourism and the Physical Environment*. Pergamon.

Fladmark, M. (1995). *Cultural Tourism*. Dunhead.

Forsyth, T. (1996). *Sustainable Tourism: Moving from Theory to Practice*. World Wildlife Fund/Tourism Concern.

Gearing, S. E., Swart, W. W. and Var, T. (eds) (1976). *Planning for Tourism Development*. Praeger.

Gee, C. Y. (1988). *Resort Development and Management*. AH&MA.

Getz, D. (1991). *Festivals, Special Events and Tourism*. Van Nostrand Reinhold.

Glasson, J., Godfrey, K. and Goodey, B. (1995). *Towards Visitor Impact Management: Visitor Impacts, Carrying Capacity and Management Responses in Europe's Historic Towns and Cities*. Avebury.

Glyptis, S. (1993). *Leisure and the Environment*. Wiley.

Gold, J. and Ward, S. (1993). *Place Promotion: The Use of PR to Sell Places*. Belhaven.

Goodall, B. and Ashworth, G. (eds) (1988). *Marketing in the Tourism Industry: The Promotion of Destination Regions*. Croom Helm.

Graburn, N. (1976). *Ethnic and Tourist Arts: Cultural Expressions from the Fourth World*. University of California Press.

Gunn, C. (1994). *Tourism Planning*. Taylor & Francis.

Gunn, C. A. (1997). *Vacationscape: Designing Tourist Regions*. 3rd edn. Van Nostrand Reinhold.

Hall, C. M. (1992). *Hallmark Tourist Events: Impacts, Management, Planning*. Belhaven Press.

Hall, C. M. (1994). *Tourism and Politics*. Wiley.

Hall, C. M. and Jenkins, J. M. (1994). *Tourism and Public Policy*. Routledge.

Hall, C. M. and McArthur, S. (1998). *Integrated Heritage Management*. The Stationery Office.

Harris, R. and Leiper, N. (1995). *Sustainable Tourism: An Australian Perspective*. Butterworth-Heinemann.

Harrison, L. and Husbands, W. (1996). *Practising Responsible Tourism*. Wiley.

Harrison, R. (ed.) (1994). *Manual of Heritage Management*. Butterworth-Heinemann.

Hawkins, D. E., Shafer, E. L. and Rovelstadt, J. M. (eds) (1980). *Tourism Planning and Development Issues*. George Washington University Press.

Heath, E. and Wall, G. (1992). *Marketing Tourism Destinations: A Strategic Planning Approach*. Wiley.

Henry, I. (ed.) (1990). *Management and Planning in the Leisure Industries*. Macmillan.

Herbert, D. (ed.) (1992). *Heritage Sites: Strategies for Marketing and Development*. Gower.

Hunter, C. and Green, H. (1995). *Tourism and Environment: A Sustainable Relationship?* Routledge.

Inskeep, E. (1991). *Tourism Planning: An Integrated Planning and Development Approach*. Van Nostrand Reinhold.

Inskeep, E. (1993). *National and Regional Planning: Methodologies and Case Studies*. WTO/Routledge.

Inskeep, E. and Kallenberger, M. (1992). *An Integrated Approach to Resort Development*. WTO.

Jansen-Verbeke, M. (1988). *Leisure, Recreation and Tourism in Inner Cities*. Routledge.

Jenner, P. and Smith, C. (1995). *Tourism Industry and the Environment*. Economist Intelligence Unit.

Johnson, P. and Thomas, B. (eds) (1992). *Perspectives on Tourism Policy*. Mansell.

Jubenville, A., Twight, D. W. and Becker, R. H. (1987). *Outdoor Recreation Management Theory and Applications*. Venture.

Krippendorf, J. (1987). *The Holiday Makers: Understanding the Impact of Leisure and Travel*. Heinemann.

Law, C. (1993). *Urban Tourism: Attracting Visitors to Large Cities*. Mansell.

Laws, E. (1995). *Tourist Destination Management: Issues, Analysis and Policies*. Routledge.

Lawson, F. (1995). *Hotels and Resorts: Planning, Design and Refurbishment*. Butterworth-Heinemann.

Lawson, F. R. and Baud-Bovy, M. (1998). *Tourism and Recreation: Handbook of Planning and Design*. Architectural Press.

Lickorish, L. J. (ed.) (1991). *Developing Tourism Destinations, Policies and Perspectives*. Longman.

MacCannell, D. (1992). *Empty Meeting Grounds*. Routledge.

Mason, P. and Mowforth, M. (1995). *Codes of Conduct in Tourism*. Occasional Papers in Geography, University Of Plymouth.

Mathieson, A. and Wall, G. (1989). *Tourism: Economic, Physical and Social Impacts*. Longman.

Mowforth, M. and Munt, I. (1998). *Tourism and Sustainability*. Routledge.

Murphy, P. (1997). *Quality Management in Urban Tourism*. Wiley.

Murphy, P. E. (1991). *Tourism: A Community Approach*. Methuen.

Nash, D. (1996). *The Anthropology of Tourism*. Pergamon.

Organization for Economic Co-operation and Development (OECD) (1981) *Case Studies of the Impact of Tourism on the Environment*. OECD.

Page, S. (1994). *Urban Tourism*. Routledge.

Page, S. and Getz, D. (1997). *The Business of Rural Tourism*. International Thomson Press.

Patmore, J. A. (1972). *Land and Leisure*. Penguin.

Patmore, J. A. (1983). *Recreation and Resources*. Blackwell.

Pearce, D. (1992). *Tourist Organizations*. Longman.

Pearce, D. (1989). *Tourist Development*. Longman.

Pearce, D. and Butler, R. (eds) (1995). *Change in Tourism: People, Places, Processes*. Routledge.

Pigram, J. (1993). *Outdoor Recreation and Resource Management*. Croom Helm.

Pizam, A. and Mansfield, Y. (1996). *Tourism, Crime and International Security Issues*. Wiley.

Powers, T. (1974). *Appraising International Tourism Projects*. Inter-American Development Bank.

Price, M. (1996). *People and Tourism in Fragile Environments*. Wiley.

Richards, G. (1996). *Cultural Tourism in Europe*. CAB.

Ryan, C. (ed.) (1997). *The Tourist Experience: A New Introduction*. Cassell.

Selwyn, T. (1996). *The Tourist Image: Myths and Myth Making in Tourism*. Wiley.

Shackley, M. (1996). *Wildlife Tourism*. Thomson International Business Press.

Sharpley, R. and Sharpley, J. (1997). *Rural Tourism: An Introduction*. International Thomson Press.

Smith, V. L. (1989). *Hosts and Guests*. University of Pennsylvania Press.

Smith, V. L. and Eadington, W. R. (eds) (1995). *Tourism Alternatives: Potential Problems in the Development of Tourism*. University of Pennsylvania Press.

Soane, J. (1993). *Fashionable Resort Regions: Their Evolution and Transformation*. CAB.

Swarbrooke, J. (1995). *The Development and Management of Visitor Attractions*. Butterworth-Heinemann.

Towner, J. (1994). *An Historical Geography of Recreation and Tourism*. Belhaven.

Turner, L. and Ash, J. (1975). *The Golden Hordes: International Tourism and the Pleasure Periphery*. Constable.

Urry, J. (1990). *The Tourist Gaze*. Sage.

Uzzell, D. (ed.) (1989). *Heritage Interpretation*. 2 vols. Belhaven.

Ward, T. and Dillon, M. (1991). *Guidelines to Hotel and Leisure Project Financing*. WTO.

Weiler, B. and Hall, C. M. (1992). *Special Interest Tourism*. Wiley.

World Tourism Organization (WTO) (1993). *Sustainable Tourism Development: Lessons for Local Planners*. WTO.

Ziffer, K. (1989). Ecotourism: *The Uneasy Alliance*. Ernst & Young.

Chapter 4 Climate and tourism

Hatch, D. (1989). *Weather around the World*. Amsterdam.

Morgan, M. and Moran, J. (1997). *Weather and People*. Prentice Hall.

Pearce, E. A. and Smith, C. G. (1984). *The World Weather Guide*. Hutchinson.

Trewartha, G. (1954). *An Introduction to Climate*. 3rd edn. McGraw-Hill.

Chapter 5 The geography of transport for travel and tourism

Ashford, N. (1991). *Airport Operations*. Addison Wesley Longman.

Blackshaw, C. (1992). *Aviation Law and Regulation*. Addison Wesley Longman.

British Airways (annual). *Environmental Report*. BA

Cole, S. (1987). *Applied Transport Economics*. Kogan Page.

Doganis, R. (1992). *The Airport Business*. Routledge.

Doganis, R. D. (1985). *Flying Off Course: The Economics of International Airlines*. Allen & Unwin.

Faulks, R. W. (1992). *The Geography of Transport for Tourism*. Ian Allan.

Gialloreto, L. (1988). *Strategic Airline Management*. Addison Wesley Longman.

Graham, B. (1995). *Geography and Air Transport*. Wiley.

Hanlon, P. (1995). *Global Airlines: Competition in a Transnational Industry*. Butterworth-Heinemann.

Miller, J. C. and Sawers, P. (1988). *The Technical Development of Modern Aviation*. Routledge.

Page, S. (1994). *Transport for Tourism*. Routledge.

Robinson, H. and Bamford, G. (1978). *Geography of Transport*. Macdonald & Evans.

Shaw, S. (1990). *Airline Marketing and Management*. Pitman.

Wheatcroft, S. (1994). *Aviation and Tourism Policies: Balancing the Benefits*. Routledge/WTO.

Wheatcroft, S. and Lipman, G. (1990). *European Liberalisation and World Air Transport: Towards a Transnational Policy*. Economist Intelligence Unit, Special Report, no. 2015.

Books: Part Two The Regional Geography of Travel and Tourism in the World

Barke, M., Towner, J. and Newton, M. T. (eds) (1996). *Tourism in Spain: Critical Issues*. CAB.

Burton, R. (1995). *Travel Geography*. Addison Wesley Longman.

Conlin, M. V. and Baum, T. (1995). *Island Tourism.* Wiley.

Davidson, R. (1998). *Travel and Tourism in Europe.* 2nd edn. Addison Wesley Longman.

Drakakis-Smith, G. and Lockhart, D. (1997). *Island Tourism: Trends and Prospects.* Pinter.

Farrell, B. H. (1982). *Hawaii: The Legend that Sells.* University of Hawaii Press.

Gamble, W. P. (1989). Tourism and Development in Africa. Murray.

Gayle, D. J. (1993). *Tourism Marketing and Management in the Caribbean.* Routledge.

Hall, C. M. (1994). *Tourism in the Pacific Rim.* Longman.

Hall, C. M. (1997). *Introduction to Tourism in Australia.* Longman.

Hall, C. M. and Johnston, M. (1995). *Polar Tourism.* Wiley.

Hall, D. (1991). *Tourism and Economic Development in Eastern Europe and the Soviet Union.* Belhaven.

Harrison, D. (1994). *Tourism and the Less Developed Countries.* Wiley.

Herbote, B. (1995). *World Tourism Directory. Part 1 Europe; Part 2 The Americas; Part 3 Africa, Middle East, Asia and Oceania.* Saur/Reed Travel and WTO.

Hernmann, E., Hitchcock, M. J., King, V. T. and Parnwell, M. (eds) (1992). *Tourism in South East Asia.* Routledge.

Horner, S. and Swarbrooke, J. (1996). *Marketing Tourism, Leisure and Hospitality in Europe.* International Thomson Business Press.

Hudman, L. E. and Jackson, R. (1990). *Geography of Travel and Tourism.* Delmar.

Jackson, I. (1989). *An Introduction to Tourism in Australia.* Hospitality Press.

King, B. (1989). *Tourism Marketing in Australia.* Hospitality Press.

Lavery, P. (ed.) (1971). *Recreational Geography.* David & Charles.

Lea, J. (1988). *Tourism and Development in the Third World.* Routledge.

Manuel, M., McElroy, B. and Smith, R. (1996). *Tourism.* Cambridge University Press.

Montanaria, A. and Williams, A. (1995). *European Tourism: Regions, Spaces and Restructuring.* Wiley.

Pattullo, P. (1996). *Last Resorts: The Cost of Tourism in the Caribbean.* Cassell.

Pearce, D. (1995). *Tourism Today: A Geographical Analysis.* Longman.

Pompl, W. and Lavery, P. (eds) (1993). *Tourism in Europe: Structures and Developments.* CAB.

Quinn, B. (annual). *World Travel Guide CD-Rom (Windows).* Columbus Press.

Quinn, B. (annual). *World Travel Guide.* Columbus Press.

Richter, L. K. (1989). *The Politics of Tourism in Asia.* University of Hawaii Press.

Robinson, H. (1976). *A Geography of Tourism.* Macdonald & Evans.

Shaw, G. and Williams, A. M. (1994). *Critical Issues in Tourism: A Geographical Perspective.* Blackwell.

Sinclair, T. and Stabler, M. (eds) (1991). *The Tourism Industry: An International Analysis.* CAB.

Taylor, M. (annual). *World Travel Atlas.* Columbus Press.

Williams, A. M. and Shaw, G. J. (eds) (1991). *Tourism and Economic Development: Western European Experiences.* Belhaven.

Reports, dictionaries, yearbooks and encyclopedias

In addition to books, journals and trade press coverage of the geography of travel and tourism, there are a number of useful sources to be found in consultants' reports, tourism dictionaries, yearbooks and encyclopedias. Some of the key sources include:

Collin, P. H. (1994). *Dictionary of Hotels, Tourism and Catering Management.* P. H. Collin.

Cooper, C. and Lockwood, A. (eds) (1989–). *Progress in Tourism, Recreation and Hospitality Management.* Vols 1–6. Belhaven.

Economist Intelligence Unit publications.

Euromonitor publications.

Europa Publications (annual). *The Europa World Yearbook.*

INSIGHTS, English Tourist Board (now English Tourism Council).

Khan, M., Olsen, M. and Var, T. (1993). *Encyclopedia of Hospitality and Tourism.* Van Nostrand Reinhold.

Medlik, S. (1993). *Dictionary of Transport, Travel and Hospitality.* Butterworth-Heinemann.

Paxton, J. (ed.) (annual). *The Statesman's Yearbook.* Macmillan.

Ritchie, J. R. B. and Hawkins, D. (eds) (annual). *World Travel and Tourism Review.* Vols 1–3. CAB.

Seaton, A., Wood, R., Dieke, P. and Jenkins, C. (eds) (1994). *Tourism – the State of the Art: The Strathclyde Symposium.* Wiley.

Witt, S. F. and Mountinho, L. (eds) (1994). *Tourism Marketing and Management Handbook.* Prentice Hall.

Witt, S. F. and Mountinho, L. (eds) (1995). *Tourism Marketing and Management Handbook.* Student edn. Prentice Hall.

World Bank (annual). *The World Bank Atlas.* Washington, DC.

Abstracting services

Using electronic searching and abstracting services is a very effective way of searching the available literature. The key services include:

Articles in Tourism (monthly). Universities of Bourne-mouth, Oxford Brookes and Surrey.

International Tourism and Hospitality Data Base CD-ROM. The Guide to Industry and Academic Resources. Wiley.

Leisure, Recreation and Tourism Abstracts (quarterly). CAB.

The Travel and Tourism Index. Brigham Young University Hawaii Campus.

Statistical sources

There is still a limited range of sources that draw together tourism statistics and trends. Nonetheless the WTO's increasingly user-friendly reports are well worth consulting for both global and regional trends. The key sources are:

Organization for Economic Co-operation and Development (annual). *Tourism Policy and International Tourism in OECD Member Countries.* OECD

World Tourism Organization (WTO) (annual). *Compendium of Tourism Statistics.* WTO.

World Tourism Organization (WTO) (annual). *Yearbook of Tourism Statistics.* WTO.

World Tourism Organization (WTO) (1992). *Tourism Trends to the Year 2000 and Beyond.* WTO.

World Tourism Organization (WTO) (1995–6). *Global Tourism Forecasts to the Year 2000 and Beyond.* 6 vols. WTO.

World Tourism Organization (WTO) (1999). *Tourism Market Trends.* 6 vols. WTO.

Tourism journals

The growth in tourism journals has brought with it a rich source of case study and statistical material. In addition the geographical journals are increasingly publishing tourism-related papers. Tourism journals with geographical content include:

Annals of Tourism Research
Asia Pacific Journal of Tourism Research
Australian Journal of Hospitality Management
Current Issues in Tourism
Festival Management and Event Tourism
Hospitality and Tourism Educator
International Journal of Contemporary Hospitality Management
International Journal of Hospitality Management
International Journal of Service Industry Management
International Journal of Tourism Research
Journal of Hospitality and Leisure Marketing
Journal of Air Transport Geography
Journal of Air Transport Management

Journal of Hospitality and Tourism Research
Journal of Leisure Research
Journal of Sports Tourism
Journal of Sustainable Tourism
Journal of Tourism Studies
Journal of Travel and Tourism Marketing
Journal of Travel Research
Journal of Vacation Marketing
Leisure Futures, Henley Centre for Forecasting
Leisure Sciences
Leisure Studies
Managing Leisure
Progress in Tourism and Hospitality Research
Service Industries Journal
The Tourist Review
Tourism Analysis
Tourism Economics
Tourism in Focus
Tourism Geographies
Tourism Management
Tourism Recreation Research
Tourism, Culture and Communication
Travel and Tourism Analyst
World Leisure and Recreation Association Journal

World Wide Web (WWW) site addresses of national tourism organizations

The WWW has become a rich source of material for anyone researching the geography of travel and tourism. Destinations, organizations and companies provide web pages containing information that previously was only available by contacting the organization concerned. This source of information needs to be used with care, as there is no quality control of the material available. However, the official sites such as those listed here are both reliable and comprehensive sources for the researcher.

At the time of writing these web site addresses were correct. However, readers need to be aware that sometimes addresses do change.

Country	Web site
Algeria	http://www.algeria-tourism.org/
Andorra	http://www.turisme.ad
Angola	http://www.angola.org/
Anguilla	http://net.ai/
Antigua and Barbuda	http://www.interknowledge.com/antigua-barbuda/
Argentina	http://www.sectur.gov.ar/homepage.htm
Aruba	http://www.interknowledge.com/aruba
Australia	http://www.aussie.net.au/
Austria	http://www.austria-tourism.at/
Bahamas	http://www.interknowledge.com/bahamas/

Bangladesh	http://www.bangla.org/tour/
Barbados	http://barbados.org/
Belgium	http://www.visitbelgium.com/
Belize	http://www.travelbelize.org/
Bermuda	http://www.bermudatourism.com
Bhutan	http://www.bhutan-info.org/
Bolivia	http://jaguar.pg.cc.md.us/turismo.html
Bonaire	http://www.interknowledge.com/bonaire/index.html
Brazil	http://www.embratur.gov.br/
Cambodia	http://www.cambodia-web.net/
Cameroon	http://www.compufix.demon.co.uk/camweb/
Canada	http://info.ic.gc.ca/Tourism/
Cayman Islands	http://www.caymanislands.ky
Chile	http://www.turismochile.cl
China	http://www.chinatour.com/cnta/
Colombia	http://www.presidencia.gov.co/
Costa Rica	http://www.tourism-costarica.com
Croatia	http://www.vlada.hr/
Cuba	http://www.cubaweb.cu/
Curacao	http://www.interknowledge.com/curacao/
Cyprus	http://www.cyprustourism.org/
Czech Republic	http://czech-tourism.com
Denmark	http://www.dt.dk/
Dominican Republic	http://www.dominicana.com
Ecuador	http://wwwpub4.ecua.net.ec/mintur
Egypt	http://touregypt.net/
Estonia	http://www.tourism.ee/
Ethiopia	http://www.ethiopia.ottawa.on.ca/tourism.htm
Falkland Islands	http://www.tourism.org.fk/
Federated States of Micronesia	http://fsmgov.org/
Fiji	http://www.BulaFiji.com
Finland	http://www.finland-tourism.com
France	http://www.maison-de-la-france.fr
French Guina	http://www.guyanetourisme.com/en/Default.htm
Gabon	http://www.presidence-gabon.com/a/index.html
Gambia	http://www.gambia.com
Georgia	http://www.parliament.ge/TOURISM
Germany	http://www.germany-tourism.de/
Gibraltar	http://www.gibraltar.gi/tourism/
Greece	http://areianet.gr/infoxenios/english/
Greenland	http://www.greenland-guide.dk
Grenada	http://www.interknowledge.com/grenada/
Guadeloupe	http://www.antilles-info-tourisme.com/guadeloupe/
Guam	http://www.visitguam.org/
Guatemala	http://www.travel-guatemala.org.gt
Guyana	http://www.turq.com/guyana.html
Hawaii	http://www.hawaii.gov/tourism/
Hong Kong	http://www.hkta.org
Honduras	http://www.turq.com/honduras.html
Hungary	http://www.hungarytourism.hu/
Iceland	http://www.icelandtravel.is/
India	http://www.tourindia.com/
Iran	http://www.itto.org/
Ireland	http://www.ireland.travel.ie
Isle of Man	http://www.isle-of-man.com/
Israel	http://www.infotour.co.il
Italy	http://www.enit.it/
Jamaica	http://www.jamaicatravel.com/
Japan	http://www.jnto.go.jp/
Jersey	http://www.jtourism.com
Jordan	http://www.jordanembassyus.org
Kenya	http://www.bwanazulia.com/kenya/
Korea (South) (Republic of Korea)	http://www.knto.or.kr
Laos	http://www.laoembassy.com/discover/
Lebanon	
Liechtenstein	http://www.news.li/touri/index.htm
Luxembourg	http://www.etat.lu/tourism
Macau	http://macau.tourism.gov.mo
Macedonia	http://www.infoguide.com.mk/
Malaysia	http://tourism.gov.my/
Maldives	http://www.visitmaldives.com/intro.html
Malta	http://www.tourism.org.mt/
Martinique	http://www.martinique.org/
Mauritius	http://www.mauritius.net/
Mexico	http://www.mexico-travel.com/
Micronesia	http://www.visit-fsm.org/
Monaco	http://www.monaco.mc/monaco/guide_en.html
Mongolia	http://www.mongoliatourism.gov.mn/
Morocco	http://www.moroccoweb.com/en/tourism index.html
Myanmar (Burma)	http://www.myanmar.com
Namibia	http://www.iwwn.com.na/namtour/namtour.html
Nepal	http://www.south-asia.com/visitnepal98/
Netherlands	http://www.visitholland.com/
New Zealand	http://www.nztb.govt.nz/
Nicaragua	http://www.intur.gob.ni/
Nigeria	http://www.tcol.co.uk/nigeria/nigeria.htm
Northern Ireland	http://www.ni-tourism.com
Norway	http://www.tourist.no
Pakistan	http://www.tourism.gov.pk/
Palau	http://www.visit-palau.com/
Palestine	http://www.pna.org
Panama	http://www.panamainfo.com/
Papua New Guinea	http://www.tiare.net.pg/tpa/home.html
Peru	http://www.peruonline.net/IN
Philippines	http://www.tourism.gov.ph/
Poland	http://poland.pl/
Portugal	
Puerto Rico	http://www.prtourism.com
Romania	http://www.turism.ro/
Russian Federation	http://www.interknowledge.com/russia/index html
Saba	http://www.turq.com/saba/
Saint-Pierre-et-Miquelon	http://209.205.50.254/Tourispmweb/
Scotland	http://www.holiday.scotland.net/
Senegal	http://www.earth2000.com/senegal/
Serbia	http://www.serbia-info.com/ntos/
Seychelles	http://www.seychelles.uk.com/
Singapore	http://www.travel.com.sg/sog/
Slovenia	http://www.ntz-nta.si/
South Africa	http://www.satour.org/
Spain	http://www.okspain.org/
Sri Lanka	http://www.lanka.net/ctb/
St Barthelemy	http://www.st-barths.com/

St. Eustatius (Netherlands Antilles)	http://www.turq.com/statia/
St. Kitts & Nevis	http://www.interknowledge.com/stkitts-nevis/
St. Lucia	http://www.st-lucia.com/
St. Maarten	http://www.st-maarten.com/
St. Martin	http://www.interknowledge.com/st-martin
St. Vincent & The Grenadines	http://www.turq.com/stvincent
Sudan	http://www.sudan.net/
Sweden	http://www.gosweden.org/homepage.html
Switzerland	http://www.switzerlandtourism.ch/
Syria	http://www.syriatourism.org
Taiwan	http://www.tbroc.gov.tw/e_index2.html
Tanzania	http://www.tanzania-web.com
Thailand	http://www.tat.or.th/
Tibet – China	http://www.tibet-tour.com/
Togo	http://www.afrika.com/togo/index.html
Trinidad and Tobago	http://www.visittnt.com/
Tunisia	http://www.tourismtunisia.com/
Turkey	http://www.turkey.org/turkey/
Turks & Caicos	http://www.interknowledge.com/turks-caicos
Uganda	http://www.uganda.co.ug/tour.htm
United Kingdom	http://www.visitbritain.com/
United States of America	http://www.tinet.ita.doc.gov/
Uruguay	http://www.turismo.gub.uy
US Virgin Islands	http://www.usvi.net/
Vanuatu	http://www.vanuatu.net.vu/
Vietnam	http://www.batin.com.vn/dbotweb
Wales	http://www.visitwales.com
Western Samoa	http://public-ww.pi.se/~orbit/samoa/welcome.html
Yemen	http://www.nusacc.org/yemen/tourism.htm
Zambia	http://www.africa-insites.com/zambia/
Zanzibar	http://www.zanzibar.net/zautalii/index.html
Zimbabwe	http://www.zimweb.com/Dzimbabwe.html

Bibliography

Ashworth, G. J. and Tunbridge, J. E. (1990). *The Tourist-Historic City.* Belhaven.

Brazil official tourist board: http:/www/embratur.gov.br/

Brazilinfo: http://www brazilinfo.com

Bruges: http://www.brugge. be/toerisme/en/index.htm

Buhalis, D. (1998). *Tourism in Greece: Strategic Analysis and Challenges for the New Millennium.* Studies and Reports, Planning and Development Series, vol. 18, International Centre for Research and Studies in Tourism, Aix en Provence.

Burkart, A. J. and Medlik, S. (1981). *Tourism, Past, Present and Future.* Heinemann.

Burns, P. and Cooper, C. (1997). Yemen. *Tourism Management*, **18** (8), 555–63.

Burton, R. (1991). *Travel Geography.* Pitman.

Butler, R. W. (1980). The concept of a tourist area cycle of evolution. *Canadian Geographer*, **24** (1).

Chubb, M. and Chubb, H. R. (1981). *One Third of our Time.* Wiley.

Clawson, M. and Knetsch, J. (1966). *The Economics of Outdoor Recreation.* Johns Hopkins University Press.

Cleverdon, R. (1979). *The Economic and Social Impact of Tourism on Developing Countries.* Economist Intelligence Unit.

Cohen, E. (1972). Toward a sociology of international tourism. *Social Research*, **39** (1), 164–83.

Collins, P. and Ashford, D. (1998). Space tourism. *Ada Astronautica*, **17** (4), 421–31.

Cooper, C. and Lockwood, A. (eds) (1989–). *Progress in Tourism, Recreation and Hospitality Management.* Vols 1–6. Belhaven.

Cooper, C. P. (1989). *Progress in Tourism, Recreation and Hospitality Management.* Belhaven.

Davidson, R. (1994). *Business Travel.* Addison, Wesley and Longman.

Davis, W. (1998). The Arctic. *Condé Nast Traveler*, January, 113.

Dublin: http://www.dublincorp.ie/dublin/ and http:/ /www.visit.ie/dublin/

El Niño: http://www.enn.com/elnino/news.htm

Faulks, R. W. (1982). *Principles of Transport.* Ian Allan.

France: http://www.maison-de-la-France.com

Giles, A. and Perry, A. (1998). The use of a temporal analogue to investigate the possible impact of projected global warming on the UK tourist industry. *Tourism Management*, **19**(1), 76.

Graburn, N. (1976). *Ethnic and Tourist Arts: Cultural Expressions from the Fourth World.* University of California Press.

Gray (1970). *International Travel – International Trade.* Heath Lexington Books.

Hatch, D. (1985). *Weather around the World.* Amsterdam.

Hawaii: http://www.gohawaii.com/

Hawaii: http://www.state.hi.us/dbedt/tourism.html

Holloway, J. C. (1989). *The Business of Tourism.* Macdonald & Evans.

Isle of Man: http://www.gov.im/tourism

Jackson, M. (1997). *Galapagos: A Natural History.* University of Calgary Press.

Lansing, J. B. (1960). *The Changing Travel Market.* Institute for Social Research.

Lavery, P. (ed.) (1971). *Recreational Geography.* David & Charles.

Lee, D. and Lemons, H. (1949). Clothing for global man. *Geographical Review*, **39**, 181–213.

Leiper, N. (1979). The framework of tourism. *Annals of Tourism Research*, **6** (4), 390–407.

Mandis Roberts Consultants (1996). *Developing a Tourism Optimisation Model (Tomm): A Model to Monitor and Manage Tourism on Kangaroo Island South Australia.* Mandis Roberts.

Manuel, M., McElroy, B. and Smith, R. (1996). *Tourism*. Cambridge University Press.

Mathieson, A. and Wall, G. (1982). *Tourism: Economic, Physical and Social Impacts*. Longman.

Mill, R. C. (1990). *Tourism: The International Business*. Prentice Hall.

Mowforth, M. and Munt, I. (1998). *Tourism and Sustainability*. Routledge.

Muqbil, I. (1998). The fall out from the Asian economic crisis. *Travel and Tourism Analyst*, **6**, 78–95.

New Forest District Council (NFDC) (1994). *Living with the Enemy*. NFDC.

New Forest District Council (NFDC) (1996). *Making New Friends*. NFDC.

New York City: http://www.nycvisit.com

Nile: http://www.idsc.gov.eg

Nunavut (Canadian Arctic): http://www.nunanet.com/nunatour

Pakkala, L. J. (1990). Egyptian tourism: cruising for growth. *Cornell Hotel and Restaurant Association Quarterly*, **31** (2), 56–9.

Patmore, J. A. (1983). *Recreation and Resources*. Blackwell.

Pattullo, P. (1996). *Last Resorts: The Cost of Tourism in the Caribbean*. Cassell.

Poon, A. (1993). *Tourism, Technology and Competitive Strategies*. CAB.

Poon, A. (1994). The new tourism revolution. *Tourism Management*, **15** (2), 91–2.

Railson Costa de Souza (1998). The evolution of Rio de Janeiro as a destination and its regeneration process. Unpublished MSc dissertation, Bournemouth University.

Richter Papaconstantinou, C. (1992). *Tourist Development of Rhodes*. Cahiers du Tourisme Serie B, no. 67, Aix en Provence.

Rivers, J. (1998). Thebes (Luxor, Egypt) traffic and visitor flow management in the west bank of the Necropolis. In *Visitor Management* (M. Shackley, ed.) pp. 161–81, Butterworth-Heinemann.

Rostow, W. W. (1959). *The Stages of Economic Growth*. Cambridge University Press.

Shaw, G. and Williams, A. (1994). *Critical Issues in Tourism: A Geographical Perspective*. Blackwell.

Smeral (1998). The impact of globalization on small to medium sized enterprises. *Tourism Management*, **19** (4), 371–80.

Smith, V, L. (ed.) (1978). *Hosts and Guests: The Anthropology of Tourism*. Blackwell.

Swarbrooke, J. (1995) *The Development and Management of Visitor Attractions*. Butterworth-Heinemann.

Terjung, W. H. (1966). Physiological climates of the coterminous United States: a bioclimatological classification based on man. *Annals of the Association of American Geographers*, **56**, 141–79.

Thompson J. and Perry, A. (eds) (1997). *Applied Climatology*. Routledge.

Trewartha, G. (1954). *An Introduction to Climate*. 3rd edn. McGraw-Hill.

Ullman, E. (1980). *Geography as Spatial Interaction*. University of Washington Press.

Waugh, D. (1995). *Geography: An Integrated Approach* (2nd edn). Nelson.

West Flanders Economic Study Bureau (1996). *Tourism in Brugge: Socio-Economic Aspects and Influence on City Planning*.

Wilkinson, P .F. (1997). *Tourism Policy and Planning: Case Studies from the Commonwealth Caribbean*. Cognizant.

Williams, A. V. and Zelinsky, W. (1970). On some patterns in international tourist flows. *Economic Geography*, **46** (4), 549–67.

World Tourism Organization (1995). *Global Tourism Forecasts to the Year 2000 and Beyond*. WTO.

World Tourism Organization (1998). *Tourism Highlights 1997*. WTO.

World Tourism Organization (1998a). *Assessment of the Asian Financial and Economic Crisis and Its Impact upon Tourism*. WTO.

World Tourism Organization (WTO) (annual). *Compendium of Tourist Statistics*. WTO.

Selective place name index

Aachen, 152
Abidjan, 254, 255
Acapulco, 324
Adelaide, 340, 343, 350
Aden, 46, 234, 236
Adriatic, 183, 184, 185, 186, 191, 192, 208, 215, 216
Aegean, 63, 197, 198, 199, 200, 227, 232, 233
Afghanistan, 260, 261, 262, 266, 267
Africa, 23, 26, 27, 28, 29, 46, 59, 62, 69, 195, 226, 227, 228, 240–51, 253–6, 257–8
Agadir, 242, 243
Agra, 264
Aland Islands, 130
Alaska, 43, 48, 64, 304
Albania, 206, 216–17
Alberta, 307
Alexandria, 197, 229
Algarve, 178
Algeria, 240, 241, 242, 244–5
Algiers, 244, 245
Alice Springs, 343
Alps, 29, 42, 43, 74, 75, 77, 144, 146, 147, 148, 149, 152, 155, 156, 158, 160, 163, 164, 182, 183, 184, 185–6, 208, 216
Altiplano, 49, 331–2
Alto Adige (South Tyrol), 183, 184, 185–6
Amazon, 46, 49, 326, 327, 328, 330, 331
Americas, The, *see* Central America, North America, South America, United States of America
Amritsar, 262
Amsterdam, 135, 136, 330
Andalucia, 168, 169, 172, 173–4, 177
Andes, 49, 326, 329, 330–2, 333
Andorra, 169, 174
Angkor, 278
Angola, 177, 248, 251

Annapurna, 268, 269, 270–1
Antarctica, 27, 39, 40, 48, 50, 52, 64, 333, 345, 348–50
Antigua, 319–20
Antrim, 121
Antwerp, 137, 138
Appalachians, 292, 297, 298, 299
Appennines, 183, 186, 188
Aquitaine, 156, 159, 161
Arabian Peninsula, 228, 229, 234–5
Arctic, The, 27, 39, 40, 48, 50, 52, 58, 64, 127, 128, 130, 131–3, 217, 218, 220, 308, 311–14
Ardennes, 134, 137, 138–9 , 162
Argentina, 16, 187, 316, 328, 332–3, 349
Arizona, 46, 302
Armenia, 221
Arnhemland, 343
Aruba, 321
Asia, 22, 27, 29, 47, 62, 68, 69, 135, 177, 226, 227, 228, 232, 251, 259–71, 273–91, 308, 338, 339, 340, 341, 346, 352
Aspen, 301
Assisi, 183, 187
Asturias, 168, 171
Aswan, 41, 229, 238, 239
Atacama, 333
Athens, 196, 197, 198, 199, 204
Atitlán, Lake, 325
Atlanta, 295, 298
Atlantic City, 295, 297–8
Atlantic Ocean, 27, 47, 50, 59, 63, 74, 82, 111, 120, 124, 155, 159, 161, 171, 173, 175, 177, 179, 180, 242, 243, 249, 250, 251, 254, 256, 295, 297, 298, 300, 306, 307, 311, 319, 320, 327, 328, 332, 333, 335
Atlas Mountains, 241, 242, 243, 245
Auckland, 344, 345
Australasia, 27, 46, 280, 338, 339, 346

Australia, 41, 51, 52, 64, 84, 118, 197, 265, 271, 275, 277, 278, 287, 289, 338, 339–44, 345, 347, 348, 349, 350–1, 352, 353
Austria, 74, 144, 145–7, 148, 150, 185, 197, 208
Aviemore, 82, 112
Ayers Rock (Uluru), 339, 343–4
Azerbaijan, 221, 222
Azores, 179, 180

Baden-Baden, 152
Baffin Island, 48, 313–14
Baghdad, 334
Bahamas, 318–19
Bahrain, 46, 234
Baikal, Lake, 221
Baja (Lower California), 324
Balaton, Lake, 209, 210, 224
Balearic Islands, 167, 169, 170, 175–6
Bali, 276, 285–8, 289, 340, 344
Balkans, 73, 74, 197, 203, 207, 212–14, 216–17
Baltic Sea, 64, 74, 126, 129, 144, 151, 206, 208, 211, 212, 217, 218
Baltic States, 207, 212
Baltimore, 297
Banff, 293, 305, 307
Bangalore, 201
Bangkok, 68, 274, 277–8, 359
Bangladesh, 260, 266
Barbados, 64, 317, 318, 320
Barcelona, 170, 172, 180
Basque Country, 168, 171
Bath, 100
Bavaria, 150, 151, 152
Beijing, 283, 285
Beirut, 232
Belarus, 211, 219, 221
Belfast, 88, 116, 118, 121
Belgium, 134, 137–9, 141, 142, 143, 157, 169
Belize, 315, 325
Benidorm, 172
Berlin, 149, 150, 152, 153–4
Bermuda, 46, 319
Berne, 149
Bernese Oberland, 147, 149
Bethlehem, 230, 231
Bhutan, 260, 261, 268
Bilbao, 76, 167, 171
Birmingham, 101
Black Forest, 152
Black Hills, 301
Black Sea, 206, 208, 212, 213, 214, 217, 218, 219, 220, 221
Blackpool, 102
Blue Mountains (NSW), 341
Blue Ridge, 67, 295, 298

Bodhgaya, 262
Bodrum, 232, 233
Bogotá, 329
Bohemia, 208, 209
Bolivia, 49, 330, 331–2, 333
Bologna, 183, 186
Bombay, 262, 265
Bonaire, 321
Bonn, 152, 153
Bosnia-Herzegovina, 197, 214, 215, 216
Boston, 296, 297
Botswana, 248, 250
Bournemouth, 89–96, 99, 107, 108
Bradford, 103
Brasilia, 328
Brazil, 49, 62, 69, 254, 311, 315, 316, 327–8, 335
Brecon Beacons, 113, 114
Brighton, 99
Brisbane, 341, 342
Bristol, 100, 105
Britain, 10, 40, 43, 47, 81–91, 104, 107, 117, 118, 151, 153, 157, 159, 177, 195, 197, 200, 230, 242, 243, 247, 248, 252, 262, 320, 339, 341, *see also* United Kingdom
British Columbia, 62, 64, 307–8
British Isles, 41, 47, 68, 81, 82, 84, 85, 87, 88, 89, 97, 110, 111, 135, 339
Brittany, 75, 160, 161
Bruges, 137, 138, 140–3
Brunei, 274, 276
Brussels, 77, 78, 137, 138, 141
Bucharest, 213
Budapest, 201, 210, 224
Buenos Aires, 332, 333
Bulgaria, 207, 212, 214
Burgundy, 156, 162
Burma, 274, 279
Burren, 120
Burundi, 256

Cairngorms, 111, 112
Cairns, 340, 342
Cairo, 228, 229, 238
Calais, 157, 159, 161
Calcutta, 262, 264
Calgary, 307
California, 43, 47, 51, 58, 62, 293, 295, 301, 303–4, 352, 353
Cambodia, 274, 278
Cameroon, 255
Campania, 185, 188
Canada, 40, 48, 69, 109, 118, 278, 292, 293, 294, 304–8, 310, 311–4, 320, 323, 352
Canadian Shield, 305, 306
Canal du Midi, 159

Canary Islands, 46, 54, 127, 169, 170, 175, 176, 179
Canberra, 340, 432
Cancún, 324
Cannes, 158, 164, 165
Cantabria, 171
Canterbury, 98
Cape Cod, 295, 297
Cape Horn, 63, 349
Cape of Good Hope, 63, 248
Capetown, 248, 249, 250
Cape Verde Islands, 256
Caracas, 329
Cardiff, 112, 113–14
Caribbean, 46, 64, 69, 135, 254, 293, 294, 315, 316–23,
    324, 325, 329, 334–5
Carinthia, 146
Carpathians, 74, 76, 207, 208, 209, 211, 212, 213
Cartagena de las Indias, 329
Casablanca, 243
Caspian Sea, 74, 222, 235
Castille, 174, 181
Catalonia, 168, 169, 172
Caucasus, 74, 217, 218, 220, 221
Cayman Islands, 318, 319
Central Africa, 256
Central America, 46, 316, 323, 324, 325–6
Central Asia, 206, 217, 218, 222, 232, 233, 259, 267
Chacaltaya, 332
Channel Islands, 84, 103, 116
Channel Tunnel, 23, 54, 62, 63, 83, 84, 86, 88, 89, 97,
    98, 99, 138, 141, 157, 159, 160, 161, 163, 358
Charleston, SC, 298–9
Chiangmai, 278
Chicago, 62, 295, 296, 301
Chile, 332, 333, 348, 349
China, People's Republic, 23, 47, 62, 274, 279, 282–4,
    285
China, Republic of, see Taiwan
Christchurch, 345
Churchill, 307
Cleveland, 301
Cobh, 120
Cologne, 152
Colombia, 329
Colombo, 262
Colorado (river), 302
Colorado (state), 301
Commonwealth Caribbean, 315, 317, 318–21, 334–5
Commonwealth of Independent States (CIS), 217–22
Comores, 252
Congo, 138, 240, 256
Constantinople, see Istanbul
Cook Islands, 348
Cook Strait, 58, 345
Copenhagen, 125, 126, 129
Corfu, 197, 200

Cork, 118, 120
Cornwall, 99, 100
Corsica, 156, 157, 159, 160, 162–3, 184
Costa Blanca, 170, 172
Costa Brava, 169, 170, 172
Costa Daurada, 169, 172
Costa de Estoril, 179
Costa de la Luz, 173–4
Costa de Prata, 179
Costa Rica, 325, 326
Costa Smeralda, 189
Costa del Sol, 170, 173, 177
Costa Verde, 179
Côte d'Azur, see French Riviera
Coto Doñana, 38, 174
Cotswolds, 101
Crete, 196, 197, 198, 199
Crimea, 221
Croatia, 63, 75, 145, 184, 207, 214, 215, 216
Cuba, 316, 317, 318, 321, 322–3
Curacao, 321
Cuzco, 330
Cyclades, 198, 199–200
Cyprus, 128, 195, 200–1, 230, 234
Czech Republic, 207, 208–9, 224

Dakar, 254
Dallas, 295, 302
Dalmatia, 215
Damascus, 231
Danube, 75, 144, 146–7, 152, 208, 209, 210, 213
Dead Sea, 230, 231, 245
Delhi, 41, 43, 261, 262, 264
Delmarva Peninsula (Delaware, Maryland and Virginia),
    297
Denmark, 68, 124, 125–6, 127, 129, 131, 150
Denver, 295, 301
Detroit, 301
Devon, 99, 100
Disneyland Paris, 23, 76, 157, 161
Disneyworld, 218
Djerba, 244
Djibouti, 248
Dodecanese, 200
Dolomites, 183, 185–6
Dominica, 316, 317, 319, 320
Dominican Republic, 321–2
Dordogne, 156, 158, 161–2
Dorset, 99
Dover, 98, 161
Drakensberg, 249, 250
Dubai, 234
Dublin, 116, 117, 118, 119, 121, 122–3
Dubrovnik, 208, 215

Durban, 249
Dutch Caribbean, *see* Aruba, Netherlands Antilles

East Africa, 48, 245–8
East Anglia, 100–1
East Asia, 58, 59, 86, 234, 259, 273–85, 288–91
East Asia and Pacific Region (EAP), 22, 23, 64, 259, 356
Easter Island, 333, 348
Eastern Europe, 22, 23, 47, 74, 75, 76, 77, 127, 145, 147, 151, 157, 206–17, 223–4, 322, 359
Eastern Hemisphere, 61
Ecuador, 35, 36, 37, 38, 49, 51, 330, 331
Edinburgh, 84, 109, 110–11, 112
Edmonton, 307
Egypt, 46, 184, 196, 227, 228–30, 234, 237–9, 247
Eilat, 230
El Salvador, 325
Ellesmere Island, 314
England, 43, 62, 66, 74, 81, 82, 84, 85, 87, 88, 89, 97–103, 107, 121
English Channel (La Manche), 63, 77, 86, 88, 98, 99, 155, 157, 159, 160, 161, *see also* Channel Tunnel
English Riviera, 99, 100
Ephesus, 233
Equator, 34, 39, 46, 256
Equatorial Guinea, 253, 255
Eritrea, 248
Estonia, 212
Ethiopia, 13, 16, 238, 248
Eurasia, 27, 40, 43
Europe, 7, 14, 17, 22, 23, 27, 29, 33, 34, 43, 46, 47, 54, 56, 58, 61, 63, 64, 69, 73–80, 226, 228, 232, 234, 241, 242, 248, 252, 253, 262, 265, 272, 274, 280, 283, 287, 293, 294, 295, 304, 305, 316, 317, 322, 327, 330, 332, 339, 340, 352, 356, 358, 359
Everest, 268, 269, 270
Everglades, 300

Falkland Islands, 52, 333–4
Far East, *see* East Asia
Faroe Islands, 124, 131
Fermanagh, 121
Fez, 243
Fiji, 340, 346, 347–8
Finland, 124, 125, 129–30, 212
Flanders, 137, 138, 140
Florence, 182, 183, 184, 187
Florida, 46, 64, 86, 292, 295, 299–300, 303, 305
Formentera, 175
France, 62, 74, 75, 76, 86, 87, 98, 99, 109, 123, 137, 138, 139, 148, 153, 155–166, 168, 169, 170, 177, 185, 196, 226, 232, 234, 241, 242, 243, 244, 251, 252, 254, 262, 278, 294, 305, 306, 311, 321, 324, 329, 333, 338, 347

French Antilles, 321
French Guiana, 329, 330
French Polynesia, 347
French Riviera, 43, 158, 159, 164–6
Friesland, 137
Frisian Islands, 126, 137, 151
Frostbelt, 293
Fuerteventura, 176

Galapagos Islands, 34–8, 331
Galicia, 168, 171
Galway, 118, 120
Gambia, 241, 253, 254
Garden Route, 250
Geneva, 147, 148, 149, 163
Genoa, 183, 184, 186
Georgia, Republic of, 218, 221
Georgia, USA, 298, 299
Germany, 10, 22, 62, 76, 125, 126, 128, 130, 131, 135, 139, 144, 145, 149–54, 157, 169, 177, 184, 191, 197, 201, 204, 208, 210, 212, 215, 233, 242, 245, 247, 249, 262, 265, 271, 294, 305, 311, 329, 332
Ghana, 253, 254, 255
Giant's Causeway, 121
Gibraltar, 74, 176–7, 195, 200
Glasgow, 84, 88, 109, 110, 111, 112
Glastonbury, 99, 100
Goa, 260, 261, 265
Gold Coast (Ghana), 255
Gold Coast (Queensland), 341, 344
Golden Ring (Russia), 220
Göta Canal, 129
Gotland, 129
Grampians, 111, 112
Granada, 174
Gran Canaria, 176
Grand Canyon, 302
Great Barrier Reef, 329, 342
Great Dividing Range, 339
Great Lakes, 300, 305, 306
Greece, 63, 75, 76, 87, 128, 145, 165, 184, 185, 188, 195, 196–200, 201, 202–5, 216, 230
Greenland, 48, 58, 308
Greenwich Meridian, 60, 61
Grenada, 319, 320
Grenadines, *see* St Vincent
Grisons, 149
Guadeloupe, 318, 321
Guam, 280, 293, 346
Guangzhou (Canton), 283, 284
Guatemala, 325
Guernsey, 103
Guianas, The, 315, 329, 330
Guilin, 284
Gulf of Mexico, 292, 295, 298, 300, 303, 324

Gulf States (Arabia), 10, 227, 234–5, 253
Guyana, 329, 330

Hadrian's Wall, 66, 75, 102
Hague, The, 78, 136
Haiti, 322
Halkidiki, 199
Hamburg, 150, 151
Hamilton Island, 342
Harz Mountains, 144, 151
Havana, 322, 323
Hawaii, 63, 64, 280, 281, 293, 305, 338, 346, 347, 351–4
Hebrides, 111, 112
Helsinki, 129, 130
Himalayas, 48, 259, 260, 261, 262, 263, 264, 266, 267–71
Hispaniola, 316, 321
Ho Chi Minh City, see Saigon
Hokkaido, 279, 280, 281
Holland, see Netherlands
Holyhead, 113, 118
Honduras, 325
Hong Kong, 61, 63, 274, 280, 283, 284–5, 288, 289, 308, 340, 341
Honolulu, 352, 354
Honshu, 279, 280
Houston, 302–3
Hudson Bay, 305, 307, 308, 311
Hungary, 146–7, 150, 207, 208, 209–10, 224

IATA Conference Areas, 59, 60
Iberian Peninsula, 167, 168, 315
Ibiza, 169, 170, 175
Iceland, 124, 130–1
Iguacú Falls, 328
Inca Trail, 331
India, Republic of, 13, 16, 236, 260, 261–6, 267, 271
Indian Ocean, 27, 226, 234, 245, 249, 251–3, 260, 266, 267, 271, 275, 343
Indian Sub-continent (South Asia), 23, 28, 46, 69, 259–68, 289
Indonesia, 46, 51, 135, 274, 275, 276–7, 285–8, 289, 290, 291
Innsbruck, 146
International Date Line, 61
Ionian Islands, 198, 200
Iran, 226, 235
Iraq, 235
Ireland, 40, 81, 82, 84, 87, 88, 113, 114, 116, 118–23, 296, 341
Isle of Man, 84, 114–6
Isle of Wight, 99
Isles of Scilly, 84, 103
Israel, 201, 226, 227, 228, 230–1

Istanbul, 75, 197, 207, 226, 232, 233, 234
Italian Lakes, The, 149, 185, 192–4
Italian Riviera, 184, 185, 186
Italy, 75, 76, 87, 137, 145, 147, 148, 150, 160, 166, 169, 182–94, 196, 197, 200, 203, 247, 271, 296, 311, 322, 329, 332
Ivory Coast (Côte d'Ivoire), 254–5

Jaipur, 264
Jaisalmer, 264
Jakarta, 276
Jamaica, 64, 316, 317, 318, 319
Japan, 13, 17, 22, 46, 47, 62, 84, 141, 185, 262, 271, 273, 274, 275, 276, 277, 279–81, 282, 283, 285, 287, 288, 289, 290, 294, 304, 305, 308, 311, 339, 341, 345, 346, 352
Jasper, 307
Java, 276
Jersey, 103
Jerusalem, 29, 227, 230–1
Johannesburg, 248, 250
Jordan, 227, 231, 232
Jukkasjärvi, 132
Jura Mountains, 148, 149, 162
Jutland, 124, 125, 126

Kalahari, 248, 250
Kamchatka, 221
Kangaroo Island, 343, 350–1
Karakoram Highway, 266
Kashmir, 260–1, 262, 263, 265
Kauai, 352, 354
Kazakhstan, 222
Kent, 98
Kentucky, 299
Kenya, 241, 245, 246–7
Kerala, 260, 263, 265
Kerry, 118, 119, 120
Key West, 300
Khyber Pass, 262, 266
Kiev, 217, 221
Kilimanjaro Airport, 247
Kilimanjaro, Mount, 245, 246, 247
Killarney, 120
Kjolen Mountains, 74, 128
Korea, 277, 280, 281–2, 289, 290, 345
Krakow, 208, 211–2
Kruger National Park, 249
Kuala Lumpur, 274, 275, 276, 359
Kurdistan, 227, 228, 234
Kyoto, 281
Kyrgyzstan, 222
Kyushu, 270, 280, 281

Labrador, 40, 50, 307, 308
Ladakh, 260, 264
Lagos, 254, 255
Lake District (England), 82, 87, 102
Lakshadweep Islands, 261, 266
Lamu, 247
Langkawi Islands, 275, 276
Languedoc-Roussillon, 155, 159, 162
Lanzarote, 176
Laos, 274, 275
La Palma, 176
Lapland, 48, 128, 129, 130, 131–2
Las Palmas, 176
Las Vegas, 296, 302, 357
Latin America, 28, 29, 48, 62, 69, 169, 291, 292, 299,
    315–16, 317, 323–333
Latvia, 212
Laurentian Mountains, 305, 306
Lebanon, 226, 227, 232
Leeward Islands, 319–20
Lesotho, 250
Le Touquet, 161
Liberia, 253, 255
Libya, 196, 241, 242, 245
Liechtenstein, 146
Liguria, 184, 185, 186
Lille, 159, 161
Lillehammer, 127, 128
Lima, 316, 330
Limerick, 120
Lisbon, 178, 179, 180, 256
Lithuania, 212
Liverpool, 103, 105, 113
Llandudno, 113
Loire Valley, 155, 160, 161
Lombok, 285, 286, 288
London, 33, 43, 58, 59, 61, 66, 84, 87, 88, 97–8, 99, 100,
    101, 104–7, 112
Londonderry (Derry), 121
Los Angeles, 64, 295, 303, 352
Louisiana, 299
Lourdes, 29, 156, 163–4
Lucerne, 149
Luxembourg, 134, 139
Luxor, 229, 237, 238, 239

Macau, 274, 284, 285
Macedonia, Greece, 198
Macedonia, Former Yugoslav Republic of, 214, 216
Machu Picchu, 330, 331
Madagascar, 252
Madeira, 46, 178, 179–80
Madras, 262, 265
Madrid, 170, 174, 180–1
Maine, 296

Majorca (Mallorca), 43, 169, 171, 175–6
Málaga, 168, 170, 173
Malawi, 245, 250, 251
Malaysia, 274, 275–6, 289, 290, 291
Maldives, 50, 260, 261, 267, 271–2
Mali, 254, 255–6
Malta, 75, 195–6
Manaus, 328
Manchester, 88, 103, 105, 113
Manila, 277
Manitoba, 305, 307
Marbella, 173
Maritime Provinces, 307
Marrakesh, 243
Martinique, 316, 318, 321
Masai-Mara, 246, 247
Massachusetts, 296, 297
Massif Central, 155, 156, 159, 160, 162
Matterhorn, 147, 149, 185
Maui, 352, 353, 354
Mauritania, 253, 255
Mauritius, 252–3
Maya Route (Ruta Maya), 316, 323, 325
Mecca, 29, 227, 235
Mediterranean, 32, 41, 43, 47, 50, 54, 63, 64, 74, 75, 76,
    86, 118, 125, 145, 149, 150, 155, 156, 159, 162–3,
    164, 167, 168, 170, 171, 172, 173, 175, 176, 177,
    183, 184, 185, 186, 189, 192, 193, 195, 196, 197,
    200, 204, 208, 213, 215, 216, 217, 221, 226, 227,
    228, 229, 230, 231, 232, 234, 241, 242, 243, 245,
    316, 318
Medjugorje, 216
Melanesia, 346–7
Melbourne, 340, 341, 342
Memphis, 299
Menton, 165
Meseta (Spain), 167, 168, 174
Mesopotamia, 235
México, 292, 294, 301, 302, 303, 305, 315, 316, 317,
    323–5
México City, 315, 324–5
Miami, 64, 299, 300, 318, 324, 325
Miami Beach, 295, 300
Michigan, 300
Micronesia, 50, 346
Middle East, 23, 28, 46, 58, 69, 84, 195, 196, 197, 200,
    201, 221, 222, 226–39, 240, 241, 242, 243, 245,
    247, 262, 267, 284, 291
Mid-West (USA), 300–1, 352
Midlands, The (England), 85, 101, 113, 114
Milan, 183, 184, 185, 186, 193
Minorca, 75, 175
Mississippi, 292, 298, 299, 302
Mojave Desert, 303
Moldavia, 213
Moldova, 219, 221

Mombasa, 247
Monaco, 164, 165, 285
Mongolia, 217, 282
Montana, 301
Monte Carlo, *see* Monaco
Montenegro, 214, 216
Monterey (California), 304
Monterrey (México), 324
Montevideo, 332
Montréal, 62, 305, 306
Montserrat (Caribbean), 316, 320
Montserrat (Spain), 172
Moravia, 208–9
Morocco, 169, 173, 176, 177, 240, 241, 242–3
Moscow, 218, 219, 220, 221
Mozambique, 177, 248, 250, 251
Munich, 54, 152
Myanmar, *see* Burma
Mykonos, 200

Nairobi, 245, 246, 247
Namibia, 250
Naples, 183, 185, 187, 188, 196
Nashville, 299
Nassau, 318
Natal-Kwazulu, 249
Nepal, 260, 261, 262, 267, 268–71
Netherlands, 7, 77, 128, 134–7, 139, 145, 157, 169, 197,
    249, 281, 321, 329
Netherlands Antilles, 321
Nevada, 302
New Brunswick, 307
New Caledonia, 347
New England, 47, 296–7
New Forest, 99, 107–8
Newfoundland, 307
New Mexico, 302
New Orleans, 299
Newport RI, 297
New South Wales, 340, 341
New York, 66, 296, 306, 309–11, 319
New Zealand, 43, 47, 52, 58, 64, 84, 338, 339, 340, 341,
    344–5, 347, 348, 349, 352
Niagara, 297, 306
Nicaragua, 325, 326
Nice, 156, 158, 159, 163, 164, 165, 166
Niger, 254, 256
Nigeria, 254, 255
Nile, 227, 228, 229, 237–9
Norfolk Broads, 87, 101
Normandy, 155, 156, 158, 161
North Africa, 22, 23, 75, 127, 159, 168, 173, 177, 188,
    195, 226, 240, 241–5
North America, 17, 22, 27, 29, 34, 40, 43, 46, 47, 56, 61,
    62, 65, 68, 73, 83, 84, 87, 118, 119, 120, 124, 161,

211, 262, 271, 274, 277, 279, 281, 289, 292–4, 318,
    319, 322, 323, 325, 330, 339, 345, 349, 356
North Cyprus (TRNC), 200, 201
Northern Hemisphere, 5, 27, 39, 40, 42, 46, 333, 345
Northern Ireland, 75, 81, 85, 88, 110, 117, 118, 119,
    120–1
Northern Territory, 339, 343–4
North Island, *see* New Zealand
North Korea, 281, 282
North Sea, 82, 100, 102, 111, 126, 136–7, 138, 144, 151
Northumberland, 102
Northwest Passage, 311, 312
Northwest Territories, 308
North York Moors, 66, 102
Norway, 64, 68, 112, 124, 125, 126–8, 132–3
Nova Scotia, 307
Nunavut, 308, 311–14

Oahu, 352, 353, 354
Oberammergau, 152
Oceania, *see* Australasia
Odessa, 221
Okanagan, 308
Okinawa, 281
Oman, 234, 235
Ontario, 305, 306
Oporto, 179
Oregon, 304
Orkneys and Shetlands, 111, 112
Orlando, 298, 299
Osaka, 274, 281
Oslo, 127, 128
Oxford, 98
Ozarks, 299

Pacific Ocean, 27, 47, 51, 61, 64, 207, 275, 293, 303,
    324, 325, 326, 329, 330, 331, 333, 338, 339, 341,
    344, 346, 347, 348, 351, 352, 354
Pacific Rim, 22, 303, 339
Pacific Ring of Fire, 28
Pakistan, 234, 260, 261, 264, 266
Palestine, 75, 228, 230, 231
Palma, 175
Pamplona, 169, 174
Panama, 326
Panama Canal, 63, 326, 333
Pantanal, 328
Papua-New Guinea, 338, 346–7
Paraguay, 328, 332
Paris, 77, 158, 159, 160–1, 163, 252, 321, 330
Patagonia, 333
Pattaya, 277, 278
Peak District, 66, 102
Pembrokeshire Coast, 114

Penang, 275, 276
Pennines, 82, 102
Pennsylvania, 297
Perth, Australia, 62, 340, 341, 343
Peru, 51, 330–1
Petra, 231
Philadelphia, 296, 297
Philippines, 274, 277, 290
Phuket, 277, 278
Pisa, 187
Poland, 207, 209, 210–12
Polynesia, 51, 338, 344, 346, 347–8, 352
Pompeii, 188
Portsmouth, 99
Portugal, 76, 167, 170, 177–80, 265, 284
Prague, 160, 208, 209, 224–5
Prairie Provinces, 307
Prince Edward Island, 305, 307
Provence, 155, 158, 165–6
Puerto Rico, 64, 316, 321
Punta Arenas, 333
Punta del Este, 332
Pyrenees, 74, 76, 156, 160, 163, 168, 171, 174

Québec, 305, 306
Queensland, 339, 340, 341–2
Queenstown, 345
Quito, 35, 49, 330, 331

Rajahstan, 264
Randstad, 136
Ravenna, 186
Recife, 328
Red Sea, 227, 229, 230, 231, 234, 247, 248
Reunion, 252
Reykjavik, 131
Rhine, 75, 136, 145, 149, 150, 152
Rhodes, 197, 200, 203–5
Rift Valley, 245
Rio de Janeiro, 61, 316, 327, 328, 335–7
Rocky Mountains, 292, 293, 301, 305, 306, 307
Romania, 150, 207, 212, 213, 221
Romantic Road (Bavaria), 152
Rome, 29, 75, 182, 183, 184, 185, 187
Ross Sea, 349
Rotorua, 345
Route 66, 295
Rovaniemi, 130
Rüdesheim, 152
Rügen, 151
Ruhr, 144, 152
Russia, 48, 59, 62, 74, 75, 127, 129, 130, 153, 197, 201,
    206, 207, 210, 212, 217, 218, 219–21, 233, 282,
    304, 311, 349

Ruta Maya, *see* Maya Route
Ruwenzori, 246, 247, 256
Rwanda, 256

Sabah, 275, 276
Sahara, 46, 75, 240, 241, 242, 244, 245, 253
Sahel (West Africa), 253, 255–6
Saigon, 278, 279, 290
Saimaa, 130
St Gotthard, 148, 193
St Helena, 256
St Kitts-Nevis, 320
St Lawrence, 292, 301, 305, 306
St Lucia, 320
St Maarten, St Martin, 321
St Moritz, 147, 148, 149
St Petersburg, Russia, 130, 217, 218, 219–20
St Thomas, USVI, 321
St Tropez, 165
St Vincent, 317, 320
Salou, 172
Salt Lake City, 302
Salvador (Bahia), 328
Salzburg, 146, 147
Samaria Gorge, 199
Samarkand, 222
Samoa, 347, 348
Sana'a, 236, 237
San Antonio, Ibiza, 175
San Antonio, Texas, 303
San Carlos de Bariloche, 333
San Diego, 64, 304
San Francisco, 62, 64, 303–4, 352
San José, 326
San Juan, 321
San Marino, 186
San Sebastián, 170, 171
Santa Barbara, 304
Santa Cruz, 176
Santa Fe, 302
Santiago de Chile, 333
Santiago de Compostela, 156, 171–2, 174
Santiago de Cuba, 323
Santo Domingo, 322
Santorini, 200
Sao Paulo, 315, 327, 328
Sao Tomé, 256
Sarawak, 275, 276
Sardinia, 159, 183, 185, 187, 188, 189
Saudi Arabia, 227, 232, 234, 235
Saxony, 152, 153
Scandinavia, 47, 69, 74, 101, 124–33, 176, 179, 197,
    201, 204, 212, 253
Scarborough, 102
Scheveningen, 136

Schleswig-Holstein, 151
Scotland, 50, 81, 82, 84, 85, 88, 89, 109–12, 114, 115, 121
Seattle, 296, 303, 304
Senegal, 254
Seoul, 274, 282, 290
Serbia, 75, 207, 214, 215, 216
Serengeti, 246, 247
Seville, 170, 174
Seychelles, 252, 253
Shanghai, 283, 284
Shannon, 117, 118, 119, 120
Siberia, 48, 217, 218, 220–1
Sicily, 76, 183, 184, 185, 187, 188–9, 196
Siena, 186, 187
Sierra Leone, 255
Sierra Nevada, Spain, 173
Sierra Nevada, USA, 292, 303, 304
Silk Road, 222, 284
Sinai Desert, 228, 229
Singapore, 42, 274, 275, 289, 290, 340, 341
Skiathos, 200
Skyros, 200
Slovakia, 207, 208, 209
Slovenia, 74, 207, 214, 215
Snowdonia, 112–3
Snowy Mountains, 341, 342
Sochi, 219, 220
Sofia, 214
Solomon Islands, 347
Somalia, 245, 246, 248
Somerset, 99, 100
Sorrento, 188
South Africa, 23, 41, 51, 68, 135, 179, 240, 248–50, 252, 253, 256, 271
South America, 27, 34, 46, 47, 51, 52, 59, 64, 135, 179, 292, 315, 316, 320, 321, 322, 325, 326–34
South Asia, *see* Indian Sub-continent
South Australia, 343
South East Asia, 15, 29, 51, 73, 252, 259, 273, 274–9, 289, 290
Southern Alps, 344, 345
Southern Hemisphere, 27, 39, 43, 47, 52, 340
Southern Ocean, 27, 47, 349
South Georgia, 349
South Island, *see* New Zealand
South Korea, *see* Korea
South Tyrol, *see* Alto Adige
South West Peninsula (England), 82, 85, 99–100
Soviet Union, 129–30, 149–50, 154, 206–7, 212, 218–19, 220, 221, 267, 282, 322, 349, *see also* Russia, Commonwealth of Independent States
Spain, 43, 54, 74, 76, 83, 87, 125, 128, 137, 150, 157, 167–76, 177, 178, 180–1, 184, 185, 231, 240, 242, 243, 317, 322, 329, 332, 333
Sri Lanka, 260, 261, 267

Stirling, 110, 111
Stockholm, 128, 129
Stonehenge, 75, 100, 357
Strasbourg, 78, 158, 162
Sudan, 245, 247–8
Suez Canal, 63, 195, 227, 228
Sulawesi, 277
Sumatra, 276–7
Sunbelt, 293
Sun City, 250
Surinam, 329, 330
Svalbard, 127, 132–3
Swaziland, 250
Sweden, 16, 68, 124, 125, 127, 128–9, 132, 150
Switzerland, 144, 145, 146, 147–9, 185, 193, 194, 247
Sydney, 62, 339, 340, 341, 342
Syria, 227, 231–2

Tahiti, 64, 347
Taipei, 274, 285
Taiwan, 280, 285, 289
Tajikistan, 222
Tangier, 242, 243
Tanzania, 245, 246, 247
Tashkent, 222
Tasmania, 47, 340, 342–3
Tatra (Tatry) Mountains, 209, 211
Tel Aviv, 227, 230
Tenerife, 169, 170, 176
Tennessee, 299
Texas, 301, 302–3
Thailand, 274, 277–8, 289, 290, 291
Thuringia, 152–3
Tibet, 49, 260, 270, 283, 284
Ticino, 149, 193–4
Titicaca, Lake, 331, 332
Togo, 253, 254, 255
Tokyo, 61, 68, 274, 280, 281
Toledo, 174, 181
Tonga, 347
Toronto, 305, 306
Torquay, *see* English Riviera
Torremolinos, 173
Trans-Siberian Railway, 62, 218, 220
Transylvania, 208, 213
Trinidad and Tobago, 320
Tropic of Cancer, 39
Tropic of Capricorn, 39
Tunis, 243, 244
Tunisia, 184, 241, 242, 243–4
Turin, 183, 186
Turkey, 184, 197, 200, 214, 222, 226, 227, 228, 232–4
Turkmenistan, 222
Turks and Caicos, 319

Tuscany, 185, 186–7
Tyrol, 145, 146

Udaipur, 263, 264
Uganda, 245, 246, 247, 256
Ukraine, 217, 218, 219, 221
Umbria, 186, 187
United Arab Emirates, 234, 235
United Kingdom, 13, 22, 77, 82, 83, 84, 85, 86, 87, 88,
    89, 97, 116, 117, 118, 119, 120, 126, 127, 128, 130,
    131, 137, 145, 157, 159, 160, 169, 196, 204, 211,
    233, 234, 241, 249, 265, 266, 271, 279, 294, 299,
    305, 311, 341, 345, *see also* Britain
United States of America, 7, 9, 10, 13, 14, 16, 22, 33, 41,
    46, 54, 59, 62, 64, 67, 76, 83, 87, 109, 118, 119,
    120, 121, 127, 128, 131, 137, 141, 150, 153, 154,
    157, 169, 185, 187, 197, 203, 221, 225, 230, 231,
    236, 249, 254, 255, 258, 262, 266, 274, 275, 277,
    278, 279, 280, 281, 282, 283, 285, 287, 292,
    293–304, 305, 309–11, 316, 317, 318, 320, 321,
    322, 323, 324, 325, 326, 327, 329, 331, 333, 338,
    339, 341, 346, 349, 351, 352, 353, 354, 358, 359
Uruguay, 332
Ushuaia, 333, 349
USSR, *see* Soviet Union
Utah, 302
Uzbekistan, 222

Valais, 149
Valencia, 169, 170, 172
Valle d'Aosta, 183, 185
Valley of the Kings (Thebes), 229, 237, 238, 239
Valparaiso, 333
Vancouver, 62, 306, 308
Vanuatu, 347
Varanasi, 261
Venezuela, 13, 316, 329
Venice, 182, 183, 184, 185, 186, 189–92, 195, 200, 215,
    302
Vermont, 296, 305
Verona, 185, 186, 193
Versailles, 155, 160
Vichy, 162
Victoria, Australia, 342
Victoria, BC, 308
Victoria Falls, 29, 251
Victoria, Lake, 247
Vienna, 145, 146, 147, 207, 209, 210, 224
Vietnam, 274, 278–9, 289
Virginia, 296, 298
Virgin Islands, 320–1

Volga, 218, 220
Vorarlberg, 146

Wadi Rum, 231
Wales, 81, 82, 84, 85, 87, 88, 89, 101, 112–4
Warsaw, 77, 211
Washington DC, 296, 297, 298
Washington State, 304
Wellington, 345
Weser Valley, 151
West Africa, 46, 253–6
West Bank, *see* Palestine
West Country (England), *see* South West Peninsula
Western Australia, 62, 343
Western Hemisphere, 61, 322
Western Sahara, 176, 242, 244
West Indies, *see* Commonwealth Caribbean
West Virginia, 297
Wexford, 120
Wicklow Mountains, 119, 120
Williamsburg, 293, 298
Windsor, 98
Windward Islands, 318, 320
Winnipeg, 307

Xian, 283

Yalta, 221
Yangtze, 284
Yellowstone, 293, 301
Yemen, 234, 235, 236–7, 246
York, 102–3
Yorkshire Dales, 82, 102
Yosemite, 304
Yucatán, 323, 324, 325
Yugoslavia, 86, 206, 207, 214–16, 359
Yukon, 308
Yunnan, 284

Zakynthos (Zante), 198, 200
Zambezi, 240, 251
Zambia, 250, 251
Zanzibar, 247
Zaragoza, 174
Zermatt, 149
Zimbabwe, 250, 251, 257–8
Zululand, *see* Natal-Kwazulu
Zurich, 59, 145, 148, 149

Subject index

Accessibility, 6, 30, 31, 32, 35
Acclimatization, 41, 48
Accommodation, 3, 6, 25, 32, 73, 77, 87–8, 98, 116, 120,
    126, 127, 128, 130, 135–6, 141, 146, 148, 150, 158,
    170, 178, 184, 198, 204, 207, 209, 218–19, 224,
    237, 244, 246, 249, 263, 281, 286, 290, 296, 310,
    313, 318, 320, 328, 329, 330, 334, 344–5, 346, 348,
    351
Accor, 77, 158
Activity holidays, 20, 28, 119, 356
Adventure tourism, 20, 28, 29, 131–3, 268–71
Aer Lingus, 118
Aeroflot, 218
Agenda 21, 122, 356
Agro-tourism, 120, 126, 145, 151, 169, 201, 332, 345,
    350
Air Afrique, 254
Air Canada, 69
Aircraft, 21, 22, 54, 55, 61, 105, 358
Airline alliances, 67–9, 358
Airport location, 61
Air quality, 43
Air routes, 56–7, 58–9
Airships, 61
Air traffic control, 77
Air transport, 10, 22, 32, 50, 54, 55, 56, 57, 58–61,
    67–9, 77, 79, 83–4, 86, 88, 97, 105, 116, 118, 125,
    127, 129–30, 131, 135, 138, 148, 150, 159, 168,
    170, 178, 180, 184, 196, 197, 201, 204, 218, 228,
    233, 234, 242, 243, 244, 247, 249, 250, 253, 254,
    262, 272, 274, 277, 281, 283, 284, 286, 290, 295,
    305, 310, 311, 313, 317, 327, 329, 330, 339, 341,
    345, 346, 347, 349, 352, 358
Alaska Marine Highway System, 304
Alitalia, 184
Allemansrätt, 128

All-inclusives, 157, 272, 318, 319, 320, 322
All-terrain vehicles, 303, 313, 333
Altitude, effects of, 41, 45, 48–9, 268, 269, 330, 331–2
American Airlines, 67, 68, 295
Amtrak, 296
Andean Pact, 327, 330
Antiquities, *see* Archaeological sites
Apartheid, 248
Archaeological sites, 75, 126, 161–2, 187, 188–9, 196,
    199, 200, 201, 215, 217, 228, 229, 230, 231, 232,
    233, 234, 235, 237, 239, 244, 245, 251, 264, 266,
    267, 276, 278, 283, 302, 323, 324, 325, 329, 330–1,
    332
Areas of Outstanding Natural Beauty, 98, 99, 102
Asian Currency Crisis, 22, 273, 275, 276, 282, 288–91,
    341, 345, 356
Association of South East Asian Nations (ASEAN), 274,
    359
Attractions, 5, 6, 8, 23, 30, 76, 87
    classification, 30
Australian Tourist Commission, 339, 340
Austrian National Tourist Organisation, 146
Autobahns, 150
Avianca, 329

Baby-boomers, 15, 18, 83, *see* Demographic trends
Backpackers, 29, 225, 262, 265, 277, 278, 286, 288, 326,
    330, 331
Barrier islands, 295, 298, 300, 342
Beach tourism, 8, 29, 43, 52
Blue Flag (beach scheme), 80
Blue Train, 249
Bord Failté Eireann, 119, 120, 121, 123
British Airways, 67
British Tourist Authority, 88, 121

Brownfield sites (for redevelopment), 32
Bullet Train, 280
Business travel, 4, 9, 15, 22, 23, 29, 30, 33, 61, 63, 76, 77, 87, 98, 100, 101, 102, 105, 110, 115, 116, 118, 128, 137, 139, 141, 146, 148, 149, 150, 152, 154, 158, 159, 161, 196, 201, 207, 209, 210, 216, 220, 222, 227, 230, 233, 234, 235, 243, 245, 247, 254, 255, 256, 259, 262, 263, 266, 276, 277, 278, 279, 280, 282, 284, 285, 293, 294, 297, 311, 316, 323, 327, 329, 356

Cableways, 63, 147
CAMPFIRE, 257–8
Canadian Pacific, 62, 305, 306, 307
Canadian Tourism Commission, 305
Canals, see Inland waterways
Canoe trails, 305–6
Caribbean Economic Community (CARICOM), 317, 329
Caribbean Tourism Organization, 317, 329
Car ownership, 18, 62, 65, 82, 99, 168, 208, 219, 228, 273, 295, 328, 340, 344
Carrying capacity, 26, 28
Cathay Pacific, 284, 290
Caves, see Limestone scenery
Cedok, 208, 209
Centrally planned economies, 14, 17, 207, 283, 322
CenterParcs, 87, 135
Ceylon Tourist Board, 267
Chicago Convention, 59
China International Travel Service, 283
CIT 184
CITES, 257
City breaks, 76, 140
Climate, 6, 34, 39–52, 73, 74, 76, 82, 99, 109, 117, 124, 126–7, 130, 131–2, 133, 134, 144, 155, 161, 162, 167, 169, 176, 177, 180, 185, 188, 193, 206, 211, 213, 215, 217, 221, 222, 227, 229, 230, 232, 242, 245–6, 249, 250, 253, 259–60, 267, 274, 279, 282, 283, 286, 292–3, 299, 301, 303, 304, 305, 307, 308, 313, 316, 323, 328, 329, 330, 331, 333, 340, 342, 344, 346, 348, 353
Climate and human physiology, 41, 42
Climate change, 50–2, 245, 357
Climate classification, 43–5
Climate, elements of, 41–3
Climate zones, 43–9
Climographs, 42, 43
Club Méditerranée, 156, 157, 242, 244, 254, 272, 276, 318, 347
Coach transport, 57, 62, 88, 295–6
Coastal resource, 29
Colonies des vacances, 157
COMECON, 207, 208
Comfort index, 43
Command economies, see Communism

Commercial business district (CBD), 33
Common interest tourism, 8-9
Communism, 207, 208, 209, 213, 217, 218, 219, 220, 223, 224, 278, 282, 322
Community involvement in tourism, 32, 89–90, 254, 257–8, 325
Complementarity, 53
Computer reservation systems (CRS), 20, 67, 83, 355, 356, 357, 358
Conference tourism, 85, 98, 141, 158, 293
Conservation,
    of the built environment, 140–3, 160, 189–92, 209, 293
    of the natural environment, see Ecotourism, National parks, World Heritage Sites
Continental climates, 40, 47
Conventions, 293
Coral reefs and atolls, 29, 46, 51, 230, 247, 252, 253, 266, 271, 272, 286, 300, 318, 319, 320, 321, 323, 325, 339, 342, 343, 346, 347, 348, 353
Country parks, 87, 98, 284
Cruising, see River Cruising, Sea Cruising
Cultural heritage, 29, 75, 226–7, 260–1
Cultural regions, 29
Cultural resources, 29–30, 75, 226–7, 260
Cultural tourism, 8, 29, 197
Culture shock, 242, 260
Currency controls, 17, 108
Cycling, 54, 125, 129, 135, 156
Cyprus Tourist Organisation, 201

Dachas, 219
Danish Tourist Board, 126
Day visitors, see Excursionists
Demographic transition, 15, 16
Demographic trends, 15, 20, 75, 83, 356
Deregulation, 17, 20, 59, 67, 77, 79, 83–4, 86, 125, 295, 358
Destination surveys, 6, 7
Developing countries, see Economic development
Differential pricing, 56
Discretionary income, 17
Diving, 31, 37, 41, 46, 156, 188, 196, 197, 215, 229, 230, 244, 247, 252, 271, 276, 277, 286, 300, 318, 319, 321, 323, 325, 342, 343, 346, 347, 353
Domestic age, 18
Domestic tourism, 7, 84–5, 118, 125, 127, 128, 135, 137, 145, 148, 150, 156–7, 168–9, 185, 201, 207, 208–9, 218, 233, 249, 262–3, 266, 273, 280, 283, 294, 305, 327, 332, 340
Dude ranches, 302

Earth Summit (Rio), 356
Eastern Orient Express, 274

Economic Community of West African States, 254
Economic development, 13–15
Economic impact of tourism, 26, 92, 98, 270, 286, 317
Eco-tourism, 8, 28, 34–7, 46, 130, 132, 174, 183, 201, 220, 221, 228, 246, 251, 254, 257, 263, 276, 277, 284, 304, 314, 318, 320, 325, 326, 328, 329, 330, 331, 333, 334, 335, 336, 340, 342, 344, 345, 354
Educational attainment, 18, 82
El Niño, 34, 51, 331
Embratur, 327, 336
Emigration, 4, 10–11, 29, 63, 111, 117–18, 127, 171, 187, 197, 274
Employment, 17
Enclave tourism, 200, 254, 287, 322, 323, 324
English Tourism Council, 89
English Tourist Board, 88–9
Environmental impacts of tourism, 26, 28, 29, 35–7, 43, 46, 48, 61, 74, 76, 101, 120, 139, 146, 166, 168, 174, 192, 193, 198, 224, 225, 233, 247, 252, 264, 268, 270, 287, 300, 303, 308, 318, 331, 342, 349–50, 354
Ethical tourism, 20, 26, 279
Ethnic tourism, 110, 118, 119, 211, 254, see also Emigration
European Bank for Reconstruction and Development, 32, 217
European Commission, 78, 79, 137, 138, 223
European Community see European Union
European Highway System, 77
European Union, 7, 10, 17, 46, 59, 75, 77, 78–80, 87, 101, 118, 119, 121, 122, 125, 138, 139, 141, 145, 162, 187, 196, 198, 202, 208, 346, 359
Eurostar, 138, 141, 159
Event attractions, 30
Excursionists, 3, 142
Expo (World Exhibition), 179, 342

Farm-stays, see Agro-tourism
Ferries (short-sea routes), 63, 77, 88, 99, 103, 111, 112, 113, 114, 116, 118, 126, 127, 129, 130, 135, 138, 150, 157, 159, 161, 171, 173, 175, 177, 184, 188, 189, 196, 197–8, 199, 200, 204, 212, 215, 272, 277, 280, 284, 285, 304, 307, 310, 317, 342, 345, 351–2
Festivals, 98, 110, 120, 121, 123, 147, 152, 165, 168, 169, 172, 174, 182, 201, 215, 286, 306, 318, 320, 335
Finnish Tourist Board, 130
Fly-cruise, 64
Fly-drive, 56, 178
Föhn winds, 42, 144, 307
Folk museums, 114, 115, 121, 126, 129, 210
FONATUR, 324
Forest resource, 29, 46, 144, 209, 213, 295
Forestry Commission, 87, 108

Fourth World (Minority tribal cultures), 29, 266, 274
Freedoms of the air, 58–9
Freeways, 295, 303
French State Railways (SNCF), 158–9, 163
Friction of distance, 6, 54

Gambling, 164–5, 250, 285, 298, 302, 318, 319, 324, 340
Game Reserves, see Safaris
Garuda, 276
General Agreement on Trade in Services (GATS), 359
Geothermal resources, 27, 130, 162, 180, 182, 210, 221, 280, 281, 301, 316, 345
German National Tourist Office (DZT), 151
Gites, 158
Global distribution systems (GDS), 202, 357
Globalization, 357–8
Global warming, 50, 272, 348
Golf, 31, 110, 111, 112, 116, 119, 121, 132, 156, 161, 173, 176, 178, 235, 243, 244, 275, 280, 286, 294, 298, 307, 308, 319, 326, 342, 352, 354
Grand Tour, 29, 182
Gravity model, 6
Great circle routes, 58
Greek National Tourist Office, 198
Greenfield sites, 32
Green tourism, 125, 146, 156, see also Agro-tourism, Sustainable development
Greenwich Mean Time (GMT), 61
Greyhound, 295
Guide services, see Heritage interpretation
Gulf War, 22, 85, 86, 200, 226, 228, 231, 232, 235, 243

Haj, 227, 235
Health risks, 32, 45–6, 50, 51, 52, 241
Health tourism, 27, 28, 147, 156, 213, 218, 222, 227, 230, 243, 322, 323, 326, see also Mountain resorts, Spas
Helicopters, 61, 272, 307, 349, 354
Heritage attractions, 30, 87
Heritage Coasts, 82, 100, 101, 102
Heritage interpretation, 33, 293, 342
Heritage Rivers, 305–6
Heritage tourism, 29–30, 118
Highlands and Islands Enterprise, 111
Highland (high altitude) climates, 41, 45, 48–9
High speed trains, 62, 77, 150, 158–9, 170, 184, 280, 296
Hiking trails, 87, 152, 156
Hill stations, see Mountain resorts
Holiday arrangements, 10
Holiday entitlement, 17–18, 125, 128, 134, 145, 157, 185, 210, 218, 180, 294, 327
Holiday Inns, 296

Holiday tourism, 8
Honeypots, 102
Hong Kong Tourist Association, 284
Host community, 26
Hovercraft, 63
Hub and spoke operations, 59, 295, 398
Humidity, 41
Hydrofoils, 63, 184, 204, 210, 215, 275, 341

IATA, 59–60
Iberia, 170
Ibusz, 270
Ice Hotel, 132
Inclusive tour, 10, 19, 269
Independent travel, 10, 19, 269
India Tourism Development Corporation, 263
Industrial heritage, 100, 101, 103, 113
Infrastructure, 32
Inland waterways, 29, 74, 87, 101, 120, 129, 150, 156,
    159, 208, 218, 220, 229, 237–9, 299, 328, *see also*
    River cruising
Inter-American Development Bank, 328
International Passenger Survey, 7
International tourism, 7, 21–3
Intervening opportunity, 54, 159, 192
Intourist, 219
Investimentos Comercios e Turismo de Portugal, 178
Irish Tourist Board, *see* Bord Failté Eireann
Italian State Railways (FS), 184
Italian State Tourist Office (ENIT), 183

Japan NTO, 280–1
Jet-lag, 61
Jet streams, 58

Karst, *see* Limestone scenery
Kenya Ministry of Tourism and Wildlife, 246
Kibbutz (working holidays), 230
KLM, 135

Lakes, 29, 74, 87, 102, 111, 112, 121, 128, 130, 146, 147,
    149, 185, 192–4, 209, 210, 211, 215, 216, 221, 245,
    251, 263, 288, 297, 298, 300, 306, 307, 308, 325,
    331, 333, 342, 345
Lakes and mountains holidays, 28, 74, 145, 146, 147,
    162, 192–4, 216
Landforms, 27–8
Latitude, 39, 40
Leisure, 3, 12, 294, 356
Life cycle:
    human, 18
    tourist area, 33

Lifestyles, 17, 20, 356
Life zones (habitats), 41, 45, 46, 49, 260, 323, 330
Limestone scenery, 27–8, 100, 102, 120, 139, 161–2,
    175, 209, 215, 216, 284, 299, 308, 319
Line routes (world shipping routes), 57, 63, 176, 179,
    236, 249, 253, 275, 326, 333
Link (airline alliance), 67
Load factor, 56
London Docklands Development Corporation, 105, 106
London Underground, 58, 105, 284
Long-haul tourism, 10
Lufthansa, 68, 150, 153

Maison de la France, 159
Marginal cost, 56
Marinas, *see* Sailing
Maritime climates, 40, 47
Maritime heritage, 81, 99, 106, 126, 179, 297, 310
Market segmentation, 21, 56, 356
Mass tourism, 7, 8, 19, 32, 169–70, 198, 356, 359
Media influence, 20, 30, 102, 111, 120, 339, 351
Mediterranean climate, 44, 47, 76, 155, 162, 167, 215,
    333
MERCOSUR, 315, 327, 332
Metropolitan Areas, 293
Metropolitan Transportation Authority (New York), 310
Mobility, 18, 53, 55, 358
Monorails, 66
Moslem fundamentalism, 226, 228, 230, 235, 239, 242,
    244, 261
Motorways, 61, 82, 97, 99, 101, 107, 138, 145, 150, 158,
    170, 184, 295, 303
Mountain landscapes, 28
Mountain resorts, 28, 201, 228, 231, 235, 243, 261, 274,
    323, *see also* Winter sports
Multinationals, 32
Multiple use, 25, 27, 29, 160, 295
Mundo Maya, 325

Narrow gauge railways, 63, 98, 101, 102, 113, 116, 263
National Aeronautics and Space Administration (NASA),
    300, 361
National parks, 28, 31, 34–8, 87, 99, 101, 102, 112–13,
    114, 128, 129, 131, 132, 137, 139, 146, 149, 160,
    171, 174, 176, 179, 183, 188, 199, 201, 208, 210,
    211, 212, 215, 246, 247, 248, 249, 251, 254, 256,
    257, 263, 267, 268, 270, 276, 281, 282, 285, 293,
    294–5, 299, 301, 302, 304, 306, 307, 308, 314, 326,
    331, 333, 339, 341, 342, 343, 344, 345, 353
National Park Service, 294–5, 301, 353
National tourist organizations (NTO), 30, 88–9, 119, 120,
    121, 126, 127, 129, 130, 131, 134, 138, 139, 146,
    148, 151, 159, 171, 178, 183, 198, 201, 207, 208,
    219, 246, 247, 249, 251, 266, 267, 275, 277, 281,
    305, 324, 327, 329, 330, 339, 344

National Trust, 32, 87, 98, 100, 160
New Forest District Council, 108
New York Convention and Visitor's Bureau, 310
New Zealand Tourist Board, 344
North-South economic divide, 46
North American Free Trade Agreement (NAFTA), 294, 323, 359
Northern Ireland Tourist Board, 121
Nortravel Marketing (NORTRA), 127

Ocean currents, 40, 46, 50, 51, 126, 132, 176, 242, 249, 250, 303, 307
Olympic Airways, 197
Olympic Games, 30, 152, 172, 219, 282, 298, 303, 306, 339, 340, 341, 359, *see also* Winter Olympics
Orbis, 211
Organization of Petroleum Exporting Countries (OPEC), 14
Orient Express, 191
Ozone layer, 52, 357

Pacific Asia Travel Association (PATA), 259, 283, 338
Pan-American Highway system, 62, 325, 326
Paradors, 170, 329
Park and ride, *see* Traffic management
Parkways, *see* Scenic drives
Perceptions, 18, 32
Permafrost, 48, 217, 313
Petroleum, 58, 86, 112, 127, 208, 222, 227, 228, 234, 244, 245, 255, 293, 307, 320, 329, 331
Pilgrimages, 29, 98, 102, 112, 114, 118, 139, 156, 163–4, 171–2, 174, 179, 182, 183, 187, 212, 216, 227, 230, 231, 235, 261–2, 268, 280, 306, 325
Pleasure periphery, 76
Political influences, 16–17
Pollution, 29, 43, 74, 192, 208, 264, 304, 350
Population factors, 15–16, *see also* Demographic trends
Port location, 64
Private sector, 6, 27, 32, 37
Provincial parks (Canada), 293, 305, 306
Public consultation, 89–96
Public sector, 6, 32, 37
Push and pull factors, 6

Rail transport, 54, 55, 56, 57, 61, 62–3, 77, 88, 97, 102, 105, 118, 127, 129, 135, 138, 145, 147, 148, 149, 150, 154, 158–9, 170, 184, 191, 197, 218, 228, 244, 249, 262–3, 274, 277, 283, 296, 300, 306, 326, 327, 330, 333, 341, 345
Rainfall, 43, 44, 47
Rapid transit, 61, 62, 105, 123, 295, 359
Recreation, definition, 3, 12

Recreation areas, classification:
  resource-based, 30, 31, 293
  user-orientated, 30, 31, 293
Recreational business district (RBD), 33
Recreational tourism, 8, 197
Recreational vehicles, 61, 296
Regionalism, 395
Regional nature parks, 160
Regional tourist boards, 89
Relief, influence on climate, 41, 48–9, 82, 144, 259–60, 292–3, 316, 323, 330
Resorts, 28, 29, 32–4, *see also* Mountain resorts, Spas, Winter sports
Resource evaluation, 25, 31
River cruising, 29, 129, 150, 152, 159, 237–9, 284, 299, 310, 342
River running, 29, 263, 268
Road transport, 54, 55, 56, 57, 61–2, 65–7, 77, 82, 88, 99, 105, 108, 112, 113, 126, 131, 136, 138, 145, 148, 150, 158, 170, 173, 178, 184, 197, 204, 208, 215, 217, 218, 228, 242, 244, 249, 263, 274, 275, 286, 295, 300, 306, 324, 326, 327, 329, 340, 345
Rural tourism, 119, 183 *see also* Agro-tourism
Ryanair, 118
Ryokan, 281

Safaris, 46, 246, 247, 249, 250, 254, 256, 257–8
Safari vessels, 272
Sailing, 29, 42, 54, 100, 101, 113, 120, 121, 125, 126, 130, 137, 151, 156, 165, 171, 173, 175, 177, 186, 196, 197, 215, 229, 233, 244, 296, 304, 308, 318, 319, 320, 321, 342, 345, 353
Scale, world, national or regional, and local, 4-5, 27, 30, 32
Scandinavian Airlines System (SAS), 68–9, 124, 131
Scenic drives, 67, 120, 164, 295, 307
Scottish Tourist Board, 88, 109
Sea cruising, 63–4, 125, 127, 133, 176, 184, 188, 191, 196, 197, 200, 201, 215, 221, 228, 233, 235, 243, 244, 277, 287, 294, 300, 304, 311, 317–8, 319, 320, 321, 322, 324, 326, 329, 333, 347, 349–50, 353, 357
Seaplanes, 61, 272
Sea transport, 54, 55, 57, 63–4, *see also* Ferries, Line routes
Seasonality, 39, 76, 84, 85, 99, 119, 127, 130, 135, 157, 166, 169, 185, 198, 249, 262, 269, 313, 344
Second homes, 29, 88, 113, 125, 127, 128, 129, 157, 209, 214, 219, 294, 296, 344
Sex tourism, 136, 208, 247, 277, 323, 324
Short haul tourism, 10
Short sea routes, *see* Ferries
Singapore Airlines, 275
Single European Market, *see* European Union
Ski resorts, *see* Winter sports
Snowbirds, 305

Snow cover, 43, 47, 49

Social/cultural impacts of tourism, 168, 169–70, 175, 191, 198, 225, 247, 254, 287, 318, 331, 344, 345, 347, 348, 353, 354

Social tourism, 20, 125, 137, 148, 157, 207, 218, 322

Societé Nationale Maritime Corse-Mediterranée (SNCM), 159

Son et lumière (sound and light shows), 161, 204, 278

South Africa Tourist Board (SATOUR), 249

South African Airways, 249, 256

Southern Africa Regional Tourism Council (SARTOC), 248

Spas, 27, 100, 101, 102, 110, 139, 141, 147, 149, 150, 152, 156, 159, 162, 163, 168, 171, 179, 182, 207, 208, 209, 210, 213, 214, 220, 223, 280, 281, 299, 304, 307, 325, 331

Space centres, 220, 300, 302, 330

Space tourism, 357, 361–2

Spatial interaction, 5-6, 53–4, 85

Sports tourism, 30, 98, 101, 106, 115–16, 139, 158, 165, 208, 251, 282, 285, 294, 299, 303, 336, 340, 341, 342, 343, 345

Star Alliance, 67, 68–9

State parks (USA), 293

Statistics:
  accommodation records, 6
  bank records, 7
  difficulties with, 7
  expenditure, 6, 7
  immigration, 6
  tourist characteristics, 6, 7
  volume, 6, 7

Stress, 6, 15–16

Sunlust, 19

Sunshine, 25, 39, 41–2, 52

Superstructure, 32

Supply and demand, 5-6

Surface transport, see Rail, Road and Sea transport

Surfing, 29, 41, 42, 100, 161, 243, 249, 251, 286, 287, 303, 341, 343, 345, 348, 353

Sustainable development, 20, 26, 122, 132, 175–6, 328, 330, 331, 351, 355, 356–7

Swedish Travel and Tourism Council, 129

Swiss Federal Railways, 148

Swiss NTO, 148

Syndicates d'initiatives, 159

Tailor-made travel, 10, 269, 356

Technology, 20, 54, 58, 63, 83, 355, 356, 357, 358–9

Teleconferencing, 356

Temperate climates, 44, 46–7

Temperature, 41, 42, 49
  apparent, 41, 42
  effective, 41, 42
  sea, 41

Thai Airways International, 68, 277

Thalassotherapy, 156

Theme parks, 30, 31, 76, 99, 101, 102, 129, 135, 137, 152, 161, 172, 250, 274, 293, 294, 299, 300, 303, 327, 341

Themed hotels, 302, 310

Third age tourism, 169

Third World, see Economic development

Thomas Cook, 147, 182, 229, 238

Tiger economies, 273

Time zones, 59–61, 217, 292

Tour de France, 123, 156

Touring, 7, 8

Tourism:
  definitions, 3-4
  forms of, 7-10

Tourism, benefits of, 26, 92, 93, 270, 286, 317

Tourism demand, 4, 5–6, 12–20, 39, 53, 73, 75–6, 82, 83–7, 118, 125, 127, 128, 134, 135, 137, 145, 148, 150, 156–7, 168–9, 177, 184–5, 203–4, 207, 218–19, 234, 241, 249, 261–2, 271, 274, 280, 282–3, 289–90, 294, 305, 311, 316, 322, 324, 327, 340–1, 344–5, 346, 351, 352, 355–6
  definition, 12–13
  effective demand, 12–19
  suppressed demand, 19–20

Tourism, impacts of, see Environmental impacts, Social/cultural impacts

Tourism planning, 26–7, 32, 89–96, 159, 334–5

Tourism products, 31–2

Tourism resources, 25–32
  characteristics, 25

Tourism supply, 4, see Resources, accommodation and transport for each regional chapter

Tourism Concern, 20

Tourism Council of the South Pacific, 346

Tourist area life cycle, 33

Tourist attractions, see Attractions

Tourist centres, 33

Tourist destination areas, 5, 21, 22, 23

Tourist enclaves, see Enclave tourism

Tourist flows, 5-7, 21–3
  measurement, 6-7

Tourist generating areas, 5, 22, 23

Tourist regions (WTO definition), 22, 23

Tourist routes, 151, 152, 174

Tourist typology, 7-8, 10

Tourist Authority of Thailand, 277, 278, 289

Tourist Development Authority (of Egypt), 229

Tourist Trophy (TT), 115–16

Trade fairs, 151, 152, 153, 177, 183, 209, 215, 251, 284, 301, 342

Traffic management, 65–6, 102, 108, 143

Train grand vitesse (TGV), 62, 159, 358

Transferability, 54

Transit routes, 5

Transport, 5, 8, 9, 10, 17, 22, 53–64
Transport costs, 55–6
Transport, elements of, 54–5
Transport heritage, 115–16
Transport modes, 55, 56
Transport networks, 57–8
Transport routes, 56–7, *see also* Air transport, Ferries,
    Line routes, Rail transport, Road transport
Travel, definition, 4, 10–11
Travel frequency, 13, 24
Travel motivators, 18–19
Travel propensity, 13, 24
Trekking, 31, 131, 229, 230, 243, 263, 264, 266, 269–71,
    331
Tropics, the (tropical climates), 39, 41, 42, 43, 44, 45–6

Ultraviolet radiation, 41–2, 48–9, 52
UNESCO, 30, 229, 238, 331
Unique selling proposition, 32
Union Pacific, 62
United Airlines, 68
United Kingdom Tourist Survey, 7, 84, 85
United Nations, 3, 11, 12, 32, 236
United States Forest Service, 294, 295
United States Travel and Tourism Administration, 294
Urbanization, 15–16
Urban tourism, 33

VARIG, 69, 327
VFR tourism (visiting friends and relatives), 8-9, 84
VIA Rail, 306
VIASA, 329
Villages vacance familiales, 157
Virtual reality, 357
Visitor, definition, 3, 11
Visitor management, 35, 102, 118

Visitor payback, 357
Voluntary sector, 32, 37

Wales Tourist Board, 88, 112
Wanderlust, 10, 19, 20
Waterfalls, 28, 29, 131, 146, 149, 251, 301, 304, 306,
    308, 328, 329
Water quality, 29, 32, 80, 129, 192, 193
Water sports, 29, 41 *see* Diving, Sailing, Surfing, etc.
Wave-piercing catamarans, 63
Wetlands, 29
Wilderness areas, 295
Wildlife resources, *see* National parks, Safaris
Wind-chill, 42
Winter Olympics, 127, 128, 158, 280, 302, 307
Winter sports, 28, 33, 43, 47, 48, 49, 50, 74, 82, 112,
    127, 128, 129, 130, 131, 132, 134, 135, 144, 145,
    146, 147, 148, 149, 152, 156, 160, 162, 163, 173,
    174, 182, 185, 199, 201, 208, 209, 211, 212, 213,
    214, 216, 221, 222, 228, 232, 235, 243, 249, 250,
    264, 266, 280, 282, 296, 297, 300, 301, 302, 304,
    305, 306, 307, 308, 332, 333, 340, 341, 342, 345
Winter sun destinations, 46, 173, 176, 179, 201, 229, 230,
    242, 244, 247, 253, 265, 300, 316, 324, 353
World Bank, 32
World Cup, 30, 158, 359
World Heritage Sites, 30, 34, 112, 121, 129, 234, 308,
    331, 339
World Tourism Organization (WTO), 12, 15, 21, 58, 259,
    292, 321, 356
World Travel and Tourism Council, 291, 356, 357
World Wide Fund for Nature (WWF), 37, 257

Yachting, *see* Sailing
Yield management, 25
Yugotours, 215

Zodiac landing craft, 133, 349
Zoning, 29, 32, 35, 160

THE
BUSINESS CASES
WEB SITE

BUSINESS CASES

◢ **Quality case study materials from quality authors**

◢ **Instant access to cases & tutor support material**

◢ **'Quick view' summaries & author profiles**

◢ **Download PDFs and 'copy' for use on specified courses**

◢ **No registration fee**

◢ **Pay on-line or open an account**

Check out this excellent site today
www.businesscases.org